INSTRUCTIONAL STRATEGIES FOR SECONDARY SCHOOL PHYSICAL EDUCATION

FOURTH EDITION

JOYCE M. HARRISON
Brigham Young University

CONNIE L. BLAKEMORE
Brigham Young University

MARILYN M. BUCK
Ball State University

TRACY L. PELLETT
Northern Illinois University

Brown & Benchmark
PUBLISHERS

Madison   Dubuque, IA   Guilford, CT   Chicago   Toronto   London
Caracas   Mexico City   Buenos Aires   Madrid   Bogota   Sydney

Book Team

Publisher *Bevan O'Callaghan*
Project Editor *Scott Spoolman*
Publishing Services Coordinator *Peggy Selle*
Proofreading Coordinator *Carrie Barker*
Production Manager *Beth Kundert*
Production/Costing Manager *Sherry Padden*
Production/Imaging and Media Development Manager *Linda Meehan Avenarius*
Visuals/Design Freelance Specialist *Mary L. Christianson*
Marketing Manager *Pamela S. Cooper*
Copywriter *M. J. Kelly*

Basal Text *10/12 Times Roman*
Display Type *Helvetica Condensed*
Typesetting System *Macintosh™ QuarkXPress™*
Paper Stock *50# Mirror Matte*

Vice President of Production and Business Development *Vickie Putman*
Vice President of Sales and Marketing *Bob McLaughlin*
Vice President of Business Development *Russ Domeyer*
Director of Marketing *John Finn*

 A Times Mirror Company

Consulting Editor Aileene Lockhart

Cover design by Lesiak/Crampton Design, Inc.

Cover photograph by Chicago Photographic Company with special
thanks to Donna Smith, Scott Guilfoil and the Senior PE
class of Maine East High School, Park Ridge, IL.

Copyedited by Laurie McGee; proofread by Paula Gieseman

Library of Congress Catalog Card Number: 95-76256

ISBN 0–697–23728–1

Printed in the United States of America by Times Mirror Higher Education Group, Inc.,
2460 Kerper Boulevard, Dubuque, IA 52001

10 9 8 7 6 5 4 3 2 1

Contents

Preface

The purpose of this book is to help prospective teachers acquire the skills necessary to design and implement effective instructional programs in secondary school physical education, including middle schools and junior and senior high schools. Effective programs require both effective instruction and a balanced curriculum. Either one without the other results in failure to educate students physically. Therefore, prospective teachers must be instructed in both aspects of the physical education program included in this book — curriculum and instruction.

As in the third edition, this fourth edition is closely tied to current research in education and physical education. It has been slightly reorganized to correspond with the order in which the chapters are usually taught, and each chapter has been updated.

Chapters 1 and 2 provide an introduction to the educational and teaching environment. Chapters 3 and 4 present theory essential to understand the characteristics of learners and the learning process, with implications for teaching physical education. This is followed in chapters 5 through 12 with procedures for planning, implementing, and evaluating the instructional program. Chapter 13 gives guidelines for developing accountability through teacher evaluation. Chapters 14 through 16 take the prospective teacher through the process of curriculum design and program evaluation.

This book follows the progression usually followed in teaching undergraduate physical education majors; that is, it assumes that lesson and unit planning and basic instructional skills are prerequisite to understanding the curriculum. It is suggested that students apply the principles taught by actually writing lessons and units and designing a curriculum as suggested in the various units of the text and the instructor's manual. In this way the entire process will be more meaningful to the learner.

The book is divided in such a way that portions of it can be used in several classes. For example, chapters 1 and 2 can be used in an introductory class, chapters 3 through 13 in a class on methods of teaching physical education, and chapters 14 through 16 to teach a separate unit on the curriculum. The entire text can also be used in one traditional methods course.

This text is unique in several ways. It *ties together all three of the learning domains* — cognitive, psychomotor, and affective — as a basis for the design and implementation of instructional strategies. The emphasis by the American Alliance for Health, Physical Education, Recreation and Dance on teaching students the conceptual background of physical education along with teaching physical fitness and skills requires that prospective teachers understand the cognitive and affective domains and strategies for teaching these skills. The development of positive student feelings toward physical education is the key toward continued participation by students in physical activities outside of school. Teaching traits such as sportspersonship and teamwork are also essential. Therefore, the affective domain should also be studied.

The book is *comprehensive* in nature, with a review of various models. However, in this fourth edition, we have simplified the organization of each chapter and made the book *more readable* by pruning sections commonly taught in other courses. It is hoped that instructors will use personal preferences and interpretation in using the book for specific classes and programs. In addition to *tying current research in education and physical education to curriculum design and instruction,* a large number of *practical applications and examples* are provided.

In the past, curriculum theory and design have been delayed until graduate school. However, since many beginning teachers are involved in curriculum development, an attempt has been made in the text to *integrate the process of curriculum design with that of designing instruction.* The curriculum chapters relate specifically to the entry-level teacher and can be taught most effectively by forming curriculum committees of three to five students and actually designing a curriculum.

The text includes a number of learning aids to help students focus on the concepts presented. *Study stimulators* at the beginning of each chapter are designed to introduce the main ideas of the chapter in a question format. A *step-by-step approach* helps students apply what is learned to actual school situations. *Review questions* are provided for further review and expansion of learning. For more in-depth study of a topic, a number of *suggested readings* have been included in the instructor's manual, along with some *learning activities* for both individual and class work. The book includes numerous *practical examples* in the areas of performance objectives, evaluation, preassessment, learning strategies, motivation, discipline, and classroom management.

Although the text is written on an undergraduate level, it can also be used as a resource for graduate students. It is suggested that graduate students form committees and design a resource unit and a school curriculum.

Instructor's Manual

An Instructor's Manual is available for instructors using *Instructional Strategies.* The manual contains an outline, suggested learning activities, suggested readings (annotated), and test questions for each chapter.

Acknowledgments

This text became a reality only through the encouragement and cooperation of many individuals, including family, students, colleagues, and friends. We wish to thank Elmo Roundy, former dean of the Brigham Young University College of Physical Education; Boyd Jarman, former department chair of the BYU Department of Physical Education; Dwayne Belt, formerly of the BYU Department of Secondary Education; and Marilyn Harding, Springville Junior High School, Springville, Utah; and many other colleagues for their support and encouragement throughout the development of the several editions of this text. Special thanks go to Cheryl Skousen and Lisa Boyack for typing many of the figures and tables. We also wish to thank those authors and publishers who generously consented to have their work reproduced or quoted.

CHAPTER 1

The Roles of Education and Physical Education

Study Stimulators

1. Is education synonymous with schooling?
2. What similarities exist among the various listings of educational goals? What differences are evident?
3. Have the purposes of education expressed in the past, in the present, and for the future remained the same?
4. Does the recent crisis in education forecast its death or its rebirth?
5. What global changes and trends might influence education? How might education be different in the future?
6. What characteristics do successful schools have?
7. What are the goals or outcomes of physical education?
8. How do the goals of physical education fit with the national goals of education?
9. What are the values of physical education?
10. What is the current status of physical education in the United States?
11. Describe the physical education program of the future.

> Nothing matters more—nothing. Education is the public enterprise in our country that is closest to people's hearts and most important to their lives. And education is the enterprise that is crucial to success in everything we attempt as a nation.
>
> Governor James B. Hunt, Jr.
> to the Task Force on Education for Economic Growth[1]

What Is Education?

Have you ever stopped to ponder the question "What is education?" As a high school or college graduate, do you feel "educated"? Do you think you will ever be truly educated?

Webster's New Collegiate Dictionary defines *educate* as "to provide schooling for."[2] How does this definition compare with your own definition of education? Do you think that education always results from, or even develops most efficiently through, formal schooling? Someone once said, "Don't let your schooling interfere with your education." Consider the classroom in which the students were interested in an exhibit of frogs, only to be told, "Come and sit down. We're going to have science now!" Consider, too, the following students, one listening to the driver education teacher talk about how to change a tire when the previous weekend she had rotated all the tires on the family car, or one jogging two laps of the track during physical education class when the night before he had run five miles preparing for an upcoming race.

1

Aristotle said, "All men by nature desire to know." Coming to "know" might take place in the formal classroom, but just as likely it will transpire in another setting. Historically, education occurred in the home, on the farm, or in the artisan's shop. Even today, much learning occurs on the job, in the home, or by way of the media. *Education is a process of learning, not a place.*

Today's advanced technological society requires continuous learning for effective living and working. Before the turn of the twentieth century, Spencer declared that the function of education is to prepare for complete living.[3] The living process, as characterized by society, is not constant, but ever changing. The educational process and its purposes must adapt to changes in society in order to prepare citizens to function in an effective way. Teachers play a key role in shaping society as they prepare citizens for complete living. To say that teachers and the education profession have a profound impact on society would be an understatement.

Krajewski and Pettier illustrated how education must adapt its purposes to changes in society with the following story:

> This is a story of civilization of some thousands of years ago. The people lived in the warm lands, covered by streams fed by glaciers far to the north. They supported themselves by spearing fish and by trapping tigers.
>
> The glaciers moved south. The lands became cold. The tigers left and sediment from the glaciers choked the rivers. Still, the people remained.
>
> Before the advent of the cold weather the people had prospered and in their prosperity they felt that they should embellish their society and they set up a school system. In that school system, quite logically, they taught the spearing of fish and the trapping of tigers. Then the cold came and the fish left and the tigers left. The people of this area now survived by snaring eel and hunting bear. And they prospered again. They went back to examine their school system. They asked the headmaster what he taught. And he said, "I teach spearing fish and trapping tigers." And they said, "Well, do you not teach snaring eels and hunting bears?" He said, "Well, of course, if you want a technological education; but for a well-rounded education I prefer the classics."[4]

The Purposes of Education

The educational process reflects what the people in a given society think, feel, believe, and do. Teachers in any setting are given the charge of training, disciplining, developing, and instructing. Teachers working in the formal school atmosphere must take this charge and enhance the purposes of education. In general, the purposes of education in any society include one or more of the following:

1. To preserve and maintain the desirable aspects of the society or culture by transmitting them to the young.
2. To teach the skills and competencies needed to function effectively as an adult member of society, both socially and vocationally.
3. To help the individual act in a responsible manner, both currently and in the future, and function within society so both the individual and the group attain their fullest potential.
4. To teach the individual to think critically, to constructively evaluate societal issues, and to influence the social order by contributing to ordered, purposeful change.

The purposes of education remain constant even though society, in which the educational structure operates, is an institution of change. As change occurs, the educational process adapts to meet the needs of society. Historically, American society has been a world role model, and its purposes of education have been unique in that they are intended to reach out to all Americans.

High school students socialize between classes.
© Spencer Grant/Photo Researchers, Inc.

The Current Status of Education

Throughout the history of American education in the twentieth century, groups have been organized with the charge to determine principles or goals for education. Table 1.1[5] shows many similarities in these educational goals from 1918 to 1990. All of the original seven cardinal principles have been reemphasized in at least two of the other five sets of goals. The major additions have been in the areas of respect for the environment, appreciation of beauty and achievement, economic understanding, and personal responsibility. The 1990 goals reflected a dramatic shift of emphasis from open-ended guidelines to national performance goals, with individual states determining strategies for reaching the goals. The plea was for excellence in education. The annual Gallup/Phi Delta Kappa polls on attitudes toward the public schools reveal a high priority for achieving the goals by the year 2000. However, respondents did not think it was very likely that we will achieve the goals, nor did they believe that much progress has been made.[6]

Conflicting reports exist as to the actual current status of education. Between 1983 and 1985 more than a dozen reports critical of current education practices were printed. One of the first was in 1983 when the National Commission on Excellence in Education issued its report, *A Nation at Risk*.[7] From it came the spine-tingling declaration that "the educational foundations of our

Table 1.1 A Perspective of the National Goals of Education

Cardinal Principles [1918]	Educational Policies Commission [1938–44]	Imperatives of Education [1964]
	Aims	
	Self-realization	
	Human relationship	
	Economic efficiency	
	Civic responsibility	
	Ten Imperative Needs of Youth	
Health (physical fitness)	Good health and physical fitness	Deal constructively with psychological tensions
Command of fundamental processes	Think rationally, express thoughts clearly, read and listen with understanding	
Vocation	Develop salable skills	Prepare for world of work
Civic education	Understand the rights and duties of a citizen. Develop respect for others, live and work cooperatively with others	Keep democracy working Work with other peoples of the world for human betterment
Worthy home membership	Understand the significance of the family	
Worthy use of leisure	Use leisure time well	Make the best use of leisure time
Ethical character	Develop ethical values and principles	Strengthen the moral fabric of society
	Know how to purchase and use goods and services intelligently	Make intelligent use of natural resources
	Develop capacities and appreciate beauty in literature, art, music, and nature	Discover and nurture creative talent
	Understand the influences of science on human life	
		Make urban life rewarding and satisfying

Table 1.1—Continued

National Goals [1973]	Seven New Cardinal Principles [1978]	Four Essential Goals for High Schools [1983]	National Education Goals [1990] By the year 2000:
Adjustment to change (mental health)	Personal competence and development	Develop critical thinking	
Communication skills	Skilled decision making	Prepare students for further education	*Preschool programs:* nutrition and health care, parental training
Computation skills			
Critical thinking		Increase students' career options	*Student testing:* national tests in grades 4, 8, 12
Occupational competence			
Responsibility for citizenship	Civic interest and participation	Build a spirit of community service	*Student performance:* students test first internationally in math and science
*Respect for law and authority	Global human concern		
*Appreciation of others	Family cohesiveness		*High school graduation rates:* rise to 90 percent
*Clarification of values	Moral responsibility and ethical action		
Clear perception of nature and environment	Respect for the environment		*Literacy:* every adult skilled and literate
Economic understanding			*Schools:* all safe and drug-free
*Appreciation of the achievements of individuals			*Teachers:*
*Knowledge of self			*Parents:*

* = Process goals

society are presently being eroded by a rising tide of mediocrity that threatens our very future as a nation and a people."[8] Recommendations to correct school shortcomings stemmed from this and other reports. The more important recommendations included the following:

1. The schools must stress science and math and move away from the "frills."
2. The teaching profession must be strengthened. The quality, pay, and autonomy of teachers must be improved and teacher education programs must be bolstered.
3. The school curriculum should be more related to the job market and to perceived needs of industry (including computer literacy).
4. Foreign-language instruction should be started in the elementary schools and should generally receive a high priority.
5. Students should spend more time in school, and their time should be used more effectively for instructional purposes.[9]

The 1990s began with a heightened public concern for education, including backing for a standardized national curriculum, upgraded educational outcomes, and support to increase taxes.[10] The first presidential State of the Union address of the decade highlighted societal ills affecting the educational process. Illiteracy, school dropouts, and drugs were targeted as national priorities.

On the other hand, the Sandia Report, which was commissioned by the U.S. Department of Energy, contradicts the results of the previous reports. This report, never allowed to be published, although it is supported by the research of others, stated that the schools are doing as well now as they ever have.[11] This is especially amazing "given the severe decline in other social institutions."[12] Bracey acknowledged that the schools have problems that need to be resolved. The schools most in need of help are the rural schools in low-income areas.

The preparation of children for the learning process becomes the critical factor in their ability to succeed in the current educational system. Students who come to school *prepared to learn* do well.[13] Lawson stated, "Schools cannot achieve their assigned goals if children and youth do not come to school ready and able to learn. . . . Only rarely do ['at-risk' children] come to school healthy, ready, and able to learn. All too frequently, they are hungry, need rest, and are seeking adult guidance and support. Today's schools cannot be expected to work for these young persons."[14] Herein lies the challenge for education in the future.

The Future of Education

The purposes of education in the future will be the same as the four purposes of education previously listed. How those purposes are achieved will change as society and technology change. A few of the issues that will shape schools of the future include site-based management, school choice, computer technology, needs of industry,[15] and the information superhighway.[16] The continued failing of other social institutions such as the family will place more pressure on schools to assume the roles formerly fulfilled by these institutions. It is not possible, however, to train teachers to serve all the roles demanded by society. For example, one area in which teachers are not adequately trained is serving as counselors for students who witness violent acts on a regular basis.

Although public education has been severely criticized in the past, it has always struggled to right itself. Based on past performance, the American educational system can continue to be the backbone of the nation. In the future, America will persist in its pursuit of excellence and will continue to attack the problems it faces in education. Futrell suggests that America must meet ethical as well as economic imperatives, preparing students not only for a life of earning money but also for a life of worth. She suggests that life in the schools should offer both excellence and equity enabling "every student—regardless of race, sex, or socioeconomic status—to reach his or her full potential."[17] Clearly, schools must adjust to the changes in society if they are to make progress. Futurists looking ahead to the year 2000 predict a shortage of qualified teachers and administrators,[18] and Hawley stressed that school administrators must find solutions to this problem.[19] Rising educational costs present another problem that must be addressed. Thus, most experts believe education must make dramatic changes in the future. Naisbitt stated, "we have to completely reconceptualize our educational system in order for it to survive."[20]

If American students are to keep pace with the rest of the world, the education workplace must be flexible to reflect these probabilities and meet the needs of all students. There must be academic quality, professional prestige, and wise expenditure of the tax dollar to silence the cries of "crisis in education."

Meeting Toffler's three goals for the education of the future would prepare students to meet the demands of a changing society.[21] They are

1. to learn how to learn;
2. to learn how to relate with others—to make and maintain rewarding human ties; and
3. to learn how to choose—to make decisions in an environment of too many choices.

To Learn How to Learn

Education must turn out men and women who are capable of educating themselves and their families as circumstances change. Silberman stated,

> "Merely to let children live free, natural, childlike lives," as Carleton Washburne, one of the giants of American progressivism, warned in 1925, "may be to fail to give them the training they need to meet the problems of later life." Thus Washburne insisted on a dual focus. "Every child has the right to live fully and naturally as a child," he wrote. "Every child has the right also to be prepared adequately for later effective living as an adult."[22]

To Learn How to Relate with Others

One of the goals of American education is to facilitate the fullest possible growth and development of each individual regardless of race, religion, sex, or ability. As this goal is realized each individual feels worthwhile and confident in interacting with others in society. If any person fails to develop his or her potential and to use it for worthy purposes, the educational system has fallen short of achieving its purposes.

To design educational programs that serve all students in ways adapted to their different capabilities and needs is a challenge to those who plan and conduct educational programs. The future success of America as a nation depends increasingly on the abilities of teachers to promote common concerns through cooperative problem solving that is based on fact, reason, and brotherly and sisterly love rather than authority or force. Mutual understanding and empathy for others are becoming essential in today's "pressure-cooker" society. For this reason, skills in cooperation must be emphasized in all classes, including physical education.

Another value traditionally held by American society is the freedom to interact with others while being responsible for one's own actions. Respect for the rights and feelings of others and sensitivity to the effect of one's actions on others are essential components of an individual's moral responsibility in society. Classroom management should be based on the principles of individual responsibility for one's own behavior. Chapter 10 describes how this can be done.

To Learn How to Choose

Coping with change demands that students explore possible alternatives for the future. Teachers can help students acquire these skills by reviewing ideas and skills that have helped people adjust in the past. They can also encourage students to search for generalizations or concepts that organize learning into meaningful wholes. Course subject matter needs to have wide application to everyday life, both now and in the future. Students must be taught to think seriously about why they are doing what they are doing and to learn the consequences for the decisions they make.[23] Thus, critical thinking and problem-solving skills must become important components of the educational program. The development of these skills is discussed in chapter 4.

Futrell summarizes the futurists' thoughts:

> As the intellectually demanding and precariously balanced world of the 21st century comes into view, it seems clear that the mission of education must be not to train people to serve the purposes of others, but to develop their capacity to question the purposes of others. We must bolster students' will to seek wisdom. We must enable them to think creatively about complex issues, to act responsibly, and—when necessary—to act selflessly. We must convince them that the gross national product is not a measure of our worth as a people.[24]

With all of the reform efforts, the calls to completely restructure the educational system, and increases in technology, the successful schools of the future will look much different from the schools of today. Toch[25] and Vickers[26] have proposed some characteristics of schools of the future.

1. Students will choose the schools they want to attend and will choose the programs in which they are involved based upon interest and ability.
2. Program specialization will occur, with a growth in "alternate" or "magnet schools."
3. Schools will be smaller. The large impersonal comprehensive junior and senior high schools will be dismantled and replaced with specialized schools. Several such schools may be housed within one building.
4. Schools will be academically vigorous and will have higher expectations for students within their capacity to learn.
5. "The schools will emphasize a more humane experience in learning, stressing the need for increased interaction between teachers and students in a knowledge based, academically rich environment."[27]

Physical Education and the Purposes of Education

Physical education is the study, practice, and appreciation of the art and science of human movement. It is a part of the total process of education. Movement is natural and basic to existence for most human beings. "Children . . . are prewired for movement at birth."[28] Although movement itself is spontaneous, the refinement and perfection of movement is an educational process that is often entrusted to physical educators. This charge must not be taken lightly. The body, that machine that enacts movement, should be highly esteemed. "The human body is sacred. . . . [I]t is a solemn duty of mankind to protect and preserve it from pollutions and unnecessary wastage and weakness."[29]

Physical educators today face the challenge of legitimizing physical education content in American public school curriculums, although it has been a regular part of such courses of study for many years. The worth of physical education programs and the human body was emphasized as early as 1974 by the National Association of Secondary School Principals:

> Today's physical education programs are aimed at helping students acquire constructive concepts and desirable habits regarding the preservation of our environment's most prized

natural resource: the well-tuned, efficiently functional human body and all its healthy competitive components. . . .

Furthermore, physical education has earned a role as one of the essential elements in any curriculum designed to educate the whole person.[30]

Since physical education is a part of the total education of a student, the curriculum in physical education must be based on a sound philosophy that, in turn, is consistent with the social and educational philosophies of the time and place in which it functions. The goals of physical education should be integrated with the national goals of education listed in Table 1.1. An evaluation of these lists reveals that approximately one-fourth of the goals relate directly to outcomes attained in physical education programs. Most of the remaining goals relate indirectly to outcomes of such programs. For example, physical education contributes to (1) health and physical fitness through the development of organic vigor; (2) the worthy use of leisure through the development of skills for use in leisure-time activity; (3) ethical character as one develops a sense of fair play, decision-making ability, and appreciation for both winning and losing; (4) respect for others and appreciation of achievement as one participates on a team; (5) appreciation of the arts in such areas as dance; (6) an understanding of science as the workings of the human body are demonstrated; (7) personal competence through the enhancement of psychomotor skills; and (8) respect for the environment through participation in outdoor and challenge activities.

The specific values of physical education are not always reflected in national goals of education and need to be explicitly defined. Other more indirect correlations relate to such outcomes as critical thinking, career options, making life more satisfying, dealing with psychological tensions, and knowledge of self. Specific values of physical education, while appreciated by the professional, often need application and clarification for the student and public.

The Values of Physical Education

Seefeldt and Vogel listed 20 values of physical education (activity) deemed important by the National Association for Sport and Physical Education.[31] They are summarized in the following list:

1. Promotes and assists the early growth, development, and function of the nervous system such as changes in brain structure and refinement of perceptual abilities involving vision, balance, and tactile sensations.
2. Promotes cognitive function through imitation, symbolic play, the development of language, and the use of symbols in the early years, and aids in developing learning strategies; decision making; acquiring, retrieving, and integrating information; and solving problems in the later years.
3. Fortifies the mineralization of the skeleton and promotes the maintenance of lean body tissue while reducing the deposition of fat. Obesity is regulated because energy expenditure is increased, appetite suppressed, metabolic rate increased, and lean body mass increased.
4. Leads to proficiency in the neuromuscular skills that are the basis for successful participation in games, dances, sports, and leisure activities.
5. Improves aerobic fitness, muscle endurance, muscle power, and muscle strength while improving cardiac function as indicated by an increased stroke volume, cardiac output, blood volume, and total hemoglobin.
6. Prevents the onset of some diseases and postpones the debilitating effects of old age. It is an effective deterrent to coronary heart disease due to its effects on blood

lipids, blood pressure, obesity, and capacity for physical work and is associated with a reduction in atherosclerotic diseases.

7. Provides an avenue for developing social competence, moral reasoning, problem solving, and creativity while enhancing self-concept and self-esteem as indicated by increased confidence, assertiveness, emotional stability, independence, and self-control.
8. Promotes a more positive attitude toward physical activity that leads to a more active lifestyle during unscheduled leisure time.
9. Provides an effective deterrent to mental illness and the alleviation of mental stress.
10. Improves the psychosocial and physiological functions of mentally and physically handicapped individuals.

In a study conducted with prospective physical education teachers to determine the values of physical education they considered to be most important, health and fitness and general well-being were ranked highest; social experience, recreation-relaxation, and emotional release were ranked lower. Females tended to view physical education as a social experience more than males did.[32]

Strong historical support of the value of physical education has not been enough to stop the reduction of physical education requirements and programs in the schools. The worth of exercise is not in question, but the priority or rank of courses in the curriculum most certainly is. Given the climate in schools for more academics, and the emphasis on athletics and winning teams, it is understandable that the regular physical education program is suffering. Some leaders in the profession support changes in school physical education programs. Lawson suggests that sport and exercise programs have reached unprecedented levels of popularity and the school is just one of many organizations offering opportunities for sport and exercise. He suggests that although schools offer more and different activities today in more expansive facilities using more modern equipment, our assumptions about physical education classes, teachers, and benefits "have not changed appreciably." He questions whether programs can remain unchanged with so many other opportunities for instruction and participation.[33]

The atmosphere today is right for dedicated physical educators to make a difference because Americans, many of whom may retain unfavorable attitudes about their bodies from adolescence, support the benefits of exercise and movement as a contributor to health and wellness. A 1986 survey indicated that 38 percent of American women and 34 percent of men were dissatisfied with their appearance and body dimensions, up from 32 percent of women and 15 percent of men in 1972. This same survey also revealed that 55 percent of women and 41 percent of men were dissatisfied with their current weight.[34]

Support for the benefits of physical education and the importance of physical activity has occurred on several fronts. For example, Vogel indicated that physical education can serve a unique role in a child's education: "Physical education, like no other curriculum area, lends itself to a student's total development."[35] Staffo concurred when he stated, "Physical education, *if it is taught properly*, is just as important as any other subject in the curriculum and can make just as valuable a contribution to the total growth and overall development of the student."[36] *Healthy People 2000* indicated the importance of physical activity among adolescents and young adults, stating that physical education provides the best medium for fostering and encouraging physical activity among young people.

> It is important for adolescents and young adults to lay the foundation for chronic disease prevention by the promotion and maintenance of healthy lifestyles. . . . Further, the

adoption of dietary and physical activity habits that will reduce the onset of obesity will help reduce the likelihood of coronary heart disease, diabetes, and high blood pressure. The case of physical activity is important because as students leave the school setting they lose the physical and social supports and incur time constraints that can result in decreased levels of physical activity. It is especially important for adolescents and young adults to recognize the importance of regular light to moderate physical activity in the prevention of weight gain associated with leaving the high school setting.[37]

The Purposes of Physical Education

Physical education has much to contribute to education. The American Alliance for Health, Physical Education, Recreation and Dance (AAHPERD) has taken the lead in assessing professional goals and outcomes for physical educators. Anchored to a time-tested purpose statement, updated outcomes guide professionals in generating meaningful programs. It takes the committed teacher, however, to breathe life into these written purposes, outcomes, and objectives for the benefit of all students, both casual performers and disciplined athletes.

A program *aim* or *purpose* is an ideal that acts as a compass by giving direction to the total program. It also provides a basis for designing and evaluating curricular offerings. The following statement is a purpose for physical education:

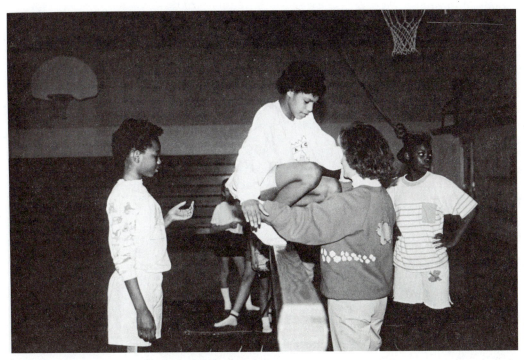

Well-planned and implemented physical education programs help students improve existing skills and experience success in physical activity.
© Martin R. Jones/Unicorn Stock Photos

Physical education is that integral part of total education which contributes to the development of the individual through the natural medium of physical activity—human movement. It is a carefully planned sequence of learning experiences designed to fulfill the growth, development, and behavior needs of each student.[38]

Since an aim is something that is usually distant (in the future) or ideal, it must be broken down into a number of *outcomes* or *goals* that, when achieved, will direct us toward the aim. These instructional goals are statements of more immediate achievements expected of students in the school. The statements shown in Table 1.2 are the instructional outcomes for physical education developed by the National Association for Sport and Physical Education. The five areas include physical skills, physical fitness, regular participation in activity, knowledge about activity, and attitudes about activity. Leaders in the profession have generally accepted these outcomes as the basic goals of physical education.

Physical Skills

The development and refinement of neuromuscular skill essential for efficient everyday movement (posture and body mechanics), as well as for efficient movement in a variety of activities, leads to less energy wasted in skill performance and more enjoyment in activity. Basic movement (fundamental) skills, sport skills, and skills in rhythmic activities are all important components of this aim.

Physical Fitness

President John F. Kennedy once said, "Fitness is the basis for all other forms of excellence."[39] The development of physical fitness and health contributes to effective living and enjoyment of life. Fitness needs to be taught with two goals in mind. Students should be expected to achieve fitness, and acquire the knowledge and desire to make it a lifelong pursuit. An important aspect of physical fitness is health-related fitness, including such components as muscular strength and endurance, flexibility, cardiovascular endurance, and body composition. Motor fitness expands the definition to include such areas as balance, agility, coordination, and speed.

Participation

Physical skills remain sharp and health is enhanced through regular physical activity. Meaningful physical education programs provide successful experiences and instill joy and motivation for physical activity, leading to lifelong participation.

Knowledge

A knowledge and understanding of the importance of physical activity and how it relates to one's health and well-being is essential. Knowledge of scientific principles related to physical activity, exercise, and health must be included in the physical education instructional program.[40] Dr. Ernest Wynder of the American Health Foundation said, "It's as important to teach kids about the body as about math and science."[41] Such an understanding must include skills in designing and implementing a fitness or weight-control program, evaluating fitness, and safe participation in activity. Knowledge about game rules, strategies, and techniques of participation enhance participation in a variety of physical activities. Game play can also increase one's ability to solve problems in highly emotional situations. Students also need to learn the processes for acquiring physical skills and the basic principles of movement such as equilibrium and absorption of force that are common to all activities.

Table 1.2   Definition of the Physically Educated Person and Outcome Statements

A Physically Educated Person:

• HAS Learned Skills Necessary to Perform a Variety of Physical Activities

1. Moves using concepts of body awareness, space awareness, effort, and relationships

2. Demonstrates competence in a variety of manipulative, locomotor, and nonlocomotor skills

3. Demonstrates competence in combinations of manipulative, locomotor, and nonlocomotor skills performed individually and with others

4. Demonstrates competence in many different forms of physical activity

5. Demonstrates proficiency in a few forms of physical activity

6. Has learned how to learn new skills

• IS Physically Fit

7. Assesses, achieves, and maintains physical fitness

8. Designs safe personal fitness programs in accordance with principles of training and conditioning

• DOES Participate Regularly in Physical Activity

9. Participates in health-enhancing physical activity at least three times a week

10. Selects and regularly participates in lifetime physical activities

• KNOWS the Implications of and the Benefits from Involvement in Physical Activities

11. Identifies the benefits, costs, and obligations associated with regular participation in physical activity

12. Recognizes the risk and safety factors associated with regular participation in physical activity

13. Applies concepts and principles to the development of motor skills

14. Understands that wellness involves more than being physically fit

15. Knows the rules, strategies, and appropriate behaviors for selected physical activities

16. Recognizes that participation in physical activity can lead to multicultural and international understanding

17. Understands that physical activity provides the opportunity for enjoyment, self-expression, and communication

• VALUES Physical Activity and Its Contributions to a Healthful Lifestyle

18. Appreciates the relationships with others that result from participation in physical activity

19. Respects the role that regular physical activity plays in the pursuit of lifelong health and well-being

20. Cherishes the feelings that result from regular participation in physical activity

Source: National Association for Sport and Physical Education. Physical Education Outcomes Committee. Definition of the Physically Educated Person: Outcomes of Quality Physical Education Programs. 1990.

Attitudes

The attitudes students have toward physical activity and toward their feelings of successful accomplishment in activity influence future participation. We need to ensure that only positive attitudes and appreciations result from physical education classes. Not only do students need to see the value in what they are doing, but they also need to derive joy and pleasure from doing it. Desirable social values—such as cooperation, commitment, leadership, followership, sportspersonship, and courtesy—can be taught through participation in physical education activities.

Physical activity also provides an opportunity for releasing emotional tension through appropriate channels. When participation occurs in a supportive environment, students can increase their feelings of self-esteem, release tension, and develop initiative, self-direction, and creativity. Hellison suggested that "our profession needs to achieve some balance between helping people and developing and promulgating the subject matter (skills, fitness, strategies, etc.)."[42]

According to Hellison, "the affective domain is not getting enough attention in today's schools, because kids are facing more personal and social problems than ever before."[43] Affective goals in physical education include: "(1) social conventions such as appropriate dress and language; (2) appreciation and affections for physical activity and its benefits; (3) psychological constructs such as self-esteem, self-efficacy, courage, motivation, and independence; (4) moral qualities such as respect for the rights of others, compassion, and justice; and (5) aesthetic qualities such as playfulness and gracefulness."[44]

Although the leaders of physical education generally agree on the goals of physical education, they differ in how they view the priority (or ranking) of these goals. To be effective, aims and goals must be worthwhile, in harmony with educational and physical educational philosophy, attainable, and incorporated in the classroom. The question that remains to be answered is whether the goals deemed important for physical education are realized in actual practice. The priority that individual teachers give each goal determines whether it is planned for and incorporated. Placek did a study to discover what influences determine planning by physical education teachers. She concluded that teachers did not view student learning or achievement to be as important as classroom environment. Teachers seemed to equate success in the classroom with keeping students *busy, happy,* and *good.*[45] One must ask whether physical educators have their priorities straight.

Objectives in Physical Education

The overall aims and purposes of physical education remain constant. Objectives, though, can more easily be adjusted to meet the needs of individual students. Therefore, the more immediate goals and objectives are continually changing to meet the needs of a changing society. Lashuk and Vickers conducted a study to examine which physical education objectives were perceived to be of the highest priority by students, parents, teachers, and teacher educators. In rank order the following objectives were the most important:

1. To develop a positive attitude toward physical activity (Attitude).
2. To acquire knowledge on how to become fit (Knowledge, Fitness).
3. To develop physical fitness (Fitness).
4. To learn a variety of sports for recreation (Physical Skills).
5. To conduct oneself in socially acceptable ways (Social Skills).[46]

Table 1.3 displays the attitudes of students in elementary, junior, and senior high schools toward physical education and other subjects in the schools.

Table 1.3 Rank Order of Students' Attitudes toward Subjects: By Level of Schooling

Liking

Upper Elementary			Junior High			Senior High		
Subject	% Like	N	Subject	% Like	N	Subject	% Like	N
Arts	93.2	1621	Arts	85.9	5130	Arts	83.6	6903
Physical ed.	86.9	1615	Voc./Career ed.	81.0	4912	Voc./Career ed.	80.8	6884
Math	81.5	1609	Physical ed.	80.1	5177	Physical ed.	79.8	6969
Reading/English	81.3	1622	Math	74.8	5160	English	72.1	7046
Science	80.9	1604	English	69.3	5231	Math	65.0	6966
Social studies	65.6	1617	Social studies	66.0	5184	Social studies	65.0	6958
			Science	66.1	5068	Science	64.1	6908
			Foreign lang.	62.0	4734	Foreign lang.	52.8	6825

Importance

Upper Elementary			Junior High			Senior High		
Subject	% Imp.	N	Subject	% Imp.	N	Subject	% Imp.	N
Math	93.9	1618	Math	95.0	5154	Math	94.3	6988
Reading/English	93.5	1617	English	91.5	5220	English	93.6	7043
Science	89.4	1593	Voc./Career ed.	85.1	4972	Voc./Career ed.	85.9	6899
Social studies	88.9	1614	Social studies	83.1	5146	Science	79.2	6863
Physical ed.	87.2	1621	Science	78.8	5045	Social studies	77.8	6961
Arts	80.2	1610	Physical ed.	75.3	5174	Physical ed.	67.4	6998
			Foreign lang.	73.5	4842	Arts	65.3	6929
			Arts	70.4	5103	Foreign lang.	65.1	6784

Table 1.3—Continued

Difficulty*

Upper Elementary

Subject	% Hard	% Easy	% Just Right	N
Social studies	19.9	47.1	33.0	1602
Math	17.7	55.0	27.3	1610
Science	14.5	54.5	31.0	1594
Reading/English	10.7	46.3	43.0	1613
Physical ed.	10.3	67.1	22.6	1609
Arts	3.4	78.6	18.0	1608

Junior High

Subject	% Hard	% Easy	% Just Right	N
Foreign lang.	23.3	29.2	47.5	219
Social studies	17.9	27.5	54.6	1420
Science	17.1	29.0	53.9	1056
Math	14.0	32.2	53.8	1670
English	12.5	31.6	55.9	1644
Voc./Career ed.	8.2	42.0	49.8	1023
Arts	7.6	45.7	46.7	1176
Physical ed.	5.0	45.8	49.2	754

Senior High

Subject	% Hard	% Easy	% Just Right	N
Science	27.8	25.2	47.0	1313
Math	26.0	28.3	45.7	1587
Foreign lang.	24.2	29.8	46.0	526
English	16.1	32.3	51.6	1793
Social studies	15.9	35.2	48.9	1749
Arts	9.3	45.4	45.3	1474
Voc./Career ed.	9.1	42.5	48.4	1726
Physical ed.	7.8	54.0	38.2	768

*As perceived only by students who were currently enrolled in each subject.

Source: Goodlad, John I. *A Place Called School: Prospects for the Future*. New York: McGraw-Hill Book Company, 1984, pp. 116–17.

Physical Education Today

The cries of "crisis in education" heard in the 1980s had a resounding and deeply felt effect on physical education programs in the schools. The *Nation at Risk*[47] report questioned the inclusion of physical education courses in the school curriculum and recommended that school boards include more "academic" subjects in course requirements at the expense of physical education and certain other subjects. Jewett acknowledged at that time that "education is receiving a great deal of attention but, unfortunately, most of this attention is not supportive of physical education."[48] As a result of the attacks on physical education, fewer teachers were needed. A surplus of physical education teachers was first reported in the 1985–86 teaching year[49] and continued into the 1990s.

Consequently, teacher morale was low at that time. Griffin outlined the following eight obstacles to excellence that face teachers of physical education:

1. Lack of teacher or program evaluation
2. Lack of formal incentive or reward
3. Lack of professional support and development
4. Inadequate facilities, equipment, and scheduling
5. Failure to include teachers in decision making
6. Compliance and smooth operations valued over teaching competence
7. Acceptance of mediocrity
8. Isolation (for the most part, working alone)[50]

At the beginning of the 1990s, Graham reviewed U.S. school physical education programs. He cited improved elementary school programs, exposure to a variety of activities rather than skill and fitness development in the middle schools, and unsatisfactory programs in the high schools.[51] Robbins represented Canadian schools much more optimistically, citing an increasing emphasis on quality, daily physical education at all levels.[52] Nevertheless, few professionals question that a major crisis exists in secondary physical education in the United States.[53] Rink suggests five reasons for this crisis:

1. Failure of the profession to articulate the goals of the program
2. Failure on the part of state and local districts to have any expectations for secondary programs or hold secondary teachers accountable for good programs or good teaching
3. Failure on the part of teachers to act professionally irrespective of a lack of accountability
4. Failure of teacher preparation programs to prepare teachers for the real world and to support the teachers in the schools
5. Conditions beyond the control of the profession such as decreased financial resources, emphasis on back-to-basics, large classes, and so on[54]

Although physical educators continue to face a struggle, a hopeless attitude is not warranted. Lambert emphasized that "there are problems in secondary physical education, but none that cannot be addressed optimistically."[55] The educational reform movement has infused hope and opportunity for change. Lovell and Reinhard declare that physical educators who seize the opportunity to get involved by demonstrating leadership are in what these researchers call the catbird seat. They feel no other subject taught has this potential.[56]

We need to think differently about secondary physical education.[57] Physical educators suggest the following guidelines to help teachers achieve excellence amid struggle: (1) Prepare for and adjust to workplace realities, (2) align goals and practices so that students master meaningful skills, (3) avoid professional isolation, (4) take full membership in the school community and involve citizens in the program, and (5) educate administrators so they can give effective support.[58] Magnotta suggests the need to reeducate physical educators as to what basic outcomes should be stressed, to motivate youth to want to be physically active, and to reeducate parents to guide their children to make proper wellness choices.[59] Mueller reminds teachers that "education is not a product, it is a process."[60] However, Finn challenges this "old" conception and emphasizes that only when the process succeeds so that the product is student achievement has education happened.[61] The foundation of such a process must be a sound curriculum based on student achievement of both cognitive and psychomotor skills. Siedentop believes that "high school physical education can be central to the adolescent curriculum and serve their developmental needs as well as any subject matter and better than most."[62] He points out that good high school programs exist all over the country and that they exhibit four commonalities: (1) Someone exerted leadership to get the program started, (2) the programs stood for something specific, such as good fitness, (3) the teachers were excited and (4) few teachers had major coaching commitments.

The current professional challenge gives educators an opportunity to proclaim the worth of what they do. On the heels of the *Nation at Risk* report, Secretary of Education William J. Bennett published *First Lessons: A Report on Elementary Education in America*.[63] It gave a real boost to the necessity of including physical education programs in the elementary school curriculum. The report pointed out that "American children are in remarkably bad shape"[64] and presented facts from The National Children and Youth Fitness Study I (NCYFS) published in 1985.[65] It revealed that 40 percent of boys ages 6 to 11 could do only one pull-up; 25 percent couldn't do any. Fifty-five percent of all girls couldn't do any pull-ups. Fifty percent of girls ages 6 to 17 and 30 percent of boys 6 to 12 couldn't run a mile in less than 10 minutes. The study also pointed out that American young people have become fatter since the 1960s. This finding was substantiated in the NCYFS II, which investigated children ages 6 to 9.[66] If we consider the amount of television children watch, usually eating junk food at the same time, these results are not surprising. The NCYFS II study pointed out differences in reported hours of television watched by children, as high as six hours per day, with most studies ranging between two hours and three-and-a-half hours per day. One thing is clear—"the amount of time a child spends in watching television seems to be related to how active the child is."[67] *First Lessons* emphasized that physical education programs belong in the elementary schools "not only because they promote health and well-being, but because they contribute tangibly to academic achievement."[68] Physical education can have an effect on the academic achievement of secondary students as well. A California school began a physical fitness program in 1972. One year later the students had gone from 55 percent to 60 percent working at grade level to nearly 80 percent.[69] *First Lessons* also stressed that today's children don't get a test of fitness when they are young because programs have been dropped.[70] George Allen, chairman of the President's Council on Physical Fitness and Sports, stated that physical education used to be a required subject in schools, just like English, math, history, and economics. He pointed out that in many states it has been almost eliminated from the curriculum.[71]

As a result of the Youth Fitness Hearings the following recommendations were made by the President's Council: All children K-12 should

1. participate in *daily* physical education that emphasizes both fitness and skills;
2. be tested twice a year in fitness;

Concurrent Resolution of the U.S. House of Representatives and the U.S. Senate.

To encourage State and local governments and local educational agencies to provide high quality daily physical education programs for all children in kindergarten through grade 12.

Whereas physical education is essential to the development of growing children;
Whereas physical education helps improve the overall health of children by improving their cardiovascular endurance, muscular strength and power, and flexibility, and by enhancing weight regulation, bone development, posture, skillful moving, active lifestyle habits, and constructive use of leisure time;
Whereas physical education increases children's mental alertness, academic performance, readiness to learn, and enthusiasm for learning;
Whereas physical education helps improve the self-esteem, interpersonal relationships, responsible behavior, and independence of children;
Whereas children who participate in high quality daily physical education programs tend to be more healthy and physically fit;
Whereas physically fit adults have significantly reduced risk factor for heart attacks and strokes;
Whereas the Surgeon General, in Objectives for the Nation, recommends increasing the number of school mandated physical education programs that focus on health-related physical fitness;
Whereas the Secretary of Education in First Lessons—A Report on Elementary Education in America, recognized that elementary schools have a special mandate to provide elementary school children with the knowledge, habits, and attitudes that will equip the children for a fit and healthy life; and
Whereas a high quality daily physical education program for all children in kindergarten through grade 12 is an essential part of a comprehensive education:
Now therefore, be it Resolved by the House of Representatives and Senate (concurring), That the Congress encourages State and local governments and local educational agencies to provide high quality daily physical education programs for all children in kindergarten through grade 12.

Figure 1.1   Concurrent Resolution of the U.S. House of Representatives and the U.S. Senate.

3. understand and be able to apply exercise science principles;
4. have posture checks, body composition assessment, routine health screenings, and appropriate follow-ups;
5. have remedial attention as needed; and
6. if disabled, be identified and provided with appropriate programs.[72]

Recommendation number one got support from the federal government in 1986 and 1987 when a concurrent resolution was adopted by the U.S. House of Representatives and the U.S. Senate. As shown in figure 1.1, this resolution stated that daily physical education programs should be required for all children, grades K–12.

Support for physical education has come in other areas as well. *Healthy People 2000*[73] stated that schools have a special role in enhancing and maintaining the health of children. "Daily school physical education programs can play an important role in helping children and youth maintain a high level of physical activity year-round."[74] Priority One of the report was titled Physical Activity and Fitness Goals. School-related objectives included the following:

1.1 Reduce coronary heart disease deaths to no more than 100 per 100,000 people.
1.2 Reduce overweight to a prevalence of no more than 20 percent among people aged 20 and older and no more than 15 percent among adolescents aged 12 through 19.
1.3 Increase to at least 30 percent the proportion of people aged 6 and older who engage regularly, preferably daily, in light to moderate physical activity for at least 30 minutes per day.
1.4 Increase to at least 20 percent the proportion of people aged 18 and older and to at least 75 percent the proportion of children and adolescents aged 6 through 17 who engage in vigorous physical activity that promotes the development and maintenance of cardiorespiratory fitness 3 or more days per week for 20 or more minutes per occasion.
1.5 Reduce to no more than 15 percent the proportion of people aged 6 and older who engage in no leisure-time physical activity.
1.6 Increase to at least 40 percent the proportion of people aged 6 and older who regularly perform physical activities that enhance and maintain muscular strength, muscular endurance, and flexibility.
1.7 Increase to at least 50 percent the proportion of overweight people aged 12 and older who have adopted sound dietary practices combined with regular physical activity to attain an appropriate body weight.
1.8 Increase to at least 50 percent the proportion of children and adolescents in 1st through 12th grade who participate in daily school physical education.
1.9 Increase to at least 50 percent the proportion of school physical education class time that students spend being physically active, preferably engaged in lifetime physical activities.[75]

AAHPERD conducted a survey during the summer of 1993 to determine physical education requirements in each of the 50 states and the District of Columbia. The survey showed only one state, Illinois, required daily physical education for all students (the requirement was later dropped). Only four states required all students to take physical education for a specific amount of time in grades K–12 (Illinois, Kentucky, Hawaii, and Rhode Island). In 1987, 42 states mandated physical education. By 1993 that number had increased to 46.[76] However, only 13 states require physical education specialists to teach elementary physical education.[77]

Although physical education programs and student outcomes were being scrutinized in the 1980s, the popularity of the classes remained high. Goodlad reported that students ranked physical education high for "liking" but relatively low for "importance" and "difficulty."[78] A survey done in 1989 revealed that 87 percent of teachers felt physical education should be required of students whether they were planning to go to college or not (up from 74 percent in 1984). Only 45 percent of the U.S. public felt this way. The majority of teachers (41 percent) felt physical education should be required for all four years of high school.[79]

Historically, physical education movements and programs have undergone significant changes in direction. At the present time the schools are dictating these changes. "Our nation's schools are currently undergoing the most far-reaching reforms and renewal processes since the turn of the century."[80] As a result of this reform movement, citizens are asking whether physical education is a viable subject in the school curriculum. If the profession is to survive in the future, physical educators must answer the critics by proving its worth and expanding its base from the schools to all citizens of the community who incorporate similar purposes as a way of life. "The reform movement in education provides a golden opportunity for a new physical education, one with the characteristics many of us have been requesting for some time."[81]

Physical Education in the Future

The physical educator of the future will have to offer programs that meet the needs of a changing American society. It has been predicted that health and fitness levels will be higher than ever in the twenty-first century. Medical technology, although costly, will enable people to maintain life almost indefinitely.[82] While people will live longer, they will also assume more of the responsibility for their own health. As Naisbitt pointed out, at least 100 million Americans, almost half the population, are now exercising in some way—up from only about one-quarter of the population in 1960. As the United States ceased to be a nation of farmers and factory workers, it became a country of joggers, bicyclists, and weight lifters. Americans have also reduced their fat intake, cut down on smoking, switched from hard liquor to wine, and increased health food sales. The corporate world has increased the number of fitness programs available to employees.[83] There is no indication that these trends will change in the future. Therefore, physical educators need to capitalize on them and guide both the young and the old in their pursuit of a healthy lifestyle.

Although conditions warrant optimism for the future public school physical education teacher, each must be a committed and dedicated professional ready to make the changes necessary to overcome the problems of the workplace. Ellis suggests that for physical educators to be employable they

> should be able to perform well at . . . teaching aerobics, weight-training and conditioning, an outdoor pursuit, a racquet sport and a team sport; organizing and publicizing a special event; refereeing a recreational sport; and creating a publicity release. They should also be able to give advice to their clients on nutrition, injury management, stress control, exercise and, through their own lifestyle, physical educators should provide a good role model.[84]

It is critical that future physical educators convince the public that they offer meaningful programs for all students and not just athletes. Each professional must communicate to society the worth of what he or she does. Freeman pointed out:

> For too long the physical educator has been cut off in the gym, with a reputation of having few interests beyond the sports pages. That type of physical educator cannot survive in the modern world, must less the future, because that type has become an educational dinosaur.[85]

Graham suggests the following changes in U.S. schools if situations are to improve:[86]

1. *Create a positive image.* Teachers must create exciting, germane, and effective programs.

2. *Point out that physical education and athletics are not synonymous.* Programs must stress their importance for all students.

3. *Identify goals and purposes of programs realistically and clearly.* Such goals should include accountability for student learning. This may involve a trimming of curriculum.

4. *Be wary of (fitness) testing.* Programs should not be evaluated only on student improvement on test items.

5. *Increase research.* The needs and problems of school programs must be studied and results used to increase quantity and quality of programs.

6. *Create more teaching opportunities.* Programs to recognize master teachers and allow them more variety will keep the best teachers teaching.

Robbins recommends that quality, daily physical education be a working goal for every school in Canada.[87]

Vickers established six guidelines for a new physical education:

1. Students will be given the opportunity to enroll in secondary programs, with two tiers of involvement, one called the lifestyle program and the other the career program. (The lifestyle program is where students learn about the human body, to be physically active, and to acquire new physical skills. The career program is for those with career aspirations such as athletes, teachers, coaches, sport psychologists, scientists).
2. Both tiers are based on a cross-disciplinary foundation.
3. Both are based on a knowledge *to* activity integration.
4. Both tiers are taught throughout the school year, with new knowledge presented continuously throughout a student's 7–12 career.
5. In both tiers evaluation is individualized for the motor skill and fitness components and occurs only in those areas where students have sustained instruction and practice.
6. Both tiers are guided by and supported by textbooks, the first developed to be placed in the hands of students in our field in North America.[88]

According to Staffo, "It is not too late to not only correct our past mistakes and re-establish our lost respect but to stand up, state, and justify the need for health and physical education taught K-12 by people degreed and certified in these areas. Too much is at stake if we don't . . . the health and fitness of a nation."[89]

Siedentop likewise has indicated the need to revitalize American secondary physical education.[90] He stated, "School physical education is still the only process that has the *potential* for educating and socializing all children and youth toward lifespan activity involvement. Schools in our society are not now achieving that potential, nor is physical education. It is time to create a new American physical education."[91]

Review Questions

1. Define education.
2. What are the four purposes of education?
3. Historically, how have the goals of education changed?
4. What are the current goals of education?
5. What are some of the issues that face education in the future?
6. What are Toffler's three goals for education in the future?
7. What are the five major outcomes that describe a physically educated person?
8. What problems exist in physical education today? How can they be resolved?
9. What should physical education be like in the future?

References

1. Task Force on Education for Economic Growth. (1983). *Action for excellence: A comprehensive plan to improve our nation's schools.* Washington, DC: Education Commission of the States.
2. By permission. From *Webster's New Collegiate Dictionary,* copyright 1981, G. & C. Merriam Co., Publishers of the Merriam-Webster Dictionaries.
3. Spencer, H. (1860). *Education: Intellectual, moral, and physical* (p. 31). New York: Appleton.
4. Krajewski, F. R., & Pettier, G. L. (Eds.). (1973). *Education: Where it's been, where it's at, where it's going* (p. 134). Columbus, OH: Merrill; Peddiwell, J. A. (1939). *The saber tooth curriculum.* New York: McGraw-Hill.
5. Commission on Reorganization of Secondary Education. (1918). *Cardinal principles of secondary education* (pp. 7–15). Washington, DC: U.S. Government Printing Office; Educational Policies Commission. (1938). *The purposes of education in American democracy* (pp. 50–123). Washington, DC: National Education Association; Educational Policies Commission. (1944). *Education for ALL American youth* (pp. 225–226). Washington, DC: National Education Association; American Association of School Administrators. (1966). *Imperatives in education.* Washington, DC: Author; Brown, B. F. (1973). *The reform of secondary education* (pp. 32–35). New York: McGraw-Hill; Gross, R. E. (1978, December). Seven new cardinal principles. *Phi Delta Kappan, 60,* 291–293; Boyer, E. L. (1983). *High school: A report on secondary education in America.* New York: Harper & Row. [The Carnegie Report]. *Goals 2000 Educate America Act.* March 21, 1994 Congressional Record, U.S. House of Representatives.
6. Elam, S. M., Rose, L. C., & Gallup, A. M. (1991–1993). The 23rd, 24th, and 25th annual Gallup/Phi Delta Kappa poll of the public's attitudes toward the public schools. *Phi Delta Kappan, 73*(1), 41–56; *74*(1), 41–53; and *75*(2), 137–152.
7. National Commission on Excellence in Education. (1983). *A nation at risk.* Washington, DC: United States Department of Education.
8. Ibid., 5.
9. Altbach, P. G. (1985). The great education "crisis." In P. G. Altbach, G. P. Kelly, & L. Weis, (Eds.), *Excellence in education: Perspectives on policy and practice* (pp. 19–20). Buffalo: Prometheus.
10. Elam, S. M., & Gallup, A. M. (1989, September). The 21st annual Gallup poll of the public's attitudes toward the public schools. *Phi Delta Kappan, 71,* 42–54.
11. Bracey, G. W. (1992). The second Bracey report on the condition of public education. *Phi Delta Kappan, 74,* 104–117.
12. Ibid., 107.
13. Ibid.
14. Lawson, H. A. (1993). School reform, families, and health in the emergent national agenda for economic and social improvement: Implications. *Quest, 45,* 293.
15. Secretary's Commission on Achieving Necessary Skills. (1992, April). *Learning a living: A blueprint for high performance.* Washington, DC: U.S. Department of Labor.
16. Boucher, R. (1994). The information superhighway: Turning the vision into reality. *National Forum: The Phi Kappa Phi Journal, 74*(2), 16–18.
17. Futrell, M. H. (1989, September). Mission not accomplished: Education reform in retrospect. *Phi Delta Kappan, 71,* 9–14.
18. Benjamin, S. (1989, March). *Educational Leadership, 12.* An ideascape for education: What futurists recommend.
19. Hawley, W. D. (1986, June). Toward a comprehensive strategy for addressing the teacher shortage. *Phi Delta Kappan, 67,* 712–718.
20. Naisbitt, J. (1985, August). Megachoices: Options for tomorrow's world. *The Futurist, 19*(4) 15.
21. Toffler, A. (1968). *The schoolhouse in the city* (pp. 367–369). New York: Frederick A. Praeger, in cooperation with Educational Facilities Laboratories.
22. Silberman, C. E. (1970). *Crisis in the classroom: The remaking of American education* (p. 116). New York: Random House.
23. Ibid., 36.
24. Futrell, Mission not accomplished, 13.
25. Toch, T. (1991). *In the name of excellence: The struggle to reform the nation's schools, why it's failing, and what should be done.* New York: Oxford University.

26. Vickers, J. N. (1993). While Rome burns: Meeting the challenge of the new reform movement in education. In J. E. Rink (Ed.), *Critical crossroads: Middle and secondary school physical education* (pp. 47–59). Reston, VA: National Association for Sport and Physical Education.

27. Ibid., 49.

28. Travers, R. M. W. (Ed.). (1973). *Second handbook of research on teaching* (p. 1210). Chicago: Rand McNally.

29. Richards, S. L. (1955). *Where is wisdom?* (p. 208). Salt Lake City, UT: Deseret Book.

30. Mesenbrink, R. (1974, December). National Association of Secondary School Principals, *Curriculum Report, 4*(2).

31. Seefeldt, V., & Vogel, P. (1986). *The value of physical activity* (pp. 1–2). Reston, VA: American Alliance for Health, Physical Education, Recreation and Dance.

32. Glair, S. (1984, December). Values of physical activity as expressed by physical education majors. *Physical Educator, 41,* 186–189.

33. Lawson, H. A. (1987). Teaching the body of knowledge: The neglected part of physical education. *Journal of Physical Education, Recreation and Dance, 58*(7), 70–72.

34. Research Works. (1986). How satisfied are Americans with the way they look? *Journal of Physical Education, Recreation and Dance, 57*(5), 7.

35. Vogel, P. R. (1991). Crisis in youth fitness and wellness. *Phi Delta Kappan, 73,* 154–156.

36. Staffo, D. F. (1990). A national K–12 health and physical education mandate is needed: But changes should be made first. *The Physical Educator, 47,* 2–6.

37. U.S. Department of Health and Human Services. (1990). *Healthy people 2000: National health promotion disease prevention objectives.* (DHHS Publication Number PHS 91–50212). Washington, DC: U.S. Government Printing Office.

38. American Association of Health, Physical Education and Recreation. (1970). *Guidelines for secondary school physical education.* Washington, DC: Author.

39. *USA Today.* (1986, May 16), p. 14A.

40. National Association for Sport and Physical Education. (1986). *Guidelines for secondary school physical education: A position paper.* Reston, VA: American Alliance for Health, Physical Education, Recreation and Dance.

41. *USA Today.* (1986, May 16), p. 14A.

42. Hellison, D. (1978). *Beyond balls and bats: Alienated youth in the gym* (p. 1). Washington, DC: American Association for Health, Physical Education, Recreation and Dance.

43. Hellison, D. (1993). Evaluating the affective domain in physical education: Beyond measuring smiles. In J. E. Rink (Ed.), *Critical crossroads: Middle and secondary school physical education* (p. 126). Reston, VA: National Association for Sport and Physical Education.

44. Ibid., 127.

45. Placek, J. H. (1983). Conceptions of success in teaching: Busy, happy and good? In T. J. Templin & J. K. Olson (Eds.), *Teaching in physical education* (p. 49). Champaign, IL: Human Kinetics.

46. Lashuk, M., & Vickers, J. (1987). The ranking of physical education objectives by four groups. *International Journal of Physical Education, 24*(4), 18–26.

47. National Commission on Excellence in Education, *A nation at risk.*

48. Jewett, A. E. (1985). Excellence or obsolescence: Goals for physical education in higher education. *Journal of Physical Education, Recreation and Dance, 56*(7), 39–43.

49. Association for School, College, and University Staffing. *Annual survey of placement officials.* Madison, WI: Author.

50. Griffin, P. (1986). What have we learned. *Journal of Physical Education, Recreation and Dance, 57*(4), 57–59.

51. Graham, G. (1990). Physical education in U.S. schools, K–12. *Journal of Physical Education, Recreation and Dance, 61*(2), 35–39.

52. Robbins, S. G. (1990). Physical education in Canadian schools. *Journal of Physical Education, Recreation and Dance, 61*(2), 34–38.

53. Rink, J. E. (1993). What's so critical? In J. E. Rink (Ed.), *Critical crossroads: Middle and secondary school physical education* (pp. 1–6). Reston, VA: National Association for Sport and Physical Education.

54. Ibid., 2–4.
55. Lambert, L. T. (1987). Secondary school physical education problems: What can we do about them? *Journal of Physical Education, Recreation and Dance, 58*(2), 30.
56. Lovell, K. C., & Reinhard, D. L. (1984). *The new recommendations for educational excellence: Catbird or hot seat for teacher educators?* Paper presented at the annual meeting of the American Educational Research Association, New Orleans, LA. In Oliver, B. (1988). Educational reform and physical education. *Journal of Physical Education, Recreation and Dance, 59*(1), 68–77.
57. Siedentop, D. (1993). Thinking differently about secondary physical education. In J. E. Rink (Ed.), *Critical crossroads: Middle and secondary school physical education* (pp. 7–10). Reston, VA: National Association for Sport and Physical Education.
58. Locke, L. (1986). What can we do? *Journal of Physical Education, Recreation and Dance, 57*(4), 60–63; Norton, C. J. (Ed.). (1987). High school physical education: Problems and possibilities. *Journal of Physical Education, Recreation and Dance, 58*(2), 19–32.
59. Magnotta, J. R. (1993). A future direction for physical education: A mandate for change. *The Physical Educator, 50,* 6–7.
60. Mueller, L. M. (1990). What it means to be physically educated. *Journal of Physical Education, Recreation and Dance, 61*(3), 100–101.
61. Finn, C. E., Jr. (1990). The biggest reform of all. *Phi Delta Kappan, 71*(8), 585–592.
62. Siedentop, D. (1987). High school physical education: Still an endangered species. *Journal of Physical Education, Recreation and Dance, 58*(2), 24–25.
63. Bennett, W. J. (1986). *First lessons: A report on elementary education in America.* Washington, DC: United States Department of Education.
64. Ibid., 37.
65. U.S. Department of Health and Human Services. (1985). Summary of findings from National Children and Youth Fitness Study. *Journal of Physical Education, Recreation and Dance, 56*(1), 43–90.
66. U.S. Department of Health and Human Services. (1987). Summary of findings from National Children and Youth Fitness Study II. *Journal of Physical Education, Recreation and Dance, 58*(9), 50–96.
67. Ibid., 87–88.
68. Bennett, *First lessons,* 37.
69. Strother, D. B. (1990). An interview with Floyd Buchanan: Building exemplary schools. *Phi Delta Kappan, 72,* 323–326.
70. Bennett, *First lessons,* 37.
71. *USA Today.* (1986, August 14), p. 9A.
72. Hayes, A. (1984). Youth physical fitness hearings: An interim report from the president's council on physical fitness and sports. *Journal of Physical Education, Recreation and Dance, 55*(9), 29–32, 40.
73. U. S. Department of Health and Human Services, *Healthy people 2000.*
74. Ibid., 102.
75. Ibid., 96–103.
76. National Association for Sport and Physical Education. *Shape of the nation 1993.* Reston, VA: Author.
77. National Association for Sport and Physical Education. (1993, November 22). *Physical educators need to justify programs.* News release. 1900 Association Drive, Reston, VA.
78. Goodlad, J. I. (1984). *A place called school: Prospects for the future* (p. 224). New York: McGraw-Hill Book.
79. Elam, S. M. (1989, June). The second Gallup/Phi Delta Kappa poll of teachers' attitudes toward the public schools. *Phi Delta Kappan, 70*(10), 795.
80. Wessel, J. A., & Kelly, L. (1986). *Achievement-based curriculum development in physical education* (p. 282). Philadelphia: Lea & Febiger.
81. Vickers, While Rome burns, 50.
82. Sherrill, C. (1983, March). The future is ours to shape. *Physical Educator, 40,* 45.
83. Naisbitt, J. (1982). *Megatrends* (pp. 146–149). New York: Warner.
84. Ellis, M. J. (1988). Warning: The pendulum has swung far enough. *Journal of Physical Education, Recreation and Dance, 59*(3), 77.

85. Freeman, W. H. (1982). *Physical education and sport in a changing society* (p. 288). Minneapolis: Burgess.
86. Graham, G. Physical education in U.S. schools, 39.
87. Robbins, S. G. Physical education in Canadian schools, 38.
88. Vickers, While Rome burns, 52–53.
89. Staffo, A national K–12 health and physical education mandate is needed, 5.
90. Siedentop, Thinking differently about secondary physical education, 7–10.
91. Ibid., 10.

CHAPTER 2

The Role of the Teacher

Study Stimulators

1. Would you advise someone to enter the teaching profession today? Why or why not? What job placement tips would you give them?
2. What teaching characteristics do effective teachers possess?
3. Is it possible to be an effective teacher of physical education and at the same time succeed as an interscholastic coach?
4. What is a code of ethics? Of what value is it to a physical educator?
5. What responsibilities to the profession of education do physical educators have?
6. Why is public relations an important role of teachers?
7. What methods can be used to enhance public relations?
8. What causes teacher stress and how does one deal with it?

What is a teacher? In response to that question, a fourth-grade student replied, "A teacher is someone who knows that you can do what you never did before."[1] A good teacher not only has the vision to see what the student is capable of doing or becoming but also can help the student achieve that goal. Most of us are aware that the mediocre teacher *tells,* the good teacher *explains,* the superior teacher *demonstrates,* and the great teacher *inspires.* Someone once said, "Your students deserve more than your knowledge. They deserve and hunger for your inspiration."

What is teaching? In one sense it is the business or occupation of teachers. In another sense it is the act of helping (inspiring) students to do that which they never did before. If teaching is an occupation, those entering the profession must make a decision to become teachers and go through the training process necessary to become qualified.

The role of a teacher has changed recently as more is expected of teachers and schools than previously. A teacher often serves as a role model, counselor, substitute parent, disciplinarian, instructor, and supporter. Each of these roles is vital to the survival of the individual student. A teacher who provides an equitable, effective learning environment, which provides each student with equal access and equal opportunity to learn, will fulfill all the expected roles.

The role of a physical education teacher generally includes the following: (1) teaching; (2) coaching; (3) advising and counseling with students; (4) administration of instructional, intramural, and extramural programs, budgets, facilities, and equipment; (5) supervision; (6) service to school and community; (7) membership in professional organizations and professional development; and (8) public relations.

In addition, physical educators have a responsibility to be role models of a physically fit, active lifestyle. Brandon and Evans found that 77 percent of physical education teachers sampled exercised three or more times a week for at least 20 minutes per session. However, the majority of the respondents (57 percent) considered themselves to be overweight.[2] Studies have shown that teachers who are overweight or inactive have a negative effect on their students and on physical education programs.[3]

Characteristics of Effective Teachers

Shulman identified seven areas of knowledge required for good teaching: (1) content or subject knowledge, (2) general pedagogical (teaching) knowledge, (3) curriculum knowledge (4) pedagogical content knowledge (specific methods for physical education), (5) knowledge of learners and characteristics, (6) knowledge of educational contexts (community, district, school, classroom), and (7) knowledge of educational purposes, history, and philosophy.[4] Effective teachers put all this together to facilitate student learning. So what makes some individuals effective teachers?

In the past, research on teaching has not answered the preceding question. As Siedentop pointed out, "Research on teaching doesn't have a good reputation. It has suffered through a long history of inconclusive results, inappropriately asked questions, and less than useful techniques."[5] Research on teacher effectiveness substantiates these claims. The first researchers isolated certain teacher personality *characteristics* as criteria for judging teacher effectiveness.[6] Some writers continue to update lists of such characteristics. However, studies fail to confirm any personal qualities possessed in common by effective teachers.[7]

Later, researchers of teacher effectiveness focused on teaching *methods*. This kind of research proved to be no more credible than centering on personality characteristics.[8] No common method used by successful teachers could be isolated because different situations often call for different methods.

Researchers then determined that effective teachers created and maintained a certain *climate* in the classroom based on teacher-student interaction. With the use of teacher observation (process–product) tools, patterns such as clarity, time-on-task, and enthusiasm could be evaluated and later modified by appropriate training. Process–product techniques tallied both teacher and student behavior, enabling researchers to describe, analyze, and explain what was actually happening in the classroom rather than portraying romantic visions of how things should be. Patterns of achievement for high-achieving and low-achieving classrooms emerged.[9] Although researchers have gained much credibility through this line of investigation, the scope of experiences that can be tallied is still limited.

Researchers next developed a model that determined that effective teachers had a large repertoire of *competencies* (such as methods of teaching, providing feedback, directing motivation, and managing the classroom) from which to draw. Teachers were evaluated by their ability to deploy these competencies appropriately to affect student achievement. In the strictest sense, teacher effectiveness refers to the ability of a classroom teacher to produce higher-than-predicted gains on standardized achievement tests.[10] Studies have shown that student achievement is significantly related to such teacher attributes as experience and educational attainment.[11]

Teacher behaviors ultimately appear to be situation-specific; that is, they are directly related to the subject matter, environment, and characteristics of students. Some factors associated with effective teaching can be identified, however. For example, the third edition of the *Handbook of Research on Teaching* emphasized the individual teacher's role as a decision maker in producing effectiveness in the classroom. The handbook pointed out that the social organization of the classroom determines teacher effectiveness and that such organization is largely the responsibility of, and determined by, the teacher. Research findings showed that successful teachers had the following cognitive skills: (1) rapid judgment, (2) *chunking* (ability to group discrete events into large units), and (3) differentiation (separating out important information).[12]

Teacher behaviors that maximize student achievement have also been identified as elements of effectiveness, including: (1) quantity and pacing of instruction, (2) whole-class versus small-group versus individualized instruction, (3) giving information, (4) questioning students, (5) reacting to student responses, (6) handling seatwork and homework assignments, and (7) context-specific findings.[13] Some other characteristics associated with successful teachers are (8) teacher warmth, (9) a positive classroom atmosphere, (10) teacher expectations, and (11) classroom management.

Quantity and Pacing of Instruction

The amount learned is related to opportunity to learn, which in part is determined by the length of the school day and the number of days of instruction. Achievement is maximized when teachers emphasize academic instruction and expect students to master the curriculum, with less "free time" spent in such activities as "student choice" or "throw out the ball." Student achievement is influenced by classroom organization and management that results in increased student *engaged* time (the amount of time the student is actively involved in instruction). Engagement rates depend on teachers' abilities to make academic activities run smoothly; orchestrate brief, orderly transitions; and spend little time getting organized or dealing with inattention or resistance. Students who learn efficiently experience success. If students are to work on assignments with high levels of success, teachers must be effective in diagnosing learning needs and prescribing appropriate activities. Finally, teachers must actively teach. Students achieve more in classes where teachers actively teach and supervise rather than expect students to work on their own.

Whole-Class, Small-Group, Individualized Instruction

Whole-class instruction is usually more effective because it is simpler and doesn't tie the teacher to a specific group. Individual and small groups are more difficult to organize, but grouping may be most effective in heterogeneous classes.

Giving Information

Achievement is maximized when teachers effectively structure lessons. They begin with overviews, advance organizers, or review objectives; they outline content and signal transitions between lesson parts; they call attention to main ideas; then they summarize subparts and review main ideas. Hunter suggests that mastery teaching will occur when lessons are structured to include: (1) stated objectives, (2) anticipatory set (questions or assignments to stimulate thinking), (3) input and modeling (lesson focus), (4) checking for understanding and guided practice, and often (5) independent practice.[14]

Student achievement is higher when information is presented with a degree of redundancy, particularly by repeating and reviewing rules and key concepts, and when presentations are done with clarity and enthusiasm. Enthusiasm is usually related to affective outcomes but often correlates with achievement, especially for older students.

Teachers who are effective at giving information allow sufficient "wait-time" for concepts to "sink in." Sufficient time must be allowed from question to answer (three seconds is suggested). Teachers may need to move at a slower pace for students to absorb information.

Questioning Students

Most good questions direct some response and elicit correct answers. They measure lower-order, factual information and exhibit clarity. Excellent teachers monitor "call outs" as answers to questions. They correlate positively with achievement in low-SES (socioeconomic status) classes but negatively in high-SES classes.

Reacting to Student Responses

Good teachers monitor student responses, such as answering a question, by acknowledging a correct reply. On the other hand, they also indicate when a response is not correct without being critical or probing for a better response.

Handling Seatwork and Homework Assignments

When students are asked to accomplish tasks more independently (often termed *seatwork*), 100 percent success rates are expected. Effective teachers thoroughly explain to students what to do, what work they are accountable for, how to get help, and what to do when they finish. Teachers or aides then circulate to provide help when needed. To be successful, students who need help must receive assistance as quickly as possible.

Context-Specific Findings

Teachers must structure different learning experiences for various groups of students. For example, in the early grades, classroom management involves a great deal of instruction in desired routines and procedures. Small-group instruction is more prevalent in early grades, whereas whole-class instruction, involving application, is more typical in later grades.

A wise teacher will distinguish between high- and low-SES students. Low-SES, low-achieving students need more control and structure, more active instruction and feedback, more redundancy, and smaller steps with higher success rates. High-SES students are more likely to be confident, eager to participate, and responsive to challenge. They usually do not require a great deal of encouragement or praise and thrive in a somewhat demanding atmosphere. Low-SES students are more likely to require warmth and support and need more encouragement. The successful teacher will remember that what constitutes appropriate instructional behavior will vary with the objectives.

Teacher Warmth

One often-mentioned characteristic of effective teachers is teacher warmth. Earls demonstrated that distinctive physical education teachers love children, suggesting that the key difference between effective and ineffective teachers may be the intention and commitment to helping students learn. The greatest dissatisfaction of the teachers studied was not being able to reach every child. Such teachers were characterized by: (1) authenticity, (2) empathy, (3) impartiality, (4) individuality, and (5) openness. The absence of discipline and motivation problems was conspicuous in their classes.[15] A study by Williams revealed that women teachers perceived themselves as being warmer, more friendly, and more comforting than did men. Student teachers for primary schools perceived themselves as more warm and supportive than did teachers for the secondary level.[16] In spite of how logical it seems that teacher warmth makes for good teaching, "data do not support the notion that efficient learning requires a warm emotional climate."[17] Negative indicators such as teacher criticism or student resistance usually show significant negative correlations with achievement, but positive indicators such as praise usually do not show significant positive correlations. As Calisch stated:

> Most books I've read about teaching indicate that the prime requisite for a teacher is a "love of children." Hogwash! . . . What you must love is the vision of the well-informed, responsible adult you can help the child become.
>
> Your job as a teacher is to help the child realize who he is, what his potential is, what his strengths are. You can help him learn to love himself—or the man he soon will be. With that kind of understanding self-love, the student doesn't need any of your sentimentality. What he needs is your brains, and enabling him to profit from them calls for decisive firmness.[18]

A Positive Classroom Atmosphere

Teachers create a positive classroom atmosphere by learning students' names, getting to know students as individuals, sharing experiences with students, and inviting students' responses. Students don't care how much teachers know until they know how much they care, or as Pullias said, "For teaching to be great, it has to be something like a love affair."[19]

The teacher who can communicate concern for each student creates a feeling of mutual respect, encouraging students to want to learn and achieve in school. Such feelings are engendered by showing courtesy and avoiding criticism, ridicule, or embarrassment. Acceptance of individual differences in backgrounds, abilities, and personalities tells students the teacher is interested in them as human beings and that they are essential to the success of the class. A willingness to listen to students and incorporate student ideas into the curriculum, when appropriate, are important factors in establishing student-teacher rapport.

Teacher Expectations

Effective teachers expect students to achieve, and they provide a firm foundation for this to occur. Teachers who expect a lot from their students tend to spend more time working with students on on-task behavior and push students to work to their full capacities. These teachers can expect that their beliefs will be rewarded. They seldom say things they can get learners to say for them. "But when they do say things, they say them loudly enough to be heard and clearly enough to be understood."[20]

Classroom Management

We also know that "teachers who are better classroom managers are more likely to produce students with better achievement test scores."[21] Physical educators are notoriously bad managers. Metzler points out that they spend from 25 percent to 50 percent of their time in management, passive observing, and organizing during class.[22] This time could be better spent in teaching for achievement gains. As it is, students are more likely to be waiting, listening, or performing unplanned tasks.

To reduce management time, effective teachers spend time during the early part of the school year discussing, practicing, and reviewing classroom rules and procedures. Administrative tasks are handled in a routine fashion and students are involved whenever possible. The teacher has clear stop–start signals and allows student input into the selection of the signals. Procedures for disseminating and collecting equipment are carefully planned for maximum efficiency.[23]

Teachers who communicate interest and concern
for students encourage student learning.
© Tracy Pellett

Teaching: An Art and a Science

It must also be recognized that part of teaching is an art rather than a science. Thomas states that as such it cannot be quantified, qualified, or conveniently duplicated:

> Teaching is an art. One becomes a good teacher in the same way one becomes a good actor, a good poet, a good musician, a good painter. One develops a unique style, a personalized method, a way of teaching that cannot be mass produced or even replicated. . . . Some teachers are great; some, average; some, poor. No one has yet been able to identify what makes one person a better teacher than another. We can recognize the art, but we cannot identify its separate common components. . . . A good teacher is one that teaches well,

much as a good surgeon operates with skill. What makes a good teacher or a good poet or a good surgeon only the stars know; and they are not, as yet, willing to tell us the secret.[24]

When the ingredients of teacher, student, and environment come together in the right mix, an educational "happening" may be the result. DeFelice calls this "magic." An individual can be a competent teacher, in that the mechanics of teaching are done well, but not inspire students. When the "magic" is present it is a "sense of vitality that seems to energize everything and everyone in the classroom. Sometimes it's a bubbling, exuberant kind of energy. Other times it's a powerful, quiet kind of energy. Either kind transforms lessons into learning and creates the charged atmosphere in which we also become transformed. . . . The teacher who is not afraid to make mistakes and who has a genuine respect for other people's ideas is filled with the energy from which magic is made. That teacher is alive, and others can't help but be affected by that vitality."[25]

The scientific foundations of effective teaching have now been discussed. The mastery of these foundation principles must be joined with the development of a successful style to produce the effective teacher. Also critical to effective teaching is the development of a personal philosophy of education and physical education.

Developing a Personal Philosophy

A philosophy is a composite of the knowledge, attitudes, beliefs, and values that forms the basis for a person's actions and provides central direction or purpose to his or her activities. Oberteuffer and Ulrich indicated that

> to understand anything one must relate all of the parts, episodes, or individual actions to the "grand plan," the overall purpose. This is sometimes called the point of view—or the philosophy underlying the effort. Without an overall plan, direction, or philosophy, a physical education program, or anything else, becomes nothing more than a series of disconnected and unrelated activities, having no unifying purpose.[26]

A sound philosophy is the basis for a sound program and effective teaching. The personal philosophies of the faculty directly affect the selection of goals and content for the physical education program. In essence, philosophy dictates what is taught, how it is taught, and how it is evaluated. A teacher whose philosophy stresses physical fitness will have a strong school physical fitness program. Another who believes strongly in student responsibility for learning will use many individualized learning methods. A philosophy that emphasizes the totality of learning might encourage a third instructor to stop activity on a beautiful spring day to point out the awe-inspiring mountains capped with snow.

Every educational institution should have a written statement of philosophy that guides curriculum development. The following is a statement of philosophy published by the American Alliance for Health, Physical Education, Recreation and Dance:

> Physical education is the study and practice of the science and art of human movement. It is concerned with why man moves; how he moves; the physiological, sociological, and psychological consequences of his movement; and the skills and motor patterns which comprise his movement repertoire. Through physical education, an individual has the opportunity to learn to perform efficiently the motor skills he needs in everyday living and in recreational activities. He can develop and maintain sound physiological functions through vigorous muscular activity. He may increase the awareness of his physical self. Through expressive and creative activities, he may enhance his aesthetic appreciations. Physical education provides situations for learning to compete as well as to cooperate with others in striving for achievement of common goals. Within the media of physical activity,

concepts underlying effective human movement can be demonstrated and the influences these have on the individual can be better understood. Satisfying and successful experiences in physical education should develop in the individual a desire to regularly participate in activity throughout life. Only through enjoyable and persistent participation will the optimum benefits of physical activity be derived.[27]

Parents, school boards, administrators, teachers, and students all want to know where physical education programs are headed. Leland Stanford used to say, "The world stands aside for the man who knows where he is going."[28] Stanford was right. If an individual knows where she or he is going, people will pay attention.

Daughtrey suggested that prospective teachers defining a philosophy ask themselves the following questions:

1. Do I know where I am headed? What is my aim?
2. Can I scientifically justify the activities I wish to teach?
3. Am I willing to abandon the teaching of certain activities if they are shown to be educationally unsound?
4. Is my program self-centered or student-centered?
5. Are the activities safe?
6. Is my program a play program or is it a teaching program?[29]

A philosophy is the result of continuously changing knowledge and experience. It is dynamic, always evolving, never static. The development of a philosophy of physical education involves the following steps:

Step 1. Study the philosophies of various leaders. Historically, three philosophies have emerged. They are education *of* the physical, education *through* the physical, and education *in* the physical. (You have undoubtedly studied these philosophies in an introduction or history of physical education class.)

Step 2. Analyze your own feelings and experiences. Many philosophies reflect an eclectic approach, in which aspects from each of the historical philosophies are merged into a personal philosophy of physical education. Through reacting to what is going on around you and questioning why things are as they are and how they should be, you can get an idea of your own feelings regarding physical education, education, and even life itself. Through struggling to define your philosophy you will also gain valuable insight into what you really believe.

Step 3. Obtain feedback from others. In addition to self-analysis, stating your philosophy orally or in writing to others and defending it will help you see areas that you have neglected to consider. You will need to reconsider what you believe over and over again as you gain knowledge and experiences throughout your life. Discussion, diversity, and disagreement should be accepted and appreciated as one's philosophy is constantly emerging.

The Role of Teacher/Coach

Though physical education and athletics are not the same, many physical education teachers also are expected to coach. This is especially true of beginning teachers, because there is a shortage of individuals qualified to coach who also desire to do so. Anyone engaged in both teaching physical education and coaching needs to be aware of the conflicts that may occur. One might ask whether it is possible to be an effective teacher while coaching an athletic team. Both roles are vitally important, but their aims, goals, and objectives are often in conflict, and a person playing both roles may tend to favor one over the other.

Typically the coach deals with relatively small numbers of highly motivated students of advanced ability who participate voluntarily. The teacher usually transmits knowledge to large numbers of students with a wide range of abilities who are required to be in class and are sometimes unmotivated or hostile.[30] It is not surprising that the role of coach might be preferred to that of teacher. The pressure to produce a winning team, the added financial gain, and the higher public credibility attributed to the coach often cause coaches to neglect physical education classes and place more importance on coaching. Begly viewed this role conflict as the rule rather than the exception:

> The crux of the teacher/coach role conflict is not that educators occupying both roles concurrently perceive them as totally different, and therefore choose the one they prefer as the dominant role. Rather . . . the core of the difficulty is mostly a matter of time. . . . The impossibility of meeting the demands of both roles simultaneously is often compounded by powerful social and personal incentives to make the coaching role pre-eminent.[31]

In a 1983 study of undergraduate physical education majors, the majority of students did not anticipate a role conflict between teaching and coaching. Fifty-eight percent of the females and 45 percent of the males were equally committed to teaching and coaching. They viewed the abilities needed for each role as similar.[32] Experienced teachers, however, are very much aware of this conflict. Earls reported that distinctive physical educators expressed concern for the interference of athletics with physical education, being intensely aware of the detrimental effects that coaching can have on physical education instruction.[33] Gender, years of experience, coaching or noncoaching assignment, undergraduate major, school socioeconomic status, and level of career aspiration were significant determiners of perceived and experienced conflict between the teaching and coaching roles.[34]

Locke and Massengale found that females perceived more, and often experienced as much, role-related conflict as their male counterparts.[35] Women may feel an added pressure to perform successfully as coaches because their numbers have declined. From 1973 to 1983, after the inception of Title IX, the percentage of women coaches at the high school level dropped from 89 percent to 38 percent.[36] This was the initial response to the implementation of Title IX, but the results have yet to change.

Many professionals believe that physical education and athletics can and must continue to coexist. Administrators, such as athletic directors and principals, can be instrumental in solving the teacher/coach role conflict. They must take the initiative to schedule classes, practices, and competition to aid the coach in fulfilling commitments, while providing an atmosphere of support. Both teaching and coaching programs are needed, and although physical educators are better trained to wear both hats, they must not allow their role as coaches to overpower their role as educators.[37] Some feel that this conflict of roles will lead to the demise of the teaching program and that a separation of coaching and teaching is needed. As early as 1968 Kneer recognized that secondary school physical education cannot survive under the present conditions and "the profession of physical education and coaching should and must begin the divorce proceedings immediately."[38]

Physical educators will often be addressed as "coach" whether that is an official title or not. Both teachers and coaches can identify with the following poem.

The Coach
Melanie A. Croy
She's the first one there in the morning
The last to leave at night
She's also the first one who catches it

When things don't go just right.
A coach is someone who wears a whistle around her neck,
Someone who teaches kids to run and jump and throw and
Kick and catch.
A job that's seldom noticed, "Oh, it's just P.E.," they say.
But I wonder? Do they really know
The things we teach each day?
Things like how to keep on trying—even though you know you
Can't win,
And how to get up when you fall and try again and again
And again.
And when the game is over and your team lost fifty to two,
To be proud because you know deep down that you did the
Best you could do.
How to give one hundred percent each and every day.
And to do the things that you know are right,
As you travel along life's way.
You see, my friend, the things we teach aren't exactly as
They seem.
For we teach kids how to set a goal and how to reach their
Dream.
And even if they try and fail, to be proud of what they've done.
Because in the end it's not the score—it's the game of life
They've won.[39]
(Reprinted by permission of Melanie A. Croy and the American Alliance for Health,
Physical Education, Recreation and Dance, 1900 Association Drive, Reston, VA 22091.)

Physical educators need to answer the question, "Do I want to be a teacher, or a coach, or both?" Once the decision is made, they must then perform with excellence. Ethical conduct on the part of the teacher/coach often solves the problem of role conflict.

A Professional Code of Ethics

A code of ethics is a statement of conduct that governs individuals within a profession. It refers to all of the relationships that occur among people and between people and institutions in the educational environment. It deals with what is right and wrong or good and bad in human conduct. Ethics deals with values as it attempts to answer the question "Why?" For the physical educator a code of ethics includes such ideals as sportspersonship, tolerance, understanding others, loyalty, fair play, cooperation, support of others, and sacrifice of self for the welfare of others. Because ethics involves conduct, a code of ethics is not complete without the decision-making process of what ought to be.[40]

Physical educators are confronted with ethical decisions on and off the playing field, and they must be prepared to take a stand and be an example for students forming their own set of values. Educators must also accept responsibilities that include belonging to professional organizations; attending conventions, workshops, clinics, and in-service meetings; acquiring and reading appropriate books and periodicals; and continuing their education. The American Alliance for Health, Physical Education, Recreation and Dance endorses the code of ethics of the National Education Association. This code consists of the expected commitment of the teacher to the student, the public, the profession, and the employer.

Commitment to the Student

The teacher must be committed to the optimum development of every student, regardless of skill level, gender, race, or disability. "Physical education should be adapted for those students who have special needs."[41] Bain indicated "teachers have an ethical obligation to act on the student's behalf when it is in the student's best interest."[42] Williamson discussed what is needed to provide an equitable environment for students. She defined equity "as creating a supportive atmosphere where students have the opportunity for successful participation and exposure to instruction regardless of gender, race, ethnicity, religion, sexual orientation, social class, or motor ability."[43] She presented six ideas to consider to establish a more equitable learning environment:

1. The teacher must believe that each student has the capacity to learn. Since one approach will work for one student but not for another, many different teaching styles need to be used.
2. The teacher needs to consider how groups are organized. Are different groups encouraged to work together? Are students needlessly categorized by sex?
3. Does the teacher interact with one group more than another? Videotaping lessons and analyzing the tapes will help determine if this is true. Also consider the use of language, using terms such as sportspersonship and player-to-player defense rather than sportsmanship and man-to-man defense. Rules can be modified according to ability level and not sex.
4. Does the curriculum offer a broad range of activities with equal opportunities for all students to participate?
5. Different standards for fitness tests for boys and girls indicate that one group is better than the other. A study of 10- to 13-year-olds indicated no differences between boys and girls.
6. To be successful in physical education the entire school must also be practicing the same values.[44]

Another issue related to commitment to the student is the establishment of a friendly but professional relationship with students. When a student and teacher become too familiar, the teacher-student link is weakened and the nature of the educational relationship is impaired. Information of a personal nature must be kept in strictest confidence and all students protected from unnecessary embarrassment.

Meaningful instructional opportunities should be available to all students. It is recommended that elementary school students have a *daily* instructional period of at least 30 minutes. The minimum instructional period for students in secondary schools is a *daily* standard class period.[45]

Commitment to the Public

Everyone in the profession must assume the role of promoting a positive image in the eyes of the public. An exemplary job of teaching must be done to sell physical education programs to the taxpayers. Those involved in athletics must work tirelessly to be sure practices are completely ethical. Crawford stressed the ethical commitment that physical educators must demonstrate:

> Physical educators have a moral responsibility to speak up, speak out, and speak at young people to stress that difficult "right" and "wrong" decisions have to be made if sport is to remain as an expressive and dramatic facet of human experience dependent on ethical behavior.[46]

Outstanding teachers participate in community affairs, promote good community-school relationships, and refrain from using school affiliation for personal gain.

Commitment to the Profession

A professional person is dedicated to providing a service to other people. Outstanding educators strive to provide a service that is highly esteemed. In the professions of medicine, law, and social work, the clients choose who to ask for service. An incompetent person in these areas is quickly weeded out. Educators are often shielded from this process, so it is even more important that they take their professional commitment seriously. In education, more often than not, students have no choice of which teacher's class to take. Moreover, tenure laws, which originated to protect teachers, now protect incompetent teachers from termination.

Teachers need to maintain relationships with other members of the profession that are based on mutual respect for one another. Teachers have an obligation to be objective, honest, and fair; to respect and defend the rights of their associates; and to hold in confidence information shared by colleagues. However, professionals also have a responsibility to confront associates who are acting unethically or are incompetent. Moreover, they also have the responsibility to follow proper administrative channels and be willing to listen to the other person's point of view.

Physical educators must never forget that they are educators and that the purpose of all programs in the school is to educate students. As such, physical education teachers and coaches share the concerns of other teachers in the school and must work together with them to promote total school unity. They can show their concern by attending general faculty meetings; serving on faculty committees; upholding school policies; and taking turns with hall, cafeteria, or bus duty. Cooperation with the school staff—secretaries, custodians, nurses, business personnel, and so on—is also essential because of the many and varied facilities necessary for physical education programs. Further, teachers must make every effort to sell themselves and the program by personal appearance, manner of speech, and enthusiasm about the program and the entire school.

Professional Organizations

Professional organizations exist to help members of a given profession work together to achieve common goals. The American Alliance for Health, Physical Education, Recreation and Dance (AAHPERD) is the national affiliate for the profession. Physical educators need to join this organization at the state, regional, and national levels and other organizations whose goals are to help its members achieve the goals of the profession.

Education associations also operate at the local, state, and national levels. The National Education Association (NEA) and the American Federation of Teachers (AFT) bring together teachers of all disciplines to capitalize on collective bargaining opportunities as well as to promote common aims and goals and enhance communication among individuals. It is at the national level that unions, such as the AFT, provide beneficial resources for teachers.

Professional organizations catering to specialized groups such as physical education teachers, athletic trainers, administrators, and coaches afford numerous opportunities for group affiliation. Members of professional organizations can share ideas with one another by speaking at conventions; writing articles in professional journals; serving on committees; holding office; or by just attending, listening, reading, or helping. In any case, the growth from such professional involvement is passed on to both students and colleagues. Professional organizations also help with employment needs by publishing job openings and providing opportunities at conventions for potential employers and employees to get acquainted.

A study to determine the commitment of elementary and secondary physical educators to professional organizations revealed that state conventions had the best support. One-third of the teachers polled attended a state Health, Physical Education, Recreation and Dance (HPERD) conference during a two-year period. Elementary and junior high school physical education teachers were twice as likely as senior high school teachers to attend state conferences. Women teachers were also more likely than men (41 percent versus 26 percent) to be in attendance. Attendance by these professionals at regional conferences dropped to 6 percent, and at national conventions attendance was 2 percent. Teachers in this survey were more likely to attend clinics and workshops sponsored by local school districts or organizations (56 percent). The lowest attenders at local meetings were the least-experienced teachers.[47]

Professional Development

Good teachers constantly improve their effectiveness through ongoing professional development. Although some states or districts require attendance at in-service workshops or college classes for recertification or salary increases, continuous updating of skills by each teacher is a matter of professional pride, whether required or not. In addition to in-service workshops and college classes, other options include (1) reading professional books and journals; (2) participating in professional organizations; (3) doing research or writing books or articles; (4) traveling to observe programs, meet other professionals, and view facilities; (5) pursuing a graduate degree; (6) speaking at clinics or professional meetings; and (7) participating on professional committees.

Commitment to Professional Employment Practices

Once a contract has been signed with a school district, the teacher is legally and ethically committed to complete the term of service specified with high-quality work and integrity in employment practices. If the contract must be terminated because of reasons beyond control, then the teacher and the district arrive at a mutually agreed upon solution to the situation.

Adherence to ethical policies and practices of the employer must always be standard procedure for teachers. Likewise, employers are expected to adhere to the same policies. Professional organizations can often assist members experiencing unethical behavior by employers.

Seeking Employment

Although competition for positions in physical education may be keen, an ambitious person can enhance his or her opportunities by incorporating definite strategies in securing a position. Lambert outlined the following systematic planning techniques for seeking employment:

1. Explore job possibilities early. Find a job or volunteer, working at as many different jobs as you can.
2. Stay current about job opportunities. Consult the school placement office regularly. Check library resources.
3. Maintain a 3.0 GPA.
4. Prepare a résumé.
   a. List all previous jobs by year.
   b. List educational background.
   c. List activities you have done that enhance credibility (i.e., Sunday School teacher, camp counselor, recreation leader, etc.).
   d. Collect letters of recommendation.
   e. Write a personal philosophy.
5. Inform relatives, friends, acquaintances, and former employers you are job hunting.
6. Follow up on all leads and advice.

7. Keep names of important contacts.
8. Start interviewing.
    a. Be positive.
    b. Find out all you can about the organization before going.[48]

The Physical Educator's Role in Public Relations

One of the activity and fitness goals established by *Healthy People 2000*[49] was daily physical education for all students K–12. Illinois was the last state requiring daily physical education.[50] Thus, physical educators need to improve the public image of physical education.[51] A marketing strategy can be used to justify to the public the need for a physical education program.[52] Marketing is matching program plans and implementation with the needs and wants of students, faculty, administrators, parents, and community. It includes advertising, communication, and public relations.[53] A quality physical education program is the first requirement. Without a quality program that meets the needs of students, all marketing strategies will fail.[54] Schneider suggests four steps for marketing physical education programs:

1. Know the product.[55] The American Alliance for Health, Physical Education, Recreation, and Dance (AAHPERD), through the National Association for Sport and Physical Education (NASPE), has developed position papers, press releases, and other materials to assist the physical educator.[56]
2. Project a good image. A physical educator's practices must be consistent with the message being presented.
3. Plan the work. Specific plans must be formulated for each target audience.
4. Work the plan. This includes being alert to new ideas and each week concentrating on a particular strategy. Personally getting to know people and meeting with as many people as possible face-to-face is very beneficial.[57]

All the various publics in the school must be part of the marketing plan. Figure 2.1 shows the interrelationships among these groups. Some ideas for motivating students, families, teachers, and the community are presented next.

Influencing Students

Students are the most important public in that they are the only ones teachers see from day to day. When students experience a sound instructional program, they will "sell" it to their parents through their enthusiasm. Therefore, physical educators must plan lessons based on sound educational goals and objectives that address cognitive, psychomotor, and affective domains. They

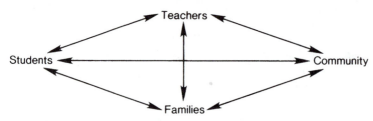

Figure 2.1 The interrelationships among the various publics of the school.

must concentrate on "constructive, positive observable student results."[58] Students grow up into community and school leaders and will have an influence on physical education in the future. Students who have a positive experience in physical education will be more supportive of it in the future. A number of ways to enhance student learning will be discussed in chapter 8. Additional ideas for student motivation are discussed in chapter 12.

Some other events that can promote public relations with students include demonstrations of physical activities in school assemblies, interdisciplinary units with teachers of other subject areas, field days such as the Super Kids' Day presented in chapter 8, and contests for the entire school.

Working with Administrators, Faculty, and Staff

Far too often, physical education teachers divorce themselves from the total school environment. Effective teachers make the effort to emerge from the gymnasium to share experiences with the rest of the faculty. They take time each year to discuss with the principal the physical education program, including an overview of the program, goals for the year, changes that have been implemented, achievements, and new trends or ideas.[59] They must help administrators understand physical education and its importance.[60] Committed physical educators also attend faculty meetings and volunteer to serve on faculty committees, from which they gain new ideas and through which they have a positive effect on the rest of the school. They attend professional workshops and become involved in professional organizations.

Teachers should use every opportunity to share program objectives with parents.
© James L. Shaffer

Figure 2.2 "Spring into Fitness" program.
Source: Artwork by Marjorie Ann McClure.

Physical educators need to be aware of opportunities to integrate physical education concepts with other subject areas in the curriculum. Implementing interdisciplinary units with teachers of mathematics, foreign languages, home economics, health, and physiology can be effective in promoting student and faculty interest in physical education activities. Additional goodwill can be initiated by inviting administrators, faculty, and staff to participate in faculty fitness programs, clinics to learn new skills, tournaments, and free-play activities.[61] One's personal appearance, manner of speech, and enthusiasm can affect the entire school.

Promoting Parent and Family Participation and Interest

A number of methods can be used to help parents understand what is happening in physical education classes. A schedule of courses to be offered is helpful for parents. A "back-to-school night" is held in many schools. Teachers could take this opportunity to point out the objectives of physical education and provide an outline of activities in which students will be involved. Samples of the students' work and minidemonstrations by students could also be provided along with a schedule of future events. Parents could also be invited to visit classes during a back-to-school day or week. Parent-teacher conferences are helpful in discussing mutual problems and goals for individual students and for the program as a whole.[62]

EASTMONT MIDDLE SCHOOL
PRESENTS
Spring into Fitness

1. Tumbling . . . . 1st Period—7th Grade
2. Pyramids . . . . 5th Period—8th Grade
3. Lummi Sticks . . . . 2d Period—7th Grade
4. Gymnastics Exhibition . . . . Special Team
5. Square Dancing . . . . 6th Period—6th Grade
6. Tinikling . . . . 2nd Period—7th Grade
7. Jump Rope Routine . . . . 3d Period—7th Grade
8. Parachutes . . . . 7th Period—6th Grade
9. Dance Aerobics . . . . 4th Period—8th Grade

Acknowledgments

Principal . . . . Mr. Glayde Hill
Vice Principal . . . . Mr. Tom Hicks
Cover Design . . . . Mrs. Marge McClure
Physical Education Department . . . . Miss Robyn Graham
Mrs. Karen Quinn
Mrs. Bell Breen
Mr. Harry Abeyta
Mr. Larry Richins

Figure 2.3 "Spring into Fitness" program.
Source: Eastmont Middle School, Sandy, Utah.

Halftime Shows and Demonstration Nights

Demonstrations are valuable in showing what students are learning and are generally well attended when all of the students participate in some way. These can be as simple as two teams playing speed-a-way or team handball during halftime at a football or basketball game, or as complex as a demonstration night for parents in which every student in the school participates. The important thing to remember is to let all students participate regardless of skill level or disability. Each class can be asked to demonstrate some aspect of the program. This provides parents with a realistic view of physical education in contrast to that of athletics. Posters in downtown stores, notices to parents, and announcements in the local paper can be used to invite the public. A public-address system is essential in most cases. The principal welcomes parents and introduces the physical education faculty, who can take turns introducing the various numbers. A simple program such as the one in figures 2.2 and 2.3 can be handed out at the door.

Family Participation

Parent or family participation in student homework can stimulate families to become more involved in outside activities, such as bike riding or jogging, and to be more supportive of student involvement in completing extra-class assignments or activities. Inviting families to participate in contests in which students earn points by participating in family recreational and fitness activities has also been very effective in some areas.

Parent-student participation nights can include everything from movement education to sports to fitness activities. McLaughlin reported a "Chip-N-Block" bowling tournament in which a parent and student form a team and compete against other teams.[63] Fitness assessment nights are popular in many areas. Likewise, aerobic activities have become increasingly popular in recent years. Other possibilities include mother-daughter, father-son, father-daughter, and mother-son activities.

Newsletters

A brief newsletter to parents or an article in the district newsletter several times a year can be valuable in describing school and community programs and promoting parent and family involvement in these programs. The newsletter might contain a description of the physical education program, objectives, evaluation, and grading; physical fitness goals and achievements; extra-class programs; programs for students with physical and mental disabilities; and special events for parents. A portion of the newsletter could provide tips for better performance in a particular activity such as tennis, bowling, or physical fitness. Newsletters that represent the best effort of the department in terms of spelling, grammar, layout, and use of pictures cast a positive image on the profession of physical education, as well as on the teachers involved. Consult with the English faculty for help if needed. In some locales the newsletter should be printed in both English and local native languages such as Spanish or Native American.

Direct Parental Communications

In addition to newsletters, letters can be sent to parents describing the physical education program,[64] the specific fitness test results of their children and what they mean, or progress in learning other skills. See figure 2.4 for an example. Schuman mentioned sending home red, green, or yellow cards each week for extremely unmotivated students. Green meant "great work," yellow meant "caution," and red said "stop and change your work habits." On the cards she listed all tasks completed during that week. Parents were asked to sign the cards and return them each Monday. Cards were stopped when students no longer needed them.[65] When students know that they will be "paid" each week, they seem to work harder.

Letters or phone calls to parents can also be used to point out students' accomplishments. The following story is told about a boy who had not had much success in school. The teacher sent home a letter to the boy's parents commending something he had done. Later the teacher asked, "Did you give the letter to your mother?" "Yes," the boy responded. "What did she say?" "Nothin'," he replied. "Nothing? Why, it was a lovely letter—and your mother said nothing?" The child nodded, "She didn't say nothing! She just bawled."[66] Generally, parents who have never heard anything good about their children are so happy to hear praise that they will do anything to cooperate with such a teacher or principal.

Junk Days

Herman suggested another practical way of gaining parents' support: Have a junk day in which parents contribute items such as old tennis rackets, golf clubs, or shuffleboard sets. Parents get rid of these space-wasters and the school gains some usable equipment. With the approval of the principal, a note can be sent to parents on which they list what they are donating. Parents sign the note to indicate that they know what their children are contributing.[67] One school's teacher asked for old brooms for broom hockey and was surprised to discover that many parents purchased new brooms just so they could help out.

Dear Parents:

One of my primary goals as a physical educator is to teach every child—from the physically gifted to the physically challenged—how and why they should keep themselves healthy and fit throughout their lifetime. In our physical education program, we provide learning experiences which are developmentally appropriate that will teach children how to be physically active in ways that increase physical competence, self-esteem and joy through lifelong physical activity. Here's how we achieve that goal:

1) Our physical education curriculum includes a balance of skills, concepts, game activities, rhythms and dance experiences designed to enhance the cognitive, motor, affective, and physical fitness development of every child.

2) We provide experiences that encourage children to question, integrate, analyze, communicate, apply cognitive concepts, and gain a wide multi-cultural view of the world.

3) Throughout the year we teach activities that allow children the opportunity to work together to improve their emerging social and cooperation skills. These activities also help children develop a positive self-concept.

4) Ongoing fitness assessment is used as part of the ongoing process of helping children understand, enjoy, improve and/or maintain their physical health and well-being.

5) Children are taught exercises that keep the body in proper alignment, thereby allowing the muscles to lengthen without placing stress and strain on the surrounding joints, ligaments and tendons.

6) Grade decisions are based primarily on ongoing individual assessments of children as they participate in physical education class activities, and not on the basis of a single test score.

7) Finally, our class is designed so that ALL children are involved in activities that allow them to remain continuously active.

I would like to invite you to come and visit our physical education class. By working together to encourage fitness, I am certain we will be able to help your children enjoy a lifetime of physical activity! I welcome your support.

Sincerely,

Your Name and Title

Figure 2.4   A letter to parents.
Reprinted from SPEAK with permission of National Association for Sport and Physical Education, 1900 Association Drive, Reston, VA 22091.

Including the Community

Two factors are involved in community–school relations. They include (1) getting the school involved in the community and (2) getting the community involved in the school.

Getting the School Involved in the Community

Teachers can take the lead in community involvement by participating in institutional, civic, and neighborhood activities or projects. Educators often participate in local business–education exchanges by touring various commercial institutions. Students can also be encouraged to participate in community-oriented projects and in work-experience programs. Youth sports provide an excellent opportunity for service in the community.

To carry out a lifetime sports curriculum, many schools must rely on resources within the community. The first step is to survey the community facilities to see what is available and appropriate for an instructional situation. The cost of a facility and the cost of transportation must then be determined. Once permission from the school and district administration is obtained, a specific legal agreement is drawn up to clarify the dates and times the facility is to be used, the cost, the roles of the school and the institution with regard to the instructional situation, and legal liability. The legal implications of transportation to and from the facility must also be considered. The use of community facilities is one more way in which schools and community can develop a better understanding of one another.

Getting the Community Involved in the School

Passive involvement of the community in the schools generally occurs through the mass media, speeches, and exhibits. The Physical Education Public Information (PEPI) program, developed by the American Alliance for Health, Physical Education, Recreation and Dance, and the newer Sport and Physical Education Advocacy Kit have performed a great service by producing materials and sharing techniques for use in the public relations effort.[68] Another organization that has played a prominent role in public relations is the President's Council on Physical Fitness and Sport. Both groups have produced films and television spots that have been well received.

Publishing articles in school and local newspapers about intramural activities, fitness projects, and class activities can stimulate community interest in physical education just as it has in athletics. The administration should approve all news articles to prevent embarrassment to the school from improper timing or undue controversy. Whenever possible, action photos should accompany the articles. Another way to inform the community about the physical education program is by speaking to parent-teacher organizations and civic groups. Talks can be accompanied by slides, videotapes, or actual performances by students. Exhibits in local stores, the public library, or other community buildings can be used to draw attention to special events.

The use of school facilities for adult education and family-oriented recreation programs is increasing in many areas. Programs range from supervised recreation to instructional programs in physical fitness and skill development. They may be sponsored by the city recreation department or the school district. Adults who become involved in these programs appear to be more supportive of school programs.

Another possible service to the community is a fitness or sports fair in which booths are set up to show what the students have learned in the various areas of sports or physical fitness. Fitness evaluation activities can be conducted at such events. It is often fun for children to test their parents. Legislative fitness days have been sponsored in Washington, D. C., as well as in individual states. Participants are tested and the results are presented in terms of actual scores as well as prescriptions for maintenance and improvement.

Citizens can provide valuable input as resource persons to school advisory committees and curriculum committees. Many districts realize the importance of these committees in discussing school problems and making recommendations, serving as "sounding boards" for new ideas or programs, and reviewing films and books for adoption into the school curriculum. Whenever these committees are used, sound policies must be established as to the purposes of the committee and the role to be played by each member.

Just as many community groups contribute to athletics through booster clubs, a number of service clubs, commercial institutions, and government agencies, along with many lay citizens, contribute to school programs either financially or by donating their time and resources. These groups have sponsored demonstrations, health and fitness fairs, safety clinics, and many other programs. For example, Clay described an "adopt-a-school" program in which various businesses each adopted a specific school and helped them with facility and equipment needs.[69] Government and other public-service agencies have donated innumerable hours teaching first aid, safety, and health skills to students.

Invitations of prominent athletes, sportscasters, sports journalists, and commercial recreation leaders to speak to physical education classes, parent-teacher organization meetings, and other school groups can extend the relationship. A file can be kept on citizens who possess skills needed by the department. Foster grandparent programs provide a double service by helping senior citizens to serve in useful endeavors and through the many services they can provide to the schools. Parents and other citizens can also serve as paraprofessional aides.

It is readily apparent that no one public relations technique works for every situation. By understanding a variety of techniques, the best one can be found for each situation. Gray suggested a number of rules that might be helpful:

1. Borrow, steal, or gain inspiration any way you can, but mainly by sharing ideas freely with teachers within your own school.
2. Never stick with a losing game plan any more than a basketball coach would.
3. "Carrot-and-stick" your classes to the limit. Reward whatever assists student progress; discourage whatever does not.
4. Don't be trapped by rules for motivation; keep them flexible.
5. Change your approach often, even when things are going well.[70]

Maggard emphasized that "physical educators everywhere should unite behind a banner of pride and energy, and work together to upgrade our national image."[71]

The last sections have examined the professional responsibilities and roles of all educators. The next section briefly looks at the special concerns of beginning teachers. The final sections of this chapter present techniques to minimize stress and avoid burnout.

The Beginning Teacher

Beginning teachers in all fields have similar concerns. When these concerns are known, steps can be taken to diminish or alleviate first-day and first-year jitters. Houston and Felder listed the following concerns of new teachers:[72]

1. Expectations about them by their principal and fellow teachers
2. Classroom management and discipline
3. Planning and preparing for the day

Despite these concerns it was noted that when beginning teachers believed in themselves as teachers, they looked forward to working with students and entered the classroom with enthusiasm. Beginning teachers must be well prepared before school starts. Textbooks must be read, materials collected, policies formulated, and a support group of caring people found. Teachers need to also recognize that once teaching has begun they will be fatigued, may develop other somatic symptoms, may become emotionally drained, or may feel they are just surviving. These symptoms will usually dissipate after three to four months. New teachers can cushion this process by anticipating it and by surrounding themselves with a support system with whom experiences can be discussed. Fellow teachers should be part of one's social experiences. More and more school districts realize the trauma of a first-year teacher and are surrounding them with a support system and easing them into full-time teaching more gradually. Some states have an organized mentor program for first-year teachers. If this is not true in your case, seek out a mentor, an experienced teacher you feel comfortable consulting about local practices and ideas for teaching. A publication titled *Transition to Teaching: A Guide for the Beginning Teacher,* published by AAHPERD, is highly recommended for those entering practice teaching or first-year teaching.[73]

Minimizing Stress

In most industrialized countries throughout the world, stress has become the main health concern of teachers.[74] Common symptoms include fatigue, nervousness, frustration, and sleeplessness. These can lead to more serious illnesses, as well as to many psychological disorders.

To prevent stress, teachers need to plan a personal lifestyle that can alleviate the stresses of teaching. It is important to begin early in the career and to maintain a lifestyle conducive to relieving stress throughout the career. Proper nutrition, exercise, and sleep are essential. Developing hobbies and interests separate from physical education is also important. Attending cultural events, engaging in interior decorating, woodworking, or other activities can release built-up tension. Involvement with people from many other walks of life is also valuable.

Pajak and Blase reported that the personal lives of teachers influenced what they did in the classroom and how they interacted with colleagues. Negative outcomes with students resulted from aspects of teachers' personal lives that took time, energy, and attention away from classroom responsibilities. They became distant from students and experienced feelings of guilt. The issues of finances (salaries, etc.) and status (poor respect for the teaching profession) were not identified as major issues in effective classroom performance.[75]

Within the school environment, teachers must learn to use time efficiently so that they do not need to work longer than necessary. Careful planning and advance organizing save last-minute wear and tear on the nerves. Knowing school policies and procedures in advance of an emergency helps one to be calm in the face of adversity. Allowing students and paraprofessionals to help also saves time and effort.

Time management techniques are a must for busy teachers who desire to avoid stress. The following time management techniques will increase efficiency and release time needed to pursue high-priority goals:

1. *Plan.* Use a large yearly calendar for school as well as personal activities. Make a list of daily tasks in order of importance and try to complete the high-priority items. Plan lessons efficiently.

2. *Put an end to putting it off.* Reduce procrastination.

3. *Get organized.* Organize and simplify your work space, filing system, materials, and so on. Develop specific class procedures that students know and follow.

4. *Consider time constraints.* Remember that it's okay to say no. Avoid the paper avalanche by setting aside a time to go through correspondence, saving only vital items.

5. *Modify teaching routine.* Team-teach by planning with other teachers and sharing facilities and equipment. Organize a physical education club that trains students to assist. Maintain a lesson plan for substitutes taking over the class.

6. *Exercise with the class.* Time to do this outside of school may not materialize.

7. *Guard against interruptions.* Shut the door or find a hideout to unwind. Play the ball; don't let the ball play you.

8. *Take time to be yourself.* Engage in recreational or social activities that are enjoyable.

9. *Develop a support system.* Ask yourself, "Who can help? How can they help?"[76]

Many of the preceding suggestions will help a teacher avoid "burnout." Burnout is real, and to avoid it prospective teachers must understand thoroughly the demands of the profession. Teacher burnout has been described as a response to a circuit overload—a result of unchecked stress on the physical, emotional, or intellectual system of the teacher.[77] With the problems facing educators today, it is no wonder they are faced with burnout. Solutions for this widely recognized malady fall into two categories. In the first category, administrators, teacher educators, supervisors, curriculum planners, and society itself solve problems by

a. expanding options for teacher behavior.
b. organizing support systems.
c. providing adequate techniques in the survival skills of
—classroom management
—public relations

In the second category, teachers themselves solve problems by

a. social contacts that revitalize.
b. physical renewal, including
—appropriate rest, nutrition, and drug use
—exercise[78]

Teacher burnout has neither a single cause nor a single solution. Physical education teachers must be alert to the reality that the dual roles of teacher/coach may lead to burnout. "Teachers must recognize the problem, look to its sources, and plan for correction."[79]

Other strategies to minimize burnout include getting involved in other activities, focusing on the positive aspects of the job, allowing fellow workers to complete their share of the responsibilities, and incorporating time management techniques into the daily routine.[80]

The teaching profession today offers many challenges, yet many exciting and creative opportunities. The prospective teacher can be optimistic about a bright future.

Review Questions
1. What are the characteristics of an effective teacher?
2. What is the teacher/coach role conflict? What can be done about it?
3. What is a professional code of ethics? What kinds of conduct or behavior are required of a professional person?

4. List the systematic planning techniques for seeking employment. When should you begin writing your résumé?
5. What is marketing?
6. Give some examples of how each of the following publics might be reached in a public relations or marketing program.
   Students
   Administrators
   Faculty and staff
   Parents and families
   Community
7. What concerns do beginning teachers have? How can you avoid many of these concerns?
8. What are the symptoms of teacher stress and burnout? How can you prevent them from occurring or relieve them when they do occur?

References

1. Fisher, E. (1970, May). What is a teacher? *Instructor, 79*(9), 23.
2. Brandon, L. J., & Evans, R. L. (1988). Are physical educators physically fit? *Journal of Physical Education, Recreation and Dance, 59*(7), 73–75.
3. Melville, D. S., & Cardinal, B. J. (1988). The problem: Body fatness within our profession. *Journal of Physical Education, Recreation and Dance, 59*(7), 85–87; Whitley, J. D., Sage, J. N., & Butcher, M. (1988). Cardiorespiratory fitness: Role modeling by P.E. instructors. *Journal of Physical Education, Recreation and Dance, 59*(7), 81–84.
4. Shulman, L. S. (1987). Knowledge and teaching: Foundations of the new reform. *Harvard Educational Review, 57*(1), 1–22.
5. Siedentop, D. (1991). *Developing teaching skills in physical education* (3rd ed., p. 19). Mountain View, CA: Mayfield.
6. Medley, D. M. (1979). The effectiveness of teachers. In P. L. Peterson & H. J. Walberg (Eds.), *Research on teaching: Concepts, findings, and implications* (p. 12). Berkeley: McCutchan.
7. Graham, G., & Heimerer, E. (1981). Research on teacher effectiveness: A summary with implications for teaching. *Quest, 33*, 14–25.
8. Siedentop, *Developing teaching skills*, 19.
9. Ibid., 20.
10. Shavelson, R. J., Webb, N. M., & Burstein, L. (1986). Measurement of teaching. Brophy, J., & Good, T. L. (1986). Teacher behavior and student achievement. Both in M. C. Wittrock (Ed.), *Handbook of research on teaching* (3rd ed., pp. 52, 339). New York: Macmillan.
11. Eberts, R. W. (1984, April). Union effects on teacher productivity. *Industrial and Labor Relations Review, 37*, 347.
12. Erickson, F. (1986). Qualitative methods in research on teaching. Clark, C. M., & Peterson, P. L. (1986). Teachers thought processes. Both in M. C. Wittrock (Ed.), *Handbook of research on teaching* (3rd ed., pp. 133, 279). New York: Macmillan.
13. Brophy & Good, Teacher behavior and student achievement, 360–365.
14. Hunter, M. (1983). *Mastery teaching*. El Segundo, CA: TIP Publications.
15. Earls, N. F. (1981, Fall). Distinctive teachers' personal qualities, perceptions of teacher education and the realities of teaching. *Journal of Teaching Physical Education*, 59–70.
16. Williams, L. R. T. (1982, Winter). Professional self-perception of physical education teachers. *Journal of Teaching Physical Education, 2*, 77–87.
17. Brophy & Good, Teacher behavior and student achievement, 336–337.
18. Calisch, R. W. (1969, November). So you want to be a real teacher? *Today's Education, 58*, 49–51.
19. Pullias, E. V., & Young, J. D. (1968). *A teacher is many things* (p. 24). Bloomington, IN: Indiana University Press.

20. Laird, D., & Belcher, F. (1984, May). How master trainers get that way. *Training and Development Journal, 38*(5), 74.
21. McCartney, K., & Jordan, E. (1990, January). Parallels between research on child care and research on school effects. *Educational Researcher, 19*(1), 25.
22. Metzler, M. (1989). A review of research on time in sport pedagogy. *Journal of Teaching Physical Education, 8,* 93.
23. Lynn, S. K. (1994). Create an effective learning environment. *Strategies, 1,* 14–17.
24. Thomas, D. (1984, October). In L. O. Pellicer, Effective teaching: Science or magic? *The Clearing House, 58,* 53.
25. DeFelice, L. (1989). The bibbidibobbidiboo factor in teaching. *Phi Delta Kappan, 70,* 639–641.
26. Oberteuffer, D., & Ulrich, C. (1970). *Physical education: A textbook of principles for professional students* (4th ed., p. 6). New York: Harper & Row.
27. American Association for Health, Physical Education, Recreation and Dance. (1970). *Guide to excellence for physical education in colleges and universities.* Washington, DC: Author.
28. Stanford, L. (1974). In C. E. Willgoose, *The curriculum in physical education* (4th ed., p. 189). Englewood Cliffs, NJ: Prentice-Hall.
29. Daughtrey, G. (1973). *Effective teaching in physical education for secondary schools* (2nd ed.). Philadelphia: Saunders.
30. Templin, T. J., & Anthrop, J. L. (1981, December). A dialogue of teacher/coach role conflict. *Physical Educator, 38,* 183.
31. Begly, G. (1987, Winter). The role of the teacher/coach. *NASPE News, 17,* 6.
32. Bain, L. L., & Wendt, J. C. (1983, June). Undergraduate physical education majors' perceptions of the roles of teacher and coach. *Research Quarterly for Exercise and Sport, 54,* 112–118.
33. Earls, Distinctive teachers' personal qualities, 59–70.
34. Locke, L. F., & Massengale, J. D. (1978). Role conflict in teacher/coaches. *Research Quarterly, 49*(2), 162–174.
35. Ibid.
36. Potera, C., & Kort, M. (1986, September). Are women coaches an endangered species? *Women's Sports & Fitness, 8,* 34–35.
37. Issues. (1985, August). *Journal of Physical Education, Recreation and Dance, 56,* 8–9.
38. Kneer, M. E. (1968, March). Physical education and athletics need a divorce. *Journal of Physical Education, Recreation and Dance, 57,* 7.
39. Croy, M. A. (1984, May). The coach. *Alliance Update.*
40. Shea, E. J. (1978). *Ethical decisions in physical education and sport* (pp. 4–8). Springfield, IL: Thomas.
41. The Society of State Directors of Health, Physical Education, and Recreation. (1985). *The school programs of health, physical education, and recreation: A statement of basic beliefs* (p. 8). Kensington, MD: Author.
42. Bain, L. L. (1993). Ethical issues in teaching (p. 73). *Quest, 45,* 69–77.
43. Williamson, K. M. (1993). Is your inequity showing? Ideas and strategies for creating a more equitable learning environment (p. 15). *The Journal of Physical Education, Recreation and Dance, 64*(8), 15–23.
44. Ibid.
45. The Society of State Directors of Health, Physical Education, and Recreation, *The school programs of health, physical education, and recreation,* 8.
46. Crawford, S. A. G. M. (1986). Values in disarray: The crisis of sport's integrity. *Journal of Physical Education, Recreation and Dance, 57*(9), 42.
47. Zakrajsek, D., & Woods, J. L. (1983). A survey of professional practices—Elementary and secondary physical educators. *Journal of Physical Education, Recreation and Dance, 54*(9), 65–67.
48. Lambert, C. (1984). Career directions. *Journal of Physical Education, Recreation and Dance, 55*(5), 40–43, 53.
49. U.S. Department of Health and Human Services. (1990). *Healthy people 2000.* Washington, DC: Author.
50. National Association for Sport and Physical Education. (1993). *Shape of the nation: A survey of state physical education requirements.* Reston, VA: Author.

51. Schneider, R. E. (1992). Don't just promote your profession— market it! *Journal of Physical Education, Recreation and Dance, 63*(5), 70–73.

52. Mize, M. (1990, June). Marketing elementary physical education. *Strategies, 3*(6), 15–18; Moore, D. B., & Gray, D. P. (1990). Marketing—The blueprint for successful physical education. *Journal of Physical Education, Recreation and Dance, 61*(1), 23–26; and Schneider, R. E. (1992). Don't just promote your profession— market it! *Journal of Physical Education, Recreation and Dance, 63*(5), 70–73.

53. Kotler, P., & Andreasen, A. R. (1987). *Strategic marketing for educational institutions.* Englewood Cliffs, NJ: Prentice-Hall.

54. Mize, Marketing elementary physical education, 15–18; Moore & Gray, Marketing, 23–26; and Schneider, Don't just promote your profession, 70–73.

55. Ibid.

56. Information can be obtained from NASPE, 1900 Association Drive, Reston, VA 22091.

57. Schneider, Don't just promote your profession, 70–73.

58. Maggard, N. J. (1984). Upgrading our image. *Journal of Physical Education, Recreation and Dance, 55*(1), 17, 82.

59. Mathieson, D. A. (1978). Interpreting secondary school physical education—Take the initiative. *Journal of Physical Education and Recreation, 49*(1), 51–52.

60. Giles-Brown, E. (1993, June). Teach administrators why physical education is important. *Strategies, 6*(8), 23–25.

61. Ward, D. S., & McClenaghan, B. A. (1980, May). Special programs for special people: Ideas for extending the physical education program. *Physical Educator, 37,* 66.

62. Henderson, H. L., & French, R. F. (1992). The parent factor. *Strategies, 5*(6), 26–29.

63. McLaughlin, R. D. (1981, June). Chip-n-block for parental involvement. *Journal of Physical Education, Recreation and Dance, 52,* 22–23.

64. National Association for Sport and Physical Education. (1994). *Sport and physical education advocacy kit.* Reston, VA: Author.

65. Schuman, M. E. (1981, November–December). Enrich the curriculum and your own style. *Today's Education, 70,* 36.

66. LaMancusa, K. C. (1966). *We do not throw rocks at the teacher!* (p. 80). Scranton, PA: International Textbook.

67. Herman, W. L. (1975). Have a junk day. *Journal of Physical Education and Recreation, 46*(8), 35.

68. For more information on the NASPE Sport and Physical Education Advocacy Kit contact AAHPERD, 1900 Association Drive, Reston, VA 22091.

69. Clay, W. B. (1981, June). First class and getting better. *Journal of Physical Education, Recreation and Dance, 52,* 19–21.

70. Gray, J. M. (1981, November–December). Enjoy yourself and be flexible. *Today's Education, 70,* 34–35.

71. Maggard, Upgrading our image, 17, 82.

72. Houston, W. R., & Felder, B. D. (1982, March). Break horses, not teachers. *Phi Delta Kappan, 63,* 457–460.

73. Wendt, J., & Bain, L. L. (1983). *Transition to teaching: A guide for the beginning teacher.* Reston, VA: American Alliance for Health, Physical Education, Recreation and Dance.

74. Trends: Teachers suffer stress around the world. (1981, November/December). *Today's Education, 70,* 6.

75. Pajak, E., & Blase, J. J. (1989). The impact of teachers' personal lives on professional role enactment: A qualitative analysis. *American Educational Research Journal, 26*(2), 283–310.

76. Virgilio, S. J., & Krebs, P. S. (1984). Effective time management techniques. *Journal of Physical Education, Recreation and Dance, 55*(4), 68, 73.

77. Horton, L. (1984). What do we know about teacher burnout? *Journal of Physical Education, Recreation and Dance, 55*(3), 69.

78. Ibid., 69–71.

79. Ibid., 71.

80. Figone, A. J. (1986). Teacher-coach burnout: Avoidance strategies. *Journal of Physical Education, Recreation and Dance, 57*(8), 60.

CHAPTER 3

Understanding the Learner

Study Stimulators

1. What common characteristics do adolescents of various ages have? What differences do they exhibit?
2. What effect do student similarities and differences have on learning and teaching?
3. How can a teacher best meet the needs of all students?
4. What effect have laws that have been enacted had on the physical education classroom?

Learning is a persistent change in behavior as a result of practice or experience. According to Woodruff, learning depends on the capacity of the learner, the degree of motivation, and the nature of the task. He perceived the process as follows:[1]

1. Internal motivation makes the learner receptive.
2. A goal is perceived as a solution to the need.
3. Inability to immediately reach the goal increases tension within the learner.
4. The learner seeks an appropriate solution to the problem.
5. Progress resulting from the selected solution results in a decrease in tension.
6. Inappropriate behaviors are discarded.

Learning occurs in three domains or areas known as the cognitive (knowledge), psychomotor (motor skills), and affective (attitudes, values, and appreciations). Influencing one domain will almost invariably affect the other two. Therefore, all three areas should be considered when planning learning outcomes. To achieve the goals of physical education, the various domains must be integrated into every aspect of instruction and curriculum planning. The student becomes the focus of the teaching-learning process as shown in figure 3.1.

Ralph Waldo Emerson once said, "The secret of education lies in respecting the pupil."[2] Respect comes from getting to know someone and appreciating that person's worth. By getting to know students, teachers can design instructional programs to help them become successful, contributing members of society. Teachers who become familiar with the characteristics of their students have a considerable advantage in planning their teaching. The investment of time in getting to know the characteristics of a learner population and students as individuals reaps a generous return in the classroom. Three areas to consider when learning about students are (1) common characteristics of children and youth, (2) significant differences among students, and (3) social forces that affect students. Educational programs must be planned that meet the needs identified in these three areas.

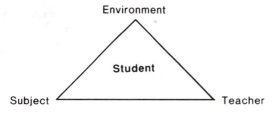

Figure 3.1 The educational system.

Students differ significantly in physical and
intellectual growth and development, social
experiences, personality, attitudes, and interests.
© Tracy Pellett

Common Characteristics of Children and Youth

Much research has been conducted in child and adolescent growth and development and is available in textbooks of educational and developmental psychology. A summary chart of the characteristics of upper elementary age children is shown in Table 3.1, with a corresponding chart for adolescent characteristics in Table 3.2. The secondary school years consist of a constantly evolving period of growth and development in which the characteristics change only in degree.[3] Exercise caution, however, in defining all students in terms of these norms. Since students are continuously growing and developing, all students do not fit the norm for a particular grade level.

Table 3.1 Characteristics and Interests of Children

Fourth, Fifth, and Sixth Grades

Characteristics and Interests	*Program Guidelines*
Psychomotor Domain	
Steady growth. Girls often grow more rapidly than boys.	Continue vigorous program to enhance physical development.
Muscular coordination and skills improving. Interested in learning detailed techniques.	Continue emphasis on teaching skills through drills, lead-up games, and free practice periods. Emphasize correct form.
Differences in physical capacity and skill development.	Offer flexible standards so all find success. In team activities, match teams evenly so individual skill levels are less apparent.
Posture problems may appear.	Include posture correction and special posture instruction; emphasize effect of body carriage on self-concept.
Sixth-grade girls may show signs of maturity. May not wish to participate in all activities.	Have consideration for their problems. Encourage participation on a limited basis, if necessary.
Sixth-grade boys are rougher and stronger.	Keep sexes together for skill development but separate for competition in certain rougher activities.
Cognitive Domain	
Want to know rules of games.	Include instruction on rules, regulations, and traditions.
Knowledgeable about and interested in sport and game strategy.	Emphasize strategy, as opposed to merely performing a skill without thought.
Question the relevance and importance of various activities.	Explain regularly the reasons for performing activities and learning various skills.
Desire information about the importance of physical fitness and health-related topics.	Include in lesson plans brief explanations of how various activities enhance growth and development.
Affective Domain	
Enjoy team and group activity. Competitive urge strong.	Include many team games, relays, and combatives.
Much interest in sports and sport-related activities.	Offer a variety of sports in season, with emphasis on lead-up games.
Little interest in the opposite sex. Some antagonism may arise.	Offer coeducational activities with emphasis on individual differences of all participants, regardless of sex.

Table 3.1—Continued

Fourth, Fifth, and Sixth Grades

Characteristics and Interests	*Program Guidelines*
Acceptance of self-responsibility. Strong increase in drive toward independence.	Provide leadership and followership opportunities on a regular basis. Involve students in evaluation procedures.
Intense desire to excel both in skill and physical capacity.	Stress physical fitness. Include fitness and skill surveys both to motivate and to check progress.
Sportsmanship a concern for both teachers and students.	Establish and enforce fair rules. With enforcement include an explanation of the need for rules and cooperation if games are to exist.
Peer group important. Want to be part of the gang.	Stress group cooperation in play and among teams. Rotate team positions as well as squad makeup.

Source: Victor P. Dauer and Robert P. Pangrazi. *Dynamic Physical Education for Elementary School Children* (New York: Macmillan Publishing Company, 1986).

Table 3.2   Characteristics and Interests of Adolescents

Junior High School

Characteristics and Interests	*Program Guidelines*
Psychomotor Domain	
Widely differing maturation levels among students:	Adjust activities for dramatic differences in sizes and skill levels of students.
Maturation of girls about 1.5 years before boys.	Distribute players to teams based on size or height.
Emergence of secondary sex characteristics.	Be aware of self-consciousness of students. Avoid awkward situations.
First girls and then boys are taller and heavier.	Consider differences in boys and girls when evaluating progress.
Differences in strength, flexibility, balance, and endurance between boys and girls.	Students must be helped to accept the dramatic differences in physical maturation they possess and understand that they are normal. Provide activities to develop health-related fitness.
Poor coordination, low strength and endurance, a greater need for sleep, and increased appetite as a result of growth spurts.	Provide opportunities for developing coordination and skill in a variety of activities. Avoid calling attention to awkwardness.
Bone ossification not yet complete.	Provide supervision to avoid injuries.

Table 3.2—Continued

Junior High School

Characteristics and Interests	Program Guidelines
Posture affected by peer pressure.	Teach correct posture and body mechanics. Guard against fatigue.
Growth rapid and uneven. Energy absorbed in growth process.	Test for structural deviations such as kyphosis and scoliosis.

Cognitive Domain

Increased attention span and ability to handle complex concepts and abstract thinking.	Teach the *why* of concepts regarding biomechanics, motor learning, exercise physiology, etc. Promote creative thinking and problem solving.
Increased interest in possible career options.	Teach the importance of physical activity throughout life.
Increased interest in societal problems.	Promote leadership and followership through cooperative, democratic living.
Wide range of experiences due to travel, TV, and family mobility.	Avoid talking down to students.

Affective Domain

Desire for independence from adults. Often critical of adults.	Help students learn responsibility, leadership and decision-making strategies, and the value of rules in their lives. Help students develop self-confidence and feelings of personal worth.
Vacillation between adult and peer-group values.	Provide approval from both peers and adults. Emphasize high ethical standards.
Interest in impressing the peer group and opposite gender.	Provide social interaction in classes and extracurricular activities to help students develop social and leadership skills. Provide success experiences in basic skills.
Interest in and self-consciousness about own bodies, appearance, and abilities.	Help students understand physiological changes, capacities, and limitations and provide help with grooming, clothes, appearance, weight control, physical fitness, weight training, and nutrition. Be aware of student self-consciousness and embarrassment dressing in front of peers.
Moody and easily angered or upset.	Help students learn strategies for emotional control and stress reduction.
Eager to try new things.	Introduce new activities. Satisfy need for adventure in socially acceptable ways.
Competitive.	Provide a balance between cooperative and competitive activities.

Table 3.2—Continued

High School

Characteristics and Interests	Program Guidelines
Psychomotor Domain	
Physical maturity results in higher levels of motor ability and fitness, with boys ending up bigger, faster, and stronger than girls.	Use different evaluation standards for boys and girls.
Large appetites continue, but some girls restrict intake.	Be aware of incidence of anorexia nervosa and bulimia among girls.
Coordination improves. Interest in personal development continues.	Develop increased specialization in lifetime activities.
Cognitive Domain	
Reaching full intellectual potential. Increased knowledge and experience base.	Teach concepts regarding the *why* of biomechanics, motor learning, exercise physiology, etc. Promote creative thinking and problem solving.
Continued interest in societal problems.	Promote leadership and followership through cooperative, democratic living.
Narrowing of career options and lifetime choices.	Teach the importance of physical activity throughout life. Provide opportunities to develop increased specialization in activities of their own choosing.
Affective Domain	
Peer-group and dating activities dominate social lives of students.	Provide appropriate social activities with opportunities to learn leadership and social-interaction skills.
Continued conflict between youth and adult values; highly critical of adults and peers.	Provide both peer and adult approval. Help students develop a personal value system.
Interest in personal appearance and social skills.	Help students with ways to improve themselves and to impress others.
Interest in new activities, adventure, and excitement.	Help students choose appropriate risk activities; avoid drugs, etc.
Emotional conflicts continue.	Help students learn stress-reduction techniques.
Increased competitiveness in dating, grades, and athletics.	Provide activities that involve a balance between cooperation and competition.

Students in one grade level may be as much as 11 months different in age, not counting older students who have been held back. Even students of the same age mature at different rates; therefore, seldom are all children or youth of a given group at exactly the same stage of growth and development. Obviously there cannot be a different school for each student; however, common characteristics of children and youth can serve as a general guide for making curriculum decisions for the school.

Significant Differences among Students

Considerable differences exist among students both within and across age and grade levels with regard to (1) physical growth and development, (2) intellectual development, (3) emotional development, and (4) social development. At the elementary school level, a span of four to five years can exist in student achievement in a single class. Greater variability exists at the secondary school level.[4] A knowledge of individual differences is essential to teachers planning to individualize instruction in their classes.

Physical Growth and Development

Growth and development depend on heredity and environment. Because of improved nutrition and better health care, today's children grow up faster. Both boys and girls are taller and heavier and mature earlier than children of previous generations. They can expect the longest life expectancy ever known.

Chamberlin and Girona describe adolescence as a "clash between culture and biology," in which "adults try to cling to and pass on the values and mores of our culture to our children while they struggle with maturing bodies and childlike emotions."[5] Although adolescence begins earlier than it used to, the economic and educational requirements of a technological society force it to end later. As a result, activities that used to be reserved for older students are now handed down to younger students. This leaves older students frustrated because nothing new is left for them to try, and yet they are not allowed to assume the privileges and responsibilities of adulthood. Teachers face the challenge of trying to help students cope with the physical and emotional changes that challenge them.

Adolescents differ widely in physical growth and capacity. Some children are early bloomers; others mature much later. They vary widely in body build and physical capacity. Although boys and girls at the elementary school level have no significant physiological differences, great variability exists between the sexes and within each sex during the middle and junior high school years. Griffin and Placek summarize these differences as follows:

> Girls have begun or are completing puberty and are growing and maturing rapidly. Most boys have not begun their growth spurt and in the early junior high years most still possess late childhood characteristics. Thus, in all the physical categories described for 7–9 graders, teachers will see a wide range of characteristics in their students. Height and weight, aerobic capacity, and body proportions will vary depending upon each individual student. With the onset of puberty girls will gain additional body fat. Hip width will also increase in girls, while boys' shoulder width will increase. In effect, boys end up with wider shoulders and narrower hips than girls, whose proportions are the reverse, with wider hips and narrower shoulders. Boys will begin to attain additional muscle mass toward the latter part of junior high.[6]

Because of the variability among students, they should not be automatically grouped by sex for physical education activities. Griffin and Placek summarize the data about students at the high school level as follows:

At this age level (14 to 18 years) most girls are physically mature and boys are rapidly growing toward adult size. Therefore, most boys will be taller and heavier and have more muscle mass. Boys' heart and lung sizes are larger than the girls', thus increasing their aerobic capacity. Most girls again have a greater percentage of body fat, wider hips, and narrower shoulders in relation to boys. Boys have longer leg length in proportion to trunk length. As adults, the average female has about 2/3 the strength of the average male. . . .

This information gives teachers guidelines about what to expect of students at different developmental levels. However, these studies also show that there is great variation within each gender from the average for each gender. Moreover, there is overlap between the comparisons of girls and boys. This means that even though there may be *average* differences between the genders on physical characteristics, in any physical education class there will also be a full range of variation and overlap in physical characteristics. There will be tall girls, short boys, strong girls, weak boys, strong boys, heavy girls and thin girls. It is important for teachers concerned with equity to teach *individual* students regardless of gender, not *average* boys or girls.[7]

Motor ability factors—such as agility, balance, coordination, flexibility, strength, and speed—predispose some students to success in some motor activities and others to success in other activities. Body build, muscle composition, and respiratory capacity help some students to be better long-distance runners and others to be better sprinters or jumpers. Other factors that vary include visual and auditory acuity, perception, and reaction time. Physical disabilities enlarge the differences among students.

Because of the wide variety of individual differences among students, excellent physical education programs include a variety of activities so that students will find some commensurate with their individual abilities. By providing different levels of activity, students are challenged to extend their abilities, yet they experience success during the learning process.

Intellectual Development

The youth of today are better informed than their counterparts of yesteryear. Nursery schools; television; scores of books, newspapers, and magazines; and widespread travel have increased the information available to today's adolescents. As a result of these experiences, children and adolescents are not easily impressed. They have seen it all. However, the abundance of information causes what Chamberlin and Girona call "over choice."[8] Young people have so much information and so many choices in dress, lifestyle, courses, occupations, and values that they are confused about what information to process and how to make the decisions that confront them. They must be helped to develop problem-solving skills if the school is going to be of value to them.

Intellectual development can be impaired by the failure of some students to take advantage of instruction. For a few students, physical or emotional disabilities disturb learning. However, even as the number of disabled students is decreasing, the number of so-called "learning disabled" students has nearly doubled since 1977.[9] Many of these learning disabled students may suffer from a late start, after which the self-fulfilling prophecy takes effect; that is, students who are labeled as "slow learners" gradually begin to see themselves as such. Bereiter concluded that:

For any sort of learning, from swimming to reading, some children learn with almost no help and other children need a great deal of help. Children whom we have been labeling as educationally disadvantaged are typically children who need more than ordinary amounts of help with academic learning. . . . From this point of view, a successful compensatory education program is one that gives students plenty of help in learning.[10]

Recent studies on the brain and learning demonstrate that students learn in different ways. *Field-dependent* individuals are much more aware of and responsive to external stimuli, whereas *field-independent* people are sensitive to internal cues. Field-dependent people are socially oriented and have high levels of self-esteem. They pay more attention to faces and social cues and choose people-oriented professions. They like to be physically close to people. Field-independent people tend toward a more impersonal orientation, have less self-esteem, and choose abstract-oriented fields.[11] Field-independent students learn better with self-selected goals, intrinsic motivation, and self-reinforcement, whereas field-dependent learners prefer externally defined goals, reinforcement from others, clearly defined structure, and a minimum of criticism.[12]

Another classification system for cognitive style utilizes methods of reasoning. Children who group a table and chairs together because they both have four legs are using an *analytic* style; those who group them together because both are used for dining demonstrate a *global* or *relational* style. Cohen hypothesized that children in an industrialized society would tend toward an analytic style, whereas many low-socioeconomic-level children would function with a relational style, thereby creating a cultural mismatch in the schools.[13] Standardized intelligence tests measure students' analytic styles.

Brain hemisphericity studies also relate to cognitive style. Students who are right-handed and most who are left-handed generally use the left hemisphere and employ an analytic style. Some left-handers, however, use a global style reflective of the right hemisphere. Other research has shown that impulsive children tend to use a global style, whereas reflective learners tend toward an analytic style. When a global strategy results in the correct answers, global children perform equally with their peers. However, when analytic processing is required, these children experience difficulty.[14]

Learning styles refer to a learner's preferred way of attending to and absorbing information. A learning style is, in reality, a group of individual preferences for working alone or in groups, in a noisy or quiet environment, in a bright or subdued environment, by doing or by listening, and so forth. Learning styles can vary across school subjects. Although more than one-half of students are right-brained and learn better through visual, holistic means, the majority of teachers teach in a left-brain or verbal mode. The implication is that all students can succeed if helped to use their own natural processes for learning.[15]

It would be difficult, if not impossible, for a teacher to match the learning styles of several hundred students a day. How can an instructor utilize information on learning styles? The answer appears to be to create an environment in which different learning styles can be accommodated and then to empower the learner to become an active participant in the learning process. Dixon suggested helping students evaluate their own learning preferences and encouraging them to expand their learning styles. She also suggested that instructors use a variety of instructional approaches and create a climate in which learners can work cooperatively to achieve learning goals by using each other as resources.[16] Sternberg suggested using a student's preferred style as a point of entry.[17]

Social Development

Adolescence is characterized by a change in social interaction patterns and a challenging of parental and authority roles. A basic need of adolescents is to learn to accept responsibility for their actions and to demonstrate self-discipline before asking for greater freedom.[18] Early adolescents are predominantly interested in groups of friends of the same sex. They are in a process of relinquishing old ties and establishing new ones in an attempt to gain independence and a new identity. Peer approval at this stage is more important than parental approval. Peers become sounding boards for ideas and controversial topics. However, adults are still important for helping adolescents test their newly formed theories. Adolescents who transfer their dependence on their parents to dependence on the group fail to develop the independence needed for mature behavior and personal self-worth. Gangs can be detrimental due to the artificial interaction patterns of the youth involved, both the leaders and the followers, as well as the failure to learn appropriate procedures for conflict resolution. Youth who are economically disadvantaged and affluent youth whose parents lavish them with material goods rather than with personal attention and love often have more difficulty adapting to appropriate interaction patterns.

The influence of the peer group, coupled with a desire for adventure, often leads adolescents into situations incompatible with their level of judgment. A lack of judgment often results in an increase in the number of accidents among this age group.[19]

During the middle phase of adolescence, same-sex peer groups decrease in size and become cliques, which emphasize certain modes of dress and behavior. Popularity and conformity to group norms is important. In the normal development process, youth gradually discard group choices for individual selection. During this phase, teenagers often identify with the parent of the opposite sex as well as develop friends of the opposite sex. Problems arise between boys and girls of the same ages because of different rates of maturation.

During late adolescence, young adults limit friends of the same sex to a few "best" friends, and they continue to develop romantic relationships with friends of the opposite sex. In addition, they become more friendly with adults on a new level. They learn to accept the flaws of friends and adults and to understand that "nobody is perfect."

Emotional Development

A critical factor in adolescent development is the ability to build and maintain feelings of personal worth and belonging. Self-esteem and self-confidence have to do with a belief in one's own worth and positive attitudes toward one's own abilities. To understand and accept other people, individuals first must learn to understand and accept themselves. The foundation for self-esteem and self-confidence is laid in infancy. Love leads to trust and a sense of being acceptable and worthwhile.

One of the tasks of adolescence is a search for a new self. Adolescents struggle with changes in physical appearance, such as being too tall, too short, too fat, too skinny, having acne, or anything else that makes them feel different or unacceptable. Hormonal changes bring on personality and mood changes, and responses vary from excitement to depression. Students fluctuate between childlike and adult emotions and behavior in an attempt to establish a new state of independence from parents while maintaining their needs for adult approval and affection. Youth spend a lot of energy "trying on" different personalities in an attempt to find the one that suits them.[20] For example, they lose or add nicknames or change from a first to a middle name. They experiment with new styles of penmanship, dress, and behavior. Unhappiness results when they fail to match up with the ideal self they envision. All of these adjustments lead to emotional stress. Thus, adolescents need time alone to reflect on and examine themselves. When a young adult learns to accept his or her physical body, public personality, and inner self, a mature personality emerges.

Once the self-concept is formed and internalized, the person tends to nurture it by seeking experiences to validate it. For example, if John feels he is a failure, he will continue to fail, since that supports his image of himself. To change a student's self-concept, significant people in the student's life, such as family, friends, neighbors, and teachers need to provide encouragement and acceptance over a long period of time. Because the self-concept is long-lasting, even minor changes for the better should be applauded. Combs stated:

> The student takes his self-concept with him wherever he goes. . . . Everything that happens to him has an effect on his self-concept.
>
> Are we influencing that self-concept in positive or negative ways? We need to ask ourselves these kinds of questions. How can a person feel liked unless somebody likes him? How can a person feel wanted unless somebody wants him? How can a person feel acceptable unless somebody accepts him? How can a person feel he's a person with dignity and integrity unless somebody treats him so? And how can a person feel that he is capable unless he has some success? In the answers to those questions, we'll find the answers to the human side of learning.[21]

Adolescents are extremely concerned about social injustices. Unless knowledge and skills are related to students' attitudes, feelings, and beliefs about themselves and their fears and concerns about the community that surrounds them, education probably will have only a limited influence on their behavior. Instruction, then, becomes a matter of linking the cognitive and psychomotor aspects of the curriculum to the intrinsic feelings and concerns of the students. When these feelings and experiences are validated for students, students believe they are worthwhile.

Various personality characteristics cause students to feel more comfortable in one activity than another. The aggressive, competitive, social student might prefer participation in a team sport, whereas the cooperative, passive loner might prefer engaging in a jogging or cycling program. Active, assertive people learn better from live instruction, whereas their less assertive schoolmates learn better from films.[22] Introverts prefer learning from self-instructional materials; extroverts prefer interacting with the instructor.[23] Some students suffer from anxiety that limits their capacity for self-fulfillment and need activities to build up their confidence and help them become self-directing.[24]

Social Forces That Affect Students

Rapid changes in society can have a detrimental effect on youth. Increased mobility has taken families away from relatives and friends. Dramatic role changes for men and women confuse some young people as to what is expected of them. Values and morals change constantly and are no longer a stabilizing force in American society.

The following statistics are evidence of how today's students are influenced by society's changes. Three to 4 million children have been exposed to damaging levels of lead. From 15,000 to 30,000 children have been infected with HIV (human immunodeficiency virus). Of the 37,000 babies born each year weighing less than three and one-half pounds who will live long enough to leave the hospital, many will face substantial learning problems. Learning capabilities will be affected for the 350,000 newborns per year that are exposed prenatally to drugs, including alcohol.[25] The American Health Foundation determined that in 1992, 17 percent of high school seniors smoked cigarettes daily. Twenty-two percent reported using marijuana, and 28 percent had five or more alcoholic drinks on one occasion over a two-week period. Per 100,000 teenagers aged 15 to 19 there were 837 new cases of gonorrhea. About 12 children per day are victims of homicide in the United States. Mental disorders afflicted about 8 million children age 18 and younger.[26] Somewhere between 14 and 27 percent of all young people drop out of school prior to high school graduation.[27] Approximately 1 million children and youth are homeless.[28]

Deterioration of the Family

Many of the preceding problems have resulted from the deterioration of the family, with one out of every four children being raised by a single parent.[29] Nearly half of our children will live in single-parent families before they reach age 18. Only about 6 percent of U.S. households consist of a "normal" family, with a working father, a housewife mother, and two school-age children.[30]

Divorce, death, and births to unwed mothers result in many mother-only households with significantly lower incomes.[31] Each year 8.7 percent of all births are to single, teenaged mothers.[32] This results in 500,000 children each year born to teenage mothers and 3.3 million children today living with teenage mothers. Approximately one in every five (12 million) children are being raised in poverty.[33]

According to a study by Dornbusch and his colleagues, adolescents in single-parent households have a significantly higher level of deviant behavior than those in families with two natural parents.[34] In many other homes, both parents work outside the home, leaving the children to fend for themselves. More than half of all mothers of children under 6 and almost 70 percent of mothers of children between 6 and 17 were working or seeking work.[35] *Latchkey* children (a term describing the house keys they often wear hanging around their necks) leave home after their parent(s) have gone to work or come home to an empty house or both. Estimates of the number of latchkey children range from 1.8 to 15 million.[36] These children come from all socioeconomic levels.

Social consequences arising from unsupervised youth include crime (especially shoplifting) and drug abuse.[37] Individual consequences include fear, loneliness, boredom,[38] accidents, child molestation, rape,[39] and teen suicide,[40] not to mention the fear and guilt experienced by parents.[41] Academic achievement may or may not be affected.

The Carnegie Council on Adolescent Development reported another consequence of the lack of adult guidance:

> Freed from the dependency of childhood, but not yet able to find their own path to adulthood,
> many young people feel a desperate sense of isolation. Surrounded only by their equally
> confused peers, too many make poor decisions with harmful or lethal consequences.[42]

Although statistics are not available, estimates indicate that about one in four adolescents in the United States is "extremely vulnerable to the negative consequences of multiple high-risk behaviors such as school failure, substance abuse, and early unprotected intercourse," and another one-fourth are at moderate risk. Thus, about one-half of the nation's youth may need strong and consistent support to avoid these problems.[43]

Some solutions to this lack of supervision include programs offered by community organizations, parent groups, social service agencies, youth groups, private industry, schools, churches, private day-care centers, and worksite centers. Some employers have offered flexible work times. Volunteer tutors after school hours, after-school playground programs, and phone-a-friend or tutor hot lines have all proven helpful. However, legal liability, money, and a lack of policies regarding these programs have limited their availability for all children.

Implications for teachers include the need to structure homework more carefully, to provide homework hot lines, and to take time to listen to the concerns of youth. Emergency procedures for contacting working parents and the establishment or support of extended-care programs enhance the working relationship between parents and the school.[44]

The remainder of this section will discuss at-risk youth, drug abuse, suicide, child abuse, and the current youth culture.

At-Risk Youth

> At-risk students are "turned off" to traditional school settings. They may be predelinquent, troubled, hostile youths with few goals—youth who have been expelled from school for a variety of reasons, are referrals from special schools, are from broken homes, are academically inferior and, many times, are among the transients who attend many different schools. These students may have a low self-concept and be alienated from society with its rules and regulations.[45]

According to Sparks, at-risk students need to know they are important. If a teacher lets the students know the teacher is glad they are in class, barriers will be broken down; students will feel good about themselves and will be motivated to participate in class. The students can be helped to develop responsible behavior and good decision-making skills once trust is established.[46]

Four steps are involved in building self-responsibility and decision-making skills. First, a positive environment is established. Second, the students are assisted in setting achievable goals. Third, the students are provided alternatives and allowed the opportunity to make choices. At-risk students need to develop a commitment to decisions that are made if they are to feel responsibility toward the outcomes of those decisions. Fourth, students examine the consequences and assume responsibility for their choices. At-risk students "often look for excuses, blame someone else, or even blame society in general for a situation they do not like or cannot control. If a teacher can create a sense of responsibility with at-risk students, the students will begin to act more responsibly."[47] Throughout this process the at-risk students must receive positive reinforcement, be treated with respect, and be praised for their efforts in reaching their goals. Rewards are preferred as motivators rather than punishment.[48]

Drug Abuse

With regard to the incidence of drug abuse, the Carnegie Council on Adolescent Development noted that many youth first experiment with tobacco, alcohol, and illicit drugs during early adolescence. Of the 92 percent of high school seniors in 1987 who began drinking before graduating, 56 percent began in the sixth to ninth grades and 36 percent in the tenth to twelfth grades.[49] "Teenagers in the United States have the highest rate of drug abuse of any industrialized country in the world."[50] Commonly abused drugs include tobacco, alcohol, narcotics, depressants, stimulants, hallucinogens, and marijuana. Although adults have been smoking less, teenagers (especially girls) have been smoking more. Other harmful practices include inhaling glue, gasoline, paint, and aerosol fumes and the use of chewing tobacco or "snuff." Synthetic drugs or analogs of controlled or illegal drugs can have potencies thousands of times those of their natural counterparts and often result in brain damage or death. Increasingly, youth are indiscriminately mixing drugs such as alcohol and barbiturates that can result in respiratory and heart failure or violent behavior.[51] Three drugs—alcohol, marijuana, and cocaine—have been singled out as those most frequently used and the "gateway" to the use of all other drugs.[52]

Drugs cripple, kill, or ruin young lives, physically and emotionally. In addition to the personal harm resulting from drug use, many drug addicts steal, assault, prostitute, and sell drugs to others to support their habits. Drugged and drunken drivers maim or kill tens of thousands of people each year. Drug use also can precipitate violent, senseless crimes.[53]

Precipitators of drug abuse are similar to those for other dysfunctional behaviors and include (1) stress, (2) skill deficiencies, (3) situational constraints, and (4) changes in the nuclear family. All of these factors interact with one another and can contribute separately or collectively to problem behavior.[54]

Adolescents today experience a great deal of stress, isolation, and alienation. Adolescence is a painful period, in which the body, mind, and emotions change drastically. New roles and increased expectations by teachers and parents create feelings of inadequacy. Postman and Elkind both focused attention on the disappearance of childhood from the life cycle.[55] Norwood added:

> Caught in this frustrated age of development, today's children experiment with behaviors thought to be adultlike with little ability to ascertain the good and bad of such behavior. . . . Thus, the role-modeling of adult behavior encouraged in today's society pressures children to engage in alcohol consumption, smoking, illicit drug use, sexual intercourse, and other roles they perceive to be adult. "Sooner is better" is a message received by our children. . . . The rationale behind pressuring children to achieve beyond their age and normal expectations must be re-examined.[56]

Youth have been superficially exposed to so many adult activities and privileges that by the time they are in their midteens they are already bored and have nothing to look forward to. Many respond by escaping to drugs, delinquency, or religious cults.

In addition to the factors just mentioned, stress may come from the loss of a parent or friend, rejection or failure, family conflict, or abuse.[57] People vary greatly in their abilities to cope with stress. The more stress they can tolerate, the less likely they are to turn to drugs.[58]

Youth who have the ability to face problems realistically and attack them systematically are not likely to get involved with drugs, whereas those who deny or blame others for their problems, run away from their problems, or expect others to solve them are especially vulnerable. Skills needed to resist drug use include problem solving, realistic self-assessment, and communication skills. Persons suffering from feelings of inferiority or powerlessness may turn to drugs for the false sense of confidence or power they create.[59]

A major situational constraint is the influence of the peer group. Initial drug use usually occurs between the ages of 12 and 18.[60] In fact, association with drug-using friends is one of the strongest predictors of drug use among adolescents.[61]

The medical revolution has led to the acceptance of drugs as chemical "miracles" and the widespread availability of prescription drugs to "cure" the ills of society. People encounter drugs everywhere they look—television, movies, newspapers, sports, and music. Television commercials and programming sell youth on drugs and alcohol and the need to look better, feel better, or escape from their humdrum lifestyle. The "me"-oriented generation focuses on pleasure, leisure activities, and winning. The need to be first in everything can result in the use of drugs to stay awake, lose weight, or ward off stress.[62] The widespread availability and the casual acceptance of drugs place people in situations in which drug use is desirable.[63] At-risk youth find themselves in many situations in which drug use is expected and supported.[64]

Children who grow up in well-adjusted, happy homes are less prone to use drugs than those who come from troubled environments. Parents who use alcohol and other drugs are poor role models for their children. Changes in the family unit have forced many youth into early independence and precipitated feelings of loneliness. These youth passively accept a way of life they see as meaningless, with a constricted expression of emotion, a low threshold of boredom, and an apparent absence of joy in anything not immediately consumable such as music, sex, drugs, and possessions. Youth who find no purpose in life and believe that life is dull, uneventful, or boring may turn to drugs for the "thrill" it affords them.[65]

The quality of parent-child interactions also has been shown to affect drug use or nonuse.[66] Another factor in whether or not children use drugs is the religiosity of the parents. "It may very well be impossible, or next to impossible to rear a child in these days with real assurance about his future unless there is some religion."[67]

Hafen and Frandsen indicated that:

> In general, people turn to drugs to fill a need—a need to relieve anxiety, a need to grow, a need to experience adventure, a need to relieve boredom, a need to cope with stress, a need to escape from problems. When drugs begin to satisfy those needs—or when a person is simply convinced that they do—the drug behavior is reinforced.[68]

Just because a person may have the needs just described does not mean that drug abuse is inevitable; however, it does indicate that the person must learn to overcome those needs by examining alternatives to meet them and turning weaknesses into strengths.[69]

Although adolescents can exhibit strange behaviors without being on drugs, some signs of drug use might include a sudden unwillingness to follow parental rules, a decline in academic achievement, increased truancy and class cutting, an endless need for money, evidence of drugs or drug paraphernalia, major changes in interpersonal relationships, inappropriate clothing habits for the weather conditions, aggressive behavior, loss of interest in former activities or friends, failure to fulfill responsibilities, and physical or mental deterioration—in short, any sudden and unexplained change in behavior, appearance, or personality.[70] Evidence of drug use could include redness of the skin and eyes; burns on the thumb and fingertips; drug particles on teeth or clothing or protruding from pockets; large numbers of matches; use of excessive deodorant, aftershave lotion, gargles, and breath fresheners to disguise telltale odors; increased illness; or emotional outbursts.[71]

When teachers suspect drug use, they are obligated, if not legally, then ethically and professionally, to do something about it. When school personnel act in good faith and show reasonable cause for concern, they are usually protected in the case of a lawsuit.[72] Towers suggested five steps that teachers can take when they suspect a student is abusing drugs:

> (1) Express concern about the youngster's failing grades, moodiness, or other observed behavior; (2) encourage the youngster to seek help and offer to assist in getting that help; (3) if the behavior is extreme or if it persists, notify the parent and similarly express concern over the observed behavior; (4) consult with colleagues about the student and refer the youngster to appropriate staff; and (5) participate in the intervention program if appropriate.[73]

However, he cautioned, if the student is currently under the influence of drugs or alcohol—glazed eyes, extreme lethargy, sleepiness, or mood swings—teachers should avoid confrontation and instead send the youth to the health room or school office.[74]

Students on some drugs may feel invulnerable to pain or injury, have delusions of great strength, or feel threatened by teachers and classmates, who may appear as monsters. In these situations they can be dangerous to themselves and others. In emergencies such as these, Towers suggested that teachers stay calm and avoid threatening the student; immediately notify the office to call for emergency help; try to keep the class quiet or remove the student to a nonstimulating environment; and speak calmly and try to reassure the student that no one intends any harm.[75]

Prevention efforts are best started in the elementary school. Towers and Swett listed three strategies for preventing drug and alcohol abuse. First, education can provide clear and accurate information about drugs and their effects on the individual and help students develop the skills needed to make responsible decisions; cope with stress, responsibility, and peer pressure; and improve their self-esteem. Second, students can be helped to find alternative ways to derive pleasure in natural, more socially acceptable, and less harmful ways by engaging in adventure activities, yoga, religion, political action groups, the arts, music, or dancing. Third, school officials can deter drug use by limiting the availability of drugs and imposing stiff, consistent penalties for use, possession, and distribution. Enforcement of school policies and the law can help students accept the consequences of drug-taking activities, rather than having them absolved by caring parents or professionals.[76]

Coalitions of school personnel, parents, students, business persons, and community agencies can work together to fight drug abuse. The National Education Association publication, *How Schools Can Help Combat Student Drug and Alcohol Abuse*, has numerous strategies and resources such groups can use to prevent drug abuse in schools.[77]

Once students are dependent on drugs, professional treatment is needed, either on a residential or outpatient basis. The sooner the treatment begins, the better the chances for success; therefore, early identification is critical.[78]

Suicide

Suicides and suicide attempts have become a major concern of parents and educators in the past few years. The number of reported adolescent suicides has jumped 300 percent in the past 30 years.[79] Reported suicides are now second only to accidents as the leading cause of death in youths 15 to 19 years of age.[80] Every 90 seconds a teenager attempts suicide, with one succeeding every 90 minutes. In addition, many suicides are not reported due to social stigma or lack of evidence. Adolescents who commit suicide tend to be highly intelligent, physically precocious, and between the ages of 15 and 24. Some are quiet and uncommunicative. Others are impulsive and delinquent. Many are driven by perfectionism.[81]

Deykin and her associates reported rates of life-threatening behavior (potentially lethal behaviors of all types) to be similar for boys and girls, although suicide attempts were nearly three times more prevalent among females.[82] However, males are three times more likely than females to actually kill themselves because they choose more lethal methods.[83] The three strongest correlates of teenage suicidal behavior are family breakdown, youth unemployment, and decreased religious observance among youth. Youth may be isolated, highly irritable, aggressive, or have maladaptive coping behaviors. Abused teenagers are at high risk for self-destructive behavior.[84] Jacobs proposed a five-stage model to explain adolescent suicidal behavior: (1) a history of problems beginning in early childhood, (2) an escalation of the problems with the onset of adolescence, (3) less and less ability to cope with stress and increasing isolation from others, (4) a "last straw" event (such as breaking up with a boyfriend or girlfriend or the loss of a family member or friend) that leaves few remaining social relationships or little hope for resolving the problems, and (5) a justification of the suicide by the adolescent to himself or herself.[85]

Garfinkel identified three clusters of identifying symptoms for potential suicide victims: (1) academic deterioration; (2) slowing down physically, such as physical complaints or illnesses, changes in eating and sleeping habits, or dropping out of athletics; and (3) withdrawal from peer involvement. Some students signal the intent to commit suicide with verbal remarks about death, suicide themes in writing or artwork, giving away personal belongings, or supposed "accidents" such as wrist-slashing or overdosing on medication.[86] Other behavioral clues include changes in dress and grooming, personality changes, depression, acting-out behaviors, alcohol or drug abuse, running away, sexual promiscuity, and belligerence. Physical educators are often the first ones to suspect a problem. Before death is finally attempted, the adolescent may be silent. Outside interference at this point is no longer desired.[87] Motto suggested several factors for assessing suicidal risk:

1. A prior suicidal attempt
2. The degree of detail in the current suicidal plan
3. The extent of feelings of hopelessness
4. The presence of a lethal weapon
5. The presence or threat of a progressively disabling physical illness
6. The presence of a psychotic disorder (including temporary disorders induced by alcohol or drugs)
7. Clues related to termination behavior, such as giving away valued objects or dropping verbal hints about not being present[88]

Hafen and Frandsen remind teachers, parents, and friends to never ignore a suicide threat. Confront the individual immediately. Listen calmly and evaluate the seriousness of the situation. Help the adolescent realize that the feelings are temporary and will clear up with time and that death is a permanent decision that cannot be reversed. Stay with the youth, eliminate possible resources for committing suicide, and get professional help immediately from a suicide prevention center or hospital. Let the youth know that you care.[89] Garfinkel emphasized establishing a support network with school counselors, psychologists, or social workers to help in this process. He also stressed the importance of teaching youth effective coping styles, including communication and problem solving.[90]

Many of the preceding problems are interrelated. Young people who smoke and drink may also experiment with sex and drugs, and these same students are prone to school failure.[91] Increasing numbers of teenagers below age 16 are becoming sexually active with high risks of pregnancy, low-birth weight infants, and school dropout.[92] Besides the risks of pregnancy, AIDS and other sexually transmitted diseases may infect 25 percent of sexually active teenagers.[93]

Hafen and Frandsen highlighted seven adolescent needs that youth leaders might consider in program planning and implementation:

1. Increased respect from adults
2. More time and involvement from adults
3. More constructive opportunities to experiment with life
4. More help in developing social competence
5. More qualified adult youth leaders
6. More opportunities for moral development
7. Help to find the meaning of life[94]

Child Abuse

Another problem of epidemic proportions is child abuse. Although the true incidence of child abuse is unknown, estimates of abuse range into millions of cases per year.[95] Cases involving adolescents are less likely to be reported.[96] Child abuse occurs among persons of all races, social classes, and religious beliefs. Most abusive parents were abused as children, thus perpetuating a cycle of abuse. In all 50 states, the law requires educators to report suspected child abuse.[97] Educators who report suspected child abuse in good faith (i.e., based on reasonable information) are immune from civil or criminal liability.[98]

Signs of abuse include bruises or other physical injuries not related to normal childhood activities; pain, especially in the genital area; nervous or fearful behavior or fear of going home; inappropriate clothing for weather conditions; malnutrition; untreated sores or cuts; and lack of hygiene.[99] Behavioral symptoms may include a decline in academic achievement, increased absence from school, explicit artwork, anger and hostility, and changes in social interaction patterns. Low self-esteem, depression, and pseudomature sexual behaviors are often seen in adolescents experiencing sexual abuse. Substance abuse and running away from home are common among abused children.[100] Most children are afraid to tell others of their experiences due to embarrassment, fear of repercussions, or fear of not being believed.[101] Victims of sexual abuse are usually girls under the age of 17. However, Harrison estimated that one out of four girls and one out of ten boys have been sexually abused before the age of 18.[102] Perpetrators are generally males known to the victim.

If you are confronted with the evidence of child abuse do not act surprised or horrified. Provide support, express concern, and praise the child for displaying the courage to tell about it.[103] Educators can follow the guidelines listed by Roscoe:

1. Show feelings of genuine concern for the student.
2. Make oneself available and provide opportunities to allow the student to talk freely about feelings, fears, etc.
3. Maintain the student's normal status within the class.
4. Reassure the student that he or she is not responsible for the assault which occurred.
5. Present learning activities which enhance the student's self-concept and self-esteem.
6. Provide experiences which allow student's self-expression and facilitate the constructive venting of emotion.
7. Respect and maintain the student's privacy.
8. Present oneself as a model for appropriate adult-child relationships.
9. Help the student keep fears and anxieties from growing out of proportion.
10. Interact closely and cooperatively with professionals who have been trained to work with sexually abused children (e.g., social workers, police, school psychologists).[104]

Educators must also notify the local department of social services.

Youth Culture

How do today's youth view society and their role in it? Workman summarized a study of youth culture, in which students wrote essays about themselves, in four themes.[105] First, students search for *family stability and communication*. Students named parents as the major influence in their lives. Even grandparents outranked idols in sports and music in terms of influence. In data collected from 11,000 eighth through tenth graders, a majority of the respondents said they rely on adult guidance to help them make important decisions about their future or about issues such as sex, drugs, and alcohol.[106] Although television ranked third in terms of influence, preferred shows dealt with family life. The second theme involved *identity problems and loneliness*. Teenagers look for connections and guidance. Third, youth live in a culture that moves at a disturbing pace. Therefore, *living with rapid change* is essential. They look forward to some stability in a changing world. The fourth theme was a *fear of failure*. With the increasing knowledge demands for employment, competition is stiff.

The effects of social forces on individual students differ in terms of their various backgrounds and experiences. For example, ethnic groups' expectations regarding the value of education differ. Likewise, families differ in the cultural experiences they provide their members, as well as in their goals and interests. Friends, neighbors, and other social groups also influence values and attitudes. Thus, experiences of individual students can be so different that generalities are no longer of use in planning educational programs.

A program has been developed by the Quest National Center in Columbus, Ohio, to help sixth through eighth graders learn about the challenges of adolescence and how to develop the skills necessary to cope with them. Called "Skills for Adolescence," the program has been adopted by more than 500 school districts. It includes units on entering the teen years, building self-confidence, learning about emotions, improving peer and family relationships, developing decision-making skills, setting goals, and developing one's potential.[107]

Meeting the Needs of All Students

The goal of education is to provide a quality educational experience for every student. There are boys and girls, low-skilled and highly skilled, slow learners and gifted students, nondisabled and disabled, and a large number of different cultural and ethnic backgrounds, including many non-English-speaking students. As students mature, differences among learners escalate. Not only must opportunities be provided, but programs must increasingly demonstrate that students achieve the goals of instruction. To meet these needs, outstanding programs include a broad spectrum of activities, with occasional opportunities for students to select their own preferences. Zakrajsek and Carnes noted that:

> Too many physical education classrooms foster and perpetuate a method of teaching that supports a singular learning concept for all students based on one kind of motivation, one style of learning, and one set of learning needs.[108]

Physical growth and development, intellectual and emotional development, social forces, and personality factors all affect the ways in which students learn. Therefore, excellent instructional programs consider various styles of learning. Some principles to consider when planning educational programs include the following:

1. Each student is unique, a result of both heredity and environment.
2. Each student learns at his or her own rate regardless of how the teacher paces the instruction.
3. Students learn many things simultaneously.
4. Students learn different things from identical experiences.
5. Learning is not a smooth, continuous process. It involves intermittent periods of growth followed by plateaus.
6. Students must learn for themselves. The teacher cannot learn for them.
7. Students learn best when
   a. learning is positively and immediately reinforced by praise or success.
   b. the learning process involves experiencing and doing.
   c. a wide variety of meaningful learning experiences are provided at the appropriate level for the maturity of the student.
   d. goals and objectives are set or accepted by the students and provide realistic standards for each student.

e. students can see the results of how well they are doing.
f. students experience many more successful experiences than failures.
g. learning is directed to the whole student.
h. the learning experience and evaluation are adapted to each student.
i. the learning environment is a comfortable place in which to make (and learn from) a mistake.

Each of these principles will be discussed in more detail in the following chapters. Doll suggested that "the challenge to education in a democracy appears much more prominently in the differences among children and youth than in their similarities."[109]

In the past, some teachers maintained stereotypes about certain groups of students. Because students performed in a certain way in the past, however, does not mean they will perform in the same way in the future. Lack of opportunities for girls and for students of some racial or ethnic groups may have hindered their performance. Programs tend to favor highly skilled students. As Dodds indicated, "No law protects students with less motor ability against the implacable laws of nature which guarantees that in the gym, as in the wider world, the rich simply get richer and the poor get poorer."[110] Programs that equalize opportunities for all students could see a decrease in performance differences. Teachers should get to know each student as a person of worth and dignity.

Mizen and Linton advocated six steps to consider when designing programs to meet the needs of all students.[111] Guidelines for specific populations will be presented at the end of this section.

1. *Prepare an environment in which individual differences are respected and valued.* This is achieved by acknowledging differences among students through class discussions and experiences in which people who are different from each other work together. Students can be taught that teasing is often caused by anxious or insecure behavior around those who are different. Wearing blindfolds or earplugs, playing with petroleum jelly smeared on the glasses, or playing with the nondominant hand or foot can help students understand the challenges others face. Focus on what the students can do rather than on what they cannot do.

2. *Eliminate established practices that unwittingly contribute to embarrassment and failure.* By adapting activities to meet the needs of all students, the teacher will help students learn faster and experience positive attitudes toward physical activity. Beware of practices that contribute to the failure or embarrassment of some students, such as elimination games, in which the unskilled children who need the most practice sit on the sidelines, or activities in which obese or disabled students cannot compete on equal terms with other students. Avoid choosing teams in front of the class. Post most-improved scores, rather than just the top scores, so low-skilled students have an equal opportunity for recognition. Change grading policies to meet the needs of the students. "Learn three new skills" would challenge all students in gymnastics, whereas "perform a somersault dismount off the balance beam" might discourage all but a few. Consider a combination of factors rather than just skill alone. All students can improve their physical fitness.

3. *Build ego strength.* Help students develop self-esteem and self-confidence by providing successful experiences, helping students set realistic expectations, and allowing students to participate at appropriate levels for their abilities. Help students to develop an awareness of their personal strengths.

Teachers can communicate their interest in students as individuals not just by words but also through feelings. Within every student lies an inner self that can be reached only when the student extends an invitation. This occurs when the student feels the sincere, unselfish concern of a caring teacher. A teacher who listens to a student sends the student a message, "I care about you. Your feelings are important to me." Listening is different from hearing. It involves putting oneself into the other person's shoes and paying attention with the heart. Stephens wrote, "I have learned . . . that the head does not hear anything until the heart has listened, and that what the heart knows today the head will understand tomorrow."[112] Listening involves patience and compassion. Hanks added:

> The time to listen is when someone needs to be heard. The time to deal with a person with a problem is when he has the problem. . . . Every human being is trying to say something to others, trying to cry out, "I am alive. Notice me! Speak to me! Listen to me! Confirm for me that I am important, that I matter."[113]

A teacher can be the one who confirms that the student matters. When talking to a student, encourage the student to express feelings. Then, listen with understanding; note the student's facial expressions, posture, and tone of voice as well as what is said.

Other ways to demonstrate an interest in students include calling them by name and recognizing each student in some way each day. A snapshot or photo can be helpful in learning names. Let the students know you want to learn their names and you want them to help you learn them. Jot down identifying characteristics in your roll book. Use games to help learn names. For example, in the name game, students introduce themselves using an adjective that begins with the letter of their name. Each student repeats the names of the previous persons and adds his or her own, for example, "Jumping Miss Jones, Singing Sally, Typing Terry, and I'm Caroling Carolyn." Another way to get acquainted is to have students create name tags. Some ideas include a collage, a personal coat of arms, or a self-commercial, such as a guitar for a student who plays the guitar or a basketball for a member of the team. When all else fails, assign students to a given court or team and learn the names of one group each day. Many other ideas can be created by both teachers and students to help class members get acquainted with one another.

Learn something about each student—interests, achievements, hobbies, favorite subject, favorite sport, or family life. Get feedback from students on how they would like their class to be run. A file card or form handed out at the beginning of the year or unit could solicit answers to such questions as:

1. Most of all, what do you like to do?
2. What is your favorite game, sport, or hobby?
3. What are your expectations of the class? The teacher? Yourself?
4. How would you like the class to be run? How will you help?
5. What would you like me to know about you?

Another technique is to ask students to pair up with a student they do not know and interview their partners for a specified period of time, then take one minute or less to tell something that impressed them about their partners.

Make it your business to be in strategic places at strategic times—such as the school play or a band concert when a student of yours is participating. Seek opportunities to say "hello" when you see students in the hall or on the street. Compliment students when deserved and appropriate. Emphasize their positive qualities. Sit with students at football games or in the cafeteria. Notice their achievements in other curricular areas such as the school newspaper, home economics, wood shop, or in out-of-school service to the community. Share student successes with other teachers and administrators.

When teaching lessons, adjust the content to student needs and interests. Encourage student involvement and sharing. Make it easy for students to ask questions and make comments. Counsel with individuals regarding fitness and skill test scores so students know where they stand with regard to class goals. Focus your attention on both the skilled and the unskilled. All of them deserve equal time and attention.

Give students an opportunity to accept leadership positions, and rotate positions often. Do not do for students what they can do for themselves. Students can be assigned to greet visitors, demonstrate skills, lead exercises, and issue and set up equipment. Know the current needs and interests of your students. Provide each student with the opportunity for success and recognition.

Sigmund Freud's niece once recalled a mushroom hunt her uncle had during a family outing. By the end of the activity each child had a prize—for the biggest, oddest, smallest, first, last, or other mushroom. Similar awards or recognition could be given to students in physical education or intramural programs. Possibilities include participant of the month, best equipment monitor, best sport, best official, most-improved player or official, or best scorer. Recognition before the class may carry more weight than individual recognition because of the need for peer approval.

Gustafson suggested that teachers construct a checklist of their strategies for enhancing self-esteem.[114] This could be used as a self-check to determine effectiveness in incorporating these items into the teaching routine.

Since self-esteem is linked to body image and skill in physical activities, a program that helps students develop physical fitness and proficiency in activity skills can increase self-esteem and enhance the development of positive attitudes toward physical activity. Since body concept is an important part of self-esteem, students can be taught to define and accept realistic body concepts and to modify factors that can be affected through physical education activities. They can also be helped to respect themselves and others, regardless of appearance.[115] When teachers occasionally engage in skills for which they have little competence or expertise, students learn that other people also have difficulty learning new and unfamiliar skills.

Harris emphasized the importance of students entering the "psychological door" through enjoyment in a specific physical activity that has meaning for them.[116] One of the main goals of physical education is to get students to incorporate physical activities into their lifestyles. When students experience successful participation in physical activities in a warm, supportive, positive environment with teachers who care, they are more likely to continue to participate outside of the school setting.

A number of different needs stimulate interest in physical activity. These needs may take the form of social affiliation, energy-release, health and well-being, or self-fulfillment. As needs change, so do interests.

4. *Provide individual assistance and keep students active.* Teachers and parents have the task of helping adolescents direct their energies into socially acceptable activities that also enhance their personal worth. Adults do this by acting as positive role models, with clearly defined values. They establish limits and define procedures so students have the emotional security that comes from knowing what is expected. Gradually, students must learn to accept responsibility for their own actions, to set personal goals, and to learn self-discipline. Adults can facilitate this process.

Peer tutors help special needs students improve
skills, fitness, and attitudes.
© James L. Shaffer

The *buddy system* and *peer tutoring* are excellent ways to help special needs students. A recent study by DePaepe found that the use of peer tutors significantly increased academic learning time and created the best environment for enhancing motor performance for moderately mentally handicapped students.[117] The Physical Education Opportunity Program for Exceptional Learners (PEOPEL) teams 15 student aides and 15 exceptional learners on a one-to-one basis in physical education classes. The aides or peer-teachers are trained to understand the problems of exceptional learners and to help their partners learn cognitive, psychomotor, and affective skills. Program results show that PEOPEL students improved significantly in physical fitness and in attitudes toward physical education, whereas similar students enrolled in traditional adapted physical education classes did not show significant improvements. Student aides improved in their understanding and appreciation of disabled students.[118]

Presenting skills in a developmentally sequential manner enhances opportunities for success. In addition, engaged learning time can be increased by using all balls and equipment available or utilizing alternative teaching stations. Some other validated programs designed to individualize learning are I CAN and Project Active.

The I CAN program is a published, individualized, instructional management system for teaching physical education and associated classroom skills to all children, disabled and nondisabled. It includes a set of sequential performance objectives, assessment instruments, instructional activities, games, class and individual records, and a Teacher's Implementation Guide. These diagnostic and prescriptive teaching resource materials are divided into four program skill areas: associated, primary, sport-leisure, and social.[119] Eight activity notebooks and accompanying films are provided to teach fundamental skills, health, fitness, body management, and aquatics.

Traditional demonstration and practice strategies may not be appropriate for all students. Teachers can learn to use a variety of teaching styles and activities to meet the diverse learning styles, needs, and interests of students. Student differences are more adequately considered by including both competitive and noncompetitive activities in the curriculum.

Project Active was developed by the Township of Ocean School District, Oakhurst, New Jersey, under the direction of Thomas M. Vodola. Materials assist teachers in the assessment, prescription, and evaluation of the physical and motor needs of disabled students.[120]

5. *Group students by ability to allow for mastery teaching.* A challenge for every physical educator is to help each student experience success by planning small, sequential steps so that all students can succeed as often as possible. Although this takes time, it is rewarding because students progress more rapidly than they would without the sequential steps, and there are fewer discipline problems. For a discouraged student, even a small success can be a boost, since these students often feel they have never experienced success before. As skills are learned and small successes become big successes, self-esteem begins to increase. Once students begin to experience success, they show a willingness to try new skills, they put forth greater effort, they obtain more success, and the circle continues as shown in figure 3.2. Conversely, failure results in an unwillingness to try and little or no effort.

Activities can be provided on various skill levels. It is sometimes advisable to group students by ability level within classes to help low-skilled students experience success while at the same time providing a challenge for the more highly skilled. Make sure skills are learned well before moving on to new skills. Provide remedial or challenge activities for students to practice the skills they are learning. Mastery learning, described in chapter 7, is an excellent

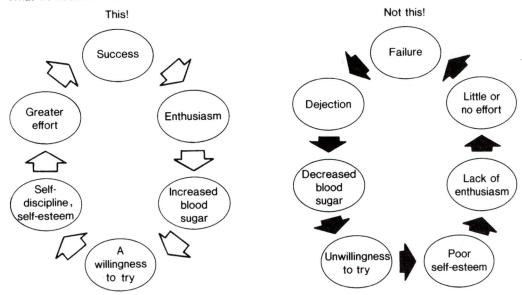

What we need is . . .

This!   Not this!

Success — Enthusiasm — Increased blood sugar — A willingness to try — Self-discipline, self-esteem — Greater effort — Success

Failure — Little or no effort — Lack of enthusiasm — Poor self-esteem — Unwillingness to try — Decreased blood sugar — Dejection — Failure

Figure 3.2 Failure and success cycles in students.
Source: Health, Physical Education and Recreation
Newsletter, Utah State Office of Education.

way to meet the diverse needs of students while giving all students an opportunity to achieve at a higher level. Individual contracts or units can also be used to individualize instruction. A number of learning activities that can be used to individualize instruction to meet the differing needs of students are presented in chapter 7.

    6. *Alter and adapt.* Most activities can be adapted to meet the needs of students of varying abilities by decreasing time periods; modifying courts, fields, and equipment; and by changing the rules. Some activities are more readily adapted than others. The best activities are those in which success or failure does not depend on the ability or performance of another person. Since many secondary schools now offer selective or elective programs, students have the opportunity to select the activities that best meet their needs.[121] Winnick suggested eight ways in which activities can be adapted so that disabled students can participate effectively with their peers:[122]

1. Modify activities to equalize competition by (a) creating "handicaps" for students, as in golf and bowling; (b) changing distance, height of basket, and so on (see the inclusion style in chapter 7); or (c) reducing skill complexity (i.e., kicking a stationary rather than a moving ball).
2. Permit "courtesy" runners (or partner runners for the blind) for students who need them.
3. Include activities in which contact is maintained with a partner, small group, or object (such as square dancing, wrestling, tug-of-war, a rail for bowling). Contact helps some disabled students know what is expected.

4. Modify the activity to require nondisabled students to assume the impairment of the disability (such as using only one leg in a relay or playing blindfolded in a game).
5. Assign positions according to the abilities of the disabled persons. (Field hockey goalies and softball pitchers do not have to move quickly and are good position choices for individuals with one leg. Catcher can be a good position for persons with one arm because they do not have to throw quickly.)
6. Change elimination activities, such as dodge ball, so that students exchange positions with the thrower or count the number of times hit rather than be eliminated.
7. Limit the size of the playing area by reducing the court size or increasing the number of players on a team.
8. Use audible goals, such as a horn or drum, to allow visually impaired students to compete in relays, basketball, archery, shuffleboard, or softball.

Other modifications might include:

1. Emphasize cooperative rather than competitive games.
2. Decrease the duration of the activity.
3. Increase or decrease the size of game objects (such as balls) or game implements (such as rackets or bats).
4. Increase or decrease the size of the target or hoop.
5. Require that players guard or block only players of the same size.
6. Require that every player on the team touch the ball before a goal is scored.
7. Allow players to choose the implement with which to hit and the object to be hit (softball-type games).
8. Make the pitcher (in softball) a member of the team at bat.

Encourage students to modify activities to ensure fair play. For the mentally and/or physically disabled student select games with simple rules and strategies. Rhythms and dance, swimming, and other individual activities are popular with these students.

The Individuals with Disabilities Education Act

The education of children with identified disabilities is protected by law. In 1975 PL 94-142 (The Education for All Handicapped Children Act) was passed. This law was renamed and updated under The Individuals with Disabilities Education Act of 1990 (IDEA), PL 101-476. The principal parts of PL 94-142 are maintained in IDEA, along with the mandates of PL 99-457 Education Amendments of 1986.

One of the main guarantees of all the legislation for disabled students is that all children, regardless of their disability, are entitled to a free, appropriate public education in the least restrictive environment.[123] This means that every disabled child must be assured a public education that will meet his or her special needs alongside nondisabled children (as much as possible) at no cost to the parents or guardian. School districts cannot deny services because of the severity of a child's disability.[124] One key factor to remember here is that the child's individual needs, not those of a grouping of students with the same disability, are to be considered in determining the education of the child.

Within IDEA, the only specific subject mentioned is physical education. The act states that "the term special means specially designed instruction, at no cost to parent or guardians, to meet the unique needs of a child with a disability, including . . . instruction in physical education."[125]

According to the law, physical education includes the development of (1) physical and motor fitness; (2) fundamental motor skills and patterns; and (3) skills in aquatics, dance, individual and group games, and sports (including intramural and lifetime sports). In addition, students receiving special education and related services must have access to extracurricular activities, including athletics, that are comparable to those received by their nondisabled classmates. Related services—such as recreation and school health services—or supportive services—such as athletics, physical therapy, or dance therapy—*must* be provided by the district or school or contracted from some other agency if such services are required to assist a disabled student to benefit from special education.

The Individualized Education Program

By law, every student with an identified disability receiving special education and related services must have an individualized education program (IEP). The IEP is used throughout the school year as a guide for teachers (and administrators) to follow in working with individual students with an identified disability. It includes the following:

1. The student's present levels of educational performance
2. Annual goals (long- and short-term) and instructional objectives for that student
3. Specific special services to be provided to the student and the extent to which the student will be able to participate in regular educational programs
4. Projected dates for initiation of and anticipated duration of services
5. Objective criteria and evaluation procedures and schedules

IEPs vary in form, length, and detail from one school district to another and from one student to another. A multidisciplinary team writes the IEP. The physical education teacher should be a part of the team when it is apparent that a particular child will need a specially designed physical education program. The physical education teacher is involved to help with suggestions of goals, modifications, and any other items that need to be addressed in developing a physical education curriculum for the student.

The Least Restrictive Environment and Mainstreaming

The *least restrictive environment* refers to the education of disabled students with their nondisabled peers when the environment is conducive to helping students reach their full potential. If a student cannot participate successfully in a regular class program, then that student can be placed in a special class or school. Most disabled students can be successfully integrated into regular physical education if their individual needs are considered.

Mainstreaming is the procedure whereby disabled students are educated in the regular classroom along with their nondisabled peers, rather than in special education classes. Mainstreamed students generally have a more favorable attitude toward physical education, adjust more adequately to the real world, and do better both academically and socially than nonmainstreamed students.[126] Their nondisabled peers also learn to understand and appreciate them. *Inclusion* is a form of mainstreaming that today is receiving a great deal of attention. In inclusion, all students are educated in the mainstream.[127] In other words, every student is in regular education classes. Miller states that inclusion has a number of positive points:

Inclusion is important because
1) Separation causes stigmatization
2) Separation leads to lowering of expectations; self-fulfilling prophesy

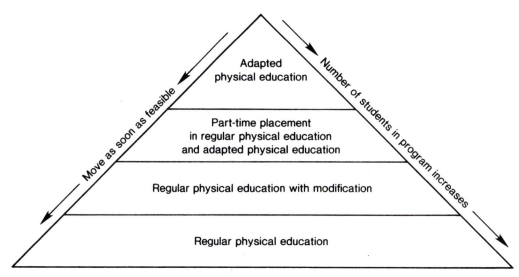

Figure 3.3 A continuum of physical education placement possibilities.

3) Inclusion provides for the benefits of peer interactions: language, social, and academic role models
4) Inclusion provides benefits to general school population: tolerance, acceptance, the valuing of differences in people.[128]

To mainstream all disabled students or to segregate all students into adapted physical education classes is to violate the principles upon which the law was based. Placement in a least restrictive environment must be made on an individual basis. Placement decisions should be based on previous physical fitness and motor ability assessments.[129] Failure to do so could result in a malpractice suit.[130] The law requires that children be placed in physical education classes according to individual needs. They must not be grouped by disabling condition (i.e., learning disabled students assigned to a class together). Physical educators must take the initiative to see that placement flexibility is maintained in IEPs so that each student participates in regular physical education activities where possible and in specially designed programs as necessary.

Alternative Placement Possibilities

Since schools are now required to enroll students who possess a wide range of individual abilities, a continuum of physical education services must be provided. This continuum ranges from the most restrictive environment to the regular physical education class, as shown in figure 3.3.

Regular physical education. Students who can safely and successfully participate in the regular physical education program should be encouraged to do so.

Regular physical education with modification. Some disabled students can participate with their nondisabled peers if appropriate modifications are made such as: (1) a buddy or peer-tutoring system, which pairs a disabled student with a nondisabled partner for specific activities as in the PEOPEL program described earlier; (2) circuit or station organizational patterns; (3) contract-learning techniques; (4) team-teaching, involving regular and adapted physical education teachers, resource teachers, or paraprofessional aides; or (5) preteaching certain activities to students with special needs. Students with special needs might work on such needs a specified amount of time each period, with the remaining time being devoted to regular activities with other members of the class.

Part-time placement. Part-time placement is an arrangement in which students spend specified days each week in an adapted physical education class, where they concentrate on special needs as delineated in the IEP, and other days in regular classes. This type of placement may be especially useful in helping students gain the skills and confidence necessary to make the transition to a regular physical education program.

Adapted physical education. Students with severe or multiple disabilities may need to be placed in an adapted physical education class to receive corrective therapy or remedial help. Only in this setting can activities be adapted enough for students with severe handicaps to participate freely and successfully. Adapted physical education can occur as a separate class within the school, in a special school, in a home, or in a hospital.

Section 504 of the Rehabilitation Act

A second federal law that affects physical education programs and facilities is Section 504 of the Rehabilitation Act of 1973 (PL 93-112); the final rules and regulations came out in 1977. This law provides that "no otherwise qualified handicapped individual . . . shall, solely by reason of his handicap, be excluded from participation in, be denied the benefits of, or be subjected to discrimination under any program or activity receiving federal financial assistance."[131]

This law requires schools to provide equal opportunities for the disabled to participate in *all* programs offered by the school, including physical education, intramurals, clubs, and interscholastic athletics. Accommodations, adaptations, and adjustments expected so that individuals with handicapping conditions can participate in regular physical education programs and activities include the following:

1. Accessible buildings and other facilities
2. Appropriate transportation
3. Appropriate curricular adjustments, such as changing competency requirements, eligibility requirements, and rules that discriminate
4. Appropriate adaptations for activities, such as a bowling ramp or beeper balls

The major impact on the schools as a result of the two laws dealing with the disabled is to modify existing curricula to include a wide spectrum of activities for the disabled. In addition, architectural, administrative, and instructional barriers must be removed to allow disabled students access to all programs offered by the schools. Eichstaedt and Kalakian suggest that schools make sure that (1) individuals with disabling conditions are not separated from those without a disabling condition and that (2) individuals with a disabling condition are not indiscriminately placed in special or segregated programs and activities. Doing so violates both federal laws and can jeopardize federal funding for the school district.[132]

Multicultural Education

Multicultural education has been defined as "education designed to promote understanding and appreciation of cultural diversity and cultural pluralism"[133] and recognizes the differences in human behavior as they are influenced by the culture and ethnicity of the individual.[134] Swisher and Swisher summarized multicultural education as it applies to physical education.[135] The

United States is a multicultural society. The number of Asian, Hispanic, African American, Native American, and Asian American citizens is increasing. By the year 2020, 48 percent of school-age children in the United States will be ethnic minorities,[136] many of them living at or below the poverty level.[137] Federal legislation and Supreme Court decisions require *equal educational opportunities* for all students regardless of gender, physical condition, socioeconomic level, racial or ethnic background, religion, or language. However, equal opportunity does not mean that all students should be treated equally. Sometimes equity requires different treatments to meet the differing needs of individual students. Multicultural education implies that teaching will capitalize on the strengths of student differences rather than on their weaknesses. This means that teachers must learn to view cultural values from each group's perspective rather than from their own. This can be done by asking questions about family life, interpersonal interaction styles, health and hygiene, and similar items. Problems arise when the interaction style of the culture differs from the style of the school. For example, the culture of Native Americans may tend to emphasize cooperation rather than competition; Mexican American children tend to learn with a global rather than an analytical cognitive style; some Asian children tend to hold the teacher in high esteem. All of these styles differ considerably from those of Caucasian children.[138]

A multicultural perspective must also exist in schools where intergroup contact is absent. Students need to examine stereotypes and misunderstandings that can result from no contact with other groups as well as from books and media.[139]

Swisher and Swisher list things that teachers can do to adopt a multicultural approach to instruction.[140] These include the following:

1. Learn students' names and pronounce them correctly.
2. Accept students' native languages while patiently helping students develop proficiency in English.
3. Use alternative teaching styles that allow for differences in students' learning styles.
4. Avoid calling attention to individual students in front of their peers.
5. Be aware of the different ways in which students of different cultures pay attention (i.e., eye contact or no eye contact).
6. Avoid the choosing of teams during class time, which can embarrass students.

Physical education is often one of the first classes in which students in the English as a Second Language (ESL) program are placed. These students, as well as their level of English proficiency, need to be identified for the physical education teacher.[141] Glakas suggested some communication techniques to use with ESL students:

1. Do not ask an ESL student to speak in class immediately.
2. Have another bilingual student help translate.
3. Use simple language with basic vocabulary.
4. Use examples, gestures, and demonstrations.
5. Do not correct ESL students who give appropriate answers in imperfect English.
6. Allow sufficient time for ESL students to respond.
7. At first ask simple yes/no-type questions, then gradually increase the difficulty of questions as their English improves.
8. Have essential written material such as departmental policies, course outlines, and form letters to parents translated.[142]

Other suggestions included teaching sports and games with which ESL students are familiar. Allow flexibility in uniforms since clothing standards are different in other cultures. Do not give timed tests to ESL students and encourage the use of bilingual dictionaries.[143]

Cultural differences also exist between students growing up in urban poverty versus suburban affluence. "These differences grow out of the many ways in which the daily world of the adolescent is structured by relationships that begin in the family and spread out from there into other social environments in the community."[144] Students with a low-income background are more likely to have learning disabilities and lower educational achievement. "They are also more likely to drop out of school, to experience teenage pregnancy and early parenthood, to become involved in criminal and delinquent acts, to be arrested and incarcerated, to be unemployed, and to continue their working lives on the lowest rungs of the work force."[145] Students from suburbia experience strong pressures to excel in areas such as sports, music, and academics. Both groups require a stable and consistent environment in which to grow and develop.[146]

Robinson stated:

> More multicultural education takes place when the white kid and the black kid sitting next to each other start making friends than in all the multiculturalist lectures in the world. The teacher is often in a position to facilitate that kind of connection, by having students work together on projects, by steering students toward projects that disturb but also strangely fascinate them, by creating an atmosphere of fun and tolerance in the classroom. Teachers who listen to their students as whole people learn from them; and when learning starts flowing in both directions, student to teacher and back, and then in all directions, everybody to everybody, barriers soon come crashing down, both inside our own heads and in society at large.[147]

Above all, teachers who accept student differences communicate to students that these differences are not problems to be remediated. Swisher and Swisher conclude that multicultural education is an attitude that communicates to students "that diversity is desirable and to be different is okay."[148] Knutson published a sensitivity index to help teachers rate themselves on their ability to help all students. She also stressed the importance of student feedback to teachers about their teaching.[149]

Gender Equity and Title IX

Historically, physical education programs have been segregated by sex. The intent of Title IX of the Education Amendments of 1972 was to provide equal educational opportunities for males and females. With regard to physical education classes, the law provided that

1. Students may be grouped by ability using objective standards of individual performance developed and applied without regard to gender.
2. Students may be separated by gender within physical education classes during participation in contact sports—wrestling, boxing, rugby, ice hockey, football, or basketball.
3. Portions of classes dealing exclusively with human sexuality may be conducted separately for males and females.
4. When use of a single standard of measurement has an adverse effect on members of one gender, then appropriate standards may be used, such as in skill and fitness test norms.[150]
5. Students whose religion prohibits coeducational physical education may be offered gender-segregated classes.[151]

In a 1984 decision by the Supreme Court (*Grove City College v. Bell*), Title IX was limited to specific programs within an institution that received federal funds. However, the Civil Rights Restoration Act of 1988 reversed the decision and restored coverage to all programs in institutions receiving any type of federal financial assistance.[152]

Geadelmann reported that the extent of implementation of Title IX has not reached the desired goal and "the content and conduct of coeducational classes . . . remain susceptible to sexist practices which perpetuate stereotypes and fail to realize the spirit of Title IX."[153] She noted that some schools have refused to offer certain activities to coeducational groups, others have eliminated controversial activities, and many offer activities on an elective basis with no previous exposure to both sexes. These same problems were confirmed by Young in a later report.[154]

Even when programs meet the requirements of the law, gender-role stereotypes are often reflected in differing teacher expectations for males and females. In a study by Geadelmann, 54 percent of the boys and 44 percent of the girls thought the teacher expected more of the boys.[155] According to Griffin, teacher expectation differences appear in programs in four ways: (1) class organization strategies, (2) teacher-student interaction patterns, (3) teacher language, and (4) teacher role modeling.[156]

With regard to *class organization,* teachers used the command style of teaching almost exclusively and picked teams publicly without using ability grouping. Studies have consistently demonstrated that participation styles of boys and girls differ, even when the teachers' purposes favor nondiscrimination.[157] Boys tend to dominate team play and girls tend to give scoring opportunities to boys. Girls and boys perceive boys as more highly skilled, even when objective tests show the girls to be more talented.[158] Boys have more contacts with the ball[159] and tend to see girls' events, such as in gymnastics, as of lower status.[160] Boys tend to sit in front of girls in squads[161] and boys have longer active learning time.[162] Low-skilled students have fewer opportunities to practice skills.[163]

However, as Griffin pointed out, "A generalized description of student interaction and participation by sex . . . can ignore or minimize differences in participation among students within the same gender group." She concluded, "To rely on gender differences in describing participation styles . . . would have presented an inaccurate picture ignoring the variety of action and attitude among the boys and among the girls observed."[164]

Even when teachers adapt games to increase participation by girls, the changes may be discriminatory, according to Geadelmann. These changes favor the girls over the boys. She emphasized that, "Without raised expectation levels regarding the physical performance of girls, it is unlikely that the girls will receive the necessary encouragement and assistance to reach new performance levels."[165]

Studies on *teacher-student interaction* patterns show that teachers interact differently with males and females. They interact more with boys in the areas of class management, discipline, physical contact, informal talk, feedback, and criticism.[166] Teachers praise boys more for their performance and girls more for their effort.[167] Boys were chosen more often as class leaders, demonstrators, role models, and equipment managers.[168] Some teachers showed condescending behavior to girls.[169] Teachers rarely corrected gender stereotyping by students in language or behavior.[170]

Studies on *teacher language* showed that teachers occasionally made stereotyped comments about "girls'" push-ups or throwing "like a boy," but they rarely made comments about girls being equal to boys. Although teachers generally used inclusive language to refer to students as a group (i.e., people, students), some stereotypical activity terms, such as "man-to-man," were used. Occasionally girls were called "ladies," but boys were rarely called "gentlemen." Some teachers used boys' last names and girls' first names.[171]

Research demonstrates that *teacher role modeling* is stereotyped in that male teachers rarely teach activities such as dance and gymnastics, whereas female teachers teach a wide variety of activities. Few teachers team-teach activities. A predominance of male athletes were pictured on bulletin boards and mentioned as role models by teachers.[172]

Sex equity depends on teachers' awareness of sex stereotyping patterns, their commitment to change, and specific action to change.[173] Effective teachers have learned that a wider range of motor abilities exists within each sex than between the sexes. Grouping students by ability can resolve the problems of students being intimidated or held back. Teachers can experiment with rules to find the best ones for both sexes. In fact, students can be challenged to experiment to find the best solution to the problem of appropriate rules.

Suggestions for increasing sex equity in physical education classes include activities to counteract the tendencies listed.[174] With regard to class organization, teachers can do the following:

1. Use a broader repertoire of instructional styles.
2. Change game rules to include all students, such as in three-on-three basketball or seven-player soccer, or by having every player touch the ball before scoring.
3. Use a variety of ways to divide students into teams.
4. Group students for instruction using simple objective tests.
5. Help students overcome gender stereotyping and learn to appreciate themselves and each other in physical education activities.
6. Since variations in abilities within the sexes are greater than between the sexes, base activities on individual needs rather than arbitrary male/female standards.[175]
7. Rather than segregate by sex for contact sports, reduce the contact in such activities so all students can participate.[176]
8. Schedule equal numbers of boys and girls into physical education classes, thus permitting equal numbers of each sex on each team. This promotes equality and fairness in participation styles.[177]

Suggestions for sex-equitable teacher-student interactions include:

1. Become aware of who receives interaction, the nature of that interaction, and possible gender-stereotyped expectations of students, and monitor teacher behavior.
2. Choose boys and girls equally as class leaders, role models, skill demonstrators, and equipment managers.

Teacher language can be improved by using the following guidelines:

1. Avoid "man" and "you guys" and consciously use inclusive language.
2. Use equivalent terms when referring to boys and girls.
3. Avoid reference to activities as boys' or girls'.

Gender-equitable role modeling includes the following:

1. Develop competencies in activities traditionally associated with the opposite sex.
2. Team-teach activities traditionally associated with the opposite sex.
3. Include male and female models participating in a variety of nontraditional activities on instructional materials such as bulletin boards.

Teachers can also elicit anonymous feedback from students about their feelings, preferences, and assessment of the results of instruction.[178] In short, when sex makes no relevant difference, boys and girls can be treated similarly; however, where relevant differences exist, boys and girls should have different, but equally valuable, opportunities.[179] Classes should be individualized according to ability level and not by sex.

In individualized instruction, students select different instructional programs to meet their various needs. Chapter 7 describes several strategies for individualizing instruction, as well as procedures for defining the tasks for differentiated instruction.

Griffin listed the factors necessary for successful coeducational programs as follows:

> In programs where coeducation is a success, where boys and girls are learning and enjoying physical activities together, students participate in a variety of competitive and noncompetitive activities, teachers spend as much time as they can helping students improve their skills, teachers step in to eliminate destructive student interactions and to change unfair game participation, and teachers frequently use ability grouping to even up competition and to match instruction to student needs. Teachers who have made coed physical education a success are enthusiastic about teaching, their students, and trying something new. They have a sense of their own power to change student behavior in their classes and know specific strategies to use in addressing problems they encounter.[180]

When planning coed programs, it is important to teach many activities in which competition is not a critical factor. Lifetime activities, such as tennis, golf, badminton, fitness, and swimming can be enjoyed on an equal basis by both boys and girls. Interest surveys will make teachers aware of students' desires for instruction in specific activities.

As Dodds indicated, "Equity is a way of looking at the world."[181] She said:

> Creating physical education classes where all children join a team without being subjected to humiliation or stress; where Blacks, Hispanics, Asians, and Whites play together peacefully; where the norms are cooperation, sensitivity to others, and appreciation of differences; and where each individual can learn in an atmosphere of encouragement and joy for every achievement is a vision held up for every teacher willing to pay the price to be fair and affirmative to all students.[182]

Some years ago, the members of the Educational Policies Commission summed up the purpose of education for all American youth, a purpose that still holds true today. They said:

> When we write confidently and inclusively about education for all American youth, we mean just that. We mean that all youth, with their human similarities and their equally human differences, shall have educational services and opportunities suited to their personal needs and sufficient for the successful operation of a free and democratic society.[183]

To implement all at once the suggestions offered for meeting the needs of all students would require a super teacher. Although it is true that excellent teachers seriously attempt to improve their teaching, they do so by tackling a few ideas at a time rather than trying to implement everything at once. Wessel noted that "Individualizing instruction does not necessarily require major changes in the class or school. Teachers can adjust existing instructional approaches to students' learning . . . within their own classrooms and within existing constraints," through the use of a variety of instructional cues, different groupings for different activities, and the modification of games and activities. Students can be given the responsibility of helping to assess, monitor, and record learning outcomes.[184]

Although the design of instruction attempts to establish conditions to facilitate learning, it is up to the learner to take advantage of them. Teachers cannot learn for their students. More and more of the responsibility for education must be placed on the learners. One seldom observes signs of friction or disorder in a classroom where the students are interested and actively engaged in meaningful school activity related to their needs and interests, especially if that schoolwork is a part of their own planning.

Studying Student Needs

Getting to know students implies taking the time to find out what the similarities and differences are among students in a particular school. Some of this information will be available in the form of school and student records. School records include data about the entire school population such as total enrollment, age and sex distributions, race or ethnic backgrounds, dropout rates, and other essential information needed for developing educational programs. Student records include health and medical status, intelligence and achievement test results, grades, results of interest and attitude inventories, and other information.

The Family Educational Rights and Privacy Act of 1974 (PL 93-380) withholds federal funds from any school denying parents (or students age 18 or over) access to student educational records or permitting third-party access to personally identifiable data in the records without prior consent. Persons permitted access to the records include teachers and school officials with legitimate educational interests and local, state, or national officials specified in the law. Parents have a right to challenge the content of the records.[185]

Observation of students in the school setting also can be a valuable source of data. Parent-teacher conferences and back-to-school nights can be helpful in getting acquainted with family backgrounds. The following questions could be used to direct your observation of students in a selected class to better meet individual needs:

1. What would you guess to be the range in height in the class? In weight? Have you observed any students for whom size may be a source of potential problems? What problems do you foresee? Record ideas for dealing with these problems.
2. What is the age range of students in the class? Does it appear that age may be a problem for any student in this class? Explain.
3. Identify the student whom you consider to be the most aggressive in the class; the least aggressive. As you think about these two and observe them, do you see a basic difference in the way they approach learning activities at school? Explain.
4. Which student, in your judgment, comes from the most affluent home? The least affluent? What implications do you see for instruction and learning?
5. What is the performance range of students in the class? The range in physical fitness? How would you adapt the instruction to meet the needs of each level?
6. Identify students who are disabled physically, culturally, or otherwise. What would you do to help them achieve success?
7. List as many other ways as you can think of in which students differ. Which of these might affect the way a student learns? Try ranking them in order of importance.

Observation of students in nonschool functions can also provide insights into student activities, interpersonal relationships, and leadership abilities. The following questions might be used as a guide:

1. Who was the group leader? How could you tell?
2. Were the leaders in these activities also leaders in school activities? Why or why not?
3. How did the boys react to the girls and vice versa?

4. Who directed the activities officially? Unofficially?
5. How was attention shown? To whom was it shown?
6. How were the students' behaviors different from their behaviors in school?
7. What motivating factors influence students when they are not in school?
8. What group or individual values were in evidence?
9. How did the group values influence the individuals?
10. How were decisions made among the students?
11. What learning was taking place?
12. What was the nature of the activity (constructive, destructive, social, religious)? How did this help determine the type of behavior considered appropriate for the situation?
13. Why were these particular students together?
14. What methods of influence did you notice being practiced?
15. How will knowing this information about students change your behavior in the classroom?
16. How do students behave differently in adult company? With different teachers?

Questionnaires can provide insight into the actual interests, attitudes, and values of students. Some possible questions are given here.

Directions: Do not write your name on this paper. Answer the questions below in the best way you know how.

1. How do you feel about yourself? I am:
2. How do you rate yourself as a student?
3. Do you have a job? If so, what kind?
4. What do you do in your free time?
5. What are your favorite sports or activities?
6. Do you play a musical instrument? Take private lessons in dance, music, sports? If so, what kind?
7. Do you have a lot of friends? A few friends? Are they close friends? Casual friends? Both?

Of course, teacher-student interaction before, during, and after classes provides one of the best opportunities for teachers and students to get to know each other on a more informal basis.

In summary Hill indicated that as a teacher it is important to "never forget:

- that failure hurts;
- that being forced to do something in front of others—particularly something 'simple'—can be humiliating;
- that failure prompts impulses to escape, distract, cheat, and attack;
- that failure can come from simply not knowing how to think about a task;
- that wanting to learn and being able to learn are two different things;
- that being forced to do something is painful but may be a necessary first step if you are going to start to improve;
- that, when you are thinking poorly, it helps if people try to understand how you are thinking;
- that taking time to talk about the way you think can change the way you think;
- that learning different specific strategies for thinking is motivating;
- that success and learning cross-fertilize one another; and
- that nothing is more important than being accepted and affirmed for who you are."[186]

Review Questions

1. What are the common characteristics of children and youth?
2. Outline the significant differences among students—physically, intellectually, socially, and emotionally.
3. Summarize the social forces that affect students and their families.
4. How can teachers meet the needs of all students in their classes?
5. Define: Public Law 101-476, Section 504 of the Rehabilitation Act, IEP, mainstreaming, least restrictive environment, adapted physical education.
6. What is multicultural education? What can teachers do to adopt a multicultural approach to teaching?
7. What is Title IX? How does it affect physical education class instruction?

References

1. Woodruff, A. D. (1951). *The psychology of teaching* (p. 241). New York: Longmans, Green & Co., Inc.
2. Pratt, D. (1980). *Curriculum: Design and development* (p. 270). New York: Harcourt Brace Jovanovich.
3. Willgoose, C. E. (1984). *The curriculum in physical education* (4th ed., p. 255). Englewood Cliffs, NJ: Prentice-Hall.
4. Wessel, J. A., & Kelly, L. (1986). *Achievement-based curriculum development in physical education* (p. 56). Philadelphia: Lea & Febiger.
5. Chamberlin, L. J., & Girona, R. (1976, January). Our children are changing. *Educational Leadership, 33,* 301–305.
6. Griffin, P., & Placek, J. (1983). *Fair play in the gym: Race and sex equity in physical education* (p. 53). Amherst: University of Massachusetts.
7. Ibid., 54.
8. Chamberlin & Girona, Our children are changing, 301–305.
9. Armstrong, T. (1985, September). How real are learning disabilities? *Learning, 14,* 45–47.
10. Bereiter, C. (1985, April). The changing face of educational disadvantagement. *Phi Delta Kappan, 66,* 538–541.
11. Grippin, P., & Peters, S. (1984). *Learning theory and learning outcomes: The connection* (pp. 125–126). New York: University Press of America.
12. Witkins, H. A., Moore, C. A., Goodenough, D. R., & Cox, P. W. (1977). Field-dependent and field-independent cognitive styles and their educational implications. *Review of Educational Research, 47,* 1–64.
13. Cohen, R. (1969). Conceptual styles, culture conflict, and nonverbal tests of intelligence. *American Anthropologist, 71,* 828–856.
14. Zelniker, T., & Jeffrey, W. E. (1976). Reflective and impulsive children: Strategies of information processing underlying differences in problem solving. *Monographs of the Society for Research in Child Development, 41*(5), Serial Number 168.
15. Jenkins, C. P. (1986, February). Brain research leads to new teaching methods. *BYU Today, 40,* 4–5.
16. Dixon, N. M. (1985, November). The implementation of learning style information. *Lifelong Learning, 9,* 16–18, 26–27.
17. Sternberg, R. J. (1990, January). Thinking styles: Keys to understanding student performance. *Phi Delta Kappan, 71*(5), 366–371.
18. Bucher, C. A., & Koenig, C. R. (1983). *Methods and materials for secondary school physical education* (6th ed., p. 57). St. Louis, MO: Mosby.
19. Willgoose, *The curriculum in physical education,* 9.
20. Bucher & Koenig, *Methods and materials,* 42.
21. Combs, A. W. (1973, January). The human side of learning. *The National Elementary Principal, 52*(4), 38–42.
22. Snow, R. E., Tiffin, J., & Seibert, W. F. (1965). Individual differences and instructional effects. *Journal of Educational Psychology, 56,* 315–326.

23. Johnson, J. R. (1974, April). *Development and implementation of a competency-based teacher education module.* Paper presented at the annual meeting of the American Educational Research Association, Chicago. Cited in Pratt, *Curriculum,* 271.
24. Pratt, *Curriculum,* 273.
25. Stevens, L. J., & Price, M. (1992). Meeting the challenge of educating children at risk. *Phi Delta Kappan, 74,* 18–20, 22–23.
26. News release from American Health Foundation. (October 4, 1993). *Youth get a poor grade on their health report card.* 320 East 43rd Street, New York, New York.
27. Woodring, P. (1989). A new approach to the dropout problem. *Phi Delta Kappan, 70,* 468–469.
28. Lawson, M. A. (1993). School reform, families, and health in the emergent national agenda for economic and social improvement: Implications. *Quests, 45,* 289–307.
29. Ibid.
30. Duckett, W. (1988, October). Using demographic data for long-range planning: An interview with Harold Hodgkinson. *Phi Delta Kappan, 70*(2), 166–167.
31. Verzaro, M., & Hennon, C. B. (1980, Fall). Single-parent families: Myth and reality. *Journal of Home Economics, 72*(3), 31–33.
32. News release from American Health Foundation, *Youth get a poor grade on their health report card.*
33. Ibid.
34. Dornbusch, S. M., Carlsmith, J. M., Bushwall, S. J., Riter, P. L., Leiderman, H., Hastorf, A. H., & Gross, R. T. (1985, April). Single parents, extended households, and the control of adolescents. *Child Development, 56,* 326–341.
35. William T. Grant Foundation Commission on Youth and America's Future. (1988). *The forgotten half: Pathways to success for America's youth and young families.* Washington, DC: William T. Grant Foundation.
36. McCurdy, J. (1985, March). Schools respond to latchkey children. *The School Administrator, 42,* 16–18.
37. Campbell, L. P., & Flake, A. E. (1985, May). Latchkey children—What is the answer? *Clearing House, 58,* 381–383.
38. Strother, D. B. (1984, December). Latchkey children: The fastest-growing special interest group in the schools. *Phi Delta Kappan, 66,* 290–293.
39. Pecoraro, A., Theriot, J., & Lafont, P. (1984, Winter). What home economists should know about latchkey children. *Journal of Home Economics, 76,* 20–22.
40. McCurdy, Schools respond to latchkey children, 16–18.
41. Pecoraro, Theriot, & Lafont, What home economists should know about latchkey children, 20–22.
42. Carnegie Council on Adolescent Development. (1989). *Turning points: Preparing American youth for the 21st century* (p. 22). Washington, DC: Author.
43. Dryfoos, J. G. (1990). *Adolescents at risk: Prevalence and prevention.* New York: Oxford University Press.
44. Strother, Latchkey children, 290–293.
45. Sparks, W. G. (1993). Promoting self-responsibility and decision making with at-risk students. *The Journal of Physical Education, Recreation and Dance, 64*(2), 74.
46. Ibid.
47. Ibid., 77.
48. Ibid.
49. Johnston, L. D., O'Malley, P. M., & Bachman, J. G. (1988). *Illicit drug use, smoking and drinking by America's high school students, college students, and young adults: 1975–1987* (DHHS Publication No. ADM 89-1602). Washington, DC: U.S. Government Printing Office.
50. Towers, R. L. (1987). *How schools can help combat student drug and alcohol abuse* (p. 18). Washington, DC: National Education Association. Order from NEA Professional Library, Box 509, West Haven, CT 06516.
51. Ibid., 29–30.
52. DuPont, R. L., Jr. (1984). *Getting tough on gateway drugs.* Washington, DC: American Psychiatric Press. Cited in Towers, *Student drug and alcohol abuse,* 28.
53. Towers, *Student drug and alcohol abuse,* 19, 26–27.

54. Norem-Heibesen, A., & Hedin, D. P. (1984, February). Adolescent problem behavior: Causes, connections & contexts of drug abuse. Reprinted from *Grassroots—Special populations* in Hafen, B. Q., & Frandsen, K. J. (1984). *Addictive behavior: Drug and alcohol abuse* (pp. 39–48). Englewood, CO: Morton; Hafen, B. Q., & Frandsen, K. J. Drug behavior: The factors behind drug abuse. In Hafen & Frandsen, *Addictive behavior.*

55. Postman, N. (1981, November/December). Disappearing childhood. *Childhood Education, 58,* 66–68; Elkind, D. (1982, January). The hurried child. *Instructor, 91,* 40–43.

56. Norwood, G. R. (1985, March/April). A society that promotes drug abuse: The effects on pre-adolescence. *Childhood Education, 61*(4), 267–271.

57. Norem-Heibesen & Hedin, Adolescent problem behavior, 39–48.

58. Hafen & Frandsen, Drug behavior, 52–64.

59. Ibid.

60. Jones, C. L., & Battjes, R. J. (1985). The context and caveats of prevention research on drug abuse. In C. L. Jones & R. J. Battjes (Eds.), *Etiology of drug abuse: Implications for prevention* (p. 3). National Institute on Drug Abuse. Washington, DC: Superintendent of Documents, U.S. Government Printing Office.

61. Hawkins, J. D., Lishner, D., & Catalano, R. F. (1985). Childhood predictors and the prevention of adolescent substance abuse. In Jones & Battjes, *Etiology of drug abuse,* 85.

62. Norwood, A society that promotes drug abuse, 261–271.

63. Hafen & Frandsen, Drug behavior, 52–64.

64. Norem-Heibesen & Hedin, Adolescent problem behavior, 39–48.

65. Zimbardo, P. Quoted in Hafen, B. Q., & Frandsen, K. J. (1985). Preventing drug use and abuse. In *Addictive behavior: Drug and alcohol abuse* (pp. 373–376 [375]). Englewood, CO: Morton.

66. Towers, *Student drug and alcohol abuse,* 45.

67. Blum, R. H. Cited in Hafen & Frandsen, Drug behavior, 60.

68. Hafen & Frandsen, Drug behavior, 58.

69. Hafen & Frandsen, Drug behavior, 52–64.

70. Ibid.; Towers, *Student drug and alcohol abuse,* 61–63.

71. Towers, *Student drug and alcohol abuse,* 64–65.

72. Ibid., 71.

73. Ibid., 186.

74. Ibid., 76.

75. Ibid.

76. Ibid.; Swett, W. E. (1984, August). Helping young people survive in a chemical world. Reprinted from *Family & community health.* (1985). In *Addictive behavior: Drug and alcohol abuse* (pp. 359–369). Englewood, CO: Morton.

77. Towers, *Student drug and alcohol abuse.*

78. Ibid.

79. Frymier, J. (1988, December). Understanding and preventing teen suicide: An interview with Barry Garfinkel. *Phi Delta Kappan, 70*(4), 290–293.

80. Hafen, B. Q., & Frandsen, K. J. (1986). *Youth suicide: Depression and loneliness.* (pp. 10–17). Provo, UT: Behavioral Health Associates.

81. Ibid.

82. Deykin, E. Y., Perlow, R., & McNamarra, J. (1985, January). Non-fatal suicidal and life-threatening behavior among 13- to 17-year-old adolescents seeking emergency medical care. *American Journal of Public Health, 75,* 90–92.

83. Hafen & Frandsen, *Youth suicide,* 26.

84. Frymier, Understanding and preventing teen suicide: An interview with Barry Garfinkel, 290–293.

85. Jacobs, J. (1980). *Adolescent suicide.* New York: Irvington.

86. Frymier, Understanding and preventing teen suicide: An interview with Barry Garfinkel, 290–293.

87. Wellman, M. M. (1984, November). The school counselor's role in the communication of suicidal ideation by adolescents. *The School Counselor, 32,* 104–109; Hafen & Frandsen, *Youth suicide.*

88. Motto, J. A. (1984, October). Assessment of suicide risk. *Medical Aspects of Human Sexuality, 18,* 134, 153.

89. Hafen & Frandsen, *Youth suicide,* 149–173.

90. Frymier, Understanding and preventing teen suicide: An interview with Barry Garfinkel, 290–293.
91. Dryfoos, *Adolescents at risk*, 96–111.
92. Hofferth, S. L., Kahn, J. R., & Baldwin, W. (1987). Premarital sexual activity among U.S. teenage women over the past three decades. *Family Planning Perspectives, 19*(2), 46–53.
93. Hayes, C. D. (Ed.). (1987). *Risking the future: Adolescent sexuality, pregnancy, and childbearing.* Washington, DC: National Academy Press.
94. Hafen & Frandsen, Preventing drug use and abuse, 375–376.
95. Straus, M. A., Gelles, R. J., & Steinmetz, S. K. (1980). *Behind closed doors: Violence in the American family* (p. 73). New York: Doubleday.
96. Solomon, G. (1979). Child abuse and developmental disabilities. *Developmental Medicine and Child Neurology, 21,* 101–108.
97. Beezer, B. (1985, February). Reporting child abuse and neglect: Your responsibility and your protections. *Phi Delta Kappan, 66,* 434–436; Hurwitz, B. D. (1985, April). Suspicion: Child abuse. *Instructor, 94,* 76–78.
98. Beezer, Reporting child abuse and neglect, 434–436.
99. Hurwitz, Suspicion: Child abuse, 76–78.
100. Roscoe, B. (1984, Fall). Sexual abuse: The educator's role in identification and interaction with abuse victims. *Education, 105,* 82.
101. Ibid.
102. Harrison, R. (1985, August). How you can help the abused child. *Learning, 14,* 74–78.
103. Hurwitz, Suspicion: Child abuse, 76–78.
104. Roscoe, Sexual abuse, 82.
105. Workman, B. (1986, May). Dear professor: This is what I want you to know. *Phi Delta Kappan, 67,* 668–671.
106. William T. Grant Foundation Commission on Youth and America's Future, *The forgotten half.*
107. Gerler, E. R., Jr. (1986, February). Skills for adolescence: A new program for young teenagers. *Phi Delta Kappan, 67,* 436–439.
108. Zakrajsek, D., & Carnes, L. (1981). *Learning experiences: An approach to teaching physical education* (p. 5). Dubuque, IA: Wm. C. Brown Publishers.
109. Doll, R. C. (1978). *Curriculum improvement: Decision making and process* (4th ed.). Boston: Allyn & Bacon.
110. Dodds, P. (1986). Stamp out the ugly "isms" in your gym. In M. Piéron & G. Graham (Eds.), *Sport pedagogy* (pp. 141–150). Champaign, IL: Human Kinetics.
111. Mizen, D. W., & Linton, N. (1983, October). Guess who's coming to physical education: Six steps to more effective mainstreaming. *Journal of Physical Education, Recreation and Dance, 54,* 63–65.
112. Stephens, J. (1942). *The crock of gold* (p. 128). New York: Macmillan.
113. Hanks, M. D. (1969, March). How to listen. *The Improvement Era, 72,* 16–19.
114. Gustafson, J. (1978, May). Teaching for self-esteem. *The Physical Educator, 35,* 67–70.
115. Haywood, K. M., & Loughrey, T. J. (1981, March). Growth and development: Implications for teaching. *Journal of Physical Education and Recreation, 52,* 57–58.
116. Harris, D. (1973). *Involvement in sport: A somatopsychic rationale for physical activity.* Philadelphia: Lea & Febiger.
117. DePaepe, J. L. (1985, October). The influence of three least restrictive environments on the content motor-ALT and performance of moderately mentally retarded students. *Journal of Teaching in Physical Education, 5,* 34–41.
118. Information about PEOPEL can be obtained from PEOPEL, 2526 West Osborn Road, Phoenix, AZ 85017. It is sponsored by the United States Education Department National Diffusion Network and National Inservice Network, Washington, DC, and the Phoenix Union High School District, Phoenix, AZ.
119. Wessel, J. A. (Ed.). (1977). *Planning individualized education programs in special education with examples from I CAN physical education.* Northbrook, IL: Hubbard. For additional information about the I CAN program, write to Hubbard Scientific Company, Box 105, Northbrook, IL 60062.
120. Annarino, A. A., Cowell, C. C., & Hazleton, H. W. (1980). *Curriculum theory & design in physical education* (2nd ed., p. 333). Prospect Heights, IL: Waveland.

121. Stein, J. (1976, January). Sense and nonsense about mainstreaming. *Journal of Physical Education and Recreation, 47*, 43.

122. Winnick, J. P. (1978, June). Techniques for integration. *Journal of Physical Education and Recreation, 49*, 22.

123. McCarthy, M. M. (1991). Severely disabled children: Who pays? *Phi Delta Kappan, 73*(1), 66–71.

124. Ibid.

125. *Individuals with Disabilities Education Act of 1990*. PL 101-476. Section 602 (a)(16)(20 U.S.C. 1401(a)(16)).

126. Seaman, J. (1970, October). Attitudes of physically handicapped children toward physical education. *Research Quarterly, 41*, 439–445.

127. Kelly, L. E. (1994, January). Preplanning for successful inclusive schooling. *Journal of Physical Education, Recreation and Dance, 65*(1), 37–39.

128. Miller, S. E. (1994). Inclusion of children with disabilities: Can we meet the challenge? *The Physical Educator, 51*, 47–52.

129. Eichstaedt, C. B., & Kalakian, L. H. (1993). *Developmental/adapted physical education: Making ability count* (3rd ed.). New York, NY: Macmillan.

130. Dunn, R. S., & Cole, R. W. (1979, February). Inviting malpractice through mainstreaming. *Educational Leadership, 36*, 302–306.

131. *Federal Register,* Vol. 42, (May 4, 1977), p. 22676.

132. McCarthy, M. M. (1991). Severely disabled children: Who pays? *Phi Delta Kappan, 73*(1), 66–71.

133. Multicultural education strategies sought. (1990, Winter). *NASPE News,* p. 6.

134. Swisher, K., & Swisher, C. (1986). A multicultural physical education approach: An attitude (p. 36). *Journal of Physical Education, Recreation and Dance, 57*(7), 35–39.

135. Ibid.

136. Duckett, W. Using demographic data for long-range planning: An interview with Harold Hodgkinson, 166–167.

137. Rittenmeyer, D. C. (1987, Winter). Social problems and America's youth: Why school reform won't work. *National Forum: The Phi Kappa Phi Journal, 67*(1), 33–38.

138. Swisher & Swisher, A multicultural physical education approach, 35–39.

139. Ibid.

140. Ibid.

141. Glakas, B. A. (1993). Teaching secondary physical education to ESL students. *The Journal of Physical Education, Recreation and Dance, 64*(7), 20–24.

142. Ibid.

143. Ibid.

144. Ianni, F. A. (1989). Providing a structure for adolescent development. *Phi Delta Kappan, 70*, 677.

145. Ibid., 678.

146. Ibid.

147. Robinson, D. (1994). Teaching whole people. *National Forum: The Phi Kappa Phi Journal, 74*(1), 36.

148. Swisher, K., & Swisher, C. (1986). A multicultural physical education approach: An attitude. *Journal of Physical Education, Recreation and Dance, 57*(7), 36.

149. Knutson, M. C. (1977, May). Sensitivity to minority groups. *Journal of Physical Education and Recreation, 48*, 24–25.

150. *Federal Register,* Vol. 40, (June 4, 1975).

151. Vargyas, E. J. (1989, February/March). Title IX today. *Strategies, 2*(4), 9–11.

152. Ibid.

153. Geadelmann, P. L. (1980). Physical education: Stronghold of sex role stereotyping. *Quest, 32*(2), 193.

154. Young, J. C. (1986). Teacher beliefs and behaviors concerning coeducational physical education. *Abstracts of research papers 1986*. Reston, VA: American Alliance for Health, Physical Education, Recreation and Dance.

155. Geadelmann, Physical education, 192–200; Young, Teacher beliefs and behaviors, 143.

156. Griffin, P. S. (1981, Spring). One small step for personkind: Observations and suggestions for sex equity in coeducational physical education classes. *Journal of Teaching in Physical Education. (Introductory Issue)*, 12–17.

157. Wang, B. M. (1977). An ethnography of a physical education class: An experiment in integrated living. Doctoral dissertation, University of North Carolina at Greensboro, 1977. *Dissertation Abstracts International, 38,* 1980A.

158. Solomons, H. H. (1980). Sex role mediation of achievement behaviors and interpersonal interactions in sex-integrated team games. In Emmy A. Pepitone (Ed.), *Children in cooperation and competition* (pp. 321–364). Lexington, MA: Heath.

159. Griffin, One small step for personkind, 12–17.

160. Griffin, P. S. (1983). Gymnastics is a girl's thing: Student participation and interaction patterns in a middle school gymnastics unit. In T. J. Templin & J. K. Olson (Eds.), *Teaching in physical education* (pp. 71–85). Champaign, IL: Human Kinetics.

161. Wang, An ethnography of a physical education class.

162. Young, Teacher beliefs and behaviors, 143.

163. Griffin, One small step for personkind, 12–17.

164. Griffin, P. S. (1985, Late Winter). Girls' and boys' participation styles in middle school physical education team sport classes: A description and practical applications. *Physical Educator, 42,* 3–8.

165. Geadelmann, Physical education, 192–200.

166. Young, Teacher beliefs and behaviors; Griffin, One small step for personkind, 12–17.

167. Solomons, Sex role mediated achievement behaviors, 321–364.

168. Griffin, One small step for personkind, 12–17.

169. Geadelmann, Physical education, 192–200.

170. Ibid.

171. Griffin, One small step for personkind, 12–17.

172. Ibid., 7

173. Ibid.

174. Ibid.

175. Melograno, V. (1979). *Designing curriculum and learning: a physical coeducation approach* (p. 216). Dubuque, IA: Kendall/Hunt.

176. Ibid.

177. Bischoff, J. (1982, Fall). Equal opportunity, satisfaction and success: An exploratory study on coeducational volleyball. *Journal of Teaching in Physical Education, 2,* 11.

178. Ibid.

179. Knopper, A. (1988, August). Equity for excellence in physical education. *Journal of Physical Education and Recreation, 59*(6), 54–58.

180. Griffin, P. (1984, August). Coed physical education: Problems and promise. *Journal of Physical Education, Recreation and Dance, 55,* 37.

181. Dodds, Stamp out the ugly "isms" in your gym, 144, 149.

182. Ibid.

183. Educational Policies Commission. (1952). *Education for all American youth* (p. 29). Washington, DC: National Education Association.

184. Wessel, *Planning individualized education programs,* 57–58.

185. *United States Statutes at Large, 93rd Congress, 2nd Session, 1974* (Vol. 88, Part 1, pp. 571–574). Washington, DC: U.S. Government Printing Office, 1976.

186. Hill, D. (1991). Tasting failure: Thoughts of an at-risk learner. *Phi Delta Kappan, 73,* 310.

CHAPTER 4

Understanding Learning and Implications for Teaching Physical Education

Study Stimulators

1. What is cognitive learning? Affective learning? Psychomotor learning?
2. What is a taxonomy? Of what advantage is it to physical educators?
3. What is the best strategy for teaching motor skills?
4. How do the methods differ for teaching cognitive information, skills, and strategies?
5. How can attitudes toward physical education, self-esteem, self-efficacy, and moral education be influenced?
6. What is ALT-PE? Why is it important in instruction? How can ALT-PE and practice trials be increased for each student?

This chapter is divided into two sections. The first part explains the three learning domains. It is followed by several strategies for increasing learning and development in these three domains.

The Three Learning Domains

Bloom and his associates are well known for dividing learning into three categories, or *domains*—cognitive, psychomotor, and affective.[1] The *cognitive domain* includes the learning and application of knowledge. The *psychomotor domain* incorporates the development of the physical body and neuromuscular skills. The *affective domain* involves the acquisition of attitudes, appreciations, and values. The learning outcomes in each area were arranged by Bloom and his colleagues into levels they considered hierarchical in nature. That means that the performance of behaviors at each level would be prerequisite to the behaviors at a higher level.

A *taxonomy* is a system for classifying something. An educational taxonomy classifies the behaviors that students can be expected to demonstrate after learning. Perhaps the most commonly known taxonomy is the cognitive taxonomy of Bloom and his associates shown in Table 4.1. Their taxonomy for the affective domain, which is shown in Table 4.2, was developed later and has also been widely accepted, although rarely implemented in physical education.[2] Bloom also constructed a psychomotor taxonomy, although he preferred to omit it in later editions of his work.[3] Several other efforts have been made to develop taxonomies in the psychomotor domain.[4] The one proposed by Jewett and associates is shown in Table 4.4.[5] Corbin outlined a separate taxonomy for physical fitness,[6] and Singer and Dick proposed one for the personal-social

Table 4.1 Bloom's Cognitive Taxonomy

Levels of Behavior

1. *Knowledge*—Involves recognition and *recall* of:
     —specific facts, terms, definitions, symbols, dates, places, etc.
     —rules, trends, categories, methods, etc.
     —principles, theories, ways of organizing ideas

2. *Comprehension*—Involves ability to use learning:
     —translating, paraphrasing
     —interpreting, summarizing
     —extrapolating, predicting effects or consequences

3. *Application*—Involves ability to use learning in a variety of situations:
     —using principles and theories
     —using abstractions

4. *Analysis*—Involves breaking down the whole hierarchy of parts:
     —identifying or distinguishing parts or elements
     —discovering interactions or relationships between parts
     —relating organizational principles (parts to whole or whole to parts)

5. *Synthesis*—Involves combining elements into a new whole:
     —identifying and relating elements in new ways
     —arranging and combining parts
     —constructing a new whole

6. *Evaluation*—Involves judgments of value of material and methods for a given purpose:
     —judgments in terms of internal standards
     —judgments in terms of external criteria

Source: Concepts taken from Bloom, Benjamin S., ed. *Taxonomy of Educational Objectives, Handbook I: Cognitive Domain.* New York: McKay Co., 1956.

area of physical education.[7] Annarino proposed an operational taxonomy for all areas of physical education—physical, psychomotor, cognitive, and affective.[8]

The Cognitive Domain

The cognitive domain includes knowledge, comprehension, application, analysis, synthesis, and evaluation as shown in Table 4.1. Each category on the taxonomy contains some elements of previous categories. Attempts to validate the hierarchical nature of the cognitive taxonomy have not been successful past the application level, at which point the taxonomy may split into a Y shape, with synthesis and evaluation on one side and analysis on the other.[9] However, the taxonomy has been useful for curriculum design and test construction.

Knowledge

The first level on the taxonomy is knowledge—the ability to recognize or recall specific facts, methods for organizing information, or theories. This level is often referred to as memorization or rote learning. Physical education content that fits into the knowledge level of the taxonomy includes

1. game rules and strategies,
2. terminology,
3. history and current events, and
4. body systems.

Comprehension

Meaningful learning includes more than just facts. Students must understand what they have learned. Comprehension is evidenced by the ability to translate or paraphrase information; to interpret or explain why something is occurring; or to summarize, extrapolate, or use facts to determine consequences and implications. Examples of items that students must comprehend include

1. game rules and strategies in specific game situations,
2. the effects of exercise on the body,
3. the benefits of exercise,
4. factors affecting exercise, and
5. social and psychological factors affecting sports participation.

Application

Once students comprehend verbal information, they are ready to use or apply the information in new problems and situations. Students use formulas, principles, theories, ideas, rules, procedures, and methods in particular situations to solve problems. For example, in physical education students must apply

1. game rules and strategies,
2. biomechanical principles to produce effective body movement,
3. processes for learning new skills,
4. techniques for relaxation and stress management,
5. safety principles, and
6. game etiquette.

Analysis

The ability to break down information into its components or parts to see their relationships is called analysis. Students learn to organize, classify, distinguish, discriminate, and clarify information by demonstrating or making explicit the relationships among ideas. Knowledge, comprehension, and application are all involved in analyzing information. Examples of analysis include relating hypotheses to evidence, relating assumptions to arguments, or creating systematic arrangements of structures and organizations. In physical education, students analyze

1. game strategies for effectiveness in specific situations,
2. articles on physical fitness for effectiveness and accuracy of information distributed,
3. the muscles stretched or strengthened by a specific exercise,
4. the reasons a particular exercise is harmful,
5. the principles involved in producing more force in skills like the volleyball or tennis serve, and
6. skills to determine whether they are performed in the most efficient way.

Synthesis

Another cognitive process based on knowledge, comprehension, and application is synthesis. It involves creating something by arranging or combining elements into patterns to form a whole, a structure or pattern not clearly there before. In synthesis, there is no "right answer." Students use their creativity to

1. create exercise programs to attain physical fitness,
2. invent new games or game strategies, and
3. choreograph dance and gymnastics routines.

Evaluation

Evaluation includes both quantitative measurements and qualitative judgments about the value of ideas, solutions, methods, or materials. It is used to determine whether methods or materials satisfy the criteria or standards specified for appraisal. Either internal or external evidence may be used to evaluate such things as policies and situations in terms of their accuracy, precision, or conclusions. Evaluation appears to involve synthesis. Students in physical education evaluate

1. the quality of sports-related consumer goods,
2. exercise programs,
3. rules and strategies and their effects on game play, and
4. how equipment affects game play.

The Affective and Social Domain

Affective learning refers to the emotional aspects of learning. It deals with how students feel about the learning experience, how they feel about the subject, and how they feel about themselves. It considers their interests, appreciations, attitudes, values, and character. Since attitudes and appreciations cannot be measured directly, they are inferred from people's tendencies to engage in certain behaviors when they have positive attitudes and in certain other behaviors when they have negative attitudes toward some subject. For example, Greta has a positive attitude toward sports events. This attitude is demonstrated by the fact that she talks about sports, attends every sporting event she can, and learns the names and characteristics of each player. Once she even took her radio to a club meeting so she could listen to a championship game. In general, people who like something keep going back for more experiences with the subject. They seek opportunities to be involved with the subject in preference to other activities. The stronger their attraction, the more obstacles they will overcome to get involved and stay involved. People who don't like something try to avoid it by changing the subject, inventing excuses, or walking away from it. When forced to become involved in instructional situations they dislike, they threaten never to have anything to do with the subject in the future. Once such an attitude has developed, the chances are slim that it will be reversed, since the opportunities to influence these people become fewer and fewer as time goes by.

The taxonomy of affective behaviors developed by Krathwohl, Bloom, and Masia describes levels on a continuum of internalization of behaviors as shown in Table 4.2.[10] It will be illustrated with an example from physical education.

Receiving

Receiving involves passive attention to the activity or event. Adam first becomes aware of what physical fitness is, begins to listen to material concerning fitness activities, and even selects and reads articles about fitness to the exclusion of other reading materials.

Table 4.2 Bloom's Affective Taxonomy

Levels of Behavior

1. *Receiving*—Involves passive attention to stimuli:
   —awareness of a fact, occurrence, event, or incident
   —willingness to notice or attend to a task
   —selecting stimuli

2. *Responding*—Involves doing something about stimuli:
   —complying, following directions
   —voluntarily involves self
   —satisfaction or enjoyment

3. *Valuing*—Places worth on something; involves display of behavior consistent with values:
   —expressing strong belief in something
   —expressing preference for something
   —seeking activity to further something and convert others to own way of thinking

4. *Organization*—Organizes values into a system:
   —seeing how the value relates to other values held
   —establishing interrelationships and dominance of values

5. *Characterization*—Acts consistently with internalized value system:
   —acting consistently in a certain way and can be described by others in terms of actions or values
   —developing a total *consistent* philosophy of life, integrating beliefs, ideas, and attitudes

Source: Concepts taken from Krathwohl, David R.; Bloom, Benjamin S.; and Masia, Bertram B. *Taxonomy of Educational Objectives, Handbook II: Affective Domain.* New York: David McKay Co., 1964.

Responding

When a person does something about the activity it is called responding. Adam responds to his information by forming an opinion about physical fitness, initially only by complying with a teacher-initiated fitness program. He participates voluntarily in a school-sponsored fitness program and begins to feel some satisfaction in doing so.

Valuing

When Adam is seen trying to convince his friends of the importance of a fitness program, he is beginning to place worth on the activity, or he is valuing it.

Organization

Adam internalizes his conviction of the importance of physical fitness and incorporates it into his hierarchy of values. His own beliefs rather than the opinions of others now guide his actions. This step involves seeing how the values relate to other values the individual holds and weighing these values to determine which ones are more important.

Characterization

When a person acts consistently with an internalized value system, the particular behavior is said to be characteristic of him. Adam becomes so committed to the importance of physical fitness that he may even decide on a career in the fitness area or do volunteer work instructing others about physical fitness.

A close relationship exists between the affective domain and the other two. By learning about something (cognitive) or doing some skill (psychomotor), instructors can produce attitudinal changes in students. By increasing positive attitudes toward physical education, students can be motivated to learn cognitive or psychomotor skills.

Singer and Dick's social domain is closely related to the affective domain and is concerned with personal adjustment and social interaction skills. These researchers included the following areas in the social domain:

1. Conduct (sportsmanship, honesty, respect for authority and rules)
2. Emotional stability in competitive situations (control, maturity)
3. Interpersonal relations (cooperation, competition)
4. Self-fulfillment (confidence, self-actualization, self-image)[11]

Teachers must ensure that positive, rather than negative, social skills are outcomes of physical education.

The Psychomotor Domain

Psychomotor learning involves learning physical or neuromuscular skills. One characteristic of psychomotor learning is that it is possible to identify distinct stages or phases that all learners seem to experience as they learn skills. An idea of how humans learn motor skills is obtained by watching a baby learn to walk. Once the baby gets an idea of what is required and has the prerequisite skills—strength, maturity, and so forth—the child makes crude attempts that are gradually refined through constant feedback from the environment—door sills, falls, carpet textures, and parents "oohing" and "ahing." Finally, a skilled performance emerges that is unique to that particular toddler.

Graham and his colleagues classified skills into four levels: precontrol, control, utilization, and proficiency. The *precontrol* level is characterized by lack of ability to control an object or the body. Every time the skill is performed, it looks different. Preschool and kindergarten children are usually at this level, although aptitude and experience determine execution, not age. The *control* level is characterized by the ability to reproduce a movement, often with intense concentration, that becomes increasingly efficient and consistent. Elementary school children are examples of performers at this level. In the *utilization* level, movements become more automatic, can be combined with each other, and can be used in different contexts, including simple games. The *proficiency* level is characterized by seemingly effortless, automatic, and flowing movements in games or activities that require adjustments to the environment or repeated exacting movements. This level is not often seen in regular physical education classes, although it should be seen more often. Older children and adolescents may be at one level in one skill and at a different level in another, depending on their experience with different activities. As they grow older, the variation in performance among children widens. Figure 4.1 is an example of a progression for throwing using these four levels.[12]

Fitts and Posner classified psychomotor skill learning into three overlapping phases: (1) cognitive—an attempt to understand the skill to be learned, (2) fixation or associative—an attempt to refine the movement by eliminating errors, and (3) autonomous—an automatic movement.[13] Gentile divided skill learning into two stages: (1) getting the idea of the movement—the cognitive stage and (2) fixation or diversification of the movement—an attempt to refine or increase the variety of response possibilities.[14]

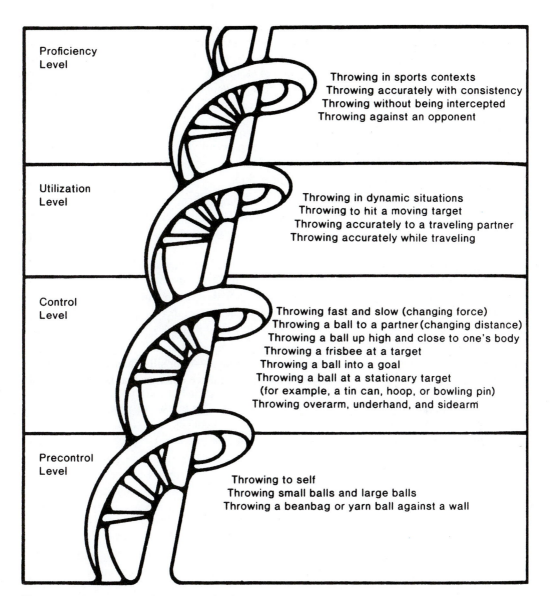

Proficiency Level

Throwing in sports contexts
Throwing accurately with consistency
Throwing without being intercepted
Throwing against an opponent

Utilization Level

Throwing in dynamic situations
Throwing to hit a moving target
Throwing accurately to a traveling partner
Throwing accurately while traveling

Control Level

Throwing fast and slow (changing force)
Throwing a ball to a partner (changing distance)
Throwing a ball up high and close to one's body
Throwing a frisbee at a target
Throwing a ball into a goal
Throwing a ball at a stationary target
(for example, a tin can, hoop, or bowling pin)
Throwing overarm, underhand, and sidearm

Precontrol Level

Throwing to self
Throwing small balls and large balls
Throwing a beanbag or yarn ball against a wall

Figure 4.1 An example of a progression for throwing in a spiral curriculum.
Source: George Graham, Shirley Ann Holt/Hale, and Melissa Parker. *Children Moving: A Teachers Guide to Developing a Successful Physical Education Program* (2nd ed.). (Mountain View, CA: Mayfield Publishing Company, 1987), p. 121

In 1971 Jewett and her colleagues introduced the psychomotor taxonomy shown in Table 4.3.[15] Bressan reformulated the taxonomy into a model to aid teachers in designing and sequencing psychomotor learning experiences.[16] She renamed Jewett's three stages of skill development, calling them (1) skill construction, (2) skill stabilization, and (3) skill differentiation, as shown in Table 4.3. Understanding these developmental stages is essential when planning the instructional sequence in physical education. Unless the teacher understands the higher levels of the taxonomy, the tendency is to stop too soon and omit some very important learning skills.

Skill Construction

Skill construction, or acquisition, includes the initial processes of receiving information and transforming it into a motor pattern. It requires establishing new or revised muscle synergies—muscles working together to create a movement pattern. The brain (cerebral cortex) incorporates the muscle synergies into motor programs that can be controlled at lower neurological levels by the brain stem (cerebellum) and spinal cord.

Perception is the basis for all learning. The student must be helped to perceive, or focus on, the important aspects of the skill to be learned. This requires active, conscious effort by the learner. The brain creates temporary neurological connections so the learner can approximate the desired performance. An example might be how a child explores throwing patterns, trying different ways of throwing, with different forces, directions, and distances. An older learner might attempt an overhead throw, again with a variety of forces, directions, and distances. The teacher must provide a balance between the efficiency of learning a prescribed pattern and the flexibility necessary for later adaptations to various sport contexts.

Patterning is the process of acquiring a specific movement pattern to create a consistent, automated motor program of muscle synergies. To achieve this, the teacher displays a model of the skill, provides for repetition through practice, and gives feedback and knowledge of results. Practice results in a permanent motor program, whether or not it is biomechanically correct. Therefore, the selection of the specific skill to pattern is critical for the next two stages of skill development.

Skill Stabilization

Skill stabilization involves generalizing the motor pattern so that it can be performed efficiently, effectively, and consistently in a variety of environmental conditions. This involves the formulation of rules or principles that can be applied flexibly for different environmental conditions.

Accommodating or adapting consists of modifying a skill to meet the needs of a variety of conditions, such as shooting from different distances at archery targets or adapting to an opponent's movements on a basketball court. Accommodating results in a motor schema, which can be compared to a computer program that governs the use of various motor programs. Lead-up games can be used to promote accommodation.

Refining a skill involves the process of practicing a specific skill, usually with skill drills, until it becomes smooth, efficient, accurate, and automatic, so that the learner can concentrate on game strategy rather than on the skills themselves. Some skills, such as archery, require mostly refining, whereas others are probably learned best with a combination of accommodating and refining experiences.

Table 4.3 Bressan's Adaptations   Table 4.4 A Psychomotor Taxonomy

Bressan's Adaptations	Learning Behavior	Definition
Skill Construction	1.0 Generic movement	Movement operations or processes, which facilitate the development of human movement patterns.
Perceiving	1.1 Perceiving	Recognition of movement positions, postures, patterns, and skills by means of the sense organs.
	1.2 Imitating	Duplication of a movement pattern or skill as a result of perceiving.
Patterning	1.3 Patterning	Arrangement and use of body parts in successive and harmonious ways to achieve a movement pattern or skill.
Skill Stabilization	2.0 Ordinative movement	Meeting the requirements of specific movement tasks through processes of organizing, performing, and refining movement patterns and skills.
Accommodating	2.1 Adapting	Modification of a patterned movement or skill to meet specific task demands.
Refining	2.2 Refining	Acquisition of smooth, efficient control in performing a movement pattern or skill as a result of an improvement process, e.g., a. elimination of extraneous movements. b. mastery of spatial and temporal relations. c. habitual performance under more complex conditions.
Skill Differentiation	3.0 Creative movement	Processes of inventing or creating skillful movements that will serve the unique purposes of the learner.
Varying	3.1 Varying	Invention or construction of unique or novel options in performing a movement pattern or skill.
Improvising	3.2 Improvising	Extemporaneous origination or initiation of novel movements or combinations of movements.
Composing	3.3 Composing	Creation of unique movement designs or patterns.

Source: Adaptations made by Bressan, E. S. "A Movement Processing Paradigm and the Curriculum in Physical Education," Journal of Teaching in Physical Education, 6 (1987): 335–343.

Source: Jewett, Ann E., L. Sue Jones, Sheryl M. Luneke, and Sarah M. Robinson. "Educational Change Through a Taxonomy for Writing Physical Education Objectives," Quest, 15 (January 1971): 35–36.

Skill Differentiation

Skill differentiation includes the processes of creating and changing movement patterns to serve the unique needs of the individual performer. At this level of skill acquisition, the learner can selectively retrieve movement or motor patterns, or even schemas, to initiate and create changes in the environment rather than reacting to the environment.

Varying occurs when the performer changes force, speed, effort, shape, or other variables to make the movement unique to the learner. Advanced players create their own grip on the racket or club, their own free-throw variation, or even a Fosbury flop (a creative high jump technique).

Improvising utilizes spontaneous movements to create new or previously untried movements or combinations of movement, such as when a student must recover from an error in a gymnastics routine or when the ball must be saved from traveling out-of-bounds.

Composing makes use of consciously planned movements to create a new movement or a movement unique to the individual performer. This occurs when a learner choreographs a dance or synchronized swimming routine or creates a new game or movement skill. Two examples of each process just identified are presented in Table 4.5.

The physical fitness domain specified by Corbin includes the following components:

1. Fitness vocabulary
2. Exercising
3. Achieving fitness
4. Establishing regular exercise patterns
5. Fitness evaluation
6. Fitness problem solving[17]

Importance of the Taxonomies in Teaching Physical Education

In spite of the classifications determined by learning theorists, it is difficult to divide outcomes of learning into *solely* psychomotor, cognitive, or affective learning. For example, driving a car may involve mental and physical skills and attitudes and values such as courtesy and respect for the rights of others. Skills can be classified on various continuums, in terms of their cognitive, psychomotor, or affective involvement.[18]

The purpose of each taxonomy is to encourage physical educators to include in instruction a progression of learning outcomes from those lower on the taxonomy through the higher-order objectives listed at the top of each taxonomy. In this way the taxonomy can be used as a checklist to ensure the entire range of behaviors is included in the curriculum or learning situation.

Corbin listed three common errors that result in failure to include the entire range of behaviors in the taxonomies. They are (1) trying to teach advanced skills and information without teaching essential prerequisites, (2) overemphasizing lower-order objectives, and (3) sacrificing higher-order objectives in the process of achieving lower-order objectives.[19] Teaching the higher-order problem-solving skills is essential so that students can learn to apply their knowledge and skills to real-life problems. The challenge, then, is to help students develop the capabilities to meet a full range of learning outcomes in each of the learning areas—cognitive, psychomotor, and affective.

A well-rounded physical education program helps students acquire a variety of physical skills, knowledges, and attitudes that contribute to students' enjoyment of physical activity and development of positive attitudes toward the body. The following sections will provide several practical strategies for developing teaching skills in each of the three learning domains.

Table 4.5 Two Examples of the Movement Behaviors Described in the Psychomotor Taxonomy

Movement Process	Balance Beam	Soccer
Perceiving	The child walks on the balance beam hesitantly, stops frequently to maintain balance; may hang onto partner or teacher. Experiments with body and arm positions. Child may use a shuffle step or slide step.	After a demonstration, the student replicates a kicking pattern. A fundamental striking pattern (swing) with the foot is the goal of performance. Neither accuracy nor distance is brought into focus.
Patterning	Child walks on the balance beam using an alternating step pattern with a well-balanced body position. Some hesitancy or slowness in performance may still exist.	The student executes a kicking pattern. The force, point of contact, and follow-through is the focus.
Adapting	Child walks on a balance beam with an alternating step pattern. He/she walks over a wand and through a hula hoop. May lack smoothness in performance.	The student adjusts his/her kicking pattern to perform an instep kick.
Refining	Each time the child walks on the balance beam, he/she performs the task smoothly with an alternating step pattern and good body position. He/she is able to move over the wand and through the hula hoop with no hesitation or loss of body control.	The student performs efficiently the instep kick in soccer. The pattern of the kick is performed smoothly with the same force and accuracy each time.
Varying	The child while walking on the balance beam varies the walk by adding a hop. The child is trying to perform a movement in a different way.	The student alters his/her kicking pattern to perform several variations. The student tries to perform the soccer kick from varying distances and positions from the goal.
Improvising	The child while walking on the beam uses a leap to go over the wand instead of a step.	The student in a game of soccer modifies the pass pattern to take advantage of his/her opponent's being pulled out of position.
Composing	The child designs and performs a series of moves on the balance beam.	The student designs an offensive strategy (kick at goal), responding to a set pattern of play developed with teammates.

Source: Gotts, Sheryl L., unpublished paper, Purdue University, 1972, 1976. Cited in Jewett, Ann E. and Marie R. Mullan. *Curriculum Design, Purposes and Processes in Physical Education Teaching-Learning,* Washington, D.C.: American Association of Health, Physical Education and Recreation, 1977.

Psychomotor Strategies

Although physical education has the same concerns relative to the domains of learning as do other subject areas, the unique contribution of this field is in the psychomotor area. Skills can be taught by creating environmental conditions in a microcosm of the total game or by learning the most basic skills, then playing the game and teaching related skills as they arise. For example, a simple game of soccer can be played with the dribble and pass, with throw-ins, goalkeeping, corner kicks, and other skills, rules, and strategies added as the need arises. Telling students what will be encountered is less effective.

Psychomotor development depends on several factors. Three of the most important factors, determined from research on psychomotor learning, will be discussed: perception, practice, and feedback.

Perception

Perception is the process of entering information into the brain.[20] The sense organs receive information from the environment that is processed in terms of its relationship to previously learned data. Only a small part of the information received by the senses is processed.

A model of the skill is extremely important so that students gain a correct perception of the desired performance. A good demonstration is worth a thousand words. Complete demonstrations should be performed several times (3–5) from different angles to enhance their effectiveness. The demonstration may be done by the teacher, a student, a film, or a videotape. Teachers

A correct model of the skill to be taught is
essential to successful performance by students.
© James L. Shaffer.

should decrease factors that can interfere with the learner's visual, auditory, or internal attention on the model. Visual difficulty might be caused by poor lighting, sighting into the sun or against a similarly colored background, or other activities occurring in the background. Yelling or talking by other students can interfere with the student's auditory perception. Internal factors include sleepiness, fatigue, boredom, or discouragement. "Formulating an accurate motor plan may be the most important stage of skill learning" next to motivation.[21] Students must perceive what the skill should look like and feel like while they are performing it.

Two or three short verbal cues should be given to help the student perceive the demonstration's key points without being distracted by nonessential movement. Too much verbiage or too many cues can be distracting. Verbal directions or cues can also help learners recognize or recall facts, skills, or strategies needed for current learning. This may involve reviewing previously learned concepts or engaging in a brief practice, perhaps as a warm-up. Concentrating on cues one at a time facilitates absorption by the learner. By thinking of potential problems for the learner and counteracting them with positive cues, the most important points will be reinforced. Pease indicated that the sum of all the cues for a skill should describe the entire skill performance from beginning to end.[22] Some cues for the volleyball set might be (1) look through the triangle, (2) keep your seat down, and (3) extend. For the badminton clear, the cues might be (1) scratch your back, (2) reach for the shuttle, and (3) make the racket whistle.

The kinesiological or biomechanical analysis of a skill should be used as a basis for developing cues that focus students' attention on relevant parts of the skill and provide feedback during the guided practice following the demonstration. In no case should the kinesiological or biomechanical analysis itself be presented to a student learning a new skill. This overloads the learner's limited capacity with irrelevant details. The ability to select the best cues is learned by experience. However, beginning teachers have access to expert experience in reference books, classes, and clinics.[23]

Students must also be helped to identify and attend to regulatory stimuli such as ball direction, speed, height, spin, angle or distance from the goal, or the location of other players. With skills like golf, the focus is on the position of the body and the implement and the learner's kinesthetic awareness. Students need to know such items as where to position themselves in relation to other objects, where to look for relevant cues, how to discriminate the object from the background, and how to use the cues to predict changes in the environment. At the same time, learners need to learn to disregard irrelevant aspects such as the spectators, environmental conditions, and anxiety. Although learners may simply be told this information, a demonstration or guided discovery may be more effective.

Practice
Following the demonstration, students should practice the skill in the most appropriate environment. Motor skill practice is essential for skilled movement. In general, motor learning and field-based research have shown that practice is highly related to achievement. The following are factors that teachers should consider when designing practice for the psychomotor domain: (1) learner involvement, (2) type of skill, (3) task appropriateness, (4) whole versus part practice, (5) massed versus distributed practice, (6) mental practice, (7) transfer, and (8) retention.

Learner Involvement
In the mid-1970s researchers conducted the Beginning Teacher Evaluation Study (BTES). The research team concluded: "Teachers who find ways to put students into contact with the academic

curriculum and to keep them in contact with that curriculum while maintaining a convivial class-room atmosphere are successful in promoting achievement."[24]

From these findings, the research team identified and studied three measures of time, each of which correlated more closely with academic achievement.[25] *Allocated time,* the amount of time provided for instruction in a given subject area, depends on the district, school, or department philosophy and on school finances. *Engaged time,* the amount of time the student attends to instruction in a given subject, primarily depends on the teacher's goals and managerial skills. *Academic learning time* (ALT) is the number of minutes the student is engaged with activities and instructional materials at an easy level for that student (generally an 80 percent success level). Although the BTES study showed a strong correlation between ALT and achievement, it varied for different subjects, objectives, grade levels, and teachers.[26]

Metzler modified the BTES instrument to measure ALT in physical education; he then measured ALT-PE in a variety of physical education contexts.[27] He defined ALT-PE as "the amount of time students spend in class activity engaged in relevant overt motor responding at a high success rate."[28] Far less ALT was found in physical education than had been imagined and much of it was cognitive rather than psychomotor.

In 1989 Metzler reviewed the research on time in physical education. He concluded that teachers (1) spend 25 to 50 percent of class time in noninstructional activities, (2) conceptualize time for classes, not individual students, (3) do not plan for maximum student participation, and (4) are inconsistent in their use of time during a class period or from lesson to lesson. He also noted a relationship between what teachers do and how students spend time in classes. With regard to students, he summarized that (1) students spend only about 20 to 50 percent of their time in activities that contribute to intended learning outcomes; (2) students differ in the amount of time they spend on achievement-related learning; (3) student time varies with the activity in which students are engaged; and (4) student ALT is low regardless of who the teacher is. Although boys and girls get approximately equal amounts of ALT, elementary pupils get more than secondary students, and college students get more than twice that of younger students. Students in individual sports get more time on-task than those in team sports. Time also varies with student ability, with students with disabilities in regular physical education classes receiving the least of all.[29]

ALT-PE is an indirect strategy for evaluating teacher effectiveness. ALT-PE research is based on the assumption that ALT in physical education correlates with student achievement as it does in academic subjects. Metzler noted at least 11 studies in physical education that reported correlations between practice time on the criterion task and increased student learning, and none of the studies suggested a negative or no relationship.[30] In any case, students' constructive use of time is more important than allocated time.[31] Although ALT-PE is essential for learning, it is not sufficient by itself to cause learning. One example of this is when students are engaged in playing a full 6-versus-6-player volleyball game. Although all the players may be actively participating in the game, players receive relatively few opportunities to actually "practice" the skill.

Silverman found that the number and appropriateness of practice trials correlated significantly with student achievement.[32] Buck and Harrison suggested that ALT-PE might not exist under Siedentop's definition, which required student engagement "in such a way that [the student] has an appropriate chance to be successful . . . usually about 80% of the time."[33] Students *appeared* to be motor appropriate,[34] but videotape analysis of learning trials showed that very few students achieved an 80 percent success level.[35] Buck and Harrison further showed that game play did not increase the performance level of students; in fact, student skill levels regressed during game play. Contrary to popular belief, sport skills are not acquired merely by playing games.[36] Neither the number of contacts per serve nor the ratio of correct trials to total trials improved during the semester. As emphasis turned to strategies, the level of play decreased. Regression occurs when students have not learned basic skills or when they are unable to apply the skills in a game setting. Finding themselves unsuccessful, some students become "competent bystanders" like Griffin's invisible players and lost souls. They develop "a strategy for appearing to be involved in game play without actually coming in contact with the ball."[37] They back off and expect someone else to step in and hit it. The high-ability students are aggressive and take over for the low-skilled students. Low-skilled students talk to the teacher about how to perform the skill rather than actually practicing it.[38]

This discussion leads to one conclusion—*physical education teachers need to increase the number and quality of learning trials if students are to become proficient in motor skills.* Research indicates that instruction should be provided in a way that allows maximum participation by each student. Some relatively simple changes in teacher behavior have been shown to increase ALT-PE. Programs that teach teachers to reduce management and student nonengagement time and to increase feedback to students result in more engaged skill learning time. Landin, Hawkins, and Wiegand reported success in helping teachers increase motor appropriate responses by using additional equipment and facilities to decrease waiting, clearly communicating class procedures, and challenging students with more demanding instructional objectives.[39] One study discovered that pupils of student teachers with early field experiences had significantly greater ALT than pupils of student teachers with no prior experience.[40]

With the reduction in funding for education, teachers must creatively manage large classes in limited spaces with inadequate equipment. The organization of time, space, equipment, rules, and group size all affect the amount of time each student has to participate in the activity and, therefore, to achieve success. Table 4.6 provides some suggestions for dealing with these variables. The book *Changing Kids' Games* also outlines different ways to analyze and modify many contemporary activities taught in physical education to increase learner involvement.[41] A games approach can also be used to teach wall/net games, invasion games, and striking/fielding games. Games are adapted so students can play real games at their level of competence and then play at progressively more complex levels until the official game is played.[42]

Type of Skill

When a learner is acquiring the motor pattern of a movement, the teaching emphasis and practice environment should differ depending on the type of skill to be learned. Gentile, who adapted a system used in industry to classify skills into open and closed skills, indicated that skills actually exist on a continuum.[43]

A *closed skill* is done in a relatively stable environment. Examples of closed skills are archery, bowling, gymnastics, golf, the basketball free throw, the placekick in soccer, and hitting a ball from a batting tee. For closed skills, fixation of the motor skill is the goal. Learning involves concentrating on the identical elements in the body and the environment and striving for consistency in executing the motor plan. Closed skills are not necessarily easier than open skills because they require extraordinary kinesthetic awareness. Students should learn to "feel" the correct movements through kinesthetic perception of their own body movements.

In an *open skill*, the environment is unpredictable, the players keep changing places, and objects move through space. Adjustments must be made in speed, timing, and space, such as in the height and speed of a softball pitch or the interaction of players on a basketball court. Other

Table 4.6 Guidelines for Increasing Learner Involvement

I. Time

    A. Keep talk short and provide demonstrations/cues.

    B. Eliminate unnecessary showering or dressing. Reduce roll-call time.

    C. Keep waiting in lines to a minimum.

    D. Plan drills to minimize transition time (i.e., 3-player drill to a 6-player drill).

    E. Use inactive time to work on study sheets; learn rules or fitness concepts; take written, skill, or fitness tests; study films or videotapes; work on skill checklists, etc.

II. Space

    A. Use alternative teaching areas (hallways; multipurpose rooms, community facilities) when feasible.

    B. Teachers could share a gym and a classroom and take turns teaching concepts and activities.

    C. Adjust class sizes among instructors when facilities are small (i.e., 60 students in soccer, 20 in tennis).

    D. Provide alternative activities (fitness) for those waiting for turns.

III. Equipment

    A. Use modified equipment (i.e., lighter balls and implements, shorter net heights and baskets, shorter serving distances).

    B. Increase the number of equipment pieces so all students have access to equipment.

    C. Design drills that involve learners in different roles at the same time—dribbling and guarding in basketball.

    D. Use one piece of equipment for every two or three students and have one student tutor or one toss and one retrieve.

    E. Use stations, at which students practice using different pieces of equipment or apparatus.

IV. Rules

    A. Design games to increase trials—require three hits on a side; use underhand volleyball serves; have softball pitchers pitch to their own team; eliminate jump balls and free throws.

    B. Change nature of drill or game from competitive to cooperative (award points for the highest number of volleys, pass-set-spike sequences, lay-ups, etc.

    C. Use a games approach to teach wall/net games, invasion games, and striking/fielding games.

V. Group Size

    A. Keep teams small so the number of contacts with equipment is increased.

    B. Keep playing areas small.

    C. Use both homogeneous and heterogeneous grouping patterns to motivate students to improve skills.

examples include tennis, racquetball, soccer, and the martial arts. Skill diversification is required to meet a multitude of environmental conditions. Decisions must be made in split seconds. Therefore practice must include a variety of situations and the learner must be informed about the range of possibilities. At first, combinations of two or three variables may be practiced, but later practice must include all possible variables. If only three speeds, three directions, three ball heights, and three distances were considered, 81 different combinations must be rehearsed. Imagine how many might exist in an actual game.[44] Practice for open skills should not consistently occur with any particular combination or a fixation might occur. Schmidt indicates that learning tasks under different conditions from those required in the actual game situation requires a shift in ability.[45] Thus, the complex nature of many games almost ensures a regression to less desirable movement patterns.[46]

With both open and closed skills, practice should be as gamelike or competition-like as possible, with a changing, unstable, unpredictable environment for open skills or a stable, predictable environment for closed skills.

Task Appropriateness

Effective teaching requires the selection of appropriate learning tasks. Students should possess prerequisite knowledge and skills, and activities should challenge students to improve existing skill levels. Instruction must be adjusted to challenge students who have high skill levels or to correct deficiencies so that poorly skilled students can benefit from instruction. Unit and lesson plans should include skill progressions from simple to complex. Harter proposed using *optimum challenges* to match task difficulty with learners' developmental capabilities.[47] Tasks that are too easy are boring, whereas tasks that are too difficult produce learner anxiety. Neither results in learning.

Fitts classified psychomotor skills into difficulty levels based on the degree of body involvement and the extent of external pacing of the activity. The simplest skills and activities are done with the body at rest. Intermediate skills and activities would involve movement of the body or an external object, but not both. The most complex skills and activities involve simultaneous movement of the individual and the external object.[48] Merrill divided skills into four areas as shown in Table 4.7,[49] but there appears to be no difference in difficulty between types II and III.[50] An example of a type I skill is a placekick in soccer. In a type II task, a stationary player

Table 4.7   Merrill's task classification system

		Object	
		At Rest	*In Motion*
Learner's Body	*At Rest*	Type I task	Type II task
	In Motion	Type III task	Type IV task

Concepts from M. David Merrill. "Psychomotor Taxonomies, Classifications, and Instructional Theory." In Robert N. Singer (ed.) *The Psychomotor Domain: Movement Behaviors* (Philadelphia: Lea & Febiger, 1972), pp. 385–414.

kicks a moving ball, and a type III task consists of a moving player kicking a stationary ball. The most difficult task involves a moving player receiving and redirecting a moving ball.

Students should begin with skills at their present level and gradually move to higher skill levels. This requires preassessing current performance levels and starting instruction at the appropriate level for each learner. Rink suggested manipulating practice in the following ways to increase task difficulty:[51]

1. Increasing the size of the "whole" to be handled by the learner
2. Adding movement to a stationary skill
3. Increasing the force requirements such as the height or distance involved in producing or receiving force
4. Receiving an object at different levels or from different directions, such as to the side of the receiver
5. Decreasing the size of the target or goal
6. Requiring a higher degree of accuracy in the placement of a hit or throw
7. Involving more interaction with other people (e.g., offensive or defensive players)
8. Using larger or heavier equipment (e.g., bowling ball, racket, bow)
9. Increasing the speed of the object to be received or redirected
10. Involving sideways or backward movement
11. Receiving an object from one location and redirecting it to another location
12. Increasing the speed of the body movement
13. Combining skills
14. Using the skills in competitive or self-testing situations

Once the concept of the skill has been acquired, the learning environment should include as many situations as possible in which students will actually use the behavior (e.g., a moving rather than a stationary ball, as close to the real speed as possible). In activities involving a ball, speed and accuracy should be stressed rather than just speed or just accuracy. In most situations, the movement should be practiced at a moderate speed.[52]

A major mistake that is made while teaching skills is to jump directly from practice drills into competitive games before students have had time to refine their skills. According to Earls, few teachers really make a difference in skill development, because they present an ideal model that students cannot or do not follow and because they ask students to participate in complex games before students are ready.[53]

Barrett emphasized that the development of game-playing ability is in reality a three-phase process, in which constant flow between adjacent phases is essential. Phase 1 focuses on the development of game skills, phase 2 on the transition from skill development to actual game play, and phase 3 on games playing. Phase 2 "is the most critical phase and one which is often missed entirely or passed through so quickly as to have no effect."[54]

To make the transition from skill drills to game play, students need to practice in gamelike conditions early in the learning sequence. Gamelike practice increases the success of low-skilled students and results in increased student confidence to attempt skill trials in game settings. Young discussed ways to improve practice drills to make them more gamelike. She suggested cones at random rather than in straight lines for dribbling practice, with several players moving at a time so that students learn to adapt to changing circumstances. Play games called 3-on-3 or Bonus Ball rather than "lead-up games," which make students feel incapable of playing the real game. For Bonus Ball, award points for using the skill in game situations.[55]

Teachers can choose or create drills and lead-up games that force students to move to the ball, to direct the ball to a moving target, or to practice under the innumerable conditions that occur in game play. For example, rather than have students hit a volleyball back and forth to a partner, a threesome forces students to direct the ball to a place different from the point of origin. Students should not set the ball over the net or hit the ball and run under the net; neither situation occurs in a game. Team strategies should not be introduced before students feel secure with the basic skills and individual offensive and defensive tactics, such as marking or guarding, playing one's position, or shooting without being guarded have been taught.

The use of lead-up games before students play the full game may help bridge the gap between skill drills and game play. Games with fewer players per team might force low-ability students to be involved and provide more opportunities for contacting the ball. Siedentop, Mand, and Taggart observed, "The games students play must be developmentally appropriate in terms of skills required, complexity of strategy, and opportunity for participation."[56] The final result of skill learning is accurate, consistent, adaptable, coordinated motor responses. Automatic skill execution enables the learner to devote attention to the game plan and strategy. Rather than paying attention to each part of a skill, the elements are "chunked" into a skill or even a combination of skills. Performers learn where to look and what to look at, how to differentiate relevant and irrelevant information, and how to predict outcomes from cues. In essence, students learn to integrate movements and information into schemas that help them to select appropriate movement responses for a wide variety of conditions, to monitor outcomes, and to guide their own learning.[57] This occurs because the information processing system improves its ability to process information. By integrating information from the environment and the body, a rule or principle emerges to guide future behavior.

Bressan and Weiss proposed an optimal challenge model to combine the teaching of skill with psychosocial education. The optimal challenge model requires teachers to observe the needs of their students and design learning experiences at the appropriate level of difficulty, with appropriate educational support for students to gain self-confidence in movement. Observation is the central process of the model. Observing for *competence* requires concentrating on the student's proficiency in managing the activity's motor, fitness, and cognitive demands. Observing for *confidence* demands focusing on student's feelings about their perceived ability to meet the challenges at hand and their anticipation of pleasant or unpleasant sensations. Observing for *persistence* involves noting the student's ability to sustain participation under various circumstances. Confidence and persistence are psychosocial or affective components. These three sources of information become the basis for teachers' instructional decisions.[58]

Teacher behavior can modify task difficulty or the degree and type of educational support provided to the learner. Task difficulty should consider the student's competence—motor, fitness, and cognitive. Feltz and Weiss identified four instructional strategies for increasing competence: (1) Sequence activities according to the students' development, (2) break skills into meaningful practice units, (3) use appropriate performance aids, and (4) provide appropriate physical or verbal guidance. Educational support relates to the learner's confidence and persistence. Helping students set performance goals, reinforcing effort and persistence, emphasizing correct rather than incorrect performance, and selecting appropriate teaching styles for maximum learner involvement in decision making can be used to provide educational support. To be true professionals, teachers must reflect on their own performance and evaluate their teaching to determine ways to increase their abilities to educate the whole student.[59]

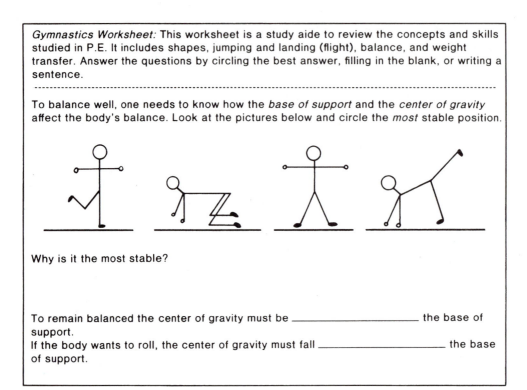

Gymnastics Worksheet: This worksheet is a study aide to review the concepts and skills studied in P.E. It includes shapes, jumping and landing (flight), balance, and weight transfer. Answer the questions by circling the best answer, filling in the blank, or writing a sentence.

To balance well, one needs to know how the *base of support* and the *center of gravity* affect the body's balance. Look at the pictures below and circle the *most* stable position.

Why is it the most stable?

To remain balanced the center of gravity must be _____ the base of support.
If the body wants to roll, the center of gravity must fall _____ the base of support.

Figure 4.2 An example of a worksheet used with upper-grade children in gymnastics.
Source: Tom Ratliffe, "Using Worksheets in Physical Education," *Journal of Physical Education, Recreation and Dance* 53 (September 1982): 48.

Practice drills used with interscholastic teams are generally not appropriate for physical education classes in which students are developing rather than refining skills. Research by Earls demonstrated a regression in skill development when students were challenged to move on to more complex patterns before their skills were sufficiently rehearsed.[60] Since most skills are learned best in a positive atmosphere, with low muscle tension, a stressful learning situation should be avoided.

Students also need help applying movement principles to a variety of situations. This can be achieved by pointing out activities in which the concepts apply and do not apply. Worksheets, such as the one in figure 4.2, can help students generalize concepts to various activity situations. Just prior to skill execution, the teacher might direct the student to focus on specific feedback processes and how they can be used to improve the skill. Through analyzing the learning process, students will learn how to learn, as well as acquire the skills themselves.

Whole versus Part Practice

Whole practice is practice of a whole task, as opposed to practice of its parts. For example, in the breast stroke in swimming, the whole method is to demonstrate the stroke and have the students imitate and practice it. In *part practice* the whole is broken down into parts, each of which is mastered separately before putting them all together. For example, the kick might be taught first until it has been mastered. Then, the arms and breathing are taught and practiced. Finally, the co-ordination of the entire stroke is demonstrated and practiced.

To overcome the difficulty the student experiences when putting the parts together, the *progressive part* method was developed. It consists of learning part one, then learning and adding part two, then part three, and so on until the whole is completed. When learning the breast stroke, for example, the student begins with a glide, then adds the arm stroke, then breathing, and finally the kick.

The majority of 30 studies reviewed by Nixon and Locke found some variation of the whole method to be superior.[61] This is in agreement with the cognitive theory of learning in unitary wholes. The basic problem seems to be in the definition of the "whole." In practical teaching situations an instructor rarely would present the whole game of basketball at once. Instead, combinations of skills, such as throwing, catching, dribbling, passing, and shooting, are combined to form play patterns. In sports that require no interaction with others, such as archery or bowling, the sport itself may be considered to be a whole for the purposes of instruction.[62] Seagoe described the characteristics of a whole as follows: "(1) It should be isolated and autonomous, an integrated entity. (2) It must have 'form' quality, a functional, coherent unit. (3) It must be more than the sum of the parts; it must be a rational structure in itself."[63]

Even though use of the whole has been shown to be advantageous, the evidence does not mean that the whole method should be used exclusively. Rather, the selection of a method should be based on the characteristics of the learner and the task and the instructional style of the teacher. Table 4.8 shows how the first two factors influence the choice of whole or part practice.

Table 4.8   Factors That Influence Choice of Whole or Part Practice

Practice Should/Can Emphasize:

	Wholes	*Parts*
If the task:	Has highly dependent (integrated) parts	Has highly independent parts
	Is simple	Is made up of individual skills
	Is not meaningful in parts	Is very complex
	Is made up of simultaneously performed parts	If limited work on parts or different segments is necessary
If the learner:	Is able to remember long sequences	Has a limited memory span
	Has a long attention span	Is not able to concentrate for a long period of time
	Is highly skilled	Is having difficulty with a particular part
		Cannot succeed with the whole method

Source: Anne Rothstein, Linda Catelli, Patt Dodds, and Joan Manahan. *Basic Stuff Series I: Motor Learning* (Reston, Virginia: American Alliance for Health, Physical Education, Recreation and Dance, 1981), p. 38.

Older and more mature learners can comprehend larger units of instruction than can younger or less-skilled students. Intelligence and cognitive style also influence the learner's ability to handle relationships in complex tasks. Several researchers have found that students with a global cognitive style learn better with whole learning, whereas students with an analytical cognitive style learn better with the part method.[64] Meaningful, connected activities are best taught with the whole method, whereas complex, independent tasks can be taught with part practice. When practices are distributed, the whole method appears to work better.[65]

Implications for teaching are that the learner should begin with a whole that is large enough to be meaningful and challenging but simple enough to achieve success. This may involve understanding a concept of the whole skill or game and the relationship of the parts to the whole. As skills are practiced, students should understand how the skills fit into the total activity. Lead-up games are "small wholes" that help learners join parts into meaningful wholes without becoming overwhelmed.[66] Meaningfulness is increased when the skill approximates the final objective sought. Work to improve portions of the performance can occur readily during practice of the whole movement. When the complete action is too complex for the beginner to handle, such as in activities in which a chance of injury exists or the learner is afraid, or the amount of information overloads the processing capability of the learner, it should then be broken into the largest subwhole that the learner can handle.

A combination of wholes and parts, including alternating from one to another, is often the best approach. Variations include *whole-part* and *part-whole* methods and the *whole-part-whole* method in which students learn the whole, then practice the parts and then put them back together into the whole.[67] In the breast stroke, the whole-part method involves practicing the whole stroke and then working on the arms, legs, and breathing. The part-whole method, in contrast, requires teaching the arms, legs, and breathing separately until they are learned and then combining them into the whole stroke. The whole-part-whole method consists of teaching the entire stroke, then working on each part, and then again practicing the whole stroke.

Massed versus Distributed Practice

Massed practice is a practice or a series of practice sessions with little or no rest between. An example is teaching one skill for the entire physical education period. *Distributed practice* is practice interspersed with rest or alternative activities. This can be done by practicing several skills for a brief period of time during each class session.

Research findings about the advantages of each type of practice are contradictory because of inconsistencies in the terminology used. With verbal skills, most research concludes that distributed practice is best except when the material is simple or can be learned in its entirety in one session.[68] Research on motor skills shows that skill learning generally occurs better with many short, distributed practice sessions rather than longer and less frequent sessions. However, on discrete tasks when boredom and fatigue are not factors, massed practice is equally effective with distributed practice, assuming that the number of practice trials is the same.[69] Massed practice has the advantage of reaching the goal sooner under these conditions (i.e., three hours on Monday versus one hour on Monday, Wednesday, and Friday).

Factors to consider when planning the frequency and length of practice sessions include: (1) the learner's age, skill level, and experience; (2) the type of skill; (3) the purpose of the practice; and (4) circumstances in the learning environment.[70] These factors are presented in Table 4.9. Distributed practice is defined in the table as shorter and more frequent, and massed practice is longer and less frequent.

Table 4.9 Factors That May Influence Your Choice of Massed or Distributed Practice Organizations

	Shorter and More Frequent	**Longer and Less Frequent**
If the task:	Is simple, repetitive, boring	Is complex
	Demands intense concentration	Has many elements
	Is fatiguing	Requires warm-up
	Demands close attention to detail	Is a new one for the performer
If the learner:	Is young or immature (unable to sustain activity)	Is older or more mature
	Has a short attention span	Is able to concentrate for long periods of time
	Has poor concentration skills	Has good ability to focus attention
	Fatigues easily	Tires quickly

Source: Anne Rothstein, Linda Catelli, Patt Dodds, and Joan Manahan. *Basic Stuff Series I: Motor Learning* (Reston, Virginia: American Alliance for Health, Physical Education, Recreation and Dance, 1981), p. 40.

Younger students and students with low ability levels fatigue easily and have shorter attention, or concentration, spans and lower interest levels. Distributed practice sessions in which several skills are practiced during a class period are usually preferred for these students. This results in less boredom, fatigue, and frustration when learning new skills. When students take turns practicing, a built-in rest interval also occurs. Older, more highly skilled students possess higher levels of concentration and motivation and can tolerate longer practice with less fatigue.

Strenuous activities often must be scheduled for shorter periods of time due to the effects of fatigue. An overview of an activity may require a different scheduling pattern than intense practice for competition or performance.

Weather conditions, such as heat, cold, smog, and rain, and school activities, such as assemblies, may interfere with a practice session. With distributed practice less time is lost when one practice must be canceled or interrupted than when a massed practice is canceled.

The time schedule for practice sessions is not nearly as important as the amount of time spent in actual activity or the number of practice trials. Too often, instructors expect a beginner to learn an entirely new activity in a two-week unit (10 days with 30 minutes of instruction per day = 300 minutes), but they spend two hours every day for months coaching talented students in the same basic skills.

Mental Practice

Mental practice is sedentary practice in which the learner imagines performing a skill and the muscles receive stimulation, but no overt movement occurs. This technique is based on the work of Köhler, in which insight plays an important role in learning. Since studies have shown that mental rehearsal increases skill performance, instruction might well include mental practice in addition to physical practice in order to efficiently use the crowded facilities and inadequate equipment in many schools. A good time for mental practice is when a student is waiting for a turn or a piece of equipment. Mental rehearsal can also be used advantageously to practice perfectly after an error and before the next response, to warm up, to increase concentration during the performance, or to practice while watching a film or videotape of a skill. Mentally rehearsing what to do in certain game situations can be helpful in developing appropriate reactions during game play. For example, in softball, students can imagine that the bases are loaded and the ball goes to third base and determine what should be done. *Reminiscence,* improvement between practice periods, may be the result of mental practice.[71] To be effective, students must understand the skill and have practiced it overtly prior to mental practice. Encourage students to *feel* the movement during practice and then during mental rehearsal.

Transfer

Transfer is the effect that learning one skill has on the learning or performance of another skill. Transfer can be positive or negative. Positive transfer occurs when previous learning has a favorable effect on new learning. With negative transfer, prior learning interferes with learning new information or skills (proactive transfer) or new skills interfere with previously learned tasks (retroactive transfer).

Transfer theories include (1) the theory that only identical elements (i.e., specific elements common to both tasks) transfer and (2) the theory that transfer occurs as a result of the ability to apply previously learned principles and insights or problem-solving strategies to new situations.[72] Laboratory research shows that very little transfer is seen from one task to another. However, the transfer of general problem-solving and learning strategies is supported when more complex tasks are studied. Transfer is probably a result of several factors, including those specific to the task and those inherent in the learning environment.[73]

An understanding of the conditions affecting transfer is essential for planning instruction. Singer listed five conditions that affect transfer. They include (1) similarity between the tasks, (2) amount of practice on the first task, (3) motivation to transfer, (4) method of training, and (5) intent of transfer.[74] Cratty added a sixth condition—the amount of time between tasks.[75] The amount of transfer depends on the complexity of the task and the capacity of the learner.[76]

Similarity between Tasks. The most important of the six conditions is the similarity between the tasks. The greater the similarity between the tasks, the greater the transfer. If there were no similar elements, there would be no transfer (either positively or negatively). In many tasks, however, some elements will yield positive transfer and others will elicit negative transfer. Thus, Cratty indicated that "the degree to which negative or positive transfer is measured depends on whether the *summation* of the negative transfer elements equals, exceeds, or fails to exceed the total of the common elements likely to produce positive transfer."[77]

Similar or identical elements can be found in the student's perception of the stimulus or in the response. Negative transfer occurs when the students are asked to respond to the same verbal or visual perception with a different response. For example, if students have practiced rebounding by batting the ball continuously against the backboard during practice, and then are expected to rebound the ball into the basket during a game, negative transfer will occur. Negative transfer may also result when the weight of an object changes, such as when changing from tennis to badminton, or when the speed of the object differs, such as in rallying a tennis ball off a backboard rather than over a net. Similar movements, such as the overarm softball throw and the overhead volleyball serve, differ in that one is a throwing pattern and the other a striking skill.

Positive transfer occurs when the two tasks have a number of identical elements, such as the names of the players in softball and baseball. Some positive transfer occurs when the same response is expected to a number of related situations. Examples include shooting at different target sizes or distances in archery, or throwing a ball fielded from many different directions to first base.

When two tasks have many elements that are similar, but not identical, negative transfer results. An example is in the rules and scoring of soccer, speedball, speed-a-way, and field hockey. Tennis, badminton, and racquetball have similarities in eye-hand coordination and agility. However, differences in wrist action and the weight of the object struck can cause negative transfer.

Amount of Practice on the First Task. Greater positive transfer occurs when the first task is well learned. Less practice on the first task may result in negative transfer. Skills involving similar movement patterns, such as tennis and racquetball, should not be taught at the same time if the learner is a beginner in both activities.

Motivation to Transfer. When motivation toward the transfer of skill or knowledge to a new task is high, greater positive transfer occurs. Increasing the motivation of students should also increase the effects of positive transfer.

Method of Training. The highest positive transfer seems to occur when the whole task is practiced rather than when the parts are practiced separately. For this reason, many current experts discourage the use of drills and progressions to teach skills. Nixon and Locke stated:

> Progression is a near sacred principle in physical education, and is taken most seriously in
> teacher education. Evidence indicates that the faith . . . may be misplaced . . .
> progressions generally appear not to be significant factors in learning many motor skills.[78]

On the other hand, research on teaching in physical education by Rink and her colleagues supports the concept of breaking down complex skills into manageable components to facilitate learning.[79]

Progressions are especially valuable when fear, danger, or lack of self-confidence are present. Drills that are not well planned may introduce elements that do not transfer to the game situation. Therefore, they should be planned so that the environment and movement relationships are as gamelike as possible. Evaluation should also be in gamelike settings.

Intent of Transfer. When the teacher points out the common elements in the two tasks, the learner will probably make greater transfer to the second task of principles and skills learned in the first task. Often, general problem-solving and learning strategies will transfer to the new situation. Understanding the principles of biomechanics should transfer to new situations, as should principles of learning.[80]

Amount of Time between Tasks. As the amount of time increases between the learning of two tasks, both negative and positive transfer decline until negative transfer disappears entirely. Since negative transfer decreases faster, a point occurs at which positive transfer is at its optimum, before it too disappears. For this reason, skills may be best learned during distributed practice sessions.

Retention
Retention, often called memory, is the persistence of knowledge. Forgetting is the opposite of retention. Behavioral psychologists believe that memory is affected by the original association of two events with each other and by the association of an event with a reward. Forgetting may be

caused by lack of use over a period of time, by unlearning due to lack of reinforcement, or by interference from other learned events, such as the learning of Spanish after French.

Information-processing research differentiates between short-term memory and long-term memory. Events are held only for a short period of time unless they are rehearsed and transferred to long-term storage. Short-term memory is limited to about seven digits, as in the ordinary telephone number. By chunking, more information can be attended to, as when phone numbers are changed to letters to form words like *car-loan*.[81] Using cues to chunk information also can help learners avoid an information overload. Once the information is encoded into long-term memory, it can be very persistent, as in the case of some motor skills, which have been known to last for many years.

Factors influencing retention include (1) the nature of the task, (2) the meaningfulness of the task, and (3) the amount of overlearning that has occurred. Tasks differ in terms of their outcomes—cognitive, psychomotor, or affective; their complexity—simple to difficult; and their effect on the learner—pleasant versus disagreeable. Fundamental skills, such as walking and bicycling and higher-order mental processing skills are relatively permanent, whereas facts are difficult to remember.[82] Pleasant tasks are more easily learned, as when an exercise series is done to music. The complexity of some learning tasks can be reduced by chaining concepts to each other, as in learning a dance, or organizing concepts into chunks of information, such as a grapevine step, which consists of a number of side and crossover steps.

Meaningful, well-organized material is remembered longer than unorganized facts. Teachers can enhance long-term memory by teaching students mental imagery, chaining concepts, and problem-solving and information-processing skills and teaching the principles underlying performance, such as the effects of ball spin and air resistance or the principles for applying and receiving force. When students know they will be held accountable for certain material, retention is also increased.[83]

That motor skills seem to be retained for longer periods of time than verbal skills may be due to the overlearning that occurs with motor skills. This fact has implications for teaching in that teachers probably spend too much time reviewing skills that have already been learned.[84]

Feedback

Feedback is information about the learner's performance or the results of performance available during or immediately following performance. Feedback may be verbal, such as "Good serve" or "Your spike is getting better," or it may be nonverbal, such as a nod, smile, glance, or merely continuing on to the next part of the lesson. Of course, visual and verbal feedback can be used simultaneously.

Feedback helps the learner decide what to do differently on the next practice trial.[85] It can also help students determine how well they are progressing toward a course objective. Information provided to the learner that tells about the quality of a performance, such as the contact position with the ball or correct arm action, is called *knowledge of performance*. Information about the outcome of the performance, such as where the ball lands on a tennis court, is called *knowledge of results*. Studies show that little or no learning occurs without knowledge of performance or results. In fact, Bilodeau and Bilodeau stated, "Studies of feedback or knowledge of results show it to be the strongest, most important variable controlling performance and learning."[86] However, it should be noted that feedback effects have not been shown to be as significant a learning variable in field-based research.[87]

Feedback is the strongest, most important
variable controlling learning.
© Tracy Pellett

Feedback can occur from the performance itself, from the performer's kinesthetic awareness of body position, or from visual or verbal cues from the teacher. Feedback directly from the
task is called *intrinsic* feedback. It can be produced internally by proprioceptors in the muscles,
joints, and tendons, or by the effects of the performance on the environment, such as a strike in
bowling or a bulls-eye in archery. *Extrinsic or augmented* feedback is provided by an outside
source such as a teacher, a coach, other student, or a videotape. Extrinsic feedback may be verbal or nonverbal. *Concurrent* feedback occurs simultaneously with the performance and may be
intrinsic or extrinsic. *Terminal* feedback occurs after the performance and may result from the effects of the performance (a made basketball shot) or from an external source.

The ability to provide meaningful feedback is one of the most important abilities a teacher possesses. Feedback is most helpful when it is specific and meaningful and provided before the next response. Feedback should be delayed briefly until the learners have had time to analyze their performances and should be matched to the individual learner's comprehension and ability to use it in subsequent practice. Too much feedback can cause an information overload and confuse the learner. Information that occurs after the next response loses its meaningfulness. In fact, teachers can speed up the knowledge of results by cuing during the performance using verbal, kinesthetic, or visual assistance. For example, having bowlers aim at a spot on the lane rather than at the pins provides feedback much sooner. Placing a hand just behind the wrist of the archer's shooting hand can keep the student from jerking the hand away from the face. Moving a student's arms in the correct swimming pattern can be useful with some students. A rope could also be strung over a badminton net to encourage correct serving technique, or a videotape replay could be provided for the student.[88] Another valuable feedback technique is a redemonstration of the skill following the students' initial skill attempts. The students' attention should be directed to the essential aspects of the skill (perhaps using the verbal cues that accompanied the initial skill demonstration) to help them correct the attempt. Gradually, as the students' skills approximate the model, patterning is complete and the cues should be changed to promote accommodation and refinement of the skill performance.

Melville used checklists of the four or five most important aspects of performance to help students and teachers focus on skill essentials.[89] Gentile proposed that the learner answer two questions about the response: "Was the goal accomplished?" and "Was the movement executed as planned?"[90] The possible answers are shown in Table 4.10. If the answer to both questions is yes, then the learner should continue to use the same motor plan. If a "surprise" is obtained, the learner must make a decision. Either the original motor plan or the incorrect but successful movement may be tried. Perhaps both plans will be tried and compared. If the "something's wrong" response is obtained, the learner may need to reevaluate the regulatory conditions to determine whether some stimuli have been ignored and establish a new plan. If the "everything's wrong" response occurs after several tries, the learner's motivation may suffer. Possible strategies include revising the motor plan, reevaluating environmental conditions, or altering the goal. Ainsworth and Fox found that students taught to use this technique to evaluate their performance

Table 4.10 Four possible outcomes for evaluating skill learning

Type of Evaluation	Was the Movement Executed as Planned?		
	Outcome	Yes	No
Was the Goal Accomplished?	Yes	Got the idea of the movement	Surprise!
	No	Something's wrong	Everything's wrong

Source: A. M. Gentile, "A Working Model of Skill Acquisition with Application to Teaching," *Quest* 17 (January 1972); p. 9.

learned skills as well as those taught using a traditional teacher-oriented technique. The advantage was that these students had learned *how* to learn as well as learned skills.[91] Lichtman suggested that helping students develop the ability to evaluate movement errors can speed up learning.[92] Pease emphasized the importance of teaching students to evaluate and interpret kinesthetic awareness or feelings during performance and performance results by comparing them with the desired results and the motor plan. In this way students can obtain immediate feedback, which would be impossible to obtain from the teacher when there are 30 or 40 or more students in a class.[93]

Cognitive Learning

Traditionally physical education teachers have emphasized skills and activities as the content of physical education. However, "being physically educated means having understandings about the body and physical activity that prepare each individual to want to live and be capable of living a physically active lifestyle."[94] Simplified concepts can be taught in elementary school with more in-depth analysis occurring in secondary schools.

Teaching the cognitive aspects of physical education is not easy. Planning is required to integrate concepts with psychomotor activity. However, knowledge gained through relevant experience lasts longer than that gained merely through reading or listening, and psychomotor learning occurs faster when students understand the principles involved in skill performance. Mohr emphasized the importance of integrating concepts with physical activity to enhance understanding and save time. She said:

> Our students do not have to stop motor activity in order to engage in cognitive activity. Students do not store their brains in their lockers. . . . To develop physical education understanding we need to guide these cognitive activities, just as we guide the motor activities. In other words, we can accomplish the intellectual, aesthetic, and social objectives without moving into the classroom. However, in some parts of the country, during inclement weather, physical education classes must be held in classrooms or other confined spaces. The resourceful teacher will take advantage of these times to plan worthwhile cognitive activities related to the body of knowledge in physical education and to the motor activities involved in the current unit. Modern audio-visual aids and numerous innovative teaching techniques are available to motivate and challenge the students to exciting cognitive achievements.[95]

Mohr concluded with the following statement:

> In your undergraduate and graduate professional preparation programs you have learned many exciting and valuable concepts about principles of movement, how the body performs desired movements, the effects of activity on these wonderful bodies of ours, and the effects of numerous factors on performance. Why keep these learnings a secret? Why not let your students share these exciting understandings so that their lives will be enriched by them just as yours have been.[96]

Cognitive Content

The knowledge explosion has dramatically increased physical education knowledge. The *Basic Stuff Series* was written to help physical educators keep up with the knowledge from an expanding research base, as well as to help teachers communicate that knowledge to students in physical education classes.[97] The series helps teachers tell students what, why, and how—knowledge about performance as well as skills and knowledge necessary to perform.[98] Series I includes six booklets on exercise physiology, kinesiology, motor development, motor learning, social and psychological aspects of movement, and movement in the humanities (art, history, and philosophy). Each booklet presents the body of knowledge in that area in a concise, readable format, with numerous examples and applications.[99] An example from the booklet on kinesiology is shown in figure 4.3. Series II *Basic Stuff in Action* has three booklets designed to help teachers apply the concepts in Series I to specific age groups (K–3, 4–8, and 9–12). An example from Series II appears in figure 4.4.

Ley listed some concept areas that should be included in instruction. They include the following:

1. Statements of description that provide information about "what"—facts, knowledge, information
2. Statements of importance that answer "why"—simple reasons, values, justifications, worth
3. Statements of scientific analysis that answer "why it happens"—principles, relationships, laws
4. Statements of problem solving (what one can do about it)—application of facts, principles, and relationships[100]

Spin in the direction of flight will cause the rebound to be closer to the surface than if the spin is opposite to the direction of flight

Balls behave in a similar fashion as they rebound from a wall or some vertical surface. A basketball with top spin around a horizontal axis will rebound farther from the backboard and one with back spin will stay closer to the board on the rebound. This is why good shooters usually release the ball so that back spin is applied. Backspin not only brings the ball down at a more vertical angle to the basket, but it will keep the ball closer to the board on a rebound and increase the possibility of the ball dropping in on the rebound. In racquetball a ball approaching the wall with top spin will rebound closer to the wall whereas a ball with back spin will rebound farther away from the wall. In games such as handball or racquetball where the rebound of the ball from the wall is altered by the type and amount of spin applied to the ball at contact, the ball frequently is spinning about a horizontal axis. However, spin about the vertical axis is also used to keep the ball closer to the wall on the rebound or to bring it back more sharply from the wall depending from which side the ball approaches the wall. These rebounds follow the same principles as those discussed earlier. If the ball tends to spin away from the performer as it comes off the wall, the ball will stay closer to the wall. If, as the ball comes off the wall, it tends to spin toward the performer, the ball will rebound farther away from the wall.

Figure 4.3 An example from *Basic Stuff Series I.*
From Ulibarri, V. Dianne. *Basic Stuff Series I.*
Volume Two, Kinesiology. (Reston, VA: American
Alliance for Health, Physical Education, Recreation
and Dance, 1987), p. 37.

> # Topic: Spins
>
> **Spin in the direction of flight will cause the rebound to be closer to the surface than if spin is opposite to the direction of flight (V2, P37)**
>
> Objects spin as a result of force applied off of their center of gravity. Spin in the direction of flight is called topspin and will cause the rebound to be closer to the surface than if the spin is opposite to the direction of flight (backspin). However, topspin off a horizontal surface will cause the ball to rebound farther from the surface than will backspin.
>
> If the spin is to the right, the ball will rebound to the left; and if spin is to the left, the rebound will be to the right. Hits with a combination of top, left, and right spin are possible. In games where the rebound of the ball from the wall is altered by the type and amount of spin applied to the ball at contact, the ball frequently is spinning on a vertical axis; and left or right spin is used to keep the ball closer to the wall on the rebound or to bring it back more sharply from the wall. A ball approaching the wall from the right will stay closer to the wall on the rebound with right spin and will rebound farther from the wall if left spin has been applied. The reverse is true for balls approaching from the left with left or right spin.

Learning Experiences:

1. Explain and demonstrate how spin is imparted and how its use can improve performance in the activity being taught.
2. Have the students apply force to an object at various angles. Have them observe the differences in rebound.
3. Complete the "Spin Task Sheet."
4. Encourage the use of spin on various appropriate skills during game play.

Conceptual Focus:

1. A ball can be spun to control rebound.
2. Placing spin on an object can improve performance.
3. Balls that spin will rebound differently depending upon the direction of force and the surface the object hits.

Materials Needed:

- equipment for the unit being taught
- pencils
- copies of the "Spin Task Sheet"

Figure 4.4   An example from *Basic Stuff Series II*.
From Kneer, Marian E. and Helen M. Heitmann.
Basic Stuff in Action, Grades 9–12. (Reston, VA:
American Alliance for Health, Physical Education,
Recreation and Dance, 1987), pp. 96–97.

Evaluation:

1. Evaluate tasks numbered 4, 5, and 6 on the "Spin Task Sheet."
2. Give a written test which includes questions on spin.
3. Observe the use of spin during game play.

References:

Broer, M.R. and Zernicke, R.F. (1979). *Efficiency of Human Movement* (4th Edition). Philadelphia. W.B. Saunders.

Related Concepts:

- The faster the topspin, the faster the rebound (V2, P36)
- An object that skids is not affected by its spin while skidding (V2, P36)
- A spinning object will rebound from a surface in the direction it is spinning (V2, P32)

SPIN TASK SHEET

NAME _____ DATE _____ CLASS _____

DIRECTIONS: Work in pairs. One person should work on Task #1 while the partner scores and retrieves objects as needed. When both have completed Task #1, go on to Task #2. Work until the criterion is met unless instructed otherwise. Record results in the right hand column.

TASK	OBJECTIVE	RESULTS
1. Hit 10 top spin shots	Ball should bounce low	
2. Hit 10 backspin shots	Ball should bounce high	
3. Hit 10 side spin shots	Ball should bounce right or left	
4. Repeat #1	Hit target at least 5 times	
5. Repeat #2	Hit target at least 5 times	
6. Repeat #3	Hit target at least 5 times	

Figure 4.4 *(Continued)*

Cognitive Learning Skills

Gagné listed three types of cognitive learning outcomes: (1) verbal information, (2) intellectual skills, and (3) cognitive strategies. *Verbal information* is stored knowledge or facts that can be utilized through *intellectual skills* that help the learner deal symbolically with the environment. The former are things learners can *tell,* whereas the skills reflect things students can *do.* Facts may be provided by the teacher prior to learning, recalled by the learner from previous learning, or learned just prior to the task at hand. When both facts and intellectual skills have been mastered, the learner is said to have the appropriate readiness for learning.[101] *Cognitive strategies* are skills used by learners to manage their own "learning, remembering, and thinking." They are used to help the learner decide what past knowledge and skills are to be used and how. During early learning experiences, the teacher cues the strategies. As the student's experience increases, the teacher may expect the learner to self-activate the strategies.[102]

Verbal Information

Verbal information includes memorization or rote learning and meaningful verbal learning. Teachers should become adept at teaching methods appropriate for both types of learning. Much information can be acquired through verbal learning in a relatively short time.

Memorization or Rote Learning. Behavioral psychologists emphasize associating items to be learned with familiar items, because repetition of paired events is assumed to create a bond or association between them. For example, almost everyone who studies music learns the lines on the staff with the sentence, "*Every Good Boy Does Fine.*" Similarly, learning fitness components can be easily done in alphabetical order—agility, balance, coordination, endurance, flexibility, speed, and strength. Rhymes such as "i before e except after c or when followed by g" are also readily remembered. Another method is using a key word, phrase, or mental image to remind the learner of the idea to be learned. Examples of mental images are the "backscratch" position in the tennis serve, the heart-shaped pull in the breaststroke, or the S pull in the freestyle. Learner-generated memory devices are generally more effective than teacher-generated devices.[103]

A common practice method is the progressive part method. The student learns part one, then parts one and two, and then one, two, three, and so forth. For example, when learning the bones in the body, start with the foot, review the foot and learn the ankle, review the foot and ankle and add the leg, and so forth. Another practice method is to respond to the entire task on each trial by using prompts such as crossing out parts of the material until the whole sequence has been learned. A third method is to use questions spaced periodically throughout the practice to increase student attention to the material. An example is to stop students during a game and have them identify the rule infraction.

Reinforcement or confirmation of correct responses is essential so the learner knows that the material has been learned correctly. Feedback must be specific so students know whether the response is correct or, if incorrect, how to change it to make it correct. Rote learning has only specific transferability. Identical elements must occur in the new situation to trigger retrieval.[104]

Meaningful Verbal Learning. Although memory devices are adequate for learning facts, they are not effective for comprehension. According to Ausubel, the key to comprehension is actively connecting new material to previously learned material to form a meaningful relationship.[105] Ausubel theorized that both subject matter and people's ideas are organized in hierarchies.

By attaching new information to old information, more information-processing space is available. Learning is enhanced by (1) presentation of an advance organizer, (2) presentation of the material to be learned, (3) anchoring new ideas to the existing cognitive structure, and (4) mastery of the new ideas.

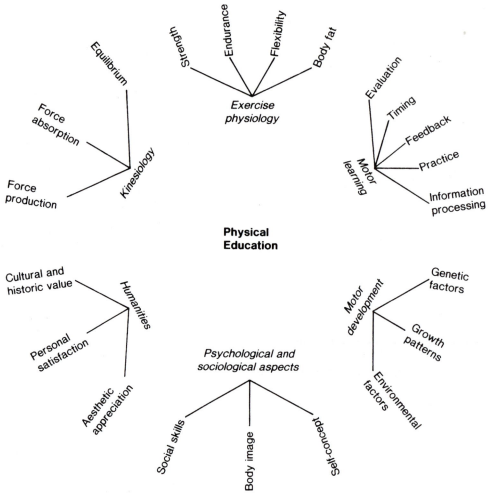

Figure 4.5 The relationship of the various components of physical education.

An *advance organizer* is a verbal or visual expression that clarifies the relationship of knowledge to be learned with previously learned material. There are two kinds of advance organizers. The *expository organizer,* shown in figure 4.5, shows the general components of physical education. Students should understand each area before proceeding to each subdivision around the outer borders of the diagram. The subdivisions may then be broken down into specific concepts, such as endurance training or measuring endurance. The expository organizer is used when unfamiliar material is to be presented. A *comparative organizer* shows the relationship of new and previously learned concepts by pointing out the similarities and differences between the two. A comparative organizer might compare the football throw with a softball throw. To facilitate learning, the teacher must refer to the previously learned skill, summarize the new material, and point out similarities and differences. Advance organizers emphasize the context within which the content fits. For this reason an excellent advance organizer is a diagrammatic portrayal of the relationships among content variables.

Content may be presented by lectures, demonstrations, class discussions, films, readings, or experiments. An outline can facilitate student organization of the material, help students understand logical relationships and maintain their attention. General information should be presented first, followed by the details. Studies show that meaningful verbal material is learned more rapidly and retained more readily with less interference than rote learning and has the potential for general transfer to many situations.

Intellectual Skills

Intellectual skills use verbal information to help the learner interact with the environment. They include discrimination learning, concept learning, rule learning, and problem solving. *Discrimination* learning involves the ability to perceive features in an object or event that are the same as or different from features in other objects or events. *Concept* learning involves organizing environmental input into categories for storage in the brain. A *rule* is a meaningful relationship between two or more concepts. *Problem solving* uses rules to help the learner interact with the environment.[106] Each skill will be reviewed briefly in the discussion that follows.

Concept and Discrimination Learning. A *concept* is an idea or picture in the brain that helps to aid understanding, as diagrammed in figure 4.6. It consists of perceptions, the meanings given them, feelings about them, and the words or symbols with which one discusses them. Most school learning involves concepts or the rules and principles created when concepts are linked together.

Concept learning entails classifying objects, experiences, processes, or configurations into a category of elements that share certain essential characteristics. A concept has the following:

1. A name or label—such as "aerobic activities"
2. Examples—instances that contain all essential attributes of the concept, such as "jogging or walking"

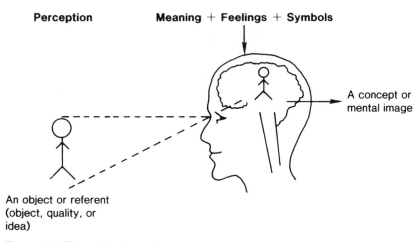

Perception   **Meaning + Feelings + Symbols**

A concept or mental image

An object or referent (object, quality, or idea)

Figure 4.6 The origination of a concept.

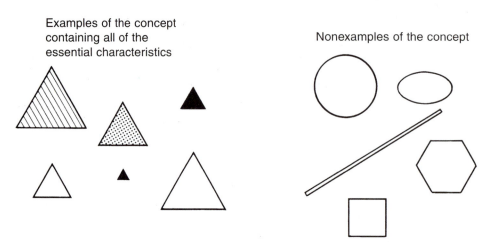

Examples of the concept containing all of the essential characteristics

Nonexamples of the concept

Figure 4.7 Concept learning involves distinguishing relevant from irrelevant characteristics.

3. Nonexamples—examples with none or only some essential characteristics, such as "sprinting or calisthenics"
4. Essential or shared attributes—common features of concept examples, such as "the constant use of oxygen without incurring an oxygen debt"
5. Irrelevant attributes—features that often accompany, but are not a required feature of, an element included in the concept, such as "when or where a person runs"
6. Definition—a statement specifying essential concept attributes, such as "Activities that develop oxygen transportation and utilization without incurring an oxygen debt are called aerobic activities"

Concept learning involves the ability to *discriminate* (1) essential characteristics from irrelevant characteristics and (2) essential characteristics of examples from essential characteristics of nonexamples, as shown in figure 4.7. Concepts can be taught by using the following steps:

Step 1. Present a variety of labeled examples that incorporate all essential characteristics of the concept—"Jogging, stationary cycling, and walking are aerobic activities."
Step 2. Compare examples and nonexamples (see preceding definitions) to identify essential characteristics and develop a hunch or hypothesis. Within the examples and nonexamples, vary the irrelevant attributes. Start with examples that are least similar, with the fewest shared characteristics. Ask "Is this an aerobic activity?": rowing—yes; sprinting—no; folk dance—yes.
Step 3. Verify the hypothesis by asking for several new examples of the concept. "List several aerobic activities."
Step 4. Have students state a definition of the concept in their own words. Check to see that the definition includes all essential characteristics of an aerobic activity.
Step 5. Reinforce correct answers.

Step 6. Apply the concept to choose appropriate examples.

Step 7. Test the concept. Can students generate examples with the essential characteristics and distinguish examples from nonexamples (e.g., aerobic from anaerobic activities)?

Concepts become more meaningful as students accumulate more experience with them. Laboratory experiences and demonstrations thus are important to help students gain the experiences needed.

Mohr provided some additional ideas for teaching concepts.[107] They are paraphrased here as follows:

1. Explain why one method of performance is better than another.
2. Omit some important feature of a skill, like stepping in the direction of the throw, to help the students see what a detrimental effect this has on the force of the throw.
3. Incorporate the learning of fitness concepts, such as exercise heart rate, recovery rate, and respiration rate, into rest periods between vigorous exercise.
4. Conduct informal experiments by comparing conditions, such as heat, cold, or smog, as they affect exercise on different days.

Rule Learning. Concepts can be linked to form rules or principles, which are taught best by application. Students who apply rules retain them more easily than those who only learn to say or write them. Rules and principles are best taught by the following steps:

Step 1. Inform the learner of the expected performance—"Traveling is a violation in basketball."

Step 2. Recall the component concepts—"Traveling is. . . . A violation is. . . ."

Step 3. Provide verbal cues that explain the relationships of the concepts—"Traveling is an unfair advantage with no body contact and is therefore a violation."

Step 4. Ask each student to demonstrate one or more instances of the rule (e.g., show various examples of traveling such as taking more than a two-step stop or moving the pivot foot).

Step 5. Ask each student to state the rule.

Step 6. Apply the rule in more complex situations (e.g., play a game and identify traveling).

Students should be taught concepts and rules at the same time the psychomotor skill is learned. For example, rules involving the volleyball serve should be taught while students are learning the serve. Principles relating to force production should be taught or recalled when hitting a tennis serve or throwing a ball. Some other ways to teach rules include:

1. Give the rule and an example. Ask students to supply a second example.
2. Give one or more examples. Have students formulate the rule.
3. Give an example. State the rule. Ask students for a second example.
4. Give the rule and ask students for an example.
5. Give the rule and ask students to restate the rule.
6. Give an example. Ask students for a second example.[108]

Problem Solving. Problem solving is the capacity to solve previously unencountered situations by combining old rules and principles into new higher-order ones. A problem is solved when previous knowledge or behavior is combined into a new relationship or added to new information to form an insight that resolves the new situation. Problem solving can be used to develop game strategies, create new games, compose gymnastic routines, choreograph dances, and for a host of other creative endeavors.

Problem solving involves the following steps:

Step 1.   Present students with a worthwhile problem.
Step 2.   Recall previously learned knowledge and behavior.
Step 3.   Provide assistance to channel students' thinking.
Step 4.   Reinforce both the process and the solution.

Step 1. Present Students with a Worthwhile Problem.   Design problems to help students apply recently learned principles. Problems must be worth solving and be capable of resolution with the time and resources available. Students should understand the problem and the expected performance. Essential features of the problem could be in the form of questions as simple as "How do I move my bowsight in archery?" or as complex as "Why are some people better performers in some activities, while others are better in other activities?"

Step 2. Recall Previously Learned Knowledge and Behavior.   Teach or recall knowledge and skills that relate to the problem. For example, have students shoot at 30 yards and ask them where they think they should place the bowsight based on their previous shooting at 20 yards.

Step 3. Provide Assistance to Channel Students' Thinking.   Teaching problem-solving strategies leads to better problem solving. Students differ in their abilities to solve problems. Bloom and Broder discovered a number of differences between successful and unsuccessful problem solvers.[109] Unsuccessful solvers

1. had low reading comprehension and failed to understand the problem. Often the problem they solved was not the one presented;
2. were unaware they possessed the knowledge necessary to solve the problem;
3. approached problems as if they had pat solutions; and
4. lacked confidence in their ability to solve problems.

To help students understand the problem, break it down into manageable components, recall relevant knowledge and skills, and reinforce the possibility of several solutions. The greater the ability to recall and apply previously learned knowledge and skills, the greater the chances of solving the problem. Listen to students' exploration of possible alternatives or provide students with cues to channel their thinking.[110] For example, ask, "What happened when you moved your bowsight up? Try moving it another direction to see what happens." Group discussion and participation appear to be superior to individual problem solving.

Step 4. Reinforce Both the Process and the Solution.   Let students know you have confidence in their ability to solve problems, and establish an environment of acceptance and self-worth in which students feel free to explore alternative solutions to problems. Make sure students have time to solve problems without pressure.

Cognitive Strategies

Cognitive strategies use networks of rules, or schemas, to achieve successful learning.[111] Teachers can help students recognize the correct strategies for given situations. A relative newcomer in the research arena is *metacognition,* which is defined by Flavell as follows:

Teaching concepts helps students apply learning
to real-life situations.
© Tracy Pellett

> Metacognition refers to one's knowledge concerning one's own cognitive processes and
> products. . . . For example, I am engaging in metacognition . . . if I notice that I am
> having more trouble learning A than B; if it strikes me that I should double-check C before
> accepting it as a fact; if it occurs to me that I had better scrutinize each and every alternative
> in any multiple-choice type task situation before deciding which is the best one; if I sense
> that I had better make a note of D because I may forget it.[112]

Metacognition involves knowing *when* you know something and when you do not, *what*
you need to know and what you already know, and *how* to use learning strategies to acquire the
information needed. Metacognition also helps you decide what information should be stored,
how much information can be handled at a time in short-term memory, and how to link the new
information with previously stored information. Metacognition increases as children mature.[113]

Learning strategies are closely related to metacognition. They are behaviors designed to influence how the learner selects, organizes, and integrates new knowledge with already existing
knowledge.[114] Norman summarized the importance of helping students learn how to learn:

> It is strange that we expect students to learn yet seldom teach them anything about learning.
> We expect students to solve problems yet seldom teach them about problem solving. And,
> similarly, we sometimes require students to remember a considerable body of material yet
> seldom teach them the art of memory. It is time we made up for this lack.[115]

Helping students develop effective ways to handle information should be a major educational
goal. Goals should be concerned with the products, as well as with the processes, of learning.[116]

Learning strategies range from the basic association strategies used for rote learning
(such as key words or mental images) to complex strategies for organizing material (such as
paraphrasing, summarizing, creating analogies, using advance organizers, underlining, listing,

notetaking, question asking or answering, outlining, diagramming, and comprehension monitoring).[117] Miller suggested some cognitive strategies useful in physical education. Problem solving can be used to explore and improve game strategies, relate skills to one another, and apply theory to practice, such as in analyzing the spin on a ball. Teachers can ask students questions that demand application to various situations (rather than present facts) and encourage students to ask and answer their own questions. Students can be encouraged to study their own performance and the performance of their opponents and to change their performance to match changes in the environment. Miller also suggested using bulletin board displays, worksheets, a sport newspaper, locker-room libraries, and reading-interest inventories to awaken students' minds. Learning centers can be used to enhance learning about activity and fitness.[118] A learning center is a station at which students work individually or as teams to discover psychomotor or cognitive principles and skills related to sport.[119] Students should rotate into games at planned intervals. (Other cognitive strategies are considered in chapter 8.)

Students should be encouraged to make a conscious effort to apply learning to life's problems. Homework assignments might be used to apply school learning to problems in the home or community. Homework can inform the family about physical education and even involve them directly in physical education activities. It can be used to practice skills, to learn or apply concepts, to increase physical fitness, to solve problems, and to develop self-discipline. Students can be encouraged to work together to complete assignments. French, Arbogast and Misner, and Docheff listed the following possibilities for homework in physical education:[120]

1. Practicing skills using task sheets or mental practice
2. Attending sports events or watching them on television
3. Coaching or officiating youth sports
4. Tutoring another student in a skill
5. Watching films or other media in a learning resource center
6. Studying for tests and quizzes or completing take-home tests or quizzes
7. Interviewing well-known sports figures
8. Reading books on sports and physical activities and writing book reports
9. Reporting on current events
10. Participating in fitness or activity programs
11. Completing study guides, worksheets, or concept games (such as crossword puzzles or scrambled word games)
12. Completing a fitness journal
13. Charting skill improvement on a progress chart
14. Reacting to situations involving sportsmanship, feelings, or attitudes

Since one objective of physical education is to encourage people to exercise on their own, why not reward students who make a habit of self-directed fitness activity?[121] Students can also be asked to solve problems, such as creating a gymnastics routine, a modern dance composition, strategies for a sports event, or a new game. Cameron tried a bonus incentive plan with extra-credit points earned for an optional out-of-class assignment each week. A maximum of three points could be earned based on the level of the problem selected. Problems consisted of self-testing and problem-solving activities, concept-related experiences, analysis of readings, and the interpretation and design of learning materials.[122]

Affective and Social Learning

Affective strategies are used to focus attention, maintain concentration, establish and maintain motivation, manage anxiety,[123] develop self-esteem, and learn ethical and social behavior. The primary purpose of teaching in the affective domain is to help students learn how to deal with their emotions and attitudes toward physical activity and toward others.

Compared with cognitive and psychomotor learning, little affective learning has been deliberately introduced into the curriculum because it is much easier to teach knowledge and skills than to influence attitudes, feelings, and character.

Developing Positive Attitudes toward Physical Activity

One's tastes, preferences, attitudes, and values will ultimately affect how one chooses to behave. Because students are both thinking and feeling beings, no learning can possibly occur without feelings being involved—feelings about themselves, the subject matter, and the situation. These feelings and values are powerful forces that sometimes block learning and on other occasions enhance it. When teachers are aware of students' feelings about physical education, they can provide appropriate learning situations. When teachers ignore the affective domain and pressure students to learn apart from their feelings and interests, students often end up disliking physical activity.

Since activity enjoyment is prerequisite to continued engagement in activity, teachers should help students develop favorable attitudes toward physical activity. To achieve this it is imperative that when students are in any physical education instructional or extracurricular activity, they are at the same time (1) in the presence of positive conditions and consequences and (2) in the presence of as few negative conditions and consequences as possible. This does not mean that all instruction should be fun, but it does mean that students will work harder and learn more when given the appropriate conditions. Although it is not always possible to determine whether a given condition is positive or negative for a certain student, Mager suggested a number of conditions or consequences that are generally considered to be positive or negative.[124] Examples are shown in Tables 4.11 and 4.12.

A supportive classroom environment is one in which students are treated as individuals and in which they know that help is available. Brophy summed up the research by saying:

> Effective teachers maintain a strong academic focus within the context of a pleasant, friendly classroom. Highly effective teachers clearly stress . . . objectives, but they do not come across as slave drivers, and their classrooms do not resemble sweatshops. They maintain high standards and demand that students do their best, but they are not punitive or hypercritical. Instead, students perceive effective teachers as enthusiastic and thorough instructors whose classrooms are friendly and convivial.[125]

Improving Self-Esteem

Felker developed five keys for improving students' self-concepts based on helping students develop the language necessary to enhance and maintain the self-concept.[126] They include: (1) adults, praise yourselves, (2) help students evaluate realistically, (3) teach students to set reasonable goals, (4) teach students to praise themselves, and (5) teach students to praise others.

Because students learn by imitating a model, teachers must learn to praise themselves. Express how good it makes you feel that you accomplished something. Later, expand to praise of your personal qualities. Try to use a variety of phrases for praising. Students need to learn to

Table 4.11 Positive conditions and consequences

Content-Oriented Conditions

1. Providing challenging instruction that leads to success most of the time.

2. Helping students know what the course objectives are and where they are in relation to the goal.

3. Preassessing students and providing instructional tasks that will help students achieve course objectives.

4. Providing immediate, specific feedback in a positive way.

5. Helping students develop confidence in their performance by overlearning skills.

6. Keeping verbal instruction to a minimum.

7. Using only relevant test items for the specified objectives.

8. Allowing students to select some learning activities.

9. Basing grades on each student's achievement, not on how well the other students performed.

Student-Oriented Conditions

1. Expressing genuine interest in the students and in their individual successes.

2. Treating each student as a person.

3. Acknowledging students' responses as legitimate learning attempts even when incorrect.

4. Allowing students to learn without public awareness of errors.

Environment

1. Providing an environment in which students feel accepted, supported, and trusted.

2. Providing a wide range of activities in which students can choose to involve themselves with appropriate counseling.

3. Focusing on what students can do rather than on what they cannot do.

---

evaluate realistically in terms of actual achievement. One way to help students do this is to have them check off skills or grade and record test scores. See chapter 9 for examples of check-off charts and other useful techniques.

Research shows that students with poor self-esteem tend to set goals too high or too low. They perceive themselves as failures when they fail to achieve goals that are too high or when they achieve a goal that anyone, even they, could reach. When students are taught to set realistic goals, their commitment to reaching them is increased. Goals should be set slightly higher than prior performances for effective learning. Short-term goals geared toward success lend themselves to appropriate praise and reward for achievement. Students should then move step-by-step up the ladder toward long-term goals.

By teaching students to praise themselves, the teacher is released from the role of behavior reinforcer. Teachers can help students learn to reinforce their own behavior by beginning with group praise, such as "Didn't we do well at . . . ?" and then moving to "Don't you think you did a great job on . . . ?" Students could also be helped to evolve from such self-encouraging

Table 4.12 Negative conditions and consequences

Pain (Physical Discomfort)

1. Forcing students to overdo in a physical fitness program, resulting in nausea, sore muscles, etc.
2. Failing to provide adequate safety, with resulting injury.
3. Making students sit for long periods of time when dressed for activity.
4. Allowing the classroom to be too hot or too cold or forcing students to participate outside when the temperature is too hot or cold, on wet grass, or when it is smoggy.
5. Forcing students to rush from one class to another or to dress more quickly than is reasonable.
6. Using subject matter as an instrument of punishment.

Anxiety (Mental or Emotional Discomfort or Anticipated Unpleasantness)

1. Being unpredictable about what is expected or how it will be graded.
2. Expressing that the student cannot possibly succeed.
3. Using vague, threatened punishment.

Frustration (Interference with Goal-Directed Activities)

1. Presenting information or skills faster or slower than the student can learn them or forcing all students to learn at the same pace.
2. Teaching one thing and testing another.
3. Failing to provide immediate and/or adequate feedback.
4. Stopping an activity just as the students are beginning to enjoy and be absorbed in it.
5. Overemphasizing competition during class time.

Humiliation and Embarrassment (Lowered Self-Respect, Pride, or Painful Self-Consciousness)

1. Making a public spectacle of a student, such as making the student do push-ups while the class watches or belittling the student's attempts to do well.
2. Allowing repeated failure.
3. Labeling students — "special ed.," "handicapped," etc.

Boredom

1. Repeating instructions that students have already had.
2. Failing to challenge students.
3. Failing to use variety in presenting course content.

statements as "I am trying hard" or "I am improving" to such self-praise as "I did a good job" or "I am a good sport." As students praise themselves, they attach the label of "worthwhile" to themselves and their behavior, and their self-esteem rises.

Felker pointed out that self-praise and praise of others are positively correlated. Praising others tends to result in satisfying responses from others, but students should be taught how to handle the few negative responses that might result. They also should be taught how to receive praise sometimes by praising in return and sometimes by a simple "thank you."

Developing Self-Efficacy

Self-efficacy is a person's belief in his or her ability to execute the behavior needed to produce a specified outcome, or, in simpler terms, it is situation-specific self-confidence. Efficacy expectations determine a student's activity selection, effort expenditure, and task persistence. Teachers should focus on developing competence, which in turn develops self-confidence. Romance suggested three ways teachers can detect students who lack confidence in physical education:

1. Performer uses extraneous or protective movements.
   a. Performer spends an inordinate amount of time warming up before trying a gymnastic trick.
   b. Performer goofs around—does not perform seriously—so as to mask unconfidence.
   c. Novice diver constantly reverts to a jump into the water at the moment of execution.
2. Performer uses inappropriate choice of tempo for moving.
   a. Performer rushes through a dance step, not staying with the music.
   b. Performer *walks* through the hurdling motion again and again.
3. Performer fixates on single element in environment.
   a. Performer continues to measure his or her jump rope and trade for new one.
   b. Performer is constantly tying shoe.
   c. Performer complains about condition of equipment (balls too slippery).[127]

Students who possess self-confidence persist in activities even when not directly supervised by the teacher. Confident performers believe they can handle new tasks and that the tasks will be satisfying, whereas those who lack confidence anticipate unpleasant consequences. Students who think they can accomplish a task may achieve tasks the teacher thinks are too difficult. However, students who think they cannot do something may avoid a task they could easily do. Dangers arise when students try activities beyond their capacities, resulting in injury or defeat.[128]

According to Feltz and Weiss, self-efficacy can be increased through (1) ensuring performance success, (2) communicating effectively, (3) modeling techniques, (4) encouraging positive talk, and (5) reducing anxiety-producing factors.[129] Performance accomplishment results from challenging activities at a level that permits student success early in the learning experience. Success yields motivation; therefore, teachers should choose activities for which students have the prerequisite skills and ensure a progression of activities from simple to complex. If tasks are too easy or performed with outside help, students attribute success to outside forces, resulting in boredom and a lack of self-efficacy. If tasks are too difficult, anxiety and failure may occur. Only success attributed to student effort results in self-efficacy.

Personally selected, specific, challenging but realistic goals result in self-efficacy. Process-oriented goals under the learner's control, such as the ability to use specified strategies in a game situation or perform a certain skill in a gymnastics routine, should be emphasized rather than winning, over which the learner may have no control (see also chapter 12). Teachers and coaches should evaluate communication to determine if it is positive and equitable to all students. One means of effective communication involves complimenting correct technique, then providing feedback on how to improve, followed by encouragement to keep trying. This "sandwich" technique was developed to the pinnacle of success by Coach John Wooden at UCLA.[130]

Modeling is important for developing self-efficacy, especially when the models are similar in age, sex, and athletic ability, and when they demonstrate the ability to achieve success through effort. To promote task persistence, however, models must exude confidence. Appropriate role modeling by teachers and coaches wins student respect, encourages confidence in teachers' abilities to help students learn, and encourages students' desire to achieve the modeled behavior.

Positive self-talk by students should be directed toward effort rather than winning. Students who perceive that effort yields success persist longer than those who focus on ability. Mental imagery can be used to envision successful performance in sport situations (see chapter 12).

Promoting Moral Development

Recent Phi Delta Kappa/Gallup polls show that a majority of the American people want schools to teach values and ethical behavior.[131] As an agent of society, the school is obligated to transmit societal values to the young. Historically, values cherished by the American people include loyalty, self-discipline, honesty, and hard work. The existing morality of a society is called the *moral consensus*. Each individual must develop a personal value system by applying rules and principles to moral situations and making decisions that result in a *moral sense*. Oser, paraphrasing Durkheim, stated that

> Values like the protection of life, the procedural forms of a democracy, and the dignity of a person cannot be reconsidered in such a way that everybody is free to choose or not to choose them.[132]

Oser concluded that moral education has been greatly neglected in the schools.[133] He said:

> The inescapable reality is that the school setting is always a moral enterprise; the inescapable fact is that social and political life is filled with moral content, and that history encompasses millions of moral decisions with which we as educators have to deal.[134]

Oser found conflicting strategies for moral learning.[135] Values education usually refers to helping people become aware of their own values. Exercises designed to help students achieve this awareness lack the ability to help students develop a moral consensus. Moral education commonly refers to a Kantian concept of justice. According to Rest, morality includes behavior that internalizes social norms, helps others, puts their interests ahead of one's own, arouses guilt or empathy, or includes reasoning about justice.[136] One must base decisions on the universal principles that guide moral behavior.

Kohlberg's *cognitive development approach* is probably the most well-known moral development model.[137] He proposed six levels of moral judgment, and he encouraged teaching moral judgment by stimulating a moral crisis or disequilibrium to guide the person to the next higher stage of moral judgment. This procedure is called a *plus-one strategy*. Kohlberg's system has been shown to be more effective than values clarification, probably due to the lack of clarity of values clarification strategies.[138]

Moral discourse is the common denominator of moral learning. Members participate in discussions about problems of justice, through which each person learns to develop a personal point of view and, at the same time, consider the point of view of others.[139] Any solution to a moral problem must be understood in terms of the following four principles governing moral discourse: (1) justification of one's course of action, (2) fairness, (3) the consequences of actions and omissions, and (4) universalization, which is a desire to take the role of a concerned person.[140]

A moral educational situation is created for an educational purpose. It demands a moral decision and has real consequences. The situation must look at the circumstances, needs, motives, and interests of the person involved and apply the four principles just outlined. Hersh, Paolitto, and Reimer described a 9-year-old boy with cerebral paralysis whom the other students teased. One day when Brian was absent the teacher explained that some people are born with conditions that prevent them from using their muscles in a normal way. She wondered what it would be like to be Brian. The children empathized and reacted. When Brian returned, they were much more receptive and helpful.[141]

The discussion helped students evaluate previous actions in terms of what was just, and the children changed their behavior as a result. The interaction allowed the children the freedom to react openly and listen to the point of view of someone else. Students need to consider a justification for the correct action, the means for carrying out the action, the responsibility they are willing to accept, the psychological and social obstacles they might confront, and the social consequences of the action.[142] To accomplish the goals of moral education, students must have a warm, accepting atmosphere in which conversation rules are maintained and aggression is minimized. Students should be led to analyze their own values and then the values of their peers, families, schools, and places of employment.

Physical education is an especially appropriate place to teach moral education. A position statement by the American Academy of Physical Education urged physical educators to encourage and support the following:

1. that the development of moral and ethical values be stated among the aims of the physical education program;
2. that the educational preparation of physical education teachers and athletic coaches emphasize moral and ethical values;
3. that the emphasis on the teaching of moral and ethical values by physical education teachers and athletic coaches be encouraged; and
4. that the profession of physical education establish criteria for the selection of appropriate ethical and moral values, develop formal plans of instruction, and methods for the assessment of results.[143]

Leona Holbrook, a prominent philosopher in physical education, espoused the following 12 action values for physical education:

1. Enjoying life
2. Realizing self
3. Helping others
4. Practicing honor—sportsmanship
5. Using moderation—emotional control
6. Developing excellence
7. Establishing personal habits—physical fitness

8. Cultivating breadth—aesthetics
9. Applying conservation
10. Esteeming work
11. Increasing productivity
12. Living spiritually[144]

Other values that have been proposed include cooperation and teamwork, tolerance and respect for others, loyalty, fairness, integrity, dependability, unselfishness, self-control, responsibility for the consequences of one's behavior, and friendliness.

Several research studies have shown that the use of moral dilemmas in physical education classes can effectively promote moral development. Preston used the Kohlbergian process to teach moral education in once-a-week sessions in health and physical education, with positive results.[145] Romance, Weiss, and Bockoven used moral dilemmas and other techniques successfully with fifth graders.[146] Bredemeier, Weiss, Shields, and Shewchuk used Bandura's social learning principles and moral dilemmas in physical education classes and found both to be effective.[147] Giebink and McKenzie utilized three strategies (instruction and praise, modeling, and a point system) to promote sportsmanship in a softball class. They demonstrated that sportsmanship can be taught in physical education classes, with unsportsmanlike behaviors decreasing dramatically. Since the phases followed each other, the three techniques undoubtedly had a cumulative effect. The learned behavior, however, did not transfer to a recreational basketball setting. They concluded, therefore, that sportsmanship training must occur over a long period of time and in a variety of settings.[148]

Wandzilak suggested five steps for constructing a social learning and moral development model to affect values through physical activity. The steps are: (1) Identify and define the specific values to be developed in terms of the behavior to be observed, (2) identify the physical activities and the dilemmas most appropriate for achieving the values and place them in a sequential order in terms of difficulty, (3) reward higher stages of moral reasoning with extra playing time, a sportsmanship trophy, or other reward rather than winning, (4) evaluate by using various observational techniques (see chapter 13), and (5) use the evaluation data to evaluate the success of the model.[149]

The following techniques have proven useful to promote moral or character development:

Moral dilemmas—real or hypothetical.[150] Sport provides its own moral dilemmas in which disequilibrium exists between the actual and desired behavior of students. Physical educators acting in a warm, accepting environment can guide or facilitate student discussions about these dilemmas. Interacting with an individual, small group, or class, the teacher can help students understand (1) why the action was taken, (2) alternative behaviors that might have been used, (3) the feelings of all persons involved in each of the alternative solutions, and (4) the most just solution to the situation the students are ready to accept. Real dilemmas can be created by allowing students to form their own teams for a game or relay, play as long as they want before substituting themselves out of a game, or by teacher-imposed rules that are unfair. Help students discuss and change the rules or procedures to improve the situation for all concerned.

Reciprocal teaching strategies[151] (see chapter 7). As partners teach each other, they learn to empathize with and encourage each other and look at situations from another person's perspective.

Game creating.[152] Interpersonal communication, learning to consider the perspective of others, cooperation, and problem solving are involved in creating games. The teacher might prescribe a limited amount of equipment, space, skills to be used, and safety procedures and ask students to develop a game in which all players have an equal chance to succeed. Games can be cooperative or competitive.

Class rules.[153] Students in each class can participate in a discussion at the beginning of the school year to establish class rules and the consequences for nonconformance to rules. As part of this process, students can be asked to make a list of their rights and responsibilities.

Challenge and initiative activities. Students work together to solve problems and achieve specified goals (see chapter 8).

Sharing.[154] Students are given a task and some of the resources necessary to complete the task. They must bargain with other groups for the resources they are missing. A time limit is imposed.

Listening bench.[155] When two students disagree, send them to a specified place to discuss their feelings and come up with potential solutions. A time limit and specific dialogue instructions can facilitate the process. Students should report their results to the teacher before resuming activity.

Review Questions

1. What is learning?
2. Define the three learning domains: cognitive, psychomotor, affective/social. What other learning domains might exist?
3. Define taxonomy.
4. Explain Gentile's model for teaching motor skills.
5. Why is perception important in all kinds of learning?
6. Define allocated time, engaged time, academic learning time (ALT), and ALT-PE.
7. What did Buck and Harrison discover about learning trials in physical education classes?
8. How can teachers maximize student involvement in instruction?
9. Summarize the various kinds of feedback and their effects on learning.
   a. Knowledge of performance
   b. Knowledge of results
10. What is an optimum learning task for students? How can a task be adjusted to increase or decrease its level of difficulty?
11. What kind of practice is best for beginners? For advanced players?
   a. Massed versus distributed
   b. Whole versus part
   c. Progressive part
   d. Mental practice
12. What conditions are necessary for positive transfer?
13. What can you do to promote retention?
14. What differences exist between rote learning and meaningful verbal learning? Which type of cognitive learning is best for learning facts? For learning principles?
15. What is an advance organizer? How should it be used to increase student learning?

16. List some concepts you might teach when explaining a sport or game.
17. List some examples of problem solving that might help students learn the principles of biomechanics in sport activities.
18. Why is it important to teach the *why* along with the *how* of physical activity? How can this be accomplished?
19. How can you tell whether a student feels good about physical education? How can you increase the chances of a student feeling good about physical education?
20. Why is self-efficacy important in learning motor skills? How is it acquired?
21. How can moral and character education be increased? What values might best be taught in physical education?

References

1. Bloom, B. S. (Ed.). (1956). *Taxonomy of educational objectives, handbook I: Cognitive domain.* New York: McKay.
2. Krathwohl, D. R., Bloom, B. S., & Masia, B. B. (1964). *Taxonomy of educational objectives, handbook II: Affective domain.* New York: McKay.
3. Bloom, Benjamin S. (1982). Personal communication.
4. Simpson, E. J. (1966/1967). The classification of objectives, psychomotor domain. *Illinois Teacher of Home Economics, 10,* 110–144; Harrow, A. J. (1972). *A taxonomy of the psychomotor domain: A guide for developing behavioral objectives.* New York: McKay; Corbin, C. B. (1976). *Becoming physically educated in the elementary school* (2nd ed., pp. 52–66). Philadelphia: Lea & Febiger; Thompson, M. M., & Mann, B. A. (1977). *An holistic approach to physical education curricula: Objectives classification system for elementary schools.* Champaign, IL: Stipes.
5. Jewett, A. E., Jones, L. S., Luneke, S. M., & Robinson, S. M. (1971, January). Educational change through a taxonomy for writing physical education objectives. *Quest, 15,* 35–36.
6. Corbin, *Becoming physically educated in the elementary school,* 52–56.
7. Singer, R. N., & Dick, W. (1980). *Teaching physical education: A systems approach* (2nd ed., p. 119). Boston: Houghton Mifflin.
8. Annarino, A. A. (1978, January). Operational taxonomy for physical education objectives. *Journal of Physical Education and Recreation, 49,* 54–55.
9. Miller, W. G., Snowman, J., & O'Hara, T. (1979, Summer). Application of alternative statistical techniques to examine the hierarchical ordering in Bloom's taxonomy. *American Educational Research Journal, 16,* 241–248; Seddon, G. M. (1978, Spring). The properties of Bloom's taxonomy of educational objectives for the cognitive domain. *Review of Educational Research, 48,* 303–323.
10. Krathwohl, Bloom, & Masia, *Taxonomy of educational objectives, handbook II.*
11. Singer & Dick, *Teaching physical education,* 119.
12. Graham, G., Holt/Hale, S. A., & Parker, M. (1993). *Children moving: A teacher's guide to developing a successful physical education program* (3rd ed., pp. 38–41). Palo Alto, CA: Mayfield.
13. Fitts, P. M., & Posner, M. I. (1967). *Human performance.* Belmont, CA: Brooks-Cole.
14. Gentile, A. M. (1972, January). A working model of skill acquisition with application to teaching. *Quest, 17,* 3–23.
15. Jewett, A. E., & Mullan, M. R. (1977). *Curriculum design: Purposes and processes in physical education teaching-learning.* Washington, DC: American Alliance for Health, Physical Education, Recreation and Dance.
16. Bressan, E. S. (1987). A movement processing paradigm and the curriculum in physical education. *Journal of Teaching in Physical Education, 6,* 335–343.
17. Corbin, *Becoming physically educated in the elementary school,* 52–56.
18. Oxendine, J. B. (1984). *Psychology of motor learning* (pp. 14–15). Englewood Cliffs, NJ: Prentice-Hall.
19. Corbin, C. B. (1981, June). First things first, but, don't stop there. *Journal of Physical Education, Recreation and Dance, 52,* 12–13.

20. Travers, R. M. W. (1982). *Essentials of learning: The new cognitive learning for students of education* (5th ed., p. 25). New York: Macmillan.

21. Pease, D. A. (1977). A teaching model for motor skill acquisition. *Motor Skills: Theory into Practice, 1*(2), 104–112.

22. Ibid.

23. Rink, J. E. (1993). *Teaching physical education for learning* (2nd ed., p. 89). St. Louis, MO: Times Mirror/Mosby.

24. Berliner, D. C. (1979). Tempus educare. In P. L. Peterson & H. J. Walberg (Eds.), *Research on teaching: Concepts, findings, and implications* (pp. 120–135). Berkeley, CA: McCutchan.

25. Brophy, J. E. (1979). Teacher behavior and its effect. *Journal of Educational Psychology, 71*, 733–750.

26. Fisher, C., Filby, N., Marliave, R., Cahen, L., Dishaw, M., Moore, J., & Berliner, D. (1978). *Teaching behaviors, academic learning time, and student achievement: Final report of phase III-B, beginning teacher evaluation study.* San Francisco: Far West Laboratory for Educational Research and Development.

27. Metzler, M. W. (1979). *The measurement of academic learning time in physical education.* Doctoral dissertation, Ohio State University, Columbus (University Microfilms No. 8009314).

28. Metzler, M. W. (1982). Adapting the academic learning time instructional model to physical education teaching. *Journal of Teaching Physical Education, 1*, 44–55.

29. Metzler, M. W. (1989). A review of research on time in sport pedagogy. *Journal of Teaching in Physical Education, 8*, 87–103.

30. Ibid.

31. Wittrock, M. C. (1986). Students' thought processes. In M. C. Wittrock (Ed.), *Handbook of research on teaching* (3rd ed., pp. 297–314) New York: Macmillan.

32. Silverman, S. (1985). Relationship of engagement and practice trials to student achievement. *Journal of Teaching in Physical Education, 5*, 13–21.

33. Siedentop, D. (1991). *Developing teaching skills in physical education* (3rd ed., p. 25). Mountain View, CA: Mayfield.

34. Siedentop, D. (1987). *Academic learning time—physical education coding manual.* Columbus: Ohio State University.

35. Buck, M. & Harrison, J. M. (1990, September). Improving student achievement in physical education. *Journal of Physical Education, Recreation and Dance, 62*(7), 40–44.

36. Parkin, D. (1981). Comments on skill development and competition by Mandle and Pang. *Australian Journal of Health, Physical Education and Recreation, 65*, 7–8.

37. Griffin, P. S. (1985, Late Winter). Girls' and boys' participation styles in middle school physical education team sport classes: A description and practical applications. *Physical Educator, 42*, 4–5.

38. Buck & Harrison, Improving student achievement in physical education, 40–44.

39. Landin, D. K., Hawkins, A., & Wiegand, R. L. (1986). Validating the collective wisdom of teacher educators. *Journal of Teaching in Physical Education, 5*, 252–271.

40. Harrison, J. M. (1987). A review of the research on teacher effectiveness and its implications for current practice. *Quest, 39*(1), 36–55.

41. Morris, G. S. D., & Stiehl, J. (1989). *Changing kids' games.* Champaign, IL: Human Kinetics.

42. Werner, P. (1989, March). Teaching games: A tactical perspective. *Journal of Physical Education, Recreation and Dance, 60*(3), 97–101.

43. Gentile, A working model of skill acquisition, 15. Concepts orginally from Poulton, E. C. (1957). On prediction in skilled movements. *Psychological Bulletin, 54*, 467–478.

44. Rothstein & Wughalter, *Basic stuff series I: Motor learning*, 50.

45. Schmidt, R. A. (1988). *Motor control and learning: A behavioral emphasis.* Champaign, IL: Human Kinetics.

46. Earls, N. F. (1983). Research on the immediate effects of instructional variables. In T. J. Templin & J. K. Olson (Eds.), *Teaching in physical education* (pp. 254–264). Champaign, IL: Human Kinetics.

47. Harter, S. (1978). Effectance motivation reconsidered: Toward a developmental model. *Human Development, 21*, 34–64.

48. Fitts, P. M. (1962). Factors in complex skill training. In R. Glaser (Ed.), *Training research and education* (pp. 177–197). Pittsburgh: University of Pittsburgh Press.
49. Merrill, M. D. (1972). Psychomotor taxonomies, classifications, and instructional theory. In R. N. Singer (Ed.), *The psychomotor domain: Movement behaviors* (pp. 385–414). Philadelphia: Lea & Febiger.
50. Hoffman, S. J., Imwold, C. H., & Koller, J. A. (1983, March). Accuracy and prediction in throwing: A taxonomic analysis of children's performance. *Research Quarterly for Exercise and Sport, 54,* 33–40.
51. Rink, *Teaching physical education for learning,* 104–108.
52. Rothstein, A., & Wughalter, E. (1987). *Basic stuff series I: Motor learning* (p. 30). Reston, VA: American Alliance for Health, Physical Education, Recreation and Dance.
53. Earls, Research on the immediate effects of instructional variables, 254–264.
54. Barrett, K. R. (1977, September). Games teaching: adaptable skills, versatile players. *Journal of Physical Education and Recreation, 48,* 21.
55. Young, J. E. (1985, October). When practice doesn't make perfect—Improving game performance in secondary level physical education classes. *Journal of Physical Education, Recreation and Dance, 56,* 24–26; Gabbard, C. (1984). Teaching motor skills to children: Theory into practice. *Physical Educator, 41,* 69–71.
56. Siedentop, D., Mand, C., & Taggart, A. (1986). *Physical education: Teaching and curriculum strategies for grades 5–12* (p. 201). Palo Alto, CA: Mayfield.
57. Young, When practice doesn't make perfect, 93.
58. Bressan, E. S., & Weiss, M. R. (1982, Fall). A theory of instruction for developing competence, self-confidence and persistence in physical education. *Journal of Teaching in Physical Education, 2,* 38–47; Weiss, M. R., & Bressan, E. S. (1985). Connections—Relating instructional theory to children's psychosocial development. *Journal of Physical Education, Recreation and Dance, 56*(9), 34–36.
59. Feltz, D. L., & Weiss, M. R. (1982, March). Developing self-efficacy through sport. *Journal of Physical Education, Recreation, and Dance, 53,* 24–26, 36.
60. Earls, Research on the immediate effects of instructional variables, 254–264.
61. Nixon, J. E., & Locke, L. F. (1973). Research on teaching physical education. In R. Travers (Ed.), *Second handbook of research on teaching.* Chicago: Rand McNally.
62. Oxendine, *Psychology of motor learning,* 304–305.
63. Seagoe, M. V. (1936). Qualitative wholes: A re-valuation of the whole-part problem. *Journal of Educational Psychology, 27,* 542.
64. Oxendine, *Psychology of motor learning,* 304–306.
65. Ibid., 312.
66. Ibid., 310.
67. Ibid., 313.
68. Travers, R. M. (1977). *Essentials of learning.* (4th ed., pp. 286–289). New York: Macmillan.
69. Magill, R. A. (1993). *Motor learning: Concepts and applications* (4th ed., pp. 371–380). Madison, WI: WCB Brown & Benchmark.
70. Lawther, J. D. (1977). *The learning and performance of physical skills* (2nd ed., p. 139). Englewood Cliffs, NJ: Prentice-Hall.
71. Oxendine, *Psychology of motor learning,* 280–299.
72. Magill, *Motor learning: Concepts and applications,* 76–78.
73. Cratty, B. J. (1975). *Movement behavior and motor learning* (3rd ed., pp. 387, 396–397.). Philadelphia: Lea & Febiger.
74. Singer, R. N. (1980). *Motor learning and human performance: An application to motor skills and movement behaviors* (3rd ed., p. 471). New York: Macmillan.
75. Cratty, *Movement behavior and motor learning,* 398.
76. Oxendine, *Psychology of motor learning,* 154.
77. Cratty, *Movement behavior and motor learning,* 389.
78. Nixon & Locke, Research on teaching physical education, 1217.
79. Rink, *Teaching physical education for learning,* 51.
80. Oxendine, *Psychology of motor learning,* 154.

81. Ibid., 164.
82. Ibid., 176–177.
83. Ibid., 176.
84. Oxendine, *Psychology of motor learning*, 179, 185.
85. Rothstein, A., & Wughalter, E. (1987). *Basic stuff series I: Motor learning* (p. 77). Reston, VA: American Alliance for Health, Physical Education, Recreation and Dance.
86. Bilodeau, E. A., & Bilodeau, I. M. (1961). Motor-skills learning. *Annual Review of Psychology, 12,* 243–280.
87. Magill, R. (1994). Augumented feedback in skill acquisition. In R. N. Singer, M. Murphey, & L. K. Tennant (Eds.), *Handbook on research in sport psychology*. New York: Macmillan.
88. DelRey, P. (1972). Appropriate feedback for open and closed skill acquisition. *Quest, 17,* 42–45; Melville, S. (1983, May). Process feedback made simple. *Physical Educator, 40,* 95–104.
89. Melville, Process feedback made simple.
90. Gentile, A working model of skill acquisition, 15.
91. Ainsworth, J., & Fox, C. (1989, September/October). Learning to learn: A cognitive processes approach to movement skill acquisition. *Strategies, 3*(1), 20–22.
92. Lichtman, B. (1984, March). Motor schema: Putting theory into action. *Journal of Physical Education, Recreation and Dance, 55,* 54–56.
93. Pease, A teaching model for motor skill acquisition, 104–112.
94. Lockhart, B. D. (1982, September). The basic stuff series: Why and how. *Journal of Physical Education, Recreation and Dance, 53,* 18.
95. Mohr, D. R. (1971, January). Identifying the body of knowledge. *Journal of Health Physical Education Recreation, 42,* 23.
96. Ibid., 24
97. American Alliance for Health, Physical Education, Recreation and Dance. (1987). *Basic stuff series.* Reston, VA: Author.
98. Lawson, H. A. (1982, September). Change, controversy, and criticism in the profession. *Journal of Physical Education, Recreation and Dance, 53,* 30–34.
99. Heitmann, H. M. (1981, February). Integrating concepts into curricular models. *Journal of Physical Education, Recreation and Dance, 52,* 42–45.
100. Ley, K. (1971, January). Teaching understandings in physical education. *Journal of Health Physical Education Recreation, 42,* 21–22.
101. Gagné, R. M. (1985). *The conditions of learning and theory of instruction* (4th ed., p. 47). New York: Holt, Rinehart & Winston.
102. Ibid., 48.
103. Grippin, P., & Peters, S. (1984). *Learning theory and learning outcomes: The connection* (pp. 194–197). New York: University Press of America.
104. Ibid., 208.
105. Ausubel, D. P. (1963). *The psychology of meaningful verbal learning: An introduction to school learning* (p. 16). New York: Grune & Stratton.
106. Grippin & Peters, *Learning theory and learning outcomes,* 177.
107. Mohr, Identifying the body of knowledge, 24.
108. Rink, *Teaching physical education for learning,* 258–264.
109. Bloom, B. S., & Broder, L. J. (1950). *Problem-solving processes of college students: An exploratory investigation.* Supplementary Educational Monographs, no. 73 (p. 25). Chicago: University of Chicago Press.
110. Hudgins, B. B. (1966). *Problem solving in the classroom* (p. 43). New York: Macmillan.
111. Grippin & Peters, *Learning theory and learning outcomes,* 179.
112. Flavell, J. H. (1976). Metacognitive aspects of problem solving. In L. B. Resnick (Ed.), *The nature of intelligence* (p. 232). Hillsdale, NJ: Erlbaum.
113. Grippin & Peters, *Learning theory and learning outcomes,* 137.
114. Weinstein, C. E., & Mayer, R. E. (1986). The teaching of learning strategies. In M. C. Wittrock (Ed.), *Handbook of research on teaching* (3rd ed., p. 315). New York: Macmillan.
115. Norman, D. A. (1980). Cognitive engineering and education. In D. T. Tuma & F. Reif (Eds.), *Problem solving and education: Issues in teaching and research* (p. 97). Hillsdale, NJ: Erlbaum.

116. Weinstein & Mayer, The teaching of learning strategies, 315.
117. Ibid., 316.
118. Miller, D. M. (1987, October). Energizing the thinking dimensions of physical education. *Journal of Physical Education, Recreation and Dance, 58*, 76–79.
119. Espiritu, J. K., & Loughrey, T. J. (1985, Late Winter). The learning center approach to physical education instruction. *Physical Educator, 42*, 121–128.
120. French, R. (1979, May). The use of homework as a supportive technique in physical education. *Physical Educator, 36*, 84; Arbogast, G., & Misner, J. (1990, September-October). Homework "how-to's": Guidelines for designing out-of-class assignments. *Strategies, 4*(1), 12, 15; Docheff, D. (1990, September–October). Homework . . . in physical education? *Strategies, 4*(1), 10–11, 13–14.
121. Klappholz, L. A. (Ed.). (1980, November). Half the PE grade is based on outside activity. *Physical Education Newsletter.*
122. Cameron, D. A. (1986, Late Winter). Who plays basketball? Bonus incentive plans—A learning stimulus. *Physical Educator, 42*, 151–155.
123. Weinstein & Mayer, The teaching of learning strategies, 324.
124. Mager, R. F. (1965). *Developing attitude toward learning* (pp. 50–57). Palo Alto, CA: Fearon.
125. Brophy, J. (1982). Successful teaching strategies for the inner-city child. *Phi Delta Kappan, 63*, 527–530.
126. Felker, D. W. (1974). *Building positive self concepts.* Minneapolis: Burgess.
127. Romance, T. J. (1985, August). Observing for confidence. *Journal of Physical Education, Recreation and Dance, 56*, 47–49.
128. Bressan & Weiss, A theory of instruction for developing competence, self-confidence and persistence in physical education, 38–47.
129. Feltz, D. L., & Weiss, M. R. (1982, March). Developing self-efficacy through sport. *Journal of Physical Education, Recreation and Dance, 53*, 24–26, 36.
130. Tharp, R. G., & Gallimore, R. (1976, January). Basketball's John Wooden: What a coach can teach a teacher. *Psychology Today, 9*, 75–77.
131. Elam, S. M., Rose, L. C., & Gallup, A. M. (1993, September). The 25th annual Phi Delta Kappa/Gallup poll of the public's attitudes toward the public schools. *Phi Delta Kappan, 75*(2), 145.
132. Durkheim, E. E. (1961). *Moral education: A study in the theory and application of the sociology of education.* New York: Free Press of Glencoe. Cited in Oser, F. K. (1986). Moral education and values education: The discourse perspective. In M. C. Wittrock (Ed.), *Handbook of research on teaching* (3rd ed., p. 144). New York: Macmillan.
133. Oser, Moral education and values education, 919.
134. Ibid., 935–936.
135. Ibid., 917–941.
136. Rest, J. R. (1983). Morality. In J. H. Flavell & E. M. Markman (Eds.), *Handbook of child psychology, Volume 3: Cognitive development* (p. 556). New York: Wiley.
137. Kohlberg, L. (1985). The just community approach to moral education in theory and practice. In M. W. Berkowitz & F. Oser (Eds.), *Moral education: Theory and application* (pp. 27–87). Hillsdale, NJ: Erlbaum.
138. Leming, J. S. (1981, May). Curricular effectiveness in moral/values education: A review of research. *Journal of Moral Education, 10*, 147–164; Lockwood, A. A. (1978, Summer). The effects of value clarification and moral development curricula on school-age subjects: A critical review of recent research. *Review of Educational Research, 48*, 325–364.
139. Oser, Moral education and values education, 919.
140. Keller, M., & Reuss, S. (1983). The process of moral decision-making: Normative and empirical conditions of participation in moral discourse. In M. W. Berkowitz & F. Oser (Eds.), *Moral education: Theory and application* (p. 110). Hillsdale, NJ: Erlbaum.
141. Hersh, R. H., Paolitto, D. P., & Reimer, J. (1979). *Promoting moral growth: From Piaget to Kohlberg* (p. 4). New York: Longman.
142. Oser, Moral education and values education, 929.
143. American Academy of Physical Education. (1981, October). *The academy papers: Reunification* (pp. 107–108). Reston, VA: American Alliance of Health, Physical Education, Recreation and Dance.

144. Griffin, J. (1981). *Developing ideas for teaching values in the physical education curriculum.* Unpublished master's thesis, Brigham Young University, Provo, UT.

145. Preston, D. (1979). *A moral education program conducted in the physical education and health education curriculum.* Unpublished doctoral dissertation, University of Georgia, Athens, GA.

146. Romance, T. J., Weiss, M. R., & Bockoven, J. (1986). A program to promote moral development through elementary school physical education. *Journal of Teaching in Physical Education, 5*(2), 126–136.

147. Bredemeier, M., Weiss, M., Shields, D., & Shewchuk, R. (1984). *The development and consolidation of children's moral reasoning in response to three instructional strategies.* Unpublished manuscript.

148. Giebink, M. P., & McKenzie, T. L. (1985, April). Teaching sportsmanship in physical education and recreation: An analysis of interventions and generalization effects. *Journal of Teaching in Physical Education, 4,* 167–177.

149. Wandzilak, T. (1985). Values development through physical education and athletics. *Quest, 37,* 176–185.

150. Figley, G. E. (1984). Moral education through physical education. *Quest, 36,* 89–101; Romance, T. J. (1988, May). Promoting character development in physical education. *Strategies, 1*(5), 16–17; Wandzilak, Values development through physical education and athletics.

151. Horrocks, R. (1980, December). Sportsmanship moral reasoning. *Physical Educator, 37*(4), 208–212.

152. Ibid.; Romance, Promoting character development in physical education, 16–17.

153. Romance, Promoting character development in physical education, 16–17; Morrison, C., Reeve, J., & Mielke, D. (1989, September/October). Teaching ideas for the affective domain. *CAHPER Journal, 55*(5), 13–16.

154. Ibid.

155. Romance, Promoting character development in physical education, 16–17.

CHAPTER 5

Planning the Instructional Program — Unit and Lesson Planning

Study Stimulators

1. What components are important in designing, implementing, and evaluating instructional programs? Where can you get help on each of these components?
2. Why is it important for teachers to write unit plans and daily lesson plans? How detailed should they be?
3. What components are included in a unit plan?
4. What components are included in a daily lesson plan that are not found in a unit plan? How should a daily lesson plan be written?
5. What is reflective teaching? How can it help you improve your teaching?

There once was a teacher
Whose principal feature
Was hidden in quite an odd way.
Students by millions
  Or possibly zillions
  Surrounded him all of the day.
When finally seen
By his scholarly dean
And asked how he managed the deed,
He lifted three fingers
  And said, "All you swingers
  Need only to follow my lead."
"To rise from a zero
To Big Campus Hero,
To answer these questions you'll strive:
Where am I going,
  How shall I get there, and
  How will I know I've arrived?"[1]

This poem emphasizes the importance of planning the instructional program. Mosston described teacher behavior as "a chain of decision making."[2] Hunter defined teaching as a "constant stream of professional decisions made before, during and after interaction with the student; decisions which, when implemented, increase the probability of learning." She stated, "When those professional decisions are made on the basis of sound psychological theory and if those decisions also reflect the teacher's sensitivity to the student and to the situation, learning will be increased."[3] Hunter found that, regardless of who or what is being taught, all teaching decisions fall into three categories: (1) what *content* to teach next, (2) what the *student* will do to learn and to demonstrate that learning has occurred, and (3) what the *teacher* will do to facilitate the acquisition of that learning. Errors made when making any of these decisions can impede student learning.

Clark and Peterson summarized the research on teacher planning.[4] Their research demonstrates that beginning teachers use a linear model for planning instruction such as the one shown in figure 5.1. They work best from daily lesson plans. Just as a traveler uses a map to reach a certain destination, teachers can use the model to plan the best route toward student learning. By following the model, teachers can be sure they do not leave out an essential part of the planning process. As teachers become more experienced, they tend to visualize the outcomes of the instructional process and construct a framework designed to fit the unique circumstances of the teaching situation. Experienced teachers tend to plan in weekly intervals. They consider student needs and the context of teaching, then subject matter, and finally goals and teaching methods.

Because teachers operate in a demanding, complicated environment, decision making is difficult. Teachers must plan carefully for students to successfully reach the goals of physical education. Effective instruction and learning should be based on the needs of individual students as well as the demands of a changing environment; teachers should avoid doing the same things year after year.

Designing the Instructional Program

The instructional designer must organize the elements of instruction in the most effective way possible to achieve the goal, which is student learning.[5] All decisions should be made with regard to whether they facilitate student learning. Teachers are in the best position to act as instructional designers because of their knowledge of the subject matter and their experience with students. However, to produce or improve learning, the teacher must understand each of the components of the system and how they interact with one another to achieve the goal, as well as the context of the environment surrounding the system.[6]

Davis, Alexander, and Yelon defined the first step in designing instruction as "describing the current status of the learning system." Such a description would include "purposes, resources and constraints, the students entering the program, their skills, expectations and needs, and [the teacher's] own capabilities."[7] Other factors include school time and facility restraints and the freedom to innovate. These aspects were presented in chapters 1 through 4.

Once the current status of the system has been defined, the instructional designer must next consider ways in which students will use knowledge, attitudes, and skills to achieve the desired outcomes. Step two is writing *performance objectives,* which set the stage for each successive step. Chapter 6 explains the process of writing objectives. To write appropriate objectives for a given group of students requires the use of content analysis and preassessment. *Content analysis* presents the content in a manner that facilitates the appropriate selection of content and activities for specific learners. *Preassessment techniques* tell the teacher where the students are at the beginning of instruction.

The third step is to utilize the objectives to select specific instructional styles and strategies. The main charge of physical educators is to help young people improve their movement skills. But all children, schools, and school environments differ. Thus, for all children to succeed at improving their movement skills, the effective teacher must use a variety of teaching skills,

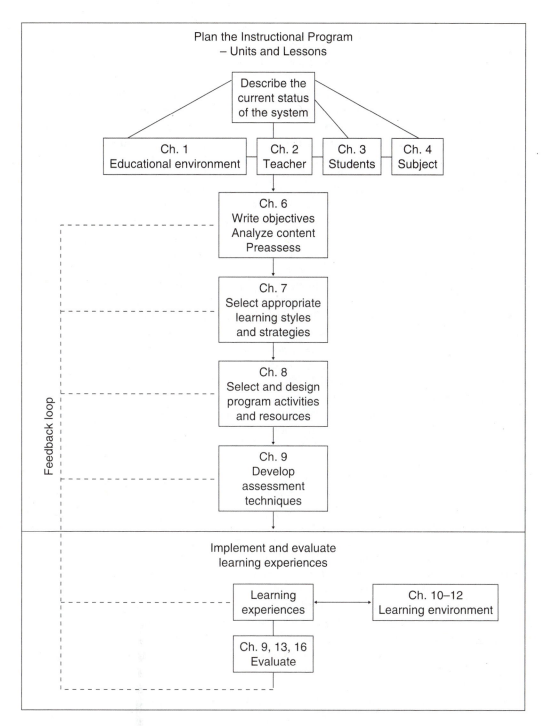

Figure 5.1 A model for designing instructional programs.

strategies, and activities while interacting with the environment.[8] A unit of instruction may incorporate several styles and strategies to ensure learning by individual students. Chapter 7 presents several such alternatives. The Spectrum of Teaching, mastery learning, individualized instruction, and other instructional strategies will be discussed.

The fourth step is to select or develop resources to take students from where they are at the beginning of the instructional process to achievement of the unit or lesson objectives. Chapter 4 presented the theory and knowledge base necessary to make sound decisions. Chapter 8 presents instructional resources, materials, and activities for various aspects of the instructional program.

The last step in the planning process is to develop assessment materials and techniques. Evaluation techniques tell whether the students have achieved the stated objectives. A variety of techniques that can be used for evaluation are described in chapter 9. An explanation is also given as to how these techniques can be combined into a grading system.

Teachers must remember that effective planning also involves modification of existing plans. Teachers may return to a stage many times before the planning phase has been completed. Teachers must continually move back and forth among the stages of the model to include items that were inadvertently omitted or change items that are later considered to be inappropriate. A continual check is necessary to make sure the elements of the system fit together properly.[9]

Planning to Implement and Evaluate the Instructional Program

Once teachers have planned the instructional program, they are ready to plan for its implementation and evaluation. An appropriate environment for learning is essential to achieve the goals of physical education. In the broadest sense of the term, the environment is a product of many factors that may be determined by legislation, school boards, administrators, parents, and circumstances that are beyond the control of the teacher. Once the general environment for learning has been established within the context of the school, however, the classroom emerges as the specific environment for learning. The classroom is the domain of the teacher, who must make many decisions that directly affect student learning. These decisions become the essence of teaching and learning.

The model for designing instructional programs illustrates that the actual content of any instructional program is determined by the planned learning experiences and the learning environment.

Chapters 10 and 11 discuss the organization and management of the instructional environment for effective learning. The areas of legal liability, department policies and procedures, class management techniques, and record keeping will be presented. Effective classroom management is the ability to organize the components of the classroom so that effective instruction occurs.

Chapter 12 deals with one of the major problems of public school teachers—class control or discipline—and its corollary—motivation. The chapter reviews various motivational and preventive discipline techniques and tells how to develop an appropriate discipline model and select a specific technique for a given situation.

One of the purposes of an instructional model is to provide a structure for reviewing and analyzing instruction so that it can be improved. Once the program has been implemented, an evaluation can determine weaknesses in each of the preceding levels of the model. Chapter 13 delineates a number of ways in which teachers can evaluate their effectiveness in providing instruction. Teachers must be open to change during the implementation stage. Anderson pointed out that if teachers are to continue to develop competence in teaching, they must develop skill in the analysis of teaching.[10] Chapter 16 details methods for program evaluation.

Chapters 14 and 15 provide assistance in developing the curriculum for a school program. Once the yearly curriculum has been designed, the teacher must follow up with two kinds of instructional plans—unit plans and daily lesson plans. Although each of these phases of planning serve a different function, they are mutually interdependent. Basically, these plans include the answers to the three questions expressed by Mager as follows: (1) Where am I going?, (2) How will I get there?, and (3) How will I know I've arrived?[11]

Where am I going? The plan should specify the performance objectives of the lesson plan or unit in the cognitive, psychomotor, and affective domains.

How will I get there? The plan should delineate the learning experiences that will be used to help students meet the objectives specified.

How will I know I've arrived? Evaluation techniques must be included that will help the teacher determine whether the students have achieved the objectives.

In this chapter, we will preview how to write unit and lesson plans. The chapters that follow will provide the detailed information needed for effective planning. You may expect to return to this chapter often as you study the remaining chapters in this text.

How to Write a Unit Plan

Unit and lesson planning involve planning to teach specific content to a specific group of students. Unit and lesson planning combine two elements of effective instruction—the educational environment and the subject matter—to best meet learners' needs.

The unit plan directs the teacher in providing purposeful chunks of learning for students; that is, it centers class work around meaningful patterns and focuses the work of different days around a central theme until some degree of unified learning is attained. The amount of time spent on the unit and on various aspects of the unit are based on curricular objectives, as well as on the previous experience and expertise of the students. Teachers can take advantage of the possibilities of transfer from previous units and teach units concurrently that provide transfer. The teacher must decide the teaching emphasis of each unit so that the result at the end of the school year is not low levels of student proficiency in most skills. Rather, sufficient time must be provided in some units so that students can learn the necessary skills to achieve *high* levels of performance and retention. A few units may be taught solely to introduce students to various skills.

Before a unit plan can be devised and Mager's questions can be answered, certain preliminary considerations must be identified. The following considerations must be listed on the unit plan form shown in figure 5.2.

1. An identification of subject matter and teaching time.
2. An identification of student characteristics. Teachers may need to identify special considerations, such as physical limitations, non-English-speaking students, and low-ability students, through surveys, school guidance materials, or informal assessment.
3. An identification of skills and concepts to be taught (see content analysis in chapter 6).
4. An identification of instructional materials and preparations.
5. An identification of preassessment techniques, if any. Teachers may need to determine interests and needs through surveys or informal assessment (review chapter 6).

The teacher who fails to plan, plans to fail.
© Tracy Pellett

Where Am I Going?

Before any learning experiences are planned, performance objectives are formulated. Write down what the student is expected to *do* at the completion of the unit. Objectives should be included for the psychomotor, cognitive, and affective domains. Objectives might include the following outcomes:

1. *Skills:* These are psychomotor skills that the student will be able to do, such as

- shoot three types of shots.
- bat and bunt successfully.
- bowl a score of 120.
- play safely.
- officiate a game (both psychomotor and cognitive).
- achieve or maintain "good or excellent" on the 1.5-mile run.

2. *Knowledge:* These are cognitive skills or ideas that the student will be able to use in some way, such as

- select the proper golf club for each distance.
- demonstrate a knowledge of the rules.

Preliminary Considerations

Unit: Beginning Volleyball   Number of days: 20

Class: Size <u>40</u>   Grade <u>7th</u>   (Boys _____   Girls _____   Coed <u> X</u>)

Skill Level: Beginning

Special considerations: None

Skills/principles to be taught: Forearm pass, set, underhand serve, spike, volleyball rules, pass-set-spike strategy

Facilities needed: Gym, 3 volleyball courts

Equipment needed: 40 VolleyLite volleyballs, 3 volleyball nets, net markers to divide nets into 2 half courts per court

Media or other materials needed: Videotape, VCR, and monitor

Preassessment: Students will be asked about their previous experience in volleyball. After each skill is demonstrated, the teacher will have the students practice and make an assessment of the skill level of the class and how fast to move to the next skill.

Objectives

Objectives	Evaluation
Psychomotor performance objectives	
The student will:	
1. Hit 10 consecutive legal hits alternating a set and a forearm pass.	Skills test
2. Serve 8 legal underhand serves anywhere in the court area.	Skills test
3. Execute the skills (pass, set, spike, serve) correctly in game play.	Subjective evaluation (5 point scale)
4. Complete 80% of all tasks on task sheets.	
Cognitive performance objectives	
1. Pass a written test with 80 percent or better on minivolley rules.	Written test
2. Pass a written quiz with 75 percent or better listing the 3 cues for each skill—pass, set, serve, spike.	Written test
Affective performance objectives	
1. Exhibit a desire to become a more skilled volleyball player by participating in drills and attempting new skills in game play at least once each day.	Record of participation in practice drills
	Incidence charts of game play

Figure 5.2   Unit plan.

Physical fitness objectives

1. Complete physical fitness contract as written.   Contract log

Day-by-Day Decisions

Day (When)	Content (What)	Learning Activities (How)	Evaluation
1	Model volleyball skills Preassessment	Videotape of youth volleyball championships.	Skills test Play minivolley
2-3	Forearm pass	Pass from partner toss.	10 times
		Pass from partner toss to side.	10 times
		Consecutive passes with partner.	15
		Consecutive passes with threesome.	10
		Toss over net, pass to hoop on floor.	5 into hoop
		Play 3-pass game starting with toss.	Try to keep it going
4-5	Set (Review pass, including quiz on pass cues)	Review pass drills above.	See above Quiz score
		Catch ball in proper position from toss.	5 times
		Set ball from partner toss.	15 times
		Consecutive passes with partner.	15 times
		Consecutive passes with threesome.	10 times
		Consecutive alternating passes and sets with threesome.	15 times
		Pass and set to hoop.	5 into hoop
		Play 3-hit game (pass-set-hit over).	Try to keep it going

Figure 5.2   *(Continued)*

Day (When)	Content (What)	Learning Activities (How)	Evaluation
6	Underhand serve (Review pass and set, including quiz on set cues	Review.	See above
		Hit serves, 15' from net; work on force production, moving back with success to service line.	Quiz score Distance from net
		Serve to partner who forearm passes to hoop on floor.	5 into hoop
		Play serve game. Serve in court = 1 point Ace serve = 1 bonus point Receiver scores for Pass-Set-Spike Play to 5 points and rotate	Number of points
		Play 3-hit game with serve; 1 point per 3 hits on side.	Try to get as many points as possible
7-8	Spike (Review other skills, including quiz on serve cues)	Review above drills.	See above Quiz score
		Hit ball out of hand toward wall.	10 times
		Toss ball & hit toward wall.	10 times
		Jump forward, jump up & scratch back of head.	10 times
		Practice approach footwork.	5 times
		Approach net, jump & scratch back of head.	10 times
		Approach net, jump & throw tennis ball over net.	5 times
		Approach & hit ball out of partner's hand (use chair).	10 times
		Approach & hit tossed ball.	25 times

Figure 5.2   *(Continued)*

Day (When)	Content (What)	Learning Activities (How)	Evaluation
		Approach & hit set ball.	15 times
		Toss ball over net, pass, set, spike	10 times
9-12	Increase proficiency in all skills. Quiz on spike cues.	Serve in order to positions 1-5 on court.	Quiz score All 5 positions hit
		Serve at targets on floor.	5 reachable hits
		Partner keeps 1 foot in hoop and forearm passes back.	
		Set—run to position and set ball. Set ball coming from different directions.	10 times
		Pass—retrieve ball from net.	10 times
		Practice setting a ball gone astray.	10 times
		Spike—Toss ball over net, pass, set, spike.	10 times
		Game—Play cooperative volleyball.	Points scored
13	Quiz on minivolley rules and pass-set-spike strategy.	Play minivolley with bonus points for pass-set-spike sequences.	Quiz score pass-set-spike sequences
14-18	Minivolley Tournament and skills tests (repeatable each day)	Play games. Practice skills tests.	Pass-set-spike sequences Skills test scores
19-20	Play official volleyball game. Introduce simple offensive and defensive strategies.	Play games, try W defense and 4-2 offense if ready.	

Figure 5.2   *(Continued)*

Motivational Techniques

Tournament the last week of the unit. Players will be selected as tournament Most Valuable Player and Most Inspirational Player by students in the class. Minivolley increases opportunities for response. VolleyLite balls decrease pain and increase success.

Grading policies

Physical fitness		40 pts
Physical fitness contract		
Completed =	40	
Almost complete =	30	
Some completed =	20	
Physical skill		80 pts
Serve test	10 pts max	
Volley/bump test	20 pts max	
Game play	25 pts max (score × 5)	
Task sheets completed	25 pts max (5 pts/sheet)	
Knowledge	————	30 pts
		~~150 pts~~

Bonus points:

25 pts = Tournament MVP (Most Valuable Player)
25 pts = Most Inspirational Player (team player, tries hard, encouragement, leadership)
10 pts = Most Improved Player
10 pts = Team whose members cooperate with each other the best

Grading breakdown

150–128 = A 85%
127–105 = B 70%
104–75 = C 50%
74–53 = D 35%
Below 53 = F

Skills test

1. Students will stand in 15′ × 15′ area and alternately hit legal forearm passes and sets as many times consecutively as they can; no time limit.
2. Students will serve 10 times legally into the court.

Figure 5.2 *(Continued)*

- use correct strategy in game play.
- describe a fitness program for a given situation.
- keep a log of his or her strength training program.

3. *Attitudes, appreciations, and social skills:* These are affective skills that will be realized, such as

- demonstrate sportspersonship in game play.
- act as a squad or other leader when requested.
- express a joyful feeling about participating in physical education activities.

Preassessment techniques, if appropriate, should be included and specified for each of the objectives—cognitive, psychomotor, and affective. Such screening devices might include questioning, skills tests, written tests, interest inventories, or goal-setting activities.

Once the objectives have been stated, unit grading policies can be formulated. Grading and reporting procedures include what to grade, the emphasis on each area, and the process (specific percentage or points) to be used. See chapter 9 to determine how to grade students in the unit of instruction.

How Will I Get There?

Certain *preliminary considerations* must be determined before a unit plan can be formulated and desired learning outcomes achieved. Such considerations include an appropriate facility, adequate equipment, length of the unit, and qualified faculty. Class size may have an effect on these factors. Weather may determine the facility and the dress requirements.

When preliminary considerations for the unit have been completed, the teacher is ready to make day-by-day decisions. Remember that unit plans are skeleton plans. Such plans simply list a meaningful progression of learning experiences that will be taught in a unit, stating when, what, and how. Organizational strategies and specifics for skill analysis are included later in daily lesson plans.

The teacher might want to include specific activities in the plan to introduce the unit. These might consist of a videotape replay or film, a demonstration by several advanced players, results of recent college or professional competition, highlighting well-known performers, or playing the game the way it was played in years past.

A *daily progression of content* (what and when) must be planned that is appropriate and logical. Such a progression provides for the following:

1. Progression from simple to complex
2. Maximum student participation
3. Successful learning
4. Safety
5. Motivation
6. Pacing of instruction compatible with individual skill levels

Learning activities (how), which translate content into meaningful learning experiences for students, can now be added to the unit plan beside the appropriate daily content. Considerations for selecting learning activities include the following:

1. Student needs and learning characteristics
2. Subject matter to be taught
3. Teacher characteristics
4. Learning environment—facilities, equipment, weather
5. Principles of learning
6. Teaching styles
7. Variety of learning activities

Examples of learning activities include the following:

1. Psychomotor
   a. Demonstration with cues
   b. Skills check-off chart

   c. Drills
   d. Games
   e. Practice with feedback
2. Cognitive
   a. Brief explanation
   b. Visual aid
   c. Question-answer session
   d. Study sheet
   e. Programmed unit
   f. Quiz
3. Affective
   a. Role-play
   b. Brainstorming
   c. Case study
   d. Questionnaire

A variety of teaching and learning activities will keep students involved and meet individual needs. Review chapters 3, 4, 7, and 8 for additional learning activities. Include a short description of each activity in the unit plan in the order of presentation. In addition, prepare a contingency plan for inclement weather (a rainy-day plan) or an emergency situation. This plan should be formulated as part of the unit plan.

Units are often terminated with formal culminating activities such as tournaments, field trips, interclass games, or faculty-student activities. Students are often more motivated when they know from the onset of the unit what these activities will be.

Motivational techniques that will enhance the day-by-day learning experience can be identified at this stage of unit planning. Such techniques might be intrinsic or extrinsic. The following examples list the end result of both types of techniques:

Intrinsic:

1. Success
2. Challenge
3. Self-confidence
4. Self-fulfillment

Extrinsic:

1. Competition
2. Ribbons for winners
3. Unique drills
4. Unusual warm-ups
5. Challenging learning strategy

(See chapters 8 and 12 for specific ideas.)

How Will I Know I've Arrived?

After planning the teaching and learning activities, the teacher is ready to write down the techniques to be used to determine when the performance objectives have been achieved. Plan now for evaluating the unit and the teacher (see chapter 13). The following examples of *evaluation techniques* may be used and might be based on norm-referenced or criterion-referenced standards (see Table 9.1).

1. Skills tests—on skills such as baserunning, batting, throwing, and fielding
2. Teacher observation—of form, use of strategy, officiating, playing ability
3. Checklist or rating sheet—in such activities as swimming or gymnastics
4. Game scores—in individual sports, such as bowling, archery, badminton
5. Time—in activities such as track or fitness testing
6. Written test—on rules and strategy
7. Incidence chart—recording the number of correct spikes, free shots made, or hits landing out of bounds
8. Tournament results
9. Accumulative record—of miles run or swum in a "stay fit" program
10. Attitude or effort inventory, questionnaire, or interview

Once the unit plan has been completed the teacher can finalize preparations for the learning experiences. Teaching stations such as the gym, field, classroom, and community facility must be reserved or scheduled, films ordered, and guest speakers secured. Handouts and examinations may be prepared. With all of this preparation completed, the teacher can feel secure about the unit of instruction that will be presented to students.

Unit plans vary in their specificity or inclusiveness. Some contain much more material and information than would be used in a single unit of instruction. The resources they include give teachers many ideas from which to make choices for their own unit plans. The following are generally included in a unit plan:

1. Title page and introduction
2. Table of contents
3. Specific performance objectives
4. Details to consider before teaching
5. Preassessment techniques
6. Introductory activities
7. Subject matter content
8. Teaching and learning activities
9. Culminating activities
10. Evaluation techniques and grading
11. Resources
12. Index (if needed)

How to Write a Daily Lesson Plan

"Teaching is an act, and teachers are actors."[12] If one accepts this premise, then it follows that teachers need a script. The script teachers use in their daily performance is an instructional plan, and the better the script, the better the performance. As Siedentop stated, "Planning is crucial to effective teaching."[13] Although effective planning does not guarantee a flawless show, the chances for success are much greater when the teacher has adequately prepared to teach a lesson.

A daily lesson plan is written for each specific day of a unit plan. It is an expanded version of a unit plan, providing a detailed analysis of each activity described in the unit plan. Each daily lesson plan fits into a scheme derived from the unit plan and based on unit objectives, but it provides "for the realities of day-to-day teaching."[14] As shown in figure 5.3, teacher considerations and performance objectives, along with their evaluation techniques, are listed. A detailed analysis of the learning experience is the main thrust of the daily lesson plan.

Lesson Plan

Name _____

Date _____

Activity _Softball-batting_

Preassessment _____ In plan (Pepper-Self Scoring)

Objectives	_Evaluation of Objectives_
1. Students will use correct batting form to hit 3 out of 5 balls during pepper drill.	1. Results/Score sheet
2. Students will demonstrate teamwork by scoring 12 points on the Teamwork checklist	2. Teacher observation

Equipment needed: All softballs, gloves, eight tees, eight bases, eight to sixteen bats

Play space needed: Field—two diamonds

Special markings: Bases

Media to be used: None

Sources of Information: Dynamic PE Curriculum and Instruction for Secondary School Students, Pangrazi and Darst

Handout—"Rules for One-Swing Softball"

Time	Teaching and Learning Experiences	Teacher and Student Class Organization	Skill Analysis—Description of Skills and Activities	Teaching Cues
5 minutes	1. _Warm-ups_	Before class—throwing and catching X ——— X X ——— X X ——— X X ——— X		Safety, Motivation, and Individual Differences, etc. Adequate space between groups All throwing north and south Vary distances and balls for various skill levels.

Figure 5.3 An example of a lesson plan.

No time	II. Roll call	Student assistant marks each student as they enter the field.			Facing away from sun or other distractions.

2 to 3 minutes	III. *Batting with cues* Demonstration	Sitting-squad order
		X X X X X X
		X X X X X X T
		X X X X X X
		X X X X X X
			Batting
			A. Grip
			  1. Right hand above and close to left, 2 to 3 inches from end of bat.
			  2. Trademark up—even with "v's."
			B. Stance
			  1. Body and knees easy, feet apart comfortably, left shoulder to pitcher.
			  2. Right foot opposite the back corner of the plate.
			C. Contact
			  1. Elbows away from body, wrist cocked.
			  2. Bat is back as far as left arm can reach easily across chest.
			  3. Step simultaneously with left foot.
				1. Grip firmly at end of bat
				2. Check trademark.
				
				Remember
				B – Body comfortable
				A – Arms away from body
				T – Tilt bat up
				
				1. Keep eye on ball.
				2. Swing level.
				3. Step and swing.
				4. Extend bat across chest.	

Figure 5.3 *(Continued)*

| 10 minutes | IV. *Pepper (drill)* | 8 Groups: rotate after every 5 hits. A. With tee.

[C] X Tee ___ X [P]
X [B]

B. Without tee as students show proficiency.

X [B]———X
X

C. Work-up game on nearby field as they reach objective. Those still practicing drill combine groups. | See above. | Meet the ball. Guide it to a teammate. | Spaced far enough to avoid collisions, but in same direction. Gloves for retrievers. Keep eye on ball.

Success. Individual help. Peer tutor for Mary. Have different balls to choose from. Play game when successful. |
| 15 minutes | V. *Play "One-Swing Softball"* | Teams 1 and 2 play on Diamond 1.
Teams 3 and 4 play on Diamond 2. | Rules on handout (attached). | Use teamwork. | No bat throwing. Do not block baseline. Call for fly balls. No sliding. Choose best pitcher to pitch for you. Have different balls to choose from. Competition, fun, different. |

Culminating Activities (Lesson Conclusion):
Review teaching cues
Report scores
Gather equipment

Figure 5.3 *(Continued)*

This analysis provides a maximum of student activity through efficient use of facilities, equipment, and time so the learner can achieve and retain what is being taught.

A daily lesson plan must be easy to follow and understand because teachers sometimes refer to it during a class. After the completion of a lesson, immediate revision of any unsatisfactory area will make the plan more usable in the future. It can then be filed for future reference.

Where Am I Going?

The daily lesson plan contains a more detailed version of unit performance objectives that once again answer Mager's question of "Where am I going?" The teacher should state what the students will be able to *do* after instruction. It is better to concentrate on only one or two objectives that can be accomplished in a class period. Although all three domains are represented in unit objectives, a daily lesson plan may focus on only one.

The following examples of performance objectives might be included in a daily lesson plan:

1. The student will hit correctly three out of five balls during a pepper drill.
2. The student will use correct rules 100 percent of the time during tournament play.
3. The student will perform one layup with correct form during practice drills, as specified.
4. The student will refrain from arguing with the official during all class game play.

Failing to have a clear lesson focus is one of the obstacles to effective teaching that beginning teachers encounter.[15] They often try to keep students busy, happy, and good, rather than learning.[16] As Ratliffe indicated:

> Unfortunately, many times this results in a series of haphazard activities with no clear purpose and with no allowance for different ability levels. Without a clear objective, the teacher is unable to make the goals of a task clear to students and is unable to provide specific feedback to students. . . . Effective teachers plan lessons which get students involved in activities that all contribute significantly toward achieving a specific lesson objective.[17]

Preassessment techniques can be included in a daily lesson plan so the teacher will know whether students have already achieved the objective or are ready to begin learning what has been planned (see chapter 6). The following examples of preassessment techniques may be used by the teacher:

1. Pretest—a written or skills test is given before instruction.
2. Observation—the students are observed performing the desired behavior.
3. Questioning—students are asked about their experience or whether they can perform a skill.

Preassessment may take an entire class period. The results may then be analyzed and used as the basis of a later daily lesson plan; or, preassessment may be incorporated into a single daily plan. In this case, the teacher can include several choices of activities in the plan to be selected based on the results of the preassessment. For example, if the teacher finds out from a pretest that swimming students will not put their faces in the water, instructional strategies must begin with activities in which students learn to function with water covering their faces. On the other hand, if students are already comfortable with their faces underwater, instruction could begin with breathing drills for the front crawl. Both options would be included in the lesson plan, and the appropriate one would be selected after the results of the pretest were known.

How Will I Get There?

The core of the daily lesson plan methodically progresses through the learning experiences of one class period in the order they will be taught. This part of the plan may be outlined, including enough detail that a substitute teacher could teach the lesson. Each teaching/learning experience in the plan is handled as an *episode*. Anyone reading the plan should be able to read directly across the plan to include all components of each episode. The following components of the plan are illustrated in figure 5.3:

1. *Time allotment:* Write down the *approximate* amount of time to be spent on each teaching or learning activity. Remember to plan time for a maximum amount of activity. Students learn by doing, not by being told. For example:
   a. 8:05–8:07—Roll Call
      8:07–8:15—Warm-ups
   or
   b. Two minutes—Roll Call
      Eight minutes—Warm-ups
      Three minutes—Demonstration

2. *Teaching and learning activities:* Briefly state a description of what will be taught in each episode. Hunter recommends that the following seven steps be included in the model: anticipatory set, objective, key information, model, check of student understanding, guided practice, and independent practice.[18] Some specific examples of teaching and learning activities include:
   a. Warm-ups
   b. Skill or activity being taught (e.g., forehand stroke, 2-1-2 zone defense)
   c. Drill
   d. Game
   e. Mimetic drill (pantomime)
   f. Practice with feedback
   g. Skills test
   h. Written test
   i. Check-off chart

3. *Class organization:* Diagram or explain each separate pattern of organization that will be used during the period. Use *x*'s for students, *T* for teacher. For example:

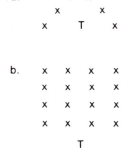

c.

```
x  x  x | x  x  x | x  x  x
x  x  x | x  x  x | x  x  x
_____|_____|_____

x  x  x | x  x  x | x  x  x
x  x  x | x  x  x | x  x  x
```

Tell how the class will be moved from each formation shown into the one following (transitions). For example:

a.
```
x  x  x  x        Squad 1 go to
x  x  x  x            court 1,
x  x  x  x        Squad 2 go to
x  x  x  x            court 2,
1  2  3  4            etc.
```

b.
```
xxxxxxxxxxxxxxxxx    one's stay
1234 1234 1234 1234  two's take 5 steps
| | | | | | | | | | | | | | | | |
| | | | | | | | | | | | | | | | |
| | | | | | | | | | | | | | | | |
| | | | | | | | | | | | | | | | |     three's take 10 steps
x | | x | | x | | | x | | |
| | | | | | | | | |
x | | x | | x | | x | |               four's take 15 steps
| | | | | | | |
x | x | x | x |
| | | |
x     x     x     x
```

4. *Content analysis:* Describe a complete analysis of the skill or activity to be taught. Attach a copy of the content analysis (see chapter 6). Remember to describe these in enough detail that a substitute teacher would feel confident teaching. The components can be written down in outline form to conserve space. For example:
   a. Forehand drive:
      1) Starting position
         Face net
         Racket in front of body
         Racket head up
      2) Backswing:
         Racket back
         Pivot
         Shoulder to net
      3) Contact:
         Eyes on ball
         Transfer weight to forward foot
         Contact ball even with body
         Swing, do not hit
         Keep ball on racket as long as possible
      4) Follow through:
         Face net
         Weight forward
         Racket reaches in direction of ball

5. *Teaching cues:* Write a brief (one to four words) cue for each skill or activity that expresses what the performer should do. Limit the cues to three or four per skill. For example:
   a. Overhead pass—volleyball
      1) Look through the triangle
      2) Get under the ball
      3) Extend
   b. Badminton—overhead clear
      1) Scratch your back
      2) Reach for the birdie
      3) Make it whistle
   c. Swimming—breast stroke
      1) Pull
      2) Kick
      3) Glide

Cues may be visual, verbal, or kinesthetic. For example:
   a. Moving a student's arms in front crawl motion
   b. Placing a hand on the student's string hand to prevent jerking to the side in archery
   c. Visual diagram of how to change lanes when league bowling
   d. Visual cues for footwork drill in badminton

6. *Safety, motivation and individual differences:*
   a. Safety: Write in appropriate safety provisions. For example:
      1) Safe spacing
      2) Rules enforced
      3) Surfaces free from obstacles, such as around walls that might be run into, or balls, pinnies, or other objects on the floor that might be stepped on
      4) Glasses guards
      5) No jewelry, long nails
      6) Shoelaces tied, shoes on
      7) Equipment in good repair and used properly
   b. Motivation techniques: Write down appropriate motivation techniques. For example:
      1) Fun! (How will this be promoted?)
      2) Competition
      3) Grades—sometimes
      4) Written or skills tests—sometimes
      5) Success! (How will this be ensured?)
      6) Recognition and feedback (see Table 5.1)
      7) Extrinsic rewards—treats, ribbons
      8) Desire for activity
      9) Playing the game (not drills, but the real thing)

      It may be helpful for the teacher to think of himself or herself as one of the students and write down items that would make the teacher want to participate in the learning activities if not required to do so.

Table 5.1 Feedback for student performance that merits recognition

The following terms link general to specific feedback. The *general* terms give *recognition.* The *specific feedback* states *why* the performance was recognized.

AMAZING!—The toss was straight up rather than angled.

NO!—Work on a straight-up toss. Hang on to the ball longer.

BETTER!—You made a soft landing with knees bent.

BACK UP!—Stand 3 inches back and more to the side.

EXCELLENT!—You rocked over the forward leg this time.

GOOD!—Just where I wanted your arm to go on the follow-through.

CORRECT!—Feet together made the difference.

FLAWLESS!—You shifted the weight forward at the right time.

GREAT!—Looking back longer helped the weight shift.

HANG ON!—That was too slow. Speed up on the curve.

IMPROVED!—Keep the elbow at shoulder level and the wrist back.

OH, NO!—The elbow was dropped below the shoulder.

MARVELOUS!—You were on your toes all the way.

MUCH BETTER!—The follow-through made the difference.

NOT RIGHT!—The bird is almost pushed over the net. Guide it.

NEAT!—Looking to the right helped a lot.

NO!—Toes were pointed. Keep them back.

PERFECT!—Did you feel the downward extension of the wrist?

INCORRECT!—You must extend the wrist downward.

RIGHT ON!—The added speed of release increased the distance.

SUPER, JUST SUPER!—Palm position moves down and out.

STOP!—Your palm was up. It must be down on the release.

TERRIFIC!—Always release just below the hip.

TOO LONG!—You held on too long.

WAY TO GO!—You took a full step with the trail leg.

WONDERFUL!—Your head was down this time.

WRONG!—Keep your head up to correct the problem.

WOW!—A backswing made the difference.

Source: Nena Rey Hawkes, Brigham Young University.

c. Individual differences: Write in how individual differences will be dealt with. For example:
   1) Handedness—Help left-handers with converting bowling leaves, because the switch is not exactly opposite to that of right-handers.
   2) Disabilities—In a swimming unit, the blind student will be placed next to the outside wall (to get bearings by feel) when swimming across the pool.
   3) Skill level—Students who can already do the underhand volleyball serve will move to court three and practice overhead serves.
   4) Social abilities—Try to promote group acceptance of Robbie.
   5) Mental abilities—Assign partners so that Mary can help Dwayne with drills.

7. *Culminating activities:* Conclude the class in a meaningful way. Assignments for equipment collection and class dismissal might be given at this time. Examples of culminating activities are:
   a. Review basic teaching cues, game rules, strategies.
   b. Ask questions about activities performed.
   c. Collect scores.
   d. Highlight good play or performance.
   e. Make assignments for participation outside class.

How Will I Know I've Arrived?

Evaluation of performance objectives determines whether the teacher has accomplished what he or she set out to do. Techniques for accomplishing this must be incorporated into the plan at the time objectives are written or at the conclusion of fashioning the learning experience. The teacher should write how he or she will know when the behavior specified in the objective has been achieved. If more than one objective has been included, it will be necessary to include more than one evaluation technique. For example:

1. Skills test—The student will hit 8 out of 10 serves into the back of the court as scored by a partner.

2. Teacher observation—The teacher will evaluate each student on layup form using a criteria checklist.

3. Game scores—The game scores will indicate a knowledge of how to pick up leaves in bowling.

4. Written test—A written test will indicate knowledge gained by the student.

5. Check-off chart—A check-off chart will be used to record negative comments to officials.

Once the class period has been planned, several final steps are included in the preparation of a daily lesson plan. First, write in the equipment needed for that day. Be sure to plan for maximum activity for each student. For example, list the following:

1. Balls
2. Bats
3. Cones
4. Scoresheets

Next, write in the facilities or playing area that will be needed. Make a note of any special markings or preparations needed to facilitate instruction. For example:

1. Three volleyball courts, tape line 15 feet from net on north side.
2. Two basketball courts, no markings.
3. Four badminton courts, tape lines at six-inch intervals from short service line back.

Finally, write in any media to be used. For example:

1. Videotape, VCR, monitor
2. Magnetic chalkboard, chalk, magnets

Scheduling equipment, facilities, and media immediately after the unit plan is completed ensures their availability for the lesson. When the daily lesson plan is formulated, remember to double-check the availability of these items and to secure them for class.

The daily lesson plan is now complete. One final item will aid the teacher in the future. Write down *sources of information,* listing where the material for this lesson was acquired. For example:

1. Book—Allsen and Harrison, pp. 36–37
2. Handout—"Defensive Strategy: Marking" (in-service training, Sept. 1986)
3. Colleague or teacher—Ms. Jones
4. Resource file—pictures from magazine

If no sources were used or needed, write "previous experience."

With the daily lesson plan completed, the teacher should feel secure and ready to face a class of eager students.

Becoming a Reflective Teacher

Irwin defined a reflective teacher as one who

> makes teaching decisions on the basis of a conscious awareness and careful consideration of (1) the assumptions on which the decisions are based and (2) the technical, educational, and ethical consequences of those decisions. These decisions are made before, during and after teaching actions. In order to make these decisions, the reflective/analytic teacher must have an extensive knowledge of the content to be taught, pedagogical and theoretical options, characteristics of individual students, and the situational constraints in the classroom, school and society in which they work.[19]

Reflective teachers are decision makers. They make conscious and rational decisions based on technical and content knowledge, organized and interpreted according to their unique experiences.[20] These decisions occur during planning, in the classroom, and following the teaching experience. They also occur in interactions both within the school and in other professional settings. These reflections, and the decisions based on them, serve as guides to future action. Reflective teaching helps teachers improve their own teaching and become better and more thoughtful professionals. Figure 5.4 provides ten questions to consider after teaching each lesson.

Reflection may occur in talking with others or writing about teaching experiences. As teachers weigh alternatives and make selections based on criteria, they justify their actions in the classroom to themselves and others. It is the intent of the authors that teachers will discuss the ideas presented in these chapters with others and expand or modify ideas to fit their own situations. Research shows that students benefit academically when teachers share ideas, cooperate in

1. Did the *activity* you planned actually occur? If not, why not?
2. Were your *objectives* realistic? Did other ones emerge during the lesson?
3. Did the *learners' actual knowledge and skills* correspond to your expectations? Did any discrepancies cause you to modify the lesson?
4. Did you cover what you planned? Did you plan too much or too little *content* to cover?
5. Did the *procedures* work? If not, what went wrong?
6. Did the *results* you anticipated occur? If not, what went wrong?
7. Did you provide sufficient *resources*? What else was needed?
8. Did you get adequate *feedback* on the lesson? What did you learn from the feedback? Did the learners get sufficient feedback?
9. Was the *time* adequate? Was the time used efficiently?
10. Were the *follow-up* activities done? Were they effective?

Figure 5.4 A lesson postmortem: Questions for
reflecting on your teaching.
From FIELD EXPERIENCE: METHODS OF
REFLECTIVE TEACHING, 2nd Ed., by George J.
Posner. Copyright © 1989 by Longman Publishers.
Reprinted by permission.

activities, and assist one another's intellectual growth.[21] Research also points out that teachers welcome professional suggestions about improving their work, but they rarely receive them.[22]

Feedback loops in figure 5.1 indicate revisions that might need to be made in the various steps of the model following the reflective process.

Teachers who follow the model for designing and implementing instructional programs soon realize that "teaching is, after all, as much science as it is magic."[23] Skill in making wise decisions based on the model increases with experience and is validated by one's creativity or "spark of magic."

Review Questions

1. Briefly discuss the importance of each of the steps involved in designing, implementing, and evaluating the instructional program.
2. What is the difference between a unit plan and a lesson plan?
3. Write a unit plan for a selected activity. Include a contingency plan (rainy-day plan).
4. Prepare three daily lesson plans to be used in a formal unit plan in which skills are reviewed and taught.
5. Practice reflective teaching by writing about what you are doing in a teaching assignment and why; then follow up the assignment by reflecting on what you did, what succeeded or failed, and why.

References

1. Mager, R. F. (1969). *Developing attitude toward learning* (p. vii). Palo Alto, CA: Fearon.
2. Mosston, M., & Ashworth, S. (1994). *Teaching physical education* (4th ed.). New York: Macmillan College.
3. Hunter, M. (1982). *Mastery teaching* (p. 3). El Segundo, CA: TIP.
4. Clark, C. M., & Peterson, P. L. (1986). Teachers' thought processes. In M. C. Wittrock (Ed.), *Handbook of research on teaching* (3rd ed., pp. 260–268). New York: Macmillan.

5. Davis, R. H., Alexander, L. T., & Yelon, S. L. (1974). *Learning system design: An approach to the improvement of instruction* (p. 304). New York: McGraw-Hill.
6. Ibid., 305.
7. Ibid., 309.
8. Graham, G., Holt/Hale, S. A., & Parker, M. (1987). *Children moving: A teacher's guide to developing a successful physical education program* (2nd ed.). Palo Alto, CA: Mayfield.
9. Davis, Alexander, & Yelon, *Learning system design,* 313.
10. Anderson, W. G. (1980). *Analysis of teaching physical education* (p. 2). St. Louis: Mosby.
11. Mager, *Developing attitude toward learning.*
12. Lawson, H. A. (1983). Paradigms for research on teaching and teachers. In T. J. Templin & J. K. Olson (Eds.), *Teaching in physical education* (p. 345). Champaign, IL: Human Kinetics.
13. Siedentop, D., Mand, C., & Taggart, A. (1986). *Physical education: Teaching and curriculum strategies for grades 5–12* (p. 322). Palo Alto, CA: Mayfield.
14. Hoover, K. H. (1982). *The professional teacher's handbook* (3rd ed., pp. 23, 26). Boston: Allyn & Bacon.
15. Ratliffe, T. (1987, April). Overcoming obstacles beginning teachers encounter. *Journal of Physical Education, Recreation and Dance, 58*(4), 18–23.
16. Placek, J. H. (1983). Conceptions of success in teaching: Busy, happy and good? In T. J. Templin & J. K. Olson (Eds.), *Teaching in physical education* (pp. 46–56). Champaign, IL: Human Kinetics.
17. Ratliffe, Overcoming obstacles beginning teachers encounter, 20.
18. Batesky, J. (1987, September). In-service education: Increasing teacher effectiveness using the Hunter lesson design. *Journal of Physical Education, Recreation and Dance, 58*(7), 89–93.
19. Irwin, J. (1987). *What is a reflective/analytical teacher?* Unpublished manuscript, University of Connecticut, School of Education. In J. W. Brubacher, C. W. Case, & T. G. Reagan. (1994). *Becoming a reflective educator* (p. 24). Thousand Oaks, CA: Corwin Press.
20. Brubacher et al., *Becoming a reflective educator,* 16–25.
21. U.S. Department of Education. (1986). *What works: Research about teaching and learning* (p. 51). Washington, DC: Author.
22. Ibid., 52.
23. Pellicer, L. O. (1984, October). Effective teaching: Science or magic? *Clearing House, 58,* 56.

CHAPTER 6

Performance Objectives, Content Analysis, and Preassessment

Study Stimulators

1. Define and give an example of a goal, an objective, and a performance objective for each of the instructional domains. Why are both goals and objectives important?
2. What three elements must be included in a performance objective? How do these differ when evaluating affective objectives?
3. What is the difference between an explicit and an implicit performance objective? Which is more commonly used in education today?
4. What is the difference between open and closed objectives? When would it be appropriate to use each of these?
5. List at least 10 acceptable verbs and 10 unacceptable verbs that could be used when writing performance objectives.
6. Define and give examples of extension, refinement, and application for a sports skill. How does content analysis apply to game skills? Choose a concept or principle and analyze it.
7. What is preassessment? Why is it important in the instructional setting?

Education has been defined as "a process that changes learners." This being the case, someone must decide what changes are "possible" and "desirable."[1] This charge most often falls to the teacher, who may be contributing ideas to a curriculum guide or determining course direction for his or her class. Determining what is possible in education is not the prime consideration, because if teachers are convinced of the need and are provided with the necessary training and experience, they can effectively teach most of the important objectives. The more difficult problem is determining objectives that are desirable.[2] The process for doing this is the same for a district curriculum guide, a school handbook, or an individual unit or lesson plan. General aims or purposes are shaped into goals, and goals are further refined into specific objectives that determine educational outcomes.

Defining Educational Outcomes

An *aim* or *purpose* is a broad statement of an ideal that is directed toward the total program. The following is an example of an educational aim:

Physical education will contribute to the total education and development of each child as a complete program of physical activity is integrated into the school day.

An *instructional goal* is more specific than an aim. It is a broad, general outcome of instruction expressing the common learning expected of all students. However, it does not tell what the learner is to do at the end of instruction.[3] Goals are used as a basis for curriculum planning and for summarizing the purposes of a school or a specific program to the public. The following examples are instructional goals:

1. Students will be physically fit; have a desire to maintain physical fitness; and possess an understanding of how to assess, develop, and maintain physical fitness.
2. Students will develop skills sufficient to participate in several recreational activities of their own choosing, understand how to learn new skills, and have an appreciation for the value of participating in physical activity.

An *objective,* sometimes called a program objective, is a relatively specific outcome of instruction that can be achieved within a short time. Objectives answer the question, "What is worth teaching?"[4] Objectives are derived logically from goals and serve as "stepping stones to the achievement of a broader goal."[5] The following are examples of objectives:

1. The student will demonstrate cardiovascular fitness.
2. The student will execute sufficient skill proficiency and knowledge of the game of tennis to participate in a competitive match if desired.

Objectives may be of two types: instructional or performance.[6] An *instructional* (process) objective tells what the teacher or coach will do during the lesson. The following is an example of an instructional objective:

The teacher will demonstrate the overhead smash.

A *performance* objective is a statement of an outcome that is attainable and is stated with enough specificity to identify what the learner is to do or produce, or what characteristics he or she should possess at the end of instruction.[7] The teacher and student can then determine whether a student has achieved the objective. Performance objectives are used more often than instructional objectives because they personalize learning for individual students. The following are examples of performance objectives:

1. The student will achieve the "good" or "excellent" category on the 1.5-mile run given several opportunities to do so.
2. The student will execute correctly three out of five tennis serves into the service court (given a racket, balls, and an official tennis court).

These examples emphasize that students' actions should be directly observable. Performance objectives have three characteristics:

1. A statement of behavior (what the learner will be able to do at the conclusion of instruction)
2. The conditions under which the learner will perform the task
3. The criteria for successful performance

The following example illustrates these characteristics:

The student will execute correctly three out of five tennis serves into the service court.

1. Behavior—*serve*
2. Conditions—*into the service court*
3. Criteria—*three out of five correct serves*

As shown in Table 6.1, statements of educational outcomes usually progress from an aim or purpose produced at the federal, state, or district level down a hierarchy to the grassroots level at which the teacher is responsible for integrating performance objectives into the instructional process. The definition of a physically educated person and the outcomes statements listed in chapter 1 are examples of national purposes and goals for physical education that might well be adopted as instructional goals for a district or school curriculum. Because of their specific nature, performance objectives may be incorporated at any level of the hierarchy.

Advantages of Performance Objectives

Performance objectives serve as a base for the entire process of instructional design. Without objectives, preassessment would be unnecessary, learning activities would be like a map without a destination, and effective evaluation techniques could not be prepared. Expressing objectives in terms of performance provides the criteria for selecting and organizing the content and learning activities for the program of instruction into a manageable, meaningful sequence. Nonessential items can be removed from lessons, thus providing more time to achieve the most important objectives. When a teacher has written performance objectives for a lesson or unit of instruction, clear purposes for both the teacher and students emerge.

Objectives also increase teacher accountability by focusing on specific behaviors that can be evaluated. Objectives convey to the parent, administrator, student, or teacher exactly what is to be accomplished. Parents and administrators are assisted in their understanding of school programs and their ability to gauge student progress. Clearly stated objectives help students evaluate their own progress toward instructional goals and therefore serve as a motivating factor toward success. Pupils are more secure because they know what is expected and can spend more time on important items. They can readily focus on their strengths and weaknesses. Students who know they need to shoot 200 points in five ends on a 48-inch target at a given distance in archery can evaluate their own progress in class better than students who are told only to shoot a round each day. Students missing a class know exactly what skills and knowledge were missed and can take steps to make up the work.[8] Teachers incorporating performance objectives are more secure because they know that what they are teaching has been carefully planned and that evaluation is appropriate and specified. With clearly defined objectives and content, teachers can

Table 6.1 Statements of Educational Outcomes and Their Uses

Statement	Use
Aim or purpose	Federal, state, district General policy statement
Instructional goal	District or school Curriculum guide
Objective	Department Program guide
Performance/instructional objective	Teacher Unit or daily lesson plan

preassess student behavior in relation to the objectives, evaluate progress toward the objectives, and determine the extent to which students have achieved the objectives.

Defining Performance Objectives

Performance objectives were formal and complex through the 1970s when *explicit* (behavioral) objectives were used. In the 1980s teachers began writing much more simplified *implicit* (experience) performance objectives. The following are examples:

1. *Explicit*—The student will correctly perform the overhead volley 10 consecutive times against the wall above the eight-foot mark.
2. *Implicit*—The student will correctly perform the overhead serve, pass, and bump in a game situation.

Educators today do not agree on the necessity of writing precise objectives.[9] Critics imply that objectives may be fallible, too many details hamper learning, and precision is emphasized at the expense of reaching new or untried applications.[10] Rink suggested that implicit objectives are more common in education today. She stated:

> Educational objectives should be specified to the degree that they provide direction for the design and evaluation of educational experiences without narrowing those experiences to what is most easily measured. Objectives still include the components of behavior, conditions, and criteria, but . . . the learning outcomes are more implicit than explicit.[11]

On the other hand, physical educators today are calling for more program accountability. Griffey stated, "We have failed to provide an experience that our students perceive as meaningful. The sense of mastering something important is denied most students in secondary physical education programs."[12] Precise objectives lead programs toward meaningful experiences and accountability. Annarino favored more precise performance objectives over "traditional" or nonexplicit objectives.[13] This text takes a formal approach to writing performance objectives that includes both explicit and implicit objectives.

Writing Performance Objectives

Performance objectives are generally divided into three types—cognitive (learning and application of knowledge), psychomotor (learning physical skills), and affective (concerned with interests, attitudes, appreciations, and values).

Performance objectives must describe the behavior of the learner. The key to writing objectives is the selection of the verb. Bloom[14] recommended using verbs that are directly observable. The following are examples of observable and nonobservable verbs:

Observable (Appropriate)
Match (duplicate, equal, agree, fit)
Translate (decipher, interpret, explain, simplify)
Compute (calculate)
Name (identify, label, designate)
Diagram (draw, illustrate, picture, design, chart)
Classify (rank, rate, arrange, categorize)
Apply (pertain to, relate to, employ)
Construct (assemble, make, produce, build)
Identify (distinguish, recognize, associate, know)

Clearly stated performance objectives help
students evaluate their progress toward
instructional goals.
© Tracy Pellett

Explain (define, decipher, illustrate)
Demonstrate (evidence, prove, be-able-to, perform)
Pass (or shoot, dribble, serve, catch, hit)
Improve (enhance, enrich, better)
List (catalog, index, enumerate, specify)

Nonobservable (Not Appropriate)
Comprehend
Understand
Learn
Respect
Think
Grasp
Take an interest in
Have knowledge of

The taxonomies for each domain are reviewed in Table 6.2 along with appropriate verbs for each level of behavior.

Since the general principles of writing objectives apply to both cognitive and psychomotor objectives, these two types will be considered simultaneously. Affective objectives will be considered later in the chapter.

Steps for Writing Cognitive and Psychomotor Performance Objectives

As stated earlier, writing performance objectives involves a statement of behavior, conditions of performance, and criteria for successful performance. Some performance objectives are *closed* in that they demand a single correct response of all learners.[15] For example, an objective that asks the student to name the thigh bone has only one answer—the femur. Some objectives are *open*. Each learner could have a different response and yet meet the behavior specified in the objective. An example of an open objective might be to perform three new skills on a chosen piece of gymnastics equipment.

Writing performance objectives requires practice. The following steps are designed to develop competence in properly stating performance objectives. Each step will add another piece to the soon to be completed objective.

Step 1. Define the area of instruction.
Step 2. Define what the student will be able to do (behavior) at the conclusion of instruction.
Step 3. Describe the conditions under which the student's performance will be evaluated.
Step 4. Specify the criteria for acceptable performance.
Step 5. Evaluate the objective.

Step 1—*Define the area of instruction.*
Choose a lesson or unit of instruction that is relevant to the student population in terms of real-world utility or preparation for future educational needs. Specify the target population in terms of age, sex, and previous experience in the unit. Some examples are:

1. Archery—seventh-grade boys and girls, no previous experience
2. Volleyball—ninth-grade boys and girls, two years experience
3. Physical fitness—high school, coed, varied experience

Step 2—*Define what the student will be able to do at the conclusion of instruction.*
In clear and concise terms, state what the student will be able to *do* at the conclusion of instruction. Include only those behaviors or products of behavior that can be observed through one or more of the five senses. Some examples of behaviors are:

1. Archery
    a. The student will define archery terms.

Table 6.2 Appropriate Verbs for Performance Objectives Within Each of The Domain Taxonomies

Cognitive Domain

Levels of Behavior	*Verbs for Objectives*
1. Knowledge	Define Match Spell Recite Who, what, where, when, why
2. Comprehension	Translate Paraphrase Tell in your own words Summarize Compare or contrast Predict
3. Application	Solve Apply
4. Analysis	Analyze Examine Break down Delineate Determine Identify
5. Synthesis	Compose Write Design Invent Hypothesize Plan Create Produce Organize
6. Evaluation	Judge Evaluate Defend

Table 6.2—Continued

Affective Domain

Levels of Behavior	Verbs for Objectives
1. Receiving	Notice Select Tolerate Be aware or conscious of Listen
2. Responding	Comply Follow Volunteer Enjoy Be satisfied Agree or disagree React Give opinion Sympathize with Demonstrate appreciation for Attend Read Accept responsibility
3. Valuing	Prefer consistently Support consistently Pursue activities Involve others Debate Argue Value Purchase Improve skills
4. Organization	Discuss codes, standards Formulate systems Weigh alternatives against standards Define criteria Base decisions on values
5. Characterization	Demonstrate consistent behavior or methods Integrate total behavior or values

Table 6.2—Continued

Psychomotor Domain

Levels of Behavior	Verbs for Objectives
1. Generic movement	
Perceiving	Identify Recognize Discover Discriminate Imitate Replicate Duplicate Pantomime
Patterning	Perform (shoot) Demonstrate (pass) Execute (swim) Coordinate (jump)
2. Ordinative movement	
Adapting or Accommodating	Adjust, alter Apply Employ Utilize
Refining	Control Synchronize Improve Synthesize Regulate Perform rhythmically (smoothly, efficiently) Integrate Coordinate
3. Creative movement	
Varying	Alter Change Revise Diversify
Improvising	Interpret Extemporize Improvise Anticipate Discover
Composing	Design Compose Symbolize Create Plan

b. The student will pass a test on the rules, etiquette, and basic skill techniques of archery.

c. The student will shoot with correct form.

2. Volleyball
   a. The student will serve a volleyball.
   b. The student will set a volleyball.
   c. The student will write a paper on the history of volleyball.

3. Physical fitness
   a. The student will create an aerobic dance routine.
   b. The student will improve his or her 1.5-mile run score.
   c. The student will engage in a strength and flexibility program.

Step 3—*Describe the conditions under which the student's performance will be evaluated.*

Include where, when, and with what equipment or materials and what set of rules the student's performance will be evaluated. In informal units (i.e., those not programmed or written out for student use), some conditions may be implied and not stated. Implicit objectives often have implied conditions. Some examples of conditions follow:

1. Archery
   a. Given a list of definitions of archery terms, the student will write the correct terms.
   b. The student will pass a test on the rules, etiquette, and skills of archery. (Implied conditions are that the student will have a copy of the test, a pencil, an answer sheet, and that the test will be closed-book.)
   c. The student will shoot using correct form as rated on the rating sheet by the instructor. (Implied conditions are the use of a bow, arrows, and target.)

2. Volleyball
   a. Using an overhand serve, the student will serve into the back half of the court. (A regulation ball and court are implied.)
   b. Using a legal volley, the student will volley a volleyball continuously against the wall so that it touches above the head. (A regulation ball is implied.)
   c. The student will write a one- to three-page paper on the history of volleyball. (Handwriting is implied, since typing has not been specified.)

3. Physical fitness
   a. Given class time daily, the student will join with two or three other students to create an aerobic dance routine to any music provided by the student or teacher.
   b. Given practice time for jogging, the student will improve his or her 1.5-mile run score. (A track or running area is implied.)
   c. The student will engage in a strength and flexibility program during class.

Step 4—*Specify the criteria of acceptable performance.*

State the criteria in such a way that a qualified person could use it to successfully choose students meeting the standard. Describe the performance or the result of performance in terms of the number of trials, the number of successful completions, the number of repetitions within a given time allotment, improvement on a given scale, percent or percentile achieved, raw score, or other observable standard. Describe a subjective performance in terms of the degree or quality of performance required. Criteria for implicit objectives are less specific. The following objectives are now complete performance objectives with behavior, conditions, and criteria:

1. Archery
   a. Given a list of definitions of 25 archery terms, the student will write in the correct term with fewer than four errors.
   b. The student will pass a multiple-choice test on the rules, etiquette, and skills of archery with a score of 80 percent or better.
   c. The student will shoot using effective form as rated by the instructor on a rating scale, with a minimum of two errors.
2. Volleyball
   a. Using the correct technique for an overhand serve, the student will serve 8 out of 10 serves into the back half of the court.
   b. Using the correct technique, the student will volley 15 consecutive times against the wall so that it touches above a line marked seven feet from the floor.
   c. The student will write a one- to three-page paper on the history of volleyball that includes the origin, early rules and changes in the game, recent changes in the style of the game, and indications of current interest in volleyball.
3. Physical fitness
   a. Given 20 minutes of class time the student will create, with two or three other students, a two-minute aerobic dance routine to music that includes activities that raise the heart rate to the target heart rate (refer to formula given in class).
   b. The student will improve his or her 1.5-mile run score by at least one level or will maintain his or her endurance at the "good" or "excellent" level.
   c. Given 20 minutes three times per week, the student will demonstrate participation in a strength and flexibility program three times a week for six weeks by turning in a log of activities on the form provided by the instructor.

Step 5—*Evaluate the objectives.*

Evaluate the objectives by asking the following questions: (1) Is the expected behavior attainable as a result of learning in the unit of instruction? (2) Is the objective relevant or is it included merely because it is easy to state in terms of performance? (3) Are good objectives omitted because they are difficult to state in performance terms? (4) Can another competent person understand the objective well enough to use it to evaluate learners in the unit of instruction? (5) Are facilities and materials available for the attainment of the objective? (6) Is the objective motivating to the student? (7) Are both short-range and long-range objectives included for the unit of instruction?

If some students are functioning within all levels of a domain, write objectives to include all of these levels. An example of objectives for each level of the cognitive and psychomotor domains is shown in Tables 6.3 and 6.4.

Self-Check on Performance Objectives

Directions: Classify the following statements as (A) properly stated performance objectives, or (B) improperly stated performance objectives or not a performance objective. If the objective is classified as (B), identify the part of the objective that is incorrect or missing.

1. The student will bat.
2. The student will list five historically prominent persons in physical education.
3. The student will learn the rules of badminton.
4. The student should learn the reasons for using correct safety procedures in archery.

Table 6.3 A Sample of Objectives for Each Level of the Cognitive Domain

Knowledge

1. Match bowling terms and definitions on a written test at the 80 percent level.

2. Given a diagram of the human body, list the names of the bones and muscles shown.

3. List the six basic rules of archery.

Comprehension

1. Given 10 game situations in a specified sport, select the correct referee's decision from a criteria sheet.

2. Describe in writing (define) the meaning of "intensity" in a physical fitness program.

3. Diagram a two-one-two zone defense in basketball.

Application

1. List the criteria you would use to purchase a quality tennis racket for yourself based on the characteristics explained in class.

2. List the situations in which you would use a zone defense and those when you would use a player-to-player defense in basketball.

3. Write a physical fitness program for an individual who was rated "poor" after completing the AAHPERD tests. Include specific recommendations for intensity, duration, and frequency.

Analysis

1. Analyze 10 exercises in *The Readers Digest* article handed out in class. List the muscles used for each exercise and determine if the exercise develops strength or flexibility.

2. Using the criteria sheet handed out in class, analyze the offensive player of your choice by watching a videotape of the NBA Championship game. List the strengths and weaknesses of this player during five consecutive plays executed by his team.

Synthesis

1. Create five new plays for flag football.

2. Choreograph a new dance lasting five minutes for three to six participants using music of your choice.

3. Create a gymnastics routine on the balance beam that includes at least five new stunts.

Evaluation

1. Using the criteria sheet, evaluate three fad diets from the following list to determine whether they meet minimum nutritional standards.

2. Judge a list of specific behaviors exhibited by the spectators at the league championship volleyball match to determine sportspersonlike behavior based on the following criteria (recognized values of society).

Table 6.4 A Sample of Objectives for Each Level of the Psychomotor Domain

Perceiving

1. Identify the tumbling skills performed by the teacher.

2. Discover how the lay-up shot is performed by asking questions after a demonstration of the skill.

Patterning

1. Perform a gallop.

2. Demonstrate a backward volleyball set into the basketball hoop.

3. Execute a headstand in good form (as determined by the criteria sheet) for 10 seconds.

Adapting

1. Dribble a basketball in control from one side of the court to the other while being guarded.

2. Shoot five arrows at 10 yards, 20 yards, and 30 yards on the archery field.

3. Bat a pitched ball to right, left, and center field.

Refining

1. Perform a bowling approach and release until it is smooth, meeting the criteria listed on the checklist.

2. Improve a softball accuracy score at a target on the wall, until a score of 50 points in 10 throws is achieved.

3. Perform a series of forward rolls in a straight line until three in good form can be executed from standing to standing.

Varying

1. Alter the forward roll until a straddle, pike, or other variation can be performed.

2. Modify the bowling stance to increase the speed of the ball three seconds from release until the pins are contacted.

3. Hit three pitched balls past the infield from the right batter's box and three from the left.

Improvising

1. Change offensive pattern #5a to involve the center more often and exploit the lack of height by the defense.

2. Add two new steps to the "That's Cool" aerobic routine.

Composing

1. Create a floor exercise routine using at least five stunts already learned.

2. Design five new flag football play patterns.

5. The Red Cross standards will be the model for student performance in swimming the five basic strokes.
6. The student will compute the percentage of body fat.
7. Given the specific data needed on a written test, the student will be able to solve six out of seven problems on body composition.
8. The student will understand physical fitness.
9. Given a pencil and paper, the student will pass a true–false quiz on the rules of bowling.
10. The student will appreciate the value of physical activity.
11. The student will shoot free throws from the foul line.
12. The student will understand basketball strategy.
13. The student will learn the overhead clear in badminton.
14. The student will demonstrate progress in weight training by keeping a progress log as specified in the handout.
15. The student will demonstrate the serve in racquetball.

Answers to Self-Check

1. B, no stated conditions or criteria.
2. A
3. B, not stated in terms of observable performance.
4. B, not stated in terms of observable performance.
5. B, not stated in terms of observable performance.
6. B, no stated conditions or criteria.
7. A
8. B, not stated in terms of observable performance.
9. B, no stated criteria.
10. B, not stated in terms of observable performance.
11. B, no stated criteria.
12. B, not stated in terms of observable performance.
13. B, not stated in terms of observable performance.
14. A
15. B, no stated conditions or criteria.

If you had difficulty with the self-check, review the preceding pages in this chapter before proceeding. Practice writing objectives until you feel that you have mastered the art of writing objectives. Have two of your classmates analyze your objectives in terms of the three criteria for writing objectives and the questions in Step 5.

Steps for Writing Affective Objectives

Performance objectives in the affective domain differ from cognitive and psychomotor objectives in that attitudes, appreciations, and values cannot be measured directly but must be inferred by the behaviors of students toward or away from the desired behavior. These behaviors are called *approach* or *avoidance* behaviors. Lee and Merrill delineated a method for writing affective objectives.[16] Their ideas have been incorporated into the following steps for writing affective objectives:

Step 1. Describe the attitude the student should acquire.
Step 2. List specific student approach or avoidance behaviors.
Step 3. Describe the conditions under which the approach or avoidance behaviors will occur.
Step 4. Specify the criteria under which the approach or avoidance behaviors will occur.
Step 5. Evaluate the objectives.

Step 1—*Describe the attitude the student should acquire.*
Write a descriptive statement describing the attitude, including interests, desires, or appreciations.

1. Physical fitness—The student will have a desire to maintain physical fitness.
2. Dance—The student will enjoy participating in dance activities.
3. Sportspersonship—The student will demonstrate good sportspersonship.

Step 2—*List specific student approach or avoidance behaviors.*
Approach behaviors. List the behaviors that students will most likely be expected to say or do that bring them into closer contact with the subject. These behaviors are called approach behaviors. Some examples of approach behaviors are:

1. Physical fitness
   a. Reads fitness books, articles
   b. Exercises daily
   c. Tells people how exercise can improve their lives
   d. Is always checking own heart rate during activity
   e. Tries to get others to engage in fitness activities
   f. Attends lectures about fitness
2. Dance
   a. Reads the fine arts section of the newspaper
   b. Subscribes to a dance magazine
   c. Participates in dance instruction or activity outside of class
   d. Knows the names and performance characteristics of professional dance performers
   e. Watches dance events on television
   f. Attends local dance events
3. Sportspersonship
   a. Volunteers to officiate intramural basketball games
   b. Reads an article or attends a lecture on sportspersonship
   c. Calls own fouls during a competitive game
   d. Controls own temper and behavior during any sports competition
   e. Shakes the hand of all opposing players after the game or match

In most school-related activities, approach behaviors are adequate for evaluating affective objectives and can be used exclusively if desired.
Avoidance behaviors. List the behaviors that students will most likely exhibit that will detract from or lead them away from the desired attitude. These behaviors are called avoidance behaviors. Some examples of avoidance behaviors include:

1. Physical fitness
   a. Tries to convince physical education teacher that he or she is not supposed to run but plays basketball later in the period
   b. Does not dress for activity on days that fitness activities are conducted

    c. Asks to substitute marching band for fitness unit
    d. Refuses to turn in a record of eating kept for one week
2. Dance
    a. Says "This is a dumb/sissy activity"
    b. Tells the teacher this is the only time the counselor is available and asks to be excused during dance class
    c. Is often tardy to class or fails to attend class
    d. Fails to study for quiz or turn in paper
3. Sportspersonship
    a. Gets involved in a fight during a game
    b. Refuses to come out of a game to allow other team members to play
    c. Blames others for unsportspersonlike behavior
    d. Constantly argues with the referees

Eliminate activities that cannot be observed either directly or indirectly. Direct observation includes student activities that are actually seen. Eliminate activities that are not commonly expected to occur among students or are inappropriate.

Step 3—*Describe the conditions under which the approach or avoidance behaviors will occur.*

A testing situation for affective objectives must include a set of alternatives presented to the student that allow the student to make a free choice, unhindered by what the teacher wants the student to do. Stating the conditions or circumstances under which the behavior will take place is the hardest part of writing an affective objective. Only when the conditions are known can the behavior be interpreted as a true approach or avoidance behavior. Students should be asked to choose between two behaviors, one of which is the behavior in question.

1. Physical fitness—Each student may run a mile and a half, swim three minutes, or play basketball.
2. Dance—Each student may choose to join the square dance group or play badminton.
3. Sportspersonship—Each student may shake hands with the opposing team or gather up the equipment.

Another possible set of alternatives would be to ask the student to choose between an approach or an avoidance activity, for example, "Each student can choose to play basketball or fail the course." In this situation, no one would feel free to sit out. Free choice is an essential component of the testing situation. Teachers must do as little as possible to influence the alternative chosen by a student in the testing situation. Some other examples of teacher influence might include extra credit, praise, or special privileges. Although these might be appropriate in a learning situation, they are inappropriate in a testing situation because they cause the student to approach the subject because of the teacher rather than because of a favorable attitude toward the subject.

When using questionnaires or other direct observation techniques, allow students to express their true feelings, perhaps through anonymity or by assessing feelings after the course grades have been submitted.

Step 4—*Specify the criteria under which the approach and avoidance behaviors will occur.*

The criterion statement indicates how well, how often, or how much of the approach or avoidance behavior must occur for the objective to be achieved. Two types of criterion statements can be used to indicate a complete objective:

A. This kind of criterion statement indicates the number of activities in which each student will participate.
  1. Physical fitness—Each student will engage in a fitness activity at least three times a week for one semester.
B. This kind of criterion statement indicates the number of students who will demonstrate the specified behavior.
  1. Dance—Eighty percent of the students will participate regularly (not more than three absences) in the dance class for a six-week unit.
  2. Sportspersonship—All of the students will shake the hands of the opposing team after a game whether they win or lose.

One advantage to using the number of activities as a criterion is that it allows students with several interests or extenuating circumstances to demonstrate approach behaviors that might not occur in a single instance. For example, a student who exhibited a large number of approach behaviors had her tonsils out and could not participate in intramural basketball, although basketball was her favorite activity.

In either kind of criterion statement, the number indicates how much of the behavior will occur for the objective to be achieved. This number should be based on some realistic goal in terms of what is already known about students, perhaps through a preassessment of student behaviors. Do not expect miracles to occur by stating numbers that are impossible for students to achieve. In addition, avoid using numbers of students so large that it is impossible to tabulate the responses or activities. Teachers can get a general idea of achievement of the objectives by selecting only one class to evaluate each semester. Words such as *several, most,* or *often* should also be avoided because they are too vague to demonstrate goal achievement.

Because behavior in the affective domain is evaluated on the basis of inferred behavior, teachers may not need to tell students what the performance objective says. A knowledge of the general objectives in the affective domain is usually sufficient for students.

An example of objectives for each level of the affective domain is shown in Table 6.5.

Step 5—*Evaluate the objectives.*

After writing several objectives, check them by referring to the following checklist, which incorporates each of the steps described by Lee and Merrill:[17]

1. Attitude
   a. Is there a descriptive statement of interest, desire, or appreciation?
2. Behavior
   a. Is a student approach or avoidance behavior specified?
   b. Can the behavior be directly or indirectly observed?
   c. Is the behavior a high-probability behavior (likely to occur often)?

3. Conditions
   a. Is a situation described in which the approach or avoidance behavior may occur and can be observed?
   b. Are at least two alternatives presented to students?
   c. Is the situation a free-choice situation in which the teacher does not directly influence the student's choice?
   d. Are cues eliminated that might indicate the expected behavior?
   e. Do students feel free to express their true feelings if direct observation is used?

Table 6.5   A Sample of Objectives for Each Level of the Affective Domain

Receiving

1 Listens attentively to an analysis of the volleyball spike.

2. When asked (following a demonstration), identifies the position of the feet in a tennis serve.

3. Selects a position to play in soccer, given a choice of three positions. . . .

Responding

1. Voluntarily assists in setting up apparatus equipment before a gymnastics class.

2. Responds to a request to work on a subject-related project, such as designing and organizing a football bulletin board.

3. Remains after a class in wrestling takedowns for additional instruction or practice. . . .

Valuing

1. Attends an optional class session to practice high jumping for the Spring meet.

2. Risks being late for the next class by continuing a discussion concerning a certain defensive strategy in basketball.

3. Volunteers to organize an intramural swimming meet during his or her free time. . . .

Organization

1. Volunteers to play for the opposing softball team so that there are an even number of players on each team.

2. Following instructional units in judo and karate, organizes and supervises a self-defense club for girls.

3. Proposes alternative safety and spotting techniques to be used when gymnastics equipment is available during a free-time activity period. . . .

Characterization by a Value or Value Complex

1. Requests additional information on ways to improve physical skills following each instructional unit.

2. Volunteers free time on Saturday mornings to coach an elementary school basketball team.

3. Participates in all intramural events either as a player, team representative, council representative, official, scorekeeper, or equipment manager.

Source: Melograno, Vincent J. "Evaluating Affective Objectives in Physical Education," *The Physical Educator*, 31 (March 1974): 8–12.

    4. Criteria
        a. Is a number of students or approach behaviors specified?
        b. Are indefinite words avoided?
        c. Is the criterion a realistic estimate of changes that can be expected in the students?
        d. Will the results indicate a trend or pattern of approach or avoidance?

Self-Check on Affective Objectives

Directions: Classify the following statements as (A) properly stated affective performance objectives or (B) improperly stated affective performance objectives or not a performance objective. If the objective is classified as (B), identify the part of the objective that is incorrect or missing.

1. The student will show responsibility by coming to class properly dressed each day of the unit.
2. The student will value dance.
3. The student will value sport by participating in at least one after-school intramural sport during the year.
4. The student will respect others.
5. The student will listen attentively to instructions.
6. The student will volunteer to help others.
7. The student will attend an athletic contest outside of class at least twice during the year.
8. The student will like others in the class.
9. The student will display sportspersonship.
10. The student will show responsibility by collecting any equipment used by him/her after class each day.

Answers to Self-Check

1. A
2. B, not stated in terms of observable performance.
3. A
4. B, not stated in terms of observable performance.
5. B, no stated conditions or criteria.
6. B, no stated conditions or criteria.
7. A
8. B, not stated in terms of observable performance.
9. B, not stated in terms of observable performance.
10. A

Concerns about Performance Objectives

Now that guidelines for writing performance objectives have been explored, some concerns about the use of objectives can be examined. Since writing performance objectives at the lowest levels of the taxonomies is easiest, teachers have a tendency to leave out many worthy objectives that cannot be easily evaluated. Often these objectives are among the most important ones.[18] Knowing this is the case, teachers can avoid a deficiency by using the taxonomies to check their objectives. Some teachers complain that writing objectives before instruction prevents them from taking advantage of "the teaching moment." This is especially true in the affective domain in which it is impossible to plan the teaching of such behaviors as good sportspersonship at a scheduled time and place.[19] These unintended effects of education may be as important or more important than many of the specified objectives.[20] Specifying the objectives of instruction does not tell the teacher when something is to be taught. It can, however, make the teacher aware of the need to teach the behavior when the opportunity arises. Good teachers will continue to take advantage of the teaching moment to aid student learning rather than limit themselves to only those behaviors that will be evaluated.

Innovative efforts can be frustrated by an attempt to specify objectives too early in the program, thus limiting the range of exploration.[21] Teachers can specify minimal objectives and add new objectives that are discovered to be worthwhile.

Specifying measurable student behaviors is difficult in fields such as dance. However, teachers do have criteria they use for evaluation, and it is only fair that students be told the criteria on which they will be evaluated.[22]

The use of performance objectives has been said to dehumanize learning. Actually, for many students, performance objectives serve to humanize learning by telling students what is expected.[23] The use of the open forms of objectives can also be used to individualize learning.

Content Analysis

Once instructional goals and objectives have been specified, learning activities must be selected to help students achieve these outcomes. Learning activities are determined by the skills or concepts to be learned and the readiness of the learners. The objectives state the performance standard expected of the learners at the conclusion of instruction. To help students achieve each objective, good teachers sequence learning experiences, beginning with less difficult or less complex skills or concepts and gradually adding difficulty and complexity.[24] This is accomplished for each skill within a lesson or lessons, as well as for the skills within an entire instructional unit or school curriculum. This process is called content analysis. It includes analyzing motor skills, both closed and open; and games skills.

Analyzing Motor Skills

Skillful performance consists of effective, efficient, adaptable performance. Rink suggests that teachers analyze motor skills by asking three questions:

1. What does it mean to be skilled with this content?
2. What does a skilled performer look like?
3. What must the performer do to adjust to the conditions of the game or event?[25]

The first question deals with the student's ability to use the skill to accomplish its intended purpose, its effectiveness. After defining the desired performance, the teacher must develop a progression or sequence of learning experiences called *extension tasks*, manipulations of the movement that will lead to successful student learning at all stages of the learning environment. This is done by changing or manipulating the difficulty or complexity of the skill as shown in Table 6.6.

The second question is concerned with the quality or efficiency of the performance. Rink calls this *refinement*. The performance should be mechanically correct for the performer for the given situation. Quality of performance is important at all levels of skill development and often indicates readiness to move to higher levels of difficulty or complexity. The teacher concentrates on performance cues to refine performance.

The third question asks the student to adapt or apply the skill to a game or event. This is called *application*. It is the ability to adjust to different conditions of game play.

Content analysis begins with extension (manipulation)—a list of progressively more difficult or complex skills. These are created by adapting such factors as equipment, skill instruction, spatial arrangements, players, desired outcomes, and game play or performance (see Table 6.6). Table 6.7 shows content analysis for the volleyball forearm pass.

Table 6.6 Techniques for Decreasing or Increasing Complexity or Difficulty of Skills

	Less Complex	More Complex	Examples
Equipment Modifications			
Weight, size, or hardness of object	Lighter, smaller, softer ball or object (discus, shot)	Regulation ball or object, hard ball or object	Volleyball, basketball, archery, bowling, tennis
Height of net or goal	Lower net or basket	Regulation height of net or goal	Volleyball, basketball
Height of equipment	Lower balance beam, etc.	Official equipment	Gymnastics, hurdles, high jump
Length of implement	Shorter racket, club, ski, bat (or choke up)	Official equipment	Tennis, golf, skiing, softball
Size of target or goal	Increased size of target or goal	Official size or decreased size	Basketball, soccer, softball
Shape of object	Round	Oblong, flat, or irregular	Football, frisbee
Skill Modifications			
Part vs. whole practice	Whole-part-whole, progressive part, backward chaining, etc.	Whole skills	Swimming, folk or square dance, basketball lay-up, tennis serve
Use of implement	Hand-eye coordination without implement	Use of implements (implement-eye coordination)	Tennis, racquetball, badminton
Player stationary or moving	Stationary or forward movement of performer	Sideward or backward movement of performer	Badminton, volleyball, softball, basketball
Ball or object stationary or moving	Stationary ball or object	Moving ball or object, moving performer and object	Soccer, basketball, golf
Direction of oncoming object	Receiving ball or object from straight ahead	Receiving from different directions	Volleyball, basketball, soccer, softball
Direction of intended movement	Sending ball or object straight ahead	Redirecting pass to a different space	Volleyball, basketball, soccer
Level or distance of object from body	Object in most desired position for easy play (use of ball machine or tosser)	Object on ground, overhead, or away from body (pitched or served ball)	Volleyball, softball, basketball, tennis

Table 6.6—Continued

	Less Complex	**More Complex**	**Examples**
Speed or force of oncoming object	Decreased speed or force (hitting to fence or partner)	Increased speed or force (hitting to backboard or wall)	Folk or social dance (with music), volleyball serve reception, softball pitch and batting, tennis
Speed or force of intended movement	Decreased speed or force	Increased speed or force	Tennis, volleyball, racquetball
Dominant or nondominant hand	Dominant hand or side	Nondominant hand or side	Basketball dribble, lay-up
Skill combinations	Isolated skills	Combinations of skills	Volleyball—pass, set, spike; Softball—field and throw; Basketball—pass, shoot, rebound
Spatial Arrangements			
Distance between players or from target	Shorter distances between players or from basket or net requires less force or speed	Longer distances between players or from the target requires more force or speed	Softball, volleyball, basketball, soccer, football
Number of players in space	Playing area of moderate size for keep-away games	Smaller playing area increases player interaction and skill difficulty	Basketball, soccer
Number of Players			
Relationship of offensive players	One or two stationary players	Three or more requires receiving from one direction and passing or throwing to another moving player	Volleyball, softball, basketball
Relationship of defensive player or players	No defense or stationary defense	With moving defensive player(s)	Basketball, field hockey, flag football
Desired Outcome			
Direction Distance Speed Accuracy Strategy	Focus on the skill itself	Focus on placement, or accuracy, distance, speed, or an opponent	Tennis, softball, archery, bowling, golf, volleyball, track and field events, football, field hockey

Table 6.6—Continued

	Less Complex	More Complex	Examples
Game Play or Performance			
Simple vs. complex games	Modified games; simulated performances	Official game; actual performances	Pickleball vs. tennis; three on three vs. basketball; minivolley vs. volleyball
Use of strategies or choreography	Effective and efficient use of the skills themselves	Complex strategies and choreographies	All ball games, dance, gymnastics
Cooperative vs. competitive	Cooperative play	Competitive play	All ball games, dance, gymnastics

Table 6.7 Example of Content Analysis for the Forearm Pass in Volleyball

Extension	Refinement	Application
Develop arm position	—Back of one hand in palm of other. —Forearms as flat as possible. —Elbows locked and arms straight.	—Proper position done on command. —Do arm position with eyes closed.
Stance	—Feet at least shoulder width apart. —90° at hip, back at 45° to floor. —Knees bent. —Heel to toe position. —Head up. —Seat down. —Weight on balls of feet.	—Position on command. —Move while in position (forward, right, left, back).
Hitting mechanics	—Ball will contact midforearms. —"Shrug" shoulders. —Contact will be made waist high at midline of body. —Head still. —Hands will separate after contact. —Keep arms straight. —Force.	—Practice hitting without ball. —Pretend to hit the ball to each other.

Table 6.7—Continued

Extension	Refinement	Application

Stationary hitting using Volley Lite
  from hold
  from drop
  from toss
	—Forearm contact.
	—Controlled straight direction of ball.
	—Hit will be equal to height of drop/toss.
		—Hitter must do three in a row correctly.
		—Tosser forms circle with arms at shoulder height and hitter will hit ball through circle seven out of ten times.

Movement
  forward
  lateral
  backward
	—Step-slide-jumpstop to ready position.
	—Stay low.
		—Direction drills (teacher indicates direction of movement).
		—Touch floor at each step.

Hitting with movement forward lateral backward	—Same as above hitting mechanics and movement. —Eye contact with ball.	—Hit five out of ten back to partner.
Controlled hitting between partners	—Correct arm position, stance, and hitting mechanics (see cues for each of these above). —Control.	—Volley six times between partners. —Continuous volley 30 seconds.
Hitting in a threesome	—Same as above. —Face direction of receiving the ball, then angle arms on contact to redirect the ball.	—Volley six times within threesome. —Continuous volley 30 seconds.
Pass from increased distance	—Check hitting mechanics. —Stopped before contact.	—Two of five tosses returned to target area.
Increase speed	—Same as above.	
Toss across net; decreased target area	—Eye contact with ball. —Concentration.	—Pass from toss across net to target. Team point scored for each pass caught by target.
Receiving serve as a team	—Communication.	(diagram) Teacher tosses randomly to passers who hit to target (⊗). One point for each catch.
Toss, then three forearm passes across the net	—Communication. —Hitting mechanics.	—Winners stay drill.
Three pass game	—Communication. —Hitting mechanics.	—Game. Start with toss. Score points for three hits on a side and hit over the net.

Diagram in Application column (Receiving serve as a team):

```
3          o       o

2        o           o

1    ⊗         ⊗          ⊗
              T
```

Source: Developed by Brent Duncan, Kim Duncan, Chris Neideck, David Wagner, Tom Terlep, and Doug Haynes at Ball State University.

Performance objectives should focus on skill
refinement and application.
© James L. Shaffer

Quality of movement or skill refinement must be monitored at all levels of skill development to ensure correct performance. Students often regress to a less mature or incorrect movement pattern in order to be successful. For each task listed in the extension (manipulation) column, the expected quality of good performance is identified. These qualities clarify performance expectations for the skill and are usually used as teaching cues at each level of instruction, as cues to direct teacher observation of student success, and as feedback cues.

The application column focuses on how to use the skill in a self-testing, competitive, or performance setting, rather than how to do the skill. These activities usually dominate class time. This setting must be congruent with each student's level of performance and the type of skill to be taught. These activities may be as simple as "How many consecutive hits can you have in your threesome?" or "How many free throws can you make out of ten tries?" Application activities should occur throughout skill learning, not just as a game at the end of the learning sequence. Several applications may be operating simultaneously to meet the needs of all students.

Analyzing Closed Skills

Closed skills are done in a relatively stable environment. Examples of closed skills are archery, bowling, gymnastics, golf, the basketball free throw, the placekick in soccer, and hitting a ball from a batting tee. For closed skills, fixation of the motor skill is the goal. Learning involves concentrating on the identical elements in the body and the environment and striving for consistency in executing the motor plan. Students can learn to "feel" the correct movements through kinesthetic perception of their own body movements. Occasionally, removing knowledge of results (such as by removing an archery target or bowling pins) is valuable to force students to focus on refining the skill first. Targets can be large at first and then gradually reduced in size until students acquire accuracy. Teacher aids, such as having students dive over a stick or putting a towel on the bowling lane for students to aim at, can also be helpful.

Some closed skills must be adapted to different conditions such as the amount of oil on bowling lanes, wind or rain in archery, or spectators during a basketball free throw. Others must be adapted to different environments such as sand traps in golf, different pin set-ups in spare bowling, and defensive player positions such as for a serve in volleyball or tennis. Closed skills should be practiced until they are efficient and consistent and then practiced in the different environments in which they might be used.

To develop extension (manipulation) activities for closed skills, the identification might look like this:

Volleyball serve

1. To serve a volleyball
   a. to different places on the court—long or short; left, center, or right.
   b. with or without spin.
2. To decide where on the court to serve the ball and what kind of spin based on the position of the opponents and their strengths and weaknesses.

Bowling strikes

1. To adjust the stance, approach speed, and release point to adjust to variations of oil on the lanes.
2. To determine
   a. whether there is too much oil on the lane or too little and where it is on the lane.
   b. whether to use the same or a different ball.
   c. whether to adjust the stance, the approach speed, the release point or several of these factors together.

Practice of each of the skill responses suggested above will help students learn to make correct decisions about which adaptations to make in a given situation.

Analyzing Open Skills

Open skills take place in unpredictable environments in which the players keep changing places, and objects move through space. Adjustments must be made in speed, timing, and space, such as in the height and speed of a softball pitch or the interaction of players on a basketball court. Skill diversification is required to meet the multitude of environmental conditions. Therefore, practice must include a variety of situations. At first, combinations of two or three variables may be practiced, but later practice must include all possible variables. Practice should not consistently occur with any particular combination, or a fixation might occur. Students can be helped to set goals for accuracy, distance, speed, quality of movement, and reduction of errors.

To develop extension (manipulation) activities for open skills, teachers must identify the skill responses and decisions that will be required in game play. For example:

Volleyball forearm pass

1. Receives the serve and passes it (changing direction) to the setter in the front row so that the setter can get under it for a good set.
   a. Receives ball from many directions.
   b. Moves in all directions to meet ball.
   c. Absorbs and redirects force of balls of various speeds.
   d. Moves to offensive position for next skill.
2. Decides when to play the ball and when to allow a teammate to play the ball.

Teachers have a responsibility to ensure safe and successful practice conditions and to keep students from developing bad habits. Practice makes skills permanent, whether or not they are correct. When students practice parts of skills too long, they lose the rhythm of the entire movement and have difficulty putting the parts together. Sometimes open skills are taught as closed skills, such as teaching children to bat from a tee prior to learning to bat a pitched ball. If practiced too long as closed skills, learners may not be able to adapt to the different environmental conditions of a pitched ball, since new motor patterns must be learned in the new environment. The teacher must decide whether it is better to begin with the closed skill and then spend the time to learn the skill in the open situation, or to begin with the open skill. Similarly, equipment modifications may be used to allow learners to achieve success or to overcome fear. Consideration must be given to both student success and correct performance. Rules may be adapted to increase time spent on skills, such as playing cooperative volleyball or eliminating free throws in basketball or huddles in flag football.

Analyzing Games Skills

A common mistake is to jump from practice drills directly into competitive games before students have had time to refine their skills.[26] The complex nature of the game almost ensures a regression to less desirable movement patterns[27] because skills required in game situations require a shift in ability.[28]

Rink proposed a four-stage process[29] to ready students for participation in games. Stage 1 involves the *ability to control the object,* including:

a. Consistently *directs objects* (throws, strikes) to a specified place with the intended force.
b. *Obtains possession of an object* (catches, collects) from any direction, level, or speed.
c. *Maintains possession* moving in different ways with different speeds.

These activities include the following:

1. Stationary to moving performer
2. Stationary to moving object
3. Stationary to moving receivers
4. Changing levels, directions, and force of object sent or received

Stage 2 involves *combining skills and adding rules.* The focus is on controlling the object in simple gamelike play. Stage 3 involves using the skills with simple offensive and defensive strategies in *less complex game situations* (lead-up games) such as keep-away games (e.g., one on one, one on two, two on two). Players, boundaries, scoring, and rules can be changed to gradually increase the complexity of the games. Stage 4 consists of *sport games,* modified at first to keep the play continuous by eliminating free throws, huddles, free kicks, volleyball serves, jump balls, and so on. At this level students may learn specialized player positions, rules, penalties, scoring, and out-of-bounds plays. These stages agree with Barrett's three-phase process of game playing (stages two and three are combined)[30] and Graham's levels of precontrol, control, utilization, and proficiency.[31] All agree that the middle stages are critical and often "missed entirely or passed through so quickly as to have no effect."[32] Table 6.8 highlights content analysis for the game skill of volleyball.

Studies show that teachers often place students in game situations before they have sufficient skill to be successful.[33] To make the transition from skill drills to game play, students should practice all possible skill combinations in less complex situations prior to using them in game play. Teachers can choose or create drills and lead-up games that force students to move to the ball, to direct the ball to a moving target, or to practice under the innumerable conditions that occur in game play. For example, rather than have students hit a volleyball back and forth to a partner, a threesome forces students to direct the ball to a place different from the point of origin. Elementary physical education textbooks often include self-testing or modified games and activities that are appropriate for the intermediate stages of learning. Examples include:

Do correct skills.
Do correct skills (hits, shots) in a row.
How far can you throw, jump, and so on?
How long can you keep the ball in the air?
How many consecutive hits, shots, and so on can you get?
How many hits, shots, and so on can you get in the goal?
How fast can you dribble to a specified place without losing control?
Can you dribble without looking at the ball?
Maintain possession as long as possible without losing control (play dribble tag).
Move the ball to a goal with a partner without losing control.
Do the skill so quietly we can't hear you hit the ball.
Do as few elementary back strokes as possible in 25 yards.
See how many pass-set-spike sequences you can do.

Young discussed ways to improve practice drills to make them more gamelike. She suggested placing cones at random rather than in straight lines for dribbling practice, with several players moving at a time so that students learn to adapt to changing circumstances.[34] Lead-up games before playing the full game help bridge the gap between skill drills and game play. Games with fewer players per team force low-ability students to be involved and provide more opportunities for contacting the ball. (See chapter 4 for more ideas on how to modify games.)

Team strategies should not be introduced before students feel secure with the basic skills and individual offensive and defensive tactics, such as marking or guarding, playing one's position, or shooting without being guarded, have been taught.

The final result of skill learning is accurate, consistent, adaptable, coordinated motor responses. Automatic skill execution enables the learner to devote attention to the game plan and strategy. Rather than paying attention to each part of a skill, the elements are chunked into a skill or even a combination of skills. Performers learn where to look and what to look at, how to

Table 6.8 Example of content analysis for game skills: Volleyball

Extension	Refinement	Application	Concepts
Stage 1			
	Skill: Forearm Pass		
See Table 6.7			Legal pass Cues for pass
	Skill: Set or Overhand Pass		
(similar progression to Table 6.7)			Legal set Cues for set
Stage 2			
	Skills: Forearm Pass and Set		
Alternate passes and sets with movement—forward, laterally, and backward. Hit to other players.	Work on legal, accurate passes and sets to another player.	Fifteen consecutive.	Legal hits. Cues for passes and sets
Receiving a tossed ball and passing to a setter who sets into a hoop attached to a pole.	Legal, accurate passes to center front and accurate sets to side front hoop.	Hit ball through hoop seven out of ten times.	Positions for setter and hitter in relation to passer.
Increase force of toss.			
As above, receive and pass from different positions on court.	Same as above. Face ball, angle arms.	Hit ball through hoop seven out of ten times.	Same as above.
Three on three, last player hits it over.	Same as above.	Start with a toss. Score one point for three hits on a side—pass, set, hit over.	Pass-set-hit sequence.
Stage 1			
	Skill: Spike		
(Teach toss, hitting action, footwork, and spike from held, tossed, and set ball on low net with Volley Lite ball.)			
Stage 2			
	Skills: All Skills Except Serve		
Spiker sets ball to setter, who sets for spiker to spike.	Work on accuracy and getting ball over net.	Ten spikes over net.	Net rules involving spike.
Toss ball over net, pass, set, spike.	Same as above.	Ten spikes over net.	Net rules.

Table 6.8—Continued

Extension	Refinement	Application	Concepts
Play three on three using pass-set-spike sequence.	Work on accuracy and getting ball over net on spike.	Start with a toss. Score one point for three hits on a side—pass, set, hit over.	Pass-set-hit sequence.
Increase height of net gradually to regulation height out of games and then in games.	Same as above.	Same as above.	

Stage 1

Skill: Serve

(Teach toss, hitting action, footwork, and serve from close, medium, and regulation distance with Volley Lite ball.)

Stage 3

Skills: Serve, Pass, Set, Spike

Play cooperation volleyball.	Work on accuracy and pass-set-spike sequences.	Score one point for each pass-set-spike sequence. Team making an error serves. Try to score as many points as possible.	Pass-set-spike sequence.
Play minivolley on half courts (two games on each court).	Work on accuracy and pass-set-spike sequences.	Regular scoring, with bonus points for pass-set-spike sequences or spikes or whatever skill needs emphasis.	Rules.

Stage 4: Game Play

Play official volleyball games.	Maintain accuracy of skills.	Play as above.	Official rules.
4–2 offense.	Every player must set and spike; rotate setters and spikers.	Play as above.	4–2 offense.
2–1–3 defense.	Same as above.	Play as above.	2–1–3 defense.
Play tournament.	Every player must set one full round; every player must spike successfully once a day.	Play official rules.	All listed above.

Note: In the interests of space, this table does not include all aspects of the game of volleyball.
Sources: Cooperation volleyball: Madden, G., & McGown, C. (1989). "The Effect of the Inner Game Method versus the Progressive Method on Learning Motor Skills." *Journal of Teaching in Physical Education, 9,* 39–48. Minivolley: Kessel, J. (1988). *Coaches Guide to Beginning Volleyball Programs,* United States Volleyball Association/Boys Clubs of America.

differentiate relevant and irrelevant information, and how to predict outcomes from cues. In essence, students learn to integrate movements and information into schemas that help them to select appropriate movement responses for a wide variety of conditions, to monitor outcomes and to guide their own learning.[35] The teacher must continually reflect on the teaching process and make necessary corrections and adjustments. Figure 6.1 illustrates this process (see also chapter 5).

Preassessment

Preassessment is used at the beginning of instruction to determine where the learner is in relation to each course or unit objective. Preassessment techniques can be used to determine the following:

1. Whether each learner can or cannot already perform the behavior stated in the objective and, therefore, whether the objective is appropriate for that learner
2. Whether the learner possesses the knowledge or skills necessary to succeed in learning the behavior specified in the objective

Why is preassessment important? It gives the teacher information needed to personalize instruction to the student or class. Preassessment aids the instructional process in the following ways:

1. Provides diagnosis or screening information to the teacher for the purposes of grouping and individualizing instruction
2. Clarifies objectives for students while helping them increase their self-awareness of and reevaluate their own skills, knowledges, and attitudes
3. Evaluates objectives for accuracy and application to the specific situation
4. Assists in the determination of student achievement and the effectiveness of teaching methods when the difference between pre- and posttests are calculated

REFLECTIVE TEACHING

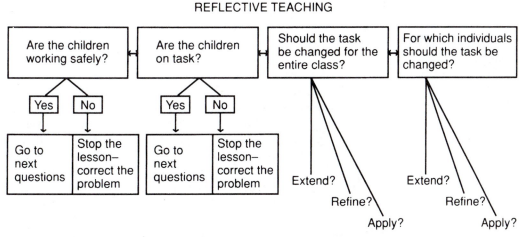

Figure 6.1 Reflective teaching.
Source: George Graham, R. Tait McKenzie Symposium on Sport, University of Tennessee. Knoxville, 1989.

Students who have already achieved the objective, as evidenced by preassessment results, should be allowed to practice the behavior at a more-advanced level or move on to other activities. For example, if the objective states that students will perform the layup shot in basketball successfully and with correct form, the teacher can quickly identify those students who can already perform successful layups with correct form. These students can be sent to a separate court to work on consecutive layups, left-handed or reverse layups, or layups in a game while the rest of the class learns to perform a basic layup successfully. In team-teaching situations or during individualized instruction these advanced students can move on to other objectives.

Students who cannot perform the behavior specified in the objective, as determined by the preassessment technique, can be given help to develop the prerequisite skills. For example, students who do not have hand-eye coordination necessary to hit a badminton shuttle are not ready to learn the overhead and underhand clears. Special help must be given to these students so they learn to connect with the shuttle before instruction can take place on the strokes.

Preassessment techniques help instructors evaluate performance objectives. For example, suppose that the class average (mean) on a pretest is 55 and the mean on a posttest is 60. A class that showed very little improvement in performance from the beginning to the end of a unit might need to be challenged to achieve more difficult levels of knowledge or skill. On the other hand, the test could be too hard, indicating that performance standards were set too high. The teacher would need to carefully analyze the results of assessment in such a situation.

Preassessment results also help teachers or administrators evaluate teaching methods. For example, Teacher A brags that her students can shoot 200 points at 40 yards and, therefore, she is an excellent teacher. Without some other information, no judgment of her teaching ability can be made. Since 200 points at 40 yards is a good score for a beginning student, we can assume either that she taught the class well or that she began the class with students who were already highly skilled in archery. Teacher B, on the contrary, indicates that in his class no student scored 200 points or better on the pretest at 20 yards, yet now all students can shoot 200 points at 40 yards. Because of the pretest scores, we know that Teacher B can be pleased with the results of his teaching.

Preassessment can be done formally through written or performance tests or informally through observation, asking questions, or analyzing student records of previous work. Some preassessment techniques fall within the realm of instruction (i.e., some can occur following the demonstration of the skill). Whatever the method, the preassessment should precede each new objective in the lesson or unit.

Because of the safety factor in some cases, do not allow students to take a pretest until a certain level of fitness or skill has been achieved. For example, in tumbling, do not evaluate students on higher-level skills such as the roundoff until they have demonstrated the ability to perform prerequisite skills such as the cartwheel. Do not ask students to run continuously in a 12-minute run/walk without engaging in a cardiovascular endurance program that gradually develops the ability to run that long without incurring adverse physical effects. The instructor should also stress that such a test is actually a run/*walk*.

The information that follows is designed to help teachers develop practical preassessment techniques for instruction.

Steps in Developing Preassessment Techniques

Step 1. List what the students will have to be able to do or know to perform the objective.

Step 2. Write down how the teacher will know whether some or all of the students have achieved the objective.

Step 1—*List what the students will have to be able to do or know to perform the objective.*

The key to a determination of prerequisite knowledge and skills is the question: "What will the students have to be able to do or know to perform the objective?" For example, if the objective of the course is, "The students will be able to play tennis at a beginning level," then what will the students need to be able to do to play tennis? Teachers would probably agree that the students will be able to use (1) a forehand stroke, (2) a backhand stroke, and (3) a serve; that they would know how to (4) score, and (5) follow game rules; and (6) enjoy playing tennis.

Content analysis allows teachers to pretest students to determine where they are in the sequence of experiences. For example, can the student do the forehand stroke from a dropped ball, a tossed ball, or a hit ball? This helps the teacher know where to start the teaching process.

Most performance objectives require some adjunct knowledge or skill in order to benefit from instruction designed to reach the objective. For example, to perform the serve correctly students must know the area of the court where balls are legally served (service court) and what constitutes a foot fault when serving. As the teacher preassesses serving ability, student knowledge of a legally served ball can also be determined.

Knowing where students are helps teachers choose activities that are challenging yet still within the realm of success for them. It eliminates the need for starting over with beginning basketball each year. By deciding on prerequisite knowledge and skills, students who are deficient in these areas can be diagnosed and remedial help provided. Students who already have these skills can move on to practice skills in a way that will be challenging and motivating. A teacher who preassesses student abilities can plan and carry out a meaningful course of study for each individual class.

Step 2—*Write down how the teacher will know whether some or all of the students have achieved the objective.*

The preassessment technique used to determine whether students have achieved the objective will often be the same technique as that used for evaluating the objective. However, other less formal techniques will be useful in conjunction with formal evaluation or when preassessment is utilized for a single lesson. An explanation of some of the more common forms of preassessment is given here. Examples of formal evaluation techniques are included in chapter 9.

Pretest

A formal test before instruction is a very accurate preassessment tool. A written test may be utilized to preassess knowledge or a skills test to check on skill achievement. These tests may be equivalent forms of a posttest or a simplified version if time is a factor. If a student passes an equivalent of the posttest, reason demands that the student not be asked to repeat the evaluation.

Teacher Observation

Students are asked to perform a skill as they have previously learned it and the teacher observes to see which students can already perform the skill according to the criterion established in the instructional objective. This can be informally done while students are engaged in a learning activity.

Question or Questionnaire

A formal questionnaire or an informal question asked of the student by the teacher is often sufficient to tell the teacher which students at least think they have achieved the objective. For example, "How many of you can do a feet-first surface dive?" If no one thinks he or she can, then it is probably a waste of time to use a more formal preassessment technique.

After performance objectives have been specified, the content analyzed, and the teacher knows the capabilities of the learners, unit and lesson plans can be written to plan the learning experiences for students.

Review Questions

1. Define and give an example of:
   aim or purpose
   objective
   instructional objective
2. Name the three components of a performance objective.
3. Write an aim or purpose for physical education. Develop it into a goal, the goal into an objective, and the objective into at least two performance objectives in each of the three domains.
4. Write three or more performance objectives for a lesson or a unit of instruction that are clearly stated and include the three essential components—behavior, conditions, and criteria. Include the cognitive, psychomotor, and affective domains.
5. Discuss the advantages and disadvantages of performance objectives from your point of view. How can some of the disadvantages be overcome?
6. Write a performance objective for each level of the taxonomy in each of the three domains for a specified unit of instruction.
7. Name and give examples of the three components of Rink's content analysis system.
8. Name and give examples of Rink's four stages of game play.
9. What is preassessment? Why is it important? What techniques can be used to preassess?
10. How can content analysis facilitate preassessment?

References

1. Bloom, B. S., Madaus, G. F., & Hastings, J. T. (1981). *Evaluation to improve learning* (p. 5). New York: McGraw-Hill.
2. Ibid., 8.
3. Burns, R. W. (1972). *New approaches to behavioral objectives* (p. 3). Dubuque, IA: Brown.
4. Bloom, et al., *Evaluation to improve learning*, 17.
5. Lawson, H. A., & Placek, J. H. (1981). *Physical education in the secondary schools: Curricular alternatives* (p. 80). Boston: Allyn & Bacon.
6. Dougherty, N. J., & Bonanno, D. (1987). *Contemporary approaches to the teaching of physical education* (2nd ed., p. 144). Scottsdale: Gorsuch Scarisbrick.
7. Mager, R. F. (1975). *Preparing instructional objectives* (2nd ed., p. 2). Belmont: Pitman Learning.
8. Shockley, J. M. (1973, April). Needed: Behavioral objectives in physical education. *Journal of Health, Physical Education and Dance, 44*, 44–46.
9. Ibid.
10. Ibid.
11. Rink, J. E. (1993). *Teaching physical education for learning* (2nd ed., p. 209). St. Louis, MO: Mosby.
12. Griffey, D. C. (1987, February). Trouble for sure: a crisis—perhaps: Secondary school physical education today. *Journal of Health, Physical Education, Recreation and Dance, 58*, 21.
13. Annarino, A. A. (1977, October). Physical education objectives: Traditional vs. developmental. *Journal of Health, Physical Education, Recreation and Dance, 48*, 22–23.
14. Bloom, et al., *Evaluation to improve learning*, 33.
15. Burns, *New approaches to behavioral objectives*, 58–59.

16. Adapted from Lee, B. N., & Merrill, M. D. (1972). *Writing complete affective objectives: A short course.* Belmont: Wadsworth.
17. Ibid., 98–99.
18. Worthen, B. R., & Sanders, J. R. (1973). *Educational evaluation: Theory and practice* (p. 240). Worthington: Jones.
19. Ibid., 241.
20. Davies, I. K. (1976). *Objectives in curriculum design* (p. 66). New York: McGraw-Hill.
21. Ibid.
22. Worthen & Sanders, *Educational evaluation: Theory and practice,* 243.
23. Ibid., 243.
24. Rink, *Teaching physical education for learning,* 101.
25. Ibid., 100–116; see also Rink, J. E. (1985). *Teaching physical education for learning* (pp. 98–122). St. Louis, MO: Times Mirror/Mosby.
26. Earls, N. (1983). Research on the immediate effects of instructional variables. In T. J. Templin & J. K. Olsen (Eds.), *Teaching in physical education* (pp. 254–264). Champaign, IL: Human Kinetics.
27. Ibid.
28. Schmidt, R. A. (1988). *Motor control and learning: A behavioral emphasis.* Champaign, IL: Human Kinetics.
29. Rink, *Teaching physical education for learning,* 244–253.
30. Barrett, K. R. (1977, September). Games teaching: adaptable skills, versatile players. *Journal of Physical Education and Recreation, 48,* 21–24.
31. Graham, G., Holt/Hale, S. A., & Parker, M. (1987). *Children moving: A teacher's guide to developing a successful physical education program* (2nd ed., pp. 38–41). Palo Alto, CA: Mayfield.
32. Barrett, Games teaching, 21.
33. Earls, Research on the immediate effects of instructional variables; Buck, M., & Harrison, J. M. (1990). An analysis of game play in volleyball. *Journal of Teaching in Physical Education, 10*(1), 38–48.
34. Young, J. E. (1985, October). When practice doesn't make perfect—Improving game performance in secondary level physical education classes. *Journal of Physical Education, Recreation, and Dance, 56,* 24–26; Gabbard, C. (1984). Teaching motor skills to children: Theory into practice. *Physical Educator, 41,* 69–71.
35. Ibid., 93.

CHAPTER 7

Instructional Styles and Strategies

Study Stimulators

1. What are direct and indirect instruction? When would each be used?
2. What factors influence the selection of a teaching style?
3. What is the Spectrum of Teaching? Describe a situation in which you would use each of the styles.
4. How would you incorporate individualized instruction into your teaching?
5. What is mastery learning and what are its components?
6. What is cooperative learning? How is it implemented?
7. How do problem-solving strategies fit into the physical education learning environment?
8. Which instructional strategies would you feel comfortable using in a class?

"Great instructors nourish individual differences."[1] They are aware that each student has unique aptitudes and needs that must be addressed. Teaching is said to be both an art and a science. It is an art in that each teacher decides what will best guide students to learn, while adding a personal touch to the process. It is a science in that when certain principles of learning are operating, a distinct outcome is usually the result.

Excellent teachers become experienced at making wise decisions. They select objectives at the correct level of difficulty for students; they select and use teaching activities that are directly relevant to daily objectives; they monitor student learning continuously; and they apply known principles of learning.[2] No teaching strategy or behavior has been shown to enhance learning for all students. The best physical educators develop a repertoire of styles and strategies to aid them in the teaching process. Many such options are presented in this chapter to give teachers alternatives to maximize the efficiency with which all their students achieve the desired objectives of the program.

Teaching Styles

Styles can range on a continuum from those designated as *direct instruction,* or teacher-centered, to those designated as *indirect instruction,* or student-centered. Direct instruction styles are used when the acquisition of basic skills is the goal.[3] Indirect instruction styles are selected to enhance creativity and independence, or change the attitudes of students.[4] Teachers most often use the direct style of teaching. Research findings have consistently substantiated that direct instruction (lecture/demonstration, drill, practice, feedback) is more effective than indirect instruction for students learning basic academic skills in elementary schools.[5] Direct instruction creates a structured teaching-learning environment that contains the following:

1. A focus on appropriate academic goals and content
2. Teacher-controlled coverage of extensive content through structured learning activities and appropriate pacing
3. Sufficient time on-task for student success
4. Monitoring of pupil performance
5. A task-oriented but relaxed environment
6. Immediate, academically oriented feedback

Selecting a Teaching Style

The selection of a teaching style depends on a thoughtful evaluation of the learning situation, including (1) the students, (2) the subject matter content to be taught, (3) the teacher, (4) the learning environment, and (5) time.

Students

One consideration in choosing a learning activity is the total educational needs of students—physical, intellectual, emotional, and social. Younger children will need a much more structured learning environment than older children, with the teacher directing most of the activities. Sooner or later, however, the students must learn to take the initiative for their own learning. Since it is the individual student who does the learning, consideration must be given to the different ways in which students learn best. Different personalities, aptitudes, experiences, and interests combine to make each learner unique in the way he or she responds to a given style of teaching. Tyler emphasized that a teacher must have some understanding of the interests and background of students to set up the desired learning environment.[6] Rink pointed out that low-ability students, as well as those who are unmotivated, unsociable, and nonconforming, seem to perform better in unstructured environments, whereas high-ability, motivated, sociable, conforming students perform better in structured environments.[7] Teachers must consider the variety of needs of individual students when planning both the environment of the learning situation and the learning task.

Hawley suggested that using a variety of teaching styles increases the likelihood that the learner will find one suited to his or her own learning style and will be motivated to achieve class goals. He also suggested that many students are only familiar with traditional styles of teaching and will have to be taught that learning can occur in a variety of ways.[8]

Subject Matter Content

A second consideration in planning instruction is the specific ideas or skills to be taught. Obviously, some methods work best for some activities while other methods work better with other activities. For example, teaching an idea or skill at the lower levels of the cognitive or psychomotor taxonomy (refer to chapter 4) might require a more-structured approach, whereas the upper levels of the taxonomies might incorporate student experiences utilizing creativity and problem solving. Affective behaviors suffer under some teaching styles and blossom with others. A knowledge of the concepts and skills in various activities can help the physical education instructor select appropriate teaching strategies.

Teacher

The teacher is a major consideration in the selection of learning activities. Some methods work better for some teachers than for others. Each teacher selects a comfortable teaching style in terms of his or her own personality and talents. The best teachers experiment with many styles until they are comfortable with a wide range from which they can choose as the learning situation changes. They must also learn to be sensitive to feedback from the students and the learning environment and use that feedback to modify their teaching behavior.

Learning Environment

A fourth consideration is the learning environment. A school or class that focuses on basic skills would predominantly use a direct instructional style. Brophy concluded that students who receive most of their instruction from the teacher do better than those who are expected to learn on their own or from each other.[9] Each teaching style establishes a unique social environment for a specific group of learners. The social system becomes a part of the learning experience along with the subject matter to be taught. Students learn competitiveness, cooperation, democratic processes, and other social skills as environments change within the school. The teaching style influences the way students react to each other, to the teacher, and to others outside the class environment.

Time

Time is the fifth consideration. Early in the school year or in a new unit of activity, the teacher may choose to use a structured teaching style. Later on, as the teacher gets to know the students' capabilities and learning styles, the teacher may choose a more informal approach. Another time variable is the allocation of practice minutes built into the teaching style. Graham substantiated that students who learned more had teachers who provided them with more time to practice the criterion skill.[10]

The Spectrum of Teaching Styles

A useful way of classifying teaching styles according to "direct" or "indirect" is Mosston's spectrum.[11] The spectrum describes a number of alternative teaching styles that provide teachers with a knowledge of the roles of teacher and learner and the objectives that can be achieved with each style. This permits teachers to move back and forth along the spectrum as needed to meet the changing needs of students, environments, and subject matter.

Mosston described teaching behavior as a "chain of decision making." As can be seen in figure 7.1, the anatomy of a style categorizes decisions as being made before (pre-impact), during (impact), or following (post-impact) the interaction between teacher and learner. The teaching style is identified by specifying who—teacher or learner—makes which decisions. Each style has been identified by name and letter and is called a "landmark" style. Eleven styles have been identified so far, ranging from style A (command), which is a complete teacher decision-making style, to style K (self-teaching), which is a complete learner decision-making style. An infinite variety of other styles exhibit characteristics of two adjoining styles and fall under the "canopies" of these landmark styles.

Each style of teaching creates different conditions for learning founded on the decision-making process. Figure 7.2 illustrates who makes decisions at what stage of impact. Based on who makes these decisions, the styles then appear to form organized clusters along the spectrum. The spectrum is organized into two clusters of styles on either side of the discovery threshold.

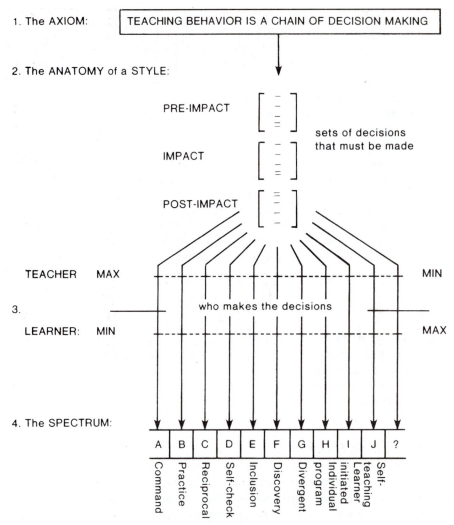

1. The AXIOM: TEACHING BEHAVIOR IS A CHAIN OF DECISION MAKING

2. The ANATOMY of a STYLE:

PRE-IMPACT

IMPACT   sets of decisions
                that must be made

POST-IMPACT

TEACHER   MAX   MIN

3.   who makes the decisions

LEARNER: MIN   MAX

4. The SPECTRUM:

| A | B | C | D | E | F | G | H | I | J | ? |

Command / Practice / Reciprocal / Self-check / Inclusion / Discovery / Divergent / Individual program / Learner initiated / Self-teaching

Figure 7.1 An overview of the theoretical structure of the spectrum of teaching styles.
SOURCE: Muska Mosston and Sara Ashworth.
(1994). *Teaching Physical Education* (4th ed.). New York: Macmillan College Publishing Company.

Styles A to E represent reproduction styles. Styles F to K represent discovery and production of the unknown. Figure 7.3 lists the characteristics of each cluster.

Research validating specific application of the spectrum is sparse and sometimes conflicts with other studies. Very little research has been conducted on the discovery and production cluster.[12] Goldberger and his associates found in studies of fifth-grade children using the direct styles of B, C, and E that all of the styles facilitated learning. In one study, style B produced the most effective results.[13] Another study revealed that average-aptitude children responded best to the

Style	Pre-impact	Impact	Post-impact
Command style (A)	T	T	T
Practice style (B)	T	L	T
Reciprocal style (C)	T	D	O
Self-check style (D)	T	L	L
Inclusion style (E)	T	L	L
Guided-discovery style (F)	T	T-L	T-L
Convergent discovery (G)	T	L-T	L-T
Divergent production style (H)	T	L-T	L-T
Learner-designed style (I)	T	L	L
Learner-initiated style (J)	L	L-T	L
Self-teaching style (K)	L	L	L

T = Teacher   D = Doer
L = Learner   O = Observer

Figure 7.2   Pre-impact, impact, and post-impact decisions in each of the learning styles on the Spectrum of Teaching.
SOURCE: Concepts from Muska Mosston and Sara Ashworth. (1994). *Teaching Physical Education* (4th ed.). New York: Macmillan College Publishing Company.

conditions provided by style B, whereas exceptional children, the combination of children with above and below average aptitude, profited more from the conditions provided by style E.[14] Beckett determined that style B was the most effective way to teach a soccer skill to college students.[15]

Salter and Graham found that when elementary school children were taught a novel golf task using the command, guided-discovery, and no instruction methodologies, no significant differences existed between the groups on skill improvement or self-efficacy. However, cognitive understanding improved significantly for the groups taught by the command and guided-discovery approaches.[16]

Pettigrew and Heikkinen reported that on 12 measures of achievement for students taught using a variety of spectrum styles, as compared with those taught by one style, 9 measures showed significantly higher achievement by students. The authors suggested that teachers who effectively accommodate the learning needs of students use a variety of instructional styles.[17]

Teachers incorporating the spectrum move freely along the spectrum as students are ready to make more and more decisions, selecting one or more applicable styles for use during each episode of a particular lesson or unit of activity. An episode is defined as "a unit of time during which the teacher and learner are in the same style, heading toward the same objective."[18] A lesson is composed of one or more episodes of varying lengths of time. Often several styles may be employed in a single lesson. Students should be involved as much as possible in the selection of methods that affect them and in the application of methods on the higher cognitive levels. Using a variety of methods provides students with different learning styles and the opportunity to find their niche in the learning experience. It also prevents boredom and the "inverted U" phenomenon

Common characteristics (objectives) of styles A–E	Common characteristics (objectives) of styles F–J
1. Re-production of knowledge and skills (known to the teacher and/or the learner)	1. Production of knowledge and skills new to the learner and/or the teacher.
2. The subject matter is concrete, mainly containing facts, rules, and specific skills. (Basic knowledge, Fixed knowledge)	2. The subject matter is variable, mainly containing concepts, strategies, and principles.
3. There is one correct way to perform the task—by emulation of the presented model.	3. Alternatives in design and performance are called for. There is no single model to emulate.
4. Time is needed for practicing and learning to adhere to the model.	4. Time is needed for the cognitive processes involved.
5. The cognitive operations mainly engaged are memory and recall.	5. Time is needed to evolve an affective climate conducive to producing and accepting alternatives and options.
6. Feedback is specific and refers to the performance of the task and its approximation to the model.	6. The cognitive operations engaged are comparing, contrasting, categorizing, problem solving, inventing, and others.
7. Individual differences are accepted only within the learner's physical and emotional boundaries.	7. Discovery and creativity are manifested through these cognitive operations.
8. The class climate (the spirit of the learning environment) is one of performing the model, repetition, and reduction of errors.	8. Discovery by the learner is developed through convergent and divergent processes or a combination of both.
	9. Feedback refers to producing alternatives and not a single solution.
	10. Individual differences in the quantity, rate, and kind of production are essential to maintaining and continuing these styles.
	11. The class climate (the spirit of the learning environment) is one of searching, examining the validity of alternatives, and going beyond the known.

Figure 7.3 Characteristics of the clusters of teaching styles.
Source: Muska Mosston and Sara Ashworth. (1994). *Teaching Physical Education* (4th ed.). New York: Macmillan College Publishing Company.

that can result from overuse of a single style. (The *inverted U phenomenon* refers to a teacher behavior or strategy that has a positive effect on learning but, if continued past a certain point, has a negative effect.)[19]

The following pages present a brief description of the landmark styles of the Spectrum of Teaching. A teacher using each style should be able to incorporate the appropriate decisions of the anatomy.

The Command Style (A)

In the command style, the teacher makes all of the decisions on what, where, when, and how to teach, and on how to evaluate learning and provide feedback. The teacher should tell the class that "the purpose of this style is to learn to do the task accurately and within a short period of time."

Pre-impact decisions:

1. Identify subject matter (i.e., swimming, soccer).
2. State the overall lesson objectives.
3. Design the episode (learning experience).

Impact decisions:

1. Explain roles of teacher and learner.
2. Deliver subject matter.
3. Explain logistical procedures.

Post-impact decisions:

1. Offer feedback to learner about performance and role in following the teacher decisions.

The command style capitalizes on the teacher's expertise through such teaching/learning strategies as lecture and other verbal presentations, demonstration, and drill. Homogeneous grouping can be used advantageously during drills to individualize learning. Instructional games can also be used to drill students on such items as terminology and rules. Students are expected to respond as they have been "commanded" to do. This style achieves the objectives of precision, synchronization, and uniformity. It is especially applicable when safety, efficient use of class time, and teacher control are essential.

The Practice Style (B)

In the practice style, the teacher determines what is to be taught and how the activity will be evaluated. The students are then given a number of tasks to practice and each learner decides which task to begin with, where to do it, when to begin and end the practice of a particular task, how fast or slow to work, and what to do between tasks. Style B is the one most often used by physical educators.[20] In style B, students are encouraged to clarify the nature of the tasks by asking questions as needed. The teacher moves around the class, offering feedback to each individual. The teacher should state, "The purpose of this style is to offer you time to work individually and privately and to provide me with time to offer you individual and private feedback."

Pre-impact decisions:

1. The same as style A.

Impact decisions:

1. The same as style A.
2. Student—practice tasks.

Post-impact decisions:

1. Teacher—offer feedback individually to all learners.

By using a variety of tasks, including fitness activities and testing activities, and employing stations, the teacher and students can make use of all of the available space. Tasks sheets, skill checklists, study guides, workbooks, journals, and progress charts are some of the teaching/learning strategies that can be used within this style.

The Reciprocal Style (C)

In the reciprocal style, students provide the feedback for each other. One student performs while the other observes and provides feedback. Then the students exchange roles. The teacher decides what tasks are to be accomplished, designs the criteria sheet that will guide the observer in giving feedback, gives the assignments to the students, and helps the observers improve their ability as observers and their ability to communicate with their partners. The teacher states, "The purposes of this style are to work with a partner and to offer feedback to your partner."

Pre-impact decisions:

1. The same as style A.
2. Design and prepare criteria sheet for observer.

Impact decisions:

1. Teacher—set up logistics; set scene for new roles.
2. Student—understand and perform role of doer and observer.
3. Student—perform the task.

Post-impact decisions:

1. Student—(observer) receive criteria; observe doer's performance, compare and contrast performance with criteria, conclude correctness of performance; communicate results to doer; initiate communication with teacher, if necessary.
2. Teacher—answer questions of observer (do not usurp role of observer).

Socialization between students is an inherent part of the reciprocal style. Students also develop feedback skills and enhance learning in the cognitive domain.

The Self-Check Style (D)

In the self-check style, the feedback is provided by the individual learner instead of by the teacher or another student. The selection of tasks is important so that students can evaluate their own performance. Events that provide external feedback—such as making baskets, kicking a football over the goalposts, or hitting a target with an object—facilitate student self-evaluation. The role of the teacher is to help the students become better self-evaluators. The teacher should state, "The purpose of this style is to learn to do a task and check your own work."

Pre-impact decisions:

1. The same as style A.
2. Prepare subject matter.
3. Prepare criteria sheet for self-check.

Impact decisions:

1. Teacher—set up logistics; set scene for new role; answer questions.
2. Student—understand role as a doer.
3. Student—perform the tasks.

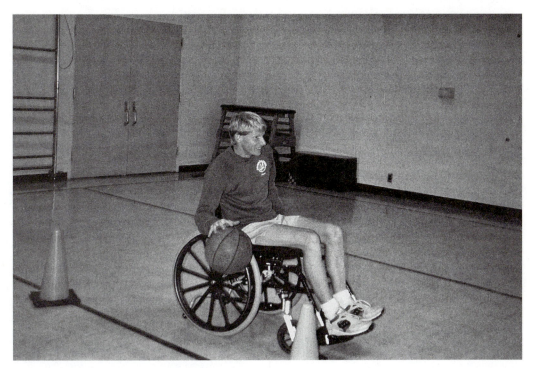

The inclusion style permits all students to be successful in the task to be performed.
© Tracy Pellett

Post-impact decisions:

1. Student—assess one's performance against criteria.
2. Teacher—offer feedback to learner about his or her role in self-check.

The self-check style can increase self-esteem for students who are comfortable working independently. One disadvantage of this style is that student interaction with the peer group and with the teacher is at a minimum. A computer can be used to monitor student progress in the self-check style. A number of different teaching/learning strategies can be used within the self-check style: testing activities used as learning activities, computer-assisted instruction (CAI), individualized learning packets, and contract learning.

The Inclusion Style (E)

The major difference between the inclusion style and the styles previously discussed is that in this style the learner selects the level of performance for each task and alters it according to each self-assessment of the performance. The teacher selects the task and defines the various levels of difficulty. The learner performs the skill at a level at which it is possible to achieve success. Some factors that contribute to differences in difficulty include distance, height of basket or net, size of ball or implement, weight of ball or implement, size of the target or hoop, angle of shot or kick, quantity of tasks to be done, and body positions. The task to be done must remain the same (e.g., all push-ups or all striking skills). Only degree of difficulty varies. The teacher should state, "The purpose of this style is for everyone to be successful."

Pre-impact decisions:

1. The same as style A.
2. Prepare the individual program for the tasks.

Impact decisions:

1. Describe the role of the learner.
2. Present the subject matter.
3. Explain logistics.

Post-impact decisions:

1. Teacher—observe class; offer feedback to individual learners.
2. Student—assess performance using criteria sheet.

The inclusion style permits all students to be successful at the task to be performed, thereby increasing each student's self-esteem and enjoyment of physical activity. For this reason, the inclusion style is especially important when teaching coed classes or classes that have mainstreamed disabled students. The inclusion style can be combined with other styles. Students choose from an inclusion skill checklist, which is a list of skills that can be performed at many levels. The checklist increases students' awareness of their own abilities and the ability to set realistic goals. Because students select their participation levels, learner anxiety is reduced. Some examples include:

1. Archery—Shoot 200 points in five consecutive ends at
   a. 20 yards.
   b. 25 yards.
   c. 30 yards.
   d. 35 yards.
2. Badminton—Do 10 consecutive underhand drop shots with a partner under a rope placed
   a. 20 inches above the net.
   b. 16 inches above the net.
   c. 12 inches above the net.
3. Volleyball—Volley the ball consecutively against the wall above a line eight feet high
   a. 5 times.
   b. 10 times.
   c. 15 times.
4. Swimming—Tread water
   a. 15 seconds.
   b. one minute.
   c. two minutes.

Procedures for creating the checklist are:

1. Determine the tasks.
2. For each task, determine one or more factors that change the level of difficulty of the skill.

3. Make a checklist of the tasks, quantity to be done, multiple performance levels, and criteria for successful performance.
4. Have students circle or put an X through the starting level and the level completed.

The Guided-Discovery Style (F)

The guided-discovery style leads the learner to discover a concept by answering a sequence of questions that the teacher presents. The teacher's role is to determine the concepts and principles to be taught and the best sequence for guiding the students to the specific response. As the students are involved in these strategies, the teacher varies the size and interrelationship of the steps and the speed of the learning sequence so that students are constantly moving toward the desired objective. The teacher should state, "The purpose of this style is to evoke the correct answer or response."

Pre-impact decisions:

1. Determine objectives.
2. Select concept to be discovered.
3. Design sequence of questions leading to the concept.

Impact decisions:

1. Teacher—present questions or clues to elicit the desired response; never tell the answer; maintain a climate of acceptance and patience.
2. Student—respond to sequential questions or clues.

Post-impact decisions:

1. Teacher—provide feedback.
2. Student—discover correct response.

The guided-discovery style requires a warm, accepting environment in which students are allowed time to think through their questions or responses and are helped to experience success in the discovery process. This style also requires a certain amount of risk on the teacher's part. The teacher must be able to trace backward from the desired objective to get the first question and the sequence from which to proceed. Whenever a student response deviates from the desired response, the teacher must be able to ask a question that brings the students back into the desired sequence. The advantage of the discovery style is its ability to help students understand the basic concepts of physical activity.

The Convergent Discovery Style (G)

In the convergent discovery style the teacher presents a question or problem and the student—through the use of logic, reasoning, critical thinking, and trial-and-error—discovers the single answer or solution. This style is different from guided discovery in that the student rather than the teacher determines the questions to be answered in solving the problem.

Pre-impact decisions:

1. Design the problem.

Impact decisions:

1. Teacher—observe learners.
2. Student—searches for solution to problem.

Post-impact decisions:

1. Student—verify solution
2. Teacher—ask questions to assist in verification.

The teacher's role is much different in the convergent discovery style. The teacher must have patience and allow the learner's ideas to evolve. This process takes time and the teacher must not interfere with the process.

The Divergent Production Style (H)

In the divergent production style, the student is encouraged to find multiple solutions to a given problem. The teacher selects the subject and designs the problem. The student discovers alternative solutions to the problem and evaluates them in terms of their effectiveness in solving the problem. In some situations in which the quality of the movement is part of the solution, verification must be done by the teacher. The teacher should state, "The purpose of this style is to engage in producing multiple responses to a single question. There is not one correct answer. It is all right to produce different responses." Individual problems can be offered to students, or problems can be clustered in groups. Finally, students can be allowed to select from a list of problems those that are relevant to their own interests.

Pre-impact decisions:

1. What is the general subject matter (i.e., tumbling, golf, modern dance)?
2. What is the specific topic (i.e., headstand, putt)?
3. What is the specific problem or series of problems that will elicit solutions (variations, downhill lie, in groups)?

Impact decisions:

1. Student—discover alternative answers to the problem.
2. Student—decide which multiple and divergent solutions are applicable to the problem.

Post-impact decisions:

1. Teacher—observe solution.
2. Student—evaluate the solution by asking, "Is my solution answering the question?"
3. Teacher—offer feedback about the learners' role in producing divergent ideas.

The divergent production style requires an environment in which the teacher feels secure enough to accept a wide variety of alternative solutions to problems. The teacher should respond to the *process* of discovery, not to the *value* of the particular response. Students must have time and a supportive environment in which to work out solutions. The major advantage of the divergent production style is its ability to help the student develop creativity. Social development depends on whether the student is working in a group or individually.

Styles I, J, and K

These styles increase the creativity of the student by allowing the learner to choose the problem and design the learning activities. These styles can be used only with individual students who are ready to take the initiative for their own behavior. The teacher's role is to facilitate the student's formulation of the problem, the learning activities, and the final presentation and evaluation. During learning, the student checks in periodically to keep the teacher up-to-date on the learning process.

In the learner's individual designed program, style I, the teacher selects the general subject matter area; the learner designs, develops, and performs a series of tasks in consultation with the teacher. An example would be a fitness unit in which the students design, conduct, and evaluate their own fitness programs. The learner-initiated style, style J, could occur when a student has a schedule conflict with physical education class and requests an alternative. The learner would select an activity, design the experiences, perform them, and then evaluate the experiences with the teacher's assistance. Style K, self-teaching, is rarely, if ever, used in school. The learner takes full responsibility for the learning process without input or consultation with the teacher.

Teaching Strategies

As teachers utilize teaching styles in the classroom they also incorporate various teaching strategies or instructional delivery systems to enhance the process of learning. The word *strategy* originally described the placement of an army in an advantageous position in relation to the enemy. As adopted by business and industry, strategy means the advantageous relationship of an organization to its environment. An instructional strategy is a particular arrangement of the teacher, learner, and environment to produce desired learning outcomes. Hurwitz defined an instructional strategy as "a plan for a pattern of actions aimed at one or more students achieving and demonstrating mastery of a specific goal or objective."[21]

The best teaching strategy is one that "pulls" the learner toward greater capacity without overstressing the capabilities of the learner.
© Tracy Pellett

Since learners respond differently to various strategies and since distinct strategies produce diverse outcomes, a number of strategies are presented to help in selecting the appropriate one for the subject, the learner, the teacher, and the instructional environment.

Selecting a Teaching Strategy

Consideration must be given to selecting appropriate strategies for students who lack self-motivation or discipline and for situations in which large classes are taught in limited facilities. There is no one best strategy for any one teaching style on the spectrum. Thus teachers should select strategies that best meet the needs of the instructional situation, and adapt each strategy to the parameters of that particular style. When selecting strategies to amplify the learning process, the prime consideration is high engaged time and large numbers of correct learning trials for students (refer to chapter 4).

Many strategies fit nicely into the physical education instructional process. Included for further discussion will be (1) lecture, (2) individualized instruction, (3) cooperative learning, (4) simulation, (5) problem solving, and (6) affective learning strategies.

Lecture

A lecture is a verbal presentation to an audience of a defined segment of information by one or more persons. Lectures include special reports, outside speakers, and panel discussions. A teacher might use a lecture to present rules, a panel discussion to elaborate on health concepts, or a police officer to speak on the dangers of drugs. Lectures can introduce, summarize, explain, or create interest in a topic. They can be used to impart information to a large group of students in a short time. When classes are large, limited student–student and student–teacher interactions may result in students misunderstanding the information. When using the lecture method in the classroom, prepare in such a way that the experience is meaningful and not limited to memory learning.

Procedures

1. Know the material.
2. Define the segment of material to be presented.
3. Organize the material to fit the time available.
4. Proceed from simple or familiar to complex or abstract.
5. Present the information in a motivational way.
    a. Use visual aids to support the topic.
    b. Relate the lecture to real life.
    c. Use humor.
    d. Repeat important points.
    e. Pace the material at the middle-level student.
6. Speak clearly and succinctly.
7. Be sensitive to feedback from listeners and modify the delivery accordingly.

Procedures for Special Reports or Outside Speakers

1. Make assignments well in advance.
2. Define the assignment clearly. Explain the topic and information wanted (and the ages and background of the class for outside speakers).

3. Help students make reports interesting by suggestions of topic, tips for presentation, and so forth.
4. Thank the speaker.

Procedures for Panel

1. Select and define the problem.
2. Choose and prepare panel participants in advance. All class members can be assigned to prepare and the panel can be chosen extemporaneously, or panel members can be assigned in advance.
3. Select a moderator who can stimulate questions and guide the discussion.

Individualized Instruction

Individualized instruction programs enable each learner to progress at his or her own pace. Such programs assume that students are capable of learning independently with minimum direction from teachers. "A major goal of individualization is to promote self-directed learners who are capable of engaging effectively in the process of decision making."[22] Teachers are then free to act as consultants to students who need or desire their assistance. Educators conceiving individualized methodologies must consider what the student already knows, what the student wants to know, and what the student needs to know.[23]

Familiarity with mastery learning, task sheets, contract learning, quests, and computer-assisted instruction are helpful when teachers attempt to individualize learning in physical education.

Mastery Learning

Mastery learning, as conceptualized by Benjamin Bloom,[24] is a theory of school learning based on the premise that almost all students can learn at a high level what the schools have to teach if given sufficient time and instructional help. Bloom asserted that children in schools are being taught as "good and poor" learners rather than "fast and slow" learners, and when students are provided with favorable learning conditions most of them become very similar with regard to learning ability. Students taught using mastery learning techniques are expected to succeed. Torshen suggested that this is the case because in mastery learning individual differences are taken into account.[25] Bloom's Learning for Mastery (LFM) is a group-based teacher-paced approach. It differs from Keller's Personalized System of Instruction (PSI), which is an individually based, student-paced model. Both systems employ many of the same components, but Bloom's model will be discussed in detail because it has been more widely used.

Mastery learning is not a new concept. Its roots go back to the Jesuit schools before the seventeenth century. Bloom and other twentieth-century theorists have structured the concepts into a well-known educational paradigm. Others have varied the model to suit their specific situations. The mastery model includes the following components:

1. *Performance objectives,* including criterion levels for student achievement that are set high enough to be demanding and challenging for all students. These objectives are made known to the students prior to instruction.
2. *Instructional activities,* including demonstration, explanation, and learning tasks that emphasize skill acquisition and application to the point of overlearning.
3. *Diagnostic assessment,* using formative tests that students repeat until mastery is achieved. Either the formative tests or a summative test administered at the end of a unit may be used for grading purposes.

4. *Feedback,* including test results so students know how they are progressing.
5. *Prescription,* including "correctives" for students who did not attain mastery and "enrichment activities" for those who did.

"Correctives" are activities engaged in by students who did not attain mastery, which enable most of them to do so on future formative tests. Such activities include practicing the tests, practicing the test skills in other ways, and personalized instruction from the teacher or a peer.

"Enrichment activities" are activities provided for students who have passed mastery tests and are waiting to move on to the next task. Such activities include probing deeper and more completely into the instructional task at hand, peer tutoring between students, and independent learning.

Students engage in learning activities involving correctives and enrichment activities until a certain percentage (usually 80 to 95 percent) of the class has attained mastery before moving on to a new task. More time to learn is needed in the initial phases of instruction because some students take longer to learn than others. Block pointed out that this time is reduced by the end of the course.[26] Students use time more efficiently as they become familiar with mastery learning procedures, and they also learn more-advanced skills faster once basic skills are mastered. Short units of one or two weeks are not sufficient for mastery learning principles to take effect.

Over the years, research on mastery learning has produced an impressive legacy of positive results. A number of literature reviews have consistently reported the beneficial effects of mastery approaches on a variety of learning outcomes.[27] However, most of the research has been done in the cognitive and affective domains. There is a lack of research documenting the effects of mastery learning on the acquisition of psychomotor skills.

Both Annarino[28] and Heitmann and Kneer[29] have emphasized mastery learning principles in physical education; however, very few studies have been done to substantiate their theories. Edwards determined that performance standards help individuals achieve significantly higher motor skill achievement scores.[30] Chambless, Anderson, and Poole demonstrated that stunts and tumbling achievement for mentally retarded children was significantly higher when mastery learning techniques were used.[31] Ashy and Lee found no significant differences on summative scores of throwing for kindergartners and first graders in mastery and nonmastery groups, although the mastery group did better.[32] Metzler showed that students in mastery classes benefited from higher intervals of ALT-PE than those in traditional classes.[33] Metzler and his colleagues used Keller's PSI model to teach college students enrolled in beginning tennis courses. They demonstrated that PSI students scored significantly higher than the conventional students on four measures of playing ability.[34] Blakemore reported that students using mastery learning techniques performed better than nonmastery learners, low-aptitude students and males performed better when using mastery techniques, and male and female performance was equalized in the mastery group. She also found that the results of mastery learning did not take effect until at least the fourth week of the unit. Thus, teachers must allot sufficient instructional time for mastery techniques to be productive.[35] Boyce demonstrated that a mastery criterion significantly influenced the acquisition and retention of a selected shooting task.[36]

Procedures

1. Complete a unit plan that is at least six weeks long.
2. Divide the unit of instruction into small teaching segments or subunits including tasks to be learned (i.e., volleyball: volley and bump, serve, spike and block). Decide on a hierarchical order to teach these tasks (see chapter 6 for content analysis procedures).

3. Preassess students on each task to determine entry levels and mastery criteria.
4. Devise specific objectives stating performance standards (scores) for each task based on preassessment results and previous testing (if possible).
5. Design formative tests to assess student competence for each task.
6. Teach the first subunit and allow students to practice.
7. Test all students to determine who mastered (passed) the formative tests included in the first subunit.
8. Provide feedback to each student based on the results of the formative tests.
9. Prescribe correctives or enrichment activities for each student. Provide individualized corrective activities to improve skill for those who have not mastered a task. Direct students who have mastered or passed a task to expand their performance of the specific skill in game situations, in more-advanced drills, and in peer tutoring circumstances.
10. Monitor students carefully as they engage in corrective or enrichment activities. Repeat the formative tests regularly for those who have not passed.
11. Teach a new subunit when 80 percent of the students have mastered the tasks of the present subunit.
12. Repeat this process of direct instruction, practice, diagnostic testing, mastery, and enrichment activities or correctives until the unit is complete.
13. If the formal model of Bloom is followed, administer a summative test.

Task sheets similar to the example shown in figure 7.4 could be used to monitor each student's progress toward mastery of the subunit tasks. The task sheet includes mastery scores and spaces to record results for several evaluations. It also includes corrective procedures (tasks 1–4), enrichment activities (tasks 5–7), and skill execution tips. Because this sheet allows the student to work independently, engaging the teacher only when specific help is needed, the teacher is free to interact with students requiring assistance.

Teachers often find teaching for mastery very time-consuming at its inception but discover that the rewards in the end are worth the effort. The rewards of mastery learning include (1) individual student success, (2) student willingness to practice, (3) progress easily identified, and (4) high levels of achievement.

Teachers incorporating mastery learning or other individualized learning techniques often desire to group students homogeneously by dividing students into smaller groups of similar ability levels. The following examples point out the practical application of such a strategy and its advantages and limitations.

Example (Layups):

1. Demonstrate layups to the class.
2. Have all students go to baskets to practice the layup progression.
3. As soon as it is determined that a student can do successful layups, have the student put on a pinnie but continue to practice using various types of layups.
4. As soon as enough students are wearing pinnies, start a half-court game with these players and move players without pinnies to other baskets.
5. Continue with 3, 4, and 5 until all players are successful.

Example (Archery):

1. Have all students shoot at 20 yards and score the best five consecutive ends.

```
                    Mastery Learning
          Racquetball Forehand/Backhand Task Sheet

  Name _____

                   Mastery Test Results

             30 Second Wall Volley Behind Short Line

  Passed:
  _____ A. Long Wall Volley: MASTERY is 15 points for FOREHAND
               (Record score and date)
               1. _____ 2. _____ 3. _____ 4. _____ 5. _____
            Date:
  _____ B. Long Wall Volley: MASTERY is 13 points for BACKHAND
               (List score and date)
               1. _____ 2. _____ 3. _____ 4. _____ 5. _____

            Date:
  IF YOU HAVE PASSED A AND B, GO TO TASK 5 BELOW:
  Check Off Tasks as They Are Passed

  Passed:
   1. Drop 20 balls; hit 15 correctly (as stated below). You or a
      partner may drop the balls. Catch the ball after each hit. The
      ball should hit the wall at the same height and straight ahead
      of where it is contacted. It should rebound to within an arm's
      length of where you are standing. An assistant should evaluate
      consistency/control, slicing, hooking, and height of ball.
   _____ 15 correctly hit balls with forehand standing mid-court.
   _____ 15 correctly hit balls with backhand standing mid-court.
   _____ 15 correctly hit balls with forehand standing 6 feet from
              the back wall.
   _____ 15 correctly hit balls with backhand standing 6 feet from
              the back wall.
   2. Stand at the side court and move to hit 20 balls that come to
      center court. Hit 15 correctly (as stated below). Your partner
      should hit or throw the ball to the front wall so it bounces
      to center court. Catch the ball each time it is hit.
   _____ 15 correctly hit balls standing mid-court with the
              forehand.
   _____ 15 correctly hit balls standing mid-court with the
              backhand.
```

Figure 7.4 Example of a mastery learning task sheet.

3. Drop the ball from behind the short line and continuously hit it off the front wall as stated below.

_____ 10 continuously hit balls with forehand.

_____ 10 continuously hit balls with backhand.

_____ 25 continuously hit balls with forehand in 2 minutes.

_____ 25 continuously hit balls with backhand in 2 minutes.

4. Practice the Long Wall Volley Test using either the forehand
_____ or backhand for 1 minute. Retake the test when you are ready.

5. With a partner, rally the ball continuously off the front wall using either forehand or backhand 25 times. Alternate hits
_____ with your partner.

6. With two or three other people, rally the ball continuously, establishing a sequence of hitting that is followed each time
_____ (e.g., John, Sally, Bill; John, Sally, Bill).

7. With a partner, play a modified game. The server stands between the red lines and puts the ball into play by bouncing it and then hitting so it rebounds off the front wall. The ball must then bounce on the floor beyond the red lines. The receiver may stand anywhere beyond the red lines to receive the ball. The server scores a point if the receiver makes an error. The receiver becomes the server if the server makes an error. The receiver does not score points. Play continues to 15 points.

Forehand Form

1. Face side wall, with racquet arm away from front wall. The feet are a shoulder's width apart with the left foot slightly closer to the side wall (right-handed player).

2. Bend knees comfortably.

3. Hold racquet arm back and perpendicular to body with the racquet head pointing to ceiling about shoulder level.

4. Contact ball between waist and knee as you step forward (skilled players will contact the ball at the knee).

5. Snap wrists and follow through to opposite shoulder so body now faces the front wall.

Backhand Form

1. Face side wall, with racquet arm close to front wall. The feet are a shoulder's width apart with the right foot slightly closer to the side wall (right-handed player).

2. Bend knees comfortably.

3. Bring racquet across midsection of body with elbow bent to form a 90 degree angle with the upper arm (L) a few inches from the body.

4. Point the racquet head to the ceiling near the shoulder.

5. Contact the ball between the knee and waist as described above for the forehand.

6. Snap wrists and follow through to head height away from the body.

Figure 7.4 (Continued)

2. Have students who score 200 points at a given distance move back five yards if there is enough room to do so safely (or move the target back five yards).
3. Students will soon be shooting at various distances designated by the teacher. The students at the closest distances need the most help.

Uses:

1. To identify students needing help with skill development.
2. To enrich the learning of advanced students.
3. To enhance safety.

Advantages:

1. The teacher can work with students who need the most help.
2. Advanced students can move on to new objectives.
3. Student effort increases.
4. Student effort is rewarded.

Limitations:

1. Advanced planning is necessary.
2. Supervising many groups doing different things at the same time may be difficult.
3. The testing situation is often emphasized rather than game play.

Task Sheets

Task sheets are used to motivate students to practice tasks and keep a record of learning activities. They shift some of the decisions for learning to the student, thereby involving students in on-task behavior and eliminating standing around or "goofing off." Some students require extra help to succeed in working on their own, but they will grow by doing so, and students will learn to accept the consequences for their learning decisions. The task sheets include lists of tasks to be done, with instructions for performance, such as quantity, quality, and use of equipment. Two examples of task sheets are shown in figures 7.5 and 7.6.

Although extra preparation is necessary to create task sheets, they can be extremely valuable for preclass activities, as well as during class time. Task sheets can be issued to each student, and items can be checked off by partners, team captains, student assistants, or the teacher. A composite list can be maintained by the teacher. Task sheets may form part of the grade for a unit.

Procedures

1. Select appropriate instructional objectives.
2. Select activities in terms of objectives and learning problems. Tasks should be relevant to group members.
3. Create task sheets that include:
   a. A description of the tasks, including diagrams or sketches.
   b. Specific points to look for in the performance.
   c. Samples of possible feedback.
4. Check to be sure students understand the purpose of the tasks and the criteria for correct performance.
5. Provide for facilitation of the observation by incorporating a system of:
   a. Comparison of the performance with the criterion for correct performance.

```
                    SKILL REQUIREMENTS FOR TENNIS

Rally Rascals—C Grade                    Name _____


      Exercises
_____  1. Fifty down bounces using forehand grip.
_____  2. Fifty up bounces using forehand grip.
_____  3. Twenty-five reverse bounces using forehand grip.


   Wall or Backboard Practice
_____  4. Return at least ten consecutive forehands. One bounce only from
          baseline.
_____  5. Return at least five consecutive backhands. One bounce only from
          baseline.


   Tossed Balls
_____  6. Return five moving forehands in a row from no man's land to no
          man's land without an error. Repeat three times.
_____  7. Repeat above for backhand.
_____  8. Return eight out of ten moving forehands from baseline to
          baseline.
_____  9. Return five out of eight moving backhands from baseline to
          baseline.
_____ 10. Return five out of eight moving forehand volleys to no man's land.
_____ 11. Return five out of eight moving backhand volleys to no man's land.


   Self-Tossed Balls
_____ 12. Put ten consecutive forehands into play from the baseline to the
          baseline.
_____ 13. Put five out of ten backhands into play from the baseline to the
          baseline.
_____ 14. Serve five out of ten fast serves into either court.


   Rally Practice
_____ 15. Short court rally for at least ten times.
_____ 16. With an experienced player, play a pro set.
```

Figure 7.5 A skill checklist—tennis.
Source: Ann Valentine, Brigham Young University.

    b. Communication of the results to the performer during and after the completion of each task.

6. Select partners or groups. Have students select a partner they have not worked with before.

Contract Learning and Quests

Contract learning is the use of an individual learning packet in which a student contracts (or agrees) with the teacher to complete specified objectives in order to receive a specified grade.

```
                        BADMINTON SKILL CHECKLIST

Name _____

_____   20 consecutive underhand drop shots in a rally with a partner.

_____   8 out of 10 short serves between short service line and white
           line.

_____   Score 25 short serves on court with rope 12 inches above net and
           target in right court.

_____   8 out of 10 long serves on court with target in right court.

_____   Score 20 long serves on court with target in right court.

_____   8 out of 10 smashes with partner setting up (shots that can be
           returned with some effort by the partner cannot be counted).

_____   8 out of 10 clears (overhead) with partner setting up (must land
           between the two back boundary lines).

_____   8 out of 10 clears (underhand) with partner setting up (must land
           between the two back boundary lines).

_____   Read the handout on scoring and score one game.

Complete the following play patterns with a partner (you should be player A
and player B in each case).

_____   Player A—Serve
                   B—Clear to deep backhand
                   A—Drive down sideline
                   B—Clear to deep forehand
                   A—Clear to deep backhand
                   B—Drive cross court

_____   Player A—Serve
                   B—Clear to deep backhand
                   A—Drop to the forehand
                   B—Clear to the deep forehand
                   A—Clear to the deep backhand
                   Repeat
```

Figure 7.6   Badminton skill checklist.

Contracts individualize learning by allowing students to select different tasks or learning activities and to take responsibility for their own learning and self-assessment. They permit students to work at their own pace on clearly defined tasks. Types of contracts include (1) teacher-controlled contracts in which the teacher determines the tasks and reinforcers, (2) transitional contracting in which the student and the teacher share decision making, and (3) student-controlled contracts in which the student determines the tasks and reinforcers. If the student writes the objectives as well, the contract is called a quest. An example of a contract is the gymnastics grade contract shown in figure 7.7. Some limitations of contracts might include the necessity of

```
Gymnastics Grade Contract

     Please read the following contract carefully and ask any
questions you may have. Remember: Teachers do not give students
grades; students earn the grades they receive.

              * * * * * * * * * *

Name _____ Period _____

I contract for an A B C (circle one) based on the criteria below:

Starting date _____ Ending date _____

Student signature _____ Teacher signature _____

Requirements for an A:
  1. Attend class regularly, be dressed, and participate each day.
  2. Actively participate in all activities taught by your
     instructor.
  3. Earn a minimum score of fourteen out of twenty on the written
     examination.
  4. Learn and perform for the instructor fourteen stunts from any
     or all of the events at the advanced level.
  5. Select and complete fourteen Learning Experience points from
     the class list.

Requirements for a B:
  1. Attend class regularly, be dressed, and participate each day.
  2. Actively participate in all activities taught by your
     instructor.
  3. Earn a minimum score of twelve out of twenty on the written
     examination.
  4. Learn and perform for the instructor twelve stunts from any or
     all of the events at the intermediate level.
  5. Select and complete twelve Learning Experience points from the
     class list.

Requirements for a C:
  1. Attend class regularly, be dressed, and participate each day.
  2. Actively participate in all activities taught by your
     instructor.
  3. Earn a minimum score of ten out of twenty on the written
     examination.
  4. Learn and perform for the instructor ten stunts from any or
     all of the events at the beginning level.
  5. Select and complete ten Learning Experience points from the
     class list.
```

Figure 7.7 A gymnastics contract.
Source: Linda Fleming and Joyce M. Harrison,
Brigham Young University.

using additional media and outside facilities, the time-consuming preparation involved, and the fact that some students are not ready to work on their own without constant teacher direction.

Quests allow students to set and pursue their own goals at their own pace and to take responsibility for their own learning. They encourage individual initiative and creativity and decrease unhealthy competition between students, since each student has different goals. However,

---

A Quest Contract

1. My objectives

2. My learning activities

3. My plans for evaluation
   _____ videotape recording
   _____ expert or professional
   _____ other:

4. I plan to present evidence of my achievement of each objective by

   _____
   (Date)

5. My contract is for an _____ grade.

   _____   _____
   Signature of student   Date

   _____   _____
   Signature of instructor   Date

Figure 7.8 A quest contract.

since students are doing different types of projects, teachers may find it difficult to state or measure the quality of each quest. Some teachers have difficulty letting students do their own thing. An example of a quest contract is shown in figure 7.8.

Procedures

1. Specify the performance and/or process objectives for a given unit of study. Identify levels (e.g., A, B, C).
2. Specify possible learning activities and learning materials.
3. Devise the contract. The teacher may do this, or the teacher and student may work together.
4. Develop evaluation methods and materials, including progress checks that tell students when performance objectives have been accomplished. (They also serve as reinforcers.)
5. Divide the instructional unit into blocks that provide ample time for activities to be taught, practiced, and evaluated.
6. Meet together as teacher and student or teacher and class to discuss the conditions of the contract and specify proposed dates for the completion of various phases of the contract.
7. Begin the instruction or activity phase with the teacher serving as a resource person when needed.

8. Evaluate progress with the criteria agreed upon. The teacher and student may need to revise the contract along the way. Performance that does not meet acceptable standards should either be redone or receive a lower grade.
9. Submit completed contract and award a grade based on the specified criteria.

Computer-Assisted Instruction

Computer-assisted instruction (CAI) is rapidly assuming the roles formally played by individualized learning packets and programmed learning. CAI is usually used for learning in the cognitive domain. It can be used to learn material, review previously learned material, or test the level of learning. The use of CAI may occur during class time but is most beneficial when used as a required assignment to be completed outside of class.[37] More class time is then available to work on psychomotor skills.[38]

CAI consists of the following characteristics: (1) Content is divided into small steps and carefully organized into a logical sequence with each step building on the preceding step; (2) the student is presented with and actively responds to one question at a time; (3) the student receives immediate knowledge of results; (4) each student can progress at his or her own rate; and (5) programs are written or created to ensure a minimum of error.

Computers encourage student responsibility for learning. Immediate knowledge of results yields higher learner motivation and confidence. Programs insist that each point be thoroughly understood; therefore, CAI works well for slower students and results in learning efficiency per unit of time.

Programs are usually written using one of two formats. In one format each student reads the same material but at a speed the individual chooses. In the other format each student begins with the same material. However, the computer selects the next material depending on the student's responses. A student who correctly answers a question will be presented with different material than an individual who needs further study of the concept. This method ensures a thorough understanding of material prior to being exposed to new material. Computers can also be programmed to keep a record of each student's progress.

A current disadvantage of this strategy is the lack of computer programs available. Use of this technique requires computer programming knowledge or the availability of authoring programs. A few easy-to-use authoring programs are available.

Procedures
1. Define the concept, rule, or strategy.
2. List as many examples of the concept as possible.
3. List as many nonexamples of the concept as possible.
4. Create a question that tests understanding of the concept.
5. Determine the next step depending on the answer selected.
6. Try out and revise.

Cooperative Learning

A current trend in the academic classroom is toward more cooperative learning strategies. In cooperative learning a team of students work together to help its members achieve a certain goal, progressing only as fast as all members have learned each skill or passed each quiz. Cooperative learning is based on the philosophy that students make no effort to learn unless schools satisfy student needs to belong. Glasser believes that to the extent that we can satisfy our needs to survive and gain love, power, fun, and freedom, we gain effective control over our lives. Ultimately, students get the idea that knowledge is power.[39] Cooperative learning "places the responsibility for learning where it belongs, on the students."[40] As students gain a greater sense of control, their attitudes toward school learning and classmates improve,[41] and a larger percentage of students work on-task, resulting in better classroom behavior.[42] Although more time-consuming than teacher-directed strategies, cooperative learning significantly increases student academic performances, social interaction, and group participation, communication, and leadership skills. It also makes teaching and learning more fun.[43] All these benefits can lead to a more effective learning environment.

Cooperative learning increases student involvement in learning and motivates slower learners to improve their performance while reinforcing the learning of faster learners. Heterogeneous grouping increases learning for all students. Low-skilled students benefit by observing high-skilled students. High-skilled students gain greater insight through teaching.

The physical education classroom is an ideal setting for cooperative learning. In his reciprocal style, Mosston assigned pairs of students to work cooperatively together, with each student given responsibility as either the observer or the doer. Cooperative learning can help students internalize and apply physical education principles. For example, the lesson focus may be to perform a proper free throw in basketball. The students need to understand the biomechanics of body alignment, the impact of spin on ball rebound patterns, the appropriate angle of ball projection, and so forth. The teacher provides this information using a lecture format, written materials, appropriate group work, or some combination of these. While practicing free throws in small groups the social skills needed are (1) observing student practice, (2) evaluating performance based on correct mechanics, (3) communicating to the performer what the skill looked like, and (4) providing accurate feedback to the performer for skill improvement. When students learn and teach each other, they will be more likely to apply these concepts in their own lives.

Students need time to learn how to work together, how to communicate effectively, and how to take responsibility for their own learning. Therefore, teachers should not be discouraged early in the process. The hard work the teacher does at the beginning of the learning process will pay large dividends in student performance later on. Preplanning is necessary, including planning for specific group dynamics. Students must be taught cooperation skills, just as they are taught psychomotor skills or classroom management skills, by modeling, practice, feedback, and more practice. "For true cooperation to take place, students must realize that they will sink or swim together."[44]

Procedures[45]

1. State lesson objectives clearly:
   a. Information required for students to understand and apply the concept or to understand the mechanics of the skill.
   b. Social skills necessary during group work (i.e., cooperation, listening, communicating, supporting, evaluating, giving feedback).
   c. Psychomotor skills to be mastered.
2. Group students heterogeneously into learning "teams." Make sure best friends are not grouped together, otherwise the activity may become entirely social.
3. Communicate goals and expectations clearly to enhance group skills, ensure responsible learning of materials, and attain appropriate skill performance levels. Use task sheets if desired.

a. Model the appropriate performance.
b. Give directions and/or task sheet, including evaluation cues. Structure activities to establish a feeling of positive interdependence among group members. To do this:
   1) Give only one copy of information to each group (e.g., rules or strategies sheets, task sheet).
   2) Give each group member part of the information or a specific part of the assignment to be shared with others. Each student studies his or her information with students from other groups who were assigned the same information. The student then shares what was learned with his or her own group. This is called *jigsawing*.
   3) Instruct the group to produce one report, game strategy, and so on (e.g., the risk factors for cardiovascular disease), with each member researching one area to contribute to the final report.
   4) Give the groups complex tasks to complete while keeping the group relatively small. Ask groups for a complex report such as identifying offensive strategies and their rationale based on their own strengths and weaknesses and the strengths and weaknesses of the opposition.
   5) Make the group responsible for reciprocal instruction, that is, students should model for and teach each other. Teachers must model positive ways of providing feedback and provide students with specific techniques.
c. Assign specific group roles. Keep groups small. With two to three students in a group, the student roles are performer, observer, and leader/timekeeper. Instruct students in effective group techniques. Give each student a specific group role or assignment. Roles should change regularly. For example, while practicing dribbling one student performs the dribble, one gives feedback, and one acts as the leader who makes sure everyone gets a turn. Each person has a designated time with the ball and time for specific feedback. Roles are designed to facilitate the group and give responsibility to each group member. Groups can be trained to automatically establish group roles for every group assignment. Roles can be posted on a wall for quick referral.
   1) *Performer:* Performs the established skill.
   2) *Recorder:* Records the number of trials, key points of the group discussion, report to be presented to class, and so on.
   3) *Observer:* Observes and evaluates individual or group performance and gives recommendations or feedback. Makes sure all members are involved.
   4) *Presenter:* Reports group progress or report to the class or teacher.
   5) *Timer:* Keeps track of practice or discussion time.
   6) *Leader:* Keeps the group on-task, makes assignments, follows through with teacher directions.
d. Set time limits. The teacher is then free to work with problems instead of playing the role of whistle-blower or timekeeper.
4. Move throughout the class, monitoring each group's progress and giving individual instruction where needed.
5. Evaluate all objectives.

a. Give grades or feedback based both on how the group performed as a unit and how students performed individually. Students can be held accountable for doing their share by means of the individual quiz. Encourage cooperation by giving bonus points if everyone in a group scores at least 85 percent on the individual quiz.[46] Occasionally use group quizzes, in which each person is responsible for leading the discussion for a question; the group must reach a consensus for each answer.

b. Have each group member write a brief evaluation of the group about halfway through the project and at the conclusion of the project. If the group is not working well together, do not intervene immediately; encourage them to work together and do their own problem solving. Provide helpful hints, but do not coerce compliance. Have the group take responsibility for itself. Removal of a group member is the last resort and should be used only when serious trouble is erupting. Reorganize groups for the next project.

Several strategies that use cooperative learning in physical education have been reported in the literature. Baseline Basketball and Class Team Tennis are two round-robin tournament strategies reported by Eason. They are described in chapter 8. Sterne also used the team, game, tournament strategy to teach skills.[47] Glover and Midura call cooperative learning "team building." They use physical challenges, which are described in chapter 8, to accomplish their goals.[48]

Simulation

An excellent teaching aid is a simulation of an event. Once again the "doing" aspect of learning is built into the learning experience. Students not competing on an athletic or intramural team may never have the experience of playing with official rules, referees, and scorers. Simulation activities are selective simplifications or representations of real-life situations in game or laboratory-type settings. They can be used to promote the learning of game skills, knowledge, attitudes, strategies, and social skills. Possible experiences include a simulated track or gymnastics meet. Figure 7.9 illustrates a simulation of a diving meet that also involves students in the administration of the event.

Activities not usually performed in a gymnasium can be adapted to the school site. For example, tennis and bowling can be simulated in a gym to provide students a fairly authentic experience.[49] Cross-country skiing can be taught during the winter months, utilizing both the outside playing fields and the gymnasium.[50] One teacher designed a nine-hole golf course in the locker-room areas of the physical education building by contacting local carpet stores for pieces of carpet and using discarded or broken pieces of sports equipment. A floor plan of the course was first designed and then transferred to the carpet. The carpet was then cut to fit the appropriate area. Scorecards, similar to those on a regulation golf course, were duplicated, and golf course courtesy was observed. The course design was limited only by the imagination of the individual.[51] The same type of ingenuity might create a course outside on a grassy playing area using whiffle or Cayman (short-flight) balls for safety.

Disadvantages of simulation are the increased time needed for preparation and learning and the expense involved in providing actual equipment in some instances. Some teachers complain that simulation activities oversimplify real situations.

Procedures for Simulation Activities

1. Counsel students on how to accomplish the objectives of the assignment.
2. Tell what the results have to do with real life.

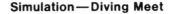

Simulation—Diving Meet

There are three students at each station. The rotation from station to station is illustrated here. Students change stations after three divers have each performed two dives. The teacher roves back and forth between the two scoring tables to offer needed assistance. Eighteen people can participate at one time, and more can be added.

Scorers   XXX   Announcer

XXX Judges

XXX

Divers

XXX

XXX Judges

Announcer   XXX   Scorers

Equipment Needed

1. Extra diving forms
2. Ten sharp pencils with erasers
3. Two diving calculators
4. Six judges scoring cards
5. Two tables and twelve chairs
6. Extra towels
7. Instructions taped to the announcer's and scorer's tables (in case they have trouble remembering their duties).

There are six teams (assigned by the instructor to assure the teams are evenly divided according to diving ability). Each team (consisting of three members) should select a captain and a name. Each team captain has the responsibility of writing each team member's two (2) dives on the diving sheet with their names in the left margin.

Figure 7.9 A simulated diving meet.
Source: Jack Romine and Joyce M. Harrison,
Brigham Young University.

3. Supervise student activities.
4. Progress from simple to complex.
5. Emphasize the meaning of the simulation activity through preassessment and follow-up.
6. Assign heterogeneous teams.
7. Allow teams to select their own positions in the group.
8. Place faculty in legitimate roles, not as advisers to teams.
9. Define rules.
10. Play the game.
11. Evaluate the results and provide feedback.
12. Discuss principles involved.
13. Allow students to create their own games.

Problem-Solving Strategies

Problem-solving strategies can be used to develop the ability to solve problems and verify solutions to problems. They can also be used to encourage the application of concepts already learned. If done in a group, they can encourage student interaction and teamwork. They encourage the use of cognitive processes other than memory and increase retention. However, they are more time-consuming than teacher-dominated instruction and can take time away from practicing psychomotor skills.

The problem-solving techniques that will be discussed further include (1) questioning, (2) inquiry learning, and (3) brainstorming and buzz sessions. Other examples of problem-solving strategies are choreographing dance or gymnastics routines, developing new games with given parameters, or thinking up and sharing new plays for games. Most of the affective learning activities also fall into the category of problem solving. Problem solving has been discussed previously in chapter 4.

When problem-solving strategies are used, keep in mind that it is difficult to meaningfully involve some students (e.g., slow learners, culturally disadvantaged, and students who lack the knowledge necessary to solve the problem) in problem-solving situations.

Procedures

1. Define the problem in a few words.
2. State conditions necessary for the problem to be considered solved.
3. List possible solutions.
4. Find the best solution based on the desired outcomes.
5. Evaluate success in solving the problem.

Questioning Strategies

Teachers use questions to arouse interest and hold attention, to help learners perceive the referent of a concept or discover a specific relationship or principle, to stimulate thought, develop understanding, apply information, develop appreciations and attitudes, or to emphasize a point or clarify a misconception. Questioning can also be used to evaluate student understanding and learning. Its use during a lecture increases individual student participation and understanding. Questioning requires considerable skill on the part of the teacher to accomplish the objective without embarrassing students or limiting the responses to only a few students. Some examples of questions at the various levels of the cognitive taxonomy include the following:

1. *Knowledge or fact questions:* who, what, where, when. Involves recognition or recall of facts, events, places, or names.
2. *Comprehension:* Compare the belief in (subject) of . . . and . . . Explain in your own words. Involves understanding of what was expressed.
3. *Application:* If you were . . . , what might you do? How does this apply in our lives? Involves using knowledge in new ways.
4. *Analysis:* Give evidence. . . . Explain. . . . What caused . . . ? What effect was caused by . . . ? Tell why. . . . Involves breaking information into parts.
5. *Synthesis:* Write a journal of your reactions to your fitness program. Describe how physical education makes a difference in your life. Involves combining parts to make a whole.
6. *Evaluation:* Should people . . .? Judge whether behavior was right or wrong. Defend the . . . Involves making judgments based on standards.

Procedures

1. Preparation. Prepare questions that:
   a. Relate to the purpose of the lesson.
   b. Are clear, definite, and easily understood.

    c. Engage the attention of the whole class.

    d. Relate to the student's world and interests.

    e. Cause students to stretch their minds.

    f. Take into account individual differences in such areas as intelligence and background experiences.

    g. Avoid manipulation of student responses.

    h. Build on knowledge students now have.

    i. Can be answered in the time available.

    j. Are phrased in such a way as to provoke a discussion rather than a simple yes or no.

2. Inform students prior to instruction that they will be expected to answer questions. To stimulate thinking, the teacher may want to introduce the discussion session with a story, diagram, chart, video, compact disk, object, case study, or a well-planned question written on the chalkboard.

3. Ask questions by:

    a. Directing the question to the entire class, pausing, and then calling on volunteers.

    b. Directing the question to the entire class, pausing, and then calling on a specific student.

    c. Directing a question from one student to another student or the entire class.

4. Encourage student involvement by:

    a. Pausing after each question to encourage thoughtful and meaningful responses (at least three seconds). Say, "Think carefully before you answer," wait, then call on someone.

    b. Using nonvolunteers. Inform students that they will be encouraged to contribute and that they might be called whether or not their hands are raised. If a student hesitates, say, "Think about it for a minute and we'll come back to you."

    c. Redirecting questions. Ask one question, then ask, "Jane, can you add anything else?" or just nod at another student. Encourage students to direct questions to other students.

    d. Rephrasing. Listen to the student's answer and then restate what was heard. For example, "Barry, do you mean . . .?" Avoid inserting personal reactions into the answer.

    e. Probing. Accept the student's initial response and then ask the student to extend, justify, or clarify it by asking, "Can you tell me more, Nathan?" Probing helps the student think more carefully and express a more complete answer.

5. When answers are off the subject, only partially complete or correct, or wrong, treat responses with courtesy and tact.

    a. Say something like, "That's not quite right. Let's think it through together."

    b. Avoid rejecting good ideas that were not the hoped for answer. Instead, rephrase the question.

    c. Avoid negative responses that might lower the student's self-esteem or discourage future responses. Always attempt to make the student feel good about responding.

    d. Avoid praising answers excessively. Other students may assume their answers were no good.

6. Keep the discussion organized by relating questions to previous answers or to questions students raise about the topic under discussion.
7. Summarize often to show students the progress they are making toward a solution, to focus the class on the solution, and to emphasize truths students are learning. Give credit to students who make important contributions. Use students to summarize when appropriate, and list the main points on the chalkboard.
8. Show how the solution can be applied to real life. Challenge the students to apply it.
9. Evaluate any questions against the following criteria:
   a. Did the sequence of questions display a logical development of ideas leading students directly to the heart of the problem and to its solution?
   b. Was each question related in some useful way to the problem statement?
   c. Was the question accurately stated, specific, and to the point?
   d. Was the question within the ability of the student to whom it was addressed?
   e. Was the question relevant to students?
   f. Did the question stimulate students to think and investigate?[52]

Inquiry Learning

Inquiry learning is a process through which students learn how to seek out answers scientifically by asking thought-provoking questions. The most commonly used example is the game Twenty Questions. Although inquiry learning is more time-consuming than conventional learning, it tends to help students learn how to learn by putting the responsibility for learning directly on them, thereby providing more meaningful learning.

Procedures

1. Provide and introduce the focus of the lesson—a puzzling or unfamiliar object, event, or situation.
2. Define the rules of questioning.
   a. All questions must be answered by yes or no.
   b. Ask only one question at a time.
   c. One student may ask a series of questions until a train of thought has been completed.
   d. Students may confer or call for a summary at any time.
3. Answer questions to help students gather data and verify information, reminding students of the rules when necessary.
4. Help students organize the information they have obtained, identify relationships among the variables, and create hypotheses to explain the situation. For example, if x is true, then would y be so?
5. Summarize the questioning procedure and identify how it can be improved.

Brainstorming and Buzz Sessions

Brainstorming means generating solutions to a defined problem by stating any relevant idea that comes to mind. For example, a small group of students might generate ideas for a new game or dance. In a buzz session, a large group is divided into small groups of people who generate ways to solve a problem. Group members can be rotated to increase the diversity of ideas. Both techniques can be used to solve a specific problem or to define creative approaches to problem solving. They can result in individual creativity, maximum group participation, and unique, creative solutions to problems.

Procedures

1. State the problem clearly.
2. Establish a time limit of five to ten minutes.
3. List ideas about the subject on a chalkboard or paper as they come to mind with no attempt to evaluate them. Try to list as many ideas as possible.
4. At the end of the time specified, the teacher restates the problem and helps students evaluate the ideas.

Affective Learning Strategies

Although attitudes are part of the teaching-learning process at all times, some specific strategies can be used to enhance the teaching of affective behaviors. Many of these activities can take time away from physical activity, but they are important to the acquisition of affective skills.

Affective behaviors can be learned during actual situations that arise during classroom interaction or during planned activities. The preferred method in physical education is to teach affective behaviors through actual experience in situations as they arise. However, some affective activities can be used on rainy days, during assembly schedules, and on other days when time does not permit dressing for activity.

Developing attitudes toward activities necessitates knowing something about the activity; therefore, students should first learn the skills and knowledge relevant to that activity. By pairing a new skill or bit of knowledge with a preferred or rewarding activity, students may acquire a liking for the new skill or knowledge. Gagné generalized that "success in some learning accomplishment is likely to lead to a positive attitude toward that activity."[53]

A number of techniques for learning affective behavior have been included with the teaching strategies in chapter 4. Their use will be more effective in a democratic classroom environment. Additional techniques are presented here.

Reaction and Opinion Papers

Reaction and opinion papers are papers submitted by students expressing their feelings, opinions, or reactions to something. They can be used to increase student awareness of their own feelings, as well as to increase teacher awareness of student feelings. Since there is no one right answer, every student can be included. However, some students may not feel free to express their true feelings when names are included on papers or when students are graded on their responses. Writing can sometimes be done as homework to decrease time spent in lieu of physical activity. Some examples of reaction and opinion papers include:

1. "I Urge" telegrams: Send a "telegram" urging someone to do something, change something, or stop doing something. For example, "To Mother, I urge you to stop smoking. Your loving daughter."[54]
2. "I Learned" statements: Write a brief statement of what you learned by doing a specific activity, for example, going on a field trip or participating in a challenging activity such as rappelling.[55]
3. Write reactions to a statement or quote such as "It's not whether you win or lose, but how you play the game," or "Winning is not the most important thing; it is the only thing," or "When the going gets tough, the tough get going," or "They didn't really lose the game; they only lost the score."

Procedures

1. Establish a nonthreatening, supportive environment in which students feel free to express their feelings.
2. Have students write their feelings about some specific topic.
3. Avoid grading reaction papers.

Goal Setting

Students learn to set realistic goals through practice. Since students have various abilities and backgrounds, they should be helped to set goals that are challenging and yet can result in successful achievement. Students will often set goals lower than their true expectations so they will not be penalized by failure to meet their goals. Some ideas for goal setting are as follows:

1. The Goalpost:[56]
   a. Decorate the bulletin board in the form of a goalpost.
   b. Have students record goals on footballs (use 3″ × 5″ cards) and post them below the crossbar.
   c. Each day students achieve their goals, they can move the football above the goalpost.
   d. Allow students time to share their successes with the class.
2. The Envelope:
   a. Have students record long-term goals.
   b. Place them in a sealed envelope for each class.
   c. Open the envelope at the end of the unit and redistribute them so students can see their progress.
   d. Allow students to share their successes.

Procedure

1. Help students think of ideas for goals using the following or other techniques:
   a. Questions.
      1) What skill would you like to be able to do better when we complete this unit?
      2) What talent do you wish you had?
   b. Suppose a doctor just told you that you have only one year to live. What would you do differently? How would you change your life? What is stopping you from doing these things now? Let's set a goal to achieve some of them.[57]
2. Help students clarify goals. Goals should be:
   a. Clearly defined.
   b. Desirable, worthwhile, challenging.
   c. Achievable.
   d. Measurable in terms of time and quantity.
   e. Controllable (goals involving another person require that person's permission).
   f. Designed so that achievement results in a better self.[58]

Discussion

Group consideration of a question or real-life problem can help students clarify values and concepts. Students can discuss the implications of the problem and how it is similar to and different from other problems they are familiar with. Through individual participation, students have opportunities to organize and communicate their thoughts and to learn respect for the viewpoints of others. Care must be taken, however, to encourage everyone to participate, rather than allowing a few talkative students to monopolize the conversation or reverting to a question-answer session. The following ideas can help to initiate a discussion:

1. Continuum.
   a. Draw a continuum on the chalkboard.
   b. Label 0 in the center, degrees toward the ends, and name the ends:

Cooperative									Competitive
Clark	40	30	20	10	0	10	20	30	40	Connie

   c. Have students place themselves on the continuum. (Do not let them position themselves in the center.)
   d. Discuss where the most popular, happiest, or capable student would be and why.
2. Priority or ranking.[59]
   a. Rank a list of three to five situations from best to worst.
   b. Think of a situation that is better than and one that is worse than the situations given.
   c. Discuss the rankings.
   d. Example: Rank the actions you might take when you see another student cheating off your paper on a test.
      1) Do nothing.
      2) Hide your paper.
      3) Tell the teacher.
3. Value voting.[60]
   a. Read questions and have the class vote for or against each one.
   b. Sample questions:
      1) Would you try rappelling?
      2) Would you turn in a friend who cheated on a test?
      3) Case studies or moral dilemmas. Discuss situations that require a decision and a plan of action (see example in chapter 4).
      4) Devil's advocate. Take a nonpopular view of an issue and encourage reactions from students.
      5) Incomplete sentences. Have students complete sentences such as the following and discuss them: Competition is . . . Winning is . . .

Procedures

1. Make sure students have the knowledge on which the discussion will be based.
2. Define the topic.
3. Work from an idea such as a visual aid, demonstration, quote, provocative question, or film.
4. Keep to the topic.
5. Involve everyone who wants to participate; avoid required participation.
6. Summarize periodically.
7. Draw conclusions.

Role Playing

Role playing is an exploration of interpersonal relations problems by re-creating or acting out real-life situations and then discussing them. Problems can include social events, personal concerns, values, problem behaviors, or social skills. Some examples are the following:

1. A coach kicks a player off the team for not conforming to the rules regarding length of hair. The student threatens the coach's safety.
2. A football player fails a test in English and is ineligible for the championship game this weekend. You are the player's best friend and the English teacher is your aunt.

Sensitivity modules, such as staying in a wheelchair for a day to see what being handicapped is like or swimming without the use of the legs, can increase student empathy for others. Through playing the roles of other people, students can explore and begin to understand the feelings, attitudes, and values of others in social situations, as well as the consequences of their behaviors on others. As they become more aware of the values of society, they also develop an awareness of alternative ways to solve problems. Some students are comfortable with role playing because they can act out their own feelings without fear of reprisal. Others have difficulty portraying feelings, so avoid embarrassing these students.

Procedures

1. Define the problem situation, which might include social problems, personal concerns, values, problem behaviors, or social skills. Choose easy problems first.
2. Prepare role sheets that describe the feelings or values of the character to be played (optional).
3. Introduce students to a problem through a real-life situation far enough away from the students to remove threat or stress yet close enough to draw out the relationship between the behavior in the problem and parallel behavior within the class or school. Ask students to think about what they would do under the same circumstances.
4. Select participants from volunteers. Avoid assigning roles based on peer pressure or the natural role of the student. Assign minor roles to shy individuals. Use role sheets if desired.
5. Clarify the setting, that is, place, time, situation, roles.
6. Assign observers specific things to look for, such as feelings of certain players or alternative endings.
7. Role-play several times if needed to bring out possible alternative behaviors and their consequences.
8. Discuss behaviors and feelings. Relate the role-playing situation to students' actual behavior in a nonthreatening way.
9. Discuss the role-playing situation, successes and failures, and how it could be improved.

Summarizing and Reviewing Lessons

A carefully prepared summary at the end of a lesson ties together the loose ends and highlights the important points. It also gives the students an opportunity to ask questions and provides the teacher with an opportunity to correct any inaccuracies acquired by the students. Some ideas for summarizing a lesson include the following:

1. Summarize the main idea of the lesson with a short statement and tell what the students should realize as an outcome.

2. Assign one or two students to listen carefully and tell the class afterward what the lesson was about.
3. Have students write or tell in their own words what they think the main idea is.
4. Use a worksheet to help students summarize the main idea of the lesson.
5. Have several students in turn tell one thing learned from the lesson.
6. Divide the class into small groups. Each group in turn acts out a part of the lesson while the other groups try to guess what is being depicted (charades).
7. Present a real-life situation that could be resolved by using lesson ideas.
8. Give an oral or written quiz.
9. Use instructional games to test the information taught.

Some ways to review a lesson include:

1. Have students keep records of their progress with lesson objectives.
2. Have students write briefly on a previous lesson topic.
3. Have students perform any specific skill previously taught.

The way is clear for each and every physical education instructor to be creative and design "new" styles and strategies for teaching in the future. The committed teacher is limited by only one criterion—is it successful in teaching students?

Review Questions

1. What factors should be considered in the selection of a teaching style?
2. Describe Mosston's spectrum of teaching styles. Give an example of each "landmark" style:

Command (A)	Convergent Discovery (G)
Practice (B)	Divergent Production (H)
Reciprocal (C)	Learner's Individual Designed Program (I)
Self-check (D)	Learner-Initiated (J)
Inclusion (E)	Self-teaching (K)
Guided-discovery (F)	

3. What is an episode?
4. What is the difference between a style and a strategy?
5. What variations are possible within the lecture strategy?
6. Describe mastery learning. What are corrective and enrichment activities?
7. What is the purpose of a task sheet? A contract? Computer-assisted instruction?
8. What is cooperative learning? How can cognitive, psychomotor, and social skills be learned through the use of this strategy?
9. What is simulation? Give an example of a simulation experience in physical education.
10. List and give examples of problem-solving strategies.
11. What affective strategies can be used to affect student attitudes and values?
12. How can lessons be summarized and reviewed?

Suggested Readings

Adams, T. M., Kandt, G. K., Throgmartin, D., & Waldrop, P. B. (1991). Computer-assisted instruction vs. lecture methods in teaching the rules of golf. *The Physical Educator, 48,* 146–150.

Adams, T. M., Waldrop, P. B., & Justen, J. E. (1989). Effects of voluntary vs. required computer-assisted instruction on student achievement. *The Physical Educator, 46*, 213–217.

American Alliance for Health, Physical Education and Recreation. (1976). *Ideas for secondary school physical education: Innovative programs from project IDEA.* Washington, DC: Author.

Beckett, K. (1990). The effects of two teaching styles on college students' achievement of selected physical education outcomes. *Journal of Teaching in Physical Education, 10,* 153–169.

Carlson, R. P. (1984). *IDEAS II for secondary school physical education.* Reston, VA: American Alliance for Health, Physical Education, Recreation and Dance.

Franks, B. D. (Series editor). (1992, January). The spectrum of teaching styles: A silver anniversary in physical education. *Journal of Physical Education, Recreation and Dance, 63*(1), 25–56.

Goldberger, M. (1984, October). Effective learning through a spectrum of teaching styles. *Journal of Physical Education, Recreation and Dance, 55,* 17–21.

Hurwitz, D. (1985, April). A model for the structure of instructional strategies. *Journal of Teaching in Physical Education, 4,* 190–201.

Metzler, M. W. (1983). On styles. *Quest, 35*(2), 145–154.

Mosston, M., & Ashworth, S. (1994). *Teaching physical education* (4th ed.). New York: Macmillan College.

Zakrajsek, D., & Carnes, L. A. (1986). *Individualizing physical education: Criterion materials* (2nd ed.). Champaign, IL: Human Kinetics.

Contracts and Task Sheets

Arrighi, M. A. (1985, September). Equal opportunity through instructional design. *Journal of Physical Education, Recreation and Dance, 56,* 58–60, 64.

Beale, J. C. (1982, May). Task sheets for badminton and racquetball. *Physical Educator, 39,* 87–90.

Darst, P. W., & Model, R. L. (1983, September). Racquetball contracting: A way to structure your learning environment. *Journal of Physical Education, Recreation and Dance, 54,* 65–67.

Gray, D., & Moore, D. (1990, February–March). PSI: Application to racquetball. *Strategies, 3*(4), 20–23.

McBride, R. E. (1989, February). You, too, can be a task master—Using task sheets in the physical education program. *Journal of Physical Education, Recreation and Dance, 60*(2), 62–66.

Morton, P. J. (1989, April/May). Contract teaching. *Strategies, 2*(5), 13–16.

Viera, B. L., & Ferguson, B. J. (1986, September). Teaching volleyball: A competency based model. *Journal of Physical Education, Recreation and Dance, 57*(7), 54–58.

Youngberg, L., & Jones, D. D. (1980, November–December). Performance contracts help teach tumbling. *Journal of Physical Education and Recreation, 51,* 63.

Cooperative Learning

Glasser, W. (1986). *Control theory in the classroom.* New York: Harper & Row.

Glover, D. R., & Midura, D. W. (1992). *Team building through physical challenges.* Champaign, IL: Human Kinetics.

Johnson, D. W., Johnson, R. T., Holubec, E. J., & Roy, P. (1984). *Circles of learning: Cooperation in the classroom.* Alexandria, VA: Association for Supervision and Curriculum Development.

Kagan, S. (1989, December/1990, January). The structural approach to cooperative learning. *Educational Leadership, 47*(4), 12–15.

Sprenger, J. (series editor). (1993, February). Special focus: Cooperative learning. *Strategies, 6*(5), 5–15.

Sterne, M. L. (1990, April–May). Cooperative learning. *Strategies, 3*(5), 15–16.

Mastery Learning

Boyce, B. A. (1989, Fall). Utilization of a mastery learning strategy in physical education: Guidelines and considerations for implementation. *Physical Educator, 46*(3), 143–148.

Reaction Papers

Wentzell, S. R. (1989, November/December). Beyond the physical—Expressive writing in physical education. *Journal of Physical Education, Recreation and Dance, 60*(9), 18–20.

References

1. Laird, D., & Belcher, F. (1984, May). How master trainers get that way. *Training and Development Journal, 38*(5), 73.
2. Francke, E. (1983, September). Excellence in instruction. *Journal of Physical Education, Recreation and Dance, 54*, 55–56.
3. Gage, N. L. (1978, November). The yield of research on teaching. *Phi Delta Kappan, 60*(3), 229–235.
4. Peterson, P. L. (1979). Direct instruction reconsidered. In P. L. Peterson & H. J. Walberg (Eds.), *Research on teaching: Concepts, findings, and implications* (pp. 57–69). Berkeley: McCutchan.
5. Goldberger, M. (1984, October). Effective learning through a spectrum of teaching styles. *Journal of Physical Education, Recreation and Dance, 55*, 17.
6. Tyler, R. W. (1949). *Basic principles of curriculum and instruction* (p. 64). Chicago: University of Chicago Press.
7. Rink, J. E. (1993). *Teaching physical education for learning* (2nd ed., p. 46). St. Louis, MO: Mosby.
8. Hawley, R. C. (1973). *Human values in the classroom: Teaching for personal and social growth.* Amherst, MA: Education Research Associates.
9. Brophy, J. (1982, April). Successful teaching strategies for the inner-city child. *Phi Delta Kappan, 63*, 527–530.
10. Graham, G. (1983). Review and implications of physical education experimental teaching unit research. In T. J. Templin & J. K. Olson, *Teaching in physical education* (pp. 244–253). Champaign, IL: Human Kinetics.
11. Mosston, M., & Ashworth, S. (1994). *Teaching physical education* (4th ed.). New York: Macmillan College.
12. Goldberger, M. (1992). The spectrum of teaching styles: A perspective for research on teaching physical education. *The Journal of Physical Education, Recreation and Dance, 63*(1), 42–46.
13. Goldberger, M. (1983). Direct styles of teaching and psychomotor performance. In T. J. Templin & J. K. Olson, *Teaching in physical education* (pp. 211–223). Champaign, IL: Human Kinetics.
14. Goldberger, M., & Gerney, P. (1985, September). The effects of direct teaching styles on motor skill acquisition of fifth grade children. *Research Quarterly for Exercise and Sport, 57*, 215–219.
15. Beckett, K. (1990). The effects of two teaching styles on college students' achievement of selected physical education outcomes. *Journal of Teaching in Physical Education, 10*, 153–169.
16. Salter, W. B., & Graham, G. (1985, April). The effects of three disparate instructional approaches on skill attempts and student learning in an experimental teaching unit. *Journal of Teaching in Physical Education, 4*, 212–218.
17. Pettigrew, F. E., & Heikkinen, M. (1985, Fall). Increased psychomotor skill through eclectic teaching. *Physical Educator, 42*, 140–146.
18. Mosston & Ashworth, *Teaching physical education*, 19.
19. Goldberger, Effective learning through a spectrum of teaching styles, 17.
20. Goldberger, The spectrum of teaching styles, 42–46.
21. Hurwitz, D. (1985, April). A model for the structure of instructional strategies. *Journal of Teaching in Physical Education, 4*, 190–201.
22. Zakrajsek, D., & Carnes, L. A. (1986). *Individualizing physical education: Criterion materials* (2nd ed., p. 33). Champaign, IL: Human Kinetics.
23. Ibid.
24. Bloom, B. S. (1976). *Human characteristics and school learning.* New York: McGraw-Hill.
25. Torshen, K. P. (1977). *The mastery approach to competency based education.* New York: Academic Press.
26. Block, J. H. (1974). Mastery learning in the classroom: An over-view on recent research. In J. Block (Ed.), *Schools, society and mastery learning.* New York: Holt, Rinehart & Winston.
27. Block, J. H., & Burns, R. B. (1977). Mastery learning. In L. S. Shulman (Ed.), *Review of research in education.* Itasca: Peacock; Bloom, *Human characteristics and school learning;* Cotton, K., & Savard, W. G. (1982, June). Mastery learning. Topic Summary Report. (ERIC Document Reproduction Service no. ED 218 279); Ryan, D. W., & Schmidt, M. (1979). *Mastery learning: Theory, research and implementation.* Available from Ontario Department of Education, Toronto; Torshen, *The mastery approach to competency based education.*

28. Annarino, A. A. (1981, March). Accountability—An instructional model for secondary physical education. *Journal of Physical Education and Recreation, 52,* 55–56.

29. Heitmann, H. J., & Kneer, M. E. (1976). *Physical education instructional techniques: An individualized humanistic approach.* Englewood Cliffs, NJ: Prentice-Hall.

30. Edwards, R. (1988). The effects of performance standards on behavior patterns and motor skill achievement in children. *Journal of Teaching in Physical Education, 7,* 90–102.

31. Chambless, J. P., Anderson, E. R., & Poole, J. H. (1980). *Mastery learning of stunts and tumbling activities for the mentally retarded.* Oxford, MS: Mississippi University, North Mississippi Retardation Center.

32. Ashy, M., & Lee, A. M. (1984, March–April). Effects of a mastery learning strategy on throwing accuracy and technique. *Abstracts of Research Papers—1984.* Reston, VA: American Alliance for Health, Physical Education, Recreation and Dance.

33. Metzler, M. W. (1984). Analysis of a mastery learning/personalized system of instruction for teaching tennis. In M. Pieron & G. Graham (Eds.), *Sport pedagogy.* Champaign, IL: Human Kinetics.

34. Metzler, M., Eddleman, K., Treanor, L., & Cregger, R. (1989, February). *Teaching tennis with an instructional system design.* Paper presented at the Eastern Educational Research Association Annual Meeting, Savannah, GA.

35. Blakemore, C. L. (1985). *The effects of mastery learning on the acquisition of psychomotor skills.* Unpublished doctoral dissertation, Temple University, Philadelphia, PA; Blakemore, C. L. (1986, May 30). *The effects and implications of teaching psychomotor skills using mastery learning techniques.* Paper presented at the International Conference on Research in Teacher Education and Teaching in Physical Education, University of British Columbia, Vancouver, BC; Blakemore, C. L., Hilton, H. G., Harrison, J. M., Pellett, T. L., & Gresh, J. (1992). Comparison of students taught basketball skills using mastery and nonmastery learning methods. *Journal of Teaching in Physical Education, 11*(3), 235–247.

36. Boyce, B. A. (1990). *The effect of instructor-set goals upon skill acquisition and retention of a selected shooting task. Journal of Teaching in Physical Education, 9*(2), 115–122.

37. Adams, T. M., Waldrop, P. B., & Justen, J. E. (1989). Effects of voluntary vs. required computer-assisted instruction on student achievement. *The Physical Educator, 46,* 213–217.

38. Adams, T. M., Kandt, G. K., Throgmartin, D., & Waldrop, P. B. (1991). Computer-assisted instruction vs. lecture methods in teaching the rules of golf. *The Physical Educator, 48,* 146–150.

39. Gough, P. B. (1987, May). The key to improving schools: An interview with William Glasser. *Phi Delta Kappan, 68*(9), 656–662.

40. Smith, R. A. (1987, May). A teacher's views on cooperative learning. *Phi Delta Kappan, 68*(9), 663–666.

41. Ibid.

42. Gough, The key to improving schools.

43. Smith, A teacher's views on cooperative learning.

44. Ibid.

45. Johnson, D. W., Johnson, R. T., Holubec, E. J., & Roy, P. (1984). *Circles of learning: Cooperation in the classroom.* Alexandria, VA: Association for Supervision and Curriculum Development.

46. Smith, A teacher's views on cooperative learning.

47. Sterne, M. L. (1990, May). Cooperative learning. *Strategies, 3*(5), 15–16.

48. Glover, D. R., & Midura, D. W. (1992). *Team building through physical challenges.* Champaign, IL: Human Kinetics.

49. Krumm, M. (1984). Tennis, despite weather and site restrictions. In R. P. Carlson (Ed.), *Ideas II: A sharing of teaching practices by secondary school physical education practitioners* (pp. 38–39). Reston, VA: American Alliance for Health, Physical Education, Recreation and Dance; Fairman, L. S., & Nitchman, D. (1984). A bowling program in the gymnasium. In R. P. Carlson (Ed.), *Ideas II: A sharing of teaching practices by secondary school physical education practitioners* (pp. 66–68). Reston, VA: American Alliance for Health, Physical Education, Recreation and Dance.

50. Nelson, J. E. (1984). Teaching cross-country skiing. *Journal of Physical Education, Recreation and Dance, 55,* 58–64.

51. Wright, K., & Walker, J. (1969, November–December). Rainy day golf. *Journal of Health Physical Education Recreation, 40,* 83.

52. Hobbs, C. R. (1972). *The power of teaching with new techniques* (p. 117). Salt Lake City, UT: Deseret Books.
53. Gagné, R. M., & Briggs, L. J. *Principles of instructional design* (p. 64). Chicago, IL: Holt, Rinehart & Winston.
54. Harmin, M., & Simon, S. B. (1972, March). How to help students learn to think . . . about themselves. *The High School Journal, 55*(6), 256–264.
55. Ibid.
56. Canfield, J., & Wells, H. C. *100 ways to enhance self-concept in the classroom* (p. 187). Englewood Cliffs, NJ: Prentice-Hall.
57. Ibid., 72.
58. Ibid., 188–189.
59. Hawley, *Human values in the classroom*, 16.
60. Ibid., 60–61.

CHAPTER 8

Program Activities and Materials

Study Stimulators

1. What learning resources and materials should the teacher consider when planning the instructional program?
2. What media would you feel comfortable using in your program?
3. How might you incorporate the computer into your teaching?
4. How might you structure a content unit on fitness?
5. What motivation techniques would you use to encourage students to perform up to their potential in a unit of movement skills?
6. Design the playing schedule for eight teams in a round-robin tournament.
7. How would you encourage students to learn concepts about physical activity?
8. How would you justify incorporating a "risk activity" into your program?
9. How might interdisciplinary units or special days contribute to your physical education program?

Committed, innovative teachers have many resources available for implementing an instructional program to achieve the goals of physical education stated in chapter 1—to develop physical skills, physical fitness, knowledge and understanding, social skills, and attitudes and appreciations. Teachers must be willing to teach traditional activities in nontraditional ways and incorporate innovative activities such as adventure and challenge activities or integrated units into their curriculum. Teachers are always expected to make learning meaningful and motivating even on rainy days, shortened days, days before vacations, or any other circumstance that may hinder the normal operation of the class. This chapter will present numerous resources and ideas to help physical education teachers plan programs that meet the needs of all students in a variety of circumstances.

Selecting General Program Aids and Materials

The purpose of instructional aids and materials is to achieve instructional objectives effectively and economically. They can increase student motivation and create heightened interest and enjoyment in learning by increasing visual involvement and reducing the amount of teacher talk. They can be used to introduce a lesson, present new material, clarify a subject or discussion, or summarize a lesson. It has been said that approximately 83 percent of all learning occurs through sight, only 11 percent through hearing, and less than 6 percent through the other senses. Retention is increased fourfold over hearing only by the use of visual involvement and nearly sevenfold by combining the use of visual and auditory senses. Instructional aids and materials accomplish these tasks by involving the students in the learning process. An old Chinese proverb points this out very well. It said:

I hear, I forget.
I see, I remember.
I do, I understand.

Sources of instructional materials include catalogs of instructional aids, and printed materials such as texts, journals, newspapers, and commercial learning packets. Professional persons, parents, and friends are excellent sources, as are many students. A college or university media center or a district or school instructional materials center can provide access to many sources. The American Alliance for Health, Physical Education, Recreation and Dance also publishes catalogs of instructional materials. A summary of various types of instructional materials with their advantages and disadvantages is shown in Table 8.1.

When selecting instructional aids and materials, teachers should attempt to choose experiences as close to real life as possible. Other considerations—such as student safety, money, and practicality—will, of course, restrict the teacher in making a selection. The process of selecting costly materials is best shared by teachers, students, parents, and administrators so that the needs of all are considered.

The use of a systematic evaluation guide facilitates the selection of materials. The guide helps the teacher consider the learning potential of the materials by asking the following questions about them:

1. Do they make a meaningful contribution to the topic under study?
2. Do they develop concepts that are difficult to convey through another medium?
3. Are they true to fact and life, accurate, and authentic?
4. Are they up-to-date?
5. Are they worth the time, cost, and effort involved?
6. Do they develop critical thinking skills?
7. Are they appropriate for the age, intelligence, and experience level of students?

A second consideration is the technical quality of the materials. Examine the picture and sound for quality. Is the mode of communication adequate for the intended purpose and the message unbiased and free from objectionable propaganda or distractions?

Ease of presentation is the third consideration. Often, management problems associated with the use of instructional materials renders them useless when, in fact, it is the management system that is ineffective. An evaluation of the ease of operation, ease of maintenance, quality, durability, and portability is best made before purchasing equipment. The following examples of instructional aids and materials may be helpful to teachers seeking ways to enrich programs.

Examples of Instructional Aids and Materials

Three general types of aids and materials commonly used in schools are (1) media of various types, (2) personal resource files, and (3) computers.

Media

Although instructional materials can be used effectively to enhance motivation and learning, research often reveals no increase in learning. Students are media saturated. Teachers compete

Table 8.1 A Summary of the Various Types of Instructional Materials

Medium	Uses	Advantages	Disadvantages
Videotapes	Evaluation of student performance. Self-evaluation of student or teacher. Magnification of small objects. Students can make own videos.	Instant replay. Can save for future use. Can prerecord. Inexpensive. Portable. Ease of operation.	
8-mm films and loops	Individual study. Homework. Stimulates verbal communication and creativity.	Portable—compact. Inexpensive. Ease of operation. Replay without rewinding.	Silent.
Videodiscs	Same as 16-mm films.	Quick accessibility to any frame on disk. Replay instantly. Can be interfaced with a computer for individualized instruction.	Availability currently limited.
16-mm films	Present meanings involving motion. Compel attention. Heighten reality. Speed up or slow down time. Enlarge or reduce size. Bring past or present into class. Build common denominator of experience. Influence and change attitudes. Promote understanding of abstract concepts.		Sound film is costly. Need skilled production staff. Requires darkened room. Internally controlled pacing. Fixed sequence. Outdated soon after purchase.
Models Mock-ups Exhibits Displays Objects, specimens	Examples of real-life situations. Comparisons.	Enlargement or reduction. High reality—3-D.	

Table 8.1—Continued

Medium	Uses	Advantages	Disadvantages
Computers	Computer-assisted instruction. Record keeping. Word processing	High interest. Fast.	Relatively expensive unless terminals can be hooked up to a main computer. Software is currently limited.
Tape recorders Audiotapes Records Compact disks	Authority resource. Create a mood. Grading comments. Student interview. Exams.	High reality. Ease of production of tapes. Low cost, accessible.	
Slides or filmstrips	History, geography. Concepts.	Magnification or reduction. Inexpensive. software Availability. High reality. Flexible sequence and pacing (slides). Can be combined with audio.	Requires darkened room. Fixed sequence (filmstrips).
Overhead transparencies	Graphic presentations.	Inexpensive software. Availability. Project in light room. Flexible sequence. Base of operation at front of room. All advantages of chalkboard plus.	
Duplicated materials	For important information: as a quiz; as a guide; as a reminder. To emphasize a point. For a complete explanation.	Can be prepared in advance. Can be retained for future reference and review.	
Opaque projections	Still pictures.	High reality. Flexible sequence.	
Magnetic boards	Sequence material. Tell stories with simple illustrations. Illustrate hard-to-understand concepts. Display materials. Strategy talks.	Inexpensive. Easy. Creative. Attention-getting.	

Table 8.1—Continued

Medium	Uses	Advantages	Disadvantages
Chalkboards	Clarify sequence of events. Focus attention. Stimulate discussion.	Flexibility and versatility. Availability. Size.	
Still pictures: Charts Posters Bulletin boards Flipcharts Graphs Maps Diagrams Cartoons	Attract attention. Arouse interest. Reinforce and add dimension. Provide concrete meaning to abstract ideas.	Very inexpensive. No equipment needed. Easy to use and store. Readily available.	Too small. Limited to two dimensions. No motion.

with the multimillion-dollar budgets of television and movies. Media used in class have to be exceptional for students to respond positively. Instructional media are of the most value when they are closely correlated with instructional objectives, so they can supplement and increase teacher effectiveness. Media must never be used just to take up time on a rainy day or when the teacher is unprepared. No medium can substitute for a concerned, well-prepared teacher.

A live demonstration is often more effective than a visual aid. However, a video, motion picture, or film loop can give the entire class the view obtained by the observer in the most advantageous position. Close-ups afford all members of a large class the opportunity to see the motion clearly. Another benefit of this type of media is that it can reproduce action that the observer rarely sees, such as an underwater view of a swimming stroke or a slow-motion view of a complex skill. Through the use of slow motion, it is possible to analyze sports skills in terms of body position, timing, and the relationship of skills to game play.

The instant replay feature of the videorecorder makes it a terrific teaching aid because players can see themselves in action. Videotaping shows learners their own mistakes or successes. (This is also true of students learning to teach.) By helping students compare their own performance with the performance of a model, videotape feedback can be even more valuable. Videotapes can be retained over a period of time to show achievements and progress in learning. Some videocameras can also take a series of timed snapshots, which can then be analyzed for feedback purposes. Polaroid pictures can be used to provide feedback on posture in activities such as archery.

Personal Resource File

A personal resource file is a file of instructional materials that can be easily located and replaced for future reference and use. A practical filing system is one that functions effectively in the situation in which the teacher is working. Materials might include pictures, items for lesson and unit planning, skill analyses, evaluation materials, handouts, study sheets, instructional media lists, books, and pamphlets. Labeling each item allows it to be returned to its location when not in use. Files might include community resources and lists of people willing to assist in developing or conducting learning activities, or for special reports or projects.

One of the simplest methods of filing is to have a file folder for each sport or topic. This might be expanded later as in the following examples of file titles:

Archery—Unit Plans
Archery—Equipment
Archery—Skill Evaluation
Archery—Knowledge Evaluation

Of course, the filing system must agree with the teacher's personal style and use materials that are readily available.

Computers

"The computer has been termed the most powerful tool in educating people since the development of the printing press."[1] In fact, computers have had the impact of a cultural mutation that affects not only our way of living but also our very way of thinking.[2] In 1991 more than 2.5 million microcomputers existed in the schools. The ratio of students to computers was 19:1.[3] The number of computers is increasing exponentially.[4] More than 95 percent of all schools have invested in computer hardware and software.[5] An explosion of computerization during the 1980s and 1990s resulted in the manufacture of hundreds of different computers and tens of thousands of software products for every conceivable application.[6] Networks are providing a means of communication for teachers and administrators that was previously unavailable. Communication through computers not only is available for a single school district but also is an avenue for sharing ideas and information among teachers in a state, the nation, and throughout the world. Computers may someday change the structure of a typical physical education class.[7]

Judith Edwards developed a model in 1978 for instructional computer uses that has proven to be visionary.[8] Edwards's model still directs the overall use of computers in education. The model pictured in figure 8.1 indicates five instructional uses of the computer. They include (1) an instructor/teacher, (2) a laboratory, (3) a calculator, (4) an object of instruction, and (5) an instructor/teacher aide. In accordance with Edwards's model, the computer is used in physical education primarily as an instructional aid and data management tool. Available software is used by teachers, coaches, and researchers to enhance the quality and efficiency of their work. Available software in the areas of sport science, health, and dance have been indexed and the titles may be retrieved from such sources as AAHPERD,[9] King and Aufsesser,[10] Donnelly,[11] and Softshare.[12] Existing programs to aid in the learning process are scarce and often not of good quality. Computer literacy helps physical educators incorporate existing programs or create their own.

Computer as Instructor

The microcomputer in the classroom was first used as an aid in cognitive instruction. Programmed learning or drill and practice programs produced a volume of software, most of which was extremely poor.[13] Computer-assisted instruction (CAI) allows students to progress at their own pace by interacting with programmed learning sequences on a computer. CAI can be used to teach concepts (including sport history, terminology, rules, safety, strategies, physiology, psychology, and biomechanics), teach skills (such as officiating and athletic training), provide demonstrations, simulate real-life experiences, and prescribe individualized programs.[14] However, workbooks or textbooks can accomplish many of these things with less money.

Computers have been lauded for their infinite patience. Very little research has been conducted to determine the value of computers in providing sports skill instruction. A study by

Students use the computer in the Learning
Resource Center to individualize their fitness
programs.
© Tracy Pellett

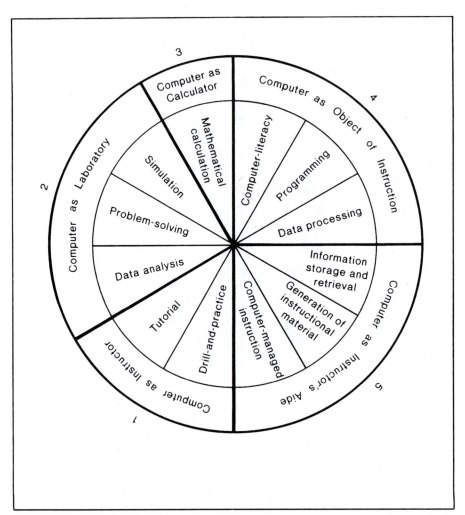

Figure 8.1 Model of instructional uses of the
computer.
Source: Adapted from Judith B. Edwards, et al.,
Computer Applications in Instruction, Hanover, New
Hampshire: Time Share (Houghton Mifflin), 1978,
p. 30.

Steffen and Hansen compared the teaching of bowling to college students using a traditional approach and a CAI approach.[15] In the CAI approach the computer lessons covered history, equipment, rules, scoring, and spare conversions. At the end of instruction there were no significant
differences in cognitive skills, but there were significant increases in the bowling skills of the
CAI group. This is probably because the computer instruction was done outside of class and so
allowed more practice time in class. The students involved perceived CAI as an excellent teaching approach.

Kerns found that students learned equally well with direct and computer-assisted instruction and recommended that CAI outside of the classroom could leave more time for teaching motor skills during class time.[16] Adams and Waldrop stated, "To realize the full potential of CAI, it must be recognized as a supplement to, rather than a replacement for other means of instruction."[17] Students could also check their understanding of concepts and principles by using a computer available during dressing time before and after class.

Physical educators can incorporate the computer as an instructional tool most effectively by interfacing it with other modern technology such as the videotape player, videodisc, or CD-ROM technologies to produce quite sophisticated programs. "Linked to a microcomputer, the videodisc is potentially the ultimate delivery system for instructional materials, combining the attributes of overhead projection transparencies, slides, film, and videotape."[18] For example, a videodisc, computer, and electronic manikin in combination have been used to teach cardiopulmonary resuscitation (CPR). Programs for skill analysis have also been produced using videodisc and computer. Stein indicated that an individual's imagination is the only limiting factor in the use of computers in physical education.[19] Cicciarella cautioned, however, that

> Although these programs can and have been developed for teaching sport strategy, rules, and skills such as refereeing, the physical setting of gymnasium, pool, or athletic fields does not adapt easily to the use of electronic equipment for instruction. It seems probable that the computer will not be heavily used for instruction in motor skills.[20]

Computer as Laboratory

In addition to its use as a tutorial tool, computers are being used by professionals in specialized areas and in the laboratory to analyze human performance and behavior. Microcomputers assist specialists in motor learning, exercise physiology, sport psychology, and biomechanics.[21] Through the use of film motion analysis, significant and objective interpretation and comparison of selected sport skill techniques are possible.[22] The use of computer technology has also been applied to programs for dance notation.[23]

Computers greatly aid research by controlling time intervals for accurate data collection and facilitating analysis of large amounts of data.[24] Teacher and student observation systems are facilitated with portable computers.

Computer as Calculator

Coaches find the computer advantageous for statistical analysis of game play in basketball, baseball, football, and other sports and for scouting reports on opposing team play. Computers are cost efficient, reducing time spent on paperwork and increasing the accuracy of data collected. This frees the coach or teacher for quality time with students.[25]

Computer as Object of Instruction

Students learn about computers by using them. Computers allow students to access sport databases and learning packages that are constantly being developed.

Computer as Instructor's Aide

Computers help instructors in three ways: (1) as producers of instructional materials, (2) as devices for information storage and retrieval, and (3) as managers of instruction.

Producers of Instructional Materials. The generation of instructional materials is proving to be of great assistance. The kinds of materials that can be printed out range from tests and games to individualized worksheets, text materials, course outlines, and reading lists.[26] Countless graphics and word processing software packages are available to help teachers create classroom materials. They are constantly being improved and updated.

Information Storage and Retrieval. The most practical and widespread use of the computer for physical educators is to assist with data generated from instructional activities. The mammoth organizational and record-keeping tasks of physical education programs warrant the use of the computer in data management. Kelly indicated that

> The average physical educator may be responsible for teaching between 250 to 500 different students each week. If a physical educator wanted to distribute quarterly progress reports to the students and their parents, this would entail computing and preparing somewhere between 1,000 and 2,000 separate reports a year. This could be done in a matter of hours with a microcomputer.[27]

Database management programs are written for either generic or specialized applications. Generic programs require computer expertise and time. Specialized programs can be used by novices, but the user has less control over what can be managed by the program. Kelly listed a number of factors to consider when selecting a database management program:[28]

1. Program parameters
   a. What are your objectives (fitness, skills, concepts, etc.), and how many do you want to manage?
   b. How many scores can be entered for each objective?
   c. How many students can be managed? The combination of these three items is determined by RAM and disk memory.
2. Data entry
   a. How efficiently and conveniently can the database be defined and student performance data entered?
   b. How are data entry mistakes detected and corrected?
   c. Are data collection worksheets available?
3. Output
   a. What type of reports can be produced?
      1) Individual student reports for students and parents
      2) Summary reports—provide feedback to document instructional effectiveness
      3) Statistical reports—allow data analysis
      4) Status reports—provide a printed copy of the data in the database
   b. Are the reports of high quality, accurate, and easy to interpret? "Preparing a 'How to read and understand this report' handout will avoid a lot of confusion and potentially hundreds of phone calls." [29]
   c. Can the teacher decide what should be included in the report and individualize report labels?
   d. Can the teacher tell the program what reports are wanted and what should be included and then have the computer produce them quickly and without continuous interaction?

Software should be selected to provide necessary, adequate, sufficient, and valid information to communicate to and educate students and parents. Pilot-test reports for readability, validity, and reliability. "Too much information is just as useless as too little. Parents review many reports from schools; experts can assist developers in determining which reports have the greatest impact and are most likely to be read and utilized."[30]

Excellent software is available to record and process grades and fitness data and provide immediate feedback and results. Most fitness tests today have computer software designed to save teacher and administrator time in evaluating fitness scores and preparing reports for distribution. They can be obtained from the sources listed in Table 8.2. Several software packages furnish class and individual reports similar to the printouts shown in figures 8.2 and 8.3. Engelhorn has made available input programs for fitness testing allowing teachers to program their own packages.[31]

Fitness testing and management programs usually have a statistical analysis package that can be used to evaluate which objectives were taught effectively and whether instruction resulted in significant gains in student performance. "This information, compiled into reports and distributed to administrators, would document the effectiveness of the physical education program."[32] Another idea for use in fitness testing would be to roll the computer into the gymnasium and have the students input their scores as their tests are completed. They could then obtain a written evaluation of their performance in a matter of seconds.[33] Entering the data into the computer can be time-consuming unless some type of scanner or individualized card is used.[34] Secretaries or student aides can help with this task so that meaningful personalized data are available to the teacher, student, and parent at the conclusion of the testing.

Although they are not often thought of when discussing computers, heart rate monitors provide another information storage and retrieval system. The students wear a chest strap that includes electrodes and a transmitter. A receiver similar to a wristwatch is worn to receive and store the heart rate data. Information on the heart rate during the class or exercise session can be manually downloaded or downloaded and saved on a computer. The information can be used to evaluate the effort of each student as well as the effectiveness of the class activities, especially if cardiovascular fitness is a goal. Timing and recording of fitness tests such as a mile run are simplified through use of heart rate monitors.

Manager of Instruction. Computer programs are available for efficient sign-up in selective physical education programs. Teachers can set the maximum number of students per class and students can sign up outside of physical education class time for the class they desire. The computer prints the selected class information for the student and also prints class lists for the teachers.[35] Intramural scheduling, tournament planning, and workout scheduling can be accomplished in a similar manner.

Computers are here to stay and they can be a tremendous aid to the teacher. Teachers must learn to use computers as any other media to enhance achievement of the goals and objectives of the physical education curriculum.

Selecting Hardware and Software

Whenever possible, hardware and software selections should consider the needs and objectives of your program and the available resources. However, in many instances the school or district will adopt one specific type or brand of computers. More and more computer software programs that facilitate learning are becoming available to physical educators, and the quality of the programs has improved.[36] Since hundreds of software programs are produced each year, skills in scrutinizing software for purchase are essential. Students must also be taught wise selection and use of physical education-related software beyond the school environment. Kelly outlined a number of considerations for selecting software:[37]

Table 8.2 Fitness Programs and Software Packages

Program Developer/ Sponsor	Grades	Test Items	Printouts	Norm- or Criterion- Referenced	Computers	Motivation Awards	Cost	Other/
Prudential Fitnessgram (1993) Cooper Institute for Aerobics Research, 12330 Preston Rd., Dallas, TX 75230 (214) 701–8001 The Prudential Insurance Company of America	K–12 and College	1-mile walk/ run curl-ups pull-ups, flexed-arm hang, or push-ups sit and reach or shoulder stretch skinfold or BMI trunk extensor	Student report card with fitness profile Individualized exercise prescription Cumulative record of test results Statistics— student; class; school Award qualifiers Group summaries	Criterion-based	Apple IIe IBM Macintosh Non-computer version Electronic scanning capability Toll-free technical support Extensive documen-tation	Get Fit and Fit for Life Awards— complete activity program I'm Fit Award— meet criteria on 4/5 items or 5/6 items SMARTCHOICE Award— perform assessment and do activities at school, home, community	Manual and software free with order of 200 Fitness-gram cards, $22	Teaching Strate-gies book, $21.95

Table 8.2—Continued

Program Developer/ Sponsor	Grades	Test Items	Printouts	Norm- or Criterion-Referenced	Computers	Motivation Awards	Cost	Other/
Chrysler Fund AAU Physical Fitness Program (1989) Poplar Building Bloomington, IN 47405 (812) 855–2059 Chrysler Corporation Fund	K–12	1/4–1-mile endurance run sit-ups pull-ups or flexed-arm hang sit and reach *Optional* (1 required) standing long jump isometric or modified push-up sprints isometric leg squat shuttle run	Individual fitness reports Group profiles Record keeping No prescriptive information	Criterion- and norm-referenced	Apple IBM Phone number for assistance	Outstanding Achievement certificate— above 80th percentile for 4 + 1 optional items Attainment certificate 45th–80th percentiles for 4 + 1 optional items Participation certificate 0– 45th percentiles	$15 0–599 certificates, $8 shipping	Instructional/ motivational video (rental or purchase) Instructors manual Activity card file *Test-Tips* newsletter Letter to parents (available in Spanish)

Table 8.2—Continued

Program Developer/Sponsor	Grades	Test Items	Printouts	Norm- or Criterion-Referenced	Computers	Motivation Awards	Cost	Other/
President's Council on Physical Fitness and Sports Fit America Fitness Management	Ages 6–17	1-mile run/walk; curl-ups; pull-ups or flexed-arm hang; V-sit or sit and reach; shuttle run	Individual student profiles—scores, percentiles; Class composites; Top 25 scores for any or all events; No exercise prescription; Must be ordered	Presidential—norm-referenced; National—criterion-referenced	Apple; IBM; Limited documentation; Card reader; Phone number for assistance	Presidential Physical Fitness Award—85th percentile on all 5 items; National Physical Fitness Award—50th–84th percentile on all 5 items; (test available for students with physical disabilities); State Champion Award—schools with highest percent of students above 85 percent; Presidential Sports Award—recognizes participation in specific sport or activity	Disk and limited documentation $85	
President's Challenge Poplars Research Center, 400 E. 7th St., Bloomington, IN 47405 (812) 855-8946		Optional; 2-mile run/walk; skinfolds; standing broad jump	List of students about 85th percentile; Statistics and data management with transfer to other programs					
For program information— PCPFS 450 5th St., NW, Suite 7103 Washington, D.C. 20001								

Table 8.2—Continued

Program Developer/ Sponsor	Grades	Test Items	Printouts	Norm- or Criterion-Referenced	Computers	Motivation Awards	Cost	Other/
Dino*Fit™ Software System. ARA/Human Factors 15312 Spencerville Court (301) 384-0800	Ages 6–18	Cognitive, affective, fitness test options	Individual profiles, class profiles Class average profile Class roster Awards list for Physical Best or Fit America	Both	IBM Apple Allows configuration to various fitness tests or customized testing Phone number		None	

Sources: Stroot, Sandra and Bumgartner, Shan. (1989, August). Fitness Assessment—Putting Computers to Work. *Journal of Physical Education, Recreation and Dance*, 44–49. Brochures from each organization listed above.

```
                        GROUP'S TEST RESULTS

CLASS NAME: PERIOD 2
TEST NUMBER: 2
TEST DATE: OCTOBER 1996
RUN TYPE: 1 WHICH IS A 1 MILE RUN
SKINFOLD TYPE: 1. . . .TRICEP ONLY
```

NO.	NAME	AGE	SEX	HT	WT	RUN TIME	SKINFOLD TRI	SUB	SIT-UPS	REACH
1	Byron Anderson	13	M			12:24		0	40	33
2	George Burke	13	M			11:54		0	28	34
3	Paula Conlin	13	F			9:09		0	35	35
4	Alecia Dayton	13	F			8:21		0	41	41
5	Paige Evans	13	F			8:51		0	31	29
6	George Fairchild	13	M			7:34		0	48	43
7	Andres Garcia	13	M			8:42		0	42	31
8	Jim Glass	13	M			10:43		0	35	38
9	Bob King	14	M			9:37		0	34	35
10	Kirsten Knight	13	F			12:45		0	33	28
11	Glen Lott	13	M			10:45		0	31	44
12	Tom Marks	13	M			7:34		0	45	26
13	Jeff Matthews	14	M			11:26		0	36	20
14	Erin McLaughlin	13	F			8:55		0	42	38
15	Nina Monsen	13	F			8:22		0	35	36
16	Kevin Moon	13	M			8:48		0	43	21
17	Brad Norman	12	M			9:02		0	33	33
18	Terri O'Connor	14	F			8:20		0	45	40
19	Kathy Stevens	13	F			8:26		0	36	35
20	Vicki Peterson	13	F			8:01		0	37	28
21	Ferrill Rowley	12	M			8:48		0	35	37
22	Carlos Sousa	13	M			8:56		0	38	38
23	Claudia Taylor	13	F			8:54		0	42	39
24	Tina Vickers	13	F			8:26		0	39	40
25	Scott Walker	13	M			9:09		0	37	38
26	Diane Zabriskie	14	F			8:29		0	34	40

Figure 8.2   A class fitness score computer printout.

1. *Technical considerations*

   Brand and model of computer compatible with software (i.e., IBM-compatible 486 or Macintosh)

   Random Access Memory (RAM) required (Is it adequate?)

   Type and number of disk drives required

   Disk operating system (DOS) (Is it compatible with computer and program?)

   Brand, type, and model of printers supported

   Error-free programming

FITNESSGRAM

COMMITTED TO HEALTH RELATED FITNESS

Jane Jogger
FITNESSGRAM Jr. High
FITNESSGRAM Test District
Instructor: Bridgman
Grade: 09   *Period:* 09   *Age:* 09

Test Date	Height	Weight
MO - YR	FT - IN	LBS
09 - 96	4 - 10	102
09 - 97	4 - 10	103

AEROBIC CAPACITY

HEALTHY FITNESS ZONE   Current   Past

One Mile

Needs Improvement	Good	Better
* * * * * * * * *	* * * * * * * * * * * * * *	* *
* * * * * * * * *	* * * * * * * * * * * * * *	* *

11:00   8:30

min:sec	
8:00	9:15

ml/kg/min	
45	43

Max VO₂   *Indicates ability to use oxygen. Expressed as ml of oxygen per kg body weight per minute. Healthy Fitness Zone = 40 + for girls & 42 + for boys.*

Jane, your aerobic capacity was very good. Try to maintain your fitness by doing 20-30 minutes of vigorous activities at least 3 or 4 times each week.

MUSCLE STRENGTH, ENDURANCE & FLEXIBILITY

HEALTHY FITNESS ZONE

The Curl-up (Abdominal)

Needs Improvement	Good	Better
* * * * * * * * *	* * *	
* * * * * * * * *	* * *	

18   32

# performed	
27	23

Improve your upper body strength by doing push-ups against the wall, push-ups, horizontal ladder and other climbing activities.

Push-up (Upper Body)

Needs Improvement	Good	Better
* * * * * *		
* * * * * *		

7   15

# performed	
5	5

Improve your flexibility by doing slow stretches and holding the stretch 20-30 seconds.

Trunk Lift (Trunk Extension)

Needs Improvement	Good	Better
* * * * * * * *	* * * * * * * * * *	* *
* * * * * * * *	* * * * * * * * * *	*

6   12

inches	
12	12

The test of flexibility is optional. If given, it is scored pass or fail and is performed on the right and left.
Test given: Back Saver Sit and Reach

Right	P
Left	F

BODY COMPOSITION

HEALTHY FITNESS ZONE

Percent Body Fat

Needs Improvement	Good	Better
* * * * * * * *		
* * * * * * * *		

32   17

% fat	
33	33

To improve your body composition remember to do some aerobic activity each day and follow a balanced nutritional program eating more fruits and vegetables and fewer fats and sugars. Improvement on this item would most likely improve your scores on other test items.

To parent or guardian: *The Prudential FITNESSGRAM is a valuable tool in assessing a young person's fitness level. The area of the bar highlighted in yellow indicates the "healthy fitness zone." All children should strive to maintain levels of fitness within the "healthy fitness zone." By maintaining a healthy fitness level for these areas of fitness your child many have a reduced risk for developing heart disease, obesity or low back pain. Some children may have personal interests that require higher levels of fitness (e.g. athletes).*

Recommended activities for improving fitness are based on each individual's test performance. Ask your child to demonstrate each test item for you. Some teachers may stop the test when performance equals upper limit of the healthy fitness zone* rather than requiring a maximal effort.

Developing good exercise habits is important to maintaining lifelong health. You can help your son or daughter develop these habits by completing the activities on the back of this report together and by encouraging regular participation in physical activity.

Developed by The
Cooper Institute for
Aerobics Research
Dallas, Texas

Sponsored by The
Prudential Insurance
Company of America

Figure 8.3   Diagram of The Prudential
FITNESSGRAM computer output.
Reprinted with permission from The Cooper
Institute for Aerobics Research, Dallas, Texas.

Text easily read, and graphics contribute to the purpose of the program
Anticipation of user errors (with help screen)
Independent student operation with little teacher intervention

2. *Instructional considerations*
   Methods of instruction—drill and practice, tutorials, problem solving
   Feedback—guides students to correct answers or reinforces correct answers
   Amount of user control of rate and sequence of information

3. *Program content*
   Appropriate to age and ability of students
   Accurate
   Compatible with goals and objectives

4. *Managerial considerations*
   Management—storing, sorting, calculating, and reporting data
   Program testing capabilities suitable for formative and/or summative evaluation

5. *Documentation*
   Clear instructions
   Toll-free telephone number?

Computers definitely have a place in physical education. Careful planning can ensure that they meet curricular, instructional, and managerial needs.

Selecting Program Aids and Materials for Specific Content Areas

The general instructional aids and materials just presented are designed to help teachers plan meaningful physical education programs. An awareness of available options can help teachers enhance the instructional experience. Specific instructional ideas for the content areas of fitness, movement skills, concepts, adventure, and interdisciplinary units are included in this section. Also included are special days. In a concentrated effort to meet the goals of physical education, teaching plans should include the following components: (1) instruction and practice, (2) motivational techniques, and (3) evaluating progress.

Fitness

"Fitness is the capacity to achieve the optimal quality of life." [38] Health-related fitness is defined as the ability "to work with vigor and pleasure without undue fatigue, with energy left for enjoying hobbies and recreational activities, and for meeting unforeseen emergencies." [39] Health-related fitness is built upon a foundation of five major factors—cardiovascular endurance, muscular strength and endurance, flexibility, body composition, and relaxation.

Studies clearly show the health benefits of regular physical activity in reducing the risk of heart disease, diabetes, osteoporosis, some forms of cancer,[40] ulcers, and mental health disorders such as depression.[41] Persons with good cardiovascular endurance have a lower risk of premature development of hypokinetic diseases (those associated with inactivity).[42] Muscular strength and endurance and flexibility are generally associated with a reduced risk of low back and other musculoskeletal problems.[43] Desirable body composition is associated with reduced risk of adult onset diabetes.[44]

In 1991 more than 58.1 percent of adults in the United States reported having a sedentary lifestyle.[45] Blair has indicated that for individuals who are extremely sedentary, adding even a little physical activity can reduce the risk of coronary heart disease as much as smoking cessation.[46]

In 1990 only 37 percent of high school students reported being vigorously active at least three times per week.[47] Schools are the logical starting points for changing future physical activity patterns,[48] but 44 percent of males and 52 percent of females were not enrolled in physical education in high school in 1990. Only 22 percent of students grades 9 through 12 were attending physical education daily.[49] Pangrazi and Corbin stated that students must be taught the importance of fitness and the process of gaining fitness even if sufficient time is unavailable to get fitness gains in physical education classes.[50] People who are trying to reduce coronary heart disease risk factors usually have to pay professionals to learn what they should have been taught in physical education.

Whether American children and youth are declining in fitness levels has been a subject of considerable discussion recently.[51] However, the National Children and Youth Fitness Study (NCYFS) data clearly indicates that children have become fatter in the last 20 years. Increased physical activity would help cardiovascular fitness as well as body fat control.[52]

Physical educators should play a major role in health and fitness promotion for the citizens of tomorrow. To do so will take a full-scale effort. Physical education programs must do more to "turn kids on" to their bodies. Students must have the opportunity to learn the joys of fitness and psychomotor accomplishment. Such insights have prompted fitness experts to evaluate physical education programs, revise fitness tests, and design fitness-specific curricula. They have created fitness tests that assess student performance, require individual goal setting, recognize the accomplishments of each student and emphasize a lifestyle of physical activity. Past fitness tests were designed to encourage recognition of the student who performed well according to norm-referenced criterion charts. This change of focus still leaves some questions unanswered:[53]

1. What are the health benefits for children and youth and do these carry over into adulthood?
2. What motivates children and youth to adhere to an activity program?
3. Do activity patterns in childhood and adolescence persist into adulthood?
4. How much of each fitness component is necessary to reduce the risk of health problems? We know the amount of exercise necessary to produce training effects in adults, but are these same amounts necessary to achieve health benefits? Do higher scores on fitness tests indicate better fitness, or can too much exercise be counterproductive?
5. Is it the level of fitness or an active lifestyle that results in benefits? Both the Harvard alumni study[54] and the Institute for Aerobics Research study[55] show that regular low-intensity exercise is enough to provide a protective effect in adults for cardiovascular disease and cancer. Regular total caloric expenditure seems to be the critical factor. The physical education instruction program can be the key to lifelong involvement. Students must learn why as well as how to exercise.

Instruction and Practice

Fitness programs must be carefully planned and structured to include opportunities to learn basic concepts and principles as well as to increase fitness. Table 8.3 illustrates a plan for implementing fitness instruction, assessment, and development. A number of fitness textbooks are available to teach physical fitness in the secondary schools, including *Fitness for Life* by Allsen, Harrison, and Vance; *Fitness for Life* by Corbin and Lindsey; and *Personal Fitness: Looking Good/Feeling Good* by Williams et al.

Fitness activities may be planned for part or all of a period. Such activities might include exercise routines, circuit training, obstacle courses, aerobic dance, jogging, cycling, swimming, and weight training. Changes can also be made in traditional drills and games to increase the

Table 8.3   A Teaching Schedule for a Fitness Unit

Design for a Lifetime Fitness Scope and Sequence Chart

Episode: 1
  Introduction to
  Physical Fitness
	Episode 2:
	  Improving Physical
	  Fitness
		Episode 3:
		  Flexibility: Meaning
		  and Values
			Episode 4:
			  Flexibility: Assessment
			  and Safety

Episode 5:
  Flexibility:
  Development
	Episode 6:
	  Muscular Strength:
	  Meaning
	  and Values
		Episode 7:
		  Muscular Strength:
		  Assessment and
		  Weight Training
			Episode 8:
			  Muscular Strength:
			  Development

Episode 9:
  Muscular Endurance:
  Meaning and Values
	Episode 10:
	  Muscular Endurance:
	  Assessment and
	  Activities
		Episode 11:
		  Muscular Endurance:
		  Development
			Episode 12:
			  Cardiorespiratory
			  Endurance: Meaning
			  and Values

Episode 13:
  Cardiorespiratory
  Endurance: Safety
  and Aerobic Activities
	Episode 14:
	  Cardiorespiratory
	  Fitness: Assessment
		Episode 15:
		  Cardiorespiratory
		  Fitness: Development
			Episode 16:
			  Body Composition:
			  Meaning, Values, and
			  Assessment

Episode 17:
  Body Composition:
  Control
	Episodes 18, 19, and 20: Personal Program Development and Activities		

amount of vigorous activity during physical education classes.[56] Some schools have a fitness room adjacent to the gymnasium (often a former equipment closet) and allow students to rotate to the fitness station during the period to work on those body areas that show the greatest need of improvement. Equipment such as that used in corporate fitness centers might be donated by community businesses.[57]

A written questionnaire that is not graded but is used to stimulate interest and point out needed areas of instruction is an effective way to introduce a unit on fitness. Questions might include the following:

1. The emphasis in the United States today on healthy lifestyles has resulted in a more physically fit nation, especially the youth.   __T__F

2. Exercising three days per week will maintain an adequate level of physical fitness.   __T__F

3. Children and youth under the age of 18 need not worry about coronary heart disease.   __T__F

4. A person burns more calories jogging one mile than walking the same distance.   __T__F

5. One must exercise at least 60 minutes per session to develop and maintain adequate physical fitness.   __T__F

6. Performing exercises involving the hips and waist will reduce the fat in those areas.   __T__F

7. Children who engage in a vigorous exercise program score higher on academic tests.   __T__F

8. Exercise increases the appetite.   __T__F

9. One should not exercise outside when temperatures reach zero degrees because the lungs may be damaged.   __T__F

10. Golf is a good aerobic exercise for those walking the course.   __T__F

Teachers themselves need to be examples of fitness. *Keep yourself physically fit!* Exercise with the students. Point out how other prominent people, such as movie stars and astronauts, stay physically fit.[58] Be enthusiastic about physical fitness. The success of any fitness program lies with the teacher. "Excellent leadership can overcome poor equipment and facilities but the opposite is seldom true."[59] Nothing can substitute for the example and enthusiasm of a good teacher. Teachers must adhere to and teach the principles of exercise: frequency, intensity, and duration.

Offer planned units of instruction focusing on health-related fitness. Teach students why physical fitness is important, the facts about exercise, how to evaluate their own fitness, how to plan their own programs, and guidelines for choosing activities, thus helping students become independent. Effective teachers provide programs that encourage success for all. "To continually force children into activities in which they don't succeed may promote temporary fitness improvements, but may not foster a lifetime of exercise."[60] Several aerobic activities can be conducted simultaneously, such as jump rope or aerobic dance, in the center of the gym while other students jog around the perimeter. Fitness routines such as circuit training, teacher-led exercises, student-led exercises, and astronaut drills can be included in each lesson.[61] Students are usually more willing to be active for longer periods of time when music is used. Let students choose their own fitness activities, invent or name their own exercises, bring their own music, and develop aerobic dance or other exercise routines. Use varied and exciting ways to develop fitness and promote a healthy lifestyle. Children and youth must first learn to participate because it is fun and thus learn to value participation in regular physical activity.[62]

Provide supplementary activities to encourage fitness. If all types of fitness are to be developed, the entire class time cannot be spent on cardiovascular endurance. Fitness is only one objective of physical education. Thus, some type of out-of-school physical activity must be included.[63] Homework using a program such as the Fitnessgram Fit for Life or Presidential Sports Award programs stimulates students to earn points by participating in physical activity with their families or friends.

Motivational Techniques

Although it is possible to hide one's scores on academic tests and assignments, it is usually impossible to hide one's fitness performance. Most students anticipate the physical fitness part of physical education based on their perceptions of their own bodies. Fitness testing can be a sensitive issue. The results of a fitness evaluation can bring up a variety of self-esteem issues if test results and realistic achievement are not understood and dealt with appropriately. Skinfolding is an especially sensitive issue, but it is important to do body composition testing.[64] Each student should be tested privately.

Fox indicated that "a focus on personal fitness improvement through carefully planned behavioral goal setting will allow children of all fitness abilities to experience a sense of mastery and competence," which tends to increase the importance students place on fitness.[65] Fox further points out that students with initially low self-esteem appear to receive the greatest benefits from successful fitness activities. Teachers must promote student success by rewarding small increments

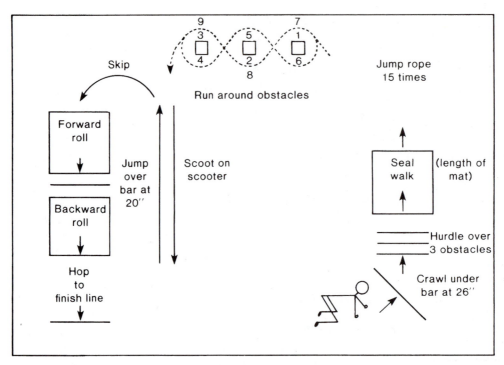

Figure 8.4 An example of an obstacle course.

of improvement without comparison to anyone other than the student being evaluated. Self-achievement can be taught as worthy of celebration—whether finishing a road race, lowering one's heart rate, or recognizing what it feels like to be fit rather than sluggish. Testing must not be taken lightly. To inch toward any fitness goal is significant and merits praise.

Which type of fitness award is best—performance awards, exercise behavior awards, or a combination of both? Or perhaps no awards should be given. What we do know is that very few youth (less than 2 percent) earn performance awards and that those who do are most likely to receive recognition for athletic accomplishments. "Certain children will have difficulty in attaining 'high' level performances regardless of exercise involvement."[66] Motor or skill-related fitness items, perhaps because they tend to test maturation and heredity, tend to eliminate youth from earning awards. "Late maturing children who have inherited low physiological and anatomical fitness capabilities may learn to believe that exercise is a waste of time because no matter how hard they try they still cannot match the scores of their more precocious and genetically fortunate peers."[67] Thus, process awards, such as completing a contract, are recommended. If performance awards are given, they should be criterion-referenced rather than norm-referenced. Improvement awards may be effective with special populations.

Do not forget to include some fun. "Without fun the program and the kids get the blahs."[68] Physical educators need to make running fun so students associate running with fun. *Running must never be used as a form of punishment.* Some fun running activities include the following runs: Scavenger, Predict, and Follow the Leader.[69] A fun, but challenging, obstacle course can also be set up inside the gymnasium or at an outside station to develop fitness (see figure 8.4).

Name _____			Date Begun _____								
Event	1-min Score	Training Dose	Workout Score								
			1	2	3	4	5	6	7	8
Jump rope — forward	40	20								
Jump rope — backward	35	18								
Push-ups	18	9								
Curl-ups	21	12								
Burpees	22	11								
Trunk twister	30	15								
Running in place (count each foot)	53	27								
Shuttle run (count laps)	13	7								

Completion Date of First Circuit _____

Completion Date of Second Circuit _____

Figure 8.5 Ten-minute circuit training record sheet.

Circuits are another fitness activity that can be challenging and motivating.[70] Tasks are performed either for time or by work load. An example of a circuit set up by work load and time is shown in figure 8.5. The work load or "training dose" for each task is the score obtained after performing the task for one minute and dividing the score in half. For example, if the student performs 10 curl-ups, the training dose is five. After the training dose is determined for each task, students perform the circuit for a specific amount of time. The time of the circuit is equal to one minute for each task (eight tasks require an eight-minute circuit). The student attempts to perform the circuit three times at the training dose for each task. At the end of eight minutes the student records how many times each task was performed. When the student is able to complete the circuit three times in the allotted time (which may take several weeks), the training dose is recalculated by once again obtaining a one-minute score for each task. If weight-training equipment is available, the circuit could employ that equipment.

Hester and Dunaway suggested developing fitness using stations, alternating activities using the upper body and legs. Each station has three color levels. Students are encouraged to try for the highest level. Activities include curl-ups with a ball, sit-and-reach with colored lines on the floor, shuttle runs with beanbags, push-ups with one hand while dribbling or moving beanbags with the other, and a partner tug-of-war.[71]

Other motivational techniques include the following:

1. *Goal setting.* Students should be involved in setting what they believe are reasonable goals for improving their fitness scores. They can be helped to set specific, measurable, challenging yet realistic goals. Students must be given help in devising strategies for reaching their goals, along with indications of their progress to help them evaluate themselves.[72] Fitness contracts could be used in conjunction with goal setting.[73]

2. *Special award programs.* Award programs recognize participation and achievement. The teacher may decide to award certificates or other awards to students who achieve their own predetermined goals in jogging, bicycling, or swimming, who achieve predetermined standards, or who participate in physical activity regularly.

3. *Fitness club.*[74] Fitness can be further promoted in a club devoted exclusively to engaging in and learning about physical fitness.

4. *Posters, charts, and banners displaying test results and improvement.* A chart, such as the one shown in figure 8.6, is unique and very motivational. Each class has a chart with a square block area for each student. Stickers or dots may be earned by students participating in acceptable fitness activities for 30 minutes outside of class. (Flexibility participation must be 30 minutes in the same week.) Students may earn stickers in any way they choose and arrange them on the chart. Other stickers may be earned in ways decided on by the class or the teacher (e.g., complete a three-day self-study of dietary habits and list appropriate changes).

5. *Unusual events.*
   a. Have a team jogging meet. Divide the class into teams of two or three people. Set a timer for a given time period, such as 15 or 30 minutes. Team members alternate laps, one runner at a time, and report to a scorer at the conclusion of each lap. Joggers are allowed to walk, skip, run, or move as they wish, but the team with the most laps completed within the time period wins the meet.
   b. Have competition among classes to see who can run the farthest in one month's time. Students record their laps each day. Awards may be given to individuals with the highest distance in each class and to all students who completed the goal.[75]
   c. Have a treasure hunt in which students run from point to point as directed by a series of clues. Students can pick up a marker at each point to show that they covered the entire course.[76]
   d. Sundberg suggested participation races in which students run to a given point and back, picking up a marker at the midpoint. Students are encouraged to pace themselves so they do not have to stop and walk.[77] Only those who finish are eligible for awards. Awards could be given for the fastest times as well as the team with the most finishers (divide the number of finishers by the number of starters). This type of race might be used at the end of a fitness unit after students have learned to pace themselves and have the endurance to last the entire distance.

Fitness Activities Chart

Fitness Activities

30 Min. CV = 1 △(with dot)   30 Min. Strength = 1 ▣

30 Min. Flexibility = 1 ●   Other = 1 ▣

Bill	Donna	Jane	Lane	Nancy	Rochelle	Tiff
△ ▫ ▫ ●			▫ ▫ ● ● ▫ ▫			
Bob ▫ ▫ ▫ ▫ ▫	**Eddy** ● ▫ ▫ △	**Jean**	**Linda**	**Neal** ▫ ▫ ▫ △ ▫ ▫ ▫ ▫	**Sandy**	**Tom**
Brenda △ ▫	**Elizabeth**	**Jim**	**Lori** ● △ ● ▫ ● ▫	**Patty**	**Sondra**	**Tracy**
Cindy △ ● ▫	**Freddy**	**John** ▫ ▫ ▫ ▫ △ ▫ ▫	**Lynn**	**Peter**	**Stacy** ▫ ▫ ▫ ▫ ▫ ● ●	**Vance**
Cory	**Gina**	**Kerri**	**Mark**	**Polly** ▫ ▫	**Steve**	**Violet**
Dave	**Hank** △ ▫ ▫ △	**Kurt**	**Mary** ▫ ▫ ▫ ▫ ▫ ▫	**Randy**	**Stewart**	**Wanda**
Debbie	**Hillary**	**Lana**	**Mitch**	**Rick**	**Tana**	**William**

Figure 8.6 Fitness activities chart.

e. Corbin suggested prediction races in which students attempt to run as close as possible to their predicted times. Individuals or teams can be used. The individual or team coming closest to its predicted time wins.[78]

f. Stein described a "Run for Fun" in which students run a specified distance and then record their overall finish place and category on a card. Awards are given to those finishing first in each category. Although Stein suggested age and gender for the categories, many other categories could be selected, such as eye color, color of tennis shoes, or birth month.[79]

g. Elsey suggested organizing walking clubs or having class "walks out of town." The class establishes a goal and records the mileage of each class member. An announcement is made when the class arrives at its goal (i.e., walked to Disneyland).[80]

6. *Fitness programs involving the school and community.*
   a. Fair: including displays, lectures, testing.
   b. Contest: involving runners, walkers, cyclers, swimmers, wheelchair participants (e.g., Jump Rope for Heart).[81]
      Family fitness program: This program combines nutrition and fitness. Students receive points when an adult family member exercises with them. Recipes are sent home and the student gets points if his or her family uses the recipe. All family members are encouraged to participate together and T-shirts are given to each participant.[82]

The real test of student motivation is the continued pursuit of health-related exercise. Lambert suggested a self-management model that uses goal-setting, attainment of goals, evaluation, and the setting of new goals to ensure continued participation by students.[83]

Evaluating Progress

"Fitness testing which reveals whether students are healthy or at risk is a meaningful practice. It allows students to decide whether or not they need to improve their health status. Students need meaningful information to make thoughtful decisions about the quality of their lives."[84]

Pangrazi and Corbin suggested three types of fitness testing:

1. Self-testing programs: Partners work together to test each other. Each person produces his/her own fitness profile, which is private property. The student can set goals and regularly monitor her/his progress toward those goals. This approach allows testing several times a year.
2. Personal best testing programs: formal testing for the purpose of receiving awards. This testing could be scheduled before or after school or at any other time for anyone who was interested. Not everyone in the school would be required to participate.
3. Institutional testing programs: used to evaluate attainment of institutional goals and objectives. Parents could be trained to help administer these formal tests. The tests could be given at certain levels such as 5th, 8th, and 10th grades.[85]

Several fitness test batteries are available for use by the physical educator. The components of each test are listed in Table 8.2. (Physical Best has merged with Fitnessgram and therefore is not listed in the table.)

Although the test batteries are similar, the programs differ in how the results are interpreted. All of them present a single fitness standard for each test. However, the standards vary with each program, so the teacher should know what the standards mean. The PCPFS National Award sets standards at approximately the 50th percentile. The Fitnessgram has standards at a level of fitness determined for good health. The Presidential Award sets standards at the 85th percentile. Table 8.4 shows an analysis of 6,959 Utah elementary school children, ages 6 to 12, on two tests—sit-ups and mile run—which are used in both programs. Data are presented showing the percentage of children who met or exceeded the standards for fitness as determined by each test battery. In addition, the percentage of children who met or exceeded the 50th percentile on the National Children and Youth Fitness Study[86] are presented to give a basis for comparison.

Table 8.4   Percentage of Children Who Met or Exceeded the Standards for Fitness as Determined by Five Different Criteria

Test	Sex	Pres. National	Fitnessgram	Pres. Challenge	NCYFS
Sit-up	M	43	72	13	57
Sit-up	F	40	59	9	54
Mile	M	56	80	19	50
Mile	F	53	73	10	43

Statistics: L. Gill Hilton, Brigham Young University.

The physical education teacher selecting a fitness program must first determine what outcomes are important and then select a program or programs to achieve those outcomes. These fitness testing programs can be expected to produce some of the following outcomes: (1) evaluate student health and fitness, (2) provide information for student goal setting, (3) recognize superior or excellent performance, (4) confirm improvement, and (5) verify a record of results to motivate students, inform parents, and place in school files.

Fitness objectives must meet the needs of *all* students and prepare each of them for lifelong participation. To meet all goals and expectations of fitness, it may be necessary to combine components of several, or all, of the programs discussed. For example, the teacher might administer the Fitnessgram or PCPFS test battery for screening and evaluation purposes. Students can then set personal goals, and teachers can design curricula to teach and practice fitness and wellness concepts. The teacher could choose a motivational recognition system from any of the programs.

Educate students about weight control, but be sensitive to individual needs. This is an emotional issue for many students. Keep in mind that the clinical definition of obesity varies. Standards will depend on the definition used.[87] Going, Williams, and Lohman have suggested critical levels for youth body fat percentages. A greater risk of coronary heart disease occurs for males with a percent body fat of 25 percent or higher and females at 30 percent or higher. They suggest that continued body composition testing is important.[88]

Sensitive teachers hold the key to healthy lifestyles for today's youth. Keep accurate records of participation, both in and outside of class. Figure 8.7 is an example of a physical fitness record-keeping form. Use the records as guidelines for program development, encouragement, and praise. Keep in mind that "most experts now agree that students should not be assigned grades based upon fitness test performance."[89]

Teachers, and the fitness programs they incorporate in the schools, can have a profound effect on students for a lifetime. Thoughtful consideration of program objectives and selection of a program based on these objectives will help students treat their body as the wonderful instrument it is.

Movement Skills

The major emphasis of most physical education programs is the development of movement skills. Whether the thrust is sport skills or rhythms and dance, teachers spend the majority of program time concentrating on improving skill execution. Despite this, many students are not

Philadelphia Physical Fitness Test Score Report

School _____ Class _____ Instructor _____

Student Gender _____ (make a separate list for boys and girls)

S = score (number, time, distance)   % = percentile rank

Students	1st Test										2nd Test									
	S&R		Jump		Sit-Up		Chin/Hang		Run		S&R		Jump		Sit-Up		Chin/Hang		Run	
	S	%	S	%	S	%	S	%	S	%	S	%	S	%	S	%	S	%	S	%

Figure 8.7 Philadelphia physical fitness test score report.
Source: Philadelphia Public Schools.

learning effective motor skills. Graham reviewed two studies in the United States and Canada in which experts rated students as "weak" or "marginally satisfactory" in motor skills. Both studies found girls consistently less skilled than boys.[90] Reasons given for the low skill level were the lack of time spent in physical activity, failure to perform the skills correctly, lack of specific feedback, time spent playing games instead of improving skills, and failure to teach skills for game conditions.

The skill emphasis over the past two decades has been that of "lifetime sports," primarily individual or dual activities that students can continue to enjoy after their school years. It is estimated that 75 percent of the nation's secondary schools emphasize lifetime sports such as bowling, badminton, tennis, frisbee, and racquetball in their physical education programs.[91] The concept of team sports has expanded from the traditional favorites to games like team handball,[92] New Games,[93] and modified games such as Speed-a-way[94] or volley tennis.[95] Team sports have also been taught using a professional league model.[96] Aerobic dance gained popularity in the 1980s and is popular in physical education programs. These exercises set to music emphasize cardiorespiratory fitness, strength, and flexibility. Although the popular activities change from time to time, the basic thrust in physical education programs still remains that of teaching movement skills. Effective teachers need useful program aids and materials to enhance these curricular offerings.

Instruction and Practice

Movement skills should be taught in an orderly teaching progression with activities chosen according to student ability. The teacher may decide to use any or all of the following activities to teach physical skills:

1. *Warm-up:* Use skills previously taught to warm up.
2. *Demonstration:* Students are shown the movements they are expected to reproduce. Demonstrations are used to create interest or to show how something is to be done, such as a sports skill or safety procedure. They help students avoid misconceptions. Procedures include the following:
   a. Plan a meaningful demonstration.
   b. Practice the demonstration or acquire a good demonstrator. Demonstrations can involve the use of live models, films, videotapes, or other media. When demonstrating sports skills, remember to use the mirror-image technique—that is, say "right hand" to the students and use the left hand—or face away from the students so they will see the image as they will be doing it.
   c. Assemble and set up equipment and the seating arrangement so all students can see and hear.
   d. Briefly explain the purpose of the demonstration.
   e. Demonstrate using key points to enhance perception.
3. *Drills:* Drills are contrived situations used to learn or to review skills. They provide a large number of practice trials in a short amount of time. Skills tests can be used as drills when students are allowed to repeat the tests to achieve higher levels of skill. Examples of drills are a partner volley in volleyball, a three-person weave in basketball, or a toss-and-hit drill in tennis. Procedures include:
   a. Demonstrate and/or explain the learning activity.
   b. Organize small groups for maximum participation.

c. Make drills as gamelike as possible to ensure transfer to game situations.
d. Provide continuous feedback to ensure correct learning of skills.
e. Adjust or change drills to provide for individual differences in student learning.
4. *Lead-up games:* Students need transitions from drill practice to game situations so they feel comfortable in game play. Lead-up games bridge this gap by allowing students to practice skills in gamelike settings, in which interest can be maintained while learning to refine and apply skills. Lead-up games are modified team games that involve one or more of the fundamental skills, rules, or procedures used in a major team game.[97] Procedures are as follows:
a. Present games from simple to more complex.
b. Use games to complement drills, not replace them.
c. Organize the game to provide maximum participation.
d. Provide evenly matched competition.
e. Match the game to the ability of the students.
f. Make maximum use of time and space.
g. Rotate players so all students get an opportunity to play all positions.[98]
5. *Game or team play:* Games are played using official or simplified rules. Metzler suggested a number of strategies for teaching using competitive games, including:[99]
a. Chalk talks.
b. Walk-through on the field.
c. Taking advantage of situations that occur in the game.
d. "Instant replays" allowing students to play the action again.
e. Player-coach manipulation of events forcing students to concentrate on certain skills and guiding play toward players who are not being included.
f. Acting as a sports analyst by making observations and guiding play through questions.
g. Making a call and then asking students to supply the reason or solution.
6. *Competition:* Competitive game situations are provided with an expected winner and loser.

Graham encouraged teachers to ask themselves five questions concerning instruction for motor skill development. They are:

1. How much time are the students spending in productive practice?
2. Am I refining the qualitative aspects of the motor skills?
3. Am I providing appropriate amounts of specific feedback?
4. How much time do the students in my classes spend playing games? Is the low-skilled student getting as much practice as the high-skilled player?
5. Am I providing the appropriate transitions so students can actually practice open skills in dynamic environments that aren't "official" games so students can try again and again without fear of penalty or harassment?[100]

Do not be fearful of straying from traditional curricular offerings. Valuable learning experiences can result for students engaged in the following nontraditional activity units:

1. *Work:* Students are taught certain tasks that facilitate the performance of work in lifting, carrying, pushing, pulling, striking, and the like. The topics of stability, force, leverage, momentum, and friction are taught through such activities as "tray relay

races." In this activity students weave in and out of markers carrying various objects (an empty bottle, a bottle one-third full of water, and a bottle three-quarters full of water) on a tray to determine the differences they feel.[101]

2. *Stress Management:* The topics of stress are discussed. Students are taught relaxation responses and techniques of exercise, recreation, and diet to cope with stress.[102]

3. *Self-defense:* Students are taught skills and strategies to protect themselves when physically attacked.[103]

4. *Movement Awareness:* Activities such as yoga, karate, aikido, or t'ai chi ch'uan are taught.[104]

5. *Cycling:* Students are taught about equipment, safety, and riding.[105]

As mentioned previously, activities not usually performed in the gymnasium can be adapted to the school site. For example, tennis and bowling can be simulated in the gym so students get a nearly authentic experience.[106] Where adequate room exists, a miniature golf course can be set up so students get the experience of keeping score and learning the rules and etiquette of the game. Whiffle balls are used to ensure safety. Cross-country skiing can be taught during the winter months using both the outside playing fields and the gymnasium.[107]

Motivational Techniques

Carron[108] cited many factors affecting motivation. One that applies to learning movement skills is reward. The following examples are inexpensive, easy-to-administer incentives to motivate students:

1. *Recognition clubs* such as the Bull's-eye Club for archery students or the 100-Mile Club for swimmers or joggers.

2. *Skill charts* used in multievent activities such as gymnastics or track and field. Students choose from a list what skills they wish to practice and progress at their own rate. Skills are checked off on the charts as they are completed.

3. *Spotlight board* recognizes individuals or teams for performance, sportsmanship, leadership, or honors.

4. *Awards* such as certificates, trophies, or T-shirts are given to outstanding performers.[109]

A second motivational factor mentioned by Carron was the introduction of novelty or change in routine. One means of incorporating novelty is through the introduction of nontraditional games such as team ball[110] or quad ball,[111] middle-school games developed to teach students skills and strategies.

Students can create games if the teacher provides sufficient structure. Kraft suggests that teachers include stipulations regarding any or all of the following: (1) purpose—the objectives and possible outcomes of the game, (2) grade level, (3) motor skills needed, (4) kind of game (ball, tag, etc.), (5) number of players, (6) organization—procedures, formations, boundaries, (7) rules, (8) scoring, and (9) equipment. Challenges might include: "Create a new game in which each team attempts to get another team's objects, while defending their own objects."[112] Hedlund mentioned that affective goals can be taught using these nontraditional sports.[113]

Nothing motivates students more than success, thus it is important to select instructional strategies that ensure success for all students. Instructional strategies were discussed in chapter 7.

Tournaments

If students have attained a sufficient level of playing ability, tournaments can be motivating for all students. Adaptations of tournament structures can also aid instruction[114] and improve cooperative skills.[115] Learning communication skills and accepting responsibility can be enhanced by having the students officiate the games. The following are types of tournaments that may be incorporated into a unit of instruction or used for league or intramural play.

Round Robin. In the round robin tournament each player competes against every other player. The victor is the player who wins the most games and loses the fewest. This structure is very time-consuming but provides maximum participation for participants. After players or teams have been ranked by previous competition, a smaller ability-grouped round robin competition is effective for participants of like ability. A round robin schedule for six teams is shown here:

1−6	1−5	1−4	1−3	1−2
2−5	6−4	5−3	4−2	3−6
3−4	2−3	6−2	5−6	4−5

This schedule was easily formulated by keeping team 1 stationary and moving every other team one place counterclockwise on the schedule. This procedure is repeated for each round until the teams rotate back to their original positions. To compute the number of games, use the following formula:

N (N − 1) divided by 2

$$\frac{6(6-1)}{2} = \frac{6 \times 5}{2} = \frac{30}{2} = 15$$

Another representation of a round robin tournament illustrates the standings of each player or team. This structure allows players or teams to select the order in which they play opponents and permits longer or shorter games to be played (see figure 8.8).

Team	1	2	3	4	5	6	Wins	Losses	Rank
1				15−8	6−15		1	1	
2									
3									
4	8−15							1	
5	15−6						1		
6									

Figure 8.8 A round robin tournament chart.

Several adaptations of the round robin tournament that overcome limitations of time, facilities, absences, and scheduling were suggested by Eason. Baseline Basketball, a unit-long activity, involves earning points for acquisition of skill, knowledge, attitude, and game play. Class Team Tennis involves teams of four boys and four girls who play other teams in singles, doubles, and mixed doubles. A team wins a point for each game won by a team member. This tournament can be used for all racket sports. Computer Softball uses computer-generated teams, which change daily. An individual point system is based on the hits, runs, and defensive plays of each player during the tournament.[116] Veal suggests playing for time and recording points scored by each player rather than wins and losses.[117]

Elimination. When elimination tournaments are used, all competitors except the winner are eliminated after one or two losses depending on the type of tournament selected. Tournaments are set up with a standard number of open slots, with the total number of teams being divisible by two (e.g., 2, 4, 8, 16, 32). If the exact number of teams needed for the brackets is not available, some teams must be given a *bye* (an exemption from playing a game in a round). To determine who gets the byes, teams are *seeded* (ranked according to how they are expected to finish based on their record from previous play). Byes are placed as far apart as possible on the tournament chart so seeded players are not playing each other in the first round and byes occur only in the first round.

Single Elimination.. A single elimination tournament is a short tournament with half of the teams being eliminated in the first round. The winner is determined quickly, but it may not be the best team. An example of a single elimination tournament with six entries is shown in figure 8.9. Figure 8.10 shows an example of 13 entries.

Consolation. A consolation tournament allows teams to compete for third place after losing in the first round. When a team loses one game after the first round, it is eliminated. Winners move to the right on the bracket tournament chart and losers move to the left. An example of a consolation tournament with four teams is shown in figure 8.11. Figure 8.12 shows an example of a tournament with 16 teams.

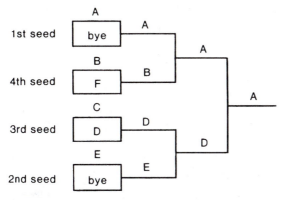

Figure 8.9 A single elimination tournament for six entries.

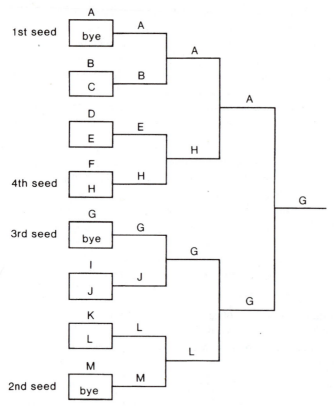

Figure 8.10 A single elimination tournament for 13 entries.

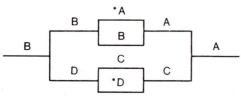

*Seeded players or teams

Figure 8.11 A consolation tournament for four entries.

Double Elimination. A double elimination tournament requires that each team must lose two games before being eliminated. It is nearly as effective in producing a true winner as a round robin tournament and is less time-consuming. Examples of double elimination tournaments for 4 and 14 teams are shown in figures 8.13 and 8.14. Note that for 14 teams, 16 slots are required.

To determine the number of games to be played, compute 2N − (1 or 2). For example, 2 × 14 = 28 − 1 or 2 = 27 or 26 games.

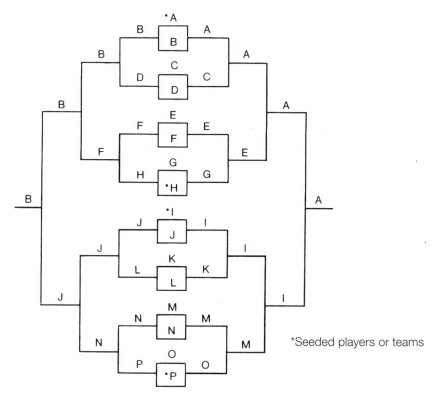

Figure 8.12 A consolation tournament for 16 entries.

*Seeded players or teams

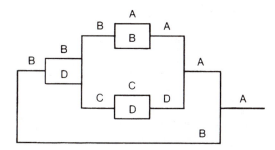

Figure 8.13 A double elimination tournament for four entries.

Challenge. In challenge tournaments each student challenges as many other players as possible within the class or group. A win allows students to change places with the loser. The best players or teams move to the top of the tournament chart. Players can be placed in an initial order by a draw, seeding, or in the order they signed up. It is sometimes fun to put the best players at the bottom of the charts so they have to win to advance to the top.

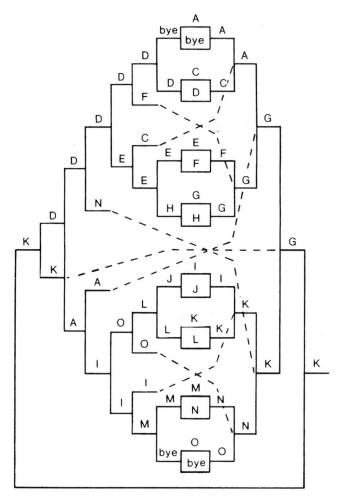

Figure 8.14 A double elimination tournament for up to 16 entries.

Ladder. A ladder tournament places teams directly above one another on a chart. Challenges are generally limited to one or two places above. Usually the team judged to be the best will be placed at the top of the ladder (see figure 8.15).

Spider Web. A spider web tournament, as shown in figure 8.16, is a unique variation of a ladder. Participants in each section of the web engage in their own challenge. Challenges are made one level above. Winners advance toward the middle of the web. On an ending date winners are placed in an elimination tournament. Participants at each level can also be placed in their own elimination tournament.

Pyramid. A pyramid tournament is designed to accommodate large numbers of participants. A team may challenge any team on the same line with it on the tournament chart as well as those to the immediate left or right on the line above. See figure 8.17 for an example.

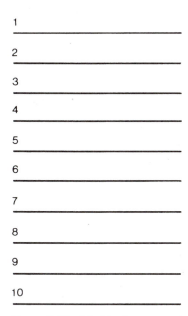

1 _____

2 _____

3 _____

4 _____

5 _____

6 _____

7 _____

8 _____

9 _____

10 _____

Figure 8.15 A ladder tournament.

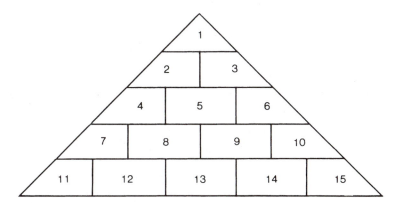

Figure 8.16 A spider web tournament.

Figure 8.17 A pyramid tournament.

Funnel. A funnel tournament combines the best features of both the ladder and the pyramid by accommodating large numbers of participants while also ranking them. The lower half of the funnel is governed by the rules for a pyramid and the upper half by the rules of a ladder. An example is shown in figure 8.18.

Clock. A clock tournament is an animated version of a challenge tournament. Participants challenge no more than two numbers ahead. The tournament ends when any player advances full circle. More or fewer numbers may be used. See figure 8.19.

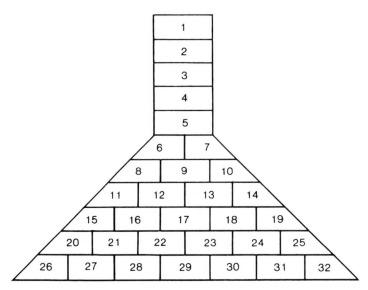

Figure 8.18 A funnel tournament.

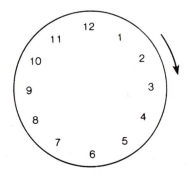

Figure 8.19 A clock tournament.

Evaluating Progress

Teacher evaluation of students' playing ability is the most accurate way to check skill performance. When skills tests are used, they should simulate the game situation as closely as possible. A volleyball skills test in which the participant executes the bump, set, and spike sequentially is an example of this principle. Upon receiving the ball, students alternate a bump and a set to themselves, working the ball into spiking position, until six series have been completed. The ball is spiked over the net to complete the test.[118]

In addition to the evaluation procedures discussed in chapter 9, teachers might also consider a feedback checklist when evaluating student performance of movement skills. For example, specific proficiencies are checked off when they are executed. Students are expected to have all proficiencies checked off. Figure 8.20 illustrates such a checklist.

```
┌─────────────────────────────────────────────────────────────────────┐
│                          Racquetball                                  │
│                    Rally Form Task Sheet                              │
│   Name _____                       │
│                                                                       │
│   _____ Passed                                                       │
│                                                                       │
│        The instructor will mark YES if student is consistent          │
│   in doing the following:                                             │
│                                                                       │
│                          1       2       3       4       5            │
│                       YES│NO  YES│NO  YES│NO  YES│NO  YES│NO          │
│    1. Waits for the                                                   │
│       ball to drop.                                                   │
│                                                                       │
│    2. Moves with the                                                  │
│       ball.                                                           │
│                                                                       │
│    3. Keeps opponent                                                  │
│       in view.                                                        │
│                                                                       │
│    4. Assumes                                                         │
│       position facing                                                 │
│       side wall                                                       │
│       before hitting                                                  │
│       the ball.                                                       │
│                                                                       │
│    5. Assumes the                                                     │
│       proper attack                                                   │
│       position to                                                     │
│       play the ball.                                                  │
│                                                                       │
│             Date:                                                     │
│   Comments:                                                           │
└─────────────────────────────────────────────────────────────────────┘
```

Figure 8.20 A feedback checklist for evaluating
student performance of movement skills.

Concepts

To be physically educated means that students must understand concepts "about the body and physical activity that prepare each individual to want to live and be capable of living a physically active lifestyle."[119] Teaching concepts is not easy. It requires planning; however, learning occurs faster when students understand the principles involved in skill performance.

Instruction and Practice

The knowledge explosion has dramatically increased knowledge in physical education. The *Basic Stuff Series* can help physical educators teach concepts in physical education classes.[120] Series I contains an explanation of the concepts, and Series II, *Basic Stuff in Action,* has three booklets designed to help teachers apply the concepts to specific age groups (K–3, 4–8, and 9–12). Examples from both booklets appear in chapter 4 in figures 4.3 and 4.4.

Study guides in the form of study sheets, workbooks, or journals are also useful in promoting cognitive learning. Students involved in completing a study sheet, a workbook assignment,

ARCHERY STUDY SHEET

INSTRUCTIONS: Briefly answer the following questions.

1. List *two* important factors about each of the following:
   Stance:

   Nock:

   Draw:

   Anchor:

   Aim:

   Release:

   Follow through:

2. Describe aiming techniques with a bowsight, including how to correct errors.

3. State how to score the following: liners, rebounds, pass-throughs, perfect end, shooting seven arrows.

4. Fill in the necessary information for the arrows shown below.

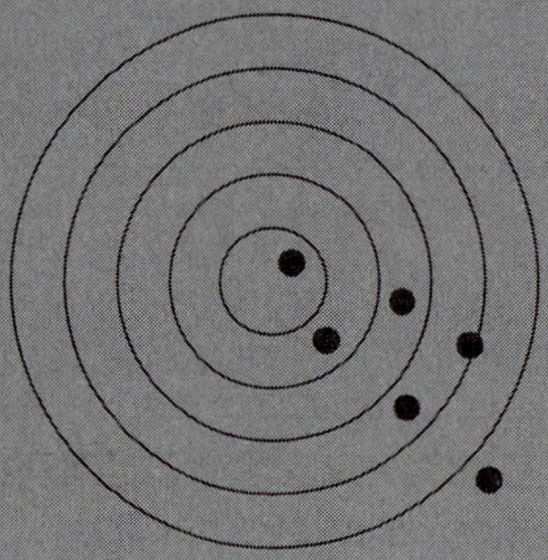

Figure 8.21   Archery study sheet.

or a journal entry have moved to the "I do, I understand" level of learning. These aids provide another chance for information to be remembered and are a good review for a test or before competing in tournament competition. An example is the archery study sheet shown in figure 8.21.

Study guides can be used for individual study or review or as an adjunct to class instruction. They can focus student attention on important instructional points. Simplify instructions and use variety in their construction to prevent boredom. Procedures include the following:

1. Use appropriate vocabulary and reading level for students.
2. Eliminate nonessential items.

3. If possible, write so that the student is actively involved in learning by filling in the blanks or working through the material to be learned.
4. Answers to study guides can be provided through class instruction, individual units, "A Rule a Day" bulletin boards, or individual study of text materials or media.

Some study guides can be used to help students excused from active participation to learn concepts by reading articles and answering questions pertinent to the sport or activity being taught.

Motivational Techniques

Several techniques can be used to increase student motivation to learn concepts. Colorful posters with a thought, term, or rule for the day can be posted on a bulletin board for students to read as they enter the activity area.

Instructional games add a new dimension to the learning process. They are also a viable option for involving students who do not normally like to participate. They can be used individually or in groups and are especially effective when regular lesson plans cannot be used due to bad weather, scheduling changes, or facility unavailability. Design games to meet specific course objectives and to keep the activities at the appropriate learning level of the students (e.g., vocabulary, spelling, content). Remember also that instructional games can lose their effectiveness if used too often.

The following games could be used as study sheets, as activities for extra credit, as activities to be done after completing regular assignments, or just for fun. Instructional games can be found in resource books, magazines, or at conventions and workshops. Creative teachers will not hesitate to make up original materials.

1. *The crossword puzzle* (figure 8.22). A crossword puzzle can be created by printing terms in the squares on a piece of graph paper and working out interlocking words. A ruler is used to draw around the squares. The numbers are added. Computer programs are available for creating crossword puzzles. The puzzle must be proofread for accuracy before it is used. Answers can be listed alphabetically for use by students who have difficulty spelling. Students can also design crossword puzzles and word search puzzles.
2. *Pyramid* (figure 8.23). Another puzzle-type study aid or motivational device is the pyramid. The longest terms for recall are placed at the bottom of the pyramid, which is built upward to the shortest terms. This works well for a test of knowledge of rules and terminology.
3. Other examples of instructional games are:
   a. Soccer Scrambled Words (see figure 8.24).
   b. Hidden Terms (see figure 8.25).
   c. Bingo Lingo (see figure 8.26).
   d. Sports Bowl (see figure 8.27).
   e. Baseball (see figure 8.28).

Evaluating Progress

Both study guides and instructional games can be used for informal evaluation. The construction and administration of written tests is discussed in chapter 9.

Instructions: Fill in the puzzle using the list of possible answers given below.

Across

2. The amount of force required to pull the bow to full draw.
4. The practice of shooting with bows and arrows.
9. An arrow that strikes the scoring area and bounces off the target.
10. The third ring outside the gold, counting four or three points.
11. To sight for hitting the target with the left eye closed for right-handed archers.
12. To pull the bowstring back to the anchor point.
14. Plastic "feathers" on an arrow.
15. A device that provides force for shooting arrows.
16. Six arrows shot in a row.
17. The fiberglass, aluminum, or wooden portion of the arrow.
18. A term for archery equipment.
21. The second ring outside the gold, counting six or five points.
22. Two feathers on the arrow shaftment that are not at right angles to the nock and are the same color are called _____ feathers.
23. To place the tip of the index finger of the string hand on the anchor point and hold it steady until the release.
27. The outer ring on the target face, counting two or one point.
28. A certain place on the face to which the index finger of the string hand is brought consistently (every time) on each draw (two words).
30. The round object, marked with circles, at which the arrows are shot.
31. The side of the bow away from the string.
34. The upper and lower parts of the bow, divided by the handle.
35. Colored stripes used for identification that are placed near the feathers on an arrow.
37. The plastic portion of the arrow into which the bowstring is fitted.
39. A leather protection worn on the forearm to keep the string from hurting the arm (two words).
40. The arm, the hand of which holds the bow during shooting.
41. A device for holding arrows.
42. A leather piece worn on the shooting hand to protect the fingers (two words).
43. The center of the target, counting ten or nine points.
44. The side of the bow toward the string.

Down

1. The edge of the target face beyond the white ring, counting zero points, sometimes marked "P" on the scorecard.
3. The center part of a bow that the archer grips with his or her hand.
5. The first ring outside the gold, counting eight or seven points.
6. To shoot the arrow from a position of full draw by straightening the fingers of the string hand.
7. Vanes are substitutes for this material.
8. The feather on an arrow that is set at right angles to the nock; usually of a different color from the hen feathers (two words).
13. To stand ready to shoot.
19. The middle section of an arrow.
20. Archery "games."
21. The string of the bow.
24. The part of the bow on which the arrow rests while shooting.
25. The line upon which the archer stands while shooting at a target.
26. The metal point of an arrow, on the forward end.
29. To brace the bow.
32. The object that is shot.

Figure 8.22 An archery crossword puzzle.

33. A method of recording hits and the total score on a score card.
36. The thread wrapped around the bowstring to keep the arrow or the fingers from wearing out the string where the arrow is nocked.
38. An archery ground.
40. To string a bow.

Possible Answers

Address	**Belly**	**Crest**	**Hen**	**Red**	**Shooting line**
Aim	**Black**	**Draw**	**Hold**	**Release**	**String**
Anchor	**Blue**	**End**	**Limbs**	**Rest**	**Tackle**
Anchor point	**Bow**	**Face**	**Nock**	**Rounds**	**Target**
Archery	**Bowarm**	**Feathers**	**Petticoat**	**Quiver**	**Tip**
Arm guard	**Bowstring**	**Finger tab**	**Pile**	**Scoring**	**Vanes**
Arrow	**Brace**	**Gold**	**Range**	**Serving**	**Weight**
Back	**Cock feather**	**Handle**	**Rebound**	**Shaft**	**White**

Figure 8.22 *(Continued)*

Pyramid Volleyball Quiz

Name _____

Period _____

Date _____

Instructions: Fill in the pyramid with the appropriate word or words to complete each sentence.

1.

2.

3.

4.

5.

6.

7.

8.

9.

10.

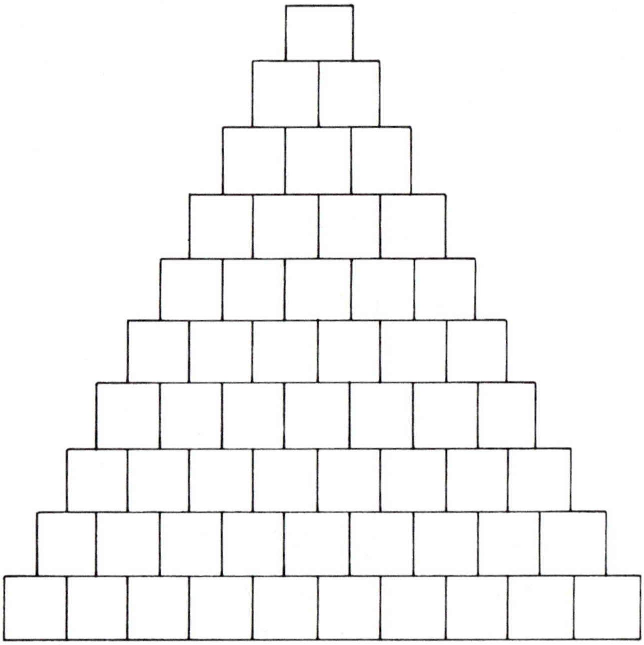

1. The winner of an official game must have at least a _____ point lead. (number)
2. The player in the _____ _____ position is the server. (initials)
3. An official team has _____ _____ _____ players.
4. A ball that lands on a court line is _____ _____ _____ _____ .
5. Except on a _____ _____ _____ _____ _____ the ball may be played out of the net.
6. To _____ _____ _____ _____ _____ _____ , is the moving of all players into position to begin serving.
7. _____ _____ _____ _____ _____ _____ _____ is called when the serving team loses turn of service.
8. The plan of attack used by a team to score points is called _____ _____ _____ _____ _____ _____ _____ _____ .
9. When the _____ _____ _____ _____ _____ _____ _____ _____ _____ team loses the rally, a point is scored.
10. In playing the ball, a player may step on but not over the _____ _____ _____ _____ _____ _____ _____ _____ _____ _____ .

Figure 8.23 A pyramid test.

Soccer Scrambled Words

Instructions: Unscramble the following words. The circled letters will give you a message.

1. L Y E A R P S   ___ ___ ___ ___ ___ ___ Ⓞ
2. N R U   ___ Ⓞ ___
3. N W I   ___ ___ Ⓞ
4. C R O E S   Ⓞ ___ ___ ___ ___
5. B H A C A L F K   Ⓞ ___ ___ ___ ___ ___ ___ ___
6. I K C K   ___ Ⓞ ___ ___
7. T N P U   ___ ___ Ⓞ ___
8. R E E F I K K C   ___ ___ Ⓞ ___ ___ ___ ___ ___
9. S S A P   Ⓞ ___ ___ ___
10. B B E L I R D   ___ ___ ___ ___ Ⓞ ___ ___
11. R E O S C C   ___ ___ ___ Ⓞ ___ ___
12. L A O G   ___ ___ Ⓞ ___
13. S L U O F   ___ ___ ___ Ⓞ ___
14. D F I L E   ___ ___ Ⓞ ___ ___

Figure 8.24 Soccer scrambled words.

Hidden Terms—Track and Field

Instructions: Circle the terms that have to do with track and field. Words may read horizontally, vertically, or diagonally, and forward or backward.

```
B R A K O S T S H O T A R T A L B U F A
T A R T A N B A U V A B A T O N A L I L
S T R O M M I N R A V E N D S Y L V N C
T J A V E L I N D U L I L I T A L S I R
E L S T R O M B L I A E X S R W S U S O
E X R I S T A H E F I I S C O N T N H S
P I T A N D R O S F H U L U N U A D A S
L E V A B E L D D A M O F S P R I N T C
E R I K M A D N U M C I T A O S D T R O
C I A M A M A D I K B A T L L I Y U I U
H U A N A K I L O L R O R O E L A T P N
A H S O C I T R O T K O N F V A R T L T
S T I A X L V Y E F H G N F A D D A E R
E L R E L A Y R G H J K L I U N S W J Y
B T A P E X S T V U O L N C L R T E U H
G N I R U S A E M Y N L O I T U T I M E
M E T E R U S P O U N D S A P S T G P J
D A M A R K E R N U O D F L A Y D H M D
S K C O L B G N I T R A T S R L C T D U
```

Bar	Pit
Baton	Polevault
Clock	Pounds
Cross Country	Relay
Discus	Runway
Distance	Shot
Finish	Sprint
Hammer	Starter
High Jump	Starting Blocks
Hurdle	Steeplechase
Javelin	Tape
Kilo	Tartan
Long Jump	Time
Marker	Track and Field
Measuring	Triple Jump
Meter	Weight
Officials	Yards

Figure 8.25 Hidden terms.

Bingo Lingo — Diving

Instructions: The teacher draws a card one at a time and reads the definition. The first student to circle five terms in a row—either vertically, diagonally, or horizontally—wins.

Approach	Back Dive	Backward Take-off	Cutaway Dive	Degree of Difficulty
Entry	Forward Dive	Header	Hurdle	Free
Inward Dive	Jackknife	Layout	Lift	Opening
Pike	Press	Rotate	Somersault Dive	Spin
Swan	Straight	Takeoff	Tuck	Twist Dive

Figure 8.26 Bingo Lingo.
Source: Jack Romine and Joyce M. Harrison.
Brigham Young University.

Sports Bowl

Instructions: Follow the procedure below to play "Sports Bowl."
1. Divide class into two teams of equal size.
2. Read a question.
3. The first person to raise his or her hand gets to answer the question. If the question is answered correctly, a bonus question is directed to the answering team; if it is answered incorrectly, the other team may attempt the answer (and the bonus).
4. There is a thirty-second time limit on questions.
5. The scoring is as follows:
   Correct answer—10 points
   Correct bonus answer—5 points
   Incorrect bonus—no penalty

Questions can be created from sports, history, current events, game rules, etc. Typical questions and bonus questions might be:

Q. Who holds the record for lifetime home runs?

B. What is the record?

Q. How many points can be scored on a penalty bully in field hockey?

B. When is a penalty bully awarded?

Figure 8.27 Sports bowl.

Baseball

Instructions: Follow the procedure below to play "Baseball."

1. Mark a diamond on the floor of a classroom or locker room area or use a magnetic board.
2. Write a list of questions about a sport.
3. Divide the class into two teams—designating one as the batting team and the other as the fielding team.
4. Ask the first batter a question. If correctly answered, the batter moves to first base. If incorrectly answered, the fielding team is allowed to answer. If the fielding team answers correctly, the batter is out. If not, the batter sits down and the next batter is up.
5. Continue until three outs are made or all batters have been up, then exchange teams.
6. Points are scored as runs are "batted" in.

Figure 8.28 Baseball.

Adventure Activities

Adventure activities are relative newcomers to the physical education program. They include activities that invoke the emotions of excitement, challenge, apprehension, and fear. They are included in the curriculum to meet the need for adventure and to build self-confidence, self-reliance, and independence.[121] Such outcomes are possible because students learn to think clearly and make wise decisions, to have the courage to act, and to control the emotion of fear.[122] Most of these activities require teamwork. See Glover and Midara for several ideas for developing teamwork.[123] Several ideas include:

1. Doing exercises as a team.
2. Creating a game.
3. Describing each team member using positive adjectives.

Instruction and Practice

Instruction and practice in adventure activities must be geared to the level of the students so they have the necessary skills and abilities to participate safely. Some students are ready to immediately engage in risk activities, but individual students should have the option of deciding whether they want this type of experience.

Challenge Activities. Students participating in challenge activities develop the ability to cooperate in a group, learn to solve problems, and improve individual fitness.[124] Games are one means of offering adventure and challenge to students. The nature of some games equalizes competition and makes everybody a winner. The New Games Foundation pioneered this concept. From this beginning cooperative sports and games and the multicultural physical education approach has emerged. Examples of challenge activities include the following:

1. *Knots*—Approximately 12 players stand in a circle, shoulder-to-shoulder, and place hands in the center of the circle. Everyone grabs a couple of hands of people who are *not* next to them. They cannot grab both hands from the same person. The objective of the game is to untie the knot, without releasing hands. The game is complete when all players are standing in one circle facing each other holding hands.[125]

2. *All on One Side*—A team of four or five players on one side of a volleyball court (with no one on the other side) attempts to move back and forth to the other side of the net as many times as possible without the ball touching the floor. Using a balloon for a ball, each player volleys the balloon to another player on the same side of the net and then scoots under the net to the other side. The last player to touch the balloon taps it over the net and scoots under. The receiving players try to keep the balloon in play on the new side of the net as they repeat the process. As the players improve, two balloons may be put into play at one time.[126]

Teachers might want to vary the components of an activity to cause students to perceive risk and feel a sense of fear while actually participating in a safe environment. For example, the group is divided into pairs. One person in each pair puts on a blindfold and stands behind a starting line. The partner stands 10 feet behind. Other pairs are at least 6 feet away. On the starting signal the blindfolded persons are guided by the verbal directions of their partners around an obstacle course, or they may be guided to perform certain activities such as walking backward.[127]

Initiative Activities. Group initiative activities are designed to provide adventure while incorporating problem-solving experiences that require a cooperative effort. Participants get to know and understand one another while developing trust and a sense of group belonging. Groups should include no more than 20 participants. Success is measured by group accomplishment rather than individual achievement. Simulation of the activity setting is stressed and little sophisticated equipment is required. The following are examples of initiative activities:

1. *Prisoners of War*—Participants are brought into a dimly lighted handball court. A 5-foot-high badminton net is stretched across the court to represent a fence. A 6-foot pipe or 15-foot rope is on the floor on the prisoners' side of the net. A mat is under the net for safety. Participants are told that guards are coming to execute them in 20 minutes. The task is to get all prisoners over the fence and up a 15- to 18-foot-high wall into the observation gallery before the guards arrive. Anyone touching the net is electrocuted. The mat may be moved to the wall for safety, but it may not be used to aid in the escape.[128] Teachers must supervise carefully and suggest safety techniques such as spotting when appropriate.
2. *River Crossing*—Participants are brought to a stream of water or a gap between two platforms, representing a 14-foot-wide river. Materials available are three 2-inch by 8-inch planks with lengths of 6, 9, and 11 feet. Participants are told the enemy is pursuing 20 minutes behind. The task is to successfully get everyone across the river using only the three planks. The water (or ground) may not be touched. The group is successful when all participants and the three planks are on the opposite bank.[129]
3. *The Chain Gang*—Participants form a circle around a stationary tetherball or volleyball standard (or a 10-foot pole set in a tire filled with cement). Short ropes or strips of cloth are used to tie team members' hands together (right hand to left hand). Mats may be placed around the base of the pole. The group is being held for ransom by international terrorists who have left momentarily, giving them time to escape. The object is to become free of the pole in the center while the pole remains upright and fixed to the ground and all members' hands remain tied together[130] (see figure 8.29).

Figure 8.29 The chain gang.
Source: Allan C. Boyer, Brigham Young University
Master's Thesis, 104 E. State Highway, Copperton,
Utah 84006.

Risk Activities. "Risk sports are characterized by physical and psychological challenges encountered by participants as they confront elements of the environment."[131] These activities usually take place in a natural setting and contain an element of perceived risk or physical danger.[132] Although some aspects of teaching these activities can be done during a regularly scheduled class period, they are often conducted after school, on weekends, and during vacations.

Activities range from low risk (fishing, cycling, orienteering) to medium risk (backpacking, cross-country skiing, horseback riding) to high risk (rock climbing, white water canoeing, winter camping).[133] Other activities of varying degrees of risk include scuba diving, cross-country cycling, rafting, field archery, high ropes courses, indoor or outdoor climbing walls, and camping.

Such activities are performed in a noncompetitive atmosphere sparked by intrinsic motivation. The activities are active, not passive, and this component alone has the potential to increase physical skills and physical fitness. The development of social skills such as leadership, trust, cooperation, *esprit de corps,* and enhanced interpersonal relationships are inherent in risk activities. Knowledge of personal limits, pride in achievement, increased problem-solving ability, and enjoyment are listed as personal development benefits. Other values include an appreciation of nature, an experiential knowledge of survival and emergency care skills as well as the application of nutrition and personal health information. The teacher must weigh the benefits against the risks of a particular activity and decide whether a safe environment can be created. Rademacher and Cruse stress that risk management is perhaps the most important key to the success of all such programs.[134]

Risk activities present physical and psychological challenges to participants.
© Bill Bachman/Photo Researchers, Inc.

Successful protection of participants in risk activities, as well as the success of the program itself, hinges on two guidelines:[135]

1. Reduce or eliminate programs with a high potential for accidents. Activities with a high accident potential include hang gliding, ice climbing, parachuting, sky jumping, mountaineering, and spelunking.[136]
2. Maintain well-planned, carefully carried out, safe activities.
   a. Publish policies and procedures of operation.
   b. Continually analyze trip goals versus the limitations or abilities of participants and leaders.
   c. Screen participants.
   d. Provide in-service training for staff, maintaining experienced, well-trained personnel. Be committed to readiness and rescue training. Provide a carefully defined progression of activities.
   e. Inspect equipment and facilities regularly.
   f. Keep track of accidents and near misses and publish records of safety. Analyze the primary causes of accidents, such as unsafe conditions, unsafe acts, or judgment errors.
   g. Establish a program leader who provides direction and expertise (consistent, directive, nonpermissive).
   h. Repeat operations in known areas.[137]

Motivation

The adventure activity itself is often motivation enough for student participation. However, some students will be overwhelmed by the risk or challenge of the activity and must be carefully directed until they gain the necessary confidence, trust, and skill to participate. All students must be diligently supervised so that the apprehensive student develops trust and the fearless student learns to exercise caution. Motivation is enhanced by letting students choose the activities in which they participate. The teacher might further ensure motivation and participation by following a systematic progression. First, challenge activities would be introduced, followed by initiative activities, and finally several choices of risk activities.

Evaluating Progress

Objectives inherent in adventure activities are often from the affective domain and are best evaluated by affective methods (see chapter 9). Cognitive concepts may be tested through written exams or other appropriate means. Certain psychomotor skills are often formally evaluated using skill tests, checklists, or other testing procedures, especially when risk activities are the focus. Evaluation of adventure activities is often informal, however, and the teacher may use successful completion of the activity as the method of evaluation.

Interdisciplinary Units

Gaff indicated that around the turn of the twentieth century specialization occurred and separate disciplines became the primary means of conducting education. The separate disciplines became a barrier to learning because the problems of the world are not isolated in these disciplines. Therefore, it is absolutely essential that the disciplines work together to improve learning.[138] Cummings stated "academia may be divided into disciplines, but the world is not."[139]

Physical education can play a vital role in the success of interdisciplinary units as well as initiate these coordinated efforts. Some ideas generated by physical education teachers follow. Young worked with math, health, language arts, visual arts, and gifted and talented teachers to develop a yearlong project for fifth graders. In physical education class the students learned about five health-related fitness components. They then learned how to test these components and tested the first through fourth grades. The math class used this data to develop math problems. The health classes also studied health-related fitness and research and developed a family fitness guide that was distributed to all families in the school. For language arts the students wrote journal entries related to their experiences and their attitudes toward personal fitness. In the visual arts class illustrations were prepared for inclusion in the family fitness guide. The gifted and talented classes used word processing to prepare the guide and proofread and edited the guide.[140]

Kirkpatrick has developed two interdisciplinary activities. One is the Heart Adventure[141] and the other is the Tropical Rainforest.[142] For the Heart Adventure the gymnasium is set up as a giant heart. The students are the blood cells that flow through the heart and the rest of the body. In physical education class the students learn about and experience how the blood circulates throughout the heart. In math class the students determine target heart rates and calculate the number of times the heart may beat during a given activity. In social studies classes the students learn what countries have the most coronary heart diseases and which ones are lowest. The differences in the cultures are then studied. Coronary heart diseases and their causes are studied in the health class. The science classes study how the heart functions. Writing assignments can be made in language arts.

The Tropical Rainforest is used at the beginning of a school year. First the gymnasium is set up as a tropical rainforest. Then the students are put in groups and told they are the sole survivors of a plane crash on an island in a tropical rainforest. They have several problems relating to survival to solve. All of the teachers in the school serve as the students' guides throughout this activity. Other activities occurring in other classes include determining where the rainforests are in the world and what is happening to them in social studies. The effects of the loss of the rainforest are studied in science. The math classes can determine how long the forests will survive at the current rate of destruction. Students can write about their feelings in language arts classes.

Another interdisciplinary idea is a time machine.[143] The gymnasium is set with a time machine in the middle and four to eight activity modules surrounding the center. Events and subjects being studied in other classes can also be designed for inclusion. Examples of modules include the Roman Empire and the Civil War. In the Roman Empire the students participate in chariot races with scooters or flying turtles becoming the chariots. Students also wear a bicycle helmet for safety. For the Civil War the students participate in the Battle of Gettysburg. Each side has different colored balls. The participants try to get their own balls into a large donut mat while removing the opponents balls from the area. At the end the balls are counted in the various areas much as the dead and wounded were counted during the Civil War. Other types of interdisciplinary units are possible. The only limitation is the imagination and creativity of the teachers involved.

Special Days (or Weeks)

A special theme may serve as the basis for conducting activities as a special event, such as a "Sports Day" or "Olympics." Such events might be held in the regular class or as a schoolwide project. When such events are conducted as a school activity they become an excellent public relations tool.

A fun type of field day for students is a "Super Kids' Day" in which students compete as partners, rotating from one event to another.[144] Each student has a Super Kids' Day certificate (see figure 8.30) on which the event and place—first or second—is recorded at each station.

Tenoschok listed a number of schoolwide contests that might be conducted during National Physical Education and Sport Week or at another appropriate time. He included a physical education essay contest; a poster coloring contest; a sports-in-action drawing contest; a physical education slogan contest; an invent-a-game contest; and a sports safari contest, which asks students to identify athletes by their animal nicknames. These activities can stimulate an overall school awareness of the objectives of physical education while encouraging students to achieve in other areas in the curriculum.[145] The National Association for Sport and Physical Education has developed several ideas to enhance a physical education curriculum.[146] All-school activity days or weeks can be designed to include all curriculum areas of the school. In this case they can be both fun and profitable for students and faculty alike.

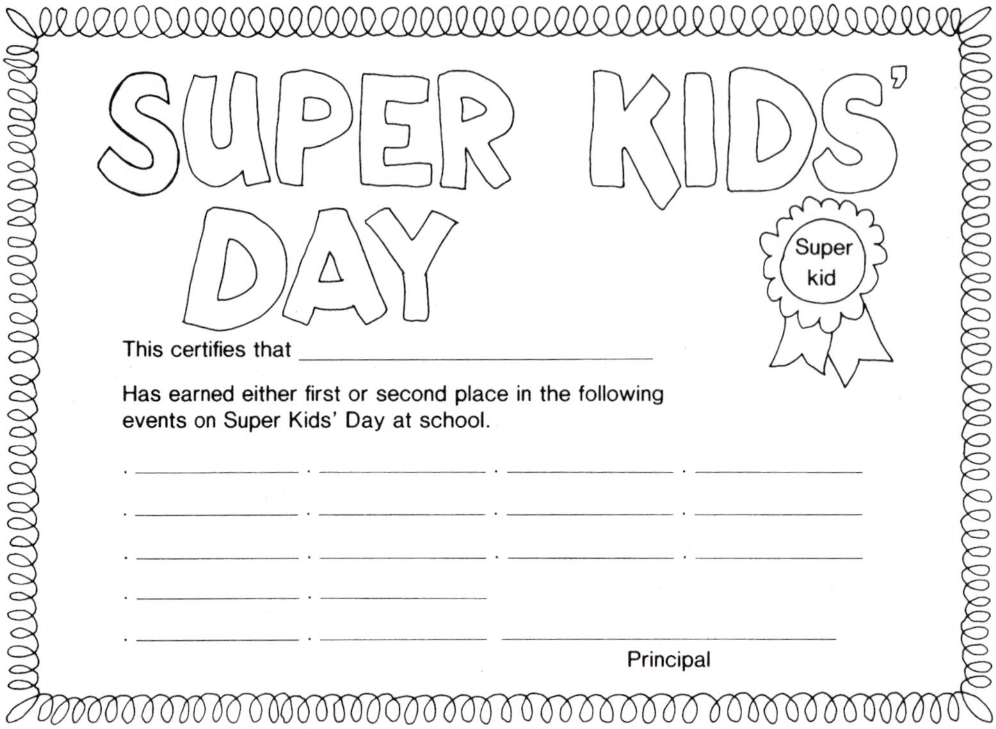

Figure 8.30 A "Super Kids' Day" certificate.
Source: Pat Sawley, Woods Cross High School,
Woods Cross, Utah.

Review Questions

1. How can instructional media help teachers teach more effectively and efficiently?
2. How can computers help physical education teachers? What factors should be considered in purchasing a computer and selecting software?
3. Briefly outline some resources for instruction in the following areas:

	Instruction	Motivation	Evaluation
Fitness			
Movement skills			
Concepts			
Adventure activities			

Suggested Readings

Barry, P. E. (Ed.). (1976). *Ideas for secondary school physical education*. Reston, VA: American Alliance for Health, Physical Education, Recreation and Dance.

Carlson, R. P. (1984). *Ideas II: A sharing of teaching practices by secondary school physical education practitioners*. Reston, VA: American Alliance for Health, Physical Education, Recreation and Dance.

Glover, D. R., & Midura, D. W. (1992). *Team building through physical challenges*. Champaign, IL: Human Kinetics.

National Association for Sport and Physical Education. *101 ways to promote physical activity and sport.* Reston, VA: Author.

National Association for Sport and Physical Education. (1994). *Sport and physical education advocacy kit.* Reston, VA: Author.

Pate, R. R., & Hohn, R. C. (Eds.) (1994). *Health and fitness through physical education.* Champaign, IL: Human Kinetics.

Adventure, New Games, and Outdoor Recreation

Attarian, A. (1989, September). Artificial rock climbing walls—Innovative adventure environments. *Journal of Physical Education, Recreation and Dance, 60*(7), 28–32.

Darst, P., & Armstrong, G. (1980). *Outdoor adventure activities for school and recreation programs.* Minneapolis, MN: Burgess.

Ewert, A. (1986, May/June). A new dimension. *Journal of Physical Education, Recreation and Dance, 57*(5), 56–57, 60.

Fluegelman, A. (1974). *The new games book.* Garden City, NY: Headlands.

Ford, P. (Series Ed.) (1989, February). Outdoor education. *Journal of Physical Education, Recreation and Dance, 60*(2), 30–46.

Orlick, T. (1976). *The cooperative sports & games book.* New York: Pantheon.

Outdoor Adventure Activity Programs. (series of articles). (1986, May/June). *Journal of Physical Education, Recreation and Dance, 57,* 56–69.

Rohnke, K. *Cowstails and cobras.* Project Adventure, Box 157, Hamilton, MA 01936.

Spencer, S., Edwards, W. H., & Spencer, D. (1991, Winter). Practical suggestions for implementing nontraditional/adventure education into the high school curriculum. *Physical Educator, 48,* 206–210.

Computers

Cicciarella, C. F. (1984, April). Getting into the computer game: Guidelines and pitfalls. *Journal of Physical Education, Recreation and Dance, 55,* 46–47.

Donnelly, J. E. (1987). *Using microcomputers in physical education and the sport sciences.* Champaign, IL: Human Kinetics.

Kelly, L. (1987, April). Computer assisted instruction: Applications for physical education. *Journal of Physical Education, Recreation and Dance, 58,* 74–79.

Kelly, L. (1987, October). Computer management of student performance. *Journal of Physical Education, Recreation and Dance, 58*(8), 12–85.

King, H. A., & Aufsesser, K. S. (1986, Spring). Microcomputer software to assist the school physical education teacher. *Physical Educator, 43,* 90–97.

Londeree, B. R. (Series Ed.) (1983, November/December). Microcomputers in physical education. *Journal of Physical Education, Recreation and Dance, 54,* 17–50.

Research Consortium, AAHPERD. *Directory of computer software with application to sport science, health, and dance.* Reston, VA: AAHPERD.

Taylor, M. S., & Saverance, D. P. (1990, September). Computers, physical education, and the year 2000. *Journal of Physical Education, Recreation and Dance, 62*(7), 38–39.

Wendt, J. C., & Morrow, J. R., Jr. (1986, February). Microcomputer software: Practical applications for coaches and teachers. *Journal of Physical Education, Recreation and Dance, 57,* 54–57.

White, S. W. (Series editor). (1991). Computers and society. *National Forum, 71*(3), 2–46.

Fitness

Deal, T. B., Updyke, W., & Gallahue, D. L. (1993). Curricular effectiveness in promoting physical fitness in fifth and seventh grade students. *Physical Educator, 50*(3), 136–144.

Elsey, S. C. (1991). Extracurricular fitness. *Strategies, 5*(3), 13.

Going, S. B., Williams, D. P., & Lohman, T. G. (1992). Setting standards for health-related youth fitness tests; Determining critical body fat levels. *Journal of Physical Education, Recreation and Dance, 63*(8), 19–24.

Hawkins, J. D. (1983). An analysis of selected skinfold measuring instruments. *Journal of Physical Education, Recreation and Dance, 54,* 25–27.

Howley, E. T., & Franks, B. D. (1989). *Health/fitness instructor's handbook*. Champaign, IL: Human Kinetics.

Jenkins, D., & Staub, J. (1985). Student fitness: The physical educator's role. *Journal of Physical Education, Recreation and Dance, 56*, 31–32.

Kuntzleman, C. T. (1978). *Fitness discovery activities*. Spring Arbor, MI: Arbor Press.

Lacy, A. C., & LaMaster, K. J. (1990, Winter). Analysis of fitness activities in junior high school physical education. *Physical Educator, 47*, 176–179.

Lacy, E., & Marshall, B. (1984, January). Fitnessgram. *Journal of Physical Education, Recreation and Dance, 55*, 18–19.

Levitt, S. (1992). Making a pact for fitness. *Strategies, 5*(7), 5–6, 8.

Morrow, J. R. (Ed.). (1992, June). Are American children and youth fit? *Research Quarterly for Exercise and Sport, 63*(2), 95–136.

Mosher, P. E., & Underwood, S. A. (1992). Circuit training: Exercise that counts. *Strategies, 5*(8), 5–8.

Pangrazi, R. P., & Corbin, C. B. (1993). Physical fitness: Questions teachers ask. *Journal of Physical Education, Recreation and Dance, 64*(7), 14–19.

Pangrazi, R. P., & Hastad, D. N. (1986). *Fitness in the elementary schools: A teacher's manual*. Reston, VA: AAHPERD.

Pemberton, C., & McSwegin, P. J. (1989, January). Goal setting and motivation. *Journal of Physical Education, Recreation and Dance, 60*(1), 39–41.

Spindt, G. (1985, September). Fitness is basic. *Journal of Physical Education, Recreation and Dance, 56*, 68–69.

Whitehead, J. R. (1992). A selected, annotated bibliography for fitness educators. *Journal of Physical Education, Recreation and Dance, 63*(5), 53–64.

Wolfe, P., & Sharpe, T. (1991). Making running fun. *Strategies, 5*(3), 8–12.

Games

Glakas, B. A. (1991). Teaching cooperative skills through games. *Journal of Physical Education, Recreation and Dance, 62*(5), 28–30.

Torbert, M. & Schnieder, L. B. (1986, September). Positive multicultural interaction: Using low organized games. *Journal of Physical Education, Recreation and Dance, 57*, 40–44.

Zakrajsek, D. (1986, September). Premeditated murder: Let's 'bump-off' killer ball. *Journal of Physical Education, Recreation and Dance, 57*, 49–51.

Interdisciplinary Units

Carpenter, G. (1993). The web: Creating an interdisciplinary unit. *Strategies, 6*(8), 26–29.

Cummings, R. (Series editor). (1989, Spring) Interdisciplinary studies defining and defending. *National Forum, 69*(2), 2–41.

Tournaments

Eason, R. L. (1990, April). Tournaments that work for physical education classes. *Journal of Physical Education, Recreation and Dance, 61*(4), 68–75.

Johnson, M. (1993). Cooperative round robin tournaments: An effective way to teach sports skills. *The Journal of Physical Education, Recreation and Dance, 64*(9), 10.

Jones, S., & Lamsden, K. (1993). The mix 'n match class structure. *Strategies, 6*(6), 5–7.

McGhie, S., & Oliver, J. W. (1993). The professional league model. *Strategies, 6*(6), 12–14.

Veal, M. L. (1991). A badminton tournament that motivates students. *Journal of Physical Education, Recreation and Dance, 62*(9), 34–37.

Wilkinson, S. (1993). Rotation play for maximum participation. *Strategies, 6*(6), 27–29.

References

1. Johnson, M. L., Loper, R. K., & Cordain, L. (1986). Computer applications and directions in university level physical education: A survey. *Physical Educator, 43*, 86–89.

2. Arsac, J. J. (1985). Teaching informatics: A French experiment. In K. Duncan & D. Harris (Eds.), *Computers in education*. New York: Elsevier Science.

3. O'Malley, C. (1991). The revolution is yet to come. *National Forum: The Phi Kappa Phi Journal, 71*(3), 12–14.

4. White, S. W. (1991). The universal computer. *National Forum: The Phi Kappa Phi Journal, 71*(3), 2.

5. O'Malley, The revolution is yet to come, 12–14.

6. Research Consortium, AAHPERD. *Directory of computer software with application to sport science, health, and dance* (p. 3). Reston, VA: American Alliance for Health, Physical Education, Recreation and Dance.

7. Taylor, M. S., & Saverance, D. P. (1990). Computers, physical education, and the year 2000. *Journal of Physical Education, Recreation and Dance, 62*(7), 38–39.

8. Edwards, J. B., Ellis, A. S., Richardson, D. E., Holznagel, D., & Klassen, D. (1978). *Computer applications in instruction.* Hanover, NH: TimeShare (A Houghton Mifflin Company).

9. Research Consortium, *Directory of computer software.*

10. King, H. A., & Aufsesser, K. S. (1986, Spring). Microcomputer software to assist the school physical education teacher. *Physical Educator, 43,* 90–97.

11. Donnelly, J. E. (1987). *Using microcomputers in physical education and the sport sciences.* Champaign, IL: Human Kinetics.

12. Many public domain and shareware programs are available from SOFTSHARE, Physical Education and Human Performance, California State University, Fresno, CA 93740–0028. (209) 294–2016. Disks are $5.00 for 5$\frac{1}{4}$″ and $7.00 for 3$\frac{1}{2}$″ disks (plus sales tax in California). Send for a list of programs available.

13. King & Aufsesser, Microcomputer software to assist the school physical education teacher, 90–92.

14. Cicciarella, C. F. (1983, November/December). The computer in physical education: Its promise and threat. *Journal of Physical Education, Recreation and Dance, 54,* 18, 32.

15. Steffen, J., & Hansen, G. (1987). Effect of computer-assisted instruction on development of cognitive and psychomotor learning in bowling. *Journal of Teaching in Physical Education, 6,* 183–191.

16. Kerns, M. (1989). The effectiveness of computer-assisted instruction in teaching tennis rules and strategies. *Journal of Teaching in Physical Education, 8*(2), 170–176.

17. Adams, T., & Waldrop, P. (1985). Computer-assisted instruction in teacher education: Making the technology work. *Physical Educator, 43,* 156–160.

18. Breckon, D. J., & Pennington, R. M. (1986). Interactive videodiscs: A new generation of computer-assisted instruction. *Health Values, 10*(6), 52–55.

19. Stein, J. (1984). Microcomputer uses to promote physical proficiency and motor development of students with handicapped conditions, *Physical Educator, 41,* 40–42.

20. Cicciarella, The computer in physical education, 18.

21. Donnelly, *Using microcomputers in physical education and the sport sciences.*

22. Barlow, D. A., & Bayalis, P. A. (1983, November/December). Computer facilitated learning. *Journal of Physical Education, Recreation and Dance, 54,* 29.

23. Sealy, D. (1983, November/December). Computer programs for dance notation. *Journal of Physical Education, Recreation and Dance, 54,* 36–37.

24. Engelhorn, R. (1983). Motor learning and control: Microcomputer applications. *Journal of Physical Education, Recreation and Dance, 54*(9), 30–32.

25. Wendt, J. C., & Morrow, J. R., Jr. (1986, February). Microcomputer software: Practical applications for coaches and teachers. *Journal of Physical Education, Recreation and Dance, 57,* 54.

26. Cicciarella, The computer in physical education, 18.

27. Kelly, L. (1987, October). Computer management of student performance. *Journal of Physical Education, Recreation and Dance, 58*(8), 12–13, 82–85.

28. Ibid.

29. Ibid.

30. Franks, B. D., Morrow, J. R., Jr., & Plowman, S. A. (1988, December). Youth fitness testing: Validation, planning, and politics. *Quest, 40*(3), 191.

31. Engelhorn, R. (1987). In J. E. Donnelly (Ed.), *Using microcomputers in physical education and the sport sciences* (pp. 81–90). Champaign, IL: Human Kinetics.

32. Kelly, Computer management of student performance, 12.

33. Wendt & Morrow, Microcomputer software; Dauer, V. P., & Pangrazi, R. P. (1995). *Dynamic physical education for elementary school children* (11th ed., p. 222). Minneapolis, MN: Burgess.

34. Dauer & Pangrazi, *Dynamic physical education for elementary school children*, 222.

35. Stein, J. (1987). Physical education selective activities: Computerizing choices. *Journal of Physical Education, Recreation and Dance, 58*(1), 64–66.

36. King & Aufsesser, Microcomputer software to assist the school physical education teacher, 90–92.

37. Kelly, Computer management of student performance, 12–13, 82–85.

38. Howley, E. T., & Franks, B. D. (1986). *Health/fitness instructor's handbook* (p. 4). Champaign, IL: Human Kinetics.

39. Allsen, P. E., Harrison, J. M., & Vance, B. (1993). *Fitness for life: An individualized approach* (5th ed., p. 4). Dubuque, IA: Brown.

40. Meredith, M. D. (1988, December). Activity for fitness: Is the process or the product more important for public health? *Quest, 40*(3), 180.

41. Corbin, C. B. (1987). Youth fitness, exercise and health: There is much to be done. *Research Quarterly for Exercise and Sport, 58*(4), 308–314.

42. Pate, R. R. (1988, December). The evolving definition of physical fitness. *Quest, 40*(3), 174–179; Franks, Morrow, & Plowman, Youth fitness testing, 191.

43. Corbin, C. B., & Lindsey, R. (1985). *Concepts of physical fitness.* Dubuque, IA: Brown.

44. Eisenman, P. (1986). Physical activity and body composition. In V. Seefeldt (Ed.), *Physical activity and well-being.* Reston, VA: American Alliance for Health, Physical Education, Recreation and Dance.

45. Centers for Disease Control. (1993, July 30). Prevalence of sedentary lifestyle—Behavioral risk factor surveillance system, United States, 1991. *Morbidity and Mortality Weekly Report,* 576–579.

46. American College of Sports Medicine (1993, July 29). *New recommendation to fight America's epidemic of physical inactivity.* (News release). 401 West Michigan Street, Indianapolis, IN.

47. Centers for Disease Control. (1992, January 24). Vigorous physical activity among high school students—United States, 1990. *Morbidity and Mortality Weekly Report,* 33–37.

48. Experts offer new recommendation regarding physical activity. (1993, October). *Journal of Physical Education, Recreation and Dance, 64*(8), 13.

49. Centers for Disease Control. (1991, September 6). Participation of high school students in school physical education—United States, 1990. *Morbidity and Mortality Weekly Report, 607,* 613–615.

50. Pangrazi, R. P., & Corbin, C. B. (1993). Physical fitness: Questions teachers ask. *The Journal of Physical Education, Recreation and Dance, 64*(7), 14–19.

51. Morrow, J. R. (1992). Are American children and youth fit? Review and commentary. *Research Quarterly for Exercise and Sport, 63,* 95. See June 1992 issue of *Research Quarterly for Exercise and Sport, 63,* 95–136 for complete discussion of this topic.

52. Corbin, Youth fitness, exercise and health, 309.

53. Ibid.; Meredith, Activity for fitness, 180–183.

54. Paffenbarger, R. S., Hyde, R. T., Wing, A. L., & Hsieh, C. (1986). Physical activity, all-cause mortality, and longevity of college alumni. *New England Journal of Medicine, 314,* 605–613.

55. Blair, S. N., Kohl, H. W., III, Paffenbarger, R. S., Jr., Clark, D. G., Cooper, K. H., Gibbons, L. W. (1989, November 3). Physical fitness and all-cause mortality: A prospective study of healthy men and women. *Journal of the American Medical Association, 262*(17), 2395–2401.

56. Rink, J. E. (1994). Fitting fitness into the school curriculum. In R. R. Pate & R. C. Hohn (Eds.), *Health and fitness through physical education* (pp. 67–74). Champaign, IL: Human Kinetics.

57. Institute for Aerobics Research. (1990, March). Around the country. *Campbell's Kids Fitness News, 1*(3), 3.

58. Ziatz, D. H. (1977, March). How do you motivate students to learn? *Journal of Physical Education and Recreation, 48,* 26.

59. Misner, J. E. (1984, November/December). Are we fit to educate about fitness? *Journal of Physical Education, Recreation and Dance, 55,* 27.

60. Corbin, Youth fitness, exercise and health, 311.

61. Hastad, D. N., & Lacy, A. C. (1988, November/December). An emerging learning domain in physical education: Health related fitness. *Strategies, 2*(2), 14–16.

62. Meredith, Activity for fitness, 180–183.

63. Corbin, Youth fitness, exercise and health, 310.
64. Going, S. B., Williams, D. P., & Lohman, T. G. (1992). Setting standards for health-related youth fitness tests—Determining critical body fat levels. *Journal of Physical Education, Recreation and Dance, 63*(8), 19–24.
65. Fox, K. R. (1988, December). The self-esteem complex and youth fitness. *Quest, 40*(3), 240.
66. Corbin, Youth fitness, exercise and health, 310.
67. Whitehead, J. R. (1989, August). Fitness assessment results: Some concepts and analogies. *Journal of Physical Education, Recreation and Dance, 60*(6), 43.
68. Jenkins, D., & Staub, J. (1985, February). Student fitness: The physical educator's role. *Journal of Physical Education, Recreation and Dance, 56,* 31–32.
69. Wolfe, P., & Sharpe, T. (1991). Making running fun. *Strategies, 5*(3), 8–12.
70. Mosher, P. E., & Underwood, S. A. (1992). Circuit training: Exercise that counts. *Strategies, 5*(8), 5–8.
71. Hester, D., & Dunaway, D. (1990, May). Beyond calisthenics: Fitness and fun in elementary school physical education. *Strategies, 3*(5), 25–28.
72. Pemberton, C., & McSwegin, P. J. (1989, January). Goal setting and motivation. *Journal of Physical Education, Recreation and Dance, 60*(1), 39–41.
73. Levitt, S. (1992). Making a pact for fitness. *Strategies, 5*(7), 5–6, 8.
74. Romance, T. (1986, April). The century club: Beyond the fitness test. *Journal of Physical Education, Recreation and Dance, 57,* 14–15; Munson, C. B. (1982, September). A club-oriented incentive program. *Journal of Physical Education, Recreation and Dance, 53,* 40, 42, 55.
75. Marquardt, R. (1978, November/December). Voluntary jog-a-thon. *Journal of Physical Education, Recreation and Dance, 49,* 68.
76. Gallery, J. A. (1983, May). Orienteering with a map and clues. *Journal of Physical Education, Recreation and Dance, 54,* 73–74.
77. Sundberg, H. E. (1981, July/August). A running program that works. *Alliance Update, 7.*
78. Corbin, D. E. (1979, June). Prediction races and relays. *Journal of Physical Education, Recreation and Dance, 50,* 58–59.
79. Stein, E. L. (1978, November/December). Run for fun: A program for all ages. *Journal of Physical Education, Recreation and Dance, 49,* 70.
80. Elsey, S. C. (1991). Extracurricular fitness. *Strategies, 5*(3), 13.
81. American Heart Association & American Alliance for Health, Physical Education, Recreation and Dance, 1900 Association Drive, Reston, VA 22091.
82. Hopper, C., Manoz, K., Gruber, M. B., Herb, R. A., MacConnie, S., & Shunk, T. (1992). A family fitness program. *Journal of Physical Education, Recreation and Dance, 63*(7), 23–27.
83. Lambert, L. (1985, September). A self-management model for health related fitness instruction. *Journal of Physical Education, Recreation and Dance, 56,* 47–50.
84. Pangrazi & Corbin, Physical fitness: Questions teachers ask, 17.
85. Ibid., 18.
86. Department of Health and Human Services. (1985). National children and youth fitness study I. *Journal of Physical Education, Recreation and Dance, 56*(1), 43–93; Department of Health and Human Services. (1987). National children and youth fitness study II. *Journal of Physical Education, Recreation and Dance, 58*(7), 49–96.
87. Going, S., & Williams, D. (1989, August). Understanding fitness standards. *Journal of Physical Education, Recreation and Dance, 60*(6), 34–38.
88. Going, Williams, & Lohman, Setting standards for health-related youth fitness tests, 19–24.
89. Franks, Morrow, & Plowman, Youth fitness testing, 191.
90. Graham, G. (1987, September). Motor skill acquisition—An essential goal of physical education programs. *Journal of Physical Education, Recreation and Dance, 58*(7), 44.
91. Pangrazi, R. P., & Darst, P. W. (1991). *Dynamic physical education curriculum and instruction for secondary school students* (2nd ed.) (p. 7). New York: Macmillan.
92. Homsy, M. (1984, May/June). Team handball: A budget sport for any program. *Journal of Physical Education, Recreation and Dance, 55,* 90.
93. Fluegelman, A. (1974). *The new games book.* Garden City, NY: Headlands.
94. Larsen, M. S. (1960). *Speed-a-way: A new game for boys and girls.* Minneapolis: Burgess.

95. Kostick, A., & Gehler, D. (1984). Volley tennis. In R. P. Carlson (Ed.), *Ideas II: A sharing of teaching practices by secondary school physical education practitioners* (pp. 99–100). Reston, VA: American Alliance for Health, Physical Education, Recreation and Dance.

96. McGhie, S., & Oliver, J. W. (1993). The professional league model. *Strategies, 6*(6), 12–14.

97. Blake, O. W., & Volp, A. M. (1964). *Lead-up games to team sports* (p. 1). Englewood Cliffs, NJ: Prentice-Hall.

98. Ibid., 3.

99. Metzler, M. W. (1990, October). Teaching in competitive games—not just playin' around. *Journal of Physical Education, Recreation and Dance, 61*(8), 57–61.

100. Graham, Motor skill acquisition, 48.

101. CEC Publishers, 6 Lexington Avenue, Merchantville, NJ 08109 (1987).

102. Koehler, G. (1984). Teaching stress management. In R. P. Carlson (Ed.), *Ideas II: A sharing of teaching practices by secondary school physical education practitioners* (pp. 108–109). Reston, VA: American Alliance for Health, Physical Education, Recreation and Dance.

103. Ibid., 117–120.

104. Linden, P. (1984, September). Aikido: A movement awareness approach to physical education. *Journal of Physical Education, Recreation and Dance, 55,* 64–65.

105. Mountain Bicyclists' Association, Inc. (1981). *Comprehensive bicyclist education program: course guide.* 1290 Williams Street, Denver, CO 80218.

106. Krumm, M. (1984). Tennis, despite weather and site restrictions. In R. P. Carlson (Ed.), *Ideas II: A sharing of teaching practices by secondary school physical education practitioners* (pp. 38–39). Reston, VA: American Alliance for Health, Physical Education, Recreation and Dance; Fairman L. S., & Nitchman, D. (1984). A bowling program in the gymnasium. In R. P. Carlson (Ed.), *Ideas II: A sharing of teaching practices by secondary school physical education practitioners* (pp. 66–68). Reston, VA: American Alliance for Health, Physical Education, Recreation and Dance.

107. Nelson, J. E. (1984, March). Teaching cross-country skiing. *Journal of Physical Education, Recreation and Dance, 55,* 58–64.

108. Carron, A. V. (1984). *Motivation implications for coaching and teaching.* Sports Dynamics: 11 Ravenglass Crescent, London, Ontario, N6G 3X7.

109. Whiddon, S. (1984). Reward incentives. In R. P. Carlson (Ed.), *Ideas II: A sharing of teaching practices by secondary school physical education practitioners* (pp. 52–53). Reston, VA: American Alliance for Health, Physical Education, Recreation and Dance.

110. McCann, P. M. (1987, March). Breaking away from tradition: A new game for middle school students. *Journal of Physical Education, Recreation and Dance, 58,* 76–79.

111. Buck, M., Harrison, J., Fronske, H., & Bayles, G. (1990, February). Quad ball—A soccer, football, basketball, and pinball game. *Journal of Physical Education, Recreation and Dance, 61*(2), 7.

112. Kraft, R. E. (1988, September/October). Let the students create the games. *Strategies, 2*(1), 27–28.

113. Hedlund, R. (1990, April). Non-traditional team sports—Taking full advantage of the teachable moment. *Journal of Physical Education, Recreation and Dance, 61*(4), 76–79.

114. Jones, S., & Lamsden, K. (1993). The mix 'n match class structure. *Strategies, 6*(6), 5–7; Wilkinson, S. (1993). Rotation play for maximum participation. *Strategies, 6*(6), 27–29; Veal, M. L. (1991). A badminton tournament that motivates students. *Journal of Physical Education, Recreation and Dance, 62*(9), 34–37.

115. Glakas, B. A. (1991). Teaching cooperative skills through games. *Journal of Physical Education, Recreation and Dance, 62*(5), 28–30; Johnson, M. (1993). Cooperative round robin tournaments: An effective way to teach sports skills. *Journal of Physical Education, Recreation and Dance, 64*(9), 10.

116. Eason, R. L. (1990, April). Tournaments that work for physical education classes. *Journal of Physical Education, Recreation and Dance, 61*(4), 68–75.

117. Veal, A badminton tournament that motivates students, 34–37.

118. Barker, J. F. (1985, May/June). A simplified volleyball skills test for beginning level instruction. *Journal of Physical Education, Recreation and Dance, 56,* 20–22.

119. Lockhart, B. D. (1982, September). The basic stuff series: Why and how. *Journal of Physical Education, Recreation and Dance, 53,* 18.

120. American Alliance for Health, Physical Education, Recreation and Dance. (1987). *Basic stuff series.* Reston, VA: Author.

121. Naylor, J. H. (1975, September). Honey & milk toast. *Journal of Physical Education, Recreation and Dance, 46,* 20.

122. CEC Publishers. (n.d.) *Adventure without ropes.* 6 Lexington Avenue, Merchantville, NJ 08109.

123. Glover, D. R., & Midura, D. W. (1992). *Team building through physical challenges.* Champaign, IL: Human Kinetics.

124. Smith, L. K. (1980, August). Using challenge activities to develop group cooperation in physical education. *Physical Education Newsletter* (Box 8, 20 Cedarwood Lane, Old Saybrook, CT 06475).

125. Fluegelman, A. (1976). *The new game book* (p. 69). New York: Doubleday.

126. Orlick, T. (1978). *The cooperative sports & games book* (p. 54). New York: Pantheon.

127. CEC Publishers. 6 Lexington Avenue, Merchantville, NJ 08109.

128. Naylor, Honey & milk toast, 20.

129. Ibid.

130. Boyer, A. C. *Initiative activities,* 104 E. State Highway, Copperton, UT 84006.

131. Tangen-Foster, J. W., & Lathen, C. W. (1983, September). Risk sports in basic instruction programs: A status assessment. *Research Quarterly for Exercise and Sport, 54,* 305.

132. Latess, D. R. (1986, May/June). Physical education and outdoor adventure: Do they belong together? *Journal of Physical Education, Recreation and Dance, 57,* 66–67.

133. Ibid.

134. Rademacher, C. E., & Cruse, L. D. (1986, Autumn). Planning success for small college outdoor programs. *UAHPERD Journal, 18,* 12–14.

135. Naylor, J. H. (1986). *Recreation without litigation.* Provo, UT: Brigham Young University.

136. Tangen-Foster & Lathen, Risk sports in basic instruction programs, 306.

137. Siedentop, D., Mand, C., & Taggart, A. (1986). *Physical education: teaching and curriculum strategies for grades 5–12* (p. 223). Palo Alto: Mayfield.

138. Gaff, J. G. (1989). The resurgence of interdisciplinary studies. *National Forum: The Phi Kappa Phi Journal, 69*(2), 4–5.

139. Cummings, R. J. (1989). The interdisciplinary challenge: Connection and balance. *National Forum: The Phi Kappa Phi Journal, 69*(2), 3.

140. Young, D. B. (1994). Curriculum interfacing through physical education: Health, math, science, language arts, visual arts, and gifted and talented. In R. R. Pate & R. C. Hon (Eds.), *Health and fitness through physical education.* Champaign, IL: Human Kinetics.

141. Kirkpatrick, B., & Buck., M. M. (in press). Heart adventures challenge course: A lifestyle education activity.

142. Kirkpatrick, B. (1992). *Tropical rainforest: Survival skills.* Unpublished manuscript.

143. Bayer, D., Doyle, B., Loy, M., Jones, D., & Wilson, V. (1993). *Time machine travel.* Unpublished manuscript. Ball State University.

144. Sawley, P. Woods Cross High School, Woods Cross, Utah.

145. Tenoschok, M. (1979, November/December). Physical education appreciation. *Journal of Physical Education, Recreation and Dance, 50,* 18.

146. The National Association for Sport and Physical Education. (1994). *101 ways to promote physical activity and sport.* Reston, VA: Author.

CHAPTER 9

Evaluating Student Performance

Study Stimulators

1. Why is evaluation an important part of instructional design?
2. What is the difference between norm-referenced and criterion-referenced evaluation as they relate to test selection, test evaluation, and learner performance? Which type of evaluation is preferable?
3. Define the following terms: reliability, validity, objectivity.
4. How might you go about selecting evaluation materials for cognitive, psychomotor, and affective objectives?
5. What is the purpose of giving grades in physical education?
6. What is the process for determining grades in physical education?
7. What kind of grading system is best?

The primary purpose of evaluation is to improve instruction. Teaching, learning, and evaluation are interdependent in the educational process. Evaluation therefore plays an important part in instructional design. What is evaluated determines what will be taught and how it will be taught. Evaluation emphasizes the importance of the skills and knowledge being taught by expecting acceptable levels of comprehension and performance by students. It makes students accountable for their performance and teachers responsible for student achievement. Such accountability, vital to the credibility and effectiveness of the profession, is often lacking. Student accountability depends on teachers. However, teachers have difficulty implementing classroom testing because of large class sizes, heavy teaching loads (including coaching), lack of facilities and equipment, and peer pressure.[1] Therefore, evaluation must be carefully planned for the greatest economy in time and energy.[2] Teachers must have expectations for students and create ways for them to achieve success. They must do more than expect students to be "busy, happy, and good."[3] Students should be expected to perform certain skills, know certain concepts, and behave in certain ways. Evaluation reflects success at doing these things.

Evaluation fulfills the following purposes. It (1) confirms student completion of instructional objectives, (2) provides information concerning student abilities and progress (often for the determination of grades), (3) aids in creating a more effective instructional process, (4) aids the teacher in providing individualized help for each student, and (5) aids in communicating objectives to the public. When evaluation techniques are used effectively, students do not have to guess lesson objectives or their progress toward the objectives.

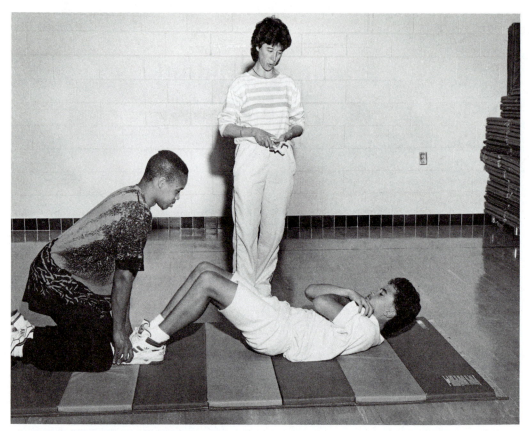

The primary purpose of evaluation is to improve student learning.

At the beginning of instruction, evaluation provides the teacher with information concerning students who have already achieved course objectives. Students who already possess the skills can be directed into more challenging activities. Students who lack prerequisite skills can be given help to improve their performance and eventually achieve course objectives.

During instruction, evaluation provides feedback to students, informing them of the course objectives and their progress toward achieving each criterion. Students who are cognizant of their progress at all times in the learning experience are more secure and can work longer on their own without difficulty. Grades should not be the means of informing students of these important factors. In effective instruction, students are prepared for tests in advance, and there are no surprises about what is required. A well-constructed test, with a broad coverage of class content, serves as a challenge for students to "put it all together" and as a summarizing experience that gives students a feeling of accomplishment by helping them realize how much they have learned.

Good evaluation also serves as a learning activity. It can arouse the student's interest, motivate class attendance, and require the learner to use or apply information and skills in real or simulated situations.

At the conclusion of instruction, evaluation helps teachers check the effectiveness of the teaching process. It tells the teacher whether each student has achieved the course objectives and the progress they made in doing so. When evaluation materials show that students are not performing well, the teacher must examine unit and lesson plans to determine whether the achievement of performance objectives was pursued in a meaningful way. Next, the teacher must critically decide whether his or her teaching techniques were effective. Because evaluation is so critical, it should be an ongoing process. One of the important roles of the present-day physical educator is that of evaluator. Evaluation will be discussed as an integral component of instructional design and as a grading procedure.

Steps in Selecting Evaluation Materials

Step 1.   Determine the purposes of evaluation.
Step 2.   Select appropriate evaluation techniques.
Step 3.   Administer the tests.
Step 4.   Evaluate the evaluation techniques.

Step 1—Determine the Purposes of Evaluation

As a vital component of instructional design, evaluation should take place informally as well as formally throughout units of instruction during the entire school year. Both norm-referenced and criterion-referenced evaluation are commonly used in education.

Norm-Referenced Evaluation

Norm-referenced evaluation refers to how well a student performs compared with others of the same age, sex, class, grade level, school, or geographic area. Standardized achievement tests are norm-referenced and provide important information regarding the general school population as it relates to national norms. Norm-referenced evaluation is based on the normal curve, which assumes that achievement is normally distributed around the average class performance. Teachers must keep in mind that norm-referenced scores may not be appropriate for all situations. It may be unrealistic to compare a particular class of students with norms derived from other students who are different in aptitude (low/high ability), environment (rural/urban, high/low economic status), and mix (all boys or all girls). It is also likely that students at one school may not fit the norm for students at another school. Students in a class one semester may not fit the norm for students in the class during the next semester. A class taught by one teacher will not fit the norm of the same class taught by a different teacher. In fact, one class taught by a teacher will not necessarily fit the norm of another class taught by the same teacher. Test scores from small classes or select populations (e.g., all athletes, all boys, or all girls) will usually not result in a normal distribution of scores. Norms are only a reference point to help teachers assess the "true" performance of students. When a test is too hard or too easy, the distribution of student performance will also deviate from the normal curve.

Norm-referenced evaluation can be used to place students into ability groups for instruction or to establish norms for criterion-based grading. Beginning teachers not yet familiar with appropriate mastery levels for a given activity or content unit sometimes find it easier to use norm-referenced evaluation as a starting point for assessing performance.

Norm-referenced evaluation is often used for *summative evaluation* at the end of a unit or course. Summative evaluation is comprehensive and allows the teacher to evaluate student progress for an entire unit of work by determining the achievement of performance objectives.

Summative evaluation is usually formal, involving such instruments as skills tests, written tests, performance records, and final projects. *Formative evaluation,* on the other hand, is administered following learning tasks or segments throughout a unit of instruction and is often informal. It usually assesses progress toward a final goal or performance objective.

Criterion-Reference Evaluation

Criterion-referenced evaluation refers to how well a student performs in comparison with a predetermined and specified standard of performance. Ideally, given enough time, each student should learn the materials and pass most of the test items. Failure to pass often indicates that the student has not had adequate time for preparation.

Criterion-referenced evaluation can be used to evaluate cognitive, psychomotor, or affective objectives. This system of evaluation is used for both formative and summative evaluation. When used for summative evaluation, the criteria should not change as students become more proficient. The initial criteria must be established with care. It is better to set standards that are too high rather than too low. Students rarely complain when standards are lowered.

With increasing frequency, educators are using criterion-referenced evaluation materials to measure student achievement because such measures demonstrate the extent to which a student has achieved competence in a given area of instruction (instead of measuring what the student does not know). However, the complaint of grade inflation often prevents educators from adopting criterion-referenced systems. One type of criterion-referenced evaluation is called a *mastery test*. Mastery learning is explained in more detail in chapter 7.

Both norm- and criterion-referenced evaluation leave no doubt in the minds of students as to what is expected of them. Some combination of criterion-referenced and norm-referenced assessment is recommended for the purpose of assigning grades.[4]

Step 2—Select Appropriate Evaluation Techniques

Selecting appropriate evaluation techniques requires attention to four essential factors—validity, reliability, objectivity, and administrative feasibility.

Validity is defined as the extent to which a test measures what it is intended to measure. *Authentic assessment* refers to "tests" related directly to the tasks and contexts encountered in the real world. Wiggins suggests that educators ask themselves "What is the equivalent of the game in each subject?"[5] Some examples of authentic assessments in physical education are as follows:

1. The ability to utilize skills in a game situation
2. The ability to assess physical fitness, develop an appropriate fitness plan, and engage in fitness activities necessary to achieve fitness
3. The ability to use the principles of motor learning to learn new skills

Content validity is increased by creating a test "blueprint" so that test items directly reflect course content. An example of a test construction blueprint is shown in figure 9.1. To determine the validity of any test, ask the following question: "Are the student behaviors asked for by the test the same as those called for in the course objectives?" A common teacher error, which destroys content validity, is writing the easiest questions or adopting the easiest skills test rather than testing the content and skills students should know or do.

When evaluating validity on a written test, the teacher asks, "What might cause the student to answer incorrectly on a test when the student knows the answer when asked orally?" Some reasons might be that the test is written on an inappropriate reading level, has vocabulary or

RACQUETBALL

1. Objectives
    A. To use the following skills successfully in game play as rated on a rating scale by the teacher: power serve, lob serve, kill shot, passing shot, lob or ceiling shot, drop shot, backwall play.
    B. To demonstrate a knowledge of the rules, history, and strategy of racquetball by passing an objective test at the 70 percent level or above.
    C. To participate in tournament play.
2. Course Content (See class handout for specific content)
    A. Skills (15)
        a. Power serve—1
        b. Lob serve—1
        c. Kill shot—1
        d. Passing shot—1
        e. Lob or ceiling shot—1
        f. Drop shot—1
        g. Backwall play—1
        h. Grip—1
        i. Skill breakdown—6
        j. Ready position—1
    B. Rules (49)
        a. Game—2
        b. Match—1
        c. Court and equipment—6
        d. Serving—9
        e. Illegal services—13
        f. Return of serve—2
        g. Hinders—6
        h. Ball hitting players—4
        i. Rallying the ball—6
    C. History (1)
    D. Strategy (10)
        a. On the serve—3
        b. Home base—1
        c. Shots to use when—2
        d. Double's play—2
        e. General—2

TOTAL   75

Figure 9.1 A test construction "blueprint" for racquetball.

instructions that are too difficult for the student to comprehend, or has a type of question that confuses the student (such as a question that asks for an official's response). Tests given to foreign or bilingual students often create problems when given in written form, but students can easily answer them in oral form.

On a skills test, the teacher might ask, "What might cause the student to perform poorly on a skills test when the student performs very well in a game situation?" Skills tests might require skills different from those needed in a real game. For example, in the tennis backboard test, the ball returns at a rate much faster than it would in a regular tennis game. Proper test selection or construction is demanding, but teachers should always strive to use valid tests. School tests such as the backboard test tend to sacrifice validity for reliability.

A *reliable* test is one on which a student would obtain similar scores on different trials of the same test. Reliability on norm-referenced tests is enhanced by increasing the number of test questions or trials or the number of students taking the test. For example, if only two questions or trials appear on the test and one day the student has a perfect score and another day misses one, the scores on the two days would be 50 and 100, a difference of 50 percent. If 100 questions or trials appear on the test, missing one would make the scores 99 and 100, a difference of 1 percent. In the same way, if 10 students take the test, a particular student might change from 9th to 10th place, whereas in a group of 100 students, a student might change in rank from 99th to 100th place.

Criterion-referenced tests, such as mastery tests, are designed for a high percentage of students to achieve the criterion; therefore, the range of scores on the test is reduced and it is very difficult to obtain a high coefficient of reliability. Reliability in such cases is determined by how consistent the test is in classifying students as masters or nonmasters.

An *objective* test is one in which a student obtains an identical score on the test regardless of who administers or scores the test. Because objective tests (e.g., true-false, multiple-choice) are easier to score, they lend themselves to increased reliability over essay or short-answer tests. Test objectivity can be increased by making up a scoring key or reporting form before administering the test.

Administrative feasibility is enhanced by choosing tests that are low in cost and free up teacher and student time. Tests that utilize equipment already owned by the school save money, and tests that can be set up easily by students and teachers and that can be administered in a short period of time maximize the time available for instruction.

When selecting specific assessment techniques, review the course objectives, including skills, knowledge, and other goals (see figure 9.1). Each performance objective in a lesson or unit states the specific performance that is to be observed (refer to chapter 6 for help in writing performance objectives). If objectives have been correctly written in terms of performance, the verb describes what the student will be expected to do to demonstrate achievement of the objective. For example, if the objective is to throw a softball, swim a distance, shoot free throws, or improve time in running, some type of *skills test* to determine skill in throwing, swimming, shooting, or running would be involved. If the objective is to define bowling terms, score an archery round, or recognize correct rules of etiquette, some type of *written test* would be necessary. Some objectives—such as writing a paper on the history of tennis or passing a multiple-choice test on the rules of badminton—are evaluated exactly as specified, by writing a paper or passing a test. Some examples of various general objectives and appropriate evaluation techniques include the following:

badminton short serve	skills test
archery form	rating checklist
swimming skills—dive, tread water	checklist
knowledge of rules	written test
dance composition	subjective evaluation by teacher using specified criteria

Many objectives would be more accurately evaluated by using several techniques:

lifesaving	skills test, essay test, personal interview
feelings about fitness	anonymous questionnaire, observation of participation in fitness activities
tennis serve	skills test on accuracy, teacher evaluation of form
challenge and risk activities	skills tests, checklist, or rating form; student journal about growth in personal and social skills

Create a class handout summarizing important content for the written tests, as well as instructions for the psychomotor and affective tests. Tests should reflect the emphasis placed on that area during class instruction or in study materials. Look for appropriate tests in tests and measurements books or professional books and journals. Some specific sources for written test items include *Test Questions for Physical Education Activities*[6] and teachers' manuals for various books on sport skills. Be sure to adapt questions to meet the specific needs of your classes. AAHPERD has skills tests for many activities. Check to see whether the norm group is appropriate for the students. It may be necessary to devise norms, which can be done once the test has been given. If no tests can be located for the objectives being evaluated, or if the tests are not practical for the teaching environment, the teacher must create tests. In this case, list the behaviors demonstrated by an outstanding player in the activity being tested and devise a means of testing for the behavior specified. Try to keep skills tests as close to a game situation as possible[7] and as simple as possible. Try out the tests with a few students to see how they work, and revise them as needed.

Affective evaluation can be used to determine student progress toward affective objectives and to assist students through individual conferences and instruction. In general, teachers attempt to assess whether student attitudes are positive or negative toward physical education or the specific activity engaged in, and how well students are applying the principles of appropriate social behavior such as good teamwork or sportspersonship. For students to answer honestly on affective evaluation instruments, they must trust that results will not be used against them.

Although evaluation in education cannot always be as precise as some statisticians would like it to be, it can certainly be much more precise than many teachers have supposed it could be. The examples on the following pages are designed to make evaluation practical and objective for the teacher, as well as providing some techniques other than written or skills tests.

Cognitive Assessment Techniques

1. *True-false test.* Develop a true-false test in which the students change the questions so the answers are all true or all false. Tell the students which of these conditions will exist.
2. *Take-home test.* Students are given questions to be answered outside of class. A deadline for submission is stated when the questions are handed out. Students may use whatever resources are available to answer questions. Students can be

asked to list resources on the answer sheet. Answers are expected to be comprehensive and will be graded accordingly.

3. *Multiple-choice test.* By labeling options of a multiple-choice test with letters other than the usual a, b, c, or d, the correct answers will be grouped into words to spell out a phrase appropriate to a given holiday or activity.[8] For example, the answer to question one might be *F;* to question two, *I;* to question three, *T,* spelling *FIT,* and so forth. Another variation is to label the responses themselves to form words, as shown in this example:

> What score would the server call out when she has scored 3 points and the opponent has scored 2 points?
> X. 30–40
> M. Ad In
> A. 40–30
> S. Deuce

4. *Nongraded exam.* Students are asked to answer questions that, when completed, serve as a study sheet. Answers are corrected but not graded. Such activities can be motivational. Examples include the crossword puzzle and the pyramid described in chapter 8.

Psychomotor Assessment Techniques

1. *Checklists (figures 9.2 and 9.3.).* Determine skills that cannot be effectively graded on a quality or quantity basis but that should be completed at a minimal level. List

SWIMMING	Sculling	Change direction	Turn over	Jump-waist deep	Jump deep	Level off	Dive	Bobbing—25 times	Rhythmic breathing	Tread water for 1 minute	Change position →↑←↓	Elementary rescues	Feet-first surface dive	Pike or tuck surface dive	
Troy	✓	✓	✓	✓	✓	✓	✓	✓	✓	✓	✓	✓	✓	✓	A
Gregg	✓	✓	✓	✓	✓	✓	✓	✓	✓	✓	✓	✓	✓	✓	A
Tracy	✓	✓	✓	✓	✓	✓	✓	✓	✓	✓	✓	✓	✓	✓	A
Gary	✓	✓	✓	✓	✓	✓	✓	✓	✓	✓	✓	✓	✓	✓	A
Jose	✓	✓	✓	✓	✓	✓	✓	✓	✓	✓	✓	✓			B

Figure 9.2 A checklist.

```
                        ARCHERY FORM CHECKLIST

                                                              NAMES

   Date _____

              Feet not positioned properly
   Address    Weight unbalanced
              Body twisted

              Arrow not perpendicular to string
   Nock       Fingers grip nock
              Archer's feet move to get arrow

              Fingers uneven on string
              Fingers or wrist curl
              Grip on bow too tight
              Forefinger above arrow rest
   Draw       Forearm, wrist, hand not even
                 with line of arrow
              Bow canted
              Bow elbow rotated downward
              Head or body moves to meet anchor

              Incorrect eye closed
   Anchor     Unsteady bow arm
   Aim        Not holding long enough to aim
              Inconsistent anchor—no anchor

              Body or head moves
   Release    Bow arm moves
              String hand jerks

   Follow     Not holding form until arrow strikes
   Through       target

                                         SCORE
```

Figure 9.3 A form checklist.

the skills to be performed and the students' names on a card or paper. Then simply check off the skills as they are achieved. The grade may consist of the number of skills completed.

2. *Scores (figure 9.4).* In activities such as bowling, track, and swimming, the score or time is the best indication of success. Fronske found that time or the number of strokes required to swim 25 yards were valid predictors of swimming skill.[9]

BOWLING	Game 1	Game 2	Game 3	Game 4	Game 5	Final average	Form	Scoring quiz	Written final	Grade
Glen	134	134	148	140	144	140 / A	B+	B	C	B
Malika	122	128	110	112	122	118 / D	B	D	B	B−
Anthony	150	168		120	168	151 / A	A−	C	A	A−
Steve	121	83	114	112	104	106 / C+	B	C	D	C
Lois	141	150	149	166	124	146 / A	B+	C	B	B+

Figure 9.4 Grading with actual scores.

ARCHERY PROGRESS RECORD

ROUND		GRADE										TOTAL POSSIBLE
	Boys	A	A−	B+	B	B−	C+	C	C−	D+	D	
	Girls	A	A	A−	B+	B	B−	C+	C	C−	D	
NAA 900		600	510	480	460	430	400	340	280	230	150	900
Columbia		500	410	360	330	300	280	240	220	180	140	648
Jr. Columbia		500	450	410	380	350	330	310	270	240	210	648
Scholastic		330	260	230	210	190	170	150	130	110	100	432
Jr. Scholastic		380	340	320	310	300	280	260	240	210	180	432

Figure 9.5 Grading with converted scores.

3. *Standard scores, percentiles (figure 9.5).* In activities such as archery, raw scores cannot be averaged because of differences in the rounds shot. In these cases, the raw scores from previous classes may be converted into standard scores that can be compared with scores on other rounds or averaged to get a composite score. Standard tests and measurements texts explain how to calculate standard scores or percentiles. Grades on each round can also be used as standard scores and can be averaged.

4. *Rating sheets (figure 9.6).* Rating sheets are checklists used to evaluate (rate) some ability. They can be constructed from a list of expected behaviors. The teacher places a check or number beside the appropriate item.

TUMBLING ROUTINES RATING SHEET

Rating to be given in each area: 4 = Very Good; 3 = Good; 2 = Fair; 1 = Poor

Group number	Entrance	Team work	Originality	Quality of skill	Stage poise	Exit	Evidence of preparation	Comments
1								
2								
3								
4								
5								
6								
7								
8								
9								
10								

Period   Date   Signature of evaluator

Figure 9.6 A rating sheet for tumbling.

5. *Incidence charts (figure 9.7).* Incidence charts list the skills performed in a given activity. The number of times each skill is used is tallied during a specified time period. Incidence charts can assist the teacher in describing game performance to the student.
6. *Tournament results.* Results of a Round Robin class singles tournament is generally a good indication of the playing ability of individual students. Avoid grading one student on his or her team's or partner's ability or lack of ability.
7. *Accumulative record (figure 9.8).* An example of a cumulative record is the Swim and Stay Fit program of the American Red Cross, in which the distance swum by each student is recorded daily. In basketball, a student can shoot 10 free throws each day and record the total number made on an accumulative record. This method of evaluation is most valuable as a motivational technique, especially for homework, fitness programs, or preclass activities. Caution should be used, however, when incorporating this technique. Students who are doing poorly may quit trying or give up. Such records can be valuable to the teacher as the low-aptitude students quickly emerge and a general indication of such factors as skill, endurance, and effort appear. Individualized programs can then be set up to meet the personal needs of each student. Scores can be averaged at the end of a unit to be used for grading purposes.
8. *Subjective evaluation of performance (figure 9.9).* Subjective evaluation by the teacher can be facilitated by evaluating a few students each day rather than evaluating all of the students at the same time. Scores for several evaluations can be averaged at the conclusion of the term. The best way to help students improve and to motivate performance is to discuss each individual rating immediately. This also opens communication for those students who may not agree with the teacher's evaluation. Several examples of skill evaluation techniques follow. Avoid using a scale so detailed that students cannot understand the difference between adjacent points on the scale.

Badminton
Grade or Points

A or 4—Correct use of all strokes.
B or 3—Correct use of clears, serves, and smash or drop.
C or 2—Correct use of clears and serves.
D or 1—Correct use of clear or serve.

Swimming
One point each for correct arms, legs, breathing, and coordination, the highest grade possible being A or 4.

Other Sport Skills

POINTS	RATING	DEFINITION
5	Excellent	Technique and form mastered. Effective, polished, confident in execution of skills and strategies.

BADMINTON INCIDENCE CHART

Name	SERVE Short Out-of-court	SERVE Short Into net	SERVE Long Too high	SERVE Long Out-of-court	SERVE Long Too short	SERVE Long Too low	SMASH Into or below net	SMASH Out-of-bounds	SMASH Missed bird	SMASH Too low	CLEAR Too short	CLEAR Out-of-court	CLEAR Out-of-position
Diane White				|||						|||		||||| |||	||	
Gregg Charlton				||||||					||||||		||||| ||||| ||||| |||||	||||| ||||| ||	|||

Figure 9.7 An incidence chart.
Source: Rudy Moe, Brigham Young University.

Jogging Record

Name	¼	½	¾	1	1¼	1½	1¾	2	2¼	2½	2¾	3	3¼
Gail													
Lois													
Karen													
Penny													

Figure 9.8 An accumulative tournament.

NAME	9/17	9/19	9/24	9/26	10/1	10/3	10/8	10/10	10/15	AVERAGE
Judy	2		2			2+		2-		2
Sally	3+			4			4-		4	4-
Vickie	2	3-			3		3	3		3
Bonnie	1		2-	2		2+				2
Kay				4				4		4

Figure 9.9 Subjective evaluation of performance.

POINTS	RATING	DEFINITION
4	Above average	Good technique and execution of skill but not highly effective or efficient. Some minor errors. Good use of strategy.
3	Average	Basic skill performed but not refined. Accuracy and effectiveness consistent enough to permit some use of strategy.
2	Fair	Executes skill with many errors that result in inconsistency, inaccuracy, and ineffectiveness. Lacks confidence and timing.
1	Poor	Basic mechanics in performance lacking. Experiences very occasional success. Fails to apply strategy.

A description of each point on the scale should contribute to a more objective and reliable grade.

Dance

Subjective evaluations in dance can be made more objective by defining the factors to be considered, as in the Modern Dance Composition Evaluation shown in figure 9.10. Specific definitions also help the student discern what is to be included in the composition.

Affective Assessment Techniques

1. *Teacher observation.* Teachers have almost unlimited opportunities to observe student behavior and attitudes. This does not necessarily mean their judgment will be objective and

MODERN DANCE COMPOSITION EVALUATION				
Period _____		Grade _____		
Names	Floor patterns (2)	Coordination of movements (3)	Variations (3)	Performance (2)
Janice				
Betty				
John				
Carlos				

Figure 9.10 Subjective evaluation in dance.

informed, however. If the assessment is to be thorough and truly useful, teachers should systematically plan both data collection and procedures for recording information. If teachers do not consciously identify the behaviors to be observed and take time to gather and record information, their impressions are more likely to be formed by extreme incidents and behavior patterns than by a less-biased sample of the behaviors of interest. Frequency counts can be used to quantify such items as absences, tardiness, failure to dress, and dropping out of school. Anecdotal records should be made of approach behaviors including participation in nonrequired club, intramural, or extramural activities or volunteering to help with physical education–related activities.

Kirkpatrick tells students they will be evaluated on effort, attitude, awareness, and expectations three times during each nine-week grading period. Because students don't know when the three evaluations will occur, they participate maximally every day. She also uses heart monitors to evaluate students' effort. She can read the heart monitors during the class period on a wristwatch monitor and also print out a copy on the computer.[10]

Kovar and Ermler remind teachers that grades should not be used for disciplinary purposes or to eliminate or reduce inappropriate behavior.[11] Behavior problems should be dealt with immediately, not at the end of the term.[12]

2. *Rating scales, inventories, and questionnaires.* Rating scales, inventories, and questionnaires can be used to provide information about the student or the object of the instrument. Several scales for rating behavior have been developed. In the Blanchard Behavior Rating Scale, the rater rates the frequency of observation of such traits as leadership, self-control, cooperation, and other personal and social qualities.[13] Cowell has developed a Social Adjustment Index to measure similar qualities, and a Personal Distance Scale to measure social acceptance.[14] Another test of group status is Breck's Sociometric Test of Status.[15] Fox has developed a tool that can be used to screen students with low self-concepts.[16] An example is shown in figure 9.11. Results of all of these scales will be influenced to some extent by the amount of trust that has been developed between teacher and students. Teachers should be aware of the possible lack of validity and reliability in these measures and exercise caution when using them.

How They See Me

Just as each part of the day is filled with positive, neutral, and negative things, each person is made up of things we like and things we do not like so much. Below are a number of circles showing persons with different amounts of positive (+) and negative (−) things about them. Which of these circles comes closest to the way you see yourself? Write the letter of the circle which most resembles you right here: _____ .

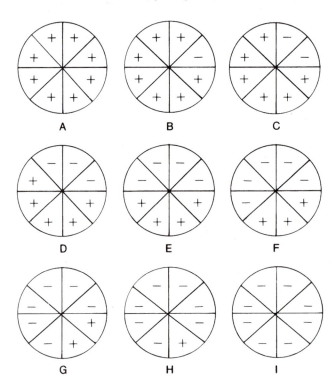

In the blank following each question, write the letter of the circle that you think each of the persons mentioned would pick for you.

1. Which circle do you think your closest friend would choose to describe you? _____
2. Which circle would the teacher in this class choose? _____

Figure 9.11 A self-concept scale.
Source: *Diagnosing Classroom Learning Environments* by Fox, Luszki, and Schmuck.
© 1966, Science Research Associates, Inc.
Reprinted by permission of the publisher.

```
Sportspersonship Checklist for _____

                          Usually  Sometimes  Seldom   Never
Knows and obeys rules,
  even when not
  observed               _____   _____   _____  _____
    Calls own violations, fouls, liners
    Plays "clean"

Respects officials       _____   _____   _____  _____
    Does not argue with officials or complain
    about misjudgments
    Compliments officials

Shows respect for
    opponents            _____   _____   _____  _____
    Applauds or congratulates good play by opponent
    Is courteous
    Shakes hands with opponents before the contest
    Congratulates opponents after the game

Maintains self-control   _____   _____   _____  _____
    Accepts victory without boasting
    Loses gracefully without complaint or alibi
    Does not make excuses
    Performs to the best of his or her ability regardless
      of the situation
    Does not use profanity
    Refrains from verbal or physical abuse of others

Shows respect for
    facilities and
    equipment            _____   _____   _____  _____
    Puts equipment away
    Respects property of others
    Takes appropriate care of equipment
```

Figure 9.12 A rating scale for sportspersonship.

Examples of rating scales that could be used for evaluating sportspersonship or teamwork are shown in figures 9.12 and 9.13.

Several attitude inventories have been created to appraise student attitude toward physical fitness, exercise, and physical education. They are referred to in a number of tests and measurements textbooks. Rating scales could also be used to evaluate student participation in adventure activities. Students could be asked to define the purposes of the activities and a rating scale could be devised much like the ones for sportspersonship or teamwork. Students could be asked to evaluate themselves or their group.

3. *Interviews.* Interviews can be structured or unstructured. Much valuable information about student feelings toward physical education can be acquired through informal discussions with individuals or groups of students. Structured interviews involve asking students predetermined questions. The effectiveness of the interview hinges on the trust between teacher and students.

```
 ┌────────────────────────────────────────────────────────────────┐
 │    Teamwork Checklist for  _____        │
 │                                                                │
 │                     Usually  Sometimes  Seldom   Never         │
 │   Shows respect for                                            │
 │     teammates         _____  _____  _____  _____     │
 │       Congratulates good play by teammate                      │
 │       Puts team before self                                    │
 │       Plays own position--does not hog ball                    │
 │       Assists play by teammates                                │
 │       Talks or signals to teammates during play                │
 │       Does not argue with team members                         │
 │       Demonstrates loyalty                                     │
 │       Is courteous                                             │
 │       Gets along with teammates                                │
 │       Works with teammates to improve skills                   │
 │   Maintains self-control   _____  _____  _____  _____ │
 │       Is punctual and in own place, does not keep others       │
 │          waiting                                               │
 │       Does not use profanity                                   │
 │       Puts in hard, honest practice                            │
 │   Shows respect for                                            │
 │     teacher or coach       _____  _____  _____  _____ │
 │       Follows instructions without arguing                     │
 └────────────────────────────────────────────────────────────────┘
```

Figure 9.13 A rating scale for teamwork.

4. *Student self-evaluation.* Student self-evaluation can be helpful in assisting students to focus on their personal effort and involvement in physical education and to learn to evaluate themselves realistically. Often students will have a different feeling about their effort and progress than the teacher does. Teacher-student conferences can be used to discuss these discrepancies and gain a better understanding of what goals each is trying to achieve. An attitude or effort inventory such as the one shown in figure 9.14 could be used for this purpose.

One of the most effective means of self-evaluation is journal keeping. Several techniques can be used to help students with their journal keeping. Students can be asked to complete a questionnaire, inventory, or rating scale, and then tell what they learned about themselves. Several of the preceding rating scales could be used in this manner. Students can complete open-ended statements such as "I wish this class . . ." or "I really like this class when. . . ." Other questions that students might answer include:

1. If I had it to do all over again, I (would/would not) take this course. Why?
2. What are the two most important things you have learned in this class?
3. To what extent will you use the things you have learned in this class?
4. Discuss what helped you most in meeting your course goals: teacher/practice drills/playing games/study sheet/individual work on skills.
5. Was the present system of grading appropriate?
6. What things would you have liked more help with in this unit?

Reaction papers or journal entries are often used to evaluate the achievement of affective objectives from participation in adventure activities.

```
SELF-EVALUATION FOR _____

INSTRUCTIONS: Answer the following questions by circling the best response
              or filling in the blank.

1. I feel  really good     good      ok      bad about myself and what I
   have done.
2. I accomplished all     almost all     most     some     none of my
   contracted objectives.
3. I completed _____ elective objectives.
              (number)
4. My efforts on the objectives would be considered: good     fair
   poor.
5. My efforts in helping others would be considered: good     fair
   poor.
6. The grade that I contracted for was _____.
7. The grade I have earned is _____.
8. If you were to grade yourself on a 10-point scale for each of the
   following items, what score would you give yourself on:
   a. Your current skill level: _____
   b. Your skill improvement: _____
   c. Your physical fitness: _____
9. How can you improve in the following areas in this class?
   a. Achievement _____

   b. Effort _____

   c. Citizenship _____
```

Figure 9.14 An attitude or effort inventory.

Step 3—Administer the Tests

After selecting or writing a cognitive test, proofread the test while making the answer key and correct any errors on the test. Then make sufficient copies for class use. Number each copy to ensure that none have been taken during the administration of the test. Provide a space on the answer sheet for students to record this number. Make sufficient copies of the test and answer sheet, and obtain extra pencils, including a red pencil or pen for correcting the tests. Be sure the answer key is in a safe place. To minimize the temptation to cheat, seat students in alternate seats or ask them to spread out through the entire room. Alternate forms of a test can also be used to discourage cheating. Review the testing procedures and the test directions orally to avoid needless questions. Include how to fill out answer sheets, how to get help if needed (e.g., raise hand or come to front desk), and what to do when finished. If possible, assign a student assistant to correct objective tests as students complete them. Also, tests can be collected when all students have completed the test and redistributed so no student gets his or her own paper. Then students correct the exam. When students are assigned to score their own tests, the test serves as a learning activity as well as a means of evaluation, because students learn the correct answer to the

BADMINTON SKILLS TEST CARD

Name _____ Period _____ Date _____

SHORT SERVE:
Equipment: Rope—20" above net
              Target

Directions: Serve 10 birds to the right court.

Scoring: Liners count higher number. (Serve must
           go between ropes. Must repeat illegal
           serves.) (Shuttle or racket above
           waist.)

5 or 3   Scored depending on area on target.
   0   For hitting net.
   0   For passing *over* rope.
   1   For hitting in service area but not on
         target.

1. _____   2. _____   3. _____   4. _____   5. _____

6. _____   7. _____   8. _____   9. _____   10. _____

Have partners score as you serve.

                                    Total _____

Figure 9.15 A skills test scorecard.

questions they missed. Make sure to collect all tests and answer sheets before dismissing the class. To increase activity time and enhance motivation, several short quizzes might be better than one long exam.

Before giving each skills test, devise some method of score keeping that allows students to quickly insert scores for each student or group of students (see figure 9.15). When administering the skills tests, demonstrate each test, read and explain the directions on the card or test sheet, and answer any questions students might have. Carefully explain trials, scoring, and recording. Mark needed areas and set up equipment for all tests in advance. Be aware of the disadvantages of grading on a single administration of a skills test. A student might be ill, anxious about the test, or just not able to perform as well some days as others. This can be remedied by allowing the student to take the test several times and use the highest score achieved. In this way, assessment activities are also learning activities, which saves time and also increases student responses and accountability.[17]

Step 4—Evaluate the Evaluation Techniques

After using the evaluation techniques with one or more classes, note how each one was implemented, whether it was effective, and why. Then make plans to remedy any problems and to increase the efficiency, validity, and reliability of the test. Look for items such as unclear directions, complex vocabulary, poor sentence structure, poorly constructed questions, and materials that do not test course content as stated on the test blueprint. Listen to students' questions as they attempt to take or correct the test and note problems with directions or test items on a master copy for use in revising the test. Record the amount of time needed to complete the test by indicating when the last student finished.

Keep a tally of questions missed. Identify those questions no one missed or that were often missed. These questions may need to be eliminated or revised. Repeat this process each time the test is given. Remember, evaluation is a means to an end, not an end in itself.

Answer the following questions about each evaluation technique:

1. Does the evaluation agree with the performance objective stated for the activity (content validity)?
2. Are the directions and vocabulary simple enough for the students' maturity and are the test items carefully selected or constructed (validity)?
3. Is the technique formulated so that another person with similar experience can use it for evaluation and get the same results (objectivity)?
4. Does the technique consistently result in the same score or grade for a student even when given on different occasions (reliability)?
5. Does the technique contribute to improved teaching-learning practices by enhancing teacher-student relations, encouraging students to devote attention to all areas of instruction, and serving as a fair and useful measure of achievement of outcomes emphasized in instruction?

When the process of ongoing evaluation has been completed, some type of reporting of results usually occurs. The assignment of a grade to each student is the most common method of reporting evaluation results.

Grading

Grading is perceived as one of the most bothersome of all teaching duties. Perhaps this is because there appears to be no consensus by members of the profession as to how or why it is to be done. In fact, many grading practices seem to be educationally unsound. Dressel pointed out:

> A grade (is) . . . an inadequate report of an inaccurate judgment by a biased and variable judge of the extent to which a student has attained an undefined level of mastery of an unknown proportion of an indefinite amount of material.[18]

In spite of the uncertainty of grading it is still a very important part of the educational process. Students, parents, employers, and institutions of higher learning all demand such accountability. Great care should be taken to ensure fairness and consistency in grading.

The Purpose of Grading

A grade informs students, parents, and administrators of the present status and progress of students toward program objectives. Grades tend to promote positive public relations with colleges, universities, professional schools, and employers, who depend on them for admission and hiring.

Grades may also serve as a motivator for teachers and students to improve the teaching-learning process. Finally, if used properly, grades help teachers evaluate the effectiveness of instruction. Under no circumstances should grades be given casually, based on the teacher's impression of the student, without evidence of student achievement.

Principles of Grading

In spite of the fact that educators have never been able to agree on how to grade, certain principles have emerged that, if followed, will make grading a more rewarding process for both teacher and student.

1. The grade should reflect individual student *achievement* as determined by declared course objectives.
2. Grades should be based on achievement of all of the stated objectives of physical education, such as psychomotor skills, physical fitness, knowledge, and social skills.
3. Grades should reflect educational aims and promote educational outcomes, not be an end in themselves. The stress placed on grades in conventional practice tends to cause the student to believe that getting good marks is the aim of education.
4. The school or district grading system should be developed cooperatively by parents, students, teachers, and school personnel so grades will be consistent with those given in other subjects in the school. A sample worksheet for developing the grading process is shown in figure 9.16.
5. The department grading system should be established collectively by all physical education teachers and be applied consistently to every physical education class in the school.
6. Students should be informed in advance of the criteria and procedures used in assigning grades and receive adequate feedback on their progress toward objectives.
7. A variety of evaluation instruments, including both objective and subjective, should be used in the evaluation process.
8. Evaluation should be an ongoing process, and students should be adequately prepared for evaluation. Grades should not depend on one test score or evaluation session.
9. Evaluation procedures should foster positive student attitudes toward physical education.
10. A grading system should be detailed enough to be diagnostic; fair as a uniform measure of achievement; and compact enough to be practical in terms of time, understandability, and ease of recording.
11. Evaluation procedures should consider individual differences such as physical characteristics, maturity, background experiences, and ability.

The Process of Grading

The process for determining grades in physical education involves the following steps:

Step 1. Select a grading system.
Step 2. Select objectives and determine the emphasis to be placed on each objective.
Step 3. Select evaluation instruments for each objective.

CRITERIA FOR GRADING

Directions:
1. Choose the criteria you will use in grading by checking either the "Yes" or "No" column.
2. Give a brief explanation for your selection or rejection of each item.
3. Indicate the items from the class roll that you will use to determine the score or grade for each criterion.
4. Indicate the total number of points representing each criterion.
5. Indicate the percent of the total points for each criterion. (This must total 100%.)
6. Under "Comments" explain how you will determine the letter grade for each student.

Criteria	Yes	No	Explanation	Items on Class Roll to Be Used in Criteria	Points	Percent
Fitness						
Game Play						
Skill Tests						
Written Tests						
Other						
				Total		100%

Comments:

Figure 9.16 Criteria for grading.
Source: Rudy Moe, Brigham Young University.

Step 4. Measure the degree of achievement of each objective.
Step 5. Determine the grade based on the original percentage specified for each objective.
Step 6. Communicate the grade to the student.

Step 1—*Select a grading system.* In the selection of a grading system or combination of systems, care should be taken to consider the advantages and limitations of each. No one method is superior in all situations; some compromises or combinations of systems may need to be made. One arrangement would be to grade all students according to prearranged standards or criteria. A second arrangement would be to group students for instruction according to skill or fitness levels and grade each group according to different criteria. The following systems of grading are presented for consideration.

Norm-Referenced Evaluation

Norm-referenced evaluation ("grading on the curve") is the measurement of individual performance as it compares with group or class performance according to a normal probability curve. Grades are distributed at different levels, usually A, B, C, D, or F. Such a system is ideal when students must be ranked.

However, several disadvantages of norm-referenced evaluation exist. First, it tends to assess the rate of learning of students rather than ability to learn; the fastest learners get A's. Second, grades are distributed over a curve whether this is appropriate or not. Third, grading on the curve is not consistent with evaluation based on performance objectives. It fails to tell whether the students have mastered the skills. In fact, some skills cannot be graded on a curve, such as "treading water" in swimming. Consequently, most grading policies do not adhere to a strict norm-referenced evaluation system. Many grading policies are modifications of the norm-referenced system, and a true curve is not strictly observed.

Criterion-Referenced Evaluation

Criterion-referenced evaluation is the measurement of individual performance as it compares with a preestablished standard of performance, such as a score, the number of tasks completed, or the difficulty of tasks completed. Grades can be expressed in percentage scores, as pass-fail, or as letter grades of A, B, C, D, or F.

Criterion-referenced evaluation makes it possible for more students to earn a good grade. Grades are not influenced by the high skill levels of others. Criterion-referenced evaluation facilitates the use of student-paced programs, competency-based instruction, and contract grading. *Contract grading* specifies the performance and criteria (quantity and quality) for which each student will receive a given grade. An example of contract grading is shown in figure 9.17. In individual contracts, each contract specifies the performance and criteria for that student and whether the student or teacher or someone else will determine when the criteria have been met.

Criterion-referenced grading reduces student anxiety and decreases subjectivity in grading. This is especially true of contract grading and mastery grading, which communicate to the student exactly what is expected in terms of performance, quantity, and quality. When students know what the objectives are, they are much more likely to achieve them.

The major disadvantages of criterion-referenced evaluation are twofold. First, accurate standards cannot always be specified before the activity or unit has been taught. Grades may become a reflection of test difficulty rather than failure to achieve. For example, if no student got 90 or above on a test, either the students did not learn or the test was too difficult. In mastery grading, it is often difficult to draw the line between what is passing and what is failing. Standards may vary from one teacher to another.

A second complaint is that criterion-referenced methods of grading encourage mediocrity. Critics maintain that grade inflation takes place when too many students receive high grades. Care must be taken to set standards high enough that the integrity of an A grade is not in question, no matter how many students earn that grade.

When *pass-fail* grading is used, students may lower their achievement to the level of the standard for passing, and motivation to excel is decreased. When pass-fail, criterion-referenced grading is used it does not differentiate between students of different abilities, except at a minimum level. In some classes, an A-pass-fail system is used to distinguish students who wish to do more than achieve the minimum specified level of performance.

Pass-no-credit grading is a variation of the pass-fail system. It eliminates the need for students to cheat in order to pass because no stigma is attached to failure. It encourages students to try new activities in which they might be afraid to fail. However, students still have to repeat the experience if they wish to receive credit.

Improvement

Grading on improvement is considered questionable at best. A grade based solely on improvement is *never* acceptable. The rationale for this is that improvement in math or science

TENNIS CONTRACT

A GRADE

I, _____ , contract with AFJH physical education instructors for an A grade. In return for this grade I will complete the following requirements on or before May 26.

_____1. Twenty-five forehand ball bounces.
_____2. Twenty-five backhand ball bounces.
_____3. Twenty-five consecutive forehand strokes against the gym wall.
_____4. Twenty-five consecutive backhand strokes against the gym wall.
_____5. Rally with a classmate at least six forehand and backhand strokes.
_____6. Serve ten consecutive serves using good form to each court.
_____7. Play a match with an *experienced* player.
_____8. Write a two-page report on the four most popular tennis tournaments and the history of the game.
_____9. Pass a quiz on scoring.

B GRADE

I, _____ , contract with AFJH physical education instructors for a B grade. In return for this grade I will complete the following requirements on or before May 26.

_____1. Fifteen forehand ball bounces.
_____2. Fifteen backhand ball bounces.
_____3. Rally against the gym wall fifteen consecutive strokes using forehand and backhand strokes.
_____4. Serve seven consecutive serves to each court using good form.
_____5. Play one game with a classmate.
_____6. Write a *short* report on the history of tennis and scoring.

C GRADE

I, _____ , contract with AFJH physical education instructors for a C grade. In return for this grade I will complete the following requirements on or before May 26.

_____1. Ten forehand ball bounces.
_____2. Ten consecutive backhand bounces.
_____3. Ten alternating ball bounces.
_____4. Serve five consecutive balls over the net to the correct court.
_____5. Read the tennis information in Mrs. Anderson's workbook and answer the corresponding questions in the test booklet.

Figure 9.17   A contract for grading.
Source: Dona Anderson, American Fork Jr. High, American Fork, Utah.

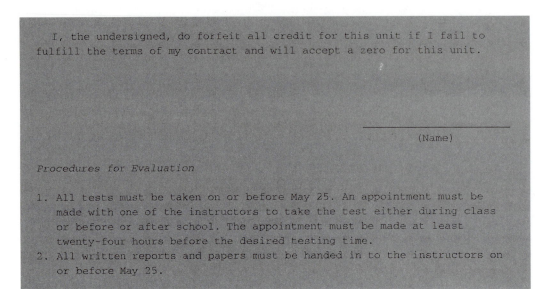

I, the undersigned, do forfeit all credit for this unit if I fail to
fulfill the terms of my contract and will accept a zero for this unit.

_____
(Name)

Procedures for Evaluation

1. All tests must be taken on or before May 25. An appointment must be
   made with one of the instructors to take the test either during class
   or before or after school. The appointment must be made at least
   twenty-four hours before the desired testing time.
2. All written reports and papers must be handed in to the instructors on
   or before May 25.

Figure 9.17 (*Continued*)

or physical education or English grammar is not worth much if the concepts needed in everyday life are missing. If students enrolled in a physical education class have not achieved the standards necessary to be considered physically educated or physically fit, grades should reflect this no matter how much improvement has occurred. Another disadvantage of grading on improvement is that many activity units do not permit adequate time for improvement to occur. Improvement scores are then unreliable. In spite of this, many physical education teachers continue to grade on improvement.

Grading on improvement is supposed to reflect individual progress, demonstrated by performance on a posttest compared with performance on a pretest. It can be used to evaluate fitness objectives when high reliability exists and in individual sports where improvement is not based on the performance of others. It can also be used when student motivation is high enough to minimize students' purposely scoring low on the pretest. Its main advantage lies in the motivation of lower-skilled students, especially when they are included in classes with students who have high levels of ability.

Deutsch suggested two ways to consider improvement in the grading process: (1) develop separate norms for each ability group based on pretest scores, and (2) calculate an improvement score as follows:

$$\frac{\textit{posttest score} - \textit{pretest score}}{\text{maximum test score} - \text{pretest score}} = \text{improvement}$$

Example: The maximum possible score on the test is 100.

Individual progress is determined by comparing performance on several occasions.
© Allen Ruid

	Pretest	Posttest	Potential Improvement	Actual Improvement
Student 1	80	90	100 − 80 = 20	90 − 80 = 10
		Student A improved 10/20 or 50 percent		
Student 2	20	60	100 − 20 = 80	60 − 20 = 40
		Student B improved 40/80 or 50 percent		

Thus both students had the same amount of improvement. The use of standardized scores yields greater accuracy for this process.

Grading on improvement favors the less-skilled students over the highly skilled students even when achievement plus improvement is included in the grade calculation. For example, a highly skilled student who scored seven baskets on a ten-shot free-throw test in basketball will probably not improve very much at the posttest. A score of eight on the posttest plus a score of one for improvement gives that student a total score of nine. A student who scored only two baskets on the pretest but scored six on the posttest receives a total score of ten (six plus four for improvement). The student making only six out of ten free throws has earned a higher score than the student scoring eight out of ten free throws. Deutsch suggests using improvement along with objective and subjective evaluation of skill for grading.[19]

Student-Assigned Grades

Some teachers perceive grades as destroying student–teacher rapport, so they favor student self-evaluation and grading. Students might be asked to write out their goals, criteria for evaluating goal achievement, ways in which the goals were achieved or not achieved, and the appropriate grade. Teachers may then add their own comments, negotiate with the student for a mutually acceptable grade, or average the student's and teacher's grades to arrive at a course grade. Student-assigned grades are most frequently used in individualized learning programs when time is available for individual student–teacher conferences, although they can be used in a group situation if students are provided with some type of form for self-evaluation.

For this type of evaluation to be used effectively, students must be taught goal-setting techniques and techniques for evaluating their own strengths and weaknesses. Often teachers will discover that students are harder on themselves than the teacher would be. However, honest self-evaluation is difficult because of the intense pressure on students to get high grades.

Step 2—*Select objectives and determine the emphasis to be placed on each objective.* List each of the objectives of physical education inherent in the unit or course of study and determine the percentage of emphasis for each one. Consistent with the unique status of physical education, skill and physical fitness should be emphasized in the weighting. (Refer to figure 9.16.) Boyce found that students who were graded on a combination of skill, knowledge, and participation performed better on skills than those who were graded on just skills or just participation.[20]

Step 3.—*Select evaluation instruments for each objective.* A comprehensive review of evaluation techniques has been presented. Appropriate instruments should be selected to evaluate each objective. A sample plan for steps 2 and 3 is shown in Table 9.1. Whenever possible, positive evaluation should be used, such as awarding points for performance instead of subtracting points for lack of performance. Both quantitative and qualitative assessments are appropriate. However, teachers should avoid the practice of grading on attitude and effort, because most techniques used to do so are not valid.

Step 4—*Measure the degree of achievement of each objective.* Student progress should be reported in terms of individual achievement of the objectives specified for each unit of activity. Care should be taken to record test scores or other data for each of the objectives. This information can be extremely valuable in interpreting student progress and grades for both students and parents. Use as many different evaluation opportunities as possible so that students are not graded on a one-time all-out effort.

Step 5—*Determine the grade based on the original percentage or points specified for each objective.* Based on the example shown in Table 9.1, if a student achieved a B+ on skill, a C on fitness, an A on knowledge, and an A on social skills, the grade would be averaged as follows:

If A + = 12 points
    A = 11
    A − = 10
    B + = 9
    B = 8
    B − = 7
    C + = 6
    C = 5
    C − = 4
    D + = 3
    D = 2
    D = 1

$$35\% \ B+ = .35 \times 9 = 3.15$$
$$35\% \ C = .35 \times 5 = 1.75$$
$$15\% \ A = .15 \times 11 = 1.65$$
$$15\% \ A = .15 \times 11 = 1.65$$

$$\overline{8.20 = B}$$

Table 9.1 A Sample Grading Plan

Objectives	Emphasis (%)	Instruments	Examples (Figures)
Skill	35	Subjective evaluation	9.9, 9.10
		Teacher observation checklists	9.2, 9.3
		Rating scales	9.6
		Incidence charts	9.7
		Skills tests	9.4, 9.5, 9.15
		Student self-evaluation	9.14
Physical fitness	35	Health-related fitness tests	9.8, Table 8.2
Knowledge	15	Written tests	9.1
		Assignments	8.21, 8.22, 8.23
		Oral discussion	
Social skills	15	Rating scales	9.12, 9.13
		Student self-evaluation	9.14
		Anecdotal records	

Students should also know and understand how the skill grade of 35 percent will be derived. If the fitness skill grade includes a run, some criteria for A, B, or C should be stated. For example:

A	=	8:29 minutes
A –	=	9:01 minutes
B –	=	9:36 minutes
B	=	10:00 minutes

Perhaps the fitness grade will be determined by the completion of an individual contract. Criteria for a grade will differ with each student. The grade might be pass-fail, or specific standards of performance could be stated in the contract for A, B, or C work.

Another efficient method of figuring grades is assigning point values to the grade components. The final grade can then be tallied by adding all points together as shown below. Each component for the total grade has a point value. For example:

Component	Maximum Points
Skills Tests	*40*

Pass (10)
Bump (10)
Serve (15)
Spike (5)

Physical Fitness   **40**

Improvement (10)
Cardiovascular (10)
Strength (10)
Other (10)

Written Work   **20**

Behavior   **20**

Improvement (10)
Social (10)

Total Grade

85–100 points	=	A
65–84 points	=	B
36–64 points	=	C
16–35 points	=	D
Below 16	=	F

All criteria for the calculation of the grade should be determined and stated before beginning instruction in any activity or unit. Caution should be used in determining grades based on a few test scores because students may be incorrectly assigned to grade groupings. The more levels of grading that are used, the larger the chance that a student will be assigned a grade that he or she does not deserve. Validity can be increased by combining the results of several different assessments of the same factor, such as using skills tests and teacher ratings for skill grades.[21]

Electronic gradebook systems can be extremely helpful in transforming scores into grades. Each score can be weighted as described earlier. The computer calculates the final grade and prints out each component and its contribution to the final grade. Some gradebook systems will alphabetize names and sort grades, calculate statistics, determine letter grade breaks from raw data, and record absences. Various types of reports can be printed for individual students, classes, and statistical analyses.

Step 6—*Communicate the grade to the student*. Many problems are eliminated by communicating grades to the students as soon as possible after the evaluation. Students are then able to see their own progress toward objectives instead of what the teacher "gave me." They can also average the grades themselves as a unit of instruction progresses. If it is possible to schedule a private moment with each student several days before the end of the grading period, the teacher can review the grades earned as well as the reasons for each grade and let the student know what grade will appear on the report card. Doing this can eliminate misunderstandings, and, if necessary, changes can be made. All grades should be communicated to the student during the course of a grading period. Nothing should come as a surprise.

Grading in Coed and Mainstreamed Classes

Since the introduction of Title IX and PL 94-142, the range of abilities within each class has widened considerably. This requires new insight into grading in order to provide equal opportunities for students to reach success. Stamm discussed three possible approaches to grading in coeducational and mainstreamed classes. These include (1) grading on improvement, (2) using separate performance standards, and (3) mastery learning.[22] All of these approaches have been discussed previously. Teachers should remember that grading males and females using separate standards may result in perpetuating the stereotype that boys are capable of better performances than are girls. Perhaps a more equitable arrangement would be to group students by ability rather than by sex and then set the standards in terms of the abilities of each group. This plan might also prove valuable in meeting the needs of disabled students in the class. Once students are divided into ability groups, objectives could be written that are broad enough for all groups, such as: Choose one piece of equipment and perform a routine on that piece (fulfilling certain criteria), in addition to checking off five new skills on each piece of apparatus. Earning tickets in track and field for meeting standards on each event, for placing in "heats" and for jogging a lap (see figure 12.3) allows students to achieve regardless of their individual differences. Balancing teams by sex and ability group and awarding bonus points for team achievements on tests, sportsperson-ship, and skill attempts in games promotes achievement for all students regardless of ability.

Record Keeping for Grading

A grading system is only as good as the records of student performance that are kept. Teachers must use a record-keeping system that facilitates calculation of the final grade and keeps track of all grade input. A comprehensive system also aids the teacher in explaining the grade to parents or administrators at a later date. Examples of record-keeping systems are shown in figures 9.18 and 9.19. Computerized grading systems are excellent for maintaining records. However, hard copy printouts should be produced to guard against computer error or crash.

Evaluation of student performance, of course, involves test and measurement theory. This chapter briefly mentions some applicable information. Excellent resource texts in the area of tests and measurement exist, including *Introduction to Measurement in Physical Education and Exercise Science* (3rd edition) by Safrit and Wood.

Review Questions

1. What are the purposes of evaluation?
2. Define:
   norm-referenced evaluation
   criterion-referenced evaluation
   summative evaluation
   formative evaluation
   validity
   reliability
   objectivity

3. Explain how to select valid, reliable cognitive, psychomotor, and affective tests.
4. Besides skills tests, what other techniques can be used to evaluate psychomotor skills?
5. What techniques can be used to evaluate affective objectives?
6. Why do teachers give grades?
7. What are the advantages or disadvantages of each grading system? What grading system or combination of systems is best?

Figure 9.18 Official class roll.
Source: Constructed by Rudy Moe and James Tyrrell, Brigham Young University.

OFFICIAL CLASS ROLL

NAMES	Fitness test	VOLLEYBALL (Best Score) V.B. Serve	Spike	Set	Wall volley	Written test	Total SKILL pts.	BADMINTON (Best Score) Long Serve	Short Serve	Clear	Drop	Smash	Written test	Total SKILL pts. bad.	Total written pts. bad.	Total SKILL pts.	COMMENTS	TOTAL POINTS	FINAL GRADE
Adams, J.	76	35	37	28	40	36	27	30	29	34	34	48	64	164	63	300			
Alder, C.	68	36	40	41	41	52	40	42	36	42	38	37	194	194	78	260			
Bennett, A.	73	30	31	26	35	26	36	34	40	40	39	25	170	170	73	304			
Boyle, D.	57	33	35	27	40	30	34	28	36	32	23	44	159	159	81	280			
Butler, N.	59	22	35	19	37	14	28	33	36	31	54	38	162	162	75	276			
Cannon, R.	64	29	34	57	38	30	25	34	28	36	20	40	154	154	78	279			
Evans, W.	75	31	34	56	51	27	32	35	35	24	33	36	157	157	71	200			
Garrick, S.	63	36	31	33	29	26	31	31	29	29	20	34	159	159	64	274			
Jensen, T.	70	40	38	57	50	57	35	30	37	36	57	53	178	178	73	316			
Jones, W.	65	37	33	30	58	52	30	28	36	28	26	34	164	164	75	294			
Madsen, G.	76	33	36	41	57	52	30	30	34	36	35	59	159	159	76	597			
Nielsen, A.	70	30	27	28	20	26	43	33	63	36	18	44	143	143	62	255			
Price, P.	82	42	41	38	56	43	40	40	46	38	39	43	206	206	80	364			
Pyne, K.	72	34	37	36	34	30	30	26	40	28	36	50	70	70	64	304			
Ramirez, N.	60	40	37	36	41	37	37	37	30	28	39	37	171	171	79	314			
Rice, V.	93	46	41	39	44	60	43	39	41	43	46	59	212	212	84	372			
Robins, E.	82	26	31	24	17	37	29	50	30	22	19	31	130	130	68	296			
Robinson, H.	93	30	35	35	35	58	16	—	—	—	—	23	0	0	72	116			
Sandberg, B.	64	34	37	29	36	36	37	37	31	57	29	38	170	170	74	291			
Saunders, P.	86	33	31	29	43	39	41	35	36	31	34	43	177	177	91	296			
Schwartz, R.	77	25	28	23	44	37	32	32	28	19	50	40	156	156	94	240			
Simons, J.	79	27	37	36	39	34	34	37	36	28	40	38	176	176	72	302			
Snow, C.	80	30	31	34	46	42	27	30	30	28	12	42	116	116	88	228			
Taylor, L.	85	29	33	30	40	42	24	28	36	18	20	41	166	166	81	296			
VanBuren, T.	74	30	34	27	35	36	36	31	39	33	30	40	165	165	75	223			
Yang, H.	71	35	28	27	29	39	19	56	37	30	27	39	162	162	76	251			

```
                        UNIT SUMMARY SHEET

  Name _____          Fourth-Term Grade
                                                Sheet
                                                Physical Education

  CLASS _____

  ROLL NUMBER _____


                        Possible       Points        Total
                                       Earned        Possible: 100
  OBSTACLE COURSE TIME
  _____   35         _____

  TRACK AND FIELD SCORES
   50-yard Dash _____     10         _____
   Standing Broad Jump
  _____           10         _____
   Running Broad Jump                                 Your Total
  _____           10         _____     _____
  Jogging _____          10         _____
                                                      Your Fourth-
                                                      Term
  TRACK AND FIELD QUIZ       10         _____     Grade _____

  WRITTEN TEST               15         _____     First _____

                                                      Second _____

                                                      Third _____

                            _____      _____     Fourth _____

              Total 100     Total _____           Final _____
```

Figure 9.19 A unit summary sheet.

References

1. Dunham, P., Jr. (1986, August). Evaluation for excellence: A systematic approach. *Journal of Physical Education, Recreation and Dance, 57*, 34–36.
2. Wood, T. M., & Safrit, M. J. (1990, March). Measurement and evaluation in professional education—A view from the measurement specialists. *Journal of Physical Education, Recreation and Dance, 61*(3), 29–31.
3. Placek, J. (1983). Conceptions of success in teaching: Busy, happy and good? In T. J. Templin & J. K. Olson (Eds.), *Teaching in physical education* (pp. 46–56). Champaign, IL: Human Kinetics.
4. Hoover, K. H. (1982). *The professional teacher's handbook* (p. 502). Boston: Allyn & Bacon.
5. Wiggins, G. (1993). Assessment: Authenticity, context, and validity. *Phi Delta Kappan, 75*(3), 200–214.
6. Mcgee, R., & Farrow, A. (1987). *Test questions for physical education activities.* Champaign, IL: Human Kinetics.

7. Bobo, M. (1978, January). Skill testing—A positive step toward interpreting secondary school physical education. *Journal of Physical Education and Recreation, 49,* 45.

8. Sullivan, L. J. (1980, November). Campus comedy. *Reader's Digest, 117,* 203.

9. Fronske, H. A. (1988, August). *Relationships among various objective swimming tests and expert evaluations of skill in swimming.* Unpublished doctoral dissertation, Brigham Young University, Provo, UT.

10. Lund, J. (1992). Assessment and accountability in secondary physical education. *Quest, 44*(3), 352–360.

11. Kovar, S., & Ermler, K. (1991). Grading: Do you have a hidden agenda? *Strategies, 4*(5), 12–14, 24.

12. Lund, Assessment and accountability in secondary physical education, 359.

13. Blanchard, B. E. (1936, May). A behavior frequency rating scale for the measurement of character and personality traits in physical education classroom situations. *Research Quarterly, 7,* 56–66.

14. Cowell, C. C. (1958, March). Validating an index of social adjustment for high school use. *Research Quarterly,* pp. 7–18.

15. Breck, J. (1947). *A sociometric test of status as measured in physical education classes.* Unpublished master's thesis, University of California, Berkeley.

16. Fox, R., Luszki, M. B., & Schmuck, R. (1966). *Diagnosing classroom learning environments* (p. 73). Chicago: Science Research Associates.

17. Lund, Assessment and accountability in secondary physical education, 359.

18. Dressel, P. L. (1957, Winter). Fact and fancy in assigning grades. *Basic College Quarterly, 2*(2), 6–12.

19. Deutsch, H. (1984, October). Sex fair grading in physical education. *Physical Educator, 41*(3), 137–141.

20. Boyce, B. A. (1990, August). Grading practices—How do they influence student skill performance? *Journal of Physical Education, Recreation and Dance, 61*(6), 46–48.

21. Hopkins, W. G., & Manly, B. F. J. (1989). Errors in assigning grades based on tests of finite validity. *Research Quarterly for Exercise and Sport, 60*(2), 180–182.

22. Stamm, C. L. (1979, January). Evaluation of coeducational physical activity classes. *Journal of Physical Education and Recreation, 50,* 68–69.

CHAPTER 10

Organization and Management of Instruction

Study Stimulators

1. What school and departmental policies and procedures are essential to a smooth operation of the department of physical education? How can these policies be communicated to students and parents?
2. What is classroom management? Why is it essential to good instruction in physical education? What governs the choice of a management technique?
3. What methods can be used to enhance classroom management?
4. Why is record keeping important? What types of records should teachers keep?

Effective physical educators stand out because of their ability to organize and manage the dozens of components that make up an effective learning environment. Effective policies and procedures must be in place on the first day of school so teachers can establish an appropriate learning environment. This will require teachers to carefully plan strategies for organizing and managing the department, locker room, and classroom instruction prior to the beginning of the school year. Suggestions for classroom management procedures, along with record-keeping tips to facilitate this process, are examined in this chapter.

Departmental Policies and Procedures

Departmental policies and procedures should be developed to regulate those elements that must be consistent for all students taking physical education. A departmental handout and handbook can be developed to include each of these elements, thereby reducing misunderstandings between home and school concerning the policies.[1] A creative example of a departmental handout is the work contract shown in figure 10.1. Signatures on these forms can also be used to verify that parental requests for excuses from physical activity have indeed come from the parent. Items that might be included in such a handout are the following:

1. The department's philosophy
2. Physical education objectives
3. Registration procedures and course offerings
4. Policies concerning uniforms, dressing, showers, locker rooms, and laundering uniforms
5. Policies for medical excuses, safety, accidents, and first aid
6. Grading standards and policies

Work Contract

Wanted—Students
Ninety days of work available

Type of Work
Preparation for lifetime physical fitness, team sports skill development, and individual sport skill development

Wage
One-half unit of physical education credit

Payroll Issued
After forty-five days and after ninety days

Qualifications
Must be willing to work, be properly dressed, be cooperative, possess the ability to get along with fellow workers, and be punctual

Hours
One hour per day at the scheduled time

Special Requirements
A uniform will be needed each day consisting of:
Shorts—White, yellow, or black—no cut-offs
Shirts—T-shirt, either white or yellow—no tank tops or bare midriffs
Gym Shoes—in good condition
Socks—preferably white
Long hair must be tied back from the face to prevent injuries
Long pants and sweatshirt for cold weather outside

Sick Leave and Vacation Time
The State of Utah requires a minimum of seventy-five class hours before credit can be issued (this would allow a maximum of fifteen days absent time). No credit will be given if exceeded.

Make-up Time
All make-up work will be due *one week* after the day you return from an illness or excused absence. No make-up will be allowed if you cut (sluff) class without being properly excused.

Figure 10.1 A work contract.

7. Policies for making up absences
8. Physical fitness appraisals
9. Policies concerning student leaders
10. Extra-class activities

Policies and procedures govern such components as (1) uniforms, (2) excuses from activity, (3) locker-room policies, (4) locks and lockers, (5) towels, and (6) showers. A discussion of each component follows.

Figure 10.1 *(continued)*

Uniforms

The use of a required uniform for physical education is a controversial issue.[2] Many states now have laws restricting the use of a special uniform. Some schools have stopped requiring students to dress in a standard outfit to participate in class activities while others still require a specific uniform to be worn. Whatever the policy, students should be required to change into clothing that allows active, comfortable, and safe participation.

Students with special needs should always be considered when establishing a dress policy. For example, students who are overweight, disabled, unable to afford a uniform, or restricted due to religious reasons should not be made to feel uncomfortable or conspicuous in class because of the uniform. It is always wise to provide several options for uniforms to teenagers who at this time in their lives are exploring their own independence.

Whatever uniform is provided should be marked with the student's name in permanent ink or on a label to facilitate recovery in case of loss. It is wise to require the uniform (whatever it is) to be kept at school and used only during the physical education class. This discourages students from participating in street clothes. Uniforms should be laundered regularly to promote good hygiene.

When a specific uniform is required by departmental policy, explain to students and parents what type of uniform is requested, why it is necessary, and possible purchase locations. An example of the uniform should be available in class for students to see. A handout could be prepared to explain the uniform, marking, and laundry policies to parents.

Teachers should also dress in appropriate clothes as an example for students to follow. Clothing should be such that the teacher can immediately be located within the activity area.

Excuses from Activity

Establish a sound policy regarding excuses from activity, and communicate the policy to students and parents at the beginning of the school year. Excuses from activity generally consist of two types: medical excuses and nonmedical excuses.

```
┌─────────────────────────────────────────────────────────────────────┐
│                                                                       │
│              Temporary physical education excuse form                 │
│                                                                       │
│   To physical education instructor:                                   │
│                                                                       │
│   Please excuse _____  Section _____       │
│                                                                       │
│   from:                                                               │
│   ☐  participation ____                                               │
│                                                                       │
│   ☐  showers ____                                                     │
│                                                                       │
│   ☐  dressing for class ____                                          │
│                                                                       │
│   From _____        To _____            │
│                                                                       │
│   Reason _____              │
│                                                                       │
│   Recommended by:                                                     │
│                                                                       │
│   Physician's note _____ Parent's note _____                  │
│                                                                       │
│   School nurse _____                                             │
│                                                                       │
│                         _____                      │
│                                            School nurse               │
│                                                                       │
└─────────────────────────────────────────────────────────────────────┘
```

Figure 10.2 A temporary physical education
excuse form.
Source: Walker, June. *Modern Methods in
Secondary School Physical Education,* 3d ed;
Boston: Allyn & Bacon, 1973.

Medical Excuses

All medical excuses should be cleared through the school nurse if possible, using a form such as
the one shown in figure 10.2. In this way a record of the frequency of illness can be kept for each
student. The nurse or the teacher should keep notes from the parent or physician for future reference. After three or four days of excuses in a row, ask the student to obtain a note from his or
her physician, or contact a parent to verify the nature of the illness.

When a student brings a note from a parent or doctor asking that he or she be excused from
activity, always honor the excuse and provide some alternate way of meeting physical education
objectives. Often students can be scorekeepers, equipment managers, or teacher aides. Later,
teachers can telephone parents if a problem other than health is suspected. When a long-term disability exists, students are often placed in a class for those requiring modified activity or excused
from the class until unhampered participation is possible. In either case, a physician should monitor all activity. No student should return to full participation until clearance is received from a
physician.

Nonmedical Excuses

When students consistently fail to dress for activity, look for the cause behind this behavior. Hardy identified three underlying causes for failure to dress for activity. They are (1) physical, (2) moral or religious, and (3) defiance of authority.[3]

Physical excuses include stomachaches, headaches, and menstrual cramps. They may also include personal embarrassment caused by, for example, obesity or peer ridicule. These excuses can often be remedied by allowing these students to dress before or after the other students or in a private area, or by allowing them to wear a different uniform, such as longer pants or a long-sleeved shirt.

A second reason students fail to dress can be moral or religious. In *Mitchell v. McCall*,[4] a student complained that the prescribed gym shorts for her physical education class were immodest. The court ruled that she was required to take the course but that she was not required to wear the uniform. The school allowed her to choose her own uniform.

A third reason for failure to dress is defiance of authority. Although very little can be done with some students, others will respond positively to activities they have had a part in choosing and to a teacher whom they know cares.

Hardy suggested some ways to encourage students to dress for class, including (1) making classes so exciting that students will look forward to participating in them, (2) setting an example of appropriate dress, (3) exhibiting a genuine desire to understand and help students resolve self-consciousness about their bodies or their performance skills, and (4) refusing to punish students who fail to dress for activity.[5]

Explain to students why dressing for activity is important. If students have forgotten their own uniforms or desire not to dress on a particular day, a system of "loaner" uniforms often solves the problem. Suits left by students at the end of the year or uniforms donated by a parents' group can be loaned to students. With this system students know that, without a medical excuse, not dressing is not an option. Loaned uniforms can be washed and returned by the students or washed in the home economics room.

Students with minor excuses can be encouraged to dress and do what they can. Do not allow students who are not dressed to participate in activities or to sit on the sidelines, where they are often an attractive nuisance. Send students who are ill, idle, or disturbing to an appropriate place such as the nurse's or counselor's office. Students who remain should be actively engaged in the class in some way. Completing a written report or answering questions on articles related to sport or physical fitness might be done during class time to encourage learning and avoid noninvolvement.

Major suggested having makeups for 45 minutes before or after school when students are encouraged to bring a friend and to run laps on the track. The schedule is printed and handed out to students at the beginning of each year. Students check in and give their names and run.[6] Each unit could also have makeup classes scheduled to work on the skills of the unit.

Dressing for activity should not be used as the chief tool of evaluation. If students fail to dress, they will usually fail to do well on written, fitness, and skills tests and in other evaluative measures. There is really no need to use dressing as a part of the evaluation system. Pease increased the percentage of students dressing for activity by rewarding students with weight training and aerobics when the percentages of students dressed reached specific goals.[7]

Locker-Room Policies

Clearly define locker-room policies to students at the beginning of each term, including (1) traffic patterns to ensure safety; (2) use of lockers (usually long lockers to secure clothing and books during class and small lockers to secure gym clothing at other times); (3) lost and found for locks, uniforms, clothing, and other items; (4) procedures for showering; and (5) guideline policies for locker clean-out, laundering of uniforms, responsibility to keep lockers locked, and valuables. In some situations, teachers will wish to have students assist in making these policies.

Check the locker room regularly for clothing and towels left out and locks left open. One teacher or a paraprofessional aide can be assigned to supervise the locker room each period. Do not give student leaders the responsibility of supervising students in the locker room. Locker rooms should be locked when not supervised.

A number of potential liability factors exist in locker rooms where students are confined in a small space among lockers, benches, trash cans, and laundry carts. In addition, floors are often wet. Students must be supervised properly to prevent horseplay and injuries. According to Hart, proper supervision involves establishing clear rules, posting signs outlining behavioral expectations, providing written and verbal warnings of all risks, enforcing rules, locking locker rooms during class time, moving students as a group from locker room to gym and gym to locker room, providing adequate time for dressing, and quieting down students before dismissing them to shower or change. Keep locker rooms clean and orderly. Where two teachers of the opposite sex are not available to supervise both locker rooms, administrators should provide a staff member to help. Student aides can also help alert teachers to problems.[8]

Locks and Lockers

Since considerable time is spent each year managing dressing facilities, sound policies should be made to reduce management time so that instructional time can be maximized.

Lockers. Two types of lockers are generally used for securing students' clothing possessions. The first is the wire basket, which is the least expensive and has the advantage of good air circulation for drying clothes. However, it has the disadvantage of being too small to include all of the students' possessions such as coats, boots, and books. Also, small items can be removed between the wires.

Metal lockers are often supplied in banks of six small lockers to one large locker to solve the storage problem, as shown in figure 10.3. Gym uniforms can be stored in the small lockers and street clothing can be placed in the long lockers during class time. Locating them together in this manner minimizes traffic in the locker room.

Locks. Locks can be built into metal lockers or combination locks can be used. Although built-in locks reduce the problem of distribution, collection, and loss of locks, they can often be opened with a knife. Because they are built in, they cannot be transferred to the large locker to secure valuables during class time. They are also difficult to repair.

Locks are available with combinations that can be changed from year to year to prevent theft. Combination locks are preferred over key locks because students tend to lose keys while participating in activity.

The school or the student can provide the locks. When locks are provided by the school, a lock deposit is often required to ensure that the locks are returned in good condition. Locks provided by the school provide easy access by the teacher in case of emergency, because a master key is usually provided. When students purchase locks, teacher access is more difficult unless locks are purchased that have a master keyhole built in for emergency use.

An accurate record of lock ownership, identification number, combination, and student locker number is vital for any physical education department. Locks get lost and students forget combinations. There must be a reliable file (discussed in the next section) to provide necessary

1		2		3		4		5		6	
1A Kristi Anderson 12-6-22		**2A** Sheila Ballard 1-10-39		**3A** Sue Boucher 7-22-14		**4A** Lida Crowder 30-15-9		**5A** Shauna Foster 5-7-25		**6A** Gloria Jensen 22-38-7	
1B Nancy Alexander 7-38-12		**2B** Sandy Andres 21-18-12		**3B** Dana Bergstrom 31-18-9		**4B** Chris Bindrup 11-36-3		**5B** Audree Dixon 8-26-17		**6B** Georgina Edwards 38-17-6	
1C Karin Cardon 8-13-29		**2C** Barbara Durrant 16-24-6		**3C** Kristin Goodwin 28-2-37		**4C** Sharane Hepworth 3-18-9		**5C** Terrie Jarvis 32-11-6		**6C** Cindy Jemmett 17-3-26	
1D Renee Baker 7-17-24		**2D** Debbie Bemis 6-4-29		**3D** Janis Brock 3-12-16		**4D** Kay Brown 3-22-6		**5D** Laura Cameron 35-9-27		**6D** Paula Campbell 20-4-33	
1E Carole Brisbin 20-13-7		**2E** Cheri Clark 18-20-36		**3E** Janiece Dee 7-19-34		**4E** Donna Dupaix 14-33-12		**5E** Kelly Fredericks 2-8-16		**6E** Jennifer Kee 8-29-16	
1F Elsie Bishop 8-23-9		**2F** Rosa De la Cruz 13-36-27		**3F** Debra Evans 29-18-26		**4F** Shelley Huber 18-23-9		**5F** Maria Vasquez 14-38-2		**6F** Alana Walker 3-36-15	

Figure 10.3 A master locker list and example of physical education lockers.

information to return lost locks, restate combinations, and locate lockers. Marking students' names on individual locks is usually difficult and temporary. It is often easier to keep track of the lock by the lock number engraved on the lock.

Assigning Locks and Lockers. It is advisable to assign lockers to students in horizontal rows by class period. This spreads students throughout the locker room each period and prevents over-crowding with its resulting safety hazards. It also facilitates dressing quickly. If the lowest rows are assigned to the lower grades and the higher rows to the higher grades, differences in height can be easily accommodated.

A master list of lockers such as that shown in figure 10.3 can be kept, showing each bank of lockers, with students' names and combinations written in pencil. Using pencil makes erasing easy when students move out.

Locker cards can be used to record the student's name, locker number, combination, and assigned locker. A sample locker card is shown in figure 10.4. A second card, shown in figure 10.5, can be used to record the combination of each lock when locks are collected for redistribution at the end of each semester or year. If students use the same lock from year to year, put a place for the name on the card. It is usually desirable to have two files. In one file, cards are filed by lock number. In the other file, cards are filed alphabetically by students' last names. The information found in either file provides access to information that is usually needed quickly.

A master lock book can be acquired from the manufacturer. This lists the lock serial numbers and their combinations. This book, in tandem with the lock card and student identification card, gives teachers a three-way system for locating locks and lockers by student name, locker number or location, or lock serial number. Lost locks can be locked on to a towel bar placed in or near the teacher's office or on the wire screen of an issue room cage. Some teachers charge students a small fee of 5 to 25 cents for retrieving their locks or telling them their combinations.

```
                            Locker Card

  Name _____ Locker # _____
  (Print)  (Last)        (First)       (Middle)

  Teacher _____      Lock # _____

  Period _____            Combination _____

  Address _____
            (Street)                        (Apt. #)

          _____
            (City)            (State)        (Zip)

  I understand and agree that I will not share the locker assigned
  to me with anyone else.

  Signed _____

  For Locker # _____ Date _____
```

Figure 10.4 A locker card.

```
┌─────────────────────────────────────────────────────────────────┐
│                    LOCKER COMBINATION CARD                        │
│                                                                   │
│    DATE ISSUED:                                                   │
│                                                                   │
│    . . . . . . . . . . . . . . . . . . . . . . . .               │
│                                                                   │
│                      LOCKER NO.  . . . . . . . . . . . . . . . .  │
│                                                                   │
│                      LOCK NO.  . . . . . . . . . . . . . . . . .  │
│                                                                   │
│                                R.  . . . . . . . . . . . . . . .  │
│                                                                   │
│               Combination: L.  . . . . . . . . . . . . . . . . .  │
│                                                                   │
│                                R.  . . . . . . . . . . . . . . .  │
│    Name: _____                 │
│                                                                   │
└─────────────────────────────────────────────────────────────────┘
```

Figure 10.5 A locker combination card.

The money collected can go into a fund for purchasing loaner suits, equipment of student choice, or adding to funds for field trips. Give students a voice in how such monies are used.

Towels

Three decisions must be made with regard to towels. They are (1) the method of acquisition of towels, (2) the laundering of towels, and (3) the distribution and collection of towels.

Acquisition of Towels. Towels can be purchased by the school or district, or leased from a towel service, or students can be asked to bring one or two towels each year for the school supply.

Laundering of Towels. Towels purchased by the school are often laundered at a school or district facility. This requires purchasing laundry equipment and hiring someone to launder towels. Leased or purchased towels may be laundered by the towel service. This requires a bid by local laundries for pick-up, laundry, and delivery. Students are often charged a towel fee for this service. Fees for indigent students are often paid by welfare or other community services or absorbed by the school.

In some cases, students are required to bring a towel each week and launder it at home. This generally results in mildew and odor problems as towels are left in lockers throughout the week. It also results in students missing showers because of failure to bring a towel. Some districts, however, prohibit charging towel fees to students, and therefore a system such as this one must be used, or the cost must be absorbed into the regular budget.

Distribution and Collection of Towels. Towels can be distributed to students by their roll call numbers and checked in after showers as in this example:

Distributed   1 2̸ 3 4̸ 5   Collected   1 X̸ 3 X̸ 5

                     6 7̸ 8 9 1̸0̸   6 7̸ 8 9 X̸1̸0̸

Note that towels were distributed to numbers 2, 4, 7, and 10, but that number 7's towel has not yet been returned. This system helps to keep stray towels off the locker-room floor and can also be used to check which students took showers. Other more informal procedures are often used. For example, a towel is issued to each student at the beginning of the school year. Each time the student showers, he or she exchanges a dirty towel for a clean one.

Showers

Required showers have often resulted in negative attitudes toward physical education. This is because some teachers require showers unnecessarily and do not consider the students' feelings when developing policies for showers. It is recommended that showers not be used as a factor for determining grades. Teach students the health-related concepts about exercise and showering and help them understand when a shower should be taken and when one is not necessary. Never require showers when students have been relatively inactive during the period, such as in archery or golf.

When showering is necessary, make certain students have enough time to do it right. The amount of time will depend on the number of students in the locker room and the number of showers available, but 10 to 15 minutes is usually adequate. More time is needed for drying hair after swimming. Efforts should be made to have private showers available for all students.

Emphasize safety and instruct students to dry off in a specified area to prevent them from slipping on water near the lockers. Prohibit the use of glass bottles in the locker room.

Effective Classroom Management

Kounin[9] identified several principles of effective management that correlated significantly with high task involvement and low deviancy of students. These were (1) "with-it-ness" and overlapping, (2) smoothness and momentum, (3) group alerting and accountability, and (4) challenge and variety. "With-it-ness" was defined as teacher's communicating to students by their actions that they know what is going on in the classroom. Overlapping refers to the ability of a teacher to attend to two activities simultaneously without neglecting one or the other. Smoothness and momentum involve the ability to move students quickly and smoothly from one activity to another at a good pace, without losing the focus on learning. Group alertness is created by using techniques that keep students actively participating in the content of the lesson. Accountability is created when students feel that they are held accountable for their time in class.

Soar and Soar[10] reviewed four studies on classroom management and concluded that effective teachers select and direct learning tasks while allowing limited student freedom to move about, gather into subgroups, and socialize. They concluded that the most effective mixture of structure and freedom depends on the complexity of the learning tasks (i.e., the more complex the tasks, the more freedom needed).

Gage[11] emphasized the importance of teachers having a system of rules to minimize direction giving and class organization while providing maximum drill and feedback. Teachers should select a variety of challenging learning activities, monitor student work closely, and ensure that students have an equal opportunity to respond.

Sanford and Evertson[12] studied the management skills of junior high school teachers and concluded that effective managers spent the first day discussing class rules and procedures and then assigned some work in which students could experience initial success. These teachers devoted some time each day to presenting, reviewing, and discussing rules and acted consistently to stop off-task behavior. Good teachers understood students' backgrounds, abilities, interests, and attention spans, provided appropriate assignments for student success, and used logical step-by-step instructions at an appropriate vocabulary level. They established accountability by monitoring work and providing appropriate feedback.

Teachers who operate a structured teaching-learning environment appear to be more effective. In addition, Brophy indicated that the most effective teachers select material at the appropriate level of difficulty for their students and move the students through the material at a rapid pace while maintaining a very high success rate.[13] Oxendine noted that physical education teachers probably spend too much time reviewing skills that have already been learned.[14] On the other hand, Earls cautioned against leaping from simple drills to complex games.[15]

The key to effective classroom management appears to be minimizing off-task and deviant behaviors by presenting appropriate learning activities, moving at a good pace, monitoring student responses, and providing instruction and practice in classroom procedures and routines.

Classroom Management in Physical Education

Good classroom management is essential to quality instruction in physical education. In fact, it is even more vital than in the academic classroom. This is partly due to the variety of activities provided, often in different facilities and with different equipment, and partly due to the larger numbers of students in physical education classes. The need for safety is an essential consideration in most of these activities. A third factor is the restricted amount of time often allotted to physical education and the additional limits imposed by dressing and showering. Because of this, it is essential that class time be carefully planned to provide the maximum instructional benefit.

Luke summarized the research on classroom management in physical education.[16] Studies of academic learning time in physical education using ALT-PE and other behavior analysis systems reveal that students spend 15 to 22 percent of class time in management activities and that managerial and organizational skills account for the very small amounts of time spent in learning. Management time varies significantly with the activity (from 7 percent in fitness lessons to 32 percent in gymnastics). The two most frequent student behaviors were inappropriate dress and being off-task. The most frequent teacher behavior was ordering students to stop doing an inappropriate behavior. Research has demonstrated that management skills can be improved by systematic intervention.

Teach students self-management skills and provide practice in using them, just as other skills are practiced. On the first day of class, teach procedures for assembly, dismissal, roll call, excuses, tardies, collecting and distributing equipment, organizing teams, and getting into formations. Tell students why each of these procedures is used. During instruction, whenever a difficulty occurs with one of the management skills, such as students getting into the proper formation, stop and review the skill or procedure before proceeding. If resistance to any policy remains, examine student feelings to determine whether modification or discontinuance would solve the problem. This attention to the problem will save instructional time in the long run and will reduce the incidence of serious discipline problems.

There is no one best way to manage a class. Each teacher must develop a wide variety of management techniques from which to choose as new situations arise. The choice of a management technique depends largely on the experience and personality of the teacher and the maturity and self-management capabilities of the students. As the style of teaching changes from more teacher-directed styles to more student-directed styles, management styles will also vary from formal to more informal techniques. Other factors that influence the selection of a management technique include the subject matter to be taught, the facilities and equipment available, the size of the class, and the school or department policies under which the teacher works. A good teacher will select the best technique for a given situation, carry it out effectively, and modify it as the need arises. When choosing a technique, a balance must be achieved between concern for the student and efficiency of instruction.

The true test of a successful management technique is whether the objectives of the lesson or unit in question have been realized. Whenever objectives are not being accomplished, select a new plan of action.

Classroom management in physical education involves (1) preparing the environment, (2) distributing and collecting equipment, (3) planning preclass activities, (4) calling roll, (5) leading warm-up and fitness activities, (6) getting students' attention and giving directions, (7) teaching and utilizing class formations, (8) organizing groups or teams, (9) supervising class activities, (10) adapting to interruptions, (11) using student leaders, and (12) increasing motivation through classroom management. Techniques for each of these activities are discussed in this chapter. Motivation and discipline are reviewed in chapter 12.

Preparing the Environment

Prior to teaching each day, inspect facilities and equipment for safety, proper lighting, adequate towels, and comfortable room temperature. Nets can be set up, baskets raised or lowered, apparatus arranged, and special markings put in place by paraprofessional or student aides before class begins or by students who come in before school or prior to class time. Avoid using instructional time to accomplish these tasks unless it is absolutely necessary.

A wise teacher will always check the equipment prior to starting a new unit or activity and make sure each day that enough equipment is available and that balls are pumped up, arrows repaired, pinnies washed, and other essentials attended to. Adequate teaching stations should be available for all instructors. If a specialized area is needed to show a film, administer a test, or present a guest speaker, make arrangements well before the activity. A plan of operations for inclement weather should be part of departmental procedures. Teachers can then make last-minute adjustments and present an uninterrupted teaching program. All teachers in a department should share these decisions so they feel they have a fair share of department facilities.

Storage facilities for loose equipment should include movable bins or racks. Plastic trash cans with wheels can be used for this purpose. Ball racks or bags that can be moved to and from the gymnasium allow for ease of distribution. To avoid loss, equipment often must be returned each hour. Student assistants or squad leaders can be assigned to assist with movement of equipment.

Distributing and Collecting Equipment

A number of techniques can be used for distributing and collecting equipment. When choosing an equipment distribution and collection technique, always consider the relationship of the technique to the safety of the students and to effective learning.

The Teacher

The teacher or an aide distributes and collects equipment as students enter and leave the gymnasium or playing area. Students can sign the roll as they pick up equipment. The system should not tie up a teacher who could be helping students with other needs. Having formal class closure as part of the daily routine can provide an opportunity to collect and properly store equipment.[17]

Squad Leaders

Squad leaders acquire the equipment needed for their individual squads and return it at the end of the practice period.

Numbers

Students are assigned equipment numbers that correspond to their roll call numbers. Student 1 picks up bow 1, arrows 1, and armguard 1. Equipment may be numbered in such a way that it would not correspond to a roll call number. In this case, the number of the assigned equipment is recorded by the roll call number. The person distributing equipment checks the roll call number of the person receiving equipment each day. Equipment can be picked up in the locker room, as students enter the gymnasium, or as they complete warm-up and fitness activities. One advantage to this technique is that students feel more responsible for returning the equipment in good condition each day. A second advantage is that students can become accustomed to a particular racket, bow, or glove.

Grab Bag

Students can be asked to get a piece of equipment and return to their space. This often results in students converging on a given box of equipment and grabbing out the best they can find. Chaos and loss of instructional time usually result and the less aggressive students may feel cheated by getting the worst equipment. This can be avoided by sending one squad or student at a time (changing squads each day) and by ensuring that all equipment is in good condition. When sending a few students at a time, it is best to have students pick up or return equipment as they enter the gym or as they complete an activity in which students finish at different times, such as after jogging or completing self-check activities.

Handing in Assignments

Assignments can be collected very efficiently by placing a basket or box for each class in a convenient location, where students can place their assignments as they enter or leave the gymnasium. Handouts for students who have been absent can be placed in a different colored or labeled box.

Planning Preclass Activities

Students often waste a good deal of time between their arrival in the gymnasium and roll call or instruction. If this is the case, students who come in last are rewarded by not having to sit around doing nothing. When students are allowed to begin activity the minute they enter the area, they begin to dress faster and come to class earlier. Motivational devices such as a preclass activity chart, listing skills that students can practice, might be posted. The accumulative tournament described in chapter 9 is an effective preclass activity, as are many other self-testing activities.

Teachers should always be close by to supervise student safety and equipment loss or damage. Teachers in larger departments can take turns supervising the locker room and the gymnasium, or a teacher aide can be used to supervise one of the two areas. At a given time or signal, students can report to roll call or to a posted or preannounced area for instruction or practice.

Calling Roll

A fast, effective roll call system gets things started on the right track. An effective roll call can take only one or two minutes at the most. Time spent in roll call reduces the learning time for students, so efficient use of time is essential. When too much time is taken for roll call, students become bored and discipline problems can arise.

A number of different roll call techniques can be used depending on the class size, maturity of students, and the learning situation. The major criteria for selection of a roll call technique are time and accuracy. Since most schools receive some funding based on the average daily attendance (ADA) of students, schools insist on accuracy in attendance taking. Five general techniques are commonly used. They include (1) numbers or spots, (2) squads, (3) student check-in, (4) silent roll, and (5) oral roll call.

A fast, effective roll call gets things started on the
right track.
© James L. Shaffer

Numbers or Spots

Each student is assigned a number or a spot. Students sit or stand in a specific spot, either in a line or in squad order. When numbers are painted on the floor, on a bench or bleacher, or on the wall, a blank number indicates an absent student. When no numbers are available, students can be asked to call out the numbers in sequence. Although this method is rather impersonal, it is very fast. Having students call their numbers and last names, as in "1-Allen," "2-Bacon," "3-Barr," can help teachers learn names.

Squads

Each student is assigned to a squad, and a leader is chosen for each squad. Each day the squad leader records the attendance of the squad members on a squad card. This could be done while students are participating in warm-ups or another squad activity.

Student Check-In

In this technique, students check in as they enter the gymnasium by signing their name and time of entry, by checking in with the teacher, by handing in an assignment, or by removing their name tags from a board or box and placing them in a specified location or wearing them. When using name tags, those remaining indicate absent students.

Silent Roll

In this technique, the teacher or teacher's aide takes roll silently while students are participating in activity. This permits students to remain active.

Oral Roll Call

In this technique, the teacher calls out the students' names and listens for a response. This technique is only effective when used with very small classes or to get acquainted with students during the first few days of instruction before rolls have been finalized. Another use is as an accuracy check by calling out only the names of those students who have been marked absent by one of the other methods.

Leading Warm-Up and Fitness Activities

A variety of warm-up techniques and fitness activities should be employed to increase student motivation. Some ideas include the following:

1. Students exercise to popular music, using prechoreographed routines or "follow the leader." Music can be taped, with cues on the tapes, to free the teacher to provide individual assistance.
2. Squad leaders direct warm-up activities for their squads. Squad leaders change regularly so many students are afforded this opportunity.
3. Students warm up on their own.
4. Students rotate through a number of fitness stations.
5. Selected student leaders direct warm-up activities for the entire class.
6. Students alternate jogging and weight training at specified time intervals (e.g., every two minutes).
7. Students run three days a week and weight-train two days.
8. Students run daily with a timed run once a week.
9. Students participate in an obstacle course.
10. Students participate in relays or games to emphasize certain fitness activities.
11. Activities related to the unit are designed to provide warm-up and skill practice.

Fitness activities can also be planned using skills from the unit.

Innumerable other techniques can be invented by the creative teacher for warm-up and fitness activities (see also chapter 8).

The following tips for leading exercises will aid the student leader or teacher who is directing the class.

1. Give a preparatory command, such as "ready-now-."
2. Give a command to begin, such as "GO" or "BEGIN."
3. During the exercise, repeat the sequence or cadence aloud so the group stays together (forward, side, forward, down; or 1, 2, 3).
4. Provide a model. If the leader is facing the class, try to mirror the actions (e.g., move the left arm when the class is moving the right).
5. Provide encouragement.
6. Have a sense of humor—smile, display enthusiasm, relax.
7. Give a command to stop. With exercises done to a cadence, a preparation to stop is also helpful (e.g., "and, stop").

Getting Students' Attention and Giving Directions

At different times teachers must get students' attention, assemble students, give directions, dismiss students, and handle emergencies. Either verbal signals such as "roll call" or "ready, go!"

Warm-up techniques using game skills increase
student motivation.
© James L. Shaffer

or nonverbal signals such as a whistle or raised arm can be used to gain attention or give directions. One teacher got effective results by calling out "HEY." The students responded with "HO." Students seemed especially responsive to this system. Be sure students understand what system will be used during class. If the whistle is used for getting attention, use it sparingly at other times so students do not tune out the sound.

Verbal Signals

Teachers of physical education should develop a "gym voice" if they expect to talk all day in large classes in open spaces. Get used to speaking with a push from the diaphragm to project the voice, as singers are taught to do. Try to keep the voice pitched low. Teachers with high-pitched voices especially need to avoid raising the pitch as they try to increase the volume. The result is a piercing sound that is hard to hear and very distracting.

A teacher who speaks softly yet loudly enough to be heard encourages students to listen carefully when he or she talks and also leaves room for a future increase in volume for the purpose of gaining attention. In contrast, when a teacher consistently shouts at students with a loud voice, they tend to increase their noise to a level that prohibits the use of verbal signals. A general rule for the teacher is to gather the students around and talk so that the student farthest away can hear clearly. If possible, try to speak with a wall behind the listeners to trap the voice.

In addition to volume, effective teachers vary speed, inflection, and vocabulary to either calm students or incite them to action. Such terms or phrases as "hustle," "quickly," and "Let's go!" are built-in motivators when used with appropriate inflection and enthusiasm. When you want students to do something do not ask, "Susie, do you want to pick up the balls?" Rather, say, "Susie, please put the balls in the basket." Save your voice by using a number of nonverbal attention-getters. An occasional lesson taught completely by gestures and written instructions can be highly effective in getting students to pay attention.

Nonverbal Attention Signals

A whistle, horn, hand clap, drum beat, or raised hand can be used effectively to gain attention once students have become accustomed to its use. Flicking the lights off and on quickly is effective for activities such as racquetball where students are dispersed in a wide indoor area. Shutting off music using a remote control is also an effective attention signal. A sharp whistle blast made by placing the tongue over the end of the whistle and quickly removing it as the air is blown is easily discernable and motivating. On the other hand, a long, drawn-out rumble denotes a lack of authority.

Teach students what behavior is expected when the attention signal is given. For example, students can be taught to sit or kneel where they are and wait for instructions or to gather to an appointed place for direction. Once the students learn the signal and the expected response, teachers can encourage them to shorten their response time by praising students who respond quickly or by rewarding them with extra time for activity. Feedback can also be provided on the amount of time spent, such as "You were ready five seconds faster than yesterday."

Giving Directions

When giving directions, gather the students close enough so all of them can see and hear and face them away from the sun and other distractions. Ask students who are not able to stand quietly to sit down.

Give directions in a clear, concise manner, telling students the location to move to, the signal for moving, and what to do when they get there. For example, you might be as specific as "On the signal 'Ready, go!' move quickly to the black line and line up facing the net." If students are given options in class procedures you might say, "On my signal, find a partner, get one ball between you, and locate a space on the floor where you can safely practice the volley." Occasionally directions can be written on the chalkboard, posted on a bulletin board, or written on a skill checklist or individual contract. Such methods may allow more student time-on-task.

When complex directions are given, the teacher might ask students whether they have any questions or ask questions to see whether students understood the directions. Avoid repeating the directions to students. They will learn not to listen the first time.

La Mancusa listed some pitfalls in giving directions.[18] They are (1) using words that students do not understand, (2) saying the same thing over and over, instead of using a few brief statements, in hopes the students will "catch on," (3) using extraneous words like "well" and "okay," and (4) failing to wait until everyone is listening before talking. She stated:

> It is the wise teacher who will *not speak* until *everyone* is listening. If it means that the teacher will be forced to stop what he is saying and wait, then by all means WAIT. If it means that the teacher will have to stop a second time, or a third time, then stop and WAIT. Silent teacher disapproval and exasperated peer disapproval is too strong a factor to override. Soon enough the offenders will understand that when *their* teacher talks, *everyone listens* because *their* teacher *means it* when he says, "I will not repeat this a second time."

There is nothing more to it than that. If a teacher allows himself to overlook rudeness, he will receive rudeness in return. Children will respond either to the *highest* or to the *lowest* of teacher-expectations.[19]

The key to avoiding these pitfalls is proper planning before speaking and careful evaluation of one's own ability to give directions. One of the best methods for evaluating one's effectiveness in giving directions is to record a class session on a tape recorder. When it is played back, ask "Would I like to be a student in my own classroom?"

Finishing an Activity

Finishing an activity or class period on a positive note is always a good idea. Include a culminating activity that capitalizes on enthusiasm and interest or reviews points taught in the lesson. This is a time when students are given an opportunity to ask questions, and it also provides the teacher with an opportunity to correct skills or reiterate important information.[20] Some ideas for summarizing a lesson include:

1. Summarize the main ideas of the lesson with a short statement and explain what the students will be expected to realize as an outcome.
2. Ask the students questions in which responses summarize the lesson.
3. Assign one or two students to listen carefully and tell the class afterward what the lesson was about.
4. Use a worksheet to help students summarize the main ideas of the lesson.
5. Have several students in turn tell one thing learned from the lesson.
6. Present a real-life situation that could be resolved by using lesson ideas.

A teacher desiring to use activities that require more time might incorporate the following:

1. Give an oral or written quiz.
2. Use instructional games to test the information taught.
3. Have students write or tell in their own words what they think the main idea is.
4. Divide the class into small groups. Each group in turn acts out a part of the lesson while the other groups try to guess what is being depicted (charades).

Noteworthy performance and effort and team or individual winners could be recognized at this time. The stage is now set for an orderly dismissal. The teacher might request that students get ready to leave in a certain fashion. For example, "The team sitting quietly in squad order will be the first to leave."

Teaching and Utilizing Class Formations

Innumerable class formations can be created to assist students and teachers in the instructional setting. Remember that the needs of the instructional situation determine the choice of a formation. For example, in the command style of teaching (see chapter 7), formal formations are used. As instruction moves toward the less teacher-dominated styles, teachers are more apt to ask students to move out, find a partner, or find a space on the floor. A number of formations follow.

Circles and Semicircles

Circles can be formed by asking students to form a circle on a painted line on the playing surface, such as a free throw circle, and then taking three giant steps backward. In folk dancing, students can be asked to join hands to form a circle. (Avoid holding hands in other activities. It usually leads to giggling and tugging.) Circles can be used for practice drills or lead-up games and for relays. Stay on the edge of the circle when giving directions so no students are behind you.

The semicircle can be formed by asking students to gather around the teacher. It is often used for giving directions to small classes or for demonstrating to a group of students.

Lines and Columns

Lines are formed by asking students to line up facing the net or wall on a particular line on the floor, or between several cones or chalk marks. Lines are often used for roll call formations and for some lead-up games, such as line soccer.

Columns are formed by selecting four to eight students as leaders and having other students line up behind one of the leaders in designated areas of the floor. Cones or other pieces of equipment can be used instead of leaders. Columns are used to create relay teams or squads.

Extended Formation

The extended formation is formed from a line. For example, students number off in fours. The ones stay where they are. The twos move forward 5 steps, threes move 10 steps, and fours move 15 steps. The extended formation is often used for warm-up and fitness activities, for demonstrations that students cannot see when grouped close together, and for mimetic drills (pantomime). Examples of this formation are shown in figure 10.6 and in chapter 5.

A variation of the extended formation is "waves," in which all the ones move (e.g., swim across the pool), then the twos, and so on. This technique permits the teacher to observe and give feedback to a small group of students at one time.

Partners or Small Groups

Partners and groups can be assigned, or students can be asked to simply find a partner or get in groups of three or four. Ask students to raise their hands if they need a partner or to sit down with their partner as soon as one is found. When there is an extra person, be specific on how that person is to be included. Partners and small groups are often used for warm-up and fitness activities and for practice drills or peer tutoring.

Whatever formations are used, teach students how to assume them quickly on a brief, consistent signal. Always tell students exactly where they are to be, such as on the red line; what formation they are to assume; and the direction they are to face. Painted lines and circles can be used when they are available. If there are none, chalk marks, traffic cones, or masking tape can be substituted.

Keep transitions between formations to a minimum. Transitions such as from a line to a circle to a line can be avoided by thinking through how students will get from one formation to another. Changing from groups of twos to threes can be particularly difficult and must be carefully planned if necessary to effective teaching progressions. X's and O's might be used to plot out formations and to help visualize the movement of the class from formation to formation. An example of an effective class transition is shown in figure 10.6.

Organizing Groups or Teams

There are as many ways to choose teams as there are teachers to choose them. However, many teachers resort to only one or two techniques. A little variety can be motivating. Some common techniques and ideas follow.

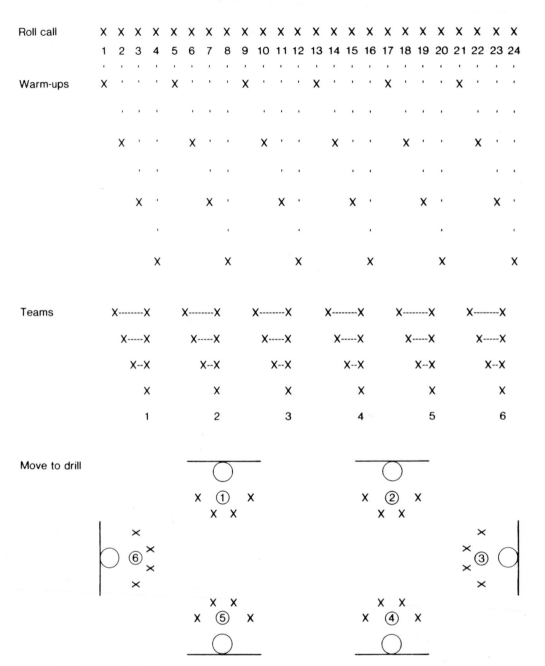

Figure 10.6 A class transition map.

Counting Off

Students line up, count off by fives, and are asked to remember their number. Then all the ones become one team, the twos another team, and so on. This method takes too much time to be recommended. Also, students tend to change their numbers or position themselves to be on the same team as their friends. It can also result in mismatched teams (see chapter 11).

Choosing Teams

Class members can elect team captains, or teachers can choose them. Rotate this responsibility among as many students as possible. Self-esteem and leadership traits can be encouraged and developed in students by wise and caring teachers.

Never allow team captains to choose teams with each captain in turn picking a member of the class until all are chosen (see figure 10.7). This results in some students always being chosen last. It ruins self-esteem and wastes valuable class time. One method is for captains to choose the teams in private using the class roll as a guide. Still another method is to have captains select team members for each other or draw a team at random from teams already chosen. Teachers can then alphabetize the list for posting.

Students within a class can select teams quickly if the following system is incorporated in an orderly manner. After the captains have been chosen, students are instructed to line up behind the captain of their choice. On the command "GO" they must *walk* to form this line. No more than a designated number of persons can be in a line. When the designated number is reached, students must go to another line. With this method, best friends, highly skilled players, and goof-offs tend to end up on the same team. It is wise to intersperse this method with other methods of choosing teams.

Dunn and Wilson proposed having each student write his or her name on a piece of paper, wad it up, and toss it into a pile. Team captains collect the number of wads needed for each team. For uneven numbers, have one captain pick up the extra wad.[21]

Assigned Teams

Teams can be assigned by the teacher and posted or read to the class. Squads can be used as assigned teams.

Figure 10.7 Always chosen last.
Source: Steven E. Dunn and Rolayne Wilson, Utah State University, Logan, Utah. Also printed in *UAHPERD Journal*, Autumn, 1990.

At Random

Students are told to "get in groups of four" or to stand behind a number of markers. A second method is to say, "You five go to court one, you five to court two," and so forth, while indicating certain students as they happen to be grouped around the teacher.

Ultra-Shuffle[22]

The Ultra-Shuffle, developed by Kirkpatrick, is a system for assigning teams that results in constantly changing the composition of each team. The result is reduced concern for the score and greater involvement of all students in the game play. Students are assigned to a row. The number of rows depends on the number and size of teams. The first person in each row steps forward and the group is assigned to a court, the skill station or to referee. When students complete the skill station, they substitute for a student in one of the games. That student goes to the skill station and when completed, substitutes into a different game. A student can substitute for a referee at any time.

Variations

Give each student a card with a color, shape, and number on it, such as:

Triangle	Circle	Square
Orange	Red	Blue
2	3	1

By varying the number of colors, shapes, and numbers, groups of different sizes can be formed. For example, if only three groups are desired, limit shapes to triangle, circle, and square. If five groups are desired, use orange, red, blue, yellow, and green. If ten groups are necessary, use the numbers one to ten. Groups can then be formed by calling out "shapes," "colors," or "numbers," and students move to join others who have the same shape, color, or number in a designated spot. Lambdin suggested using playing cards and varying groups by number, color, and suit (clubs, hearts, diamonds, spades). She also proposed assigning a permanent card and placing student names on a chart. She includes a guide for placing students on the chart by skill level and sex so that groups can be evenly balanced for activity.[23]

Other variations might include date of birth, height, eye or hair color, and right-handedness or left-handedness, depending on the size of teams wanted or the purpose for grouping students. Teachers are only limited by their ability to create other variations for special occasions.

Whatever technique is used for selecting teams, change the method often for variety and to encourage positive social interaction among students. Regularly trade leadership roles for teams so that most students are afforded this responsibility. It is also important to divide the various abilities of students as evenly as possible among the teams. When teams are used for game play, colored vests or pinnies can be used to distinguish one team from another.

Supervising Class Activities

Supervising is the part of teaching that occurs while students are practicing skills, playing games, or participating in other activities. Proper planning is essential for students to continue learning and to participate safely during this portion of the lesson.

The teacher must employ both vision and movement in supervising class activities. Use a wide range of vision as the class is scanned and that "sixth sense" or "eye in the back of the head" is called upon. Never get so involved in the subject matter that students are forgotten.

Keep moving along the edges of the class when you are not involved in direct instruction. This permits you to keep all of the students in view constantly and avoid favoring students in one part of the playing area. The center of the class is not a good place for the teacher to stand. Doing so means some students will be out of view and may also have trouble hearing. When a discipline problem exists, the teacher can easily move from the perimeter toward the offenders and stand beside them and, if necessary, quietly speak to them.

Provide students with as much freedom as possible, keeping in mind the nature of the task and the maturity of the students. As the teaching style moves toward the student-directed styles of the spectrum (see chapter 7), more and more freedom occurs, with increased student responsibility for learning. Allow students to work together as long as they work cooperatively. Keep an eye on students who cause a disturbance, separating them from other students.

Teachers are responsible for all students in the class. *Never leave students unsupervised.* Classes not working together as an entire group present problems in this regard. It is up to teachers to work out team teaching and supervising schedules or get adequate help when supervising individualized class programs.

Teachers must be sure all students are accounted for when class is in session. Some students might attempt to sneak off after roll call. If the class is a meaningful and motivational experience this should not occur, but students sometimes have behavior problems for which a teacher is not responsible. Once teachers know of such students, adequate precautions must be taken during class, or additional help from the counseling office might be secured to help with the student.

Adapting to Interruptions

A number of interruptions that reduce instructional time occur during school hours, including such things as emergencies and injuries, assemblies, school dances, field trips, testing, and fire drills. Some of these activities reduce the length of the instructional period, often making it impractical to dress for activity. Others take students away from physical education classes, thereby leaving the teacher with only a few students in class. Another deviation is caused by inclement weather.

Dealing with Emergency Interruptions

Preplanning for emergencies is essential so that when they occur the teacher can act in the most efficient manner. For example, formulate plans for action when the fire alarm sounds and students are in the shower or for serious injuries occurring in class. An accident plan might include sending one student for first aid supplies, another to the office for the principal or school nurse, and a third to call the paramedics. Of course, first aid supplies, phone numbers, and so forth must be prepared in advance so they are readily available when the emergency strikes. Be prepared to give first aid if needed, wait for the paramedics, and then make sure the parents are called. Do not allow students to stand around to witness the drama of an accident or emergency situation. Devise a plan to provide supervision for the remainder of the class. This could include what other teachers, administrators, or staff would be available to supervise during each period of the day and how those individuals are to be contacted.

When the emergency is over, complete an accident report as soon as possible while the incident is fresh in everyone's minds. A sample accident report is shown in figure 11.1 on page 396. Accident reports should be kept for many years in case of lawsuits. They should be reviewed each year to analyze problem areas that could be addressed.

Dealing with Shortened Periods or Inclement Weather

Three types of activities can be used when the planned lesson must be changed. One type includes an adaptation of the activity currently being taught to an indoor facility; a lesson on terms, rules, strategy, or other cognitive concepts related to the activity; or an evaluation activity such as a skill or written test. If the use of an activity-related lesson is not feasible, a fitness-oriented lesson could be taught. This might include teaching fitness concepts, teaching a fitness activity such as an aerobic dance or circuit training, giving physical fitness tests, or evaluating posture. A third activity is the use of a values-oriented activity from the affective domain. Chapter 7 includes several activities the teacher might use.

Dealing with a Small Class

When the teacher ends up with a small class, it is time to rejoice. This is an excellent opportunity to provide practice time for skill development, with students given individual help from the teacher. An alternative plan is to play a recreational or lead-up game using the skills that have been taught in the class.

Using Student Leaders

The physical education program should provide numerous opportunities for students to develop leadership skills. Within individual classes, students can serve as squad leaders, team captains, officials, equipment monitors, and in many other capacities. Rotate student leaders often to allow every student a chance to develop leadership skills.

In addition to these in-class leaders, student assistants can be assigned to assist the teacher with various nonteaching activities. Student assistants have proven to be an inexpensive method of improving teacher effectiveness and morale in large classes. In addition to helping teachers, student assistants can improve themselves in the following ways:

1. Develop and improve physical activity skills.
2. Develop social skills, such as leadership, followership, responsibility, and cooperation.
3. Develop improved skills in written and oral communication.
4. Learn more about the teaching profession and about physical education as a profession.
5. Grasp the significance of serving others and of working with others to accomplish stated objectives.
6. Develop a better understanding of students who are less able than others.
7. Learn how to plan and lead activities.

Select student assistants on the basis of their interest, scholarship, physical ability, character, ability to get along well with others, and willingness to do what is required. The experience afforded students is often enhanced if they can be assigned to a specific class section other than their own and if they have uniforms distinct from the other students (such as a different shirt) to set them apart.

Because student assistants are students and therefore lack professional training and experience, they must be prepared for their new role. Much of this preparation can precede the actual experience, and some of it must continue throughout the term in which the duties are performed. A leader's club or class can be used to instruct student assistants in their duties. Students should thoroughly understand the policies and procedures of the department and the duties that they will be expected to perform. The major duty of the student assistants is to assist the instructor in any way possible, consistent with their own capabilities and potential. Some other possible duties include the following:

1. Preparing the play area
2. Distributing, collecting, and caring for equipment
3. Taking roll
4. Making out squad cards
5. Checking uniforms
6. Recording tardy and absence slips
7. Checking showers
8. Leading exercises and drills
9. Demonstrating skills
10. Officiating
11. Assisting with media hardware
12. Downloading information into computers from heart rate monitors
13. Recording fitness scores on the computer
14. Turning showers on and off
15. Assisting with test administration and scoring
16. Providing individual assistance to students
17. Assisting with other duties, according to interests and abilities

Some problems have arisen from the use of student leaders. They include students being inadequately prepared for their assignments, students doing teachers' "dirty work," students being placed in situations where they "know too much," students assisting during their own physical education period and thus missing time to improve their own skills, and students losing friends by attempting to cope with grading or discipline situations. Each of these problems can be prevented by adequate preparation and by recalling that the duties of the student assistant are to assist with the class work, not to be responsible for grading or disciplining students.

Periodic evaluation of student assistants and the program should be made and the results followed up. An evaluation form that could be used for this purpose is shown in figure 10.8.

Increasing Motivation through Classroom Management

The discussion here is limited to aspects of classroom management that relate directly to motivation. See chapter 12 for other suggestions on motivation. Some teacher behaviors that can be used to enhance classroom management include the following:

1. Be efficient while keeping the emphasis on the activity rather than on the organization.
2. Keep distractions to a minimum.
3. Begin lessons promptly.
4. Be alert for boredom or inactivity.
5. Be consistent with respect to requirements.

In addition to these behaviors, norm-setting and classroom management games can be effective in many situations. Norm-setting involves students and teacher in setting rules for the health, safety, and mutual welfare of all concerned. When students participate in setting rules they are generally more responsible about implementing them. For a complete explanation of norm-setting, refer to chapter 12.

EVALUATION OF THE TEACHING ASSISTANT

Name: _____

       (Last)   (First)

Instructions: Rate the student on each of the items listed below. If there is no basis for determining a rating on an item, write "no basis."

	Strong	Average	Weak
I. *Personal Qualities*			
Adaptability, flexibility	_____	_____	_____
Initiative, originality	_____	_____	_____
Responsibility	_____	_____	_____
Well-mannered, well-groomed	_____	_____	_____
Punctual, dependable	_____	_____	_____
II. *Teacher-Teaching Assistant*			
Friendly	_____	_____	_____
Asks for and accepts suggestions	_____	_____	_____
Acts upon suggestions	_____	_____	_____
Cooperates well	_____	_____	_____
III. *Teaching Assistant-Students*			
Likes students	_____	_____	_____
Understands students	_____	_____	_____
Students respond well to her or him	_____	_____	_____
Fair and impartial	_____	_____	_____
IV. *Teaching Skills*			
Knowledge of subject	_____	_____	_____
Demonstrates well	_____	_____	_____
Officiates well	_____	_____	_____
Communicates knowledge to students	_____	_____	_____
Keeps accurate records	_____	_____	_____
V. *Class Management*			
Effective organization of groups	_____	_____	_____
Good control	_____	_____	_____
VI. *Professional Growth*			
Interest in the profession	_____	_____	_____
Growing knowledge of the profession	_____	_____	_____

The teaching assistant was:

    Valuable-a great deal of help   _____

    Some help   _____

    A burden-little or no help   _____

Comments: _____

Signature: _____

Figure 10.8 A student assistant evaluation form.

Management games are generally based on Grandma's law, which states, "First clean up your plate and then you may have your dessert." Translated into physical education terminology, it states, "By accomplishing certain classroom management tasks quickly, you will have more time for play." Clearly specify a few rules that tell what is expected to earn the reward. The reward may be based on the behavior of the entire class or of each squad. For example, all squads quiet, sitting in place, and ready for roll call within five seconds from the teacher's signal earn a point. A stopwatch can be used to record the amount of time used. A variety of reinforcers to reward appropriate behaviors often set a positive atmosphere in a class. Ideas for behavior modification are discussed in chapter 12.

Record Keeping

The main purposes of record keeping are to provide information to administrators, parents, and guidance counselors; and to help teachers evaluate students, themselves, and the curriculum. Keep only pertinent, up-to-date records, such as (1) attendance records; (2) records of achievement, including grades; (3) health and medical records; and (4) equipment and locker records.

Attendance Records

Teachers are required to keep an accurate record of the daily attendance of all students assigned to them. Keep records up-to-date each day. Because pencil tends to blur, the records should generally be kept in ink.

Attendance Register

Figure 10.9 shows a sample page from an attendance register. The top section identifies the class as Mrs. Jackson's second period physical education class at Younowhere Junior High School during the fall semester. No text is required. In the left-hand column, the students are listed in alphabetical order. Next to their names are their sex, grade, entry code, and exit code. The entry codes are as follows:

E1—Enrolled from within the state
E2—Entered from another state this school year

The exit codes are as follows:

T1—Transferred to another class
T2—Transferred to another school
D1—Dropped out of school

Attendance markings may differ from state to state or district to district. These are two common sets of markings:

Absence	—	/
Excused absence	(—)	⊘ or x
Tardy	⋅̇	ʌ
Excused tardy	(⋅̇)	ʌ̇ or Ⓐ
Excused for another school event	Ex	Ex

Days enrolled includes the total number of days each student was enrolled in the class. Absences and tardies are also summarized for the term.

Figure 10.9 An attendance register.

Period	Instructor(s)		Course Title	Text(s)			
2	Mrs. L. Jackson		Physical Education	None			
Fall Term	School: Younowhere Jr. High		Date Class Began 9/8 to Date Class Ended 1/12	Total Days Held 80			

Ref	Pupil	Sex	Grade	Entry Code	Exit Code	Term Summary — Days Enrolled	Term Summary — Days Absent	Term Summary — Times Tardy
1	Alexander, Claudia	F	8	E1		44	2	0
2	Bishop, April	F	8	E1		44	0	0
3	Carter, Susan	F	8	E1		44	2	0
4	Dixon, Lonnie	M	8	E1	E1	21	1	0
5	Dove, Jim	F	8	E1		44	0	1
6	Eden, Sherron	F	8	E1		44	0	0
7	Giles, David	M	8	E1		44	8	0
8	Herton, Giles	M	8	E1		44	0	0
9	Johnson, Kyle	M	8	E1		44	0	0
10	Killian, Teresa	F	8	E1		44	0	0
11	Lance, Cathy	F	8	E1		44	0	0
12	Limb, Susan	F	8	E1	D	44	16	0
13	Peery, Phyllis	F	8	E1		44	0	0
14	Rasmus, Jody	F	8	E1	T2	19	0	0
15	Skinner, David	M	8	E1		44	0	1
16	Sousa, Pepe	M	8	E2		26	1	0
17	Stevens, Jim	M	8	E1		44	0	1
18	Walden, Heather	F	8	E1		44	0	0
19	Wardell, Mark	M	8	E1		44	1	0
20	Wilson, Rosalie	F	8	E1		44	0	0
21	York, Ryan	M	8	E1		44	9	0

Source: Marilyn Harding, Springville Junior High School, Springville, Utah.

Period____________

Squad ____________

ATTENDANCE

Members	Roll No.	1st Week					2nd Week					3rd Week					4th Week					5th Week				
		M	T	W	T	F	M	T	W	T	F	M	T	W	T	F	M	T	W	T	F	M	T	W	T	F
1.																										
2.																										
3.																										
4.																										
5.																										
6.																										
7.																										
8.																										
9.																										
10.																										

Figure 10.10 A squad card.

Squad Cards

Squad cards are often used to take roll and the attendance record transferred to the attendance register after class. A sample squad card is shown in figure 10.10.

Records of Achievement

Records of student achievement are usually kept on class record cards and on individual permanent record cards. A discussion of each of these types of records follows.

Class Record Cards

A class record card is a record of the achievements of all students in a particular class. It provides information to the teacher and to the student on each student's progress in the class. A sample class record card is shown in figure 10.11.

Individual Permanent Record Cards

A permanent record card for each student provides a valuable source of information about student progress in the physical education program. It provides a record of the parents' names and phone numbers for emergencies, the students' fitness test results, all of the activity or content units completed by the student, and awards and honors in extra-class programs. File individual record cards alphabetically in the department office. The front and back of an individual permanent record card are shown in figure 10.12. The computer provides an alternative method of keeping information about student progress. A printout can be used to obtain information about individual or class achievement in any area of physical education.

Health and Medical Records

In the first part of this chapter, medical excuses for temporary or long-term illness or injury were discussed and forms were presented for each of these situations. Keep each of these forms on file in the physical education department office.

BADMINTON PERIOD 4	Serves	Clears	Drops	Smashes	Strategy & Positioning	FORM	Skills Test Clears	Skills Test Smashes	Skills Test Drops	Skills Test Serves	SKILL TEST	TOURNAMENT	QUIZ-RULES	FINAL TEST	SKILL	KNOWLEDGE	GRADE
Babbett, Mark R.	3	2	2	3	3	A	35	35	36	25	A-	A	B	A	A	A	A
Bagat, Devendra	2	3	1	1	2	C	13	26	20	25	C	B	C+	A	C+	B+	B-
Bushman, Virnell	3	3	3	3	3	A	36	30	17	14	C	A	B	A	B+	A-	B+
Crow, Craig J.	3	3	2	2	3	A	27	39	41	28	A-	B	A	A	B+	A	A-
Davis, Karen A.	3	2	3	3	2	A	34	38	10	43	B	B	B	B	B+	B	B+
Erickson, Craig A.	2	3	2	3	2	B	34	44	40	21	A	C	B	A-	B+	B+	B+
Gold, Lu Anne	3	3	2	2	2	B	31	40	29	38	A	B	C	B	B+	B-	B
Hansen, Marilyn A.	3	2	3	2	1	B	22	38	36	32	B	B	A	A-	B	A-	B
Hendrickson, Jan	3	3	1	1	1	C	4	30	25	38	C	C	C	B	C	B-	C+
Jackson, Linda A.	1	3	1	2	2	C	36	38	34	15	B	B	B-	A	B-	B+	B
Kramer, Terry May	3	3	2	3	2	A	20	43	24	31	C	A	B	B	B+	B	B+
Liscom, Leslie J.	3	2	2	2	1	C	24	31	13	34	B	C	C-	B	C+	C+	C+
Melner, Eric C.	3	3	2	3	2	A	27	38	29	29	B	B	A-	B	B+	B+	B+
Nielson, Lucy A.	2	3	3	1	2	B	32	29	32	14	B	A	C	C	B+	C	B-

Figure 10.11 A class record card.

AN INDIVIDUAL RECORD CARD

Name _Carol Duncan_   Date of Birth _21 June 1982_

Address _234 S. Glassell_

Parents' Names _Lloyd & Karen Duncan_   Phone _358-9308_

PHYSICAL FITNESS TESTING

Grade	1.5 mile run R.S.	%	% Fat R.S.	%	Flexibility R.S.	%	Strength R.S.	%
9 Pre	17:19	45	18	75	29	30	35	50
9 Post	16:54	55	18	75	30	35	35	50
10 Pre	16:14	60	17	55	30	20	35	40
10 Post	15:50	65	18	80	32	30	37	50
11 Pre	15:26	70	18	85	32	35	37	65
11 Post								
12 Pre								
12 Post								

Figure 10.12 An individual record card (front).

Activity	Fitness & Skills	Knowledge	Citizenship	Grade	Year Taken
Archery					
Badminton	B+	A	A	A-	1996-7
Basketball	B	A	A	B+	1995-6
Flag Football					
Folk Dance	A-	A	A	A-	1996-7
Golf	B-	A-	A	B+	1996-7
Gymnastics	A-	A	A	A-	1996-7
Modern Dance	A-	A	A	A-	1997-8
Soccer	B	A	A	B+	1995-6
Social Dance	A	A	A	A	1997-8
Softball					
Swimming	A	A	A	A	1995-6
Tennis					
Volleyball	B	A	A	B+	1995-6

AN INDIVIDUAL RECORD CARD

Intramural participation—Activities and awards:

Extramural participation—Activities and awards:

Figure 10.12 *(continued)*. An individual record card (back).

Another type of record that should be kept on hand is a record of health status for each student. The school nurse can be helpful in collating this information from permanent school records. Such conditions as asthma, allergies, diabetes, heart conditions, muscular or orthopedic disorders, and many other conditions can affect student participation in the physical education program.

Equipment and Locker Records

Locker records were discussed earlier in the chapter under school policies and procedures. A record should be kept in the department by the department head, or some other faculty member, of all departmental transactions. Equipment purchases and maintenance are especially important. Equipment records include a yearly equipment inventory, copies of purchase orders, and check-out forms for athletic equipment. For further information regarding these subjects, refer to a textbook on administration.

Review Questions

1. Explain usual department guidelines for:

    uniforms
    excuses from activity
    locker-room policies
    locks and lockers
    towels
    showers

2. Summarize the research findings about classroom management.
3. Explain how to:

prepare the environment

distribute and collect equipment

plan preclass activities

call roll

lead warm-up and fitness activities

get students' attention and give directions

teach and utilize class formations

organize groups or teams

supervise class activities

adapt to interruptions

use student leaders

increase motivation through classroom management

4. What are appropriate and inappropriate ways to choose teams?
5. What is Grandma's law? How can it be used in physical education?
6. What kinds of records should be kept by physical educators?

References

1. Cox, C. C. (1992). From handout to handbook. *Strategies, 6*(1), 7–8.
2. Issues. (1991). *The Journal of Physical Education, Recreation and Dance, 62*(3), 14–15. Issues. (1991). *The Journal of Physical Education, Recreation and Dance, 62*(4), 12–14, 63.
3. Hardy, R. (1979, December). Dressing out in physical education: Probing the problem. *Physical Educator, 36,* 191–192.
4. *Mitchell v. McCall,* 273 Ala. 604, 143 So. 2d. 629 (1962).
5. Hardy, Dressing out in physical education, 191–192.
6. Major K. (1990, March-April). *New ideas, new classes: Learning-growing-improving.* Paper presented at the AAHPERD convention, New Orleans, LA.
7. Pease, P. C. (1982, Fall). Effects of interdependent group contingencies in a secondary physical education setting. *Journal of Teaching in Physical Education, 2,* 29–37.
8. Hart, J. (1990, January). Locker-room liability. *Strategies, 3*(3), 19–20.
9. Kounin, J. S. (1977). *Discipline and group management in classrooms.* Huntington, NY: Krieger.
10. Soar, R. S., & Soar, R. M. (1979). Emotional climate and management. In P. L. Peterson & H. J. Walbert (Eds.), *Research on teaching: Concepts, findings, and implications* (pp. 97–119). Berkeley, CA: McCutchan.
11. Gage, N. L. (1978, November). The yield of research on teaching. *Phi Delta Kappan, 60*(3), 229–235.
12. Sanford, J. P., & Evertson, C. M. (1981, January-February). Classroom management in a low SES junior high: Three case studies. *Journal of Teacher Education, 32,* 34–38.
13. Brophy, J. (1982, April). Successful teaching strategies for the inner-city child. *Phi Delta Kappan, 63,* 527–530.
14. Oxendine, J. B. (1984). *Psychology of motor learning* (p. 179). Englewood Cliffs, NJ: Prentice-Hall.
15. Earls, N. F. (1983). Research on the immediate effects of instructional variables. In T. J. Templin & J. K. Olson (Eds.), *Teaching in physical education* (p. 261). Champaign, IL: Human Kinetics.
16. Luke, M. D. (1989, April). Research on class management and organization: Review with implications for current practice. *Quest, 41,* 55–67.
17. Aicinena, S. (1991). Formal class closure—An effective instructional tool. *Journal of Physical Education, Recreation and Dance, 62*(3), 72.
18. La Mancusa, K. C. (1966). *We do not throw rocks at the teacher!* (p. 166). Scranton, PA: International Textbook.

19. Ibid., 116–117.
20. Aicinena, Formal class closure, 72–73.
21. Wilson, R., & Dunn, S. E. (1990, Autumn). Creative and fun grouping strategies. *Utah Association of Health, Physical Education, Recreation and Dance Journal, 22,* 17–23.
22. Kirkpatrick, B. (1993). *The ultra-shuffle: Who's keeping score?* Grundy Center, IA: For Your Heart.
23. Lambdin, D. (1989). Shuffling the deck. *Journal of Physical Education, Recreation and Dance, 60*(3), 27–28.

CHAPTER 11

Physical Education and the Law

Study Stimulators

1. What is tort liability? How can teachers defend themselves in a tort liability case?
2. What steps can teachers take to reduce the likelihood of being sued?
3. What is the connection between students' safety and planning, organizing, and managing instruction?
4. What actions are expected of a reasonably prudent physical educator?
5. What civil rights are protected by the First, Fourth, and Fourteenth Amendments to the Constitution?

Michelle Landers was 15 years old, 5'6" tall and weighed 180 pounds. She was in a class of 40 students. Because of her size she expressed fear in her ability to successfully execute a backward roll. She was given only a brief demonstration of the backward roll. The teacher told Michelle to practice the skill with the help of another student; Michelle suffered a neck injury resulting in surgery. She sued her teacher for improper instruction.[1] Michael Mantague had successfully executed a vault approximately 33 times, including five or six vaults one day prior to falling and fracturing his arm. The suit was decided in favor of the teacher.[2]

In a survey of more than 400 recent lawsuits in the areas of recreation, instruction, and organized sports 24 percent of the cases involved accusations of faulty supervision, 40 percent were due to the selection and conduct of activities, and 36 percent resulted from accusations of failure to provide a safe environment. In the instructional area, 65 percent of the cases were due to the selection and conduct of activities. Supervision, selection and conduct of activities, and provision of a safe environment are all duties of a physical educator.[3] The nature of physical education presents an environment in which the risk of potential injuries resulting in legal action is great.[4] Table 11.1 indicates the estimated sports-related medically attended injuries during 1991. Physical educators must be familiar with issues of law to provide an environment that is as risk-free as possible.[5]

This chapter explains legal liability and discusses practices that will provide a safer environment and reduce the likelihood of a suit. Also included is a discussion of other law issues of importance to physical educators.

Legal Liability

Liability refers to a legal responsibility that can be enforced by a court of law in a civil action, which is an action involving a relationship between citizens or between citizens and an institution

Table 11.1 Estimated Sports-Related, Medically Attended Injuries during Calendar Year 1991

Sport	Medically Attended Injuries
Playgrounds	262,378
Organized football	149,527
Organized baseball	137,753
Organized basketball	120,503
Weight lifting	61,140
Track and field	58,586
Organized soccer	48,148
Wrestling	43,894
Dance	39,257
Golf	38,626
Swimming	34,748
Field hockey	31,145
Tennis	29,936
Organized volleyball	25,629
Exercise equipment	25,258
Ice hockey	23,456
Organized gymnastics	17,272
Cheerleading	11,682
Archery	7,397
Total	1,166,335

Source: Dougherty, N. J., Auxter, D., Goldberger, A. S., & Heinzmann, G. S. *Sport, Physical Activity, and the Law* (p. 236). Champaign, IL: Human Kinetics Publishers. Copyright 1994 by Neil J. Dougherty, David Auxter, Alan S. Goldberger, Gregg S. Heinzmann. Reprinted by permission.

such as a school or district. A basic understanding of the laws governing liability in physical education is essential to the preservation of physical education programs in the schools.

From 1961 to 1970 the number of lawsuits in physical education doubled from that of the previous 10 years.[6] In the 1970s the number of reported cases again more than doubled.[7] The 1980s and 1990s reflected a continuation of these escalating trends.

Baley and Matthews suggested several reasons for the increases in lawsuits. Some relating to physical education are the following:

1. Increased emphasis on lifetime sports. Teachers are teaching and supervising activities in which they have limited training or knowledge.

2. People more attuned to their individual rights. Actions once considered reasonable are now considered negligent by a court of law.
3. Increased accessibility of legal services.
4. Awareness that schools and most individuals are insured.
5. Increased valuing of individual rights.[8]

The *Sports and the Courts: Physical Education and Sports Law Quarterly* emerged to inform professionals of actual cases and court settlements. Each issue documents an average of 20 cases. The Summer Law and Sports Conference came into being in the early 1980s to prepare physical educators to deal with the issues of legal liability.[9] Settlements now reach millions of dollars, and a single case can wipe out a school district's entire year's budget.[10] In light of these facts, some states have passed legislation limiting awards to the maximum amount of insurance coverage. With this turn of events have come escalating insurance costs for school districts. Many districts report that the price of insurance is prohibitive.[11]

A Legal Liability Case

The parents of a senior high school student filed a one million dollar suit against her physical education teacher and the board of education for injuries the young woman suffered in a physical education class–related accident (in which the student disobeyed the teacher's orders and was jumping on a trampoline between classes). In the suit, the parents complained that she was required to take the class to graduate and that reasonable safety precautions were not taken to prevent injury.[12]

In the preceding incident, the injured girl and her parents were the *plaintiffs*—the person or group initiating the action against another party. The teacher and school board were the *defendants*—the person or group against whom the action is brought. The complaint summarized the reasons the plaintiff felt she was entitled to compensation for her injury. As the legal process continued, the defendant (the teacher) filed an answer stating why she felt she was not at fault. After a period of time, the case came before the court. The entire case was based on the assumption that a wrong had been committed, resulting in an injury. In this case, the parents charged the teacher with the commission of a tort.

Tort

A *tort* is a civil or legal wrong, an action that results in injury to another person or to that person's reputation or property. A tort can be caused by an act of *omission,* or the failure to perform a legal duty, such as failure to close the outside doors during a fire drill when previously instructed to do so. A tort can also be caused by intentional interference, or *commission.* There are various types of intentional tort:

1. *Negligence* is the failure to act as a reasonably prudent person would act under the same circumstances.
2. *Assault* is a threat to inflict harm on someone.
3. *Battery* is the unlawful use of physical force against another person.
4. *Defamation* involves a malicious intent to injure a person's reputation through:
    a. *Slander*—the spoken word.
    b. *Libel*—the written word.

Negligence

Most liability cases involving the schools are based on negligence. Negligence may be caused by any of the following:

1. *Nonfeasance* involves failure to do what is required, such as failure to instruct the students properly in the use of the trampoline or failure to administer first aid to an injured student.
2. *Misfeasance* involves doing something incorrectly, such as moving an injured student when it is improper to do so, thereby further injuring the young person.
3. *Malfeasance* involves doing something illegal, such as using corporal punishment in a state where it is against the law.

Negligence involves a comparison of the situation with an acceptable or established standard of conduct for persons in similar situations. To determine negligence, the courts generally ask four questions:[13]

1. Duty—Did one person owe a duty to another?
2. Breach—Did that person fail to exercise that duty?
3. Harm—Was a person actually injured?
4. Cause—Was the failure to exercise due care the direct or proximate cause of the injury?

A *duty* is a legal responsibility to act in a certain way toward others to protect them from physical or mental harm. It includes the expectation that a teacher will provide appropriate instruction, supervision, and a safe environment in which students can learn. A *breach* is failure to exercise a standard of care equal to the risks involved. However, the breaching of a duty does not constitute negligence. Cause and harm must also be shown. A causal relationship must exist between the breach of duty and the injury of another person. *Foreseeability* is involved when a teacher could have anticipated or foreseen a potential danger and failed to eliminate the danger. If a person was injured as a result, the teacher is liable. In the case just cited, the teacher could have seen that leaving a trampoline available for student use would result in students jumping on it even when advised not to do so. As another example, when teachers know that a student has exhibited violent behavior in the past, they should foresee that such acts are likely to be repeated in the future.[14]

Finally, an actual injury or loss must occur as a result of the breach. *Harm* can exist in many forms. Physical injury is most often the result, such as a broken bone, but sometimes the end result of a condition initiated by negligence is the harm. For example, permanent paralysis, death, or emotional distress may not be evidenced until a later time. These conditions are still grounds for court action.

To establish negligence, the plaintiff must demonstrate that the teacher's actions were the direct or *proximate* cause of the injury. In the case just cited, the fact that the trampoline was left out by the teacher could be considered to be the proximate cause of students jumping on it and, therefore, of the accident.

Defenses against Negligence

When defending a case involving possible negligence, lawyers generally rely on one or more of the following defenses.

Governmental Immunity. Governmental immunity is based on the English common law premise that "the king can do no wrong" and is therefore immune from suit. In a few states, the government still enjoys this privilege. Therefore, even when a school district is negligent, no damages or money can be awarded. However, beginning in 1959, when an Illinois state court abolished governmental immunity in a school transportation case,[15] most of the states have lost their immunity through legislative or court action.[16] Unlike boards of education, individual administrators, teachers, or other employees of the districts have never been immune from tort liability.

Contributory Negligence. Contributory negligence occurs when the injured person directly contributes to the injury. No damages are allowed in cases of contributory negligence. In the case discussed earlier, the student contributed directly to her injury by jumping on the trampoline despite the fact that she knew she was violating the safety rules that the teacher had established and repeatedly emphasized. Participants must act for their own protection as a reasonably prudent person of their age would act.

Comparative Negligence. Comparative negligence happens when both the injured person and the defendant are jointly responsible for the accident. The court generally determines the percentage of responsibility held by each person and distributes the money accordingly. For example, in the case involving the trampoline, the student, the teacher, and a medical doctor could be held responsible for 50 percent, 25 percent, and 25 percent of the injuries, respectively. If an award is determined, the defendants would be required to pay the percentage for which they are held responsible.

Comparative negligence has replaced contributory negligence. In most cases of contributory negligence, if the court determined the plaintiff's actions had contributed in any way to the injury, no award for damages could be given. Comparative negligence allows an award even if the plaintiff's actions did contribute to the injury. The award is reduced by the amount of the plaintiff's responsibility.

Assumption of Risk. Assumption of risk occurs when a person understands and accepts that participation in the activity involves a certain amount of risk of injury that a teacher or supervisor cannot prevent. The defense of assumption of risk can be used only when the participant knows and understands the risks involved and voluntarily participates in the activity. If coercion is present in any form, an assumption of risk by the participant has not occurred. This defense can rarely be used in physical education classes because participation in class is generally not voluntary as it is in interscholastic athletics or intramurals.[17] However, a person never assumes the risk of negligent behavior of another person in any activity.

Act of God. An act of God is an unforeseeable or unavoidable accident due to the forces of nature. If a student were suddenly struck by lightning while playing softball, the accident would be considered an act of God. However, a teacher allowing students to remain in an outdoor swimming pool during an electrical storm is undoubtedly negligent.

Legal Precedents. Legal precedents are court decisions made previously in similar cases. They are used by both the plaintiff and the defendant to defend their particular points of view. Cases often depend on previous legal decisions for their solutions.

Preventing Negligence

Because of large settlements occurring in court cases, more and more lawsuits involving physical education are being settled out of court. However, when these suits do come to court, the courts are showing less tolerance for mistakes by teachers and demanding greater responsibility than ever before.

Negligence generally arises from one of five sources. They are (1) failure to supervise students properly, (2) failure to instruct students properly, (3) unsafe facilities, grounds, or equipment, (4) failure to take proper first aid measures in an emergency, and (5) failure involving transportation. By increasing their awareness of these five areas, teachers can considerably decrease their chances of becoming a defendant in a lawsuit and the damages awarded if such a case occurs.

Supervision. More than 50 percent of all lawsuits involving physical education and sports are a result of improper supervision.[18] Henderson stated, *"By far the most crucial responsibility of physical education teachers is that of supervision."*[19] Berryhill and Jarman listed two basic questions frequently asked by the attorney for the plaintiff in a suit involving supervision:

1. If the supervisor had been present would the accident have occurred?
2. Did the supervisor perform his assigned duties or abide by the rules and regulations?[20]

Dougherty, Auxter, Goldberger, and Heinzman defined supervision as:

the quality and quantity of control exerted by teachers or coaches over the individuals for whom they are responsible. Therefore the number of supervisory personnel assigned to a group must be sufficient to effectively control the group in question, and the supervisors must have the training and skills necessary to fulfill their assigned duties.[21]

Teachers are expected to be where they are assigned on time and to provide active rather than passive supervision. Hart and Ritson stated that active supervision requires more than mere presence. Physical education personnel are expected to

1. monitor and keep activities within the skill level of individual students and athletes;
2. keep students from participating in unsafe activities;
3. enforce class and school rules;
4. keep records and be aware of the health status of individual students; and
5. provide spotting and other specific supervision in activities of elevated risk, such as gymnastics, wrestling and football.[22]

Student discipline is a critical element of supervision. Effective practices and policies must be initiated. Class and school rules, especially safety rules, must be established, communicated both in written and oral form, and enforced. Failure to enforce rules when reckless behavior occurs implies approval of the behavior.[23] Results of court cases indicate that teachers who use corporal punishment will be vulnerable to litigation. Always avoid the use of physical contact of any kind in disciplining students.[24] California and Oregon include exercise used for punishment, such as laps and push-ups, in their definition of corporal punishment, which is prohibited by law.[25]

The quantity and quality of supervision needed depends on the circumstances, including the (1) age and maturity of the students, (2) amount of risk inherent in the activity, (3) skill level of the students, and (4) previous preparation of the students.

Age and Maturity. Younger, less mature students need more supervision; older, more mature students generally need less. However, teachers should consider the tendency of older students to engage in horseplay.[26]

Amount of Risk in the Activity. Activities that involve greater risk—such as gymnastics, wrestling, swimming, archery, and initiative activities—require closer supervision and fewer students per teacher than activities with less risk. Avoid supervising two high-risk activities at one time, such as the high jump and shot put in track and field, as well as many gymnastic activities.[27]

Proper instruction and supervision help to prevent lawsuits.
© Tracy Pellett

Skill Level. Students who are just beginning to learn a new skill need more direct supervision than advanced students.

Preparation of Students. The teacher should gradually prepare students to assume responsibility for their own behavior. Students should earn the opportunity to participate in student-directed styles of learning.

Administrators have the responsibility (1) to assign qualified teachers for each activity taught in the curriculum, (2) to communicate to teachers what is expected of them, and (3) to

Table 11.2   Supervision Guidelines

The reasonably prudent physical educator:

1. Develops comprehensive class, team, and locker-room rules and procedures and effectively communicates those to students and athletes. Establishes clear rules relative to all equipment use.

2. Strictly and consistently enforces all established class, team, and school rules.

3. Provides active supervision required within the scope of his/her employment whether in the gym, on the field, in the locker room, or in the hall. The teacher is where he/she is assigned and on time. Provides general as well as specific supervision.

4. Does not unnecessarily absent him/herself from classes or practice sessions. Gives consideration to age and composition of the group, past experience with the group, the nature of the activity and the equipment being used, and the reason and duration for any temporary absence before leaving the group for any reason.

5. Assigns only qualified personnel to conduct and supervise activities.

6. Does not allow students to engage in unreasonably dangerous activities.

7. Is aware of the health status of all students under his/her charge and provides modified activity or exclusion from activity where appropriate.

8. Carefully matches students and athletes in any activity involving potential contact, giving consideration to age, size, skill, and experience differences.

9. Keeps activities within the ability level of individual students.

10. Refrains from all use of physical discipline and punishment, including the use of exercise as punishment.

11. Does not attempt to supervise more than one area at a time.

12. Immediately attends to any dangerous situations.

Source: Hart, J. E., & Ritson, R. J. (1993). *Liability and Safety in Physical Education and Sport* (pp. 97–98). Reston, VA: American Alliance for Health, Physical Education, Recreation and Dance.
Reprinted from Liability and Safety in Physical Education and Sport with permission of the National Association for Sport and Physical Education, 1900 Association Drive, Reston, VA 22091

supervise teachers to determine whether the expectations have been met. They also have the responsibility to regulate class sizes to meet the needs of the students.

Teachers have a responsibility to remain with their classes at all times. This includes positioning such that the entire class is in view at all times. When an emergency occurs, a student should be sent to the physical education or administrative office for help. The teacher should not leave the room to assist an injured student unless a second, qualified teacher is in the room. Never dismiss a class early or late without supervision. Locker rooms are one of the more potentially dangerous rooms in a school and should be supervised when in use and locked at all other times.[28] Teachers are liable for unsupervised students in gymnasiums, dressing rooms, halls, or on the school grounds. Table 11.2 provides guidelines for the behavior expected of a reasonably prudent physical educator.

Instruction. Several principles apply when designing the instructional situation. They relate to (1) the selection of the activity, (2) safety precautions, (3) planning, (4) direct instruction, and (5) grouping.

Selection of the Activity. Potential activities must be evaluated for their educational value and their appropriateness for students. Educational value is determined by the ability of the activity to help students meet the objectives of physical education. The courts have considered activities such as killer ball or war ball to be hazardous for students.[29] Appropriateness for students is determined by the age, maturity, skills, and fitness levels of students. Carefully screen students for such high-risk activities as combatives and gymnastics and for fitness activities in which students might be compelled to push themselves beyond their limits.[30] Running backward in a relay race is highly questionable for many students, although learning to move backward to reach a high clear might be acceptable in a sport like badminton.[31] A sound educational practice would be to individualize instruction for all students, not just students for whom Individualized Education Programs have been written.[32]

The use of stations is a common and appropriate practice in many situations. Extra planning is required, though, to be sure all stations are adequately supervised. If only one teacher is present, only one station should be an activity in which the risk is elevated. The teacher must be able to supervise or spot at the station of elevated risk and still maintain general supervision of the entire class. As mentioned before, the teacher must be positioned to see all students at all times.[33]

Evaluate health problems and prevent students from participating in activities that are beyond their abilities. Do not allow students to participate in activity following a serious illness or injury without medical approval. Physical education teachers must be aware of medical conditions of all students in their classes.[34] A student who complains of an illness or injury should not be second guessed.[35]

Safety Precautions. Warn students of the possible dangers inherent in the activities in which they participate and caution them not to try things that they have not yet been taught. This is especially true in gymnastics, in which the plaintiff has usually been favored in court cases.[36]

Carefully formulate and teach safety rules and regulations to students. Rules should be few in number and well enforced. To ensure that students have learned them, safety rules can be distributed to students, reviewed with students, and posted as reminders. Test students to determine their knowledge of the rules before allowing them to participate in the activity. Do not allow students who have been absent to participate in activities until they have learned the appropriate safety rules.[37] Failure to follow the rules should result in exclusion from that activity.

Safety equipment—such as fencing masks and body protectors, catcher's masks and chest protectors, helmets, and other game-related safety equipment—should be required of all participants. Eyeglass protectors should be strongly encouraged when not required by policy or law. Check to make sure all equipment is used properly and safely. Ground rules can be used to help students learn safety rules, such as requiring softball players to lay the bat in a marked area on the way to first base or be called out.

Students should be taught that they have a responsibility to be careful, to respect possible dangers, and to prevent accidents from occurring by using appropriate means of prevention. Provide a handout and review it with the class explaining the responsibility of participants to report bad equipment, to rest when fatigued, and to ask for help when experiencing difficulty in performing a new skill. Remind students that instructors cannot be present at all times to help individuals, and therefore they must accept some responsibility for their own safety.

Sufficient space must be allowed between playing boundaries and walls or other obstructions. When the space is minimal, the walls and obstructions should be padded. A wall should never be used as a boundary,[38] or be used to touch as part of a relay race.

Planning. Teachers should follow accepted procedures for instruction contained in state, district, or school courses of study or in a recognized text. Deviations from such procedures must be based on sound reasons, such as research demonstrating that the previous procedure was unsound or that a new procedure is better.

Unit and lesson plans are essential to ensure that proper progressions are followed and specific concerns regarding safe participation are provided (see examples in chapter 5). Failure to carefully plan each unit and lesson can not only result in poor teaching but will also provide no evidence to defend, in a court of law, the progressions used.[39] Careful planning of lessons and units can do much to decrease the potential for an injury and a resultant lawsuit.[40]

Never leave substitute teachers in charge of a class without a lesson plan. A substitute is at a distinct disadvantage because the individual does not know the students as well as the teacher does. Provide the substitute with information about the health status of the students, including those who are excluded from activity due to injury or illness. Also supply information about chronically disruptive or physically aggressive students, safety procedures, and the names of individuals who could help in case of an emergency. The substitute should be informed of known hazardous conditions within the facilities or grounds. Activities with an elevated risk of injury should not be planned.[41]

Direct Instruction. Instruction in proper techniques and progressions should precede participation in any activity. Students should progress gradually from less strenuous and simple tasks to more demanding, complex, and higher-risk activities. Include proper techniques for the performance of the activity, the proper use of equipment, the inherent dangers in the activity or the equipment, and information on how to avoid those dangers.[42]

Grouping. To prevent unnecessary injuries in contact sports or combative activities, group students for competition by similar characteristics such as height, size, skill, or sex; however, students cannot be grouped *solely* by sex. "Counting off" and other such methods of grouping are convenient but may result in mismatches. Teachers participating with their classes can result in the greatest mismatches and should be avoided. Failure to properly match participants has resulted in awards to students who are injured.[43]

Lehr has provided some recommendations for properly classifying students into groups.

1. Document all planning strategies.
2. Know the skill and experience levels before the student is asked to perform a skill.
3. Do not segregate on the basis of sex.
4. Do not pair/match by convenience.
5. Know the physical or emotional conditions of a student that may restrict participation.
6. Determine the most appropriate method of matching. Pair students by matching characteristics, and match the student to the activity.[44]

Table 11.3 provides guidelines for the behavior expected of a reasonably prudent physical educator in regard to instruction.

Table 11.3   Instruction Guidelines

The reasonably prudent physical educator:

1. Develops written unit plans for each unit of study or sport season to ensure that proper progressions and safety are built into each activity unit.

2. Develops daily, written lesson plans which allow for adequate warm-up, instruction and practice with both classroom management and safety considerations included.

3. Analyzes his/her teaching or coaching methods not only for their effectiveness but for their attention to student and athlete safety.

4. Provides adequate instruction before requiring student or athlete participation in any activity, including verbal instructions as well as teacher and/or student demonstrations.

5. Provides adequate safety instructions prior to any activity.

6. Provides clear warnings to students and athletes as to the specific risks involved in any activity or in the use of equipment, facilities or grounds.

7. Teaches or coaches only those activities with which he/she is familiar and qualified to teach/coach.

8. Gives proper instructions for both skill and safety which conform to recognized standards employed in the professional field.

9. Does not coerce students to perform.

10. Selects activities which are appropriate for the age of student being instructed and is familiar with any existing district or state scope and sequence documents.

11. Follows all guidelines related to program which are set forth by the school, district, state, or activity association.

12. Requires an adequate amount of practice before competition.

13. Does not attempt to instruct or supervise an excessive number of students or athletes, especially in activities involving elevated levels of risk.

14. Continues to upgrade both skill and knowledge through participation in workshops, continuing education and other inservice opportunities.

Source: Hart, J. E., & Ritson, R. J. (1993). *Liability and Safety in Physical Education and Sport* (pp. 49 – 50). Reston, VA: American Alliance for Health, Physical Education, Recreation and Dance.
Reprinted from *Liability and Safety in Physical Education and Sport* with permission of the National Association for Sport and Physical Education, 1900 Association Drive, Reston, VA 22091

Safe Facilities, Grounds, and Equipment.   Essential components of accident prevention are safe facilities, grounds, and equipment. Administrators should set policies and make plans for periodic inspection of facilities, grounds, and equipment to determine possible hazards and defects. The line of responsibility must be clearly delegated to a specific person.[45] Records listing the inspector, date, condition of the equipment, and recommendations for repair should be retained. Maintain complete inventories of equipment, including the dates of purchase and repair.

Physical educators should inspect facilities, grounds, and equipment frequently and take note of any potential hazards. Report hazards promptly to the principal and follow up with a written letter to the principal (and superintendent, if necessary) stating the date and the nature of the problem. Retain a copy of the report. Administrators are responsible for maintaining facilities and grounds and correcting defects.

While waiting for the defect to be corrected use temporary measures to protect students from injury: Post signs warning of the danger; warn students to stay away from the area; close off or lock the area; or station a supervisor nearby to keep students away. Never use a facility while unsafe conditions exist. Appenzeller sums up one of the major problems with equipment: "Too often teachers try to get by just one more day with obsolete and outdated equipment that should have been discarded years ago. These teachers are either indifferent to the needs of their pupils or are totally unaware of the serious consequences that may lay ahead."[46]

Physical education departments provide equipment for the use of students in their physical education classes. Brown listed four general responsibilities of individuals who provide equipment.

1. When providing equipment without charge, make sure that the equipment is safe. Inspect all new equipment for defects.
2. Select equipment that is appropriate for the participants' height, weight, skill and overall competence.
3. Ensure that equipment is used only for its intended purpose. A school could be liable if a participant is injured while being allowed to use equipment in ways other than were intended by the manufacturer.
4. Teach all participants how to use the equipment properly.[47]

An *attractive nuisance* is a dangerous situation that attracts the attention of children or youth. Swimming pools, gymnastics apparatus, jumping pits, and excavation areas are all attractive nuisances. To prevent injuries, teachers and administrators have a responsibility to keep such areas and equipment locked up when not in use.

Table 11.4 provides guidelines for the reasonably prudent physical educator in regard to safe equipment, grounds, and facilities.

First Aid versus Medical Treatment. The law both requires and limits the medical treatment of students to first aid—the immediate and temporary care needed to preserve the student's life or prevent further injury until medical care is available. This legal duty is imposed because the teacher stands *in loco parentis,* or "in the place of the parent," and also because physical education teachers are expected to be qualified to administer this aid.

Two common errors occur in giving first aid—doing too much or doing too little. An example of doing too much is moving an injured student before medical help has arrived. Cases of spinal injury and paralysis have resulted from this particular error. On the other hand, failure to obtain medical help for students suffering from heat exhaustion, a broken bone, or other injury can also be harmful. All head injuries should be considered serious. Any delay in treatment can be life-threatening.[48]

To help prevent accidents, proper medical examinations are often required of students at various school levels. Physical educators should take note of students who have medical problems or handicaps and may need close supervision or adapted instruction. Require students who have been seriously ill or injured to obtain a doctor's release before resuming normal physical activity.

If an accident does occur, administer first aid while sending a student to summon medical help and inform the principal. An emergency plan should be formulated and reviewed frequently so that it can be followed quickly and without further mishap. Keep an accurate report of each accident

Table 11.4 Equipment, Grounds, Facilities Guidelines

The reasonably prudent physical educator:

1. Regularly inspects equipment, facilities and grounds used by students. Does quick visual check daily with a detailed inspection monthly.

2. Keeps all inspection reports on file.

3. Reports all hazardous facility or grounds conditions immediately and refrains from using hazardous areas until these conditions are remedied.

4. Does not use defective, overly worn or broken equipment.

5. Refrains from using equipment for purposes other than those for which it was intended.

6. Provides all necessary safety equipment in those activities where appropriate such as soccer, hockey, softball, football, and gymnastics.

7. Purchases equipment of high quality; does not supply equipment that is dangerous for its intended use.

8. Does not modify factory purchased equipment.

9. Properly secures and/or stores all equipment when not in use.

10. Does not turn an otherwise safe facility into a dangerous one by improperly arranging equipment and materials for student or athlete use (e.g., placing equipment too close to walls, bleachers, or other obstructions or crowding).

11. Instructs students and athletes to also check for common safety hazards involving equipment, facilities and grounds.

12. Posts appropriate warnings and rules relative to equipment and facility use.

13. Is cautious in the use of homemade equipment.

14. Keeps locker rooms clean and orderly.

Source: Hart, J. E., & Ritson, R. J. (1993). *Liability and Safety in Physical Education and Sport* (p. 148). Reston, VA: American Alliance for Health, Physical Education, Recreation and Dance.
Reprinted from *Liability and Safety in Physical Education and Sport* with permission of the National Association for Sport and Physical Education, 1900 Association Drive, Reston, VA 22091

including a detailed report of the activity and the circumstances of the accident, the nature of the injury, the first aid treatment given, medical attention obtained, the names of persons rendering service, and the names of witnesses. A sample accident report form is shown in figure 11.1.

Appenzeller summarized the expectations of the court regarding first aid:

> As a coach, the court expects you to handle emergencies when they arise. The court will set a much higher standard of first aid for the coach than the average classroom teacher. The court will demand emergency treatment but nothing more. Do not go beyond the emergency stage; avoid attempting to treat your players; *let the professional do this!*[49]

Medical treatment includes the dispensing of any medication. Teachers and coaches should be extremely cautious in this regard and should not even give students aspirin.

Figure 11.1 An accident report form.

INJURED PERSON

NAME (last, first, middle)

TELEPHONE NUMBER

ADDRESS

AGE

SEX □ Female □ Male

CLASSIFICATION □ Student □ Faculty □ Visitor

DATE AND HOUR OF ACCIDENT

SEVERITY □ Nondisabling (loss of less than a full day of normal activity) □ Disabling (loss of one or more full days of normal activity)

DEPARTMENT SUPERVISING ACTIVITY

JURISDICTION □ On school property □ Off campus in school-conducted activity

ACTIVITY AT TIME OF ACCIDENT (e.g., driving auto, diving from low board, lifting crate, etc.).

DETAILS OF ACCIDENT (Describe fully the events, conditions, factors that contributed to the injury)

ACTION TO PREVENT SIMILAR ACCIDENTS (Indicate if taken)

ACCIDENT

TYPE OF FACILITY
□ Athletic or physical education
□ Instruction
□ Exterior walk or sidewalk
□ Other, specify _____
□ Street or highway
□ Service or maintenance
□ Undeveloped area

LOCATION
□ Gymnasium
□ Sports arena or play field
□ Swimming pool
□ Bath, shower, or locker room
□ Interior stair or ramp
□ Interior hall or corridor
□ Classroom, lecture hall
□ Auditorium or library
□ Laboratory
□ Shop (mechanical)
□ Home economics
□ Storeroom
□ Food preparation/service
□ Cafeteria or dining room
□ Public transportation
□ Private transportation
□ Bldg. exterior or grounds
□ Water area
□ Farm, field, or woods
□ Other, specify _____

NATURE OF INJURY

☐ Amputation
☐ Bruise
☐ Burn, scald
☐ Concussion
☐ Open wounds
☐ Dermatitis, infection
☐ Other, specify ____

☐ Exposure, frostbite
☐ Fracture
☐ Foreign body
☐ Heat exhaustion, sunstroke
☐ Inhalation (dust, fumes, gases, etc.)
☐ Internal injury

☐ Poisoning, internal
☐ Shock, electrical
☐ Shock, fainting
☐ Sprain, strains, dislocation
☐ Suffocation, drowning, strangulation
☐ Rupture, hernia

PART OF BODY INJURED

☐ Generalized
☐ Skull or scalp
☐ Eye
☐ Nose
☐ Mouth
☐ Jaw
☐ Other head
☐ Other, specify ____

☐ Neck
☐ Spine
☐ Chest
☐ Abdomen
☐ Back
☐ Pelvis
☐ Other trunk

☐ Shoulder
☐ Upper arm
☐ Elbow
☐ Forearm
☐ Wrist
☐ Hand
☐ Finger

☐ Hip
☐ Thigh
☐ Knee
☐ Lower leg
☐ Ankle
☐ Foot
☐ Toe

INJURY

WITNESSES AND THEIR ADDRESSES

WITNESSES

EMERGENCY CARE & PATIENT STATUS

☐ First aid only, not at hospital or by doctor
☐ Treatment by school nurse
☐ Treatment at hospital
☐ Confinement at hospital or at residence

This report prepared by (signature) _____

Title or status _____

Address _____

Date _____

TREATMENT

DISTRIBUTION: White,   Yellow, Originating Department

Figure 11.1 (Continued)

Physical Education and the Law   397

Transportation and Field Trips. When transportation is necessary to and from off-campus facilities or during a field trip, school officials should approve all travel arrangements. The preferred arrangement is to use school buses or commercial vehicles. However, in an emergency situation when these are unavailable, several precautions should be taken.

When teachers or adults drive their own cars, administrators should ensure that they have adequate liability insurance in case of student injury. They should also be aware that many automobile insurance policies do not protect the car owner who is paid for transporting passengers, even if the pay is only reimbursement for gas and oil. An insurance rider on the policy must be purchased to provide this protection.[50] School or district transportation should be used by teachers except in emergency situations.

Extreme caution should be used when allowing students to drive to and from school functions. Only when drastic circumstances arise should this be allowed. Administrators must then examine the student drivers' reputations and records for safe and careful driving and the cars for freedom from defects that might make them unsafe when student drivers are used. Such drivers should also be cautioned to obey all traffic laws and not to overload their cars or to allow students to drive who have not been approved by the administration. The students' insurance policies should be checked for adequate coverage.[51]

School boards would be wise to protect their students by establishing rules and regulations for student transportation and by securing liability insurance for their employees who transport students. It is also good public relations to let parents know exactly what is and is not covered.

Consent forms are often sent home to parents before students are allowed to go on field trips. Bucher and Koenig indicated that "waivers and consent slips are not synonymous." A parent cannot waive the rights of a child who is under 21 years of age; the parent is merely waiving his or her right to sue for damages. The child can still sue the individual, however.[52] Although these waivers do not stand up in court,[53] they serve a valuable purpose of informing parents and receiving their permission for the trip. They may also reduce the possibility of a lawsuit.[54] Any teacher who is transporting students should have an emergency treatment authorization form with them for each student, including the student's name, family physician, insurance information, allergies, current medications, and parents' names and signatures.[55]

Table 11.5 summarizes behaviors expected of a reasonably prudent physical educator.

Protection Against Legal Liability

Study the guidelines for protection against legal liability presented in this chapter and apply them to your own environment. Because of the abrogation of governmental immunity, more students are now able to recover damages for injuries caused by the negligence of school employees. Although this is a positive outcome for the injured person, it also means that teachers may be involved in more nuisance suits with resulting stress, professional embarrassment, and financial loss. School districts will also pay higher rates for insurance and sports equipment.[56] The result is a higher cost to the taxpayers for the support of their schools.

The fact that physical education teachers are held legally responsible for their actions should not cause prospective or practicing educators to throw in the towel. Rather, it should make them take their responsibilities as educators seriously and use common sense in their interactions with others. Teachers should become acquainted with the tort liability laws as they apply to their particular states.

In addition, the wise physical education teacher will also obtain liability insurance to protect against catastrophic personal loss. In some states, *save-harmless* legislation requires or permits

Table 11.5 Transportation Guidelines

The reasonably prudent physical educator:

1. Refrains from using anything other than district vehicles to transport students and athletes.

2. Never overloads a vehicle.

3. Makes sure each rider has a designated seat and uses a seat belt if one is provided.

4. Completes a visual check of a vehicle as well as a check of all lights, blinkers, tires, and wipers whenever a vehicle other than a school bus is used. Does not use any vehicle which is not well maintained.

5. Immediately reports any maintenance or safety needs of any district vehicle which he/she uses to transport students.

6. Makes sure any vehicle is equipped and supplied with adequate warning devices such as markers and flares.

7. Equips any vehicle used to transport students or athletes with a first aid kit.

8. Never arranges for students or athletes to drive.

9. Provides adequate supervision within the vehicle.

10. Makes sure any vehicle used is properly insured and that all drivers are properly licensed. In a number of states, a large passenger van full of riders requires the driver to have a chauffeur's license.

Source: Hart, J. E., & Ritson, R. J. (1993). *Liability and Safety in Physical Education and Sport* (p. 170). Reston, VA: American Alliance for Health, Physical Education, Recreation and Dance.
Reprinted from *Liability and Safety in Physical Education and Sport* with permission of the National Association for Sport and Physical Education, 1900 Association Drive, Reston, VA 22091.

districts to provide teachers with protection against financial losses resulting from a job-related liability suit. Personal liability insurance is available from some local or state education associations, the American Alliance for Health, Physical Education, Recreation and Dance, or the National Education Association.

Departmental and class procedures must be legal and safe. Policies and procedures for supervision, instruction, care of equipment, emergencies, and transportation must be documented (see Chapter 10).[57] Units and lessons must be thoughtfully and carefully planned, and student welfare should be of prime concern.

Civil Rights of Students

Clement stated, "To create a quality learning environment, professionals must foster freedom without disruption, secure individual rights without infringing on the rights of others, and establish gender equity".[58] These are protections of civil rights provided by the First, Fourth, and Fourteenth Amendments to the United States Constitution.

The First Amendment

The First Amendment allows for freedoms of speech, press, and privacy. The amendment protects an individual's right to express ideas either in speech or written form. Any language that is obscene, libelous, or slanderous is not protected. The learning environment must be protected and anything that disrupts the learning environment is prohibited. The courts will balance the needs of the public against the rights of the individual.[59] Freedom from invasion of privacy will be discussed as a part of the Fourth Amendment.

The Fourth Amendment

The Fourth Amendment provides protection against unreasonable searches. This also includes drug testing. Random drug testing should be discouraged and when drug testing is to occur, individuals involved must be made fully aware of the conditions under which the testing will take place.[60]

Searches of student's purses, lockers, and clothing have been the subjects of litigation. In each case, the searches are allowed if a reasonable suspicion exists that the search will reveal evidence to support the claim of violation of a rule.[61] The standard for school officials is different than for law enforcement professionals. It is important that policies be established and made known to the students and parents prior to the start of school or a specific school activity.[62]

The Fourteenth Amendment

The Fourteenth Amendment includes procedural due process and equal protection, which also includes Title IX. "Procedural due process is the provision of an opportunity for an individual to be heard, to defend personal actions, and be assured of fair treatment before a right or privilege is taken away."[63] The right of a student to explain or defend actions must be considered whenever punishment or discipline is implemented.

The Fourteenth Amendment and Title IX provide protection against discrimination. Title IX has been discussed in earlier chapters but it is important to note that monetary compensation for lost opportunities may now be awarded.[64] Prior to *Franklin v. Gwinnett*, complaints of violations of Title IX resulted in an investigation. If a violation was found, then the institution was required to make the necessary changes in policy, procedures, and practices. No monetary damages were allowed. Title IX cases generally occur in the area of athletics.

The Constitution of the United States protects the rights of students as well as teachers. These include a safe learning environment; freedoms of speech, press, and privacy; protection from unreasonable searches; due process; and equal protection. If efforts are made to ensure these rights are protected in the school, they are less likely to be settled in court.

Review Questions

1. Define the following terms:

legal liability	nonfeasance	plaintiff	*in loco parentis*
defendant	malfeasance	tort	misfeasance
negligence	breach	assault	duty
foreseeability	harm	defamation	battery
cause	slander	libel	proximate
attractive nuisance			

2. What four questions are asked to determine negligence? Explain negligence by omission and negligence by commission.
3. What six possibilities exist for a defense of negligence?

4. Explain the five sources of negligence and guidelines for protection against legal liability.
5. What protection is available against the costs of defending a court case?
6. What civil rights are protected by the First, Fourth, and Fourteenth Amendments to the Constitution?
7. What does Title IX have to do with the civil rights of students?

References

1. *Landers v. School District No. 203*, O'Fallon, 66 Ill. App. 3d 1978 383 N.E. 2d 645.
2. *Montague v. School Board of Thornton Fractional Township North High School District*, 215.57 Ill. App. 3d 828 (1978).
3. Dougherty, N. J., Auxter, D., Goldberger, A. S., Heinzmann, G. S., & Findlay, H. A. (1994). *Sport, physical activity, and the law* (pp. 250, 251). Champaign, IL: Human Kinetics.
4. Conn, J. H. (1993). The litigation connection: Perspectives of risk control for the 1990s. *Journal of Physical Education, Recreation and Dance, 64*(2), 15.
5. Ibid., 15.
6. Berryhill, L., & Jarman, B. (1979). *A history of lawsuits in physical education, intramurals and interscholastic athletics in the western United States: Their implications and consequences* (p. 2). Provo, UT: Brigham Young University.
7. Arnold, D. E. (1980, March). Positive outcomes of recent legislative and case law developments which have implications for HPER programs. *Physical Educator, 37*, 25.
8. Baley, J. A., & Matthews, D. L. (1989). *Law and liability in athletics, physical education and recreation* (pp. 3–4). Dubuque, IA: Wm. C. Brown.
9. *Sports and the Courts: Physical Education and Sports Law Quarterly*, Box 2836, Winston-Salem, NC 27102.
10. Appenzeller, H. (1970). *From the gym to the jury* (pp. 83–84). Charlottesville, VA: Michie.
11. Appenzeller, H., & Appenzeller, T. (1980). *Sports and the courts* (p. 4). Charlottesville, VA: Michie.
12. For a similar case, see *Smith v. Vernon Parish School Board*, 442 So. 2d 1319 (La. Ct. App. 1983).
13. Hudgins, H. C. Jr., & Vacca, R. S. (1979). *Law and education: Contemporary issues and court decisions* (p. 72). Charlottesville, VA: Michie.
14. Carpenter, L. J. (1990, May/June). Guns, knives and fists—Campus violence by third parties. *Journal of Physical Education, Recreation and Dance, 61*(5), 13–14; Holford, E. J. Physical education teachers—Liable for acts of intentional violence between students? *Journal of Physical Education, Recreation and Dance, 61*(4), 88–90.
15. *Molitor v. Kaneland*, 163 N.E. 2d 89 (Ill. 1959).
16. Arnold, Positive outcomes of recent legislative and case law developments which have implications for HPER programs, 25.
17. Hart, J. E., & Ritson, R. J. (1993). *Liability and safety in physical education and sport* (pp. 17–18). Reston, VA: American Alliance for Health, Physical Education, Recreation and Dance.
18. Berryhill & Jarman, *A history of lawsuits in physical education, intramurals and interscholastic athletics in the western United States*, 2.
19. Henderson, D. H. (1985, February). Physical education teachers: How do I sue thee: Oh, let me count the ways! *Journal of Physical Education, Recreation and Dance, 56*, 44.
20. Berryhill & Jarman, *A history of lawsuits in physical education, intramurals and interscholastic athletics in the western United States*, 3.
21. Dougherty, Auxter, Goldberger, Heinzmann, & Findlay, *Sport, physical activity, and the law*, 252.
22. Hart & Ritson, *Liability and safety in physical education and sport*, 51.
23. Ibid., 67.
24. Ibid., 52, 86–87. See *Waechter v. School District No. 14–030*, 733 F. Supp. 1005 (1991).
25. Ibid., 88. See *Metzger v. Osbeck*, 841 F. 2d 518 (1988, Pennsylvania).
26. Drowatzky, J. N. (1978, May). Liability: You could be sued! *Journal of Physical Education and Recreation, 49*, 17–18.

27. *Merkley v. Palmyra—Macedon Central School District,* 515 N.Y. S. 2d 932 (N.Y. 1987).

28. Hart & Ritson, *Liability and safety in physical education and sport,* 96.

29. *Cook v. Bennett,* 288 N.W. 2d 609 (Mich. Ct. App. 1979).

30. Appenzeller, *From the gym to the jury,* 8–9.

31. Barrett, K. R., & Gaskin, L. P. (1990, January). Running backwards in a relay race: *Brown v. Burlington City Board of Education. Journal of Physical Education, Recreation and Dance, 61*(1), 33–35.

32. Hart & Ritson, *Liability and safety in physical education and sport,* 44.

33. Ibid., 65.

34. Ibid., 53

35. Ibid., 156.

36. Appenzeller, *From the gym to the jury,* 171.

37. Hart & Ritson, *Liability and safety in physical education and sport,* 141.

38. *Brahatcek v. Millard School District No. 17,* 273 N.W. 2d 680 (Neb. 1979).

39. Ibid., 23–25. See *Larson v. Independent School District No. 314,* 289 N.W. 2d 112 (1979).

40. Gray, G. R. (1991). Risk management planning: Conducting a sport risk assessment to enhance program safety. *Journal of Physical Education, Recreation and Dance, 62*(6), 29.

41. Hart & Ritson, *Liability and safety in physical education and sport,* 141.

42. Hudgins & Vacca. *Law and education,* 84.

43. Lehr, C. (1993). Proper classification *Journal of Physical Education, Recreation and Dance, 64*(2), 24–25, 63.

44. Ibid., 63.

45. Appenzeller, *From the gym to the jury,* 174.

46. Ibid., 115.

47. Brown, S. C. (1993). Selecting safe equipment—What do we really know? *Journal of Physical Education, Recreation and Dance, 64*(2), 33.

48. Hart & Ritson, *Liability and safety in physical education and sport,* 154–155. See *Barth v. Board of Education of City of Chicago,* 490 N.E. 2d 77 (1986).

49. Appenzeller, *From the gym to the jury,* 146.

50. Ibid., 139.

51. Ibid., 137.

52. Bucher & Koenig, *Methods and materials for secondary school physical education,* 164.

53. Kaiser, R. A. (1984, August). Program liability waivers. *Journal of Physical Education, Recreation and Dance, 55,* 55.

54. Acosta, R. V. (1989, April-May). I promise I won't sue! *Strategies, 2*(5), 5–6.

55. Hart & Ritson, *Liability and safety in physical education and sport,* 149.

56. Arnold, Positive outcomes of recent legislative and case developments which have implications for HPER programs, 25.

57. Clement, A. (1988). *Law in sport and physical activity* (p. 29) Dubuque, IA: Brown & Benchmark.

58. Clement, A. (1993). Civil rights—The first, fourth, and fourteenth amendments. *Journal of Physical Education, Recreation and Dance, 64*(2), 62.

59. Ibid., 16.

60. Ibid., 16.

61. Dougherty, Auxter, Goldberger, Heinzmann, & Findlay, *Sport, physical activity, and the law,* 134.

62. Clement, Civil rights—The first, fourth, and fourteenth amendments, 16.

63. Ibid., 17.

64. Ibid., 62. See *Franklin v. Gwinnett County Public Schools,* 117 L. Ed. 2d 208 (1992).

CHAPTER 12

Motivation and Discipline

Study Stimulators

1. Why are motivation and discipline studied together?
2. What is motivation? How can understanding motivational theories help teachers teach?
3. What is discipline? Why is a study of discipline so important?
4. What motivational techniques can be used to prevent discipline problems?
5. Describe several discipline models that you might like to use in your teaching.
6. What disciplinary techniques are generally considered to be acceptable? Which ones would you use and when?
7. What disciplinary techniques are generally considered to be unacceptable?
8. What factors should be considered when a disciplinary incident arises?

According to Doyle, teaching basically involves a combination of instruction and order.[1] Assuming the teacher has the expertise to model and convey subject matter, he or she must then plan the instruction to maintain order and promote learning. Inherent in this process are both motivation and discipline.

Motivation and discipline are like heads and tails of the same coin. Fewer discipline problems occur when students are motivated through active involvement in meaningful learning and when enthusiastic teachers present material in stimulating ways. Students have neither the time nor the energy to create discipline problems. On the other hand, teachers cannot motivate when students are disruptive. Teachers who punish students or attack their dignity can't increase student motivation.[2]

Hellison pointed out that physical educators and coaches are increasingly concerned with discipline and motivation.[3] He maintained that if physical education and sport leaders want to prevent or reduce discipline and motivation problems, they must adjust to the changing world in the following ways:

1. Improve control in our classes and on our teams.
2. Help students make responsible choices.
3. Help students lead more stable lives.
4. Counter the ineffectiveness of schools.
5. Accomplish these needs without minimizing participation in physical activity.[4]

Teachers working with students who lack motivation and self-discipline and teachers who want to increase these traits in students would do well to study Hellison's model. He outlined some nontraditional goals of physical education, including teaching students to exercise self-control, to take responsibility for their own learning, to make wise choices, to develop a meaningful and personally satisfying lifestyle, and to cooperate with and support and help one another. His model for teaching involves developmental levels of progression for students involving attitudes and behavior, and interaction strategies for both teachers and students.

Teachers set the stage for both motivation and discipline. Meaningfully organizing instruction is vital to maintaining order in the classroom. Planning and consistently implementing one's plans are key elements in maintaining order. Without them teachers play a stressful guessing game in which trial and error are the dominant influences. Without some kind of systematic approach to student motivation, teachers are left not knowing what to do next.[5]

Students also contribute to maintaining or decreasing order. They come with attitudes molded by their personalities and experiences. Some live in insecure family environments in an increasingly violent society, in which they are often forced to fend for themselves. Some spend much of their time watching and listening to violence and profanity. Some students come to school with difficult temperaments. In school they may face boring lectures, powerlessness, unclear limits, attacks on their dignity, and a lack of acceptable outlets for their feelings.[6] Teachers are not responsible for students' attitudes, but they can exercise some control over the school environment.

Motivation

According to Joe Cybulski, a 10-year-old at Ballwin Elementary School in Missouri, motivation is "to convince someone he always wanted to learn something he never even knew he wanted to learn."[7] Motivation is an inner urge or desire to satisfy a need, achieve a specific goal, do one's best, surpass one's previous performance, or exceed another person's performance. It is part of the desire of humankind to improve and to excel. Achieving one's best under trying or even disappointing circumstances is a part of living one's life to the fullest. Great moments in sport, as with great moments in life, are not so much those of winning or losing but of doing one's best. Motivation is active; it is the process of initiating, sustaining, and directing activity toward a specific goal.[8] It involves both intensity and direction toward the goal. Teachers cannot motivate students or make them learn. They can only manipulate environmental variables, which may encourage students to do something that will result in learning.[9] Motivation is influenced both by personal factors within the student and by external environmental factors manipulated by the teacher.[10]

Motivated students engage in approach behaviors toward the activity or subject. Unmotivated students engage in avoidance behaviors and do not perform the desired responses; thus they learn slowly or not at all. The process of learning is more rapid when students are motivated. It works somewhat like a mathematical equation, in which skill equals performance times motivation. Learning increases geometrically as motivation increases.

Variables known to be related to the amount of motivation include the following:

1. *The degree of concern or tension that exists within the learner.* When tension increases to an undue degree because of excessive anxiety, anger, hostility, or compulsion, motivation decreases.
2. *The feeling tone* (pleasant or unpleasant). Pleasant feeling tones increase motivation to a high degree. Unpleasant feeling tones will also increase motivation, but to a lesser degree. The absence of or neutral feeling tones will not influence motivation.
3. *Interest.* People are motivated to do things that interest them.
4. *Success.* People are usually more successful in activities that interest them. Success in turn tends to stimulate interest. The degree of success becomes an important variable in motivation.

5. *Knowledge of results* (How am I doing?). The more specific the feedback, the more one becomes motivated to improve performance.
6. *Intrinsic (internal)-extrinsic (external) motivation.* Most examples of these are not completely one or the other, and both may be effective.[11]

Theories of Motivation

A number of theories have evolved in an attempt to define how intrinsic motivation develops and how it influences learners' achievements. Research has focused on (1) the need for achievement, (2) effectance motivation, (3) social learning theory, (4) movement confidence, (5) attribution theory, locus of control, and learned helplessness, and (6) teacher expectations.

Need for Achievement

Maslow identified a hierarchy of needs as the basis for all human motivation.[12] These needs are physiological, safety (and security), love (or social), esteem, and the need for self-actualization. He proposed, in general, that lower order needs must be satisfied before the next higher need can be activated. Thus, when physiological needs are met, the individual is concerned with safety and so on up the hierarchy until another physiological need must be attended to. For some persons, minimal satisfaction of a need is enough to progress upward, whereas others require satisfaction at a higher level. Occasionally a certain need takes precedence over all other needs regardless of its position in the hierarchy. Such is the case when a mother risks her life for her child.

Physiological needs such as food, water, sleep, exercise, and bodily elimination are essential for survival and when they are not met, students cannot learn effectively. Teachers see evidence of this in classes that meet right before lunch, in students after a morning of taking achievement tests, or in a student who is ill. Both physical and psychological *safety and security* are essential for learning. The threat of physical violence in some schools prevents effective learning, as does discrimination on the basis of race, sex, or ability. In physical education, students who are afraid to learn a new skill due to possible failure or ridicule are concerned about security. Some students have a high tolerance level for stress or physical risk while others have a low tolerance level and react strongly to situations in which their security is threatened.

When safety and security needs are met, the student seeks to fulfill the need for *love*. This need can be met in part through social approval from adults or peers, but it must be met for students to be successful in school. Most dropouts are students who lack acceptance from one of these sources.

Everyone needs to feel capable; therefore, each student must have some activities in which he or she feels success. Gagné emphasized the need to arrange the learning environment so students experience success and develop *self-esteem*. He said:

> Achievement, successful interaction within the learning environment, and mastery of the objectives of an educational program can themselves lead to persisting satisfaction on the part of the learner and can therefore become a most dependable source of continuing motivation.[13]

This fact underscores the value of adapting activities to meet the needs of students with a wide range of abilities so that each student experiences success and enjoyment.

Once basic needs have been satisfied, the individual can move on to *self-actualization*. Self-actualizing persons are motivated intrinsically and have an intense desire to explore, discover, and

Success in physical activities increases self-esteem.
© James L. Shaffer

create. They are aware of their strengths and weaknesses and those of their environment and resolve to improve them in a consistent, orderly manner. Maslow felt that only a small percentage of the population would become self-actualized. Schools need to create environments in which students can satisfy their basic needs so that they will be free to move on to self-actualization.

Effectance Motivation

In 1959 White proposed a motivational construct called effectance motivation, in which an intrinsic need to deal effectively with the environment propels the learner toward competent performance. Success results in feelings of efficacy or pleasure, which in turn increases effectance motivation.[14] Harter refined White's model and emphasized that effectance motivation is often domain specific. For example, a student may have a high level of self-efficacy in cognitive tasks and a low level of perceived competence in psychomotor skills.[15] Harter emphasized the importance of *optimum challenges*, matching tasks with the capabilities of learners. The most appropriate tasks are challenging, yet achievable through practice. Students with high persistence levels sustain effort over longer periods of time, whereas their low-persistence classmates need skills that can be achieved with minimal practice. Goals should also be specific. Clear expectations define the performance and effort required to achieve them and facilitate evaluation of how one is doing. Motivation is increased by focusing on specific, short-term subgoals that yield self-satisfaction, which sustains the learner's efforts along the way.[16]

Social Learning Theory

Bandura, in his social learning theory, described behavior in terms of expectations of personal efficacy (situation-specific self-confidence) and estimates of behavioral outcomes.[17] Decisions involve both (a) an efficacy expectation—the person's conviction that he or she can successfully execute the behavior required to produce the outcome and (b) an outcome expectation—the person's estimate that the behavior will result in the expected outcome and will be worthwhile.[18]

Efficacy expectations differ in (1) the magnitude or level of the task perceived to be possible, (2) the generalizability of past successes to similar situations, and (3) the strength of the expectations in the presence of disconfirming experiences. Students with high expectations will try new activities and expend more effort over a longer period of time than those with low expectations. The model for the theory is shown in figure 12.1.

A person is more likely to behave in a certain way if the resulting outcome is seen as positive and less likely to behave in that way if the result is perceived to be negative. Even if the outcome is considered desirable, the individual may feel unable to perform the behavior needed to achieve the outcome and so the behavior may be avoided. Since most behaviors result in both positive and negative outcomes, the person weighs the perceived outcomes and decides whether or not to engage in the behavior.

Bandura postulated that efficacy expectations can be altered by personal performance accomplishments (competence), vicarious experience (modeling), verbal persuasion, and emotional arousal. Competence is generally considered to be the strongest, most lasting source of self-efficacy. Perceived competence or self-efficacy can differ in the cognitive, social, and psychomotor domains. One student may have a high level of self-efficacy in the psychomotor and social areas and a very low level in the cognitive area; another may have a high level of perceived competence in the cognitive and psychomotor domains and feel ill-at-ease in social situations.

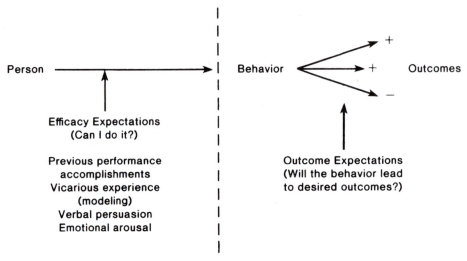

Figure 12.1 Bandura's social learning theory.
Source: Concepts from Albert Bandura. "Self-Efficacy: Toward a Unifying Theory of Behavioral Change." *Psychological Review* 84 (1977): 191–215; and *Social Learning Theory* (Englewood Cliffs, NJ: Prentice-Hall, 1977).

Modeling shows how to perform skills, which are refined through self-correction based on the consequence of the performance and feedback from others. Seeing others overcome obstacles through determined effort is more effective than viewing skilled performers who make the skill look easy.

The effectiveness of verbal persuasion depends on the credibility of the persuader. Prestige, expertise, self-assurance, and trustworthiness in the eyes of the learner affect credibility. If teachers raise expectations without arranging conditions for successful learning, the resulting failure will discredit the teacher's influence and further undermine the student's self-efficacy.

Emotional arousal can reduce perceived chances of success. Emotional anxiety, increased by fear-provoking thoughts, can exceed the fear experienced in actual situations. Anxiety is best extinguished by teaching effective coping skills.

Bandura viewed self-efficacy not as a global personality trait but as dependent on the task, situation, and previous experience of the learner. According to Bandura, motivation results from personal goal-setting and evaluation.[19] Individuals prescribe self-rewards for achieving self-prescribed standards and persist in their efforts until their performance matches the standards. After accomplishing these standards, they often make self-reward contingent on the attainment of even higher achievements. To be most effective, goals should be challenging, yet attainable. Goals that are too easy yield little effort and little satisfaction, whereas goals that are too difficult may result in failure. Frequent failure weakens efficacy expectations and therefore motivation.

Since performance accomplishments are the best predictors of self-efficacy, teachers should ensure performance success through appropriate instructional strategies. Teachers must structure the environment so that all students can perform successfully by modeling skills, providing graduated learning tasks, and varying the severity of the threat. For example, students who are afraid of the water must be gradually introduced to feeling the water on their bodies, putting their faces in the water, opening their eyes underwater, and experiencing buoyancy. The instructor usually begins by standing nearby to provide assistance and then helps the students to rely on peer tutors and finally on their own abilities.

Realistic performance standards help students gradually increase their abilities and, in turn, their self-efficacy. Students are, therefore, more willing to try new skills and to persist until they have learned them. A number of studies support this theory.[20] Feltz concluded that self-efficacy is important in explaining motor behavior and counseled coaches to learn techniques and strategies that develop and maintain self-efficacy.[21] Weinberg, Gould, and Jackson noted that high-efficacy subjects were more self-confident and predicted success more often than low-efficacy subjects. They also found that, in the face of failure, high-efficacy subjects showed increased persistence, whereas low-efficacy subjects exhibited decreased persistence. The researcher ascribed this to a temporary state similar to learned helplessness.[22] (Learned helplessness is described in an upcoming section.)

Movement Confidence

Griffin and Keogh extended and applied Bandura's and Harter's theories to physical education. They define movement confidence as "an individual feeling of adequacy in a movement situation." They believe that movement confidence results from the performer's evaluation of self in relation to the demands of the task. Two factors are considered—movement competence (skill) and the sensory experiences expected from the movement. Movement sensations may include personal or social enjoyment and potential physical or psychological harm and are more important for low-skilled learners than for the highly skilled. Movement confidence affects the person's (a) choice to become involved or not, (b) actual performance, and (c) persistence in the current task and future involvement. Individuals with high levels of movement confidence choose to participate and perform in ways that bring satisfaction, whereas those with low levels are less likely to participate and performance is less satisfying.[23]

Attribution Theory, Locus of Control, and Learned Helplessness

Attribution theorists study perceived reasons for a person's success or failure.[24] Successes and failures can be attributed to internal or external causes, which are stable or unstable over time, and are controllable or uncontrollable by the learner. Student expectations, persistence, and performance can be positively or negatively influenced by the various dimensions of attribution.[25]

Success attributed to internal causes such as ability, effort, or personality raises self-esteem and motivation, whereas attributions to external causes such as luck, task difficulty, weather, and officiating have no effect on self-esteem. Success attributed to factors over which students feel they have no control, such as the teacher's behavior, luck, or easy tasks, does not increase motivation. Success with minimal effort yields a strong sense of ability; overcoming challenging tasks through persistence results in a strong sense of self-efficacy.[26] Mastery-oriented subjects tend to take more credit for successes and more blame for failures and emphasize effort in achieving outcomes.

Failure by individuals with low perceived competence results in internal, uncontrollable, and stable attributions that lead to low expectations, a lack of persistence, and failure to improve performance. On the other hand, individuals with high perceived competence attribute failure to internal, controllable, and unstable causes leading to increased motivation, expected performance gains, and improved performance.[27]

Weinberg, Gould, and Jackson found that males displayed more positive self-talk, whereas females exhibited more negative self-talk. They suggested that failure for females may reflect on their ability, whereas males attribute failure to lack of effort.[28] Corbin and Nix discovered that girls have lower expectations than boys for motor skills.[29] These findings may explain why some students persist in the use of inappropriate responses "to camouflage their feelings of inadequacy."[30]

The theory of attribution helps us understand why some students persist and achieve with or without instruction and why others fail in spite of our help. Students with internal/stable attributions for failure consider themselves "helpless"; no matter what they do, they will not succeed. Even when they experience success, they attribute it to luck or easy tasks that anyone can do, so they don't expect success to occur again.

Maier and Seligman defined *learned helplessness* as the inappropriate conclusion that controllable events are uncontrollable after experiencing uncontrollable events.[31] Learned helplessness appears to be more likely when a subject attributes failure to achieve control to stable factors such as ability or task difficulty rather than changeable ones like lack of effort or bad luck. When faced with the same situation in the future, subjects give up, whereas in new situations they may respond normally.[32] It is important to remember that in many life situations, no control is possible and, in these instances, the best response may be to give up.[33] Learned helplessness in sport is instilled into females at an early age according to Greendorfer.[34] Teachers can help to counteract this tendency.

Martinek and Griffith provided some questions to help teachers identify learned helpless students:

1. Does the student always give up quickly when presented with a learning task?
2. Does the student fail to demonstrate a variety of strategies after an unsuccessful attempt at a learning task?
3. Does the student continually attribute his or her failure to lack of skill (e.g., "I am not good at this anyway").
4. Is the student always reluctant to take credit for any success (e.g., "I was really lucky on that shot!")
5. Does the student display an "I don't care" attitude toward various learning tasks? That is, does he or she simply "go through the motions"?[35]

They also caution teachers to verify the student's "yes" responses over a period of time and with confirmation by other teachers.

Some evidence indicates that students can be taught to attribute failure to lack of effort and thus do better on future tasks than children provided only with success experiences.[36] Various researchers have attempted to increase performance expectations, persistence, and performance in sport situations when failure is present by teaching students to attribute failure to internal, controllable, and unstable factors. Rudisill investigated perceived competence and causal dimension orientations on the expectations, persistence, and performance of junior high school-aged students. Students were divided into high or low perceived competence groups. Each group was further divided into three subgroups, which were presented with (a) internal, controllable, unstable dimensional orientations, (b) internal, uncontrollable, stable dimensional orientations, or (c) no dimensional orientations. Students were told their performance on a balancing task was below average for their age group. The high perceived competence students, regardless of causal dimension orientations, had higher expectations, persistence, and performance than low perceived competence students. Students taught internal, controllable, unstable orientations had higher expectations, persistence, and performance than the other students regardless of perceived competence. Expectancy results on the first trial suggested that females had lower performance expectations than males. Either high perceived competence or internal, controllable, unstable orientations appear to positively influence students' expectations, persistence, and

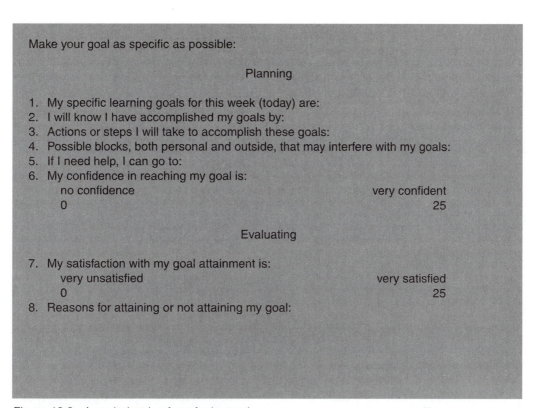

Make your goal as specific as possible:

Planning

1. My specific learning goals for this week (today) are:
2. I will know I have accomplished my goals by:
3. Actions or steps I will take to accomplish these goals:
4. Possible blocks, both personal and outside, that may interfere with my goals:
5. If I need help, I can go to:
6. My confidence in reaching my goal is:
    no confidence   very confident
    0   25

Evaluating

7. My satisfaction with my goal attainment is:
    very unsatisfied   very satisfied
    0   25
8. Reasons for attaining or not attaining my goal:

Figure 12.2 A goal-planning form for learned-helpless students.
Source: Alderman, M. Kay. (1990, September). Motivation for at-risk students. *Educational Leadership, 48*(1), 29.

performance. Thus, through causal dimension training, teachers can enhance the expectations, persistence, and performance of students who would normally drop out of motor activities due to failure.[37] Martinek and Griffith have also worked with learned helpless students and find that attributional retraining can help students succeed by trying harder.[38]

To break the cycle of failure—low expectations—helplessness, teachers must have a high sense of their own ability to influence student learning and motivation (self-efficacy), combined with high but realistic expectations for student achievement. They let students know they will be expected to achieve and that they will be taught in a way in which they will be able to achieve.

The learning environment must be structured so that student effort yields success. Alderman listed four steps to help learners achieve success.[39] Suggestions from Martinek and Griffith have been incorporated in the ideas listed to carry out these steps.[40]

Step 1. The first step is to set goals that are specific; hard, but attainable; and proximal (short-term). This can be accomplished by pretesting and analyzing student errors. A form that can be used to help students set goals is shown in figure 12.2. Students will need help with creating realistic goals.

Step 2. Several techniques can be used to help students select learning strategies to help them accomplish their goals. Mosston's inclusion style (see chapter 7) requires teachers to establish different levels for the same task. Thus, students could spike an official ball or Volley Lite ball, held or moving, over a net at 2 meters, 7'4" or 8'. As students experience success, they can progress to higher levels of the task by choosing which ball to use and where they want to practice (see Table 6.6 for ways to increase or decrease task difficulty.) Students can also be allowed to choose noncompetitive self-challenge activities rather than competitive activities in which students tend to be compared with each other. Another strategy that can be very effective with low-skilled learners is mastery learning. This was discussed in chapter 7.

A third method that appears to work with some students is the use of peer tutoring or heterogeneous learning groups, in which students help each other reach their performance goals. Whatever method is used, the teacher must be available to provide feedback and encouragement to students and helpers, and the strategy must not point out the difference of the learned helpless student. Other teachers in the school and parents also may help students who have become "helpless" in many areas of the curriculum.

Step 3. Focus is on progress made rather than on the end result. Students might graph their performance on a progress chart. The student must see that his or her own effort resulted in success (progress toward the goal). The teacher's role is to give feedback about why the student succeeded or failed.

Step 4. Once the skills have been learned well, the student may attribute success to ability. It is important for the student to see ability as something that can be learned. Once students have attributed success to effort and ability rather than to luck or easy tasks, they are on the road to increased self-efficacy—increased confidence in their ability to accomplish goals.

If failure occurs, help the student to attribute failure to an incorrect learning strategy rather than to lack of ability. Teachers who have alternative strategies can make them available as students need them.

Mastery-oriented classrooms stress progress and learning rather than performance and ability. Errors are viewed as part of the learning process, not as a lack of ability. Students in mastery-oriented classrooms have opportunities to correct errors by taking tests over or revising papers and projects.

When students succeed, teachers' self-efficacy also increases. As Alderman indicated, this type of intervention takes time and patience. The focus is on progress, not miracles.

The preceding studies indicate that increased levels of self-efficacy result in higher intrinsic motivation to participate in sport activities. Students with high self-worth tend to be intrinsically motivated, whereas students with low self-worth tend to be extrinsically motivated and were unsure of the forces responsible for their successes and failures.

Teacher Expectations or the Self-fulfilling Prophecy

Goethe is thought to have said, "If you treat an individual as he is, he will stay as he is. But if you treat him as if he were what he could and ought to be, he will become what he ought to be." The Pygmalion effect, so dramatically portrayed in George Bernard Shaw's *Pygmalion*, was demonstrated to occur in the classroom in studies by Rosenthal and Jacobson[41] and many others.[42] The studies discovered that students perform in agreement with the perceived expectations of their teachers. This was found to be especially true of disadvantaged children in urban schools. Brophy concluded that effective teachers perceive their students as being capable of learning and themselves as being capable of teaching effectively. They expect their students to learn and act accordingly.[43]

Studies of the self-fulfilling prophecy in physical education classes confirm that teacher expectations influence student performance.[44] They show that physical education teachers form expectations of students based on such factors as age or grade level, motor ability, physical attractiveness, perceived effort, and the presence or absence of a disability. For example, younger students tended to receive more nonverbal praise and encouragement (smiles, hugs, pats, and nods) than older students. However, teachers more readily accepted ideas from older students. Students with high skill levels received more praise, contact time with teachers, and criticism, perhaps because teachers felt they were more capable of capitalizing on the feedback than lower skilled learners. Teachers also had higher expectations for attractive students and students who "tried hard" or were most often on-task.

Although students are sensitive to teacher expectations, it appears that individual students interpret teacher behaviors differently.[45] Darley and Fazio described student attributions of teacher expectations as being of four types: (a) self-attributions, in which the student perceives personal factors as a cause of the problem, (b) teacher attributions, in which teacher characteristics are perceived to be the cause of the problem, (c) situational attributions, such as task difficulty or the learning environment, and (d) combinations of the three preceding categories.[46] Martinek found that the perceptions of students perceived by teachers to be low-skilled were similar to coded teacher behaviors, whereas high-skilled students perceived more teacher praise than actually existed. Low-skilled students were more inclined to explain teacher behaviors with self-attributions; high-skilled students explained them as due to teacher characteristics.[47]

Martinek cautioned that when low-skilled students internalize low teacher expectations, learned helplessness may result. He added, "For some students self-perceptions may be so strong that expectations that are counter to them may have little or no effect on the student." In fact, when teachers do give help, praise, or empathy, they may reinforce the student's perceptions of incapability.[48] Martinek and Karper found competitive environments to have a negative influence on the efforts of low-expectancy students in physical activity.[49]

Rink indicated a lack of teacher expectation for learning in physical education.[50] She suggested that teachers communicate higher expectations to students and provide learning environments that ensure student success.[51] She proposed three ways for teachers to communicate their expectations to students:

1. Present tasks holistically, concretely, and briefly using concrete examples, brief explanations, and cues.
2. Help students refine, extend, and apply tasks (rather than jumping from one skill to another)
3. Provide specific task-related feedback to students and modify tasks as needed to ensure student success.

Martinek proposed that students may not attend to teacher expectations; may misunderstand their expectations; or may not have the knowledge, skill, or motivation to respond appropriately.[52]

Hutslar pointed out that high expectations are positively correlated with achievement. Teacher expectations can be bad, however, when they negatively influence student performance or affect. She listed a number of questions teachers can ask themselves to evaluate their expectations:

1. Do I expect enough from my "low" ability students?
2. Do I present new and challenging material to my "low" as well as my "high" ability students?

3. Do I smile as frequently at my poorest students as I do at my best students, at my least favorite as my favorite student?
4. Do my nonverbal responses convey negative feelings to my "low" students (frowns, shrugs, rolling eyes)?
5. By creating a friendly environment, do I encourage all students to feel free to initiate a conversation with me?
6. Do I give as much corrective feedback on skill performance to my "low" ability students as my "high" ability students?
7. Do I praise and respond positively to appropriate behavior and good performance of my "low" students, or do I allow it to pass unnoticed?
8. Am I less tolerant of incorrect answers and inappropriate behavior of my "low" ability students?
9. Do I give my "low" ability students as much time to answer questions as my "high" ability students?[53]

She then suggested that teachers select several students and behavior categories and tally each interaction, and then set new interaction goals based on the findings. In this way teachers can make the pygmalion effect work in a positive direction by setting realistic and challenging expectations for all students.

Turner and Purkey emphasized the importance of teacher expectations with regard to student affect. They noted that "people respond best when they are invited to feel valuable, able, and responsible" and that student potential "is best realized in an environment that *intentionally* invites such development."[54] They suggested that teachers evaluate their teaching to determine whether intentional or unintentional *disinvitations* are exhibited and attempt to change them to *invitations*.

The implication for teaching is clear. Effective teachers believe that *all* of their students are capable of success and communicate that belief to their pupils. Teachers should carefully evaluate the ways they interact with students of all ability levels, all races, and both sexes.

Discipline

Of the major problems facing the public schools, discipline was ranked number one by the annual Gallup poll until 1986, when drugs took over the top position. Since then, discipline has taken the second or third spot.[55] Behavior problems are considered one of the major obstacles to successful teaching and considerably decrease student time-on-task.[56] Many teachers leave the teaching profession because of their inability to discipline.

Research shows that schools contribute to their students' academic achievement by establishing, communicating, and enforcing fair and consistent discipline policies.[57] Educators have a responsibility to organize and carry out effective discipline procedures by providing a productive learning atmosphere and teaching acceptable behavior. If a student is to behave in a disciplined manner, such behavior must be taught and learned. The schools are not solely responsible for teaching and monitoring discipline, but the results of their efforts are always in the public eye.

Students are critical of teachers who do not maintain adequate classroom control. They indicate that few teachers can teach well without establishing good class discipline. They are aware that beginning teachers often have less control than experienced teachers.

The most important concern in discipline, of course, is the establishment of a good learning environment, one in which students can grow both in knowledge and self-control. Each student has a basic right to an educational experience free from unnecessary distractions caused by a few unruly students. Good order, based on a cooperative effort of everyone involved, contributes both to the teacher's goal of optimum learning and to the student's growth as a responsible member of society.

What is discipline? Is it a set of rules, controlled behavior, a systematic method to obtain obedience, punishment, or moral and ethical behavior? Discipline is difficult to define because its meaning has evolved over the years to include many aspects of behavior. We often think of discipline as cut-and-dried standards of good versus bad. However, because each individual reacts differently to his or her environment, many variations in behavior may be accepted as disciplined.

Children go through various stages as they mature and come to understand control. Preschool children are trained to follow established rules and procedures. Children learn to relate to nonpersonal objects, becoming familiar with natural laws and governing themselves so as to use those laws for their own purposes. As children enter school, they are helped to develop a certain amount of conformity to group patterns, which we might call social control. They learn to relate to the culture and its institutions and to develop the capacity for some reciprocal adjustment with their environment. Finally, children learn to interact with others through a process of self-control. They interact on a psychological level and need no extrinsic reward or punishment.

Discipline becomes a process of helping youngsters adjust to their environment and develop acceptable inner controls. For purposes of discussion, discipline will be defined as *orderly social behavior in an atmosphere that allows meaningful learning to transpire*. It involves a slow progression from the direct, authoritative control of behavior needed by some learners to a desirable level of self-control experienced by only a few. In education today, emphasis is often placed on students' natural abilities to interpret situations and react accordingly (reaping the consequences of any undesired act) rather than on a strict code of behavior for all students.

Discipline involves both students and teachers. Teachers must know when to be authoritative, when to be permissive, and when to straddle the middle ground. Classes can change dramatically from one hour to the next or one week to another. Pep rallies, assemblies, lunchtime activities, weather, or the activities of previous classes can cause normally quiet students to stampede into a room. Success or failure with homework or previous assignments can affect the attitude of students before the lesson has even begun.

As students and teacher embark upon a day's activities, many things can happen. Ideally, both teacher and students will be successfully engaged in teaching and learning activities, neither interfering with the activities of the other. However, since teachers and students often have different personalities and values, conflict might occur, resulting in behavior unacceptable to either the teacher or the student.[58] Teachers must listen to the students' problems and attempt to understand and resolve them if possible. If the problem hinders the teacher's activities, the teacher must communicate to the student how he or she feels in an attempt to resolve the conflict. For example, the teacher might say, "I'm trying to help everyone learn . . . , but I can't when I'm constantly interrupted." Sometimes the student will understand and alter the behavior. Often the school or teacher has a specific policy for handling the behavior. If not, the teacher will be forced to (1) take a stand and authoritatively decide what to do to solve the problem, (2) allow the student to continue the behavior at the expense of the teacher and often of the other students, or (3) attempt to work out a solution that is acceptable to both parties.

A typical classroom usually consists of three groups of students: 80 percent rarely break rules or violate principles, 15 percent break rules on a somewhat regular basis and need teachers to set clear expectations and consequences for them or they will disrupt learning for other students, and 5 percent are chronic rule breakers and generally out of control most of the time. Nothing seems to work for them. They have typically experienced failure from an early age and maintain no hope for success in the future[59]

Raffini declared that teachers' ability to discipline depends on one of the following three contingencies:[60]

1. The teacher must develop student respect.
2. If respect is not possible, then the teacher must develop a reward or reinforcement system to control students.
3. If the above are not possible, the teacher must instill in students fear of the consequences for not doing as they are told.

Motivation and Preventive Discipline

The wise teacher realizes that discipline problems are most often preventable. The responsibility for discipline and motivation lies with the teacher. Preventive discipline is good teaching. It involves (1) belief in the worth of each student, (2) teacher modeling of mature behavior and appropriate ways to resolve problems, (3) a warm, supportive, well-organized environment, (4) well-planned, appropriate learning and assessment experiences, and (5) helping students learn self-direction and responsibility for their own behavior.

Belief in the Worth of Each Student

The key to classroom control comes from understanding the worth of each student and communicating that worth to them. Coloroso emphasized six critical life messages that students need to receive from teachers. They are as follows:

1. I believe in you.
2. I trust in you.
3. I know you can handle life's situations.
4. You are listened to.
5. You are cared for.
6. You are very important to me.[61]

Students need to feel self-worth and be able to say:

I like myself.
I can think for myself.
There is no problem so great it can't be solved.[62]

Teachers need to address learners' universal needs before individual differences can be attended to. One of these needs is self-esteem.[63] Self-esteem encompasses those ideas and thoughts a person has about himself or herself, which trigger strong emotions and feelings.

Learners achieve at levels in keeping with the picture they have of themselves, even when their ability shows they are capable of achieving at near-perfect levels.[64] This occurs because all persons act in ways that are rewarding and that maintain their current self as it is. Change (learning) occurs only when learners can maintain control of their lives and further support or enhance their current "self-picture." Achievement-oriented students picture themselves as capable of succeeding, whereas learned helpless students see themselves as failures.

One way to help students develop self-esteem is to focus on impact-oriented evaluation of instructional products rather than on product-oriented evaluation. Product-oriented evaluation labels a product as good or bad, right or wrong. Some students learn to play the game of discovering the teachers' and textbooks' right answers.[65] However, they may then find that their value depends on producing the "right" product, so they live in a precarious relationship with teachers. "What if I had not produced the desired product?" they ask. "Then my value would diminish. I am, therefore, subject to teacher control and lose my autonomy and identity as a person." This yields resentment and learning deterioration.[66] Impact-oriented evaluation, on the other hand, focuses on whether the product works and accomplishes its purpose. It asks such questions as:

Did it work?
Did it communicate?
Was it effective?
What effect did it have on you? On others?
Did it make a difference in someone? Feelings, ideas, actions?
If so, how? To what extent?
If not, why not?[67]

Active, cooperative learning yields a product that works.[68] Passive learning produces "right" answers.

Another way to help learners develop self-esteem is to look at students' characteristics. Look for the best in your students. Reinforce the positive characteristics by pointing them out to the students and to others. Look for positive qualities (independence) that are currently expressed by negative behavior (stubbornness). Reinforce positive, appropriate ways to express these qualities. Ignore negative items that are merely a matter of personal taste, preference, or style.[69]

Avoid comparing students with each other. Physical educators often post charts on the walls or shout out numbers during physical fitness testing. Be careful with students' fragile self-esteem. How would you feel if you were ranked number 32? Cardinal suggested creating a "bump board," in which the top three performers are listed by age, sex, or class. Students are constantly trying to get on the board, stay on the board, or move up on the board, and the names are constantly changing. This recognizes the outstanding performers, without threatening the rest of the class.[70]

Glasser maintained that "the major problem of the schools is a problem of failure."[71] He further suggested that educators need to examine why children fail and provide schools in which children can succeed. Youth who feel the concern and acceptance of a teacher can gain self-confidence, which in turn enhances self-motivation. These factors constitute the foundation for success. A student experiencing success is much more likely to anticipate each learning activity and participate in an orderly way than a student who is not experiencing success. Once the cycle of success within each student is in operation, class control is more effective. Teachers must be committed to helping students succeed and show a genuine concern for each of them. This concern for learners involves the following:

1. Caring: helping students feel they are liked.
2. Understanding: creating an atmosphere of empathy and tolerance.
3. Identification: considering students as separate, worthy individuals.
4. Recognition: appreciating students' unique contributions.[72]

All cognitive units should include corresponding affective (feeling) experiences. Retention requires an investment of feelings.[73]

A Warm, Supportive, Well-Organized Environment

The learning climate is a result of the effects of the teacher's attitudes and behavior on students' feelings and thoughts about their personal safety and self-esteem.[74] The personality, self-confidence, and attitudes of the teacher communicate to the students that the teacher cares about them and about the subject that is being taught.

Chandler suggested using an invitational approach to physical education in which physical educators "invite students to succeed." He defined an invitation as "informal or formal messages sent verbally or nonverbally to students, teachers, parents and others . . . to inform them that they, the recipients, are valuable, able, and responsible."[75] Purkey suggested some things teachers could do to achieve this.[76] Some other suggestions have also been added.

1. Teach students, not sports. A psychological insight into the background, needs, and characteristics of students and the causes of behavioral problems can be helpful. Be aware of and responsive to student interests and concerns. Try to understand their world and their heroes, fads, fashions, and interests. Be a mentor and guide for them.
    a. Learn their names, greet them at the door or in the locker room, and see them off.
    b. Create a special, caring environment.
    c. Share a thought or current event.
    d. Get to know and introduce new students.
    e. Let students know they are missed.
    f. Tell others about good things students do.
    g. Give emotional support as needed. Praise when appropriate. Provide encouragement to attain goals.
    h. Seek out opportunities to help students succeed and then point out their successes to the class.[77]
    i. Make positive comments to them about their individual improvement, effort, sportspersonship, and teamwork.
    j. Share duties with students, such as taking roll and distributing and collecting equipment.
    k. Always treat students with dignity.
    l. Involve students in decisions.
    m. Play games with no winners or losers.
    n. Touch kids (even junior high and high school kids) when talking to them. A pat on the back, high five, hug, touch on the shoulder, or handshake can help kids bond with you. Don't touch if you are angry with a student, if you are sexually attracted to a student, or if you know the student has been abused. Students can be taught the difference between good and bad touch.[78]
2. Listen to students in a way that indicates that you care. When you listen you say, "You are important!" Listen not just for the story but also for why the student is telling you something. Respond to the feelings that are expressed. Don't try to "fix it and make it better." Rather, help the student explore alternatives if there is a problem to solve.[79]
    a. Ask for student input instead of assuming you know what they want or why they did what they did.
    b. Have a gripe box. Read the gripes to the class and get their input.[80]
3. Recognize special people and times. Activities that bring social approval to students not only increase motivation but also individual self-esteem.
    a. Remember birthdays.
    b. Post a picture and historical sketch of the student of the month.

c. Post a "player of the week"-type award on the bulletin board for any specified behavior such as leadership, sportspersonship, effort, or skill performance.

d. Award fun prizes for unusual accomplishments, such as the golden arrow for the most bulls-eyes (an old arrow sprayed gold) or the belle of the ball for most matches played (a tennis ball dressed in a gown) or the sneaker award (an old sneaker) to the most-improved runner on the physical fitness test.

e. Put articles about students in the school or community newspaper.

f. Use school assemblies to showcase student talents.

g. Praise the student to other teachers.

4. Send explicit, unconditional invitations supporting students, such as "I think you can do it" rather than "You can do it *if* you . . ."

5. Get to know students' families. Have a family night in which a parent and child participate in activities together.

6. Share your personal background with the students—your spouse, children, where you are from. Allow one student each week to ask you a question and ask a question of one student each week.[81]

7. Create an inviting physical environment using neat, colorful bulletin boards and posters to brighten the surroundings and attractively displayed slogans and signs politely encouraging students to do something.

8. Encourage interest in physical education.

a. Invite students to draw posters about an activity and its history.

b. Have students bring in little known facts.

c. Ask students to bring their records or tapes to play during warm-up exercises (check tapes before using them).

d. Bertel suggested starting an activity just like it might have been played by its inventors and then adding rules, skills, and strategies as the need arises. Once the students become involved, they will want to learn more. For example, basketball can be played with peach baskets or the old rules of three dribbles before passing or shooting.[82]

e. Share inspiring sports stories.

9. Develop class spirit. Have students choose a name, motto, emblem, or color.

10. Provide opportunities for students to safely make avoidance responses and reduce aggressive behavior, such as punching a bag instead of a student or taking time out to cool off.[83]

11. Invite administrators, parents, and others to become involved in physical education by teaching special activities or skills or to be an audience for student presentations.

12. Create positive, pleasant relationships with all students. Help students develop positive interpersonal relations skills with teachers and other students. Relationships should be based on mutual respect.

13. Be professionally responsible, working through counselors and administrators to correct potential problems, confronting students professionally about their behavior, and seeing students as they *can be,* not as they are.

Motivation can also be increased by effective classroom management. When large numbers of students continually disrupt the learning environment, it typically means that something is wrong with the classroom management system. When teachers plan and implement an effective management system, students know what is expected of them and are busily engaged in achieving expectations. Some teacher behaviors that can be used to enhance classroom management were included in chapter 10.

Teacher Modeling

Teachers can model mature, effective behavior and appropriate ways to solve problems, including admitting their mistakes and accepting student's mistakes. They should also be proper role models of what they teach by incorporating good fitness practices into their lifestyles and demonstrating their enthusiasm and love for physical activity. Teachers with good discipline in their classes exhibit some similarities in their authority style, but there is no specific formula that will produce good discipline for all teachers. Effective discipline tends to emanate from teachers who

1. are positive role models. They
   a. are assertive rather than aggressive.
   b. act rather than react.
   c. are consistent rather than inconsistent.
   d. clearly communicate expectations rather than being vague.
   e. convey interest and enthusiasm rather than disinterest and boredom.
   f. set realistic goals rather than unrealistic goals.
2. are efficient planners.
3. are effective communicators.
4. are thorough assessors of
   a. their own teaching behavior, which they modify when needed.
   b. students and their learning styles.
5. are consistent in their expectations of children.[84]

Teachers should take responsibility for their own behaviors, including dressing appropriately, starting class on time, teaching in an interesting manner, returning papers in a reasonable time period, helping students learn, and ending on time.[85]

Well-Planned, Appropriate Learning and Assessment Experiences

The establishment of an interesting, relevant, challenging curriculum that is responsive to the needs of the students (e.g., love, control, freedom, fun) can be accomplished best by involving students in the planning stages. Students can be asked to survey student interests and curricular offerings that allow students to choose between several possible units. An example of a selective curriculum is given in chapter 15.

Students need programs that are well organized and related to their needs and abilities. A mismatch between student interests and abilities and instruction invites discipline problems. When students act out it may be to protect themselves against frustration or failure with a too difficult assignment or boredom with one that is too easy. Talking rather than doing also contributes to boredom, inattention, and deviant behavior. When learning is too easy, students find little value in it. Physical educators generally need to have higher expectations for student achievement. In 90 percent of research studies, specific, difficult goals produced better performance than easy, do-your-best, or no goals.[86] Involvement in challenging learning activities not only contributes to the opportunity for success but also keeps students busily engaged in positive behavior with little or no time or incentive for irrational, unruly behavior.

To determine learner readiness for certain skills, ask the questions, "Are students physically and emotionally ready to learn the material?" and "Do students have the prerequisite facts, intellectual skills, and strategies necessary for learning?" Introducing skills before a student is ready may result in failure and negative consequences on the learner's self-image. Therefore, readiness has implications regarding the sequencing of skills within the curriculum. Readiness for physical education activities depends on maturation, previous experience, and attitudes toward the subject. Readiness for a given activity differs among students and in the same student from time to time. Physical readiness depends on maturation; general motor development including strength, coordination, endurance, balance, speed, and agility; and prerequisite skills. Prerequisite skills include basic locomotor skills such as running and jumping and fundamental skills such as throwing, catching, and striking. Teachers can increase student readiness for future learning by providing a background in a wide variety of activities.[87]

Students are not unmotivated. As McKeachie indicated, "They are learning all the time—new dance steps, the status hierarchy on campus, football strategy, etc."[88] Teachers need to realize this and capitalize on "what turns students on." Students are much more motivated to learn and remember material that is meaningful. Teachers must put themselves in the shoes of their students to determine what is meaningful to them.

Wlodkowski developed the "time continuum model" to increase student motivation. Each of his three basic time phases has a motivational focus, structure, and activities. At the beginning of instruction, the focus is on developing a positive *attitude* toward the subject. This is done by discussing why the subject is important to learn and how it relates to students' needs. In the middle of the instruction, the focus is on *stimulation* of students' minds through cooperative learning, high-level thinking, and creativity (the kinds of learning *not* provided by television) while continuing to meet the affective needs of learners. At the end of instruction, helping the student achieve *competence* is paramount. *Reinforcement* of the desired learning is necessary to promote a desire to continue learning.[89]

Certain instructional techniques enhance motivation. Students generally prefer to be involved in cooperative and competitive learning activities with their friends. Stress cooperation, progress, and achievement rather than competition. Group students heterogeneously (different skill levels in the same group). Match group size with the task to be accomplished. Give clear directions about the end product required—a presentation, performance, paper, and so on. Help students develop communication and sportspersonship skills. Utilize task sheets, contracts, and other individualized learning materials to allow students some choice over their own activities while keeping them on task. Make learning fun and enjoyable. Use humor to lighten things up. Select older students who have been in trouble and need to feel good about themselves to work with younger students.[90]

Vary your presentation techniques. Adolescents have an attention span of about 15 minutes, so use at least three different teaching techniques during a 45- to 50-minute class period (e.g., lecture, small group discussions, report back to large group, short writing assignment or review previous skill, model new skill, practice new skill using task sheets, play lead-up game).

Involve students in evaluating their own performances. Students can give input on ways to assess their behavior, what to put on tests, and how to evaluate the results. They can write questions, administer and score tests, and keep plots of their progress. With teacher evaluation, students develop an external locus of control, whereas student evaluation helps students develop an internal locus of control. Helping students evaluate their own work helps them become more responsible and self-directed. Student self-evaluations can become a portion of the final grade. Both teacher and student assessment should be directed toward promoting student development.[91]

Students who have never received good grades don't believe they are possible, so they don't try; it is more rewarding to be a nuisance and get peer approval. One teacher gave all of her students As or Bs and then each quarter told them that they would have to work just a little harder to maintain that grade. Make it genuinely possible for all students to receive an A or B.[92]

Helping Students Learn Self-Direction and Responsibility

The right to be in school carries certain responsibilities. Students are responsible for coming prepared, not giving excuses, and doing their own work.[93] Teachers are responsible for teaching students how to be prepared, social skills for interacting with others, and how to solve problems that arise in the classroom.

Students need the guidance and security provided by well-defined rules of expected behavior and the knowledge that adults care enough about them to enforce those rules. Children raised without correction have lower self-esteem, are more dependent, achieve less, and have less control over their world.[94] A study of appropriate behavior in a low socioeconomic level junior high school revealed that the teacher with discipline problems failed to enforce rules and monitor behavior of students.[95] The results substantiated Durkheim's premise that "children themselves are the first to appreciate good discipline."[96] Teachers need to remember that it takes courage to discipline, but that students want it and they will respect and like the teacher who is a good disciplinarian.[97]

Until teachers and students know each other, discipline usually begins in a serious, no-nonsense manner with adult rule and pupil obedience. Good teachers establish clear, consistent direction, use routine procedures for recurring situations, practice skills with the class, and manage in a fair and predictable fashion. The teacher then attempts to work toward student self-control by planning with individuals in the class.

Teacher-directed group planning, in which the scope and area of planning are predetermined, is the next step toward self-direction. Help students set their own class rules. Define a few clear, specific guidelines that define teacher and student roles and behaviors, with a range of natural or logical consequences appropriate for the age level involved. Students learn to make choices and to gain control of their own learning situation. Encourage student involvement in solving problems that arise.

Self-management through group planning is achieved only after all of the other skills and understandings needed have been achieved. Even after self-direction in known areas has been achieved, however, some students will fail to be self-directing when a new situation presents itself. For this reason, patterns of control must be applied according to the appropriateness of the situation. At times the teacher needs to provide the students with a choice between self-direction and teacher direction and let them decide which will be more valuable to them in the specific learning environment.

Student leadership can also be used to help students develop responsibility. For example, students can be asked to serve as warm-up leaders, team and squad captains, and equipment monitors. Rotate these opportunities often so all students eventually get a chance to serve. Some students who normally would be chosen last might be selected to do this early in the year.

Discipline Models

A number of systematic approaches to discipline have been proposed, some of which may be applicable to physical education. Five models of discipline are presented in Tables 12.1 to 12.5. The first two models, Behavior Modification and Assertive Discipline are models in which teacher control is the primary factor. In the last three models, Logical Consequences, Transactional Analysis, and Reality Therapy/Control Theory, student responsibility and self-discipline are stressed. In the following pages, a number of disciplinary techniques will be discussed that are helpful in implementing these models.

Table 12.1 Behavior Modification Model

Principles

Behavior is controlled by external consequences.

Behavior that is positively reinforced is repeated.

Behavior that is negatively reinforced is avoided.

Behavior that is no longer reinforced is reduced.

Discipline Strategies

Conditioning—getting students to respond in a specific way to a specific stimulus

Shaping—rewarding behavior that comes closer and closer to the desired goal

Reinforcement—use of a thing or event following a behavior to increase the likelihood that a person will repeat the behavior

1. Competence (skill acquisition)
2. Being correct (feedback)
3. Social approval (praise)
4. Contingent activity (for example, "Do . . . and then you can have five minutes of free time.")
5. Tokens or check marks (exchanged for other reinforcers)
6. Tangibles (ribbons, trophies)
7. Edibles (food, candies)[a]

Extinction—occurs when a response or behavior is no longer reinforced (e.g., ignoring inappropriate behavior)

Punishment—applies negative consequences to a behavior to decrease its frequency

Time-out—removal from reinforcement

Advantages

Easy to learn

Immediate results

Saves class time

Works with all age groups

Compatible with teacher's need for control

Limitations

Based on extrinsic rewards, thus results may end when rewards are terminated

May be considered as bribery

Does not encourage development of student responsibility

Students and teachers may become adversaries.

Is especially helpful to teachers who have lost control of classroom behavior, since desirable behavior is rewarded and encouraged.[b] The problem with reinforcement theory is "not that it is wrong, but that it might become true; that is, that learners might start to believe that the world controls them rather than that they can control it."[c]

Source: Becker, W. C., Englemann, S., & Thomas, D. R. (1971). *Teaching: A course in applied psychology* (p. 171). Palo Alto, CA: Science Research Associates.

[a] Tillman, M., Bersoff, D., & Dolly, J. (1976). *Learning to Teach: A Decision-Making System* (p. 361). Lexington, MA: Heath.

[b] Dorr, D. (1975). "Behavior Modification in the Schools." In W. D. Gentry (Ed.), *Applied Behavior Modification* (p. 38). Saint Louis, MO: Mosby.

[c] Wittrock, M. C. (1978). "The Cognitive Movement in Instruction." *Educational Psychologist, 13,* 20.

Table 12.2 Assertive Discipline Model

Principles

Based on the premise that students have a right to learn, teachers have a right to teach, and parents have a right to know

Master teachers assertively teach students how to behave by
   establishing classroom rules and procedures to produce an optimum learning environment.
   reinforcing appropriate behaviors.
   punishing inappropriate behaviors.

Discipline Strategies

1. Establish clear rules, communicate them to students, and teach students to follow them.

2. Catch students being good. Praise each student every day. Reinforce positive behaviors. Rewards might include: (1) personal attention, (2) positive notes or phone calls to parents, (3) awards, (4) special privileges at home or at school, (5) individual or class rewards.

3. Tell students at the beginning of the year the consequences for misbehavior. Include a maximum of five consequences with which you are comfortable. For example: (1) a warning, (2) time-out, (3) loss of privileges, (4) call the parent, (5) go to the principal's office. Use firm, consistent negative consequences, but only after ensuring that students understand and have practiced the rule.

4. Be consistent and fair in applying the consequences.

Advantages

Easy to learn and use

Involves parents and administrators

Compatible with teacher's personal desire for control

Limitations

Punishment may result in undesirable behaviors.

Group misbehavior is difficult to resolve.

Students may be embarrassed.

The model fails to teach students responsibility.

Teachers often fail to include the positive aspects of this model.

Sources: Canter, L. (1989, September). "Assertive Discipline—More Than Names on the Board and Marbles in a Jar." *Phi Delta Kappan, 71*(1), 57–61; Canter, L., & Canter, M. (1976). *Assertive Discipline: A Take-Charge Approach for Today's Educator.* Seal Beach, CA: Canter and Associates; Canter, L., & Canter, M. (1981). *Assertive Discipline Follow-Up Guidebook.* Los Angeles: Canter and Associates.

Table 12.3 Logical Consequences Model

Principles

Students should have freedom of choice.

Students need to belong and be accepted. Failure to achieve acceptance results in attention-seeking, power struggles, attempts to get revenge, or displaying inadequacy.

Discipline Strategies

Encouragement for effort, rather than praise for achievement

Steps:

1. Teachers attempt to ascertain and help students understand their motives.
2. Students are helped to substitute useful goals for inappropriate ones.
3. Students and teachers use class discussions to create common goals and expectations, improve cooperation and communication skills, and develop responsibility.
4. Students and teachers use logical consequences for improper behavior (e.g., if students damage equipment, they can spend time repairing equipment or pay for a replacement).

Advantages

Helps students learn correct behavior and accept responsibility for their behavior

Promotes mutual respect between students and teachers

Relies on logical consequences rather than punishments

Limitations

Teachers may have difficulty ascertaining students' motives for their behavior.

Class discussions take time.

Teachers must be willing to allow students more control over discipline.

Sources: Edwards, C. H. (1993). *Classroom Discipline and Management* (pp. 75–98). New York: Macmillan; Dreikurs, R., Grunwald, B. B., & Pepper, F. C. (1982). *Maintaining Sanity in the Classroom: Classroom Management Techniques* (2nd ed.). New York: Harper & Row; Dreikurs, R., & Cassel, P. (1972). *Discipline Without Tears*. New York: Hawthorne Books.

Table 12.4 Transactional Analysis Model

Principles

Students and teachers have three ego-states in the subconscious mind, developed from their life's experiences, which affect everyday behavior:

Parent:	Rules, admonitions, laws issued by parents during early childhood; controlling and directing
Child:	Children's responses to gain approval of parents in early childhood; compulsive and expressive
Adult:	Examines and monitors the Parent and Child to determine useful, valid behaviors under current conditions

Four life positions evolve:

I'm OK—You're OK:	Involves self-worth and ability to deal realistically with life situations
I'm not OK—You're OK	
I'm OK—You're not OK	Involve feelings
I'm not OK—You're not OK	

Discipline Strategies

Teachers use transactional analysis principles in interacting with students:

1. Students play "games" to cover up I'm not OK feelings (using Child and Parent ego-states).

2. Teachers analyze games to determine student motives, refuse to play the games by remaining as Adults, and then provide "stroking" to help students feel accepted.

Teachers teach students transactional analysis to help them reach an I'm OK—You're OK condition.

Advantages

Can help students understand their own behavior and develop constructive interpersonal relationships both in and out of school

Limitations

Is difficult to learn and apply for teachers and/or students

Applies primarily to verbal interactions

Sources: Harris, T. A. (1967). *I'm OK—You're OK*. New York: Avon Books; Berne, E. (1972). *Games Students Play*. Millbrae, CA: Celestial Arts.

Table 12.5   Reality Therapy/Control Theory Model

Principles

Persons who can fulfill their needs through responsible behavior will have no need to act irresponsibly. These needs are the need to know that one is of worth to oneself and to others and the need to love and be loved.

Reality therapy depends on three factors: (1) acceptance of the person but rejection of irresponsible behavior; (2) a meaningful relationship between teacher and student; and (3) educating the student to fulfill his or her needs in responsible ways, thus encouraging better behavior.

Control theory is based on helping students control their own behavior so as to satisfy their needs for love, control, freedom, and fun in a legitimate way.

A "Quality School" satisfies the students' needs by providing meaningful experiences that satisfy students needs for survival, love, power, fun, and freedom, while achieving a high level of quality.

Discipline Strategies

The teacher helps the student (1) identify the inappropriate behavior, (2) identify the consequences of the behavior, (3) make a value judgment about the behavior, (4) make a plan, and (5) follow the plan. To do this, the teacher asks the following questions:

1. What is your goal? What do you want to happen?

2. What are you doing? *or* What did you do?

3. Is that what you should be doing? *or* How will that help you?

4. What is your plan? *or* What will you do that will help you?

5. What will be the consequences?

6. What can I do to help you?

Class meetings are used to develop group norms, plans, and consequences.

A quality school is established to lead rather than coerce students.

Advantages

Promotes student responsibility; helps students understand their needs and determine possible consequences of their behavior and solutions to their discipline problems

Promotes interpersonal communication skills

Limitations

Teachers may feel threatened by helping students satisfy their need for control.

Classroom meetings take time that could be used for instruction.

Teachers may find it difficult to help students work through the individual and group processes necessary.

Sources: Glasser, W. (1969). *Schools Without Failure*. New York: Harper & Row; Glasser, W. (1965). *Reality Therapy: A New Approach to Psychiatry*. New York: Harper & Row; Glasser, W. (1986). *Control Theory in the Classroom*. New York: Harper & Row; Glasser, W. (1990). *The Quality School: Managing Students Without Coercion*. New York: Harper & Row.

Choosing/Creating a Personal Discipline Model

In the beginning of this book, we discussed the importance of developing a personal philosophy of education and physical education. The discipline model that you choose to implement should match these philosophies. You may need to choose elements from several models so that your personal model will work for you. Remember that the Behavior Modification Model and the Assertive Discipline Model are teacher-centered. For this reason they may be easier for a beginning teacher to use. The Logical Consequences, Transactional Analysis, and Reality Therapy/Control Theory models will undoubtedly take more time to learn, but they will help you to develop the self-esteem and responsibility of your students. You may need to study them carefully and then role-play them with your peers to make sure you can implement the techniques associated with them in your classes. As Curwin and Mendler indicated:

> True discipline does not come from the quick mastery or the implementation of a packaged method. Effective discipline comes from the heart and soul of the teacher. It comes from the belief that teaching students to take responsibility for their behavior is as much the "job" of the teacher as teaching [the subject].[98]

Acceptable Disciplinary Practices

Henkel studied teacher control strategies and classified them into three areas. First, teachers suspected or anticipated misconduct and took precautions to avoid problems. Second, when misconduct occurred, teachers tutored students to modify their conduct. Third, when serious misconduct occurred, teachers imposed unpleasant consequences, such as time-out or loss of privileges.[99]

Each student is an individual, so it may be necessary to vary actual discipline practices or consequences according to individual needs. Students who have been disciplined should not be made to feel uneasy. Try to interact with these students in an accepting way.

Teachers must decide what discipline practices work for them. Teachers striving to incorporate acceptable practices should remember the following guidelines: (1) Solve your own problems whenever possible, (2) be available and visible, (3) admit mistakes, (4) take advantage of the teaching moment, and (5) look for causes of misconduct.

Waiting Aggressively

Waiting aggressively is a teacher tactic that lets students know they must pay attention. Such waiting should be obvious. Waiting signals can include a frown, a shake of the head, a clearing of the throat, a disapproving look at an offender, a mild reproof, or movement toward the trouble spot. Often these techniques will resolve problems before they become difficult.

Rewards

Extrinsic and intrinsic rewards are based on reinforcement theory. Extrinsic rewards are external to the learner and are result-oriented—a good grade, peer recognition, or teacher approval. Intrinsic rewards are internally perceived and controlled by the learner. They include the pleasure derived from participation or competence in the activity itself, self-confidence, self-discovery, pride, or personal progress.

Studies have demonstrated that when intrinsic motivation is present, extrinsic rewards can actually decrease satisfaction in the activity.[100] Deci, however, isolated two kinds of rewards, only one of which results in a deterioration of intrinsic motivation. Rewards that intend to make students do what the teacher wants, when and where the teacher wants it done, are called *controlling* rewards. *Informative* rewards, such as "good work" written on a student's paper, provide feedback about their competence and self-determination. Deci's results showed that when teachers stressed the informative nature of rewards rather than the controlling nature, students were more intrinsically motivated, had more positive attitudes toward themselves, and were more self-directing.[101]

Harter described two general functions of rewards. *Motivational* rewards, used as incentives, increase the chances of a child's engaging in certain activities. The degree of pleasure or satisfaction experienced also influences the child's developing self-reward system. The *informative* function tells the child what goals are worthy and appropriate and provides feedback on the child's success in achieving those goals. When deciding how to behave in complex situations, younger children appear more responsive to adult feedback, whereas older children consider social (adult and or peer) feedback and the objective consequences of their behavior as compared with their internalized standards of success and failure. As children develop, they need less extrinsic motivation. Intrinsically motivated students are capable of operating on a "relatively thin schedule of reinforcement."[102]

Harter also found that for older children, boys had significantly more intrinsic motivation, whereas girls relied more heavily on adult approval. However, tremendous variability existed within gender groups as well as considerable overlap between boys and girls. When girls are equally or more competent than boys on skills, no differences in intrinsic motivation have been found. Teachers can help students of both sexes acquire proficiency in activities and develop strong feelings of self-efficacy in movement patterns.[103]

Some teachers worry about the use of extrinsic rewards in the classroom. Remember that reinforcement is a part of life. Adults are rewarded with pay checks, recognition by society, praise from friends or bosses, and many other types of reinforcement. In fact, modifications in behavior are constantly being made by those who interact with others in the environment. It is the same in school. Teachers must take students as they are and assist them in trying out new kinds of behavior until they learn the satisfaction that comes from success in the activity itself. Students, like adults, choose whether they will respond to rewards. As La Mancusa stated, "The teacher does neither himself nor his students a favor by perpetuating the climate of failure."[104] Giving students attention for good behavior is far more desirable than giving them attention for misbehavior. Reprimands tend only to increase the behaviors they are intended to eliminate. Consistently ignored behaviors tend to increase in frequency initially and then weaken and disappear.

Becker identified three ways in which reinforcers lose their effectiveness.[105] One is *competing reinforcers*. These are reinforcers available from a source other than the teacher, such as those from the peer group. Second is *satiation,* in which the reinforcer has been used so often that it loses its effectiveness. Third is the *lack of transfer* of reinforcers to new situations. When learning a new task, the learner may fail to understand that the rules for achieving reinforcement are the same. Several solutions to these problems include withholding reinforcement for a short time to make it worthwhile again, changing the reinforcer, or strengthening the reinforcer. Reinforcement is not effective with all students. Avoid overdoing special privileges and material rewards. Sander suggests that good behavior should be the expectation and the norm rather than something done to earn a reward.[106]

Contingency Contracting

Most of us have practiced behavior modification on ourselves. You might be saying to yourself right now, "As soon as I finish reading this chapter, I'm going to eat a snack." That is an example of contingency contracting. *Contingency contracting* is reinforcement that is contingent on the performance of the desired behavior. An example of the technique is Grandma's law discussed in chapter 10. A more-sophisticated explanation was developed by Premack and is called the Premack principle.[107] It suggests that any behavior that occurs frequently can be used to reinforce a behavior that occurs less frequently. For example, "obtaining high performance scores" (a highly-desired result) becomes a reinforcer for practicing one's skills (a less-desired result).

Contingency contracting can be used along with extinction to reduce undesirable behavior, to develop new behavior, or to strengthen and maintain existing behavior. Joyce and Weil described contingency contracting as "the heart of effective classroom management."[108] According to Homme,[109] contingency contracts should be

1. *Clear*—The directions should be stated in explicit terms that are easily understood by the student, such as:
   If you do . . . , then you will get. . . .
   If you do . . . , then I will do. . . .
   If you do . . . , then you may do. . . .
   (Note: *You* is a student or a group.)
2. *Fair*—The two sides of the contract must be of relatively equal importance.
3. *Honest*—The reward should be given immediately *after* the performance but *only* for the performance specified in the contract.
4. *Positive*—The contract *should not* say, "If you do . . . , then I will *not* do . . . .
5. *Systematic*—The instructor should be consistent in reinforcing only the desired behavior.

The following procedures will help when establishing a contract:

1. Clearly specify a few rules that tell exactly what is expected. Limit rules to five or less.[110] Establish the target behavior in terms of performance and criteria for achievement. Establish what the reward will be for correct performance. Stress academic achievement rather than obedience.[111] Academic achievement is usually incompatible with disruptive behavior. Maintain a fair contract.
2. Initiate a contract with students. The contract may be a short statement by the teacher that states the consequences to be gained by certain behaviors.
3. Ignore disruptive, nondestructive behavior.
4. Reward the student immediately after completion of the desired behavior. Initial rewards are given for behavior that approximates the goal (e.g., small, simple tasks). Later, behaviors should be increasingly close to the final objective.
5. Use a variety of reinforcers to reward appropriate behaviors. Work toward the use of higher-order reinforcers and an intermittent reinforcement schedule (random or unpredictable reinforcement) to increase resistance to extinction. This reduces teacher approval to only a few times a day. The needs of each individual will determine what things or events will serve as reinforcers. Teachers can plan in advance to see what is reinforcing and what is not for their particular students. To be worthwhile, rewards must be highly desirable and not obtainable outside the conditions of the contract.[112]
6. Be consistent in following the plan.
7. Progress from teacher-directed contracts to mutually directed contracts to student-initiated contracts.

Examples of contingency management programs include the Champions program, in which students earn points for good behavior and lose points for inappropriate behavior. By accumulating a certain number of points, students are awarded a Champions sweatband of the color earned.[113] Colored chips have also been used as a behavior management tool.[114] In one school, students earn soda cards that can be redeemed in the principal's office. Students should write their names on the cards so other students do not steal them.[115]

Several studies have been conducted in physical education settings. Vogler and French used smiley face and frowny face tokens, which students could exchange for free-time activities, to successfully increase on-task behavior.[116] Paese rewarded students for appropriate dress with free gym time and choice of activities and increased the percentage of students dressed for activity from 71 percent to 92 percent.[117]

Different personalities of teacher and student, different student learning styles, and different environmental conditions can affect the success or failure of contingency contracting.

Contingent Activities

Contingent activities can be a reward for a goal fulfilled. Such activities should always be positive. Physical activity must never be negative, such as using running or push-ups as punishment for the losers of the game or for inappropriate behavior. Some possible activities include the following:

1. Reward class effort by letting students play novelty games or make up their own games.
2. Allow students who complete assigned tasks early to set up a game or match of their choice, practice on their own, or use specialized equipment (e.g., a ball machine).

Since preferred activities can serve as reinforcers, all instructors have to do is observe students to determine what activities they like to do best. Teachers can even ask students what activities are worth working for.

Social Reinforcement and Praise

How the teacher uses reinforcers frequently determines their success, because teachers themselves are one of the major sources of classroom motivation. Enthusiasm, facial expression, animation, and vocal intensity are some of the important qualities a teacher can exhibit.

Praise is used extensively in physical education even though research shows that it is often ineffective. Brophy found, however, that praise correlates positively with academic achievement for children of low socioeconomic status.

Introverts, low-skilled students, minority group students, and those with an external locus of control tend to respond to praise more than their counterparts. Students with the opposite traits are generally intrinsically motivated and may respond negatively to praise, resulting in decreased motivation. In fact, adults and high school students tend to perceive individuals who are praised for their successes, but given neutral feedback on their failures, as having lower ability levels, in contrast to those who receive criticism for their failures and neutral feedback for their successes. Praise, then, appears to convey information about teacher goals and desires and correct answers rather than serving as a reinforcer to student learning.[118]

The effects of praise vary with students' experience, personality, and previous successes and failures. Some students find praise embarrassing; others encourage and even elicit praise from teachers. Use praise only when it is sincere. However, either praise or criticism may be more motivating to many students than ignoring the student.

Praise correctly rather than often. Verbal praise can be effectively supplemented by written praise on student work and by teaching students to set realistic goals, evaluate their own performance, and provide self-reinforcement. Students also need to be taught to attribute success to their own abilities and effort rather than to external causes. As with the self-fulfilling prophecy, individual students react differently to praise.[119] Catch students being good. Praise each student every day.[120] Reinforce positive behaviors rather than focus on negative behaviors.[121] Sander suggests written reports or letters to parents and positive verbal feedback.[122]

To be effective, praise must be contingent on correct performance, specific to the performance, and sincere. Privately given praise based on specified performance criteria (including effort) is effective.[123] General, nonspecific praise is not usually regarded by students as credible. Moreover, it can create anxiety and put students into a dependent mode. When students are praised for high achievement, they may feel insecure because they don't know whether they can maintain the high achievement. In addition, they are subject to criticism from their peers. The other students feel insecure because their efforts are not of value to the teacher unless they get high marks. Thus, self-worth and achievement are equated. Self-worth should not be based on performance. Students can also see praise as manipulative and react adversely. Expressing feelings of appreciation or positive feelings about the high quality of students' work can have a good effect.[124]

Brophy stated that boys get more praise and criticism simply because they are more active; they get more of all kinds of teacher interaction. Boys tend to be praised more for achievement and girls for such traits as neatness and following directions. On the other hand, girls are more often criticized for unacceptable achievement, whereas boys are criticized for speaking out of turn and sloppy work. These factors have serious implications for self-concept, especially for girls, who apparently internalize teacher criticism as a deficiency in their abilities, since they have been praised for their effort and obedience. Boys, on the other hand, generally blame their failures on external circumstances and their successes on their own abilities and, therefore, maintain positive self-concepts.[125]

Tokens or Points

Tokens or points can be collected to be exchanged at a later time for a specific reward. The object is not only to reward behavior but also to change it. Tousignant and Siedentop found that students who were rewarded for effort or performance reduced the quantity of off-task behaviors.[126] Certificates, ribbons, stickers, special events, and other rewards might be used to motivate students. Siedentop specified a series of guidelines to implement this system:

1. Define the target in observable units.
2. Explain the target behaviors clearly to the participants.
3. Monitor the target behaviors consistently.
4. State the contingency (reward) clearly.
5. Use a simple reward system.
6. Think small. Make the system manageable.
7. Be consistent.[127]

The following examples illustrate the use of tokens or points:

1. Points are awarded during tournament play for game results. The following point system might be used:

    1 point = a loss
    2 points = a tie
    3 points = a win

At the end of round robin competition, points are totaled to award first, second, third, or other place honors. Points might also be given for acts of courtesy and sportsmanship.

2. Colored tickets are awarded for events in track and field throughout the unit (see figure 12.3).

Blue   = 1st place (Running events)
Red   = 2nd place (Running events)
White = 3rd place (Running events)
Orange = jogged a lap

Blue, red, white, yellow, and green ribbons are also awarded for designated heights or distances in field events. Students are able to earn ribbons even though they might not place first, second, or third.

At the conclusion of a unit, the point values of each ticket are calculated and students record their total score.

3. Extra-credit points or tokens are awarded for participation outside of school hours in activities from archery to water skiing. Have students keep a log of dates and hours spent in each activity.

4. Points are awarded to units within a team for outstanding plays or goals achieved. For example, on the basketball team the guards, forwards, and centers would compete as three separate units. An average unit free-throw percentage would be kept and the unit with the highest average would get points or tokens.

5. Grades are based on a point system for completing learning tasks and policy requirements. When such a system is used, students know exactly what is required of them to earn a grade.

Punishment

Punishment is negative contingency contracting—"If you do x, you will get y," y being undesirable. Punishment involves external control over a student by the teacher. It usually implies mental or physical pain or discomfort. *Restitution* of things taken and *reparation* for things damaged or destroyed willfully are generally conceded to be fair forms of punishment. To be effective, this form of punishment must teach the student that when something is destroyed it affects the welfare of the entire group. This technique also teaches the student to make amends. The teacher's responsibility lies in explaining the reasons for the punishment and in following through to see that restoration is made. If the student is financially unable to pay expenses for reparation, the school should find a way for the student to work off the debt. Where parents are too free with money, the school can solicit their cooperation in making the punishment effective by permitting the student to work out the debt to society.

Punishment has some undesirable side effects. Teachers must weigh the impact of these side effects before incorporating punishment into a system of discipline. Although a behavior may be temporarily suppressed when punishment or the threat of punishment follows behavior, it will often reappear later. One possible reason for this is that punishment tells the student what not to do but gives no direction as to the appropriate behavior, causing the student to experiment with a whole range of inappropriate behaviors while searching for the appropriate behavior. Reward, on the contrary, immediately tells the student what the appropriate behavior is. Other undesirable side effects of punishment, such as a negative self-concept or a dislike of school, the subject, or the teacher, can develop. These negative feelings may predispose the student to retaliate or withdraw. Further, punishment reduces the behavior only in the presence of

INDIVIDUAL TRACK RECORD

Staple tickets below:
Blues on top, reds
next, etc.

	Blue	Red	White	Yellow	Green	Orange	Ticket totals for each event
High jump	4	2	3	2	1	1	13
Standing long jump							0
Running long jump			2	1	2	1	6
All dashes (50-75-100)	2	2	1	1	✕	✕	6
All relays (440 and shuttle)	2	1		1	✕	✕	4
Total number of tickets for each color	8	7	5	6	2	1	29

To calculate your total score:

Count 10 points for *each* ticket.   290
Count 3 more points for each *blue* ticket.   24
Count 2 more points for each *red* ticket.   14
Count 1 more point for each *white* ticket.   5

Total score   333

Figure 12.3 Individual track record.
Source: Kathryn Alldredge and Mary Taylor.

the punishing agent. Students may learn how to avoid getting caught by more-sophisticated cheating or lying. Finally, punishment teaches students to be aggressive through imitation of the aggressive behavior of adults.

Punishment should only be used in a planned, careful way to deal with problems that cannot be resolved by the alternative measures discussed, or when students know ahead of time that certain results come from their actions. Some school districts have a discipline code that categorizes student misbehavior and identifies administrative or teacher actions that may be taken. Becker suggested two circumstances in which punishment may be needed: (1) when direct reinforcement procedures are likely to fail because the negative behavior is so frequent that there is no positive behavior to reinforce and (2) when someone might get hurt.[128]

Punishment, when it is used, should be primarily a natural consequence of the choices made by students. Students should be counseled as to the consequences of alternatives when they make their choices. Negative reinforcement must never be used to punish one student in front of a group of students. The following procedures are suggested when using punishment:

1. Allow an undesirable act to continue (or insist that it continue) until the student is clearly bored with it. For example, a teacher could insist that a student throwing spit wads continue to make spit wads until the student has clearly learned how unattractive the behavior is and can make a decision to follow a desired behavior.
2. Always accompany punishment with a suggestion of something positive to do (e.g., the desired behavior).
3. End the punishment with the student's decision to perform the desired behavior.
4. Reward the positive behavior or the student will revert to the bad behavior to get recognition, even if it takes the form of punishment.

Use of Rules and Consequences (Assertive Discipline—Teacher-Controlled)

Establish clear rules, communicate them to students, and teach students how to follow them. Rules for each type of activity should be explicit and posted for everyone to see if possible. Behavior skills can be taught in the same manner as psychomotor skills—by modeling the skill and by practice, followed by positive reinforcement. Deviations from the rule might mean a misunderstanding, requiring a review. Avoid bargaining or negotiating with students. Communicate expectations at the beginning of the year and each lesson.[129] Sander emphasizes limiting rules for younger students to not more than five, including such rules as

Traffic Rule: Stop, look, and listen when the teacher speaks or signals.
Friendship Rule: Be polite. Cooperate with classmates.
Golden Rule: Do not use rude language, fight, or argue.
Safety Rule: Handle all equipment safely and carefully.[130]

Tell students at the beginning of the year the consequences for misbehavior. Include a maximum of five consequences with which you are comfortable. For example: (1) a warning, (2) time-out, (3) loss of privileges, (4) call the parent, (5) go to the principal's office. Use firm, consistent negative consequences but only after ensuring that students understand and have practiced the rule.[131] Explain consequences for inappropriate behavior.[132] Never threaten a student with consequences unless you intend to follow through. Consequences should never be physically or psychologically harmful to students. Corporal punishment, including using exercise as punishment, must never be used as discipline.

Provide firm direction and structure. Avoid phrases like "Do you want to . . . ?" "Would you like to . . . ?" "Okay?" Use phrases like "Please do this." Make sure all students are listening when giving instructions. Do not ignore misbehavior.[133]

Be consistent and fair. Students learn to choose whether to behave or misbehave and the consequences for either choice. They learn that they control the consequences.[134] Canter emphasizes that "One day is not enough. It takes a great deal of effort and continuing training for a teacher to master the skills of classroom management."[135]

The Social Contract—Logical Consequences

Curwin and Mendler suggested the use of social contracts to achieve discipline with dignity. They noted the following components of a successful social contract:[136]

1. Sound principles, which provide guidelines for classroom behavior, such as being respectful, courteous, prepared, practicing the Golden Rule, and doing one's best.
2. Effective rules, based on the principles, which define clearly what is and is not acceptable. Rules should be brief, stated in positive terms (if possible), and specific enough that students know what is meant by the rule. Students ought to be involved in this step. They might also create rules for the teacher. Make sure you can live with their rules before agreeing to them.
3. Consequences should be clear, specific, natural or logical, reasonable, and related to the rule, including a range of alternatives to meet the needs of various students. They are not punishments. Consequences should preserve student dignity. Since students are different, different types of consequences are necessary. Four kinds of consequences that generally meet the needs of a variety of students include:
   a. Reminder of the rule. "Mary, we sit in our squads during roll call. This is your reminder."
   b. A warning. "Chan, this is the second time you have forgotten your homework. This is your warning."
   c. An action plan for improving behavior. "José, you are bothering Jackie again. I want you to write down how you intend to stop breaking this rule. List very clearly what you will do when you want to tell Jackie something." A conference with the student, parent, and teacher may be helpful in developing an action plan.
   d. Practicing the behavior. When students lack the skills to follow the rules, the teacher may demonstrate how to follow the rule and have the student(s) practice. This may be done after class in private.
   Student involvement should be solicited in deriving appropriate consequences. The more students are involved, the better they feel about the plan.
4. A copy of the contract could be sent to parents, other teachers, and administrators with a letter explaining the contract and soliciting their suggestions. You might list some rules you are having difficulty with and ask for suggestions. This could be done with parents on Back-to-School night.
5. Test the students on the contract to make sure they understand the rules and consequences. Cite class privileges that they will earn by passing the test, such as being a student leader or earning free time.

Be consistent in implementing the consequences. Simply approach the student, make eye contact, and softly but firmly state the rule and the consequence, without moralizing. Don't

An individual conference is one of the most
effective disciplinary techniques.
© James L. Shaffer

embarrass the student in front of his or her peers. This maintains student dignity. If students need help understanding the rule, teach them privately. Do not accept excuses or bargaining. Simply repeat the rule and the consequence.

Individual Conference

An individual conference with a student outside of class time is one of the most effective discipline techniques. A serious and frank talk is the logical first step in understanding behavior problems. Conferences help the teacher understand the causes of misbehavior and problems the student faces. They can also provide an opportunity for the teacher to explain school or class regulations to the student.

Group Discussion

When an entire class is disruptive, several possibilities exist:[137]

1. Meet with the ringleaders. Tell them you are tired of yelling and threatening. Ask for suggestions on how to stop the disruption.
2. Abandon your lesson plan. Tell your students what you mean by disruptive behavior. Ask for verbal or written suggestions for changing their behavior and/or your teaching style.

3. Consider mutually creating a social contract, with students and teacher working together to set rules and consequences.
4. Have students make a list of rewarding activities and privileges. Tell them that they may earn these privileges by daily or weekly record of improvement.

Loss of Privileges

The loss of privileges, particularly those of a social nature, is generally a well-accepted method of discipline. When this method is applied, it should follow the offense as a natural, logical form of correction with no retributory attitude on the part of the teacher. After the student has had time to examine the misbehavior, he or she can be restored to full privileges. Often students will plead to be allowed to work after being excluded.

Time-Out

Time-out consists of cutting off reinforcement for a period of time.[138] Usually the student is required to sit away from other students until he or she decides to engage in appropriate behavior. Some teachers use time-out to help students resolve interpersonal problems, such as fighting. Students are asked to leave the group until they have settled their differences, so that other students can continue to learn. The lack of an audience can be very effective in quieting emotions. Students may be asked to sit on a bench together and agree on what they are fighting about. This process helps children learn to resolve their own differences. Time-out is probably the most widely used technique to change behavior. When used correctly, time-out can be one of the most effective discipline tools an instructor can use for students of all ages. To make time-outs productive, Fronske recommends the following:

1. Students must enjoy the activity, the company of other students, or the teacher.
2. Use one warning before sending a student to a time-out box.
3. The student should inform the instructor when he or she is ready to return to activity and participate according to the rules.
4. On the third offense, the student loses the choice of when to return. It is now up to the teacher to make that choice.[139]

The use of time-out can be abused. The following cautions will help you implement time-out:

1. Use positive techniques before using time-out.
2. Never put a student in a time-out box for the remainder of the class.
3. Rarely put a student into a time-out box for a specified period of time on the first offense.
4. Avoid having students face the wall or stand behind a door where they cannot observe class activity. Remember, the instructor is legally liable for the activity of the student during time-out. Also, observing the fun other students are having increases the student's desire to return to activity.[140]

Reality Therapy

Reality therapy[141] requires the teacher to become involved with and care about students. The teacher must work in the present and toward the future, ignoring the student's excuses. The teacher helps the student (1) identify the inappropriate behavior, (2) identify the consequences of the behavior, (3) make a value judgment about the behavior, (4) make a plan, and (5) follow the plan. To do this, the teacher asks the following questions:

1. What is your goal? What do you want to happen?
2. What are you doing? or What did you do?
3. Is that what you should be doing? or How will that help you?
4. What is your plan? or What will you do that will help you?
5. What will be the consequences?
6. What can I do to help you?

If the student fails to apply the plan, the student should be allowed to suffer the consequences of the irresponsible behavior, but within a framework of love and understanding. The student can then be helped to reconsider the commitment that has been made.

The following example of reality therapy takes place in a 10-grade gymnastics class. The students have been assigned to develop an individual routine on a chosen piece of apparatus. The routine is to be completed by the end of the hour. A substantial portion of the student's grade will be based on the routine. Louise sits in a corner. She has not even attempted to create a routine. Instead she is staring into space. The teacher approaches Louise and confronts her. Key elements of the reality therapy are footnoted.

TEACHER:	Louise, what are you doing?
LOUISE:	I'm just sitting here.[a]
TEACHER:	What are you supposed to be doing?
LOUISE:	I don't know.
TEACHER:	What is the rest of the class doing?
LOUISE:	I guess they're working on the routine.
TEACHER:	What are you supposed to be doing?
LOUISE:	I guess I'm supposed to be working on the routine.[b]
TEACHER:	How far will sitting around get you?
LOUISE:	Probably nowhere.
TEACHER:	What will happen if you don't do the routine?
LOUISE:	I'll probably flunk the class.[c]
TEACHER:	Do you want to fail?
LOUISE:	I don't know.
TEACHER:	What will happen if you do fail?
LOUISE:	I'll probably have to take the class over.
TEACHER:	Is that what you want?
LOUISE:	No.
TEACHER:	What can you do to keep from failing?
LOUISE:	I guess I better work on the routine.[d]
TEACHER:	What can I do to help you?
LOUISE:	Tell me what skills to do.
TEACHER:	That's not acceptable. What else can I do?[e]
LOUISE:	Explain what things I'm supposed to have in my routine.[f]
TEACHER:	Okay. Will that help you?
LOUISE:	I think so.
TEACHER:	Will you be ready to perform tomorrow?
LOUISE:	I guess so.
TEACHER:	Okay.

Notes: a. Student identifies behavior.
  b. Student makes a value judgment.
  c. Student identifies the consequences of behavior.
  d. Student makes a plan.
  e. Teacher guides development of the plan.
  f. Teacher helps the student with the plan.

Norm Setting

When reality therapy is used with a group of students, it is known as *norm setting*. Norm setting is based on the principle that students are more responsible for implementing behavior expectations that they have helped select than those chosen by someone else. Teachers and students work together to formalize and publicize essential rules and regulations. Rules should be clear, brief, reasonable, easily applied to all, and enforceable by teacher observation. For norm setting to work, the teacher must recognize the worth and intelligence of students. Norm setting can be used with groups of all ages and in many different settings. The procedures include the following:

1. Help students share their goals or expectations regarding either learning or behavior. Focus on what students *need* to learn or do, not what they *want* to do.
2. State goals the teacher wants students to achieve.
3. Refine goals into one set of mutually acceptable goals by eliminating undesirable goals (those that cannot be achieved within the course) and adding any desirable goals that were omitted.
4. State goals in such a way that students and teacher will know what each goal is and when it has been achieved.
5. State what you are willing to do to help students achieve the class goals (be available, be prepared, be willing to admit mistakes, care for students, listen to students). Do not promise to do anything you will not do. Teachers who really care ask students what additional expectations they might have of the teacher.
6. Help students describe what they need to do and are willing to do to ensure attainment of class goals.
7. Identify consequences for nonattainment of goals.
8. Commit the teacher and the students to the class goals. Agreements may be written down and signed in the form of a contract.
9. Use various motivational techniques to reward behavior that is consistent with the norms or standards previously agreed upon.
10. Use reality therapy techniques to help the misbehaving student judge behavior in terms of the commitments made by the class.
11. Review goals and commitments from time to time and make changes when necessary.

Use of Videorecorders

Videorecorders are becoming more and more common to prevent crimes and driving infractions. They are currently finding their way into school hallways and classrooms. Physical educators have used videorecorders to provide feedback to students on their physical performance. Kusky recommends their use in the classroom to encourage safe practices and to help students see their own behavior. He indicates his intentions to students and mentions that he might use the tapes in counseling sessions with their parents and with the school administration. When students ask whether it is an invasion of their privacy, he assures them that they are in a public building and what they do is a matter of public record. He is just making that record more permanent and transportable. Videotapes counter the tendency of students to play a different role in the office or at home and put the blame on the teacher. Confronted by the videotape, they are much easier to get started on the correction of the problem.[142]

Cooperation between Home and School

Genuine cooperation between home and school through conferences, home visits, and social contacts can achieve remarkable results, provided both parties are willing to understand the student's behavior and are sincere about wanting to help the student. Home-school cooperation can produce fruitful information and lead to correction of misbehavior. A positive, cooperative effort is usually most successful. Keep a record of student misbehavior.[143] Written and videotape records can help to identify patterns of behavior and to provide objective data for parents.[144]

Administrative Assistance

Administrative assistance should be secured only after the teacher has been unsuccessful in correcting a disturbing situation, or after repeated incidents of misbehavior. Sending a student to the office removes the offender from the class and facilitates instruction to the other students. However, it also bars the student from necessary instruction. Occasionally it creates a scene in which the offender may be humiliated or, on the contrary, become a hero to classmates. This method appears to be justified only in severe cases. However, a principal once told a teacher, "After you've done everything you can and the student doesn't improve, don't let it bother you out of proportion. Let it give the principal an ulcer." The administration has a duty to do everything possible to help the teacher deal with discipline problems for the sake of the student, the teacher, and the school as a whole. However, the teacher should refer a student to the administration only when all the resources at hand have been exhausted. Procedures for using administrative assistance include the following:

1. Before you are faced with a need to use administrative assistance, write down the rule violations you believe to be worthy of referral to an administrator. Then set up an appointment with your administrator to discuss your list.[145]
2. Know the student. A trip to the office may be just what the individual wants at that moment to get out of a difficult assignment.
3. When it becomes necessary to send a student to the office of the administrator, send along a note (with another student) that states the difficulty and the kind of treatment expected.
4. See the administrator as soon as possible to discuss the situation.
5. Do not send more than one student to the office at a time.
6. If the student is sent back to class, calmly readmit the student and ignore any face-saving behavior the student displays.

Mediation

Sometimes disciplinary problems cannot be solved by the teacher and the student involved. One method for alleviating such a problem is called mediation. Mediation uses an outside party to help settle a classroom dispute. The mediator is not a judge or jury. His or her sole purpose is to assist both sides in airing their grievances in a manner that will resolve the difficulty. By using a mediator in difficult situations, the teacher can reaffirm respect for student rights.[146]

Handling Explosive or Violent Situations

An explosive situation is one that requires immediate action to prevent personal injury or property damage. The most extreme situations are attack, robbery, rape, and hostage taking. Although students tend to be robbed by other students, teachers are more likely to be robbed by young intruders.[147] It is best to prevent an explosive situation from occurring whenever possible by using the following suggestions:

1. Become a hard target. "Target hardening is a security concept that significantly decreases, deters, or prevents crime against specific individuals. . . . A soft target is an easy target; a hard target is a difficult one." Hard targets are much less likely to become crime victims.[148] Develop a healthy alertness about what is happening around you. Do not be distracted by reading or listening to a radio or cassette. Make eye contact with students as you pass through the halls. Walk with an erect bearing, emanating confidence. Walk down the center of empty hallways and on the street edge of the sidewalk away from buildings and shrubs where you have room to run. Better yet, don't walk alone anywhere. Do not wear expensive jewelry or carry much cash. Do not carry things in two hands; use an attaché case. Care about your students. They are not likely to injure someone they respect. "Target hardening can reduce your chances of being a crime victim by 70 percent or more."[149]
2. Do not let misbehavior go too far before attempting to handle the problem. Call for help if a situation may turn into an explosive situation.
3. Do not lose your cool. Explosive situations become volcanic when the teacher and student are not in control of themselves. Maintaining a sense of humor will keep the student-teacher relationship on a personal level and can often defuse tense situations. Many discipline problems could be easily avoided if molehills remained molehills.[150]
4. Be decisive, act quickly, and disarm the situation. Insist calmly but firmly that the behavior be stopped immediately. Suggest an alternative behavior, an "out" by which the student can save face. Use a time-out or, if possible, remove the student or students from the classroom. Do not touch the student if this can be avoided.
5. Do not use too harsh a punishment as that can result in later aggressive behaviors.
6. Avoid confrontations with students. Do not accept a challenge as a personal matter.
7. Calm the class by restructuring the incident or using it as a topic for discussion. Introduce humor.

When an explosive situation does occur, the following procedures may be helpful:[151]

1. In the case of a robbery or hostage attempt, do not resist. Do as you are told. Don't argue.
2. In case of a rape attempt, keep the intruder talking as long as possible. Negotiate without pleading. Negotiation and resistance will not work with a criminal rapist.
3. Mentally make a record of the attacker's description, especially any distinctive features.

4. Get help! If possible, send a student for another teacher, the principal, or a counselor. This may be after the robber has gone.
5. Do not touch anything the intruder has touched.

Creative Techniques[152]
1. Allow a student to play teacher. You take the student's place and act like he or she usually does. Then have a conference to discuss how you "as a student" could improve your behavior.
2. Use humor to diffuse disruptive situations.
3. When students criticize, say, "There's a lot of truth to that. There are times when I . . . Thanks for pointing that out."
4. When a student says, "You can't make me. What are you going to do about it?" say, "I'm going to finish this lesson, hop on over to the airport and take the first flight to Tahiti."
5. Make the behavior acceptable (throwing erasers—give the student a target) and ask the student to keep doing it, or tell a student he or she is not allowed to do homework. If the student stops, you win. If the student continues, he or she is doing what you said to do, so you win. If a student swears, ask him or her to define the term right now and you will write the definition on the chalkboard. The student has to behave more appropriately as a way of defying your authority. Have an eraser throwing contest to see who can throw the farthest or most accurately.
6. Throw a tantrum. Stand on the chair, knock things over, scream and yell. Save this for a few selected times a year.

Unacceptable Practices

Some disciplinary practices used by teachers are generally considered unacceptable. Often they are initiated because the teacher is feeling the stress and tension of the situation. The use of such tactics normally generates resentment on the part of the student or causes the student to withdraw. Teachers must decide ahead of time that the following practices will not be employed no matter what the intensity of a circumstance might be. These practices include (1) coercion; (2) ridicule; (3) forced apologies; (4) detention without a specified purpose; (5) imposition of schoolwork or homework for punitive purposes; (6) punishment instigated on the spot, including grades; (7) group punishment for misbehavior by one or a few; and (8) corporal punishment. Using exercise for punishment can be considered a form of corporal punishment and may be prohibited by state law or result in a lawsuit. Other methods that generally result in a teacher's lack of control include appealing to the student's sympathy; the use of vague, unfulfilled threats; and exclusion of the student from the room without supervision. To avoid unpleasant situations caused by a disciplinary action the teacher must have in mind appropriate techniques that will be triggered automatically by the situation.

Choosing Appropriate Techniques for the Situation

Teachers can be prepared to act instinctively when a disciplinary incident arises in class. Outcomes are often unpredictable. Predetermined rules and regulations might provide a solution to the problem, but the teacher still must react with a cool head and conclude the incident. Whatever problem might arise, proper action depends on (1) the teacher's philosophy and teaching style, (2) the students, and (3) the incident.

By understanding a variety of suitable techniques that match the model chosen or created by the teacher and success in carrying out different methods will allow you to select appropriate techniques for different conditions. Experiment to see what works best, because what works for one teacher may not work for another. Administrative policy may limit the choices a teacher is allowed to select. Often you must deal with the incident and at the same time direct students not involved in the action. No method of control is effective with all students. One must consider the age, sex, personality, and social values held by the student or group. Be alert to the individual needs of students. Occasionally, deafness, poor vision, or other disabling conditions create supposed discipline problems.

Try to determine the cause of the behavior and what actually happened without relying too heavily on statements made by students. Often the cause of the incident results from the classroom environment. Poor, haphazard, and unproductive instruction or a curriculum that is too easy, too hard, or not relevant to student needs may cause many discipline problems.

With these items in mind, first stop the ineffective behavior and then help the students overcome individual problems, thus preventing a recurrence of the problem. The action must be clear, definite, and one in which you truly believe. By continually being alert to early signs of trouble and dealing with them firmly, calmly, and with consistency before they become serious, major discipline problems can be avoided.

An inexperienced teacher or one new to a school must still deal with discipline problems in a confident, controlled manner. Use preventive and positive discipline to prevent discipline problems. The following hints for new teachers are aimed at avoiding beginning pitfalls:

1. Learn school policies and procedures thoroughly.
2. Be an example the students can emulate.
3. Be a teacher, not a pal, to students.
4. Plan and organize.
5. Be flexible but consistent in carrying out plans.
6. Respect and appreciate students as individuals.
7. Let students know from the start what the payoff will be for working hard in class.[153]

Review Questions

1. What is the relationship between discipline and motivation?
2. Define the following terms and tell how each is applicable to teaching:
   motivation
   Maslow's hierarchy of needs
   effectance motivation (self-efficacy) and optimum challenges
   Bandura's social learning theory
   movement confidence
   attribution theory and learned helplessness
   discipline
   extrinsic and intrinsic motivation
3. What is the self-fulfilling prophecy, the pygmalion effect? Why are teacher expectations important? How can positive expectations be communicated to students?
4. Freud once said that "No one ever does anything unless he would rather." What does this statement suggest about affective learning?

5. What can you do to prevent discipline problems in your classroom?
6. How can teachers invite students to succeed in physical education?
7. What discipline model(s) do you want to try in your classroom? Why?
8. What discipline practices are compatible with your model?
9. Why is it illegal to use physical activities as punishment?
10. What is an explosive situation? What should be done when an explosive situation arises in the classroom?
11. What practices are never acceptable disciplinary techniques?
12. What factors affect the selection of a disciplinary technique?

References

1. Doyle, W. (1986). Classroom organization and management. In M. C. Wittrock, *Handbook of research on teaching* (3rd ed., pp. 392–431). New York: Macmillan.
2. Curwin, R. L., & Mendler, A. N. (1988). *Discipline with dignity* (pp. 158–159). Alexandria, VA: Association for Supervision and Curriculum Development.
3. Hellison, D. R. (1985). *Goals and strategies for teaching physical education* (p. 1). Champaign, IL: Human Kinetics.
4. Ibid., 2–3.
5. Wlodkowski, R. (1978). *How to help teachers reach the turned off student.* Unpublished paper. Cited in Curwin & Mendler, *Discipline with dignity*, 161.
6. Curwin & Mendler, *Discipline with dignity*, 5–10.
7. Dunn, H. (1981, November-December). Listen to kids! *Today's Education, 70,* 37.
8. Wittrock, M. C. (1986). Students' thought processes. In M. C. Wittrock (Ed.), *Handbook of research on teaching* (3rd ed., p. 304). New York: Macmillan.
9. Hunter, M. (1971). *Motivation theory for teachers.* El Segundo, CA: Tip.
10. Carron, A. V. (1984). *Motivation implications for coaching & teaching* (p. 7). Kingswood, South Australia: Sports Dynamics.
11. Hunter, *Motivation theory for teachers.*
12. Maslow, A. H. (1943). A theory of human personality. *Psychological Review, 50,* 370–396.
13. Gagné, R. M. (1970). *The conditions of learning* (2nd ed., p. 288). New York: Holt, Rinehart & Winston.
14. White, R. (1959). Motivation reconsidered: The concept of competence. *Psychological Review, 66,* 297–323.
15. Harter, S. (1978). Effectance motivation reconsidered: Toward a developmental model. *Human Development, 21,* 52.
16. Ibid.
17. Bandura, A. (1977). Self-efficacy: Toward a unifying theory of behavioral change. *Psychological Review, 84*(2), 191–215.
18. Ibid., 193.
19. Bandura, A. (1977). *Social learning theory* (pp. 160–163). Englewood Cliffs, NJ: Prentice-Hall.
20. Feltz, D. L., & Weiss, M. R. (1982, March). Developing self-efficacy through sport. *Journal of Physical Education, Recreation and Dance, 53,* 24–26, 36; McAuley, E., Duncan, T. E., & McElroy, M. (1989). Self-efficacy cognitions and causal attributions for children's motor performance: An exploratory investigation. *Journal of Genetic Psychology, 150*(1), 65–73; Weinberg, R., Gould, D., & Jackson, A. (1979). Expectations and performance: An empirical test of Bandura's self-efficacy theory. *Journal of Sport Psychology, 1*(4), 320–331.
21. Feltz, D. L. (1982). Path analysis of the causal elements in Bandura's theory of self-efficacy and an anxiety-based model of avoidance behavior. *Journal of Personality and Social Psychology, 42,* 764–781.
22. Weinberg, Gould, & Jackson, Expectations and performance.
23. Griffin, N. S., & Keogh, J. F. (1982). A model for movement confidence. In J. A. S. Kelso & J. E. Clark (Eds.), *The development of movement control and coordination* (p. 213). New York: Wiley.
24. Weiner, B. (1980). *Human motivation.* Chicago: Holt, Rinehart & Winston.

25. Rudisill, M. E. (1989). Influence of perceived competence and causal dimension orientation on expectations, persistence, and performance during perceived failure. *Research Quarterly for Exercise and Sport, 60*(2), 166–175.
26. Bandura, Self-efficacy, 191–215.
27. Rudisill, Influence of perceived competence and causal dimension orientation, 166–175.
28. Weinberg, Gould, & Jackson, Expectations and performance.
29. Corbin, C. B., & Nix, C. (1979). Sex-typing of physical activities and success predictions of children before and after cross-sex competition. *Journal of Sport Psychology, 1*, 43–52.
30. Martinek, T. J. (1989). Children's perceptions of teaching behaviors: An attributional model for explaining teacher expectancy effects. *Journal of Teaching in Physical Education, 8*, 327.
31. Maier, S. F., & Seligman, M. E. (1976). Learned helplessness: Theory and evidence. *Journal of Experimental Psychology: General, 105*(1), 3–46.
32. Wortman, C. B., & Brehm, J. W. (1975). Responses to uncontrollable outcomes: An integration of reactance theory and the learned helplessness model. In L. Berkowitz (Ed.), *Advances in experimental social psychology* (Vol. 8). New York: Academic Press.
33. Ibid.
34. Greendorfer, S. (1978). Socialization into sport. In C. A. Oglesby (Ed.), *Women and sport: From myth to reality.* Philadelphia: Lea & Febiger.
35. Martinek, T. J., & Griffith, J. B., III. (1993). Working with the learned helpless child. *Journal of Physical Education, Recreation and Dance, 64*(6), 17–20.
36. Dweck, C. S. (1975). The role of expectations and attributions in the alleviation of learned helplessness. *Journal of Personality and Social Psychology, 31*, 674–685.
37. Rudisill, Influence of perceived competence and causal dimension orientation, 166–175.
38. Martinek & Griffith, Working with the learned helpless child,17–20.
39. Alderman, M. K. (1990). Motivation for at-risk students. *Educational Leadership, 48*, 27–30.
40. Martinek & Griffith, Working with the learned helpless child, 17–20.
41. Rosenthal, R., & Jacobson, L. (1968). *Pygmalion in the classroom: Teacher expectation and pupils' intellectual development.* San Francisco: Holt, Rinehart & Winston.
42. Brophy, J. E., & Good, T. L. (1974). *Teacher-student relationships: Causes and consequences.* New York: Holt, Rinehart & Winston.
43. Brophy, J. (1982). Successful teaching strategies for the inner-city child. *Phi Delta Kappan, 63*, 527–530.
44. Martinek, T. J. (1981). Pygmalion in the gym: A model for the communication of teacher expectations in physical education. *Research Quarterly for Exercise and Sport, 52*, 58–67; Martinek, T. J. (1983). Creating golem and galatea effects during physical education instruction: A social psychological perspective. In T. J. Templin & J. K. Olson (Eds.), *Teaching in physical education* (pp. 59–70). Champaign, IL: Human Kinetics; Martinek, T. J., & Karper, W. B. (1982). Canonical relationships among motor ability, expression of effort, teacher expectations and dyadic interactions in elementary age children. *Journal of Teaching in Physical Education, 1*, 26–39; Martinek, T. J., & Karper, W. B. (1983). A research model for determining causal effects of teacher expectations in physical education instruction. *Quest, 35*, 155–168.
45. Wittrock, Students' thought processes, 297–298.
46. Darley, J. M., & Fazio, R. H. (1980). Expectancy confirmation processes arising in the social interaction sequence. *American Psychologist, 35*, 867–881.
47. Martinek, T. J. (1988). Confirmation of a teacher expectancy model: Student perceptions and causal attributions of teaching behaviors. *Research Quarterly for Exercise and Sport, 59*(2), 118–126.
48. Martinek, Children's perceptions of teaching behaviors, 325.
49. Martinek, T., & Karper, W. (1984). The effects of noncompetitive and competitive social climates on teacher expectancy effects in elementary physical education classes. *Journal of Sport Psychology, 8*, 408–421.
50. Rink, J. E. (1993). *Teaching physical education for learning* (2nd ed., p. 47). St. Louis, MO: Mosby.
51. Rink, J. E. (1981). The teacher wants us to learn. *Journal of Physical Education and Recreation, 52*, 17–18.
52. Martinek, Children's perceptions of teaching behaviors, 321.

53. Hutslar, S. (1981). The expectancy phenomenon. *Journal of Physical Education, Recreation and Dance, 52*(7), 88–89.

54. Turner, R. B., & Purkey, W. W. (1983, September). Teaching physical education: An invitational approach. *Journal of Physical Education, Recreation and Dance, 54,* 13–14, 64.

55. Elam, S. M., Rose, L. C., & Gallup, A. M. (1993). The 25th annual Phi Delta Kappa/Gallup poll of the public's attitudes toward the public schools, *Phi Delta Kappan, 75*(2), 137–152.

56. Swick, K. J. (1981). *Maintaining productive student behavior.* Washington, DC: National Education Association.

57. United States Department of Education. (1986). *What works: Research about teaching and learning* (p. 47). Washington, DC: Author.

58. Gordon, T. with Burch, N. (1974). *T.E.T., teacher effectiveness training.* New York: Wyden.

59. Curwin & Mendler, *Discipline with dignity*, 27–28.

60. Raffini, J. P. (1980). *Discipline.* Englewood Cliffs, NJ: Prentice-Hall.

61. Coloroso, B. (1983). *Discipline: Winning at teaching* (p. 5). Littleton, CO: Kids Are Worth It, P.O. Box 621108, Littleton, CO 80162.

62. Ibid., 10.

63. Faust, V. (1980). *Self esteem in the classroom,* (p. 53). San Diego: Thomas Paine.

64. Faust, S. (1974). *Effects of ability-labeling on psychomotor and academic performances of selected sixth grade students.* Unpublished doctoral dissertation, University of Miami, Coral Gables.

65. Faust, *Self esteem in the classroom*, 103–106.

66. Ibid., 121–123.

67. Ibid.,144–158.

68. Ibid., 273.

69. McKay, M., & Fanning, P. (1992). *Self-esteem* (p. 244). Oakland, CA: New Harbinger.

70. Cardinal, B. J. (1991, June). Motivation: Strategies for success. *Strategies, 4*(6), 27–28.

71. Glasser, W. (1969). *Schools without failure* (pp. 6–7). New York: Harper & Row.

72. Hoover, K. H. (1982). *The professional teacher's handbook: A guide for improving instruction in today's middle and secondary schools* (3rd ed., p. 64). Boston: Allyn & Bacon.

73. Faust, *Self esteem in the classroom*, 156–157.

74. Ibid., 234.

75. Chandler, G. L. (1988, April). Invitational physical education: Strategies in the junior high school. *Journal of Physical Education, Recreation and Dance, 59*(4), 68–72.

76. Ibid., 68; Purkey, W. W. (1978). *Inviting school success.* Belmont, CA: Wadsworth.

77. Cardinal, Motivation: Strategies for success, 27–28.

78. Curwin & Mendler, *Discipline with dignity*, 16; also Stetzel, J. (1994, August). *Journal of Physical Education, Recreation and Dance, 65*(6), 13.

79. McKay & Fanning, *Self-esteem*, 248–250.

80. Curwin & Mendler, *Discipline with dignity*, 215.

81. Kovar, S. K., Ermler, K., & Mehrhof, J. H. (1992, August). Helping students to become self-disciplined. *Journal of Health, Physical Education, Recreation and Dance, 63*(6), 26–28.

82. Bertel, B. (1974, May). Try what? *Journal of Health, Physical Education, Recreation, 45,* 24.

83. Faust, *Self esteem in the classroom*, 267.

84. Gallahue, D. L. (1985, Late Winter). Toward positive discipline in the gymnasium. *Physical Educator, 42,* 14–17.

85. Curwin & Mendler, *Discipline with dignity*, 16.

86. Locke, E. A., Shaw, K. N., Saari, L. M., & Latham, G. P. (1981). Goal setting and task performance: 1969–1980. *Psychological Bulletin, 90,* 125–152.

87. Oxendine, J. B. (1984). *Psychology of motor learning* (pp. 189–195). Englewood Cliffs, NJ: Prentice-Hall.

88. McKeachie, W. J. (1978). *Teaching tips—A guidebook for the beginning college teacher* (7th ed., p. 222). Lexington, MA: Heath.

89. Wlodkowski, R. (1980). *Motivation and teaching.* Washington, DC: National Education Association.

90. Curwin & Mendler, *Discipline with dignity,* 155.

91. Edwards, C. H. (1993). *Classroom discipline and management* (pp. 217, 226). New York: Macmillan.

92. Curwin & Mendler, *Discipline with dignity*, 170.
93. Ibid., 16.
94. McKay & Fanning, *Self-esteem*, 259.
95. Sanford, J. P., & Evertson, C. M. (1981, January-February). Classroom management in a low SES junior high: Three case studies. *Journal of Teacher Education, 32,* 34–38.
96. Durkheim, E. (1961). *Moral education: A study in the theory and application of the sociology of education* (p. 152). New York: Free Press.
97. Madsen, C. H., Jr., & Madsen, C. K. (1970). *Teaching/discipline* (p. 10). Boston: Allyn & Bacon.
98. Curwin & Mendler, *Discipline with dignity*, 31.
99. Henkel, S. A. (1989, January). STP—The teacher's edge to pupil control. *Journal of Physical Education, Recreation and Dance, 60*(1), 60–64.
100. Deci, E. L., Sheinman, L., Wheeler, L., & Hart, R. (1980, May). Rewards, motivation and self-esteem. *The Educational Forum, 44,* 430.
101. Ibid., 429–433; Deci, E. L., et al. (1981, October). An instrument to assess adults' orientations toward control versus autonomy with children: Reflections on intrinsic motivation and perceived competence. *Journal of Educational Psychology, 73,* 642–650.
102. Harter, Effectance motivation reconsidered, 52.
103. Ibid.
104. La Mancusa, K. C. (1966). *We do not throw rocks at the teacher!* (p. 146). Scranton, PA: International Textbook.
105. Becker, W. C., Engelmann, S., & Thomas, D. R. (1971). *Teaching: A course in applied psychology* (p. 157). Palo Alto, CA: Science Research Associates.
106. Sander, A. N. (1989, January). Class management skills. *Strategies, 2*(3), 14–18.
107. Premack, D. (1959). Toward empirical behavior laws: 1. Positive reinforcement. *Psychological Review, 66*(4), 219–233.
108. Joyce, B., & Weil, M. (1980). *Models of teaching* (2nd ed., p. 332). Englewood Cliffs, NJ: Prentice-Hall.
109. Homme, Csanyi, Gonzales, & Rechs, *How to use contingency contracting in the classroom*, pp. 18–21.
110. Becker, Engelmann, & Thomas, *Teaching*, 171.
111. Glavin, J. P. (1974). *Behavioral strategies for classroom management* (p. 52). Columbus, OH: Merrill.
112. Homme, Csanyi, Gonzales, & Rechs, *How to use contingency contracting in the classroom*, 9.
113. Carter, J. (1989, May-June). The "Champions" program—Behavior improvement in physical education. *Journal of Physical Education, Recreation and Dance, 60*(5), 66–67.
114. Coach Chipper, Box 27843, Santa Ana, CA 92799–7843.
115. Major, K. (1990). *New ideas, new classes: Learning-growing-improving.* AAHPERD Convention session, New Orleans, LA.
116. Vogler, W., & French, R. (1983). The effects of a group contingency strategy on behaviorally disordered students in physical education. *Research Quarterly for Exercise and Sport, 54,* 273–277.
117. Paese, P. (1982). Effects of interdependent group contingencies in a secondary physical education setting. *Journal of Teaching in Physical Education, 2,* 29–37.
118. Wittrock, Students' thought processes, 300.
119. Brophy, J. (1981). Teacher praise: A functional analysis. *Review of Educational Research, 51,* 5–32.
120. Canter, L. (1989). Assertive discipline—More than names on the board and marbles in a jar. *Phi Delta Kappan, 71*(1), 57–61.
121. Ratliffe, T. (1987, April). Overcoming obstacles beginning teachers encounter. *Journal of Physical Education, Recreation and Dance, 58*(40), 18–23.
122. Sander, Class management skills, 17.
123. Brophy, Teacher praise, 26.
124. Edwards, *Classroom discipline and management*, 152.
125. Ibid.
126. Tousignant, M., & Siedentop, D. (1983). A qualitative analysis of task structures in required secondary physical education classes. *Journal of Teaching in Physical Education, 3,* 47–57.

127. Siedentop, D. (1978). The management of practice behavior. In W. F. Straub (Ed.), *Sport psychology: An analysis of athlete behavior.* Ithaca: Movement.
128. Becker, Engelmann, & Thomas, *Teaching,* 158.
129. Kniffin, M. (1988, June). Instructional skills for student teachers. *Strategies, 1*(6), 5–8.
130. Sander, Class management skills, 14–18.
131. Canter, Assertive discipline, 57–61.
132. Kniffin, Instructional skills for student teachers, 7.
133. Ratliffe, Overcoming obstacles beginning teachers encounter, 19.
134. Canter, Assertive discipline, 57–61.
135. Ibid., 60.
136. Curwin & Mendler, *Discipline with dignity,* 31.
137. Ibid., 233.
138. Becker, Engelmann, & Thomas, *Teaching,* 157.
139. Fronske, H. (1990). Personal communication.
140. Ibid.
141. Glasser, W. (1965). *Reality therapy: A new approach to psychiatry.* New York: Harper & Row; Glasser, W. (1986). *Control theory in the classroom.* New York: Harper & Row; Glasser, W. (1990). *The quality school: Managing students without coercion.* New York: Harper & Row.
142. Kusky, C. S., Jr. (1992). Turning the cameras on them. *Phi Delta Kappan, 74*(3), 270.
143. Sander, Class management skills, 17.
144. Vestermark, S. D., Jr., & Blauvelt, P. D. (1978). *Controlling crime in the school: A complete security handbook for administrators* (pp. 132, 189–190). West Nyack, NY: Parker.
145. Curwin & Mendler, *Discipline with dignity,* 227.
146. Graham, T., & Cline, P. C. (1989). Mediation: An alternative approach to school discipline. *The High School Journal, 72*(2), 73–76.
147. Quarles, C. L. (1989). *School violence: A survival guide for school staff,* Washington, D.C.: National Education Association, p. 17, 19.
148. Ibid., 12.
149. Ibid., 16.
150. Wegmann, R. G. (1976). Classroom discipline. *Today's Education, 38*(1), 18–19.
151. Quarles, *School violence: A survival guide for school staff,* 16.
152. Curwin & Mendler, *Discipline with dignity,* 15, 151–154.
153. Becker, Engelmann, & Thomas, *Teaching,* 177.

CHAPTER 13

Accountability and Teacher Evaluation

Study Stimulators

1. Who has the responsibility for worthwhile outcomes of physical education programs?
2. Why is teacher evaluation important?
3. List the steps in teacher evaluation.
4. What are the advantages and limitations of evaluation that is based on student achievement or improvement, informal analysis, informal analysis by students, descriptive analysis, and interaction analysis?

Accountability

The 1980s and 1990s will be documented in history books as the years of educational reform. The barrage of reports in the early 1980s challenging the competency of our national education system sparked improvement by the schools. The "Education Report Card" released by the U.S. Department of Education showed four years of improvement by the schools that ended with a leveling off in 1985–86. Student test scores were up, as were teachers' salaries; the number of pupils per teacher was down; and expenditures per pupil were up.[1] Even with these positive gains the cry to do better was heard. Secretary of Education William J. Bennett emphasized, "We have to do better. Our children deserve better."[2] Legislators reinforced these words. Lawsuits claiming that students were receiving inadequate education forced state legislatures to pass laws requiring schools to be accountable for educating students. The majority of the states now require students to pass minimum competency tests in order to graduate from high school.[3]

The publication of the outcomes statements by the National Association for Sport and Physical Education (NASPE) (see chapter 1) will make it easier for parents and the public to know what physical education competencies they can expect from high school graduates. Teachers, schools, and districts would do well to further define these competencies with regard to their specific programs and to establish evaluation techniques to demonstrate that students are physically educated as defined. Failure to do so could make them vulnerable to educational malpractice suits. Failure to provide programs that result in skill proficiency in lifetime activities and increased health-related fitness and knowledge expose teachers to public criticism.[4] Physical educators are responsible for the poor image they have created because of inadequate lesson preparation, poor personal appearance, failure to attend faculty and professional meetings, and inability to articulate objectives and their importance to the public, including students.[5]

Accountability, according to the law, tends to be limited to accountability of teachers and administrators for learning by students. However, accountability is more than that. Schools have a responsibility to educate students. Parents and taxpayers have a responsibility to provide the resources necessary for adequate learning experiences. Students must be accountable for their own behavior.

Enochs set forth several principles for education in his Modesto, California, district. He stated:

> The development of responsible adults is a task requiring community involvement. It cannot be left solely to the public schools. . . . Parents must consistently support the proposition that students have responsibilities as well as rights, and the schools have an obligation to insist upon both. . . . The full responsibility for learning cannot be transferred from the student to the teacher.[6]

Today the worth of physical education is being challenged as never before. Physical education programs are costly. Physical educators must face the possible elimination of their programs if outcomes cannot be demonstrated. On the other hand, the public has never been more active physically than at the present time. People are spending millions of dollars to look and feel better. More than 100 million people in the United States are actively engaged in fitness activities, an estimated 1,300 books on fitness are currently in print, and 50,000 firms spend an estimated $2 billion a year on fitness and recreation programs for their employees.[7] However, physical educators cannot claim a contribution to this increase in physical activity because their programs lag behind in teaching lifetime fitness concepts and activities. Thus, physical educators are calling for more accountability. Griffey stated, "We have failed to provide an experience that our students perceive as meaningful. The sense of mastering something important is denied most students in secondary physical education programs."[8] Students should be expected to perform certain skills, know certain concepts, and behave in certain ways. This is what teaching is all about. Evaluation reflects success at doing these things.

Accountability requires, first, that students understand the worth of physical education activities to the extent that they become committed to improving their own performance and participating in vigorous activity throughout their lives. Class instruction must be more than "free play" and organized games. Students must be evaluated and results of achievement made available to parents, administrators, the general public, and the students themselves. Chapter 9 discussed ways to assess student achievement. Second, teachers must improve their effectiveness. Teacher evaluation will be presented in this chapter. Third, the public must be convinced of the worth of physical education programs so that they will pledge their support. Public relations was discussed as one of the roles of the teacher in chapter 2.

Teacher Evaluation

Teachers must be able to state performance objectives, assess student achievement of objectives, and use strategies that help students achieve objectives. Educators must also learn to evaluate and remediate weaknesses in their own teaching and in their programs. Administrators must be able to evaluate teachers' performances and help teachers improve their effectiveness.

Effective teachers have the ability to adapt their teaching behaviors to meet the needs of their students. Studies demonstrate that teacher evaluation increases their awareness of these different instructional behaviors and helps them to improve both student achievement and teacher morale. This is true because teachers often perceive their teaching behavior as quite different from that which actually occurs. Teacher evaluation enables the teacher to retain effective teaching behaviors and eliminate ineffective behaviors, thereby making actual behavior more congruent with desired behavior. Teacher evaluation involves the following steps:

Step 1. Determine what to evaluate.
Step 2. Choose or construct specific evaluation techniques.
         Student achievement or improvement
         Informal analysis
         Systematic observation
         Interaction analysis
Step 3. Use the appropriate techniques to record information.
Step 4. Evaluate or interpret the data.
Step 5. Make changes and reevaluate.

Step 1—*Determine what to evaluate.*

The first step in any evaluation plan is to specify goals. This can be done by examining what you believe to be the most important goals of teaching and the behaviors necessary to achieve those goals.[9] Some examples of goals and related behaviors, based on some characteristics of effective teachers, are shown in Table 13.1.

Table 13.1   Goals, Behaviors, and Suggested Evaluation Techniques

Goals	Teacher Behavior	Suggested Evaluation Techniques
Teacher warmth	Calls student by name.	Event recording
	Provides more positive than negative feedback.	Event recording
	Interacts with students.	Student evaluation of instructor Interaction analysis
Teacher expectancy	Facilitates achievement of instructional objectives.	Student performance
	Facilitates improvement in student learning.	Student improvement
	Selects tasks in terms of student abilities.	Student evaluation of teacher Informal analysis
Task-oriented climate	Helps students spend a large amount of time in productive behavior.	Time analysis Spot checking Event recording
	Monitors student progress.	Time sampling
	Provides feedback on behavior.	Event recording
	Decreases time spent on class management.	Time analysis Time sampling
Effective instruction	Provides appropriate model and explanation.	Informal analysis Event recording
	Provides appropriate feedback for skills.	Event recording
	Provides opportunity for student practice.	Time analysis Time sampling
	Provides appropriate progression of content	Number of practice trials/person Event recording

Step 2—*Choose or construct specific evaluation techniques.*

Because teaching is so complex, a variety of formal and informal observation and recording techniques must be employed to describe the total teaching process. The techniques discussed in this chapter include: (1) student achievement or improvement, (2) informal analysis, (3) systematic observation, and (4) interaction analysis. These techniques generally assess either the performance of the students or the performance of the teacher.

Student Achievement or Improvement

The principal duty of teachers is to help students learn. Therefore, the key to evaluating teaching is to determine the extent to which learning has taken place. The use of performance objectives facilitates this process by providing an observable student behavior for each skill or content area to be learned. If students are learning and have positive feelings toward activity, then the teacher is effective, no matter how unorthodox the instruction appears to be. However, if students are not learning or do not have positive attitudes toward activity, then an analysis of the teacher's performance can help to pinpoint possible problem areas for remediation. Common techniques for evaluating student achievement include knowledge tests, skills tests, and various affective measurements. Each of these techniques was discussed in chapter 9.

A second method for evaluating student learning is to record student performance each day and compare it with the objectives of the daily lesson plan. This can be as simple as having students check off skills as they accomplish them (such as in gymnastics or swimming), count the number of successful attempts (such as basketball free throws or tennis serves), or turn in a score (such as in archery or bowling). See chapter 9 for examples. If the lesson has been well planned, most of the students should be able to achieve lesson objectives. An accountability log can be kept each day, which shows not only student achievement toward the objective for that day but also the achievement of previous unit objectives. This log can be a tremendous eye opener of how much review and practice students need to achieve course objectives. The log might include a list of objectives and the number of students who have completed each one.

Another method is to preassess students, teach, and then evaluate the improvement. Again, a knowledge or skills test or an affective measurement can be employed. Examples include:

1. Sprint—Check for improvement in time.
2. Knowledge—Check the number of students improving scores on a quiz, or check the class average on a quiz.
3. Attitude—Check the number of students changing from a negative to a positive attitude toward an activity. Review chapter 9 for specific suggestions on evaluating affective behavior.
4. Basketball strategy—Count the increases in successful passes per team.

There are limitations when evaluating teachers based on student performance. One of the major limitations is the difficulty of accurately evaluating student performance. Weather, time of day, illness, fatigue, and innumerable other factors can influence student performance scores. Subjective evaluation techniques and teacher-constructed tests may be unreliable. Measurements may not be sensitive enough to determine improvement during short units of instruction. A second limitation is that it is difficult to establish a cause-and-effect relationship between a specific teaching behavior and learning. Students may have learned from a parent, friend, or from private lessons. Students may have begun with the skill level being evaluated. Students may learn because of or in spite of a teacher. When they do learn, it is difficult to prove which

Teacher evaluation can be enhanced by coding
and analyzing specific teaching experiences.
© Tracy Pellett

teaching behaviors may have caused the improvement. These limitations, however, should not keep teachers from making some educated guesses about their own teaching based on student achievement. Checking for achievement or improvement each day will provide a better idea of which teaching behaviors helped to create the changes in student behavior.

Informal Analysis

The most common method of teacher evaluation is informal analysis by oneself, a supervisor or administrator, another teacher, or by students. By videotaping the class, the teacher can record observations for self-evaluation and make changes to improve teaching performance. However, such evaluations are based on the observer's subjective opinions. There is a real danger that different observers may interpret different occurrences very differently; thus it is important to use more than one observer. Some informal analysis techniques include a written or verbal description of a lesson, a checklist, or a rating scale.

A written or verbal description of a lesson is generally influenced, either consciously or unconsciously, by the biases of the observer; therefore, use several observers and explicitly define the behavior to be evaluated. The description may focus on only one portion of the teaching-learning situation, such as on discipline or on teacher-student interaction. Sometimes a recording form is used to direct the observer's attention to specific aspects of the teaching situation. An example of a recording form is shown in figure 13.1.

```
                    EVALUATION OF TEACHING
    Name_____        Activity_____

    School_____        Date_____

    Time_____

    Instruction:
        Objective clear
        Demonstration
        Practice
        Correction
    Selection of Activity:
        Success potential
        Challenging-motivational
        Progression
    Maximum Participation:
        Time
        Transitions
        Organization-space-equipment
        Opportunity for all
    Safety:
        Progressions
        Safety rules
        Equipment
    Teacher Relating to Class:
        Aware of class
        Aware of individuals
        Rapport
        Personal appearance
        Voice
```

Figure 13.1   A recording form for informal analysis.

Informal analysis serves a useful purpose because it focuses on aspects of performance that are important to the teacher in making day-to-day decisions. However, this form of evaluation is limited by its subjectivity and narrow focus (i.e., people see what they want to see). Informal analysis is most useful when comments are highly specific, such as "The color drained from Paul's face when you started the next relay before he was finished," or when a record is kept over a period of time. Written records, tape recordings, or videotape recordings can provide a valuable journal of progress when kept for periodic review.

Because of its lack of validity and reliability, informal analysis alone should *not* be used to evaluate a teacher for retention or tenure. It should be combined with the other methods of evaluation discussed in this chapter to form a profile of the teacher's instructional abilities.

A checklist can be used to direct the observer's attention to specific parts of the lesson. The observer simply checks each item that was included in the teacher's behavior during the lesson.

TEACHER EVALUATION FORM

Name _____ Date_____ Evaluator _____

Personal Qualifications
_____ Displays knowledge of the subject
_____ Projects enthusiasm and interest
_____ Maintains confidence and respect of the students
_____ Is easily heard and understood
_____ Displays self-confidence

Organization
_____ Lesson flows smoothly into activity, from activity to activity,
         (1) equipment available and ready (2) teacher doesn't talk too
         much
_____ Students know where to go and what to do
_____ Students understand the objective of the activity or lesson
_____ Available equipment and space is used effectively
_____ Time allotment is appropriate

Instruction
_____ Adequate safety precautions are taken
_____ Individual and group help is given
_____ The activity is challenging, enjoyable, and has success potential
_____ Students are motivated, interested, and involved (not standing too
         long)
_____ Teacher uses appropriate disciplinary techniques so students are
         controlled

Comments (Includes strengths, suggestions for improvement, clarification of
above)

Lesson Plan
_____ Instructional objectives stated in behavioral terms
_____ Performance cues sufficient for skill execution
_____ Estimate of instructional time is appropriate
_____ Practice situations specified in detail (with diagrams)
_____ Sufficient equipment provided to maximize participation

Figure 13.2 A checklist of teacher functions.

An example of a checklist is shown in figure 13.2. The checklist provides the appearance of scientific accuracy but vague, undefined statements or characteristics result in a very low level of reliability for most checklists. A checklist like this provides no information concerning the frequency with which a given behavior occurs.

Rating scales can be valuable as a tool for self-evaluation and goal setting by teachers. They can also be completed by both teachers and supervisors and the results compared to encourage discussion of different points of view concerning the teacher's performance. Goals can then be set to evaluate and correct specific areas needing attention. Rating scales can be developed to evaluate specific items such as execution of teaching styles, demonstrations, or questioning skills. Rosenberg and Knutson developed rating scales to investigate interpersonal relations.[10]

An advantage of rating scales is that they take a minimum of time to complete and can provide information sufficient to get a teacher started on a personal improvement plan. However, as an evaluative device, the rating scale is generally less valid and reliable than many of the other techniques that will be presented in this chapter. This is especially the case when the ratings (i.e., usually, sometimes) are not clearly defined.

When constructing a rating scale, remember that providing fewer choices increases reliability. However, enough points must be included to make the scale useful for its intended purpose. If two observers complete the scale independently and then talk over discrepancies, items can be changed so that differences in understanding of the characteristics in question can be corrected. Then it is more probable that the differences are related to teacher performance rather than to understanding the scale. Any of the types of rating scales presented in chapter 9 can be used to assess teaching performance. The choice depends on how an individual feels about a specific tool.

Many schools, districts, and universities provide rating scales of various standards of performance that can be used for self-evaluation or by peers or supervisors. The rating scale in figure 13.3 is one part of such an evaluation tool. The results can be compared to determine areas that might need improvement.

Because informal analysis relies on each person's individual perceptions, it can be used to help teachers see things as others see them. Thus, informal analysis can be especially helpful in determining how students feel about what they have learned and their perceptions about the learning situation. The most effective informal analysis by students is written, not oral, and is anonymous to allow for free and honest responses. Use caution when asking young students to analyze teacher behavior. Avoid using questionnaires with students who do not have the ability to understand the intent of the questions and to provide valid answers. Some examples of questions that might be asked on a student questionnaire include the following:

1. What are the two most important things you have learned in this class?
2. What factors helped you learn them? (Be specific. Who did what to help you?)
3. How could this class be improved to make it better?
4. List the strengths of your teacher.
5. Tell how your teacher could help you learn better.

To score the analyses, simply tally the number of times a similar response was given to each question. Then look seriously at the ones listed most often. Also take note of responses that have never been given on previous questionnaires.

Checklists can also be used to obtain an overall estimate of student feelings toward specific aspects of teacher performance. Items might include some of the following:

1. Place a check beside *each* characteristic that describes your teacher:

_____ Interesting	_____ Organized	_____ Strict
_____ Smart	_____ Pushover	_____ Disorganized
_____ Uninformed	_____ Dull	

TEACHER EVALUATION RECORD

Name _____ Date_____ Evaluator _____

Instructions: Rate yourself (or have someone else rate you) on each of the major items by placing an "X" on the lines provided.

	Always	Usually	Sometimes	Seldom or Never	Doesn't Apply
Works Well with Associates					
Is friendly and cordial	_____	_____	_____	_____	_____
Possesses tact and courtesy	_____	_____	_____	_____	_____
Gains the respect of associates	_____	_____	_____	_____	_____
Promotes cooperative action among individuals and groups	_____	_____	_____	_____	_____
Listens attentively when associating with others	_____	_____	_____	_____	_____
Has a genuine desire to help others without concern for personal benefit or credit for achievement	_____	_____	_____	_____	_____
Is sensitive to own effect on others	_____	_____	_____	_____	_____
Accepts and utilizes suggestions from others	_____	_____	_____	_____	_____
Keeps informed on policies and procedures and follows them	_____	_____	_____	_____	_____
Asks questions to clarify assignments and responsibilities	_____	_____	_____	_____	_____
Carries own share of school responsibilities willingly and cheerfully	_____	_____	_____	_____	_____
Keeps commitments reliably	_____	_____	_____	_____	_____
Serves on committees and participates in other group projects	_____	_____	_____	_____	_____
Is prompt and accurate with reports	_____	_____	_____	_____	_____
Goes through regular "channels" on matters affecting the welfare of associates or of the institution	_____	_____	_____	_____	_____
Is loyal to associates, school, and district	_____	_____	_____	_____	_____

Figure 13.3 A portion of a teacher evaluation record.

2. Place a check beside the answer that best describes your feelings toward the teacher:
   a. The teacher helps me learn or improve my skills.
      Yes_____ No_____ I don't know_____
   b. The teacher has good discipline.
      Yes_____ No_____ I don't know_____

Several different types of rating scales can be used for student evaluation of teachers. Questions using a semantic differential scale to score student attitudes toward the teacher might appear as follows:

Friendly	: : : : : : : :	Unfriendly
Boring	: : : : : : : :	Interesting

Items are scored from one to seven, with seven being the most positive. An average of the scores for the entire class on each item would undoubtedly provide the most information.

A Likert-type scale can be used to determine student attitudes toward the teacher, or to compare how the students feel versus how the teacher feels about each characteristic. For example, in the following questions, x marks how the student feels, and o marks how the teacher feels on each item.

	Mostly true	Usually true	Neutral	Usually false	Mostly false
1. The teacher is concerned about student learning.	o			x	
2. The teacher likes teaching.		x	o		

When a serious discrepancy exists between the teacher's and the students' feelings, as in item 1, the teacher becomes aware of the need to communicate feelings differently.

Students' perceptions about the instructional system can also be acquired via a rating scale. An example of this type of rating scale is shown in figure 13.4. This scale could be used as a report card for students to grade the teacher at the end of a unit of instruction or grading period. The scale could be written at a lower level of reading ability for use by younger students.

Systematic Observation

One way to avoid the subjectivity inherent in informal analysis is to use systematic observation. Systematic observation is used to collect data that describe various components of the teaching performance. The data are then analyzed to determine the extent to which the intended teaching behavior actually occurred during teaching. The primary purpose of systematic observation is to collect objective data that accurately describe events occurring in the classroom. The data must be recorded in such a way that they can be used to analyze one or more components of the teaching/learning process.

Literally hundreds of analytic systems have been developed to encode student and teacher behaviors. Some are relatively easy to learn and use; others are so complex that only trained researchers use them. In this chapter, the simpler kinds of systematic observation that can be used for self-improvement are presented. These systems require only an observer, paper and pencil, and a

STUDENT OPINIONNAIRE—
BASIC INSTRUCTION PHYSICAL EDUCATION PROGRAM
KNOWLEDGE—CLARITY—ENTHUSIASM

1. The instructor effectively explained or demonstrated the skills of the activity.
   INEFFECTIVE A_____ B _____ C _____ D _____ E VERY EFFECTIVE

2. The instructor was perceptive in diagnosing and skillful in correcting individual errors in performance.
   OBLIVIOUS/NOT HELPFUL A_____ B _____ C _____ D _____ E PERCEPTIVE/HELPFUL

3. The instructor clearly explained the rules, scoring and strategies involved in the activity. (May not apply to dance, gymnastics, skating, etc.)
   VAGUELY A_____ B _____ C _____ D _____ E CLEARLY

4. The instructor was enthusiastic and interested in teaching the subject matter.
   APATHETIC A_____ B _____ C _____ D _____ E ENTHUSIASTIC

5. The instructor demonstrated a comprehensive knowledge of the activity.
   UNINFORMED A_____ B _____ C _____ D _____ E VERY KNOWLEDGEABLE

6. The instructor encouraged and motivated you to attain a higher skill level.
   UNCONCERNED A_____ B _____ C _____ D _____ E VERY PERSUASIVE

7. The instructor seemed capable of teaching the more highly skilled performers.
   INCAPABLE A_____ B _____ C _____ D _____ E VERY CAPABLE

ORGANIZATION AND PREPARATION

8. The instructor provided, verbally or via a course outline, the course objectives, expectations, assignments, examination information, and grading procedures.
   UNDEFINED A_____ B _____ C _____ D _____ E CLEARLY DEFINED

9. The instructor's lessons reflected planned learning sessions and efficient utilization of class time.
   DISORGANIZED A_____ B _____ C _____ D _____ E WELL PLANNED

10. Within the limitations of the facilities, the instructor provided maximal active participation time for all students.
    INACTIVE A_____ B _____ C _____ D _____ E VERY ACTIVE

11. The textbook and other instructional materials were of value in the course.
    NO BENEFIT A_____ B _____ C _____ D _____ E VERY VALUABLE

12. A safe learning environment was provided for the class.
    HARMFUL A_____ B _____ C _____ D _____ E VERY SAFE

INSTRUCTOR-STUDENT INTERACTION & RAPPORT

13. The instructor provided evaluative feedback concerning your skill development.
    UNINFORMATIVE A_____ B _____ C _____ D _____ E INFORMATIVE

14. The instructor was impartial and fair in dealing with students.
    UNFAIR A_____ B _____ C _____ D _____ E VERY FAIR

15. The instructor was interested in you and your skill development.
    DISINTERESTED A_____ B _____ C _____ D _____ E VERY INTERESTED

16. The instructor was understanding of and helpful to students who experienced difficulty acquiring the activity skills.
    NO HELP A_____ B _____ C _____ D _____ E VERY HELPFUL

GENERAL EVALUATION

17. Fun and enjoyment were experienced throughout the course.
    BORING A_____ B _____ C _____ D _____ E VERY ENJOYABLE

18. Based on your experience in this course, would you enroll in another physical education course and/or recommend activity courses to others?
    ABSOLUTELY NOT A_____ B _____ C _____ D _____ E DEFINITELY

19. Considering all aspects of the course, how would you rate this course?
    POOR A_____ B _____ C _____ D _____ E EXCELLENT

20. Considering all of the instructional aspects of this course, how would you rate the instructor?
    POOR A_____ B _____ C _____ D _____ E EXCELLENT

Figure 13.4 A student rating scale.
Source: Zakrajsek, Dorothy B. and Ronald R. Bos.
"Student Evaluations of Teaching Performance,"
Journal of Physical Education and Recreation, 49
(May 1978): 64–65.

stopwatch. A tape recorder or videorecorder can be valuable if teachers wish to analyze their own teaching behavior rather than have an outside observer evaluate them. The computer is a recent tool that aids the observer in teacher evaluation. The laptop models enable on-the-spot observation. Simple programs make it possible to keep track of time (e.g., minutes spent talking to the class) and behaviors (e.g., the number of times "okay" was said). Such programs usually convert tallies to percentages immediately and allow teachers to see results while everything is fresh in their minds.

Systematic observation is generally limited to a description of what the teacher and students were doing (i.e., how much time the teacher spends giving students practice or how much feedback students receive). It generally tells little about the quality of the performance (i.e., how well a teacher demonstrates a skill). Byra is one of the few researchers to develop an instrument to accurately measure and describe qualitative aspects of the teaching process (quality of demonstration, clarity of presentation, and quality of feedback).[11] Other limitations are the limited sample size (sometimes only one student), the limited time sample, and the limited set of categories used for describing behavior. Systematic observation uses the techniques of duration recording, interval recording, spot checking, and event recording. A discussion of each technique follows.

Duration Recording

Duration recording analyzes time and is useful for determining the amount of time spent on the various functions that teachers perform.[12] Such functions include instructing students (e.g., demonstrating, explaining, or questioning); class management (roll call, organizing students, distributing equipment, discipline); active student practice with feedback from the instructor; and student practice with no feedback from the instructor. A stopwatch is used to record the amount of time spent in each category. The stopwatch is restarted each time the teacher changes functions. An example of a duration recording form is shown in figure 13.5.

At the conclusion of the lesson, the time in each category is totaled and divided by the total class time to obtain the percentage of time spent in each category. Then the results are analyzed to see whether the time has been spent in the best way. Individual functions, such as roll call or demonstrations, can also be analyzed by duration recording to determine where the time is going, and changes can be made to eliminate the nonproductive use of time.

A variation of duration recording is to record the amount of time an individual student spends in actual practice. The teacher may discover that, although the class is engaged in what appears to be a large amount of practice time, individual students spend a large amount of time waiting for a turn or standing out in right field.

Duration recording can also be done for several brief periods of time spaced throughout a lesson. For example, three 5-minute samples can provide a valid indication of the percentage of time spent in each type of behavior.[13] To obtain a percentage, merely divide by 15 minutes instead of the total class time.

Interval Recording

In interval recording, the observation session is divided into a number of equal intervals, and a specified behavior is observed and recorded at the conclusion of each interval. For example, in a 35-minute period there are 35 one-minute intervals or 70 thirty-second intervals. The number of intervals selected will depend on the behavior to be sampled.

Because interval recording occurs only at the end of each interval, considerable time is saved. Some time samples, such as checking on a student every five minutes to determine student involvement in activity, can even be done while teaching.

TIME ANALYSIS FORM

Class __Badminton__ Date __March 16__

Total class time __37 minutes__

Instruction	Management	Participation with feedback	Participation without feedback
4:30	3:06	6:18	2:06
1:10	1:24	3:50	6:00
1:10	2:50	10:08	8:06
2:00	1:50		
8:50	1:50		
	:46		
	9:56		

| 23.87% | 26.85% | 27.39% | 21.89% |

Suggestions for improvement

1. I should try to reduce the time spent organizing students during each management episode to less than 1 minute.
2. I should provide more feedback during student practice.

Figure 13.5 A duration recording form.

The easiest kind of interval recording involves only two categories, such as active or passive, productive or nonproductive. A student is selected, and at the end of each interval a check or tally indicates the behavior the student demonstrates. Several students can be observed by observing the first student during intervals 1, 4, 7, and so on; the second student during intervals 2, 5, 8, and so on; and the third student during intervals 3, 6, 9, and so on. The intervals can be recorded on a tape recorder, or a watch or stopwatch can be used to determine the end of each interval. To code a number of behaviors, the observer selects an average student and codes what the student is doing at the end of each interval. To make it easier, coding can be done for three minutes, followed by resting three minutes, and repeating the coding and resting throughout the period.

Figure 13.6 shows an interval recording form designed by Anderson to determine how students are spending their time during a class session. It uses a five-second interval for coding. The categories are the following:

1. Performs motor activity—Plays game or sport, practices skill, does exercises or calisthenics, explores movement
2. Receives information—Listens, watches demonstration, uses media, reads written material
3. Gives information or assists—Talks to teacher or student, demonstrates, spots
4. Waits—Waits for turn, waits for game or drill to begin
5. Relocates—Moves from one place or activity area to another
6. Other—Ties shoes, gets equipment, gets a drink

At the end of each three-minute period, notes can be recorded to help the teacher recall information explaining the recorded behaviors. At the end of the period, each column is totaled and a percentage calculated. The behavior is then analyzed and goals set for improving teaching. Figure 13.7 shows another type of interval recording form.

Teacher behaviors can also be coded using interval recording and the categories used for duration recording. An example of an interval recording form for teacher behavior appears in figure 13.8.

Spot Checking

Spot checking is interval recording applied to a group. It is useful when you want to know what most of the students in a group or class are doing. Spot checking involves counting the number of students engaged in a particular behavior at the conclusion of a specified interval of time, such as every two or three minutes. Limit behaviors to be checked to two or three so the spot check takes only about 10 seconds. The observer scans from left to right each time and records the number of students who are engaged in the less frequently occurring behavior. For example, in an actively involved class, the inactive students are counted and subtracted from the total number of students to get the number in the actively involved category. A sample spot-checking record is shown in figure 13.9.

Anderson suggested the use of the following categories for spot checking: active/inactive, on-task/off-task, safe/unsafe, attentive/unattentive, cooperative/disruptive, and interacting with others/isolated.[14] Most of the students should be engaged in appropriate and productive behavior for teaching to be effective. An example of spot checking is shown in figure 13.10.

At the conclusion of the class, the percentage of students in each category is calculated by dividing each column total by the sum of the two or three columns. The data are then analyzed, and changes are planned for improving teaching behavior.

Event Recording

Event recording is merely tallying the frequency with which a given behavior occurs during a specified time period. It is done by identifying one person to observe (the teacher, an average student) and one or more behaviors to tally. The observer then proceeds to put down a mark each time the specified behavior occurs. For simple behaviors, a golf counter can be used to record frequency. Five 3-minute intervals, spaced throughout the period, are usually adequate for event recording.

Sample Coding Form and Record

TIME SAMPLING OF A SINGLE STUDENT'S BEHAVIOR

RECORD A CHECK (✓) FOR EACH
5 SECONDS OF STUDENT ACTIVITY.

STUDENT'S NAME: Alice Smith

CLASS: Elementary Gymnastics

SEGMENT (3-MIN)	PERFORMS MOTOR ACTIVITY	RECEIVES INFORMATION	GIVES INFORMATION OR ASSISTS	WAITS	RELOCATES	OTHER	NOTATIONS
I 9:00- 9:03	✓✓✓ ③	✓✓✓✓✓ ✓✓✓✓✓ ✓✓✓✓✓ ✓✓✓✓✓ ㉒		✓✓✓✓✓ ✓✓✓✓✓ ⑩	✓✓ ②	✓ ①	Waited for teacher to begin Rec. info on class organization
II 9:06- 9:09	✓✓✓✓✓ ✓✓✓ ⑧	✓✓✓✓✓ ✓✓✓✓✓ ✓✓✓✓✓ ✓✓ ㉒		✓✓ ②	✓✓✓ ③	✓ ①	End instruction / began tumbling and head stand
III 9:12- 9:15	✓✓✓✓ ✓✓✓✓✓ ✓✓✓✓✓ ✓✓ ⑰	✓✓✓✓✓ ⑤	✓✓✓✓✓ ⑤	✓✓ ②	✓ ①	✓✓✓✓✓ ✓ ⑥	Cont'd. tumbling "Other" = replaced mats
IV 9:18- 9:21	✓✓✓✓✓ ✓✓✓✓✓ ✓✓✓✓✓ ✓✓ ㉒	✓✓✓ ③	✓✓✓ ③	✓✓✓✓✓ ⑤		✓✓✓ ③	Performed on ropes
V 9:24- 9:27	✓✓✓ ③	✓✓✓✓✓ ✓✓✓✓✓ ✓✓✓✓✓ ✓✓✓✓✓ ㉓		✓✓✓ ③	✓✓✓ ③	✓✓ ②	Recd. instruction on bars
VI 9:30- 9:33	✓✓✓ ③	✓✓✓✓✓ ✓✓✓✓ ⑩		✓✓✓✓✓ ✓✓✓✓✓ ✓✓✓✓✓ ✓✓✓✓✓ ✓ ㉑		✓✓ ②	Waits turn on bars and performs
TOTALS	f = 56 % = 56/216 = 26%	f = 85 % = 85/216 = 39%	f = 8 % = 8/216 = 3%	f = 43 % = 43/216 = 19%	f = 9 % = 9/216 = 4%	f = 15 % = 15/216 = 7%	

SUMMARY COMMENTS AND EVALUATION (made by Teacher of class)

Too much time spent waiting for teacher and getting organized.

Good activity levels on mats and ropes — too much waiting around on bars.

Overall, a greater proportion of time should be spent in performing activities.

Figure 13.6 An interval recording form for student behavior.
Source: From Anderson, William G. *Analysis of Teaching Physical Education,* St. Louis, 1980. The C. V. Mosby Co.

STUDENTS' USE OF TIME CODING FORM

Teacher **MRS. WARNICK**   Coder **J. BRAITHWAITE**

Date **10/22**   # of students **39**   over 50% of students **20**

Time Analysis Codes: Decision is based on what 51% of the observed students are doing at the
time and of each 15 second segment.

M = Management: Time when *most* students (over 50%) are *not* receiving instruction or involved in lesson activity, eg., changing activities; getting out or putting away equipment; listening *to* behavior rules or reminder.

A = Activity: Time when most students (over 50%) are involved in physical movement, e.g., catching a ball; throwing at a target.

I = Instruction: Time when most students (over 50%) are receiving information about how to move or perform a skill, e.g., how to move using all the space; watching a demonstration; listening to instructions.

W = Waiting: Time when most students (over 50%) are *not* involved in the other categories, e.g., group activity but only one or two are participating; waiting for a turn; off-task behavior; waiting for the teacher to give directions.

Percent of M time =	**210**	÷	**1440**	= **15**	%
	TOTAL M seconds		TOTAL LESSON seconds		
Percent of A time =	**855**	÷	**1440**	= **59**	%
	TOTAL A seconds		TOTAL LESSON seconds		
Percent of I time =	**285**	÷	**1440**	= **20**	%
	TOTAL I seconds		TOTAL LESSON seconds		
Percent of W time =	**90**	÷	**1440**	= **6**	%
	TOTAL W seconds		TOTAL LESSON seconds		

Figure 13.7 An interval recording form for student behavior.
Source: George Graham. *Beyond Ordinary: Teaching to Make a Difference,* Department of Exercise and Sport Science, University of Utah, 1990.

TIME SAMPLING OF TEACHER BEHAVIOR

Class **BASKETBALL**   Date **5/2**

Total Class Time **50 MIN.**

Instructions: Record a check (✔) for each five seconds of teacher activity. **[EVERY 10 MIN. — DO A SEGMENT]**

Segment (3 min.)	Instruction			Management Activities	Student Participation	
	Class	Group	Individual		With Feedback	Without Feedback
I	✓✓✓✓ ✓✓✓✓ ✓✓✓✓ ✓✓	✓✓ ✓✓	✓✓	✓✓✓✓✓✓	✓✓✓✓	✓✓✓✓ ✓✓
II		✓✓✓✓ ✓✓✓✓ ✓✓	✓✓✓✓✓ ✓✓✓✓✓		✓✓✓✓✓✓ ✓✓✓✓✓✓ ✓✓✓✓✓✓ ✓✓✓✓✓✓	✓✓
III	✓✓✓✓✓ ✓✓✓✓✓ ✓✓✓✓✓ ✓✓✓✓✓		✓✓✓✓✓	✓✓✓✓	✓✓✓✓✓	✓✓
IV					✓✓✓✓✓✓✓ ✓✓✓✓✓✓ ✓✓✓✓✓ ✓✓✓✓✓✓	✓✓✓✓
V					✓✓✓✓✓✓ ✓✓✓✓✓✓	✓✓✓✓✓ ✓✓✓✓ ✓✓✓✓✓✓ ✓✓✓✓✓
Totals	5¾ MIN.	1 MIN.	1½ MIN.	.80 MIN.	6÷ MIN.	3 MIN.

Summary Comments and Evaluations:

AS CLASS PROGRESSED & STUDENTS PLAYED GAMES THEY GOT LESS FEEDBACK.

Figure 13.8 An interval recording form for teacher behavior.

Class Track and Field   **Date** May 10

Time \ Categories	Off-task	On-task active	On-task waiting	Comments
8:50	1	2	7	TIEING SHOES
8:56	0	3	7	PRACTICED WHILE WAITING
9:02	0	3	7	
9:08	3	2	5	TALKING
9:14	4	3	3	PLAYING AROUND
8:52	0	1	9	COMPLIMENTED OTHERS
8:58	0	1	9	
9:04	2	1	7	TALKING
9:10	5	1	4	TALKING
9:16	4	1	5	WANDERED OFF
8:54	0	4	6	
9:00	0	4	6	PRACTICED WHILE WAITING
9:06	0	4	6	
9:12	1	3	6	GETTING A DRINK
9:18	2	4	4	TALKING
Column Totals	22	37	91	
Total of All Columns		150		
Percent of Total	14.7%	24.7%	60.7%	

Rows labeled on left margin: High Jump (first 5 rows), Long Jump (next 5 rows), Hurdles (last 5 rows).

Summary Comments and Evaluation:

on-task, active = performing or helping
on-task, waiting = watching performance
off-task = talking, wandering around, daydreaming

Students are spending a lot of time waiting
and seem bored, especially at end of period.

Figure 13.9 A sample spot-checking record.

INSTRUCTIONS FOR OBSERVATION TOOL USE

MANAGEMENT TIME

Record the amount of time spent in each management segment. Management is defined as activities such as taking roll, giving announcements, explaining procedures, giving instructions, moving to different activities.

Add each segment to determine total management time and record the total class time. Divide management time by the total time. A goal to strive for would be less than 20% management time.

ACTIVITY SCAN

Record the total number of students in attendance and able to participate for the class period being observed.

During six 1-minute segments of class do the following: Each 10 seconds scan the class and take a quick count of the number of students actively engaged in the assigned task. After each 10-second count record the number on the appropriate space. (1) is for the first 10-second interval, (2) is for the second 10-second interval, and so on to (6) for the last 10-second interval.

The activity scans should be spread out throughout the class period and occur only during activity time and not during management time.

The goal is that over 50% of the students are active during *all* 10-second intervals during each scan.

FEEDBACK

Record a C, G, or I for each item of feedback given in the appropriate box, using C for feedback given to the entire class, G for feedback given to a portion or group within the class, and I for feedback given to one individual.

Non-skill items refer to comments made which are not related to the skills being taught. A negative example would be comments relating to bad behavior, while praising good behavior would be positive non-skill feedback. Other examples could be appearance or a comment about something that occurred outside of class.

Skill items relate to the skill being taught. Corrections for improvement would be considered negative skill feedback while indicating what has been done correctly would be positive.

Count the number of feedback comments recorded and place the total for each category to the right of the corresponding box. Add the four totals together for total feedback. Divide the total feedback by the total class time. The goal should be at least two or three per minute.

Figure 13.10 An observation sheet using duration recording, spot checking, and event recording.
SOURCE: Marilyn Buck.

Name Mr. Zimmerman _ _ _ _ _ _ _ _ _ Evaluator M. Blake _ _ _ _ _

Date _ _ 10/11 _ _ _ _ _ _ _ _ Grade _ _ 9 _ _ _ _ _ Activity Basketball _ _

MANAGEMENT TIME

_ _5_ _ Min.　　　　_ _3_ Min.　　　　_ _1_ _ Min.　　　　_ _ _ _ _Min.

_ _1_ _ Min.　　　　_ _6_ Min.　　　　_ _ _ _ _ Min.　　　　_ _ _ _ Min.

Total Management Time _ _16_　　　　　　　　Total Time_ _45_ _

% Management (Management divided by total time) 35%_ _
(Should be 20% or less)

ACTIVITY SCAN

Total students _ _40_ _

1st　(1) _31_ _ (2) _30_ _ (3) _25_ _ (4) _31_ _ (5) _28_ (6) _29_ _

2nd　(1) _15_ _ (2) _16_ _ (3) _17_ _ (4) _15_ _ (5) _14_ (6) _18_ _

3rd　(1) _30_ _ (2) _27_ _ (3) _42_ _ (4) _40_ _ (5) _35_ (6) _30_ _

4th　(1) _28_ _ (2) _30_ _ (3) _33_ _ (4) _37_ _ (5) _30_ (6) _29_ _

5th　(1) _25_ _ (2) _28_ _ (3) _25_ _ (4) _29_ _ (5) _30_ (6) _27_ _

6th　(1) _31_ _ (2) _33_ _ (3) _32_ _ (4) _30_ _ (5) _35_ (6) _34_ _

(Goal: over 50% of students active during all 10 sec. intervals)

FEEDBACK

		Total
Positive Non-skill	C C C G C I	Total = _ _6_
Negative Non-skill	I I I G C	Total = _ _5_
Positive Skill	C G I I G C C I I G	Total = _10_
Negative Skill	C I I G	Total = _ _4_

C = Class　　　　G = Group　　　　I = Individual

Total Feedback _ _ _25_　　　　Total per minute (Fb/Min) _1.8_ _ _
(One feedback per minute is absolute minimum. Should be 2 or 3)

GENERAL COMMENTS Too much time spent on management. Second activity needs to be changed (too much waiting) Very negative feedback to one child caused a total class disruption. Feedback is generally positive. Need to give more feedback, generally keep class active.

Figure 13.10 (Continued)

Event recording can be used to collect meaningful data on a wide variety of teacher or student behaviors. It produces a numerical value that can be converted into rate per minute. The rate per minute on different occasions can then be compared to determine whether improvement in the behavior has occurred. Event recording can be used to record items involving instruction, class management, student practice, use of first names, and feedback.

Instruction. The extent to which the intended concepts are conveyed to the students can be determined by listing each concept and recording a check beside the concept each time it is mentioned by the teacher. An example of content evaluation is shown in figure 13.11.

Class Management. Event recording can be used to tally the number of times the students have to be told how to assume a formation for roll call, drill, or game play. For each transition from one activity to another, only one teacher behavior should be emitted. In the example shown in figure 13.12, the teacher spent 3:06 minutes organizing drills and told the students how to get organized seven times. This teacher needs to clarify instructions so that they are communicated to students on the first try.

Student Practice. The number of practice trials a student attempts or the number of times a student touches the ball or uses a piece of equipment can be easily tallied, as shown in figure 13.13. This can be done during practice drills, in lead-up games, or during actual game play. A list of skills or tasks to be accomplished, with a check by each one attempted, provides an overall view of the distribution of practice over the entire range of tasks inherent in the activity. Figures 13.13 and 13.14 show how this can be done. A study of the record aids the teacher in determining the adequacy and distribution of practice trials.

Feedback. Feedback has been defined as one of the key elements in the acquisition of psychomotor skills. Feedback also occurs in response to appropriate and inappropriate student behavior. Event recording can be used to record the extent to which both kinds of feedback occur. Both skill feedback and behavior feedback can be analyzed in the following ways by using the form in figure 13.15 (feedback is also evaluated in figure 13.10):

1. Rate of feedback per minute.
2. Ratio of positive to negative feedback. Feedback should generally be in the ratio of four positive comments to each negative comment.
3. Percentage of specific feedback.
4. Percentage of value feedback.
5. Percentage of group-directed feedback.
6. Percentage of nonverbal feedback.
7. Ratio of reinforcement of appropriate behavior to punishment of off-task behavior.

Each column of the form can be used separately, or several columns can be recorded at once. Simple computer programs make such recording less tedious. Categories can be defined as follows:

1. Positive—A tone that conveys acceptance of a student's performance or behavior.
2. Negative—A tone that conveys rejection of a student's performance or behavior.
3. General—Feedback with no specific information given about the skill or behavior.
4. Specific—Feedback with specific information given about how to perform the behavior or skill.

Sample Coding Form and Record

CONTENT OF TEACHER'S INSTRUCTIONS
A check (✓) is recorded each time the teacher refers to a listed item of content

TENNIS LESSON ON BACKHAND DRIVE	BASIC MOVEMENT LESSON ON THROWING
1. Entire stroke (general) ✓✓	1. Performance elements
	- Eyes on target ✓
2. Grip (general) ✓	- Feet apart ✓✓
- 1/8th turn ✓	- Rotate trunk
- 45° angle	- Weight to back foot
- Other (list) *too loose* ✓	- Elbow bent
	- Transfer weight to front foot
3. Back swing (general)	- Point of release ✓✓
- Short ✓	- Follow through ✓✓
- Help with left hand ✓	
- Body pivot ✓✓✓✓ ✓✓✓✓	
- Elbow position ✓	2. Major concepts
- Other (list)	- Point of release affects direction ✓✓✓✓
	- Transfer of weight gives power
4. Forward swing (general) ✓	
- Arc of racket ✓	3. Common errors
- Point of contact ✓✓✓✓✓✓✓✓✓✓	- Facing front ✓✓✓✓✓✓✓✓✓
- Angle of contact	- no rotation ✓✓✓
- Other (list) *eye on ball* ✓✓✓✓	- Pushing
5. Follow through (general) ✓	
- Racket head rises	4. Other (list)
- Top spin	*forgot to snap wrist* ✓✓
- Other (list) *smoothness* ✓	*"stride" toward target* ✓
	angle of projection ✓
6. Common errors	
- Excessive body action	
- Chopping	
- Other (list) *backswing too long* ✓✓	
elbow finish ✓	
7. Other (list)	
getting into position ✓✓✓✓✓✓✓	
anticipating flight of ball ✓✓✓✓ ✓✓✓✓✓	

SUMMARY COMMENTS AND EVALUATION	SUMMARY COMMENTS AND EVALUATION
I neglected the "follow through". I forgot to include "eye on ball" in initial plan, but covered it with individual students. "Positioning" and "anticipation" came up frequently, include in future presentations. Emphasized "point of contact" and forgot about "angle of contact".	Tried to cover too much with these third graders so purposely left out some things. Forgot to cover "weight transfer = greater power". Too many students had to be corrected for facing front, emphasize "sideward" stance next time. Performance elements were covered at beginning, but not during later practice.

Figure 13.11 A sample content evaluation record.
Source: From Anderson, William G. *Analysis of Teaching Physical Education,* St. Louis, 1980. The C. V. Mosby Co.

RECORD OF TEACHER MANAGEMENT BEHAVIORS

Length of Each Episode	Number of Teacher Management Behaviors	Types of Management Behaviors
3:06	⊬⊬ II	Organizing drills
1:24	III	Changing drills
2:50	IIII	Starting games
1:50	III	Rotating teams
:46	II	Ending class

Total Management Time = 9:56
Average Time Per Episode = abt 2 min.
Average Number of Teacher Behaviors Per Episode = 3.8

Summary Comments and Evaluation:

I need to clarify my expectations so that I don't need to repeat instructions more than once.

Figure 13.12 A sample record of management behaviors.

STUDENT PRACTICE RECORD

Class ___Soccer_____   Date ___Oct. 15_____

Skills	Student #1 Period _1_	Student #2 Period _1_	Student #3 Period _1_	Student #4 Period ___
Number of times each student touches the ball	ЖНI ЖНI ЖНI III	II	ЖНI)III	

Summary Comments and Evaluation:

Apparently student #2 rarely touches the ball. Perhaps I need to use smaller teams or rotate players so each student has an equal opportunity for skill development.

Figure 13.13 A sample record of student practice.

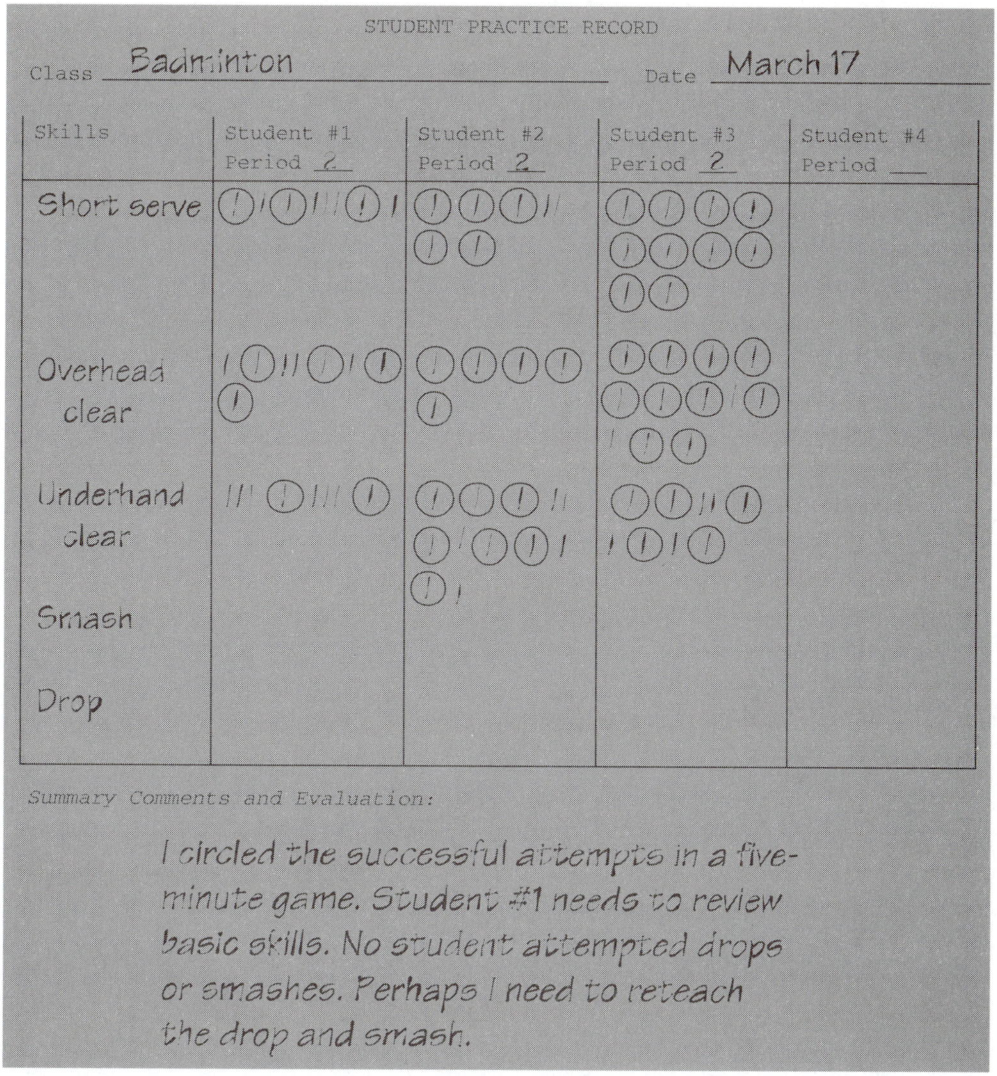

STUDENT PRACTICE RECORD

Class __Badminton__   Date __March 17__

Skills	Student #1 Period 2	Student #2 Period 2	Student #3 Period 2	Student #4 Period ___
Short serve	① / ① / / ① /	① / ① ① / / ① ①	① / ① ① / ① / ① / ① / ① /	
Overhead clear	/ ① / / ① / ① ①	① / ① / ① / ① ①	① / ① / ① / ① ① / ① / ① / ① / ① ①	
Underhand clear	/ / / ① / / / / ①	① / ① / ① / / ① / ① ① / ① /	① / ① / / / ① / ① / ① /	
Smash				
Drop				

Summary Comments and Evaluation:

I circled the successful attempts in a five-minute game. Student #1 needs to review basic skills. No student attempted drops or smashes. Perhaps I need to reteach the drop and smash.

Figure 13.14 A record of student trials on key skills.

EVENT RECORDING OF BEHAVIOR OR SKILL FEEDBACK

✓ — Skill Feedback
— Behavior Feedback

Five-minute Event Recording	Tone Pos./Neg.	Kind General/Specific/Value	To Whom Individual/Group	Skill-Feedback Type Verbal	Skill-Feedback Type Visual and Verbal	Skill-Feedback Type Kinesthetic and Verbal	Behavior-Feedback Type Reinforces Appropriate Behavior	Behavior-Feedback Type Punishes Off-Task Behaviors
I	‖ ₪			₪ / ‖						‖₪
II	/ ₪ ₪			‖ / ‖						
III	‖‖			₪‖ ‖‖ / /				‖	₪‖ ‖
IV	‖ ₪			‖ / /						‖
V	‖‖ ‖			₪ ₪ / /				‖	₪ ₪
Totals	8 | 26		29 | 5				4	27

Summary:

Feedback per minute =

Ratio of positive to negative feedback = 8/26

Percent of specific feedback =

Percent of feedback that explains why =

Percent of group-directed feedback = 14.7%

Percent of nonverbal feedback =

Ratio of reinforcement to punishment = 4/27

Comments and Evaluation:

Feedback is generally negative in tone and directed toward individuals. I need to look for what students do well and reinforce them, especially in group situations.

Figure 13.15 Event recording of behavior or skill feedback.

5. Value—Feedback that tells why a specific behavior or skill should be done in a certain way.
6. Individual—Feedback to one student.
7. Group—Feedback to more than one student.
8. Verbal—Feedback that is only verbal.
9. Visual and verbal—Feedback that demonstrates how the skill or behavior should be performed.
10. Kinesthetic and verbal—Feedback that uses touch or manipulation of body parts to correct the movement (such as spotting in gymnastics).
11. Reinforces appropriate behavior—Feedback that rewards appropriate behavior.
12. Punishes off-task behavior—Feedback that is nonreinforcing or punishing for inappropriate behavior.

Creating a Personalized Descriptive System

Often evaluation instruments are not appropriate for specific situations. Those who know the situation best can create or adapt an appropriate tool for evaluation. Once an instrument has been formulated, try it out and check it for reliability. Make modifications until it brings the desired results. When preparing a descriptive system, incorporate the following components: (1) a single behavior focus, (2) a definition of categories, (3) an observation and coding system, and (4) reliability.

The Behavior Focus. Select a single teaching component for analysis. Trying to analyze too much can defeat the system. Define the component to identify what is and what is not included in the behavior focus. An example for one teacher was to reduce the use of distracting words or phrases.

Definition of Categories. Categories within the behavioral focus must be defined so that any observable behavior can be assigned to only one category. Provide examples of behaviors falling into each category. For example, "ok" or "all right" fit into the category of distracting words or phrases.

An Observation and Coding System. Choose a technique such as duration recording, interval recording, spot checking, or event recording; then develop a form for recording the data.

Reliability. Reliability results when two observers obtain similar results after independently rating the same lesson or when one observer obtains the same results on two separate occasions from a videotaped recording. When this occurs, it reveals that the definitions of the behavior categories are sufficiently clear to ensure that behaviors are recorded accurately by the observer and reflect the actual behavior that occurred during the lesson.

Interaction Analysis

Interaction analysis provides objective feedback about the type and quality of teacher–student interaction. Most of the interaction analysis systems have been based on verbal interaction, and nearly all of them are based on teacher dominance of instruction. The best-known tool for interaction analysis is the Flanders system.[15] This system does not differentiate behaviors used most by physical education teachers. A number of adaptations of the Flanders system have been produced. However, they made the system cumbersome to use for teacher improvement.

Anderson identified a simpler method for recording the interaction of teachers and students.[16] It is based on Morgenegg's findings that interaction in physical education classes focused on the three behaviors of teacher solicitations of movement, student movement responses, and teacher reactions to the movement responses.[17] A sample coding form is shown in figure 13.16. Each entry shows who solicited the response (the teacher or the student), who reacted and how (motor activity, verbal activity, or other behavior), and the reaction caused by the behavior. For example, the teacher asks students to get ready to shoot and the students respond; or the teacher asks a student to shoot an arrow, the student responds by shooting, and the teacher replies, "Good!"

Include four or more five-minute coding periods. At the conclusion of the lesson, the amount and direction of the interactions are evaluated. Answering the following questions will help direct the teacher toward an analysis of the results. Are all solicitations initiated by the teacher or are students encouraged to seek out solutions to their problems? Is there a balance between teacher-directed instruction and student-directed instruction? Does the teacher react enough? Or too much?

Step 3—*Use the appropriate techniques to record information.*

Table 13.1 listed possible evaluation techniques for the teaching goals and behaviors specified in Step 1. The best evaluation technique is the one that provides precise feedback related to the specific teaching goal. Since only a few events can be recorded during each lesson, formulate a plan to utilize the most effective techniques for the objectives of the specific lesson. A sample evaluation plan for a lesson is shown in figure 13.17. Keep the plan simple. Two or three evaluation techniques at a time are probably as many as can be checked accurately.

Step 4—*Evaluate or interpret the data.*

So far, research has been unable to find one best way to teach. Therefore, teachers must experiment to determine the best combination of teaching skills to create the desired results for their particular students and situation. The major purpose of the evaluation is to determine how closely the actual teaching behavior matches the intended behavior. This can be done by referring back to the plan established in Step 3. Some questions to ask are as follows:

1. What teaching behaviors are satisfactory?
2. What changes in teaching behaviors might improve student learning?
3. Which changes are practical?
4. Which one or two changes in teacher behavior would result in the most important changes in student performance?
5. What will have to be done to implement these changes?
6. What target goal for the change would be indicative of a successful change effort (e.g., call 10 students by name each period)?

Anderson delineated some problems with attempting to interpret the match between actual and intended behaviors:

> There will be a natural tendency to be pleased when reality matches your plans and to be disheartened when there is a mismatch. . . . That's as it should be, most of the time—but not always. There are times when unfolding events in class signify the need for a change of plan in midstream. A teacher who is tuned in to such signals is likely to digress from his or her original plan. In such cases the record will show a mismatch. Is that bad? There are

Sample Coding Form and Record

TEACHER - STUDENT INTERACTION

CLASS: Jr. H.S. Archery

TEACHER: Dick Martin

CODES: (T) Teacher (S) Student
(M) Motor activity
(V) Verbal activity or response
(O) Other behavior

SOLICIT	RESPOND	REACT
T	S o	
T	S o	
T	S o	
S	T v	T
T	S m	
T	S m	
T	S m	T
T	S m	T
		T m
		T m
		T
T	S o	
T	S m	
T	S m	
T	S m	
T	S v	T
T	S m	T m
S	T v	
T	S m	
T	S m	T
T	S m	T m
		T m
		T m
T	S o	
T	S o	
T	S v	
T	S m	
T	S m	T
T	S m	T
T	S m	
T	S m	T m
		T m
S	T o	
T	S m	
T	S m	
T	S m	
T	S o	
T	S o	

TOTALS:

SOLICITATIONS: 32					
By teacher: 29			By students: 3		
verb.	mot.	oth.	verb.	mot.	oth.
2	19	8	2	1	0

RESPONSES: 32					
By teacher: 3			By students: 29		
verb.	mot.	oth.	verb.	mot.	oth.
2	0	1	2	19	8

REACTIONS: 16					
By teacher: 16			By students: 0		
verb.	mot.	oth.	verb.	mot.	oth.
0	15	1	0	0	0

MOST COMMON PATTERNS: $T \rightarrow S_M = 13$
$T \rightarrow S_M \rightarrow T = 6$
$T \rightarrow S_O = 8$
$T_M = 8$

SUMMARY COMMMENTS AND EVALUATION (by observed teacher)

I do virtually all the soliciting and reacting; the students do almost all the responding.
I focus on eliciting student motor responses - which is OK - but I virtually never elicit verbal responses from students - which is not OK.
I seem to be reasonably conscientious about reacting to what students do.
Overall, I'm concerned that I seem to start (solicit) and end (react) all the interactions.

Figure 13.16 A sample coding form for teacher–student interaction.
Source: From Anderson, William G. *Analysis of Teaching Physical Education,* St. Louis, 1980. The C. V. Mosby Co.

```
                        AN EVALUATION PLAN

Lesson Plan                 Evaluation Plan                 Data

Objectives
1. Students will hit        Students record
   three out of five        number of successful
   balls pitched to         hits during a
   them during drill.       specified time
                            period.

2. Students will hit        Tally number of
   100 percent of the       students at bat and
   times at bat in          number of successful
   one-swing game           hits.

Teaching and Learning Activities
1. Demonstrate and          Event recording of
   explain batting.         content of teacher's
                            instruction.

2. Pepper drill for         Event recording of
   maximum                  student trials
   participation with       during drill and
   teacher feedback.        skill feedback of
                            teacher.

3. One-swing softball       Event recording of
   game for                 student trials and
   application to           successes during
   game situation.          game.

Specific Teacher Goals
1. Reduce management        Time analysis of
   time.                    management time.

Summary Comments and Evaluation
```

Figure 13.17 A sample evaluation plan.

times when unfolding events in class signify the need for a change of plan but the teacher is *not* tuned in to such signals, and so he or she plows ahead as originally planned. (Some teachers who *are* tuned in plow ahead anyway.) Such behavior will produce a record that shows a close match with the original plan. Is that good?

Sometimes, in the midst of a lesson you come up with a brilliant idea that you hadn't thought of before. You try it out and it works. So you continue to pursue it and in the process abandon your original intentions. The lesson turns out to be a smashing success. The record shows an enormous mismatch. So? . . . Interpreting matches and mismatches can be tricky business. Be careful.[18]

Evaluating teacher effectiveness is complex and tricky. One research study concluded that the instrumentation to measure effectiveness was not sensitive to differences in how individual teachers handled individual skills. The instruments used to evaluate instruction indicated that instructional characteristics did not change from skill to skill, but student learning did.[19]

Step 5—*Make changes and reevaluate.*

Try to incorporate the selected changes into the teaching repertoire. Make only one or two changes at a time. Teach the same or a similar lesson, concentrating on the intended changes, and reevaluate the lesson to determine whether the changes produced the desired results. If not, select a new procedure to try.

An Example of Teacher Evaluation
Step 1—*Determine what to evaluate.*

For a softball unit, the teacher selected the following evaluation goals: (1) to increase student skill achievement and (2) to reduce class management time.

Step 2 — *Choose or construct specific evaluation techniques.*

The specific evaluation techniques selected were (1) student achievement, (2) duration recording and event recording of management time as shown in figures 13.5 and 13.12, (3) event recording of student practice using the technique demonstrated in figure 13.14, and (4) event recording of skill feedback as shown in figure 13.15.

Step 3—*Use the appropriate techniques to record information.*

Student assistants were used to record student achievement and practice by tallying successful trials. Several lessons were videotaped for evaluation of management time and skill feedback. A sample evaluation plan for one of the lessons is shown in figure 13.17.

Step 4—*Evaluate or interpret the data.*

The results of the data showed that students were spending too much time practicing without the help of teacher feedback and the feedback when given was primarily verbal. With regard to class management, the analysis showed that the teacher had to tell students several times before they proceeded to do what they had been told.

Step 5—*Make changes and reevaluate.*

The teacher decided to use a golf counter to keep a tally of the number of feedback attempts during one period each day to increase the frequency of feedback. Later, an event recording of skill feedback also showed an increase in the number of nonverbal feedback attempts.

The second result of the evaluation occurred in class management. The teacher told the students what they were to do, asked several questions to determine whether they understood, and then refrained from repeating instructions. Students were timed to determine how long it took to get into the next formation, drill, or game, and feedback provided on the length of time it took. The result was a rapid decrease in management time.

A Challenge to Teachers
Evaluation challenges teachers to "put it all together" and, as a summarizing experience, gives teachers a sense of accomplishment by helping them realize how much they have achieved. As a learning activity it should also focus the teacher on how to improve the transmission of

information and skills. By helping teachers check the effectiveness of the teaching process, evaluation tells the teacher whether students have achieved the course objectives and the progress they made in doing so. When evaluation materials show that students are not performing well, the teacher should examine unit and lesson plans to determine whether the achievement of performance objectives was pursued in a meaningful way. Next, the teacher must critically decide whether his or her teaching techniques were effective.

Because evaluation is so critical, it should be an ongoing process. Evaluation makes students accountable for their performance and teachers responsible for student achievement. Such accountability, which is often lacking, is vital to the credibility and effectiveness of the profession.

Review Questions

1. What is accountability? How can physical education teachers demonstrate accountability for educating students?
2. Define and give an example of each of the following teacher evaluation techniques:
   Student achievement and improvement
   Informal analysis
   Systematic observation
   Duration recording
   Interval recording
   Spot checking
   Event recording
   Interaction analysis
3. How can teacher evaluation techniques help teachers improve their teaching?

References

1. U.S. Department of Education. (1987). *Education report card.* Washington, DC: Author.
2. Staff. (1987, February 11). *The Daily Universe.*
3. Benjamin, R. (1981). *Making schools work: A reporter's journey through some of America's most remarkable classrooms* (p. 119). New York: Continuum.
4. Arbogast, G. W., & Griffin, L. (1989, August). Accountability—Is it within reach of the profession? *Journal of Physical Education, Recreation and Dance, 60*(6), 72–75.
5. Maggard, N. J. (1984). Upgrading our image. *Journal of Physical Education, Recreation and Dance, 55*(1), 17, 82.
6. Benjamin, *Making schools work,* 177.
7. Bucher, C. A., & Koenig, C. R. (1983). *Methods and materials for secondary school physical education* (6th ed., p. 184). St. Louis, MO: Mosby.
8. Griffey, D. C. (1987, February). Trouble for sure: a crisis—perhaps: Secondary school physical education today. *Journal of Health, Physical Education, Recreation and Dance, 58,* 21.
9. Siedentop, D. (1991). *Developing teaching skills in physical education* (3rd ed., pp. 302–303). Mountain View, CA: Mayfield.
10. Rosenberg, M. (1973, March). Test your HRQ (human relations quotient). *Teacher, 90*(7), 29; Knutson, M. C. (1977, May). Sensitivity to minority groups. *Journal of Physical Education and Recreation, 48,* 24–25.
11. Byra, M. (1992, March). Measuring qualitative aspects of teaching in physical education. *Journal of Physical Education, Recreation and Dance, 63,* 83–89.
12. Siedentop, *Developing teaching skills,* 298.
13. Anderson, W. G. (1980). *Analysis of teaching physical education* (pp. 23–24). St Louis, MO: Mosby.
14. Ibid., 32.

15. Amidon, E. J., & Flanders, N. A. (1971). *The role of the teacher in the classroom* (p. 14). Minneapolis: Association for Productive Teaching.
16. Anderson, *Analysis of teaching physical education,* 76.
17. Morgenegg, B. L. (1978). Pedagogical moves. In *What's going on in gym? Descriptive studies of physical education classes.* A special monograph of *Motor skills: Theory into practice.*
18. Anderson, *Analysis of teaching physical education,* 109–110.
19. Rink J. E., Werner, P. H., Hohn, R. C., Ward, D. S., & Timmermans, H. M. (1986, June). Differential effects of three teachers over a unit of instruction. *Research Quarterly for Exercise and Sport, 57,* 132–138.

CHAPTER 14

Basic Principles
of Curriculum Design

Study Stimulators

1. What is a curriculum?
2. What is the relationship between curriculum and instruction?
3. What is curriculum design? Why is it important?
4. List the steps for designing a curriculum.
5. What is the role of administrators in curriculum design? Of teachers? Of students? Of other resource persons? Why are all of these important on a curriculum committee?
6. What information should be considered before designing a curriculum?
7. Describe the influence of government legislation on curricular decisions.
8. Name the common physical education curriculum patterns and give an example of each. How are the patterns used to build physical education programs?
9. What resources are of most value in designing a curriculum for a particular school?

What Is a Curriculum?

Studying curriculum theory and design is often delayed until graduate school. However, since even beginning teachers are involved in curriculum development, this text integrates curriculum design with instructional design.

Jewett, Bain, and Ennis described the physical education curriculum as follows:

> Broadly defined, the school curriculum includes all experiences conducted under school auspices, from formal classroom instruction to interscholastic athletics. More specifically, the curriculum is defined as the planned sequence of formal instructional experiences presented by the teachers to whom the responsibility is assigned.[1]

The curriculum should reflect the society within which it operates, by considering the society's philosophy, as well as knowledge handed down by that society that influences students and how they learn. The teacher becomes the intermediary whereby the curriculum (the blueprint) is translated into the instructional strategies (the delivery system) that influence student learning. Teachers' personalities and abilities influence their capacity to transpose curricular content into student learning. Student's interests and abilities, in turn, influence their input into the instructional system. Figure 14.1 demonstrates how this interaction occurs.

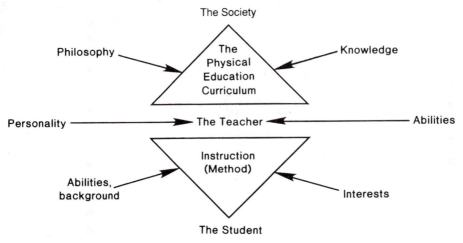

Figure 14.1 The relationship of curriculum and instruction.

The Importance of Curriculum Design

Curriculum design is the creation of an action plan or set of operating principles, based on theory, that guide faculty decision making in practical situations as they translate educational knowledge and philosophy into teaching methodology.[2] The Phi Delta Kappa Gallup poll has listed poor curriculum as one of the top five problems confronting the public schools for all but one of the past 10 years.[3] Parents and students become dissatisfied when curricular offerings lack an orderly plan for achieving educational objectives.

Until the twentieth century, social patterns and values changed almost imperceptibly from generation to generation. Now, with the accelerated rate of social change, schools are preparing youth for adulthood in a society not yet envisioned by its members. As Hawley stated:

> It's not a question of whether or not to change, but whether or not we can control the way
> we are changing. We are living in an *Alice in Wonderland* world where you have to run just
> to stay where you are. To get anywhere you have to run even faster than that. The pieces on
> the chess board keep changing and the rules are never the same.[4]

Factors that force curriculum change are cuts in financial resources, outdated and inadequate facilities and equipment, changes in student populations, changes in faculty availability and expertise, changes in student needs and interests, and other environmental and technological changes.

Progress is impossible without change. However, all change does not result in improvement. In fact, some changes may be worse than no change at all. Changes must be carefully considered and evaluated before implementing them on a full scale. At the same time, when schools continue to lag behind in curriculum development, changes may be imposed from the outside. The national governors' "1991" report on education, *Time for Results,* suggested a state intervention procedure for school systems that fail to meet acceptable performance standards.[5]

Curriculum change should be based on a well-informed evaluation of past, present, and future. This is done by considering the best thinking of professionals who have researched and tested each proposal. Effective ideas should be retained; ineffective ones discarded. New ideas ought to be tried on a small scale (perhaps with only one or two classes) prior to adoption. Planning and preparation are keys to a successful and meaningful program. Traditionally educators make two mistakes with regard to curriculum design. They either just let things happen, or they look around for a good curriculum and adopt it whether or not it fits their particular needs. Lawton described curriculum design problems as follows:

> If we wish to be completely frank we would probably say that the typical curriculum is a mess—an uneasy compromise between traditions (of doubtful pedigree) and various pressures for change; a mixture of high-sounding aims and classroom practice which could not possibly attain the aims and sometimes flatly contradicts them . . .
>
> One of the problems of curriculum, as with many other aspects of education, is the enormous gap between theory and practice . . . the difference between what teachers suggest should happen and what can be observed in the classroom.[6]

Curriculum designers must carefully merge cultural elements, old and new, into a curriculum that fits the students, school, and community. The constantly changing American society requires a continuous, systematic process of evaluating and redesigning the curriculum to achieve program objectives.

Models of Curriculum Design

An effective curriculum must be built on a solid philosophical foundation that answers the question of what educational purposes the school should seek to achieve. Bain described the value of studying curriculum theory as follows:

> Curriculum theory describes potential criteria for selection and structuring of content and predicts the impact of such criteria upon the instructional process.[7]

The classical model for curriculum design, proposed by Tyler in 1949, asked four questions of curriculum planners: (1) What educational purposes should the school seek to attain? (2) What educational experiences can be provided that are likely to help attain these purposes? (3) How can these educational experiences be effectively organized? and (4) How can we determine whether these purposes are being attained?[8] Tyler's steps for curriculum design included stating objectives, selecting learning experiences, organizing the experiences, and evaluating results. Tyler's model is most closely aligned with the educational purposes of preserving the social order and teaching skills and competencies needed to function effectively in society.

Tyler's model has been criticized for not describing the way curriculum committees actually proceed. Walker observed curriculum designers and described their actions.[9] Their first step was to establish a platform of beliefs and values to guide the planning process. The second step was to develop curriculum materials and then review these materials by identifying facts, generating alternative solutions, determining consequences, weighing alternatives, and choosing the best solutions. The result was a curriculum "design" or product. Some of the newer value orientations might fit more effectively into Walker's model.

Steps in Curriculum Design

The steps of the curriculum process presented here are based primarily on Tyler's classical design for curriculum development.

1. Identify those responsible for curriculum design and establish a curriculum committee.
2. Study basic curriculum principles and determine the philosophy, aims, and objectives of the school and of physical education.

3. Determine the program's scope and sequence.
4. Schedule.
5. Implement the program.
6. Evaluate and revise.

Figure 14.2 shows a diagram of the curriculum design process. Steps 1 and 2 are discussed in this chapter. Chapter 15 identifies how to determine the scope of the curriculum (what) and the sequence of instructional activities (when). Examples of the scope and sequence for various school levels are included. Scheduling considerations are also presented in chapter 15. Curriculum evaluation techniques are introduced in chapter 16. After evaluation in any instructional or curriculum model, the teacher or committee should follow the feedback loops back to the beginning of the cycle and reexamine the objectives and instructional programs to determine how to improve them using the new information gained. To take full advantage of the information presented here, readers are encouraged to form a curriculum committee, choose a school (real or imaginary) with which to work, and design a curriculum while studying these chapters.

Identify the Persons Responsible for Curriculum Design and Establish a Curriculum Committee

Persons responsible for curriculum decisions include administrators, teachers, students, parents, and community leaders. Most major innovations in the public schools are introduced by teachers

Program development should be a cooperative effort of all those involved in its implementation.
© Tracy Pellett

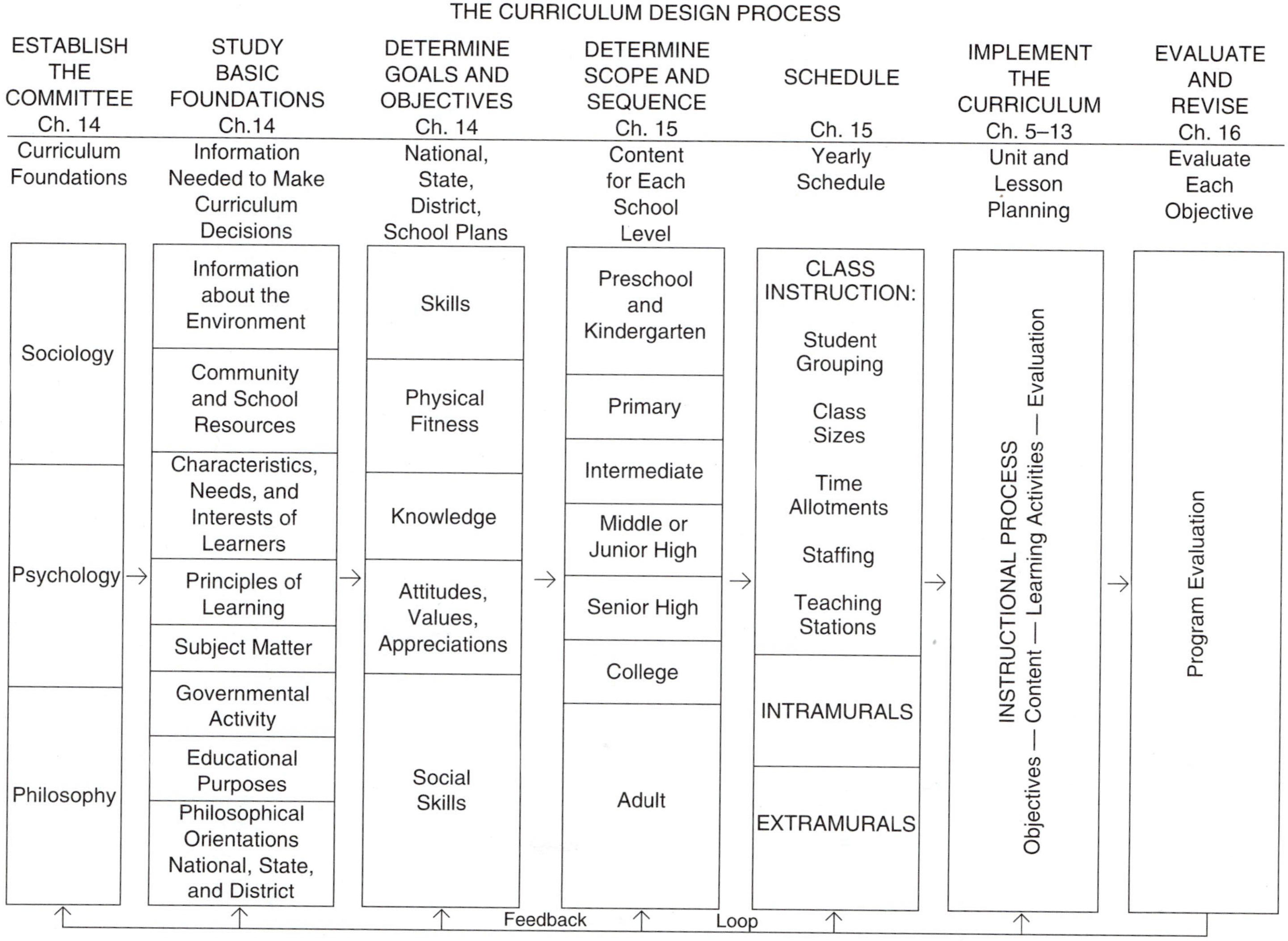

THE CURRICULUM DESIGN PROCESS

ESTABLISH THE COMMITTEE Ch. 14	STUDY BASIC FOUNDATIONS Ch.14	DETERMINE GOALS AND OBJECTIVES Ch. 14	DETERMINE SCOPE AND SEQUENCE Ch. 15	SCHEDULE Ch. 15	IMPLEMENT THE CURRICULUM Ch. 5–13	EVALUATE AND REVISE Ch. 16
Curriculum Foundations	Information Needed to Make Curriculum Decisions	National, State, District, School Plans	Content for Each School Level	Yearly Schedule	Unit and Lesson Planning	Evaluate Each Objective

INSTRUCTIONAL PROCESS
Objectives — Content — Learning Activities — Evaluation

Program Evaluation

CLASS INSTRUCTION:
Student Grouping
Class Sizes
Time Allotments
Staffing
Teaching Stations

INTRAMURALS

EXTRAMURALS

Preschool and Kindergarten
Primary
Intermediate
Middle or Junior High
Senior High
College
Adult

Skills
Physical Fitness
Knowledge
Attitudes, Values, Appreciations
Social Skills

Information about the Environment
Community and School Resources
Characteristics, Needs, and Interests of Learners
Principles of Learning
Subject Matter
Governmental Activity
Educational Purposes
Philosophical Orientations National, State, and District

Sociology

Psychology

Philosophy

Feedback   Loop

Figure 14.2 The curriculum design process.

and administrators, with accrediting agencies and local education associations also playing a direct role. Colleges and universities that train teachers indirectly provide educational leadership. Private philanthropic foundations provide teachers with released time from school to develop innovative instructional programs. Textbook publishers and instructional materials producers affect curriculum as new products are adopted. However, once adopted, they can deter change because of the cost of product revision. State boards or departments of education sometimes provide leadership for promoting educational change, but many departments are too small to enforce the changes.

The Administrator's Role in Curriculum Design

The instructional program is the most important responsibility of all school administrators—superintendents, principals, and department heads. Administrators must plan instructional programs that contribute to the intellectual, physical, and emotional growth and well-being of all young people and select and assign competent teachers.

Administrators at different levels provide leadership for curriculum initiation, planning, implementation, evaluation, and revision. Direct leadership occurs when department chairpersons, principals, or district supervisors help teachers assess program needs, define goals and objectives, and evaluate curriculum quality. Once a decision is made to develop or revise a curriculum, the department head or supervisor selects a curriculum committee and proposes goals and guidelines for action. This process is more formal at the district level or in a large department, whereas in a smaller department all teachers might compose such a committee.

Administrators should continue to work closely with the committee by providing input based on experience and knowledge and by reviewing proposals for new programs. Released time for committee meetings and provision of adequate resources, including equipment, supplies, secretarial help, and assistance by experts and consultants, is imperative.

When changes are desired, the department head presents a proposal to the principal, who interprets the program to the public or invites the department head to do so. Administrators at each level are responsible for helping to implement approved programs and direct the development of curriculum materials.

Indirectly, all administrators, and especially principals, have the responsibility to provide a climate for personal and group growth. This requires effective communication, time and resources for personal and group study, and freedom to experiment with new ideas. Communication between teachers and administrators increases when administrators work with teachers and not over them. Teachers who are given time and resources to study and experiment with new ideas and practices generally are more innovative than teachers who perceive little support for innovation. A teachers' study area with books and journals, opportunities to attend conferences or visit innovative schools, regular discussions about innovations during faculty meetings, and adequate clerical help motivate teachers to study new ideas. Freedom evolves from administrators' confidence in teachers' abilities to resolve their own problems.

The Teacher's Role in Curriculum Design

Although instructional supervision is an administrative responsibility, teachers' insights are critical for developing a successful curriculum. Teachers are the first to notice a need for change. Their intimate knowledge of learners, classrooms, and the school environment puts them in a position to make and implement practical curriculum changes. Participation in curriculum development provides them with a clearer picture of how to implement program changes. In fact, many changes occur, almost unnoticed, as teachers work together to revise course content and schedules. Unless teachers receive the responsibility and authority to make curriculum decisions, they are demoted to the role of technicians in the schools. A current trend is to assign school *curriculum leaders,* master teachers with additional training in curriculum development and leadership skills.

Physical educators have more flexibility for curriculum development than other teachers because of the unique facilities involved. Sound curriculum development principles and practices will prevent the curriculum from "just happening." Students can be grouped and regrouped by ability levels or interests more easily than in intact classrooms, and class sizes can be altered to fit the activity to be taught and the facilities available.

Teachers have a responsibility to study and keep abreast of changes in physical education and how to teach effectively. They do this by attending conventions and in-service meetings, visiting other schools, reading professional journals, and discussing ideas with other teachers in their own and in other schools. Whenever possible, teachers should serve on school or district committees to develop instructional materials, write curriculum guides, and evaluate and revise curricular offerings. Released time should be provided for professional development.

The Curriculum Committee

The number and kinds of curriculum committees depend on the extent of the curriculum project. For a large school curriculum development project, committees might include a coordinating committee and subcommittees for each grade level, as shown in figure 14.3. Representatives from each school make up the *coordinating committee.* In smaller school systems, each member of the physical education staff might serve on this committee. The coordinating committee acts as a clearinghouse for ideas and suggestions. The coordinating committee functions as follows:

1. Establishes the overall physical education philosophy for the district or school
2. Explores satisfactions and dissatisfactions with the present program
3. Schedules meetings, establishes work sequence, and coordinates activities of all committees
4. Selects members for subcommittee assignments
5. Serves as a clearinghouse for proposals from subcommittees
6. Provides for curriculum evaluation

Subcommittees can be organized to give input at specific grade levels or for intramural, extramural, and athletic programs. Such committees are usually temporary and might include the following personnel:

1. Elementary—A principal, nonphysical education teacher(s), parent, elementary physical education specialists
2. Secondary—Physical education teachers, coaches, principal, community representative, parents, students

Subcommittee functions might be as follows:

1. Establish specific grade-level objectives
2. Establish the program scope and sequence for each grade level
3. Make teaching suggestions, including specific lesson and unit plans

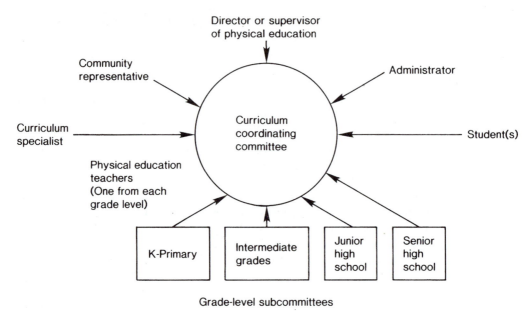

Figure 14.3 A possible organization for a district curriculum development program.

Although program development can be a product of individual teachers, administrators, or supervisors, experience shows that a curriculum cooperatively planned by all those involved in its implementation yields the best results. A sound committee includes the following individuals:

1. *Administrators,* who can provide insights into time schedules, budgets, facilities, resources, and other administrative details.
2. *Teachers,* who work daily with students and know what will or will not work.
3. *Students,* who can provide information regarding their own interests, learning obstacles, relevance of learning experiences, and recommended extra-class programs.
4. *Parents and community leaders,* who can provide varied, fresh ideas based on their experiences with school and life and their aspirations for children. These people can be influential in promoting curriculum change if they have been consulted during the planning stages.
5. *Recent graduates,* who can be especially helpful in evaluating the curriculum's relevance to real life.
6. *Curriculum specialists,* who can provide expertise in curriculum design and ideas that have worked well in other schools.
7. *Clerical assistants,* who can record, type, copy, collate, and distribute information.

Persons chosen to serve on curriculum committees should represent and have the respect and support of their peers and the administration. Small committees can achieve consensus and get the work done more effectively. Periodically rotating committee memberships avoids fatigue and promotes a fresh attack on the problems at hand. When several people from various backgrounds join together in a group effort, synergy occurs; that is, the result is greater than the sum of its members. Since curriculum development is a time-consuming process, released time or pay for extra work should be considered for committee members.

Information Needed to Make Curriculum Decisions

To make effective curriculum decisions, the committee must learn all it can about the environment, the school, the learners, and the subject matter and how it is learned. Then it must integrate this information and its implications with the educational philosophy espoused by the district and school. Governmental activity also has an influence on curriculum decisions.

Information about the Environment

A large number of social forces that affect students' lives and, therefore, the school curriculum were discussed in chapter 3. Increases in the incidence of one-parent families and mothers in the workforce has resulted in numerous latchkey children. Drug use, alcoholism, and suicide are common among American youth. Increased leisure time increases the need for individual, family, and community recreation. Other cultural forces affecting schools include racial and sexual inequalities, television and gang violence, and early unprotected sex, resulting in teenage pregnancy and sexually transmitted disease.

In spite of the increased mobility of society, most communities still share certain values, attitudes, and beliefs that influence curriculum development. The current emphasis on physical fitness and lifetime sports reflects a general commitment to the ideal of preparing students for effective adult living. Thus, schools in many areas have adopted Fitness for Life or similar courses. Local commitments to promote equality of opportunity for all students may not be strong enough to overcome the value for athletic excellence, especially if finances are limited. Thus, curriculum developers must consider local attitudes and values as well as national ones. Local resources and interests also influence the selection of learning activities.

Needs and priorities can be assessed through brainstorming, observation, interviews, questionnaires, surveys, inventories, public hearings, available statistics, prior needs assessment research, and objective tests. Asking people to indicate priorities as critical, important, or desirable can be helpful, as can asking them to classify needs as long-range or immediate. A community survey can provide information concerning the following:

1. The community's historical background
2. The philosophy of community members and their willingness to support education and physical education programs
3. Economic and tax base factors of the community, such as major employers; average family income; incidence of unemployment; and educational, recreational, health, and other services
4. Social, cultural, and political factors, such as population and prospective changes in population, age distribution, ethnic and racial makeup of the population, social and cultural attitudes, religious orientation, educational background, crime, political pressures, and form of government
5. Geographical and locational factors, including such regional factors as climate, altitude, and the availability of lakes, mountains, and seashores, that affect students' activity interests and the time that can be spent out-of-doors; and the environment (urban, suburban, or rural), which affects personal and family income and therefore the activities students can engage in outside of school

6. Community resources, including colleges and universities; private and parochial schools; public libraries; parks and playgrounds; swimming pools; cultural programs; government agencies; citizens' groups; commercial ski resorts, bowling lanes, and equestrian clubs.

Data obtained from studies of social and cultural forces in the community are analyzed for implications related to the curriculum. Students are taught to accept some problems in their community, to resolve or eliminate other problems, and to prepare to make future decisions about problems that have not yet arisen.

From community to community, and even within the same community, conditions may range from poverty to wealth. Learning more about the community increases one's understanding of its organization, as well as its lifestyle. Sensitivity to people's feelings and to the fear, insecurity, poverty, hunger, and disease that exist, as well as to individuals and groups who are trying to bring about constructive changes, will increase. The analysis of social forces leads to implications for curricular needs. Hass listed curriculum criteria to consider when dealing with social forces.

1. What social or cultural factors contribute to the individual differences of the learners?
2. How can the curriculum and the teaching take into account these differences?
3. What values are we teaching?
4. What values do we wish to teach?
5. What can the curriculum do to assist learners in their goals of social self-understanding and self-realization?
6. How can the curriculum and teaching be planned and organized so that learners are assisted in confronting personal and social problems?
7. How can learners be helped to develop the skills needed to solve problems?[10]

Information about the School

External conditions directly affect school resources, which then influence the physical education curriculum. These resources include finances, staff, facilities and equipment, school and department policies, and the total school curriculum.

Finances affect nearly every aspect of the school. Most school monies are spent for building construction and maintenance and administrator and teacher salaries. The remainder is used for equipment and supplies. When finances are low, teachers and students may be left without essential instructional materials. The number and characteristics of the administrative and instructional staff have a tremendous impact on teaching. The age, sex, socioeconomic background, and philosophies of administrators and teachers affect staff morale and cohesiveness and the ability of the staff to work together to achieve common goals. The interests and expertise of physical educators directly affect what is taught.

The type and location of facilities also affect the physical education curriculum. Note the number and size of gymnasiums, multipurpose rooms, swimming pools, dance studios, wrestling rooms, and outdoor fields, courts, and tracks. If school facilities are not available, consider local community resources such as bowling centers, skating rinks, ski slopes, and gymnastic studios. State and national parks and forests provide resources for adventure and outdoor education activities. Two problems exist with regard to facilities: trying to establish a curriculum without the proper facilities, and failing to include activities that could be provided. Facilities and equipment can be obtained if the desire is great enough. Governmental, community, business, and philanthropic agencies and foundations are often willing to aid schools in obtaining resources.

The school's organizational structure, relationships between teachers and administrators, power structure, and school policies stifle or encourage creativity in curriculum planning. Administrators' values, attitudes, and policies toward learning, student behavior, and faculty freedom affect student and teacher morale.

The school curriculum pattern, schedule, and time distribution dictate the limits within which the physical education program must operate. Local courses of study may define the boundaries of the curriculum in any given subject area.

Information about the Learners

Students' characteristics and needs at different ages were reviewed in chapter 3. Educational goals and curricular objectives arise from student needs, which are generally of two types. The first kind arises from needs within the organism itself, such as those suggested by Maslow (see chapter 12).[11] To achieve physical and psychological safety, students need a safe progression of curricular activities and self-confidence and skill in basic movement skills, which yield security to try activities requiring higher skill levels.[12] Never force students to try activities they feel are dangerous. Create standards for measuring performance that consider differences in skill level. When teachers plan group experiences to increase social approval, Kehres emphasized the use of games and activities that allow for both competition and cooperation, structured so that

Student needs and interests play an important part in the selection of curriculum content.
© Tracy Pellett

low-skilled individuals are not at a disadvantage; opportunities for experiencing both individual success and success as a member of a group; and special assistance for students experiencing social rejection.[13]

To increase students' self-esteem, teachers can adapt activities so students with a wide range of abilities experience success and enjoyment. Counsel students to select those activities best suited to their individual needs and interests. According to Maslow, the school should create an environment in which students can satisfy their basic needs so they will be free to move on to self-actualization. To develop self-actualization in physical education, Kehres emphasized the need to teach the relationship of vigorous movement to health and well-being in adulthood, place students in positions of leadership and responsibility, and allow students to make decisions.[14]

The second type of needs is determined by comparing the learner's current status with the status expected by society. The gap between these two levels defines an educational need. For example, if a society expects its members to be able to swim and students cannot swim, then a need exists that might be attended to by the curriculum. Some educational needs are common to children or adolescents of a particular age level, no matter where they might live, whereas other needs are specific to the environment in which the students live. It is easy to generalize, for example, that all 7th graders need instruction in team sports and all 12th graders need to develop skills in individual and dual sports for use in their leisure time. It is not that simple, however, since students vary considerably within a single grade level in both age and intellectual, physical, social, and emotional development. Youth in Hawaii may need to be adept at swimming and surfing, whereas children in Colorado may need to be good snow skiers.

Students who differ dramatically from group norms, including potential dropouts, bilingual students, the mentally and physically disabled, and the gifted also should be considered. In fact, the courts have ruled that schools must begin to meet the needs of all learners, whatever their differences might be. Programs must be flexible enough to adapt to learners' individual differences. Physical educators must consider the needs of the athlete as well as the quiet, sensitive student who needs activity just to have a healthy body. In his book *The Ultimate Athlete,* George Leonard expressed the idea that *every* human being has a right to move efficiently and joyfully.[15] Students' interests and purposes for enrolling in physical education must be considered. Curriculum designers should plan for a variety of learning modes to accommodate students' individual learning styles.

Data concerning both the whole student population and individual students are essential. Curriculum designers must consider the nature of the student body—the number of students, their ages, sex, grade levels, socioeconomic levels, racial composition and ethnic background, personal and family characteristics, interests, achievements, talents, and goals. Data from physical fitness, knowledge, skill, and attitude tests can be helpful in describing students' past achievements. Health assessments can also provide essential information about students. Questionnaires to determine student interests can help determine readiness for learning specific activities. Other methods for studying learners include observations, questionnaires, interviews, and school and community records concerning attendance, delinquency, health, social status, discipline, extracurricular activity, and participation in recreation programs. Hass listed questions curriculum planners can ask to test how well programs have been planned to meet students needs:

1. Does the planned curriculum provide for the developmental differences of the learners being taught?
2. Does the planned curriculum include provisions so that learning may start for each learner where he or she is?[16]

Data about students are compared with desirable norms and deviations noted as possible concerns for school attention. The curriculum committee must distinguish between needs and wants, then decide which needs can be appropriately met by the school and which would best be met through other social agencies. For instance, the school can teach appropriate health behaviors, but if facilities for maintaining proper health are unavailable, other agencies may have to resolve that situation.

The Subject Matter and How It Is Learned

Curriculum designers must consider all of the learning domains in physical education—cognitive, psychomotor, and affective—as well as the various levels of learning within each domain. Each of these domains was discussed in some detail in chapter 4. Each student selects from the subject matter those areas of perceived importance and organizes them in a meaningful way. Students should be helped to discover how physical education relates to them and how they can use the information gained to solve their problems.

Some questions to consider when planning the subject matter and instructional methodology include the following:

1. What does a physically educated student know? Do? (See outcomes statements in chapter 1.)
2. What subject matter is of most worth: physical skills? fitness? concepts? movement?
3. Does the curriculum allow students to develop at all levels in each learning domain?
4. Does the curriculum help the learner identify and organize the key concepts and principles of physical education?
5. Does the curriculum prepare the student to utilize the content of physical education to solve personal problems, now and in the future?
6. Does the curriculum provide alternative approaches to learning to accommodate individual learning styles?

Physical educators generally agree on five instructional goals for physical education, including (1) physical skills for participation in a wide variety of activities, (2) physical fitness, (3) a knowledge and understanding of fitness, principles of movement, and the importance of exercise, (4) social skills, and (5) attitudes and appreciations that encourage activity participation and enjoyment.

Curriculum designers are obligated to study trends, innovations, and research that have implications for meeting the goals of physical education and to use the ideas they learn, selecting the best of the old and the new. Avoid change for change's sake. Toffler made a strong case for this when he said:

> The adaptive individual appears to be able to project himself forward just the "right"
> distance in time, to examine and evaluate alternative courses of action open to him before
> the need for final decision, and to make tentative decisions beforehand.[17]

One societal trend that influences the school curriculum is the emphasis on preventive medicine and total health and fitness. Physical education programs should also emphasize fitness and the concepts involved in taking care of one's body through changes in lifestyle. The Fitnessgram discussed in chapter 8 is an outcome of the emphasis on fitness.

Another trend is the "back to the basics" movement with its emphasis on academic, rather than physical, achievement. Physical educators emphasize sport studies or cognitive learning, with themes developed around disciplinary concepts. Several examples are included later in this chapter. Even the name of physical education has been changed in many institutions of higher learning to kinesiological studies or exercise and sport science. Many states have adopted criteria for promotion or graduation to ensure educational accountability. The emphasis on these tests makes "teaching to the tests" a high priority.

Some recent innovations in the secondary school curriculum include outdoor pursuits such as cross-country and alpine skiing, hiking, backpacking, camping, and orienteering; new or cooperative games; and adventure or risk activities such as climbing walls and rappelling. Leisure-time activities such as scuba diving, canoeing, sailing, and bicycling are popular. One school even has its own circus. These activities involve concerns about teacher expertise, safety, transportation, and legal liability that must be dealt with before implementing the programs. However, with appropriate planning, such activities can be safely introduced in the curriculum. Professional journals and associations and state departments of education can identify programs or facilities that teachers can visit or write to for help in implementing new programs.

Research in educational psychology and motor learning, in exercise physiology, and in other areas of education have implications for curriculum development. The curriculum designer must determine the effects of research on the curriculum. Chapter 4 reviewed research in the cognitive, psychomotor, and affective domains with implications for learning. Research on academic learning time and mastery learning were reviewed in chapter 7. A knowledge of educational psychology helps educators select objectives that are attainable at certain age levels and the conditions and amount of time necessary for learning. Research indicates that learning that is applied or integrated with other learning is retained longer than isolated or compartmentalized learning.

Governmental Activity

Federal and state legislation; judicial decisions such as those on legal liability, integration, and busing; and government regulations and supervision, including the power to allot or withdraw funds, play a major role in the educational process. Three federal laws that have had a tremendous effect on school programs include PL 94-142 (The Education for All Handicapped Children Act) and its sequel, The Individuals with Disabilities Education Act of 1990 (PL 101-476); Section 504 of the Rehabilitation Act; and Title IX. These laws, with implications for teaching, were discussed in chapter 3. Policy constraints often dictate what can be done, leaving little latitude for innovation. On the other hand, legislation can provide one of the quickest forms of change. For example, by reducing the state per pupil expenditure, schools can be forced to cut programs. However, when legislation is enacted without public support, the schools or the public may resist government attempts to enforce compliance. Such was the case in some schools with PL 94-142 and Title IX. AAHPERD has prepared *Shaping the Body Politic* and the *NASPE Sport and Physical Education Advocacy Kit* to help physical educators change public opinion and influence political decisions that affect physical education.[18]

Philosophies of Education and Physical Education

The philosophical orientation of persons responsible for curriculum decisions is undoubtedly the greatest variable influencing the selection of school goals and objectives. Progressive philosophers study the learner and select curricular purposes and content in terms of student needs and interests. Essentialists derive goals and subject matter from the body of knowledge that has been handed down over thousands of years. Sociologists view the school as a means to help people deal with contemporary problems. In reality, all of the sources presented in this chapter should be considered before making decisions about the purposes of the school.

Educational philosophies attempt to answer questions such as whether to educate persons to adjust to the culture or to improve the culture, and whether to provide a general education for all students or vocational training for those who wish to leave early or immediately after high school to go to work. The board of education is generally responsible for establishing the overall philosophy and goals of the schools within its jurisdiction.

Geiger and Kizer recommended that teachers become aware of their own philosophies in order to form a philosophical base on which to build a meaningful program. To accomplish this, they suggest that teachers grapple with the following issues:

> What is the purpose of education?; what is physical education and how does it relate to education in general?; what is the role of a teacher?; should the learning situation be teacher centered or student centered?; is the purpose of physical education to teach sport skills or is there another purpose?; what is humanistic physical education?; is conceptual teaching possible in physical education?[19]

District goals should be divided into subgoals and performance objectives consistent with general educational goals. Physical education goals and objectives are formulated in the same manner. Unless goals are explicit, they will have no value in the curriculum.

Not all of the objectives suggested for the school by the preceding analyses can possibly be implemented in the time available in the curriculum; therefore, it is essential to select the most important ones and ensure that they are achieved. Pratt's criteria for curriculum objectives require that objectives identify learning outcomes, are consistent with the curriculum aim, and are precise, feasible, functional, significant, and appropriate.[20] Proposed objectives must be evaluated in terms of the values (stated or implied) in district, school, and department philosophies. Objectives that do not agree with the philosophies are deleted. Even though objectives are stated early in the curriculum process, they will undoubtedly be revised over and over again as decisions are made with regard to scope and sequence, selection of learning activities, and evaluation. They should be refined into a usable state before the curriculum is implemented, even though some may be revised after evaluating the new program.

Once the objectives have been selected, they should be stated as observable student behaviors and in a way that educators, parents, students, and other interested persons can understand what behaviors are intended. Hass listed some guidelines for evaluating goals and objectives as follows:

1. Have the goals of the curriculum or teaching plan been clearly stated, and are they used by the teachers and students in choosing content, materials, and activities for learning?
2. Have the teachers and students engaged in student–teacher planning in defining the goals and in determining how they will be implemented?
3. Do some of the planned goals relate to the society or the community in which the curriculum will be implemented or the teaching will be done?
4. Do some of the planned goals relate to the needs, purposes, interests, and abilities of the individual learner?

5. Are the planned goals used as criteria in selecting and developing learning activities and materials of instruction?

6. Are the planned goals used as criteria in evaluating learning achievement and in the further planning of learning subgoals and activities?[21]

Educational Purposes, Value Orientations, and Curriculum Patterns

Local social and environmental forces and the philosophies of educators and physical educators directly influence the purposes of education and the value orientations that are selected as the bases for local curricula. As social forces change, the demands placed on schools also change. Decisions about social implications must take into account the following purposes of education:

1. to preserve and maintain desirable social features by transmitting them to the young;
2. to teach skills and competencies needed to function effectively as an adult member of society;
3. to help the individual function within society to the fullest extent possible, both now and in the future, through intelligent self-direction, group deliberation, and action; and
4. to teach the individual to constructively evaluate social issues and influence the social order by contributing to ordered, purposeful change.

Jewett, Bain, and Ennis described five value orientations for curriculum development that match the preceding purposes.[22] They are disciplinary mastery, social reconstruction, learning process, self-actualization, and ecological integration. The chosen value orientation should be stated in the philosophy of the curriculum guide.

Disciplinary mastery emphasizes the transmission "of the cultural heritage from one generation to the next." The current "back-to-the-basics" movement reflects this emphasis, as does the traditional emphasis on physical fitness and mastery of basic movement and sport skills in physical education.

Social reconstruction stresses instruction for "creating a better society" and emphasizes interpersonal and problem-solving skills. Social reconstructionists include nontraditional activities such as outdoor and adventure education and "new games," with emphasis on cooperation rather than competition, in an attempt to broaden community recreational interests.

An example of the *learning process* is Toffler's emphasis on learning how to learn, which equips graduates with the skills needed to deal with rapid changes in knowledge and technology.[23] Content includes basic physical education knowledge, as well as learning how to acquire sport skills.

Self-actualization, as stressed by Maslow, was reviewed in chapter 12.[24] The advocates of this value orientation attempt to provide opportunities for students to explore many activities and then develop expertise in one or more chosen activities. Experiences through which students can direct their quest for personal excellence and satisfaction also include outdoor pursuits and adventure activities.

In the fifth orientation, *ecological integration,* self-actualization is sought as a means toward a holistic interaction between the individual and the environment. This orientation is directed toward a global interdependent society and emphasizes health-related fitness, skillful movement, self-confidence, creativity, outdoor education, and leadership skills designed for optimum personal development.

For learners to achieve curriculum goals and objectives, learning experiences must be selected and organized to reinforce concepts, values, and skills. Common school organizing structures include the separate subjects curriculum, the broad fields curriculum, and the core curriculum. Elementary school curricula generally follow the *broad fields* pattern, including such areas as language arts, social studies, and natural science. Middle schools often use a core curriculum, combining classes such as English, history, and science, with separate classes in physical education, art, music, and other subjects, using teacher specialists in those areas. Several high schools have adopted *core* courses in which physical education is combined with the physical and biological sciences and English. Students spend up to one-half of the school day and some weekends hiking, backpacking, and bicycling to natural environments where they study science and then write about their findings.[25] The most common secondary school organizational pattern is the *separate subjects* curriculum in which a different subject is encountered by the learner during each period of the school day. No attempt is made to relate principles learned in courses such as chemistry, biology, and health to each other. The broad fields curriculum tends to be more learner-centered and promotes greater integration of concepts learned, whereas the specific subject pattern tends to be primarily subject-centered.

No one curriculum pattern is adequate to serve the varied populations of all schools. Curriculum designers must study curriculum patterns as a basis for intelligent action and then select and combine elements from several patterns to form a curriculum pattern that suits the needs of the particular school or system within which they are working. This requires knowing the elements of each pattern and possessing the creativity to adapt them to the needs of the situation.

In physical education, curriculum patterns have evolved from either a subject-centered or a student-centered approach. Subject-centered curriculum patterns include the traditional activity-based and the more recent movement-based and concepts-based curriculum patterns. They are generally chosen to promote the purposes of transmitting the culture to young people to prepare them for effective living in society. They emphasize disciplinary mastery and learning how to learn. Student-centered patterns include the developmental needs and the student-centered curriculum patterns. These patterns tend to reinforce the purposes of self-actualization and social change, along with their respective value orientations.

Activity-Based Curriculum Patterns

In the most common pattern, the curriculum is organized around activity units, including dance, fitness, and sports. Meaningful participation in activities is the goal. It is not a means toward other goals, such as physical fitness or social development. Since all possible activities cannot be included, a percentage of the total time is usually established for each activity category. Local considerations and the school situation influence specific selections within each category. Progression is from basic skills in the elementary grades to specialization in a few selected activities at the high school level.

The foremost advocate of play for its own sake is Siedentop. He stated that "physical education derives from play, is best understood in reference to play and best defined as playful motor activity, and in its mature form is institutionalized in culture as sport and dance."[26] Play is seen as an important part of human existence. Students need instruction to develop the fundamental motor patterns needed for participation in all activities and counseling to help them match their interests and abilities to suitable activities. Although few curricula publicly advocate a play philosophy, most demonstrate adherence to the characteristics of the play pattern, with the exception that some appear to emphasize recreation rather than learning.

Sports education is an activity-based approach that stresses learning to be good sports-people through participation in competition in ways similar to athletic participation. Students participate in formal competitive schedules with pre-"season" instruction, team practice sessions, a culminating event, and publicized records and standings. Teachers become coaches. Sports education may occur in single classes, with competition between classes scheduled during the same class period or other class periods, or during intramural activity time. Sports education teaches skills, rules, strategies, appreciation for play in our society, and proper ethical principles involved in *good* sport.[27]

Another activity-oriented curriculum approach is *wilderness sports and adventure education*. Wilderness sports include activities conducted in wilderness settings, such as backpacking, canoeing, and scuba diving. Adventure education uses contrived obstacles or environments as problems or challenges for students to solve. Whereas physical skill is the primary objective of wilderness activities, group or individual problem solving under stress is the major purpose of adventure education. Although instruction is included in physical education classes, weekend or overnight outings are essential for skill application in wilderness or adventure settings.[28] Some activities for this approach were presented in chapter 8.

The advantage of activity-based patterns is ease of administration. Disadvantages include boredom, caused by repetition, and the failure to develop skills beyond basic instructional levels when programs are inadequately planned and implemented. Students often fail to develop the concepts necessary for a total understanding of the purpose of physical education throughout life. This type of program is difficult to justify to administrators and taxpayers.

Movement-Based Curriculum Patterns

The movement-based curriculum is based on the work of Laban and is used primarily in elementary school programs.[29] The curriculum is organized around themes involving the body and its interrelationship with space, time, effort, and flow. Exploration of movement concepts and a variety of movement skills in dance, gymnastics, and sports are included in the instructional process. Students use problem solving or discovery learning to create new ways of using their bodies to achieve specified goals with various pieces of equipment. Graham and his associates produced the framework shown in figure 14.4 for developing a movement-based curriculum.[30]

Concepts-Based Curriculum Patterns

Concepts approaches based on the body of knowledge about human movement are organized around key ideas or principles, broad enough to permit instruction in a wide variety of activities and meaningful enough to justify the time and effort expended. The goal is to help the students understand the what, why, and how of physical education through problem solving in laboratory and activity settings. Sport and movement skills can be used to teach concepts. Progression is from simple to more complex knowledge. Concepts approaches are based on two assumptions: (1) that concepts transfer to new skills and situations and (2) that students learn concepts better by emphasizing the concept (e.g., force production) rather than by teaching the concept within an activity unit.

Concepts-based curricula are more easily justified in an academic sense and may help physical education achieve a more-respected place in the school curriculum. They adapt readily to individual student differences and to different locales. Students who do not excel in physical education activities often like the concepts approach. Another advantage may be the carryover of basic concepts about health and fitness to real life.

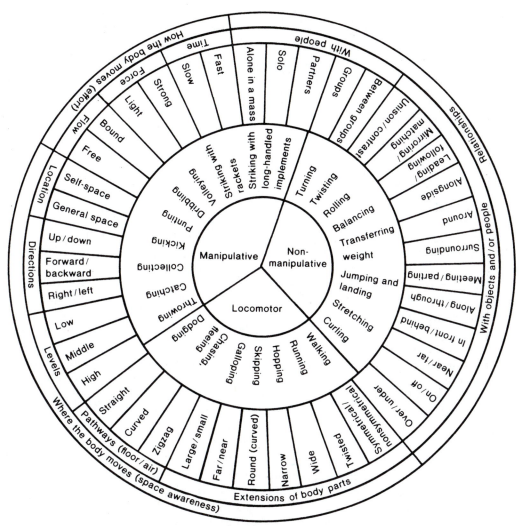

Figure 14.4 Framework depicting the interaction
of movement concepts and skill themes.
Source: Graham, George, Shirley Ann Holt/Hale,
and Melissa Parker. *Children Moving: A Teacher's
Guide to Developing a Successful Physical
Education Program,* 2nd Ed. (Mountain View, CA:
Mayfield Publishing Company, 1987), p. 121

The main disadvantage of concepts approaches is that students may not learn the skills
needed to participate in each activity. Another disadvantage is that concepts may transfer to new
skills and situations only when the application is made clear in the new situation.

In the *subdiscipline* approach to physical education, units are based on the six areas covered
by the *Basic Stuff* series—exercise physiology, kinesiology, motor development, motor learning,

social and psychological aspects of movement, and movement in the humanities (art, history, and philosophy).[31] Although there has been some controversy over the *Basic Stuff* series, teachers would do well to teach concepts along with whatever curriculum pattern is chosen. An example of a concept-oriented instructional unit for biomechanics using the subdiscipline approach might include:

Week 1: Center of gravity and base of support
Week 2: Balance
Week 3: Spin and angle of rebound
Week 4: Newton's laws of motion
Week 5: Force production
Week 6: Summary of the use of biomechanics in sport[32]

Several variations of the concepts-based curriculum pattern include (1) integrating concepts with the traditional activity-based curriculum; (2) teaching a separate unit on concepts along with the traditional activity units; and (3) teaching concepts on special occasions such as rainy days and shortened periods. An example of activities in which concepts are integrated with sport skills is shown in Table 14.1.

With the current emphasis on physical fitness, wellness, and healthy lifestyles, it is no surprise that physical educators have created a *fitness-based curriculum approach*. Most programs emphasize fitness concepts, as well as activity skills in activities for developing healthy lifestyles. *Fitness for Life,* by Allsen, Harrison, and Vance,[33] and similar programs have been popular with college and adult populations for many years. Corbin and Lindsey's *Fitness for Life*[34] was developed to teach fitness concepts to secondary school students, and several other textbooks have emerged in recent years. These programs are generally supplemented with activity units designed to encourage participation in physical activity throughout life. Several authors have proposed fitness models composed of health and fitness objectives.[35]

Developmental Needs Curriculum Patterns

The *student needs curriculum* is based on the cognitive, psychomotor, and affective developmental stages and growth patterns of children and youth. The various taxonomies and the characteristics of children and youth are studied as a basis for developmental curriculum planning. Basic skills are taught in elementary school programs, team sports are emphasized in middle and junior high school programs, and lifetime activities are taught in senior high school and college curricula, along with appropriate cognitive and affective objectives for students' developmental levels. The curriculum is often divided into activity or theme units chosen by the faculty to meet student needs. This curriculum pattern is primarily based on the assumption that students go through the same developmental stages at the same rate, although some programs attempt to offer a variety of learning experiences to provide for individual variation in these developmental levels. The developmental needs curriculum is widely accepted and often combined with the activity-based curriculum under the assumption that development will occur automatically through participation in motor activities.

Student-Centered Curriculum Patterns

Student-centered curriculum patterns are based on students' purposes for enrolling in physical education activities, including social interaction, adventure, emotional release, physical fitness, self-discipline, or personal expression. The assumption is that students can assess their own

Table 14.1 Commonalities of Fundamental Movement Skills and Related Mechanical Principles

Moving the Body through Space	+	Moving an Object through Space	=	Moving the Body and an Object through Space
(Initiating Movement, Locomotion, Absorbing Momentum)		(Altering the Pathway, Sending, and Receiving)		

Moving the Body through Space (Initiating Movement, Locomotion, Absorbing Momentum)

Activities	Locomotor Skills
Badminton	Starting (staying ready to move)
Basketball	Running
Field hockey	Sliding
Gymnastics	Jumping
Soccer	Stopping
Softball	Changing directions (flexible pathways)
Tennis	Landing
Track and field	Propulsion
Volleyball	
Swimming	

+ **Moving an Object through Space** (Altering the Pathway, Sending, and Receiving)

Activities	Manipulative Movements
Softball, Field hockey, Badminton, Tennis, Golf, Volleyball	Striking ⎱ Sending
Soccer	Kicking ⎰
Softball, Basketball, Field events	Throwing
Archery	Projecting
Softball, Basketball	Catching ⎱ Receiving
Soccer	Blocking and trapping ⎰

= **Moving the Body and an Object through Space**

Activities	Manipulative Movements	Locomotor Skills
Basketball	Dribbling (hands)	Starting
Soccer	Dribbling (feet)	Running
Field hockey	Dribbling (stick)	Stopping
Basketball	Juggle (air dribble)	Changing directions
		Sliding

Control of Body + Control of Object = Control of Body and Object

Source: From Seidel, Beverly L., Fay R. Biles, Grace E. Figley, and Bonnie J. Neuman. *Sports Skills: A Conceptual Approach to Meaningful Movement*, 2d ed. © 1975, 1980 Wm. C. Brown Publishers, Dubuque, Iowa. All Rights Reserved. Reprinted by permission.

Basic Principles of Curriculum Design   505

purposes and make appropriate choices. Counseling helps students make choices appropriate to their values and interests. A wide variety of activities with beginning, intermediate, and advanced levels of instruction are required to meet student needs. When students are allowed to concentrate on activities in which they have real interest and develop competence in activities in which they will participate outside of school hours, attendance, cooperation, and learning increase. Teachers may need to learn to teach activities that are of interest to students. If students continually shift from one teacher to another, teachers may not get to know students. Some students can get lost in such a system.

Humanistic physical education stresses the uniqueness of each individual. It uses physical activity to assist students in their search for personal meaning, self-understanding, self-actualization, and interpersonal relations. Subject matter mastery is de-emphasized. Humanistic physical education requires a caring, authentic teacher who can establish a close teacher–student relationship and facilitate student learning. Heitmann and Kneer introduced a humanistic approach to physical education instruction based on the fact that children differ in their growth rates, learning styles and rates, interests and goals, and physical and psychological makeups.[36] They emphasized the importance of teaching students the skills needed to direct their own behavior and encouraging them to accept responsibility for their own learning. They suggested that teachers facilitate instruction by providing a variety of teaching styles and resources from which the students could select those appropriate for themselves.

Hellison developed a humanistic or *social development* curriculum model for physical education. He identified and numbered five levels of awareness of students: (0) irresponsibility, (1) self-control, (2) involvement, (3) self-responsibility, and (4) caring. In *Goals and Strategies for Teaching Physical Education* he proposed strategies for helping youth progress through the five stages.[37] One of these techniques is shown in Table 14.2.

Another student-centered curriculum pattern is the *personal meaning approach,* in which the focus is on the satisfaction gained from participation in the movement experience or from the use of movement activities to achieve personal goals. The purpose-process curriculum framework (PPCF), defined by Jewett and Mullan,[38] consists of seven groups of movement purposes—physiological efficiency, psychic equilibrium, spacial orientation, object manipulation, communication, group interaction, and cultural involvement. It is assumed that students have the same purposes, but the emphasis may change from school to school depending on the students. The curriculum content can be arranged within activity or concept units emphasizing one or more selected purposes. An example of the PPCF is a program developed for a Canadian school district. The 10th-grade plan is shown in Table 14.3. Students take one unit each in fitness, personal development, and dance; two goal-type games; two net games; and one target game or combative activity. Adventure activities fit in well with the personal meaning curriculum. The major problem with the PPCF is that it is difficult to use for persons not familiar with the framework.[39]

Building a Program from Curriculum Patterns

Curriculum design involves choosing one or more curriculum patterns that meet the goals and objectives of the school or district for which the curriculum is being designed. For example, a movement approach may be chosen for the elementary schools, with activity-based programs dominating the secondary programs. Fitness-oriented concept units could be taught in the junior and senior high schools, with other concepts integrated with the appropriate activity units. The important thing to remember is that programs and patterns must be compatible with school and

Table 14.2   Big Ideas Sheet

A. Goal

Caring

B. Definition of the Goal

We are not hermits. We look to others to fill many of our emotional, social, and physical needs. Likewise, we can fill these needs for others.

C. Reasons for Valuing the Goal

Realization of the fact that you need other people will help you build ties with others. Other people will value you if you help them in meeting their goals, just as you feel a tie toward anyone who assists or helps to make you feel good.

D. Self-Inventory   (Circle One)

CODE: 5   (Very Often)

4   (Frequently)

3   (Occasionally)

2   (Seldom)

1   (Never)

I understand caring if:			I don't understand caring if:	
I'm quiet when the teacher is talking.			I talk and interfere with others' rights and responsibility to teach.	
5	4	3	2	1
I helped someone recently.			I can't remember the last time I helped someone.	
5	4	3	2	1
I let people help me learn new or difficult things in PE and other classes.			I don't let people help me because I'll look weak or inferior to that person.	
5	4	3	2	1
I compliment people on things that they do well.			I never compliment anyone because they'll think they have the one-up on me.	
5	4	3	2	1
I thank people who have helped me.			I don't thank anyone because I'm too tough and cool.	
5	4	3	2	1
I'm humble about the talents I have.			I flaunt my talents and wipe them on others.	
5	4	3	2	1
I shared something with someone recently.			I never share anything because I might not get it back or they might not repay me.	
5	4	3	2	1

Table 14.2—(Continued)

I stuck up for or found something good about someone everyone else was putting down.			I like getting into a group and tearing someone apart that everyone agrees is a jerk.	
5	4	3	2	1
I can accept compliments graciously.			I can't accept compliments because I think they're trying to get something from me.	
5	4	3	2	1

Source: Hellison, Donald R. *Goals and Strategies for Teaching Physical Education* (Champaign, IL: Human Kinetics Publishers, Inc., 1985).

community philosophies. Avoid taking the "easy way out" when, with a little effort, a more appropriate pattern could result in greater benefits to students.

Annarino and his colleagues listed the following practical considerations for designing or selecting curriculum patterns and programs:

1. The needs and interests of students
2. The number and type of students
3. The preentry skills of the students
4. The terminal objectives to be achieved
5. The type, expertise, and number of instructional personnel
6. The grouping of students
7. The availability of equipment and supplies
8. The number of teaching stations
9. Time allotments
10. School and state requirements
11. Type of instructional strategy to be employed
12. Availability and types of instructional aids
13. Seasonality[40]

Siedentop and his colleagues suggested the following considerations:

How adequate are the school facilities? How adequate are the community opportunities? How easy is it for students to get from school to the community sites? Do students have to catch buses right after school? Is the school district willing to provide supplementary compensation for faculty leadership in intramurals, clubs, and drop-in recreation? What is the state law regarding physical education? What support is there for going beyond the requirements of the state law with an elective program? *How motivated are the physical education teachers to build a program that really counts?* The answers to these questions will provide the background information for making decisions about how much a program can accomplish.[41]

Whatever program is selected, do it well. It may be worthwhile to implement program components in small steps and work with that portion until success is achieved before starting another part.

Table 14.3 Core Program Outline—Grade 10

Subject Area	Concepts	Possible Activities
Fitness: 1 unit	Circulo-respiratory efficiency Self-knowledge	Cross country running, cross country skiing, jogging
Personal development: 1 unit	Neuro-muscular efficiency (balance, agility, co-ordination) Challenge	Tumbling, floor routines Apparatus—trampolining
Games: 5 units 2 goal types	Object manipulation/projection, reception a) one using the body to manipulate object b) one using an implement to manipulate the object Group interaction, teamwork, competition	Body: a) Basketball, soccer, team handball, flag football, rugby b) Ice hockey, floor hockey, lacrosse, broomball, field hockey
2 net types	Object manipulation/projection, reception a) one net game using the hands to manipulate the object b) one net game using an implement to manipulate the object Spacial relationships	a) Volleyball b) Badminton, tennis
1 of: target or combative types	Target Object projection, catharsis Combative Maneuvering weight, neuro-muscular efficiency (agility)	Curling, golf, archery, bowling Wrestling, self defense, judo
Dance: 1 unit	Participation, joy of movement, clarification	Folk dancing, social dancing, square dancing, modern dancing

Source: Jewett, Ann E., and Marie R. Mullan. *Curriculum Design: Purposes and Processes in Physical Education Teaching-Learning* (Washington, D.C.: American Association of Health, Physical Education and Recreation, 1977).

Resources for the Curriculum Committee

Persons responsible for curriculum design should be aware of the resources available, which include people, organizations, professional journals, curriculum guides, commercial publications, facilities, and media.

People

Curriculum and instruction specialists at colleges and universities are often willing to serve as consultants. If none are available, write to authors of curriculum articles in professional journals. Researchers, housed in universities and commercial institutions, conduct basic research that is often rejected by teachers because researchers fail to make their findings adaptable to the school setting. Teachers who could do applied research often lack the time, training, or money to do so. The best solution is a collaborative arrangement in which researchers and teachers work together to identify and investigate problems and alternatives for resolving them.

Organizations

Two national organizations that can provide tremendous resources are the American Alliance for Health, Physical Education, Recreation and Dance (AAHPERD), and the President's Council on Physical Fitness and Sports. AAHPERD has four excellent position papers outlining guidelines for physical education:

Essentials of a Quality Elementary School Physical Education Program
Guidelines for Middle School Physical Education
Guidelines for Secondary School Physical Education
Guide to Excellence for Physical Education in Colleges and Universities

AAHPERD also publishes several journals; *Completed Research in Health, Physical Education, and Recreation;* and a number of other pertinent publications. The President's Council provides speakers, public relations help, bulletins, and films on various areas of interest to physical educators.

A large number of national agencies also have materials or journals of value to physical education. Check your university or local library for addresses and publications. A few of them include the following:

American Association of School Administrators (NEA)
Amateur Athletic Union
American Camping Association
American Cancer Society
American College of Sports Medicine
American Medical Association
American Heart Association
American Public Health Association
American Red Cross
American School Health Association
Association for Supervision and Curriculum Development (NEA)
Athletic Institute
Lifetime Sports Foundation
National Association of Secondary School Principals

National Federation of State High School Athletic Associations
National Education Association
National Federation of State High School Athletic Associations
National Parent-Teachers Association
National Recreation and Park Association
National Safety Council
Society of State Directors of Health, Physical Education and Recreation
United States Office of Education
United States Public Health Service

State departments of education often provide consultants, in-service activities, conferences, clinics, and workshops. Many states have a state course of study or curriculum guide. State education associations and state Associations of Health, Physical Education, Recreation and Dance can be of inestimable service. The local chamber of commerce can provide information about the resources and makeup of the local community.

Professional Journals

The number of professional journals relating to physical education has increased dramatically in the past few years. An excellent list of the scholarly periodicals in physical education appeared in the *Journal of Physical Education, Recreation and Dance*.[42] Some that relate directly to curriculum and instruction are the following:

CAHPER Journal (Canadian)
Journal of Physical Education, Recreation and Dance
Journal of Teaching in Physical Education
Phi Delta Kappan
The Physical Educator
Quest
Research Quarterly for Exercise and Sport
Strategies

Curriculum Guides

State departments of education and local school systems publish curriculum guides detailing their overall course of instruction and their requirements for specific subject areas. Curriculum guides show how schools, districts, and states have solved similar problems. They can be used as a springboard for curriculum development. Curriculum guides generally include some or all of the following: (1) philosophy, goals, and objectives, (2) characteristics and needs of students, (3) program scope and sequence with suggested units of instruction for each grade level, (4) sample schedules, (5) administrative guidelines, (6) instructional activities, (7) evaluation techniques, and (8) resources. Teachers who help write curriculum guides find them more useful than those who merely read them. Curriculum guides should suggest specific, practical helps to facilitate the teaching–learning process and provide usable resource materials. As school districts move from traditional programs to more individualized instruction, the guides become more useful to teachers. Curriculum guides enhance the articulation between programs at different school levels and ensure proper progression and development in the three domains of learning.

Commercial Publications

Textbooks and physical education equipment and media are available through various commercial companies. University libraries, salespeople, and school catalogs can be useful in locating these sources. Books on curriculum development can delineate principles and practices for effective curriculum design.

Media

Hardware catalogs are usually available at school district administrative offices or media centers. Information on software is available from AAHPERD, the NASPE Media Resource Center,[43] and commercial catalogs.

Review Questions

1. What is a curriculum?
2. What is curriculum design? Why is it important?
3. What are Tyler's four questions for curriculum design?
4. What other models exist? How do they differ from Tyler's model?
5. What are the steps in the curriculum design process?
6. Who should serve on a curriculum committee? What is the role of each of these persons?
7. What should be considered in each of the following areas before making curriculum decisions?
   a. Community
   b. School
   c. Learners
   d. Subject matter
   e. Trends, innovations, research
   f. Governmental activity
   g. Philosophy
8. Define each of the following curriculum patterns:
   Subject-centered
   a. Activity-based
      1) Sports education
      2) Wilderness sports and adventure education
   b. Movement-based
   c. Concepts-based
      1) Subdiscipline
      2) Fitness
   d. Developmental needs
   Student-centered
   a. Humanistic
   b. Social development
   c. Personal meaning
9. What resources are available for curriculum designers?

References

1. Jewett, A. E., Bain, L. L., & Ennis, C. D. (1995). *The curriculum process in physical education* (2nd ed., pp. 11–12). Madison, WI: WCB Brown & Benchmark.
2. Pratt, D. (1980). *Curriculum: Design and development* (p. 9). Chicago: Harcourt Brace Jovanovich.
3. Elam, S. M., Rose, L. C., & Gallup, Alec M. (1993, October). The 25th annual Phi Delta Kappa/Gallup poll of the public's attitudes toward the public schools. *Phi Delta Kappan, 75*(2), 137–152; see also September or October issues for each year 1986–1992.
4. Hawley, R. C. (1973). *Human values in the classroom: Teaching for personal and social growth* (p. 70). Amherst, MA: Education Research Associates.
5. National Governors' Association, Center for Policy Research and Analysis. (1986). *Time for results.* Washington, DC: Author.
6. Lawton, D. (1973). *Social change, educational theory, and curriculum planning* (p. 7). London: University of London Press.
7. Bain, L. (1978, March). Status of curriculum theory in physical education. *Journal of Physical Education and Recreation, 49,* 25–26.
8. Tyler, R. W. (1949). *Basic principles of curriculum and instruction.* Chicago: University of Chicago Press.
9. Walker, D. F. (1971). A naturalistic model for curriculum development. *School Review, 80,* 51–65.
10. Hass, G. (1977). *Curriculum planning: A new approach* (2nd ed., p. 234). Boston: Allyn & Bacon.
11. Maslow, A. H. (1943). A theory of human personality. *Psychological Review, 50,* 370–396.
12. Kehres, L. (1973, March). Maslow's hierarchy of needs applied to physical education and athletics. *Physical Educator, 30,* 24–25.
13. Ibid., 25.
14. Ibid.
15. Leonard, G. (1975). *The ultimate athlete.* New York: Hearst.
16. Hass, *Curriculum planning,* 234.
17. Toffler, A. (1970). *Future shock* (p. 420). New York: Bantam.
18. Seiter, M. M., Goffin, M., & Beach, B. K. *Shaping the body politic: Legislative training for the physical educator.* Reston, VA: American Alliance for Health, Physical Education, Recreation and Dance; For information on the NASPE Sport and Physical Education Advocacy Kit contact AAHPERD, 1900 Association Drive, Reston, VA 22091.
19. Geiger, W., & Kizer, D. (1979, March). Developing a teaching awareness. *Physical Educator, 36,* 25–26.
20. Pratt, *Curriculum,* 183–187.
21. Hass, *Curriculum planning,* 233.
22. Jewett, Bain, & Ennis, *The curriculum process in physical education,* 23–29.
23. Toffler, A. (1968). *The schoolhouse in the city* (pp. 367–369). New York: Praeger, in cooperation with Educational Facilities Laboratories.
24. Maslow, A theory of human personality, 370–396.
25. Kudlas, J. (1976). Outdoor/environment programs. In P. E. Barry, *Ideas for secondary school physical education.* Reston, VA: American Alliance for Health, Physical Education and Recreation.
26. Siedentop, D., Mand, C., & Taggart, A. (1986). *Physical education: Teaching and curriculum strategies for grades 5–12* (p. 21). Palo Alto, CA: Mayfield.
27. Siedentop, Mand, & Taggart, *Physical education: Teaching and curriculum strategies for grades 5–12 ,* 185–202.
28. Ibid., 203–228.
29. Von Laban, R. (1963). *Modern educational dance* (2nd ed.), revised by L. Ullman. New York: Praeger.
30. Graham, G., Holt/Hale, S. A., & Parker, M. (1987). *Children moving: A teacher's guide to developing a successful physical education program* (2nd ed., pp. 38–41). Palo Alto, CA: Mayfield.
31. American Alliance for Health, Physical Education, Recreation and Dance. (1987). *Basic stuff series.* Reston, VA: Author.
32. Lawson, H. A., & Placek, J. H. (1981) *Physical education in the secondary schools: Curricular alternatives.* (pp. 210–226). Boston: Allyn & Bacon.

33. Allsen, P. E., Harrison, J. M., & Vance, B. (1993). *Fitness for life: An individualized approach* (5th ed.). Dubuque, IA: Brown & Benchmark.

34. Corbin, C. B., & Lindsey, R. (1990). *Fitness for life: Physical education concepts* (3rd ed.). Palo Alto, CA: Scott, Foresman.

35. Steinhardt, M. A., & Stueck, P. M. (1986, September). Personal fitness: A curriculum model. *Journal of Physical Education, Recreation and Dance, 57*, 23–29; Gillam, G. M. (1985, Fall). Back to the "basics" of physical education. *Physical Educator, 42*(3), 129–133.

36. Heitmann, H. M., & Kneer, M. E. (1976). *Physical education instructional techniques: An individualized humanistic approach.* Englewood Cliffs, NJ: Prentice-Hall.

37. Hellison, D. R. (1985). *Goals and strategies for teaching physical education.* Champaign, IL: Human Kinetics; Hellison, D. (Ed.). (1990, August). Physical education for disadvantaged youth. *Journal of Physical Education, Recreation and Dance, 61*(6), 36–45; Hellison, D. R., & Templin, T. J. (1991). *A reflective approach to teaching physical education* (pp. 104–111), Champaign, IL: Human Kinetics.

38. Jewett, A. E., & Mullan, M. R. (1977). *Curriculum design: Purposes and processes in physical education teaching-learning.* Washington, DC: American Association of Health, Physical Education and Recreation.

39. Carnes, M., & Potter, D. L. (1987, April). Use of the movement process category system in planning instruction. *Journal of Teaching in Physical Education, 6*(3), 320–334.

40. Annarino, A. A., Cowell, C. C., & Hazleton, H. W. (1986). *Curriculum theory & design in physical education* (2nd ed., p. 220). Prospect Heights, IL: Waveland.

41. Siedentop, Mand, & Taggart, *Physical education,* 141.

42. Crase, D., & Rosato, F. Selected scholarly periodicals—A profile. (1989, November–December). *Journal of Physical Education, Recreation and Dance, 60*(9), 34–38.

43. The NASPE Media Resource Center, Department of Physical Education, University of South Carolina, Columbia, South Carolina 29208.

CHAPTER 15

Scope, Sequence, and Scheduling in the Physical Education Program

Study Stimulators

1. Explain what is included in a balanced curriculum.
2. Identify the methods to use in selecting content for a specific curriculum.
3. Should physical education credit be awarded for nonphysical education activities?
4. Describe how sequence relates to teaching activity skills or content.
5. Describe appropriate objectives and activities for each grade level.
6. Describe each of the steps in the scheduling process.
7. Tell why scheduling is so difficult to do.

The content selected for the curriculum and the order in which it is organized for presentation are called scope and sequence. Scheduling is the process of adapting the physical education program to the individual school and its community, staff, students, facilities, and time restraints.

Scope

Scope refers to the curriculum content at each grade level. It includes *what* should be taught to meet student needs and physical education objectives. Many schools have an inadequate physical education curriculum, with a narrow scope that focuses only on a few sports, plus an athletic program. In contrast, the curriculum should be broad in scope, encompassing a variety of rich and guided experiences—instructional, intramural, recreational, and athletic—to meet the wide diversity of physical, intellectual, emotional, and social needs of children and youth. Too many experiences, however, can dilute the effectiveness of each experience.

Program Balance

A balanced program emphasizes a variety of learning experiences consistent with program objectives and students' needs. To obtain balance, curriculum goals and objectives must consider the learners' needs and interests, society's needs, and the subject matter to be learned. The curriculum pattern chosen should provide a logical structure for organizing learning activities. Balance among the goals or objectives can be maintained by allocating time to each objective consistent with the value placed on that objective within the school context and the curriculum committee's philosophy. Objectives include knowledge, physical skills, physical fitness, social skills, and attitudes and appreciations. Curricula in which only sports are taught are not balanced, nor are curricula that exclude instruction in fitness or knowledge. Social skills, such as teamwork and sportspersonship, are often cited in the objectives but difficult to find in the instructional program. A "hidden curriculum" often exists, with unwritten objectives and activities. However, the proposed curriculum and the actual curriculum should be the same.

Time allotted to class instruction, intramurals, and extramurals must also be balanced. Commitment should be first to class instruction, second to an intramural program, and last to an extramural program, although in excellent programs it is often hard to distinguish between in-class and extra-class programs. Sport education and adventure education programs utilize time before and after school and on weekends to apply skills learned in physical education classes.

Intramural programs and clubs extend opportunities for students to use and refine skills learned in class instruction and to learn skills not available during class time (due to the inaccessibility of facilities during school hours) such as bowling, skiing, skating, hiking, and rock climbing.

Extramural or interscholastic athletics provide competition for highly skilled students. To meet educational objectives, athletic programs must be carefully designed and managed by dedicated professionals. Although athletic management is an administrative responsibility, the curriculum committee has a responsibility to ensure that the program is conducted to achieve planned educational values. Legislation requires equal opportunities for boys, girls, and the disabled to participate in extra-class programs.

Methods for Selecting Content

Since far more activities and experiences exist than can possibly be included in the curriculum, only the most appropriate should be selected. Many programs try to do everything and therefore do nothing well. They repeat activities and content year after year but spend so little time on each that students master none of them. Learning experiences must be selected to meet students' needs and interests, society's needs, and the program's expressed philosophy and objectives. Learning experiences are selected to obtain the objectives stated, without producing undesired side effects.

Activities are often selected based on the teachers' interests and abilities or the coaches' desire to develop skills involved in the athletic program. Such practices usually result in unbalanced programs based primarily on team sports. Parents and participants suggest the need for lifetime activities such as golf, swimming, tennis, bowling, dance, boating, camping, and fitness. Outdoor adventure and initiative activities are also increasing in popularity. Increased interest in physical fitness suggests a need for more emphasis on cognitive involvement in physical education. Content should be selected by a curriculum committee composed of educators, parents, and students, using the following steps:

Step 1. Determine broad activity or concept categories.
Step 2. List possible activities.
Step 3. Establish a systematic method for selecting curricular experiences.
Step 4. Assign weight values to criteria.
Step 5. Evaluate experiences by awarding points for each criterion.
Step 6. Arrange experiences by rank.
Step 7. Evaluate experiences by relative value.

Step 1—*Determine broad activity or concept categories.*

Categories should agree with the curriculum pattern selected in the preceding chapter. Activity categories that might be included are as follows:

Aquatics
Team sports

Gymnastics
Individual sports
Rhythms and dance
Physical fitness
Outdoor education and adventure activities

Concept areas that might be included are as follows:

Exercise physiology
Kinesiology
Motor development
Motor learning
Social and psychological aspects of movement
Movement in the humanities

Affective categories could include:

Cultural understanding
Joy of movement
Self-awareness
Cooperation

A scope chart shows the percentage of the total program to be spent in each broad activity or concept area. These percentages should reflect the philosophies of the curriculum committee, the school district, and the teachers. They should provide a balanced program of experiences that correspond with students' needs and developmental levels. An example of a scope chart is shown in figure 15.1.

Step 2—*List possible activities.*

Within each category, list all possible activities. A sample activity list for individual sports is shown in the first column of figure 15.2. The other columns will be explained in succeeding steps. In this example, an activity-centered curriculum pattern has been used. If concept categories have been chosen, select activities that help students understand the concepts to be studied. Note that some activities could be included in more than one category. For example, skiing could be included in individual sports or in outdoor education and adventure activities.

Step 3—*Establish a systematic method for selecting curricular experiences.*

Since school time is obviously limited and only the most appropriate experiences for a given situation can be considered, a systematic method for selecting relevant curricular experiences must be established. List essential criteria for including an activity in the curriculum, and keep criteria few in number and realistic. The following criteria are generally considered to be essential:

1. Is the experience consistent with each stated objective of physical education and education?
2. Is the experience consistent with students' present and future growth and developmental needs?
3. Is the activity relatively free of hazards?

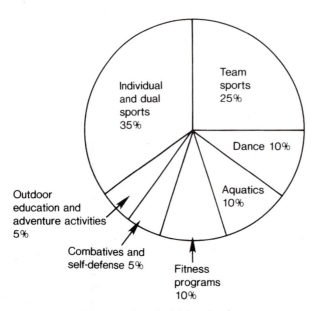

Figure 15.1 A scope chart for high school physical education.

4. Is the activity feasible in terms of local considerations? Some possible criteria for determining which activities are most suitable for a particular area include:
   a. Is the activity acceptable to the community? (For example, in some regions, dancing may be prohibited by certain religious groups.)
   b. Do students like the activity? (Regional and local factors influence students' interests and possible carryover values, e.g., surfing and snow skiing.)
   c. Are the necessary resources available in the school or community, including facilities, equipment, finances, faculty expertise or availability of resource persons, time constraints, transportation, and climate?

Step 4—*Assign weight values to criteria.*

Several possible ways exist for assigning weights to each criterion. One method involves weighing all criteria equally with each one counting a number of points. A more realistic way is to weight each criterion differently based on its importance to the selection process. This can be done by assigning a different number of points to each criterion as shown in figure 15.2. These weights should be based on the rank order of importance given to the objectives of physical education. Individual factors such as safety and feasibility may be considered separately.

Step 5—*Evaluate experiences by awarding points for each criterion.*

Make up a chart with the criteria across the top and the experiences down the side as shown in figure 15.2. Give a copy to each curriculum committee member and have them evaluate each experience by awarding points according to the plan decided on in Step 4; then, average the points from all members of the committee. Another method is to arrive at the evaluation by consensus among the committee members.

CRITERIA FOR INCLUSION

Activities by Category	Consistent with Program Objectives?					Student Interests	Consistent with Student Growth?	Safe?	Acceptable	Locally Feasible?		Include?	Comments
	Fitness	Skills	Knowledge	Social	Total					Carryover	Resources		
	1-5	1-5	1-5	1-5	4-20	1-10	Yes-No	Yes-No	Yes-No	Yes-No	F Eq Ex Tr C	Yes-No	
Individual													
Archery	1	3	4	2	RANK ⑪ 10	2	YES	WITH PROPER INSTRUCTION YES	YES	YES	✓✓✓-✓	YES	
Badminton	5	4	4	4	① 2	7	YES	YES	YES	YES	✓✓✓-✓	YES	
Bowling	1	3	4	5	④ 13	9	YES	YES	YES	YES	✓✓WALK✓	YES	BOWLING LANES NEAR SCHOOL
Cycling	5	2	3	2	⑦ 12	9	YES	WATCH TRAFFIC YES	YES	YES	✓NOV-✓	YES	HAVE STUDENTS BRING BIKES
Fencing	1	3	4	1	⑫ 9	2	YES	YES	YES	NO	✓NO NO-✓	NO	NOT FEASIBLE NO INTEREST
Golf	1	3	4	5	④ 13	5	YES	YES	YES	YES	NO/NO/✓/YES	YES	NEED BUS TO GOLF COURSE
Gymnastics	4	4	4	1	④ 13	5	YES	NO	NO	NO	✓✓✓-✓	NO	DISTRICT PROHIBITS GYMNASTICS
Racquetball	5	4	3	5	① 12	9	YES	USE EYE GUARDS	YES	YES	✓✓✓-✓	YES	VERY POPULAR
Skiing	3	3	3	3	⑦ 12	8	YES	WITH PROPER INSTRUCTION YES	YES	YES	NO NO/YES	(YES)	OFFER AS A CLUB SPORT
Surfing	4	3	2	3	⑦ 12	1	YES	NO	NO	NO	NO NO/NO	NO	NOT FEASIBLE
Tennis	3	4	4	5	③ 16	10	YES	YES	YES	YES	✓✓✓-✓	YES	VERY POPULAR
Track & Field	4	3	4	1	⑦ 12	6	YES	YES	YES	NO	✓✓✓-✓	YES	

Figure 15.2 An example of a chart for evaluating activities for inclusion in the curriculum. *Note:* F = Facilities, Eq = Equipment, Ex = Teacher expertise, Tr = Transportation, C = Climate or geographic necessity

Step 6—*Arrange experiences by rank.*

Based on the average points for each activity, arrange the experiences by rank within each category as shown in the total column. Notice that several activities are of equal value. Eliminate experiences that do not meet the criteria selected in Step 3. Some activities may satisfy the physical fitness objective but be of little value in terms of social skills. Others may contribute to students' knowledge but be of little value with regard to physical fitness. By ranking the experiences within the broader categories selected in Step 1, the committee can determine which experiences within each category best meet the selected criteria.

Step 7—*Evaluate experiences by relative value.*

Experiences that best meet program objectives and student needs are given priority. When several desirable experiences meet all the criteria for inclusion but cannot be included because of lack of time, two possibilities exist. First, experiences can be eliminated on the basis of local criteria. For example, of the activities listed in figure 15.2, tennis appears to command such an interest in the community as a leisure-time activity that the committee feels students need specific instruction in it. Surfing may be discarded due to lack of a beach and lack of student interest. Second, experiences can be organized into categories with specified amounts of time devoted to each area. Heitmann suggested several patterns for broadening curriculum scope to meet the needs of individual students while achieving curricular objectives. She suggested using the various objectives of the physical education program to establish global goals or areas into which the various activities or units can be placed. Some units might be considered essential or required and others as enrichment.[1] Figure 15.3 shows examples of how Heitmann's organizational patterns might be used in a physical education curriculum. The five areas included in the figure are health- and fitness-related courses, aquatics, dance, individual sports, and team sports. Programs are often planned so every student acquires competence in these activities. Although a minimum requirement exists, students are encouraged to explore activities of interest beyond the minimum.

Extra-Class Activities

Extra-class activities such as intramurals, sports days, play days, and club activities should be chosen in a manner similar to the preceding steps. Student interest is a major factor in selecting these activities. By using gymnasiums when athletic teams are outdoors and community facilities such as bowling centers, golf courses, skating rinks, swimming pools, and tennis courts, a wide variety of activities can be scheduled, including some that would not be possible during class time. Intramurals can be scheduled before or after school, during the noon hour, or during a scheduled activity period.

State high school activities associations generally specify interscholastic activities and send regulations to the schools prescribing seasons and game schedules. Additional activities can be added by working directly with the state association.

Should Substitute Activities Be Allowed Physical Education Credit?

In many schools and colleges, physical education credit is awarded for participation in marching band, ROTC, or varsity athletics. Is this credit justifiable? To answer this question, evaluate each activity in the same way every other experience in the curriculum is evaluated—by determining its ability to help students achieve physical education objectives. The goals of physical education, as specified in AAHPERD's *Guidelines for Secondary School Physical Education,* include

Pattern 1

Core Required

Fitness	Aquatics	Dance	Individual Sports and Combatives	Team Sports
Fitness for Life	Beginning swimming	Introduction to dance forms	Self-defense	Biomechanical concepts of sport

Select One from Each Area

Weight Training	Intermediate	Folk	Archery	Basketball
Jogging	swimming	Square	Badminton	Flag football
Aerobic Dance	Lifesaving	Modern	Bowling	Field hockey
	Water games	Jazz	Cycling	Lacrosse
		Ballet	Fencing	Soccer
		Social	Golf	Softball
			Gymnastics	Speedball
			Racquetball	Volleyball
			Skiing	
			Tennis	
			Track and field	
			Wrestling	
			Martial arts	

Pattern II

Core Required

Fitness	Aquatics	Dance	Individual Sports and Combatives	Team Sports
Fitness for Life	Beginning swimming	Introduction to dance forms	Self-defense	Biomechanical concepts of sport

Select Any Four from Any Area or from Three of the Five Areas

Weight Training	Intermediate	Folk	Archery	Basketball
Jogging	swimming	Square	Badminton	Flag football
Aerobic Dance	Lifesaving	Modern	Bowling	Field hockey
	Water games	Jazz	Cycling	Lacrosse
		Ballet	Fencing	Soccer
		Social	Golf	Softball
			Gymnastics	Speedball
			Racquetball	Volleyball
			Skiing	
			Tennis	
			Track and field	
			Wrestling	
			Martial arts	

Figure 15.3 Examples of suggested organizational patterns.
Based on information from Heitmann, Helen M. "Curricular Organizational Patterns for Physical Education," presented to the NASPE Curriculum Academy Working Symposium, St. Louis, Missouri, November 4–6, 1978.

Pattern III

Core—Select One from Each Area

Weight Training	Swimming	Folk	Archery	Basketball
Jogging	Lifesaving	Square	Badminton	Flag football
Aerobic dance	Water games	Modern	Bowling	Field hockey
		Jazz	Cycling	Lacrosse
		Ballet	Fencing	Soccer
		Social	Golf	Softball
			Gymnastics	Speedball
			Racquetball	Volleyball
			Skiing	
			Tennis	
			Track and field	
			Wrestling	
			Martial arts	

Pattern IV

Select One Track

Track 1
Fitness for Life
Swimming
Folk and square dance
Archery/badminton

Track 2
Fitness for Life
Swimming
Social dance
Tennis/bowling

Track 3
Fitness for Life
Swimming
Modern dance
Golf/racquetball

Figure 15.3 *(Continued)*

developing a variety of physical skills, achieving physical fitness, participating regularly in physical activity, knowing the principles related to physical activity, and valuing physical activity and its contribution to a healthful lifestyle.[2] District goals may, by law, specify more specific outcomes to be achieved. If an activity contributes to student development toward the goals of physical education, it might be considered as a portion of the physical education requirement. If the activity does not meet these criteria, then physical education credit should be denied. Consider also the many experiences that might be missed through continued participation in one of these substitute activities. When students are excused from physical education for four years or more, we are really saying that physical education programs are not particularly beneficial. The President's Council on Physical Fitness and Sports recommend that "no substitution of band, ROTC, athletic programs or other extra-class activities for physical education class work" be allowed.[3]

Two AAHPERD publications, *Physical Activity & Well-Being,* and the condensed version, *The Value of Physical Activity,* have been prepared by the National Association for Sport and Physical Education (NASPE) to help physical educators summarize the benefits of physical education for students, parents, school administrators, and boards of education, and to point out the relationship between activity and academic achievement.[4]

Sequence

Sequence refers to the order in which curriculum components are taught. Appropriate sequencing depends on achieving basic movement patterns such as throwing, catching, and using space prior to engagement in game skills such as fielding and guarding. Failure to provide a graduated instructional sequence in knowledge and skills is the biggest stumbling block to quality programs in physical education. For example, the same basketball unit is often taught to the same students year after year with no increased learning. This would be equivalent to teaching students "2 + 2" or similar arithmetic skills from kindergarten through the 12th grade. No matter what is written down in the curriculum, if students do not achieve the prerequisites, sequence is hindered. Thus, the number of competencies included must be limited to fit within the time available (see the discussion of appropriate time allotments later in this chapter).

Physical education programs should be organized as a continuous flow of experiences through a carefully planned, graduated sequence of ideas and skills from preschool through college. This sequence would fulfill student needs and interests and build progressively toward the attainment of a single set of physical education objectives. Preschool programs stress self-care skills and developmental tasks. Elementary school students acquire fundamental motor patterns. Proficiency in motor skills used in active team games are stressed in the middle or junior high school to meet students' physical and social needs. Lifetime activities are added during the high school years. Planning must be coordinated to provide a variety of activities at all grade levels, to develop skills required for later participation, and to avoid unnecessary overlap or omissions or undue repetition of instruction. Then students will be able to progress toward an increasingly mature utilization of their knowledge and skills to solve complex problems related to themselves and to society. An example of a scope and sequence chart for activities in grades 5 to 12 is shown in figure 15.4.

Obviously, students do not learn all there is to know or develop skill proficiency in an activity in a single encounter. Teachers are often frustrated when students absorb only the smallest part of a unit of instruction. Often teachers try to do too much and so students learn nothing well. Willgoose summed this up very well when he said:

> The chief problem facing most physical education teachers is not what to teach, but how far to go at specific grade levels. One way to get around this dilemma is to think less in terms of stereotyped grade levels and more in terms of *skill levels*. For example, in a middle school or junior high school, it would be more efficient to build a sequence of skills and knowledge in an activity through at least three levels of expectation.[5]

Table 15.1 shows examples of beginning, intermediate, and advanced levels of volleyball.

Graham and his associates suggested using a spiral curriculum in which the student progresses to a higher level of skill each time the activity is introduced.[6] An example of skill sequencing for throwing is shown in figure 4.1 on page 101. In the spiral curriculum, activities are presented several times in the curriculum, with students engaging in the activity at a higher level each time it is encountered.

Turkington and Carre suggested several ways to sequence instruction.[7]

1. Students select a specific physical education class from the school schedule based on interest and ability level.
2. Students are randomly assigned to physical education class periods but select an activity at the appropriate level from the activities offered that period.

SCOPE AND SEQUENCE CHART

Scope	5	6	7	8	9	10—12	Electives
Fitness	25%		10%			10%	
Testing	X	X	X	X			
Aerobic activities	X	X	X	X			
Weight training					X	X	
Aquatics	(optional)		10%			10%	
Water safety	X	X	X	X			
Water games	X	X					
Swimming			X	X	X	X	
Emergency water safety						X	
Dance	10%		8%			10%	
Aerobic	X	X	X	X		X	
Folk, round, square	X	X	X	X			
Creative or modern	X	X	X			X	
Social or ballroom				X	X	X	
Fundamental Skills	10%						
	X	X					
Low-organized Games	15%						
	X	X					
Team Sports	25%		40%			25%	
Basketball			X	X	X	X	
Flag football	X	X	X	X		X	
Floor hockey	X	X					
Soccer			X	X	X	X	
Softball	X	X					
Speedball	X	X					
Team handball	X	X	X				
Volleyball				X	X	X	
Individual and Dual Sports	15%		25%			35%	
Stunts, tumbling, apparatus	X	X					
Four square, tetherball	X	X					
Paddle tennis		X	X				
Archery				X		X	
Badminton				X	X	X	
Bowling			X			X	
Golf					X	X	
Gymnastics			X	X			
Racquetball					X	X	
Tennis					X	X	
Outdoor Pursuits	(optional)		5%			5%	
Hiking, orienteering	X	X					
Challenge activities			X	X			
Skiing						X	
Cycling						X	
Combatives	(included in stunts)		5%			5%	
Combative games	X	X					
Wrestling			X	X			
Self-defense					X		

Figure 15.4 An example of a scope and sequence chart for grades 5–12, with the percentage of time allocated to each category by grade level.

Table 15.1   An Example of Skill Order Sequence in Volleyball

Beginning	Intermediate	Advanced

I. Skills:
    Overhead pass
    Forearm pass
    Underhand serve
    Teamwork
	I. Review:
	    Overhead pass
	    Forearm pass
	    Underhand serve
	  Teach:
	    Overhand serve
	    Spike
	    Block
	    Team strategy
		I. Review:
		    All skills
		  Teach:
		    Rolls
		  Emphasize:
		    Advanced strategy and
		    team play

II. Concepts:
    Basic rules
    Scoring
    Basic strategy
	II. Official rules
	    Offensive strategy
	    Defensive strategy
		II. Official rules
		    Officiating
		    Offensive strategy
		    Defensive strategy

III. Minivolley to learn skills,
    brief introduction to
    official game
	III. Official game, including
	    tournament play
		III. Official game, with
		    advanced strategy and
		    tournament play

3. Students are randomly assigned to physical education class periods, with opportunities for each student to work at the appropriate level in the activity offered.
4. Students are randomly assigned to physical education classes with a teacher-selected activity. Several teachers teach the same activity and divide students into ability groupings.

Considerations for determining skill sequence or grade placement include student characteristics, the subject matter, and safety. Students' physical, mental, and social development, along with previous fitness, knowledge, and skill competencies, are the primary considerations when placing activities into grade levels. Student interests should also be considered.

Attempt to match the subject matter with student characteristics. Consider the complexity and amount of information to be presented and the difficulty of skills to be learned. Proper sequencing will result in safe, effective learning and successful student participation. The National Association for Sport and Physical Education has established "benchmarks" for specific grade levels based on the outcomes presented in Table 1.2.

Curricular Scope and Sequences for Various School Levels

Determining the scope and sequence of the curriculum from preschool through college is a complex and significant task requiring careful consideration of the correct emphases for the different developmental stages of children and adolescents. Following is an overview of recommended program emphases for the different school levels. A scope chart for one school system may or may not fit the curriculum for a different school system. Categories and percentages must be determined by following the steps presented earlier in the chapter.

Preschool and Kindergarten

For children ages three through five, the program orientation is toward the child as a unique individual. The curriculum emphasis is on developing (1) perceptual-motor skills, such as balance, eye-hand coordination, and laterality; (2) gross motor skills, such as running, walking, crawling, climbing, and pushing; and (3) self-awareness and expression through movement. Activities emphasize spontaneous, vigorous, large-muscle movement in an environment that provides freedom and opportunity for the children to explore and create their own movement patterns.

Primary Grades

For children ages six through eight, the program orientation continues to be on the individual child as a unique person. The curricular emphasis is on (1) perceptual-motor development; (2) development of fundamental and or basic movement patterns, such as skipping, walking backward, and rolling; (3) development of self-awareness and an awareness of what the body can do within its environment, including force, space, and time relationships; (4) improvement in muscular strength, endurance, flexibility, and agility; (5) basic safety; (6) development of simple concepts about physical activity; and (7) development of positive attitudes toward activity.

Activities concentrate on large-muscle and creative movement. Rhythmic activities (singing games, creative movement, and simple folk and aerobic dance movements); gymnastic skills (stunts, tumbling, self-testing activities, and apparatus); fundamental skills (throwing, catching, dribbling, striking); low-organized games; and educational movement are often combined with a movement exploration method of teaching that emphasizes each child's progress rather than comparing that child with other students in the group. Aquatics should be included where facilities permit. Physical fitness is maintained by participation in a variety of activities within the program. A possible scope chart for the primary grades is shown in figure 15.5.

Intermediate Grades

The orientation at this level, ages nine though eleven, is to the individual child as a member of a group of peers. The curricular emphasis is (1) developing and refining specific motor skills, (2) developing a high level of physical fitness, (3) developing social skills through more highly organized activities, (4) developing self-esteem through successful participation in peer groups, and (5) developing basic activity-related concepts such as rules and strategies in games.

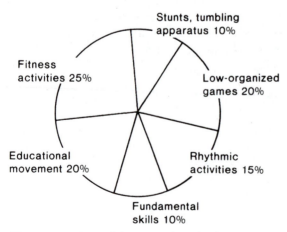

Figure 15.5 A possible scope chart for the primary grades.

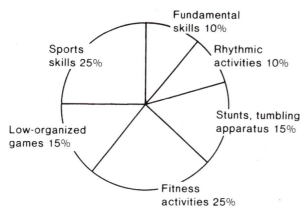

Figure 15.6 A possible scope chart for the intermediate grades.

Activities include rhythmic activities, gymnastic skills, fundamental skills, simple games and relays, and sports lead-up games. Aquatics and outdoor adventure activities should also be provided as facilities and instructor expertise permit. Physical fitness is an essential component of all program activities. A possible scope chart for this level is shown in figure 15.6.

Middle and Junior High School

The orientation at this level is on the individual student as an emerging adult with a broad exposure to the challenges facing the individual in our society and strategies for coping with those challenges. The curricular emphasis is on developing (1) physical fitness; (2) a wide variety of specific activity skills; (3) a basic understanding and appreciation of a broad variety of activity and fitness concepts that will facilitate intelligent choices regarding out-of-school and future participation; (4) physical, emotional, and social self-awareness and self-confidence; and (5) social skills leading to increased concern for others.

A variety of activities is included so that students can intelligently select those they wish to pursue in the future. In view of the physiological and emotional characteristics of adolescents, activities are selected in which students can feel successful and progress toward higher levels of skill proficiency. A minimum level of competence should be achieved in activities so that students will be able to use the skills for personal enjoyment. Team sports are important because they provide social interaction. In addition, the curriculum includes individual and dual sports, dance, aquatics, and fitness activities. Combatives, self-defense, and adventure activities should also be provided. A possible scope chart for junior high school appears in figure 15.7.

Senior High School

The orientation is on the individual as a capable, intelligent participant in activities appropriate for one's own needs and interests when given guidelines and options. The curricular emphasis is on developing (1) competencies in and appreciation for participation in selected lifetime activities; (2) knowledge and understanding essential to provide insight and motivation for a lifetime of vigorous physical activity; (3) personal physical fitness; and (4) self-confidence, individual initiative, and responsibility to self and society.

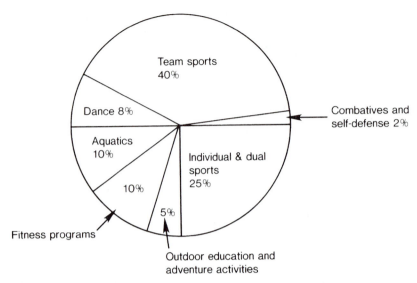

Figure 15.7 A possible scope chart for junior high school.

Senior high school programs should include a variety of outdoor pursuits.
© Joel Dexter/Unicorn Stock Photos

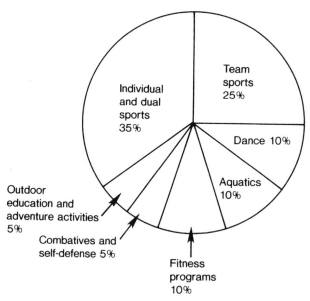

Figure 15.8 A possible scope chart for senior high school.

A wide variety of activities is provided from which to choose, including individual and dual sports, dance, aquatics, team sports, physical fitness, combatives and self-defense, outdoor pursuits, and opportunities for service and leadership development. A possible scope chart for senior high school appears in figure 15.8.

College

The orientation is on the individual student's adaptation to current and future life conditions. The curricular emphasis is on preparing the student for a lifetime of vigorous physical activity by developing (1) skills and interests in selected activities; (2) a desire for maintaining physical fitness; and (3) a knowledge and understanding of physical education and its contribution to the complete life.

The curriculum should offer a broad spectrum of activities that encourage lifetime participation, with several levels of entry for beginning, intermediate, and advanced students. Most of the activities will be the same as those found at the high school level, but with increased opportunities for developing advanced skill levels. Physical fitness courses emphasize the underlying concepts and develop the ability to design lifetime individualized fitness programs.

Scheduling

Scheduling is the process of adapting the physical education program, including classes and extracurricular activities, to the individual school and its community, staff, students, facilities, and time restraints. It is a time-consuming but essential job. Physical educators must work with local school administrators to achieve the best possible scheduling arrangement for physical education within the master schedule. Computers vastly increase scheduling possibilities based on student need and subject matter requirements.

How to Develop a Schedule

The following steps are suggested as a guide toward the achievement of a workable schedule:

Step 1. Identify the most desirable grouping pattern for class assignments.
Step 2. Determine class size.
Step 3. Determine appropriate time allotments for daily, weekly, and unit instruction.
Step 4. Determine staffing patterns and teacher loads, and assign teachers.
Step 5. Identify teaching stations and equipment.
Step 6. Develop a schedule.

Step 1—*Identify the most desirable grouping pattern for class assignments.*

Students can be grouped homogeneously or heterogeneously for physical education classes. Homogeneous grouping puts similar students together in the same group; in heterogeneous groups students differ from each other. The assignment of students to classes and learning groups should be made on the basis of individual learning needs. The ideal grouping arrangement would consider all of the factors affecting learning—intelligence, capacity, maturity, knowledge, skill, fitness, interests, and so on. However, the inability to scientifically measure such factors has generally precluded homogeneous grouping.

In most schools, students are assigned to physical education according to the period they have free in the schedule. In middle and junior high schools, students are usually assigned by grade level. Senior high school students are often scheduled in 10th through 12th or 11th and 12th grade groupings, with freshmen or freshmen and sophomores scheduled by grade level. Within these classes, teachers are generally free to rearrange students into homogeneous groups by students' interests, abilities, and needs. The physical education staff divides students according to objective skills test results or interests. Groupings should vary as activities change, since students have different interests and skill levels in different activities. Grouping persons with similar interests and skills is believed to enhance success and therefore the social and emotional development of students. Mainstreaming of disabled students and coeducational programs have considerably increased the range of abilities in physical education classes. A wide range of student abilities can be frustrating to teachers and might result in recreational rather than instructional programs.

Instruction must be provided for students with physical limitations, including those with inadequate skill development and the physically underdeveloped. Physical performance tests can be used to identify physically underdeveloped students and to appraise the motor aspects of physical fitness. Students should be placed in the least restrictive environment in which an appropriate learning situation can be provided. At Prospect High School in Illinois, students are grouped by health-related and skill performance scores. The program for each group is designed specifically to meet the needs of students in that particular group. Students can advance to the next higher group each semester.[8]

One beneficial aspect of heterogeneous grouping is highly skilled students acting as role models and peer tutors for their less-skilled classmates, thereby increasing motivation and social interaction. Teaching styles can facilitate dealing with individual differences. Peer tutoring, inclusion, task, and problem-solving activities are particularly useful when dealing with heterogeneous groups. Activities that emphasize cooperation rather than competition can also be effective with heterogeneous groups of students.

Step 2—*Determine class size.*

Identify the appropriate class size for each learning group, task, and instructional method. Class size may range from very large to only one student, depending on the aim of the instruction. For example, a film could be shown to a large group, whereas skills have to be practiced in smaller groups, and individual help or contract learning may be on a one-to-one basis. Team sport classes usually lend themselves to larger class sizes to accommodate competitive situations.

Ideally, class size should be consistent with the requirements of good instruction and safety. Appropriate class sizes ensure that students receive adequate teacher assistance and individual practice or study. For example, a tennis unit with four courts available would best be limited to 16 students if the course objectives are to be met. Since it would be impossible to schedule 16 students in a traditional class each period, a suitable alternative is to schedule a reasonable "average" class size (i.e., the same pupil-teacher ratio as for other subject areas in the school),[9] and then to adjust class sizes among the physical education teachers in terms of the units being taught. The average class size for secondary school physical education can be determined by the following formula:

$$\text{Average class size} = \frac{\text{Total students in school}}{\text{Number of teachers} \times \text{Number of periods/day taught by each teacher}}$$

The average recommended class size is usually 35.[10] Adapted physical education classes should have no more than 20. Teachers of physical education need to demonstrate the sound instructional techniques that justify reasonable class sizes and avoid "throw out the ball"-type programs.

Step 3—*Determine appropriate time allotments for daily, weekly, and unit instruction.*

In 1986 and 1987, the United States Senate and the House of Representatives passed a concurrent resolution supporting daily physical education for all students (see figure 1.1 on page 19). However, the individual states prescribe the minimum instructional time allotment per day or per week (either by law or by suggestion).

The American Alliance for Health, Physical Education, Recreation and Dance (AAHPERD),[11] the Society of State Directors of Health, Physical Education, and Recreation,[12] and the President's Council on Physical Fitness and Sports[13] recommend a daily instructional period for elementary school pupils of 30 minutes, or a total of 150 minutes per week. At the secondary school level, they recommend a minimum of one standard class period daily or equivalent class time.

One of the biggest concerns in curriculum planning is the failure to provide long enough instructional units for students to develop the skills and knowledge needed for participation in a given activity. Most teachers underestimate the time necessary to achieve mastery. Failure to achieve mastery of the objectives for one year results in the need to adjust the objectives for every year thereafter.[14] Units of two, three, and four weeks are inadequate for development of most skills. Research substantiates the fact that the beginning-level learner often experiences frustration in so short a period of time. Bain indicated that the curriculum should provide in-depth instruction in activities of particular interest to students.[15]

How much time is needed to achieve each objective? It depends on the task to be learned, the instructor's teaching skills, and the age and ability of the students. Because younger students and beginners have shorter attention spans and fatigue sooner, shorter lessons distributed daily are more appropriate. Older and more-advanced students can benefit from longer periods of time occurring less often. Simple skills can be taught in a shorter length of time than more complex skills. Wessel and Kelly reported the need to budget approximately 120 to 180 minutes to develop each fundamental motor skill, with the lower number representing the older students.[16] This translates into four to six 30-minute periods with 100 percent on-task activity. However, since students are active only 20 to 50 percent of the time,[17] 8 to 30 class periods might be necessary per objective. Obviously, this number will vary from objective to objective. Teaching the do-si-do might take only a few minutes, whereas the volleyball spike might take many hours. The number of objectives that can be achieved is a function of the time available and the amount of time required to achieve mastery of the objectives to be taught.[18]

Instructional units must be long enough to develop the skill levels necessary to enjoy participation in the activity, yet short enough to prevent boredom with the activity. Each unit consists of a cluster of objectives. If each unit had an average of five objectives or skills to be taught in 120 minutes per objective, that would be an average of 600 minutes per unit or four weeks minimum. However, at 50 percent activity rate, the unit would take a minimum of 8 weeks. Bain recommended a minimum of 10 to 12 weeks.[19] Once the number of objectives to be taught is known, they can be distributed over a unit or several years. Some units at the middle and junior high school levels may be devoted to learning basic skills so that students are introduced to activities from which they will be allowed to choose later on in the curriculum.

Scope charts with percentages of time for each area can be translated into units by multiplying the percentage by the number of weeks (or periods) in the year to get the weekly (or period) allotment for each category. Time can be allotted to specific activities or to areas for student choice within the category time allotment. However, limit the number of activities so that each unit will provide adequate time for learning to occur. Kelly suggested using the following formula to determine the number of objectives that can be achieved in each year of instruction:[20]

Number of weeks school is in session	36
Number of days per week of physical education	5
Weeks × days (5)	180
Number of minutes per period in instruction	30
Weeks × days × minutes	5400
Subtract 10 percent of time for "lost" instructional days	540
Total time available for year's instruction	4860
Total time divided by 600 minutes (approximate time per unit at the high school level) = the maximum number of units that could be taught	8

Yearly schedules include (1) the sequence and length of time of physical education activity units within a school year, (2) the sequence of physical education activities over a span of several years, and (3) the relationships of class instruction, intramurals, and extramurals. Two types of yearly plans for class instruction have emerged, the cycle and the modified cycle.

In the *cycle* plan, the course of study changes for the whole school each year as shown in figure 15.9. This means that all students participate in the same activity at the same time. Activities are usually different each year. The advantages of this system are (1) teachers have to prepare for only one class at a time and equipment can be left set up all day; (2) motivation is increased by reducing the repetition of activities from year to year; and (3) the length of time for each activity is increased, thus facilitating learning.

Cycle | | | | | | | | Modified Cycle

Cycle 1

1996
1999

Orientation	Flag football	Tennis	Folk and square dance	Archery	Swimming	Closing and testing	Sophomores
Weeks							
1/2	7	7	7	7	7	1/2	

Cycle 2

1997
2000

Orientation	Basketball	Golf	Social dance	Gymnastics and apparatus	Swimming	Closing	Juniors
Weeks							
1/2	7	7	7	7	7	1/2	

Cycle 3

1998
2001

Orientation	Soccer	Track and field	Wrestling and self-defense	Weight training and jogging	Volleyball	Closing	Seniors
Weeks							
1/2	7	7	7	7	7	1/2	

Figure 15.9 An example of cycle scheduling.

The disadvantages of the cycle plan are that students often fail to progress from lower to higher levels of skill in each activity, and teachers become bored when they teach the same activity all day long. This system works well in small schools where teachers and facilities are limited.

The second type of yearly plan is a *modified cycle* in which all of the cycles are taught each year but to different classes. For example, the sophomores receive cycle 1; the juniors, cycle 2; and the seniors, cycle 3. Advantages are that progressions in specific activities can be built into the program, and boredom is reduced because teachers generally teach more than one grade level. A disadvantage may result, however, if too many activities are taught and the program is spread so thin that students fail to learn any activity well.

Two methods of scheduling activities within the yearly plans are the block system and the alternating system. The *block* system, shown in figure 15.10, involves instructional units in

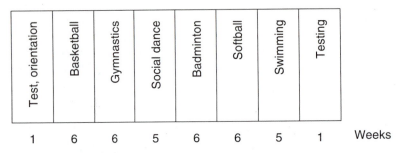

Test, orientation	Basketball	Gymnastics	Social dance	Badminton	Softball	Swimming	Testing
1	6	6	5	6	6	5	1

Weeks

Figure 15.10 An example of the block system.

Days	M	T	W	T	F
	Speedball	Square dance	Speedball	Square dance	Speedball

Figure 15.11 An example of the alternating system.

which the same activity is scheduled each class period for several consecutive weeks before another activity is scheduled. Blocks should be six or more weeks in length. Proponents argue that massed practice favors skill learning and retention and that facility scheduling is easier, especially in off-campus facilities. Opponents point out that many schools teach the same sports year after year. The greatest danger is in trying to compress activities into very short units.

A modification of the block is teaching two activities (one week each) and then allowing students to choose which activity to devote their time to for the remainder of the block, or teaching one unit until some students have mastered the material and then starting a new activity. In both of these variations, a teacher would be teaching two activities simultaneously.

In the *alternating* system, students receive instruction in more than one activity each week. For example, on Mondays, Wednesdays, and Fridays, basketball is taught; on Tuesdays and Thursdays, instruction is in golf, as shown in figure 15.11. The major advantage of the alternating system is that variety increases motivation for some students. The disadvantage is the lack of continuity in each activity and the failure to provide long enough units for skill development.

Step 4—*Determine staffing patterns and teacher loads, and assign teachers.*

Analyze staffing requirements and existing staff strengths, and assign teachers to classes based on the competencies (skills and knowledge) needed to teach the activity. Teachers of potentially hazardous activities such as aquatics, gymnastics, skiing, and adventure education need enough specialized training to be recognized and certified by the national agencies associated with these activities. Special qualifications, including the ability to work with students at various skill levels, or with particular phases of the instructional program, and preferences about classes, planning times, and related matters should also be considered.

Secondary schools may be staffed by "generalists" or "specialists" in physical education. A specialist has in-depth knowledge and skill in a few areas, such as aquatics or dance, and can usually help learners achieve higher levels of skill by anticipating and resolving potential learning problems with the subject matter. A generalist has adequate skill in most curriculum offerings. The generalist sees the student in a variety of activities and can anticipate the learning needs of individual students. Consideration of the teaching load is essential to high-quality instruction. At the secondary school level the recommendation is that class instruction per teacher not exceed five class periods or hours per day or more than 200 students per teacher.[21]

Most physical education instructors are scheduled for after-school work coaching athletic teams or cheerleaders, conducting intramural programs, and advising clubs. Two prevalent methods used by school districts to compensate teachers for these extra duties include giving the teacher additional salary for the extra work (usually not commensurate with the responsibility and time involved) or reducing the teacher's instructional load. Many physical education authorities prefer a reduced instructional load on the basis that no person, no matter how well paid, can work productively and efficiently for an excessive number of hours.

Step 5—*Identify teaching stations and equipment.*

A teaching station is an area assigned to a teacher for a class, preferably with some physical or visual barrier between two classes to cushion sound. Distance may serve as a barrier between classes. The following method can be used to calculate the number of teaching stations and teachers needed for a *secondary school* physical education program:

1. Number of sections to be offered $= \dfrac{\text{Total number of students}}{\text{Class size}}$

2. Number of teaching stations (classes per period) $= \dfrac{\text{Total number of students}}{\text{Class size} \times \text{Number of periods/day}}$

   Round off to the next higher whole number.

3. Number of teachers needed $= \dfrac{\text{Number of sections}}{\text{Number of periods taught/day/teacher}}$

An example is shown in the following chart.

Total Number Students	Class Size	Periods Per Day	Periods Per Week	Sections Offered	Teaching Stations	Teachers Needed
1,500	30	6	5	50	10	10.0
1,500	35	6	5	43	9	8.6
1,500	40	6	5	38	8	7.6

(Note: Each teacher teaches five periods. Fractions equal a part-time teacher in physical education.)

Program flexibility is increased when large numbers of students are assigned to a physical education program that has multiple teaching stations. Few schools, however, possess all the facilities

Excellent programs take advantage of community resources.
© Courtesy of the Evanston Recreation Department

they need. Multipurpose rooms, hallways, auditorium stages, theaters, and leftover classrooms can provide needed facilities for physical education. Community resources can be used to supplement school facilities. For example, bowling lanes, archery ranges, skating rinks, swimming pools, ski resorts, bicycle paths, equestrian facilities, boating marinas, dance studios, golf courses and driving ranges, tennis courts, and adventure courses can often be rented by having students pay a small fee. The use of community resources can help educators bridge the gap between school and community. Transportation may cause legal problems and should be discussed with the principal for approval before adopting any off-campus program. Elective programs can help to resolve problems with fees and transportation, since the class is not required of those who cannot afford the fees for transportation. Teachers should retain control of classes taught in off-campus facilities even when an outside professional is teaching. Courses offered before or after the normal school day can take advantage of facilities out of transportation range during regular class time.

Regarding equipment, AAHPERD recommends:

> Facilities, supplies and equipment should be provided for the instructional program in accordance with the needs, interests and number of students to be served. . . . The physical education program should have enough equipment to provide each student with an opportunity to actively participate throughout the entire class period.[22]

Equipment can sometimes be built by industrial arts classes, parents, or teachers, or purchased by parent-teacher associations. All equipment must meet established safety guidelines, however, or schools can be subject to a lawsuit. Good teaching also requires provision of appropriate books, periodicals, media, and other teaching aids.

Step 6—*Develop a schedule.*

Work out a schedule that coordinates time, teachers, and facilities. Some considerations include the following:

1. Two classes must not be scheduled in the same facility at the same time.
2. Class sizes must not exceed the space available for participation.
3. A teacher should not be assigned to teach two classes at the same time.
4. Units should be assigned to teachers based on their individual skills and interests.
5. Each teacher should be assigned a preparation period.
6. Time should be planned for all teachers in the department to meet together for department meetings.
7. Outdoor facility use depends on the weather.

Although scheduling is essentially an administrative function, the success of the program is based on its implementation by the various faculty members involved. Teachers must avoid a curriculum that attempts to do a little bit of everything with nothing done well. A possible scheduling chart is shown in figure 15.12.

An Example of Scheduling

Given: A high school (grades 9 through 12), with 800 students, four teachers, a six-period day, five days per week.

Step 1—*Identify the most desirable grouping pattern for class assignments.*

The committee decides to implement a required program in grade 9 and a selective program (required, but with student selection of activities) in grades 10 through 12. The major advantage of the selective system is that students can develop expertise in activities in which they will participate throughout their adult lives. A second advantage is the ability to meet student needs and interests within a traditional school system.

One ninth-grade class will be offered each hour and the remainder of the student body will be scheduled into the period best fitting their schedules. All classes will be coeducational. Each student will be assigned to a specific teacher who can diagnose strengths and weaknesses and provide assistance in making choices tailored to individual needs. Since students were introduced to a variety of activities in earlier grades, they will find it easier to make appropriate choices. Students will be required to select a specified number of activities in each category during each school year, as shown in this example:

Class	Team Sports	Individual	Fitness	Aquatics
Sophomore	3	1	1	1
Junior	2	3	1	
Senior	1	4	1	

Another way to balance the program might be to require a certain number of specified activities to be taken anytime prior to graduation.

Organization and record-keeping duties for the selective program will be distributed among teachers by assigning a different teacher each period as the *master teacher.* The master teacher is responsible for all of the students for that period. This includes distributing class rolls, accumulating grades, and distributing and collecting lockers and towels.

	BLOCK 1		BLOCK 2		BLOCK 3	
Period 1 Jones Garcia Lungo Platero	Golf Tennis Flag football Prep.	g f g	Aerobic dance Volleyball Swimming (beg.) Prep.	b a e	Gymnastics Basketball Wrestling Prep.	b a h
Period 2 Jones Garcia Platero Lungo	Social dance Prep. Flag football Archery/ Tennis	a g d,f	Cycling Prep. Soccer Fitness	i g b	Aerobic dance Prep. Swimming (beg.) Basketball	b e a
Period 3 Jones Platero Lungo Garcia	Rec. dance Soccer Prep. Archery/ Tennis	a g d,f	Bowling Swimming (beg.) Prep. Fitness	i e b	Aerobic dance Volleyball Prep. Basketball	c b a
Period 4 Jones Platero Lungo Garcia	Prep. Flag football Rec. dance Archery/ Tennis	g a d,f	Prep. Tennis Swimming (beg.) Fitness	f e b	Prep. Aerobic dance Volleyball Basketball	c a b
Period 5 Jones Garcia Lungo Platero	Rec. dance Tennis Soccer Badminton/ Bowling	a f g b	Bowling Aerobic dance Swimming (beg.) Fitness	i c e b	Jazz dance Outdoor pursuits Basketball Volleyball	c i a b
Period 6 Jones Lungo Platero Garcia	Golf/Softball Archery Tennis Cycling	g d f i	Fitness Basketball Bowling Flag football	b a c g	Basketball Volleyball Swimming Aerobic dance	b a e c

a--Gym A   d--Track   g--Field
b--Gym B   e--Pool   h--Wrestling room
c--Dance studio   f--Tennis   i--Community facility

Figure 15.12 A possible schedule.

On the first day of each unit, students all meet to select the next activity. Students will be told in advance the activities and the teacher who is teaching each activity. Seniors choose first, then juniors, followed by sophomores. When the class enrollment for an activity is reached, the class will be closed for that block. A card will be issued to each student on which the activity is marked for that block. The cards will be collected and processed by hand or by computer. Roll sheets for each teacher are made from the cards. A sample record card is shown in figure 15.13.

BLOCK 4		BLOCK 5		BLOCK 6	
Bowling	i	Cycling	i	Archery	d
Badminton	a	Soccer	g	Tennis	f
Swimming (int.)	e	Track and field	d	Softball	g
Prep.		Prep.		Prep.	
Badminton	b	Gymnastics	b	Golf	g
Prep.		Prep.		Prep.	
Swimming (int.)	e	Basketball	a	Tennis	f
Volleyball	a	Golf/Softball	g	Badminton/	
				Bowling	a
Gymnastics	h	Badminton	b	Cycling	i
Basketball	a	Swimming (int.)	e	Archery	d
Prep.		Prep.		Prep.	
Volleyball	b	Golf/Softball	g	Badminton/	
				Bowling	a
Prep.		Prep.		Prep.	
Bowling	i	Softball	g	Badminton	a
Basketball	a	Swimming (int.)	e	Track and field	d
Volleyball	b	Badminton/		Golf/Softball	g
		Bowling	a		
Modern dance	c	Ballet	c	Social dance	c
Volleyball	a	Badminton	b	Tennis	f
Swimming (int.)	e	Golf	g	Track and field	d
Basketball	b	Archery/		Golf/Softball	g
		Tennis	d,f		
Volleyball	b	Tennis/		Badminton/	
Wrestling	h	Archery	d,f	Bowling	a
Swimming (int.)	e	Track and field	d	Softball	m
Basketball	a	Badminton	b	Tennis	f
		Soccer	g	Golf	g

Ninth-grade activities are underlined.

Figure 15.12   (Continued)

In a selective program, class sizes can be adapted to the facilities available for instruction. Thus, instruction can be effective in activities such as tennis or racquetball where facilities are often limited.

Step 2—Determine class size.

The average class size is 40.

$$\frac{800 \text{ Students}}{4 \text{ teachers} \times 5 \text{ periods/teacher}} = 40$$

```
Name_____    Sex: M/F  Period _____

First Block            Second Block           Third Block
Tennis                 Swimming               Wrestling
Soccer                 Fitness                Volleyball
Flag football          Aerobic dance          Badminton
Social dance           Soccer                 Jazz dance
Archery                Basketball             Basketball
Fencing                Volleyball             Aerobic dance
                                              Swimming


Fourth Block           Fifth Block            Sixth Block
Basketball             Fencing                Aerobic dance
Swimming               Fitness                Softball
Fencing                Swimming               Tennis
Modern dance           Ballet                 Track and field
Volleyball             Outdoor pursuits       Social dance
Gymnastics             Basketball             Modern dance
Wrestling              Track and field        Cycling
Outdoor pursuits       Social dance           Golf
                                              Fitness
```

Figure 15.13   A sample record card.

Since approximately one-fourth of the students are 9th graders (200), the number of sections of freshmen will be five (200 ÷ 40 = 5). The remainder of the sections will have approximately 40 students per section, but all 10th- through 12th-grade students will be placed on one roll. The schedule begins to look like this:

	Ninth Graders		Tenth through Twelfth Graders	
Period 1	0 classes	= 0	3 classes	= 120
Period 2	1 class	= 40	2 classes	= 80
Period 3	1 class	= 40	2 classes	= 80
Period 4	1 class	= 40	2 classes	= 80
Period 5	1 class	= 40	3 classes	= 120
Period 6	1 class	= 40	3 classes	= 120
		200 +		600 = 800

Once the students are scheduled by period, the 10th through 12th graders will divide up into selected activities. Class enrollments may vary according to the activity.

Step 3—Determine appropriate time allotments for daily, weekly, and unit instruction.

The committee voted to have six 6-week blocks per year. This fits nicely with the 36-week school year. This will give students enough time to learn the activities, but not so much time that they get bored. Ninth-grade units will vary according to subject matter. Team sport units will be longer, since students are expected to have basic skills before advancing to the selective program. Other units are introductory to give students a basis for choosing activities later on and are, therefore, shorter.

Step 4—Determine staffing patterns and teacher loads, and assign teachers.

Teachers will be assigned to classes based on expertise, personal preference, and special qualification. All swimming instructors are certified Red Cross Water Safety instructors. The archery teacher is a certified National Archery Association instructor. All teachers can teach team sports and will rotate teaching those classes. Teachers will also teach at least one ninth-grade class each. Competencies are as follows:

Teacher	Expertise
Mrs. Platero	WSI, individual sports
Mr. Lungo	WSI, bowling, wrestling, track
Ms. Jones	gymnastics, dance, individual sports
Mr. Garcia	tennis, golf, badminton

Step 5—Identify teaching stations and equipment.

Teaching stations include the following:

Gym A	Tennis courts
Gym B	Bowling lanes (community)
Dance studio	Golf course (community)
Pool	Field space, for three classes
Balcony	Wrestling/gymnastics room
Weight room	

Equipment is available for each student in the class sizes taught.

Step 6—Develop a schedule.

The schedule might look like the one in figure 15.12. Staff schedules are such that teachers with the competencies to teach activities scheduled for certain periods are available to teach them during the periods in question.

Review Questions

1. Define scope, sequence, and balanced curriculum.
2. What activity or concept areas should be included in a balanced curriculum?
3. What determines which activities or concept areas to include in a curriculum for a specific school?
4. Should substitute activities ever be allowed physical education credit?
5. If you have to give a presentation defending the benefits of physical education, what sources could you use to find this information quickly?
6. What is the biggest stumbling block to quality physical education programs?
7. What is a spiral curriculum?
8. What factors should be considered when determining sequence?
9. What should be the emphases at each of the following school levels?
   a. Preschool and kindergarten
   b. Primary grades
   c. Intermediate grades
   d. Middle and junior high school
   e. Senior high school
   f. College or university

10. Define the following and give an example of each:
    a. Scheduling
    b. Homogeneous grouping
    c. Heterogenous grouping
11. How is class size determined? What is the recommended class size for secondary school physical education?
12. What is the recommended time allotment for physical education in elementary and secondary schools?
13. How much time is needed to achieve each instructional objective according to Kelly?
14. What is a scope chart? How can it be translated into weeks or days?
15. Define and give an example of each:
    a. Cycle plan
    b. Modified cycle
    c. Block system
    d. Alternating system
    e. Teaching station

References

1. Heitmann, H. M. (1978, November). *Curricular organizational patterns for physical education.* Paper presented to the NASPE Curriculum Academy Working Symposium, St. Louis, MO.
2. National Association for Sport and Physical Education. (1992). *Guidelines for secondary school physical education.* Reston, VA: American Alliance for Health, Physical Education, Recreation and Dance.
3. President's Council on Physical Fitness and Sports. (1983). *Youth physical fitness: Suggestions for school programs* (p. 76). Washington, DC: U.S. Government Printing Office.
4. Seefeldt, V. (Ed.). (1986). *Physical activity & well-being.* Reston, VA: American Alliance for Health, Physical Education, Recreation and Dance; Seefeldt, V., & Vogel, P. (Eds.). (1986). *The value of physical activity.* Reston: VA: American Alliance for Health, Physical Education, Recreation and Dance.
5. Willgoose, C. E. (1984). *The curriculum in physical education* (4th ed., pp. 147–150). Englewood Cliffs, NJ: Prentice-Hall.
6. Graham, G., Holt/Hale, S. A., & Parker, M. (1987). *Children moving: A teacher's guide to developing a successful physical education program* (2nd ed., pp. 38–41). Palo Alto, CA: Mayfield.
7. Turkington, H. D., & Carre, F. A. (1985, February). Individualized physical education: The British Columbia Approach. *Journal of Physical Education, Recreation and Dance, 56,* 36–38, 48.
8. Pifer, S. (1987, August). Secondary physical education—A new design. *Journal of Physical Education, Recreation and Dance, 58*(6), 50–51.
9. National Association for Sport and Physical Education. (1986). *Guidelines for middle school physical education.* Reston, VA: American Alliance for Health, Physical Education, Recreation and Dance; *Guidelines for secondary school physical education.*
10. President's Council on Physical Fitness and Sports. (1986). *Youth physical fitness: Suggestions for school programs* (p. 76). Washington, DC: U.S. Government Printing Office.
11. National Association for Sport and Physical Education. (n.d.). *Required: Quality, daily physical education; Guidelines for elementary school physical education; Guidelines for middle school physical education;* and, *Guidelines for secondary school physical education,* Reston, VA: AAHPERD.
12. Society of State Directors of Health, Physical Education, and Recreation. (1985). *A statement of basic beliefs* (p. 8). Kensington, MD: Author.
13. President's Council on Physical Fitness and Sports, *Youth physical fitness,* 76.

14. Kelly, L. E. (1989, August). Instructional time. *Journal of Physical Education and Recreation,* *60*(6), 29–32.
15. Bain, L. L. (1980, September). Socialization into the role of participant: Physical education's ultimate goal. *Journal of Physical Education and Recreation, 51*(7), 48–50.
16. Wessel, J. A., & Kelly, L. (1986). *Achievement-based curriculum development in physical education* (pp. 100–111). Philadelphia, PA: Lea & Febiger.
17. Metzler, M. (1989). A review of research on time in sport pedagogy. *Journal of Teaching in Physical Education, 8,* 87–103.
18. Kelly, Instructional time, 31.
19. Bain, Socialization into the role of participant, 49.
20. Kelly, L. E. (1988, August). Curriculum design model: A university-public school cooperative model for designing a district-wide elementary physical education curriculum. *Journal of Physical Education, Recreation and Dance, 59*(6), 26–32.
21. President's Council on Physical Fitness and Sports. *Youth physical fitness,* 76.
22. National Association for Sport and Physical Education, *Guidelines for secondary school physical education.*

CHAPTER 16

Evaluating and Revising the Instructional Program

Study Stimulators

1. Define formative and summative evaluation. What are the purposes of each?
2. Describe the process for evaluating a program in physical education.
3. Describe several kinds of data-gathering instruments and tell the advantages or disadvantages of each.

As resources diminish and academic standards receive renewed emphasis, physical education programs are cut or threatened. When programs do not produce observable results, parents and school administrators may allocate the time and resources in other ways. Rog proposed 10 questions for measuring the vulnerability of physical education programs:

1. Does your building principal hold high expectation(s) of student achievement in physical education?
2. Do you hold high expectations of student achievement in your physical education classes?
3. Are your program and its goals clearly understood by others in the school and community?
4. Are the students in your physical education program evaluated primarily on their skill performance?
5. Does your program have frequent monitoring of student progress using criterion-referenced testing based on identified objectives of student achievement?
6. Do students in all of your schools have physical education programs available to them at least 150 minutes per week?
7. Does your state require that physical education programs be made available to all students in order for your school to receive state aid?
8. Are all of your physical education classes being taught by physical education specialists or specific skill specialists?
9. If your school system's athletic program were cut, would your physical education program survive?
10. Do you have evaluation data on the achievements of your students in physical education which would demonstrate to your school committee the value of keeping your program?[1]

If your program rates high on each of these questions, your program is exceptional. If not, you will become aware of some opportunities for improvement.

The Role of Program Evaluation

Evaluation is one way to provide information to the public about the success of physical education programs. If physical educators can describe results, they are more likely to get the support needed for effective school physical education programs. Vogel and Seefeldt noted that erosion of physical education programs can only be stopped when physical educators begin to identify the anticipated outcomes and rationales of their programs and the degree to which students achieve program objectives. They noted that it is time for physical education teachers to:

1. clearly specify program intent,
2. select and implement correspondingly appropriate instructional methods,
3. evaluate the degree to which the desired outcomes are obtained, and
4. alter programs or methodology as needed so that students' achievement of stated objectives is realized.[2]

To review the entire curriculum each year is impractical. Therefore, physical education departments should select a portion of the curriculum to evaluate each year. Through constant appraisal and revision, the curriculum can be gradually improved to meet its purposes.

Program evaluation involves both measurement (quantitative) and judgment (qualitative) appraisals. For example, fitness tests are used to measure physical fitness. Knowledge tests measure concept acquisition. Questionnaires and inventories assess students' attitudes about physical fitness. The scores are then evaluated to determine whether the students achieved the objectives specified in the program.

With the increased concern for educational accountability, evaluation provides empirical data for reporting to students, parents, administrators, boards of education, state departments of education, public media, accrediting agencies, and sponsors of educational research regarding program successes or failures.

It is possible to develop an outstanding curriculum only to discover that students fail to achieve desired learning outcomes because of failure to translate curriculum development into teaching methods. Evaluation can help determine whether the program works and how its effectiveness can be increased. The two major purposes of program evaluation are (1) to provide information for program improvement during the instructional process—formative evaluation and (2) to assess the validity and effectiveness (or success) of the curriculum—summative evaluation. Both formative and summative evaluation provide feedback for improving physical education programs.

Formative Evaluation

Formative evaluation is feedback to teachers and program designers throughout the program or activity. It is used to evaluate whether students are achieving instructional objectives and to revise the program *while* it is being developed. Since most programs are only 60 percent effective the first time, they can only be improved if evaluation points out what is working or is not working and where changes can be made to improve the program. For example, if students are having difficulty learning badminton skills, it would be useless to wait until the posttest results reveal that the students did not learn. Self-testing activities conducted each day or week could expose students' specific learning problems. Perhaps the difficulty is a student's lack of hand-eye coordination or an instructional pace that is too fast. Once the cause is known, instruction can be redesigned to resolve the problems and increase student learning. Formative evaluation discloses whether the content is relevant or useless, practical or impractical. It reveals whether the instruction is too fast or too slow, too difficult or too easy. Student interest and motivation can also be checked.

Although formal evaluation techniques may be used, formative evaluation generally uses informal, criterion-referenced evaluation techniques, such as those reviewed in chapter 9, to point out strengths and weaknesses of individual lessons or short units. Informal evaluation techniques vary in quality depending on the skills of the person constructing the instruments. However, when carefully constructed, these instruments can be valid for evaluating local programs. They provide data that can help to determine instructional effectiveness and feasibility in terms of cost, teacher time, and student and teacher attitudes toward instruction. When teaching strategies are discovered to be impractical or ineffective, changes can be made at once to revise, add, or subtract lesson content or to change methods to achieve the desired results.

Summative Evaluation

Summative evaluation, which is evaluation of the final product, is used to determine the overall effectiveness of a unit or program. It takes place at the end of a unit or program and provides feedback necessary for program improvement by revealing how well students have achieved specific objectives or whether a specific educational program is worth more than an alternative approach. Unexpected outcomes, such as negative attitudes or excessive costs, should also be analyzed. Although summative evaluation may utilize informal evaluation techniques, it tends to rely on formal evaluation methods, such as standardized tests and inventories that are norm-referenced. Often an external evaluator is called in to evaluate a program. Accreditation teams serve this function by evaluating the overall school program to determine whether the school curriculum meets the goals established by the accrediting association and the school. If the program is adequate, the school is accredited for five to ten years.

Two pitfalls that occur in summative evaluation are evaluating too soon and evaluating the results of a program that teachers never really adopted. Expecting complete results from a new program in less than three years is unreasonable, and some results might be more appropriately evaluated after five years. In a similar vein, evaluators must not automatically assume that teachers have adopted the program. An evaluation plan must include some way, such as classroom observation, to verify that the program has been implemented.[3]

How to Evaluate Physical Education Programs

The following steps are suggested for evaluating programs:

Step 1. Describe the program to be evaluated.
Step 2. Identify the purposes of the evaluation.
Step 3. Establish criteria for judging quality and making decisions.
Step 4. Describe the information needed to make the decisions.
Step 5. Obtain, record, and analyze information.
Step 6. Interpret data in terms of standards.
Step 7. Make decisions and formulate recommendations.

Following a description of all of the steps, an example of the process will be presented.

Step 1—*Describe the program to be evaluated.*

The program description helps to avoid overlooking aspects that need to be evaluated. A description generally includes the following:

1. A statement of the program philosophy
2. The people involved—students, their families, faculty, and administrators

3. Performance objectives—cognitive, psychomotor, and affective—including entry behaviors, intended and unintended outcomes arranged in a hierarchy from general to specific
4. Subject matter content
5. Instructional elements such as scheduling pattern, learning activities, student-student and student-teacher interactions, media use, motivation, and evaluation and grading techniques
6. Facilities and equipment
7. Costs
8. Administrative conditions

Step 2—*Identify the purposes of the evaluation.*

Identify areas of concern about the program and anticipate decisions that will have to be made by asking questions such as: Are goals and objectives appropriate and worthwhile? Are students achieving the objectives? What problems exist? What are the reactions of various audiences to the program? and What unanticipated outcomes are there?

Vogel and Seefeldt asserted that positive responses to the following questions yield evidence of successful programs:

1. Are the important potential contributions of activity to the quality of life included in the program?
2. Is the content of the program (What is being taught? When? Why?) clearly defined?
3. Do the content and the methods of instruction match the individual needs of the students?
4. Do the graduates attain the desired objectives related to skilled performance, knowledge, fitness, and attitude?
5. Do the outcomes of the program justify the time, money, and energy expended to support the program?
6. Are there periodic evaluations and resultant program improvements?
7. Can the program continue if the current teacher(s) leave the district?[4]

Decisions to be made might include adopting a new program, discontinuing a program, changing student grouping patterns, increasing the budget, changing the staff, using community facilities, or implementing different instructional strategies. Possible alternatives should be identified in each instance. Four types of decisions included in program evaluation are (1) planning decisions, (2) organizing decisions, (3) implementing decisions, and (4) evaluating decisions.[5] Table 16.1 shows the questions that might be asked in each area, along with areas of concern.[6]

Persons responsible for making the decisions should be identified. These may include students, teachers, administrators, or the board of education. A date should be specified for making the decisions, along with policies within which the evaluation must occur.

Step 3—*Establish criteria for judging quality and making decisions.*

Two types of standards are used to judge program quality—absolute standards and relative standards. *Absolute standards* are those established by personal or professional judgment. These criteria are established in the same way that performance objectives are created. The problem with using absolute standards lies in selecting the level that indicates program success. Standards can be derived from criteria achieved in similar programs in other schools, in former programs

Table 16.1 Decisions Involved in Curriculum Evaluation

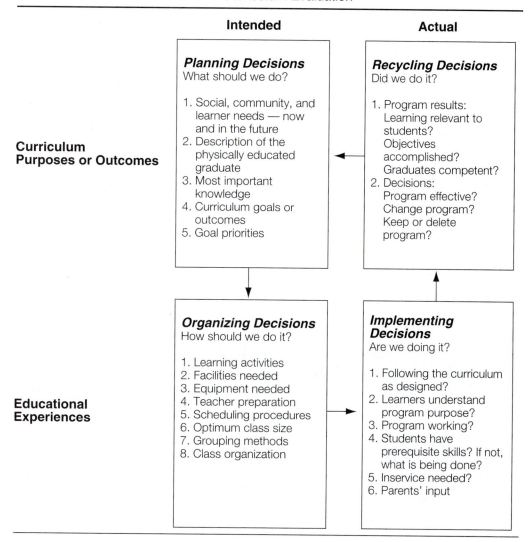

	Intended	**Actual**
Curriculum Purposes or Outcomes	**Planning Decisions** What should we do? 1. Social, community, and learner needs — now and in the future 2. Description of the physically educated graduate 3. Most important knowledge 4. Curriculum goals or outcomes 5. Goal priorities	**Recycling Decisions** Did we do it? 1. Program results: Learning relevant to students? Objectives accomplished? Graduates competent? 2. Decisions: Program effective? Change program? Keep or delete program?
Educational Experiences	**Organizing Decisions** How should we do it? 1. Learning activities 2. Facilities needed 3. Equipment needed 4. Teacher preparation 5. Scheduling procedures 6. Optimum class size 7. Grouping methods 8. Class organization	**Implementing Decisions** Are we doing it? 1. Following the curriculum as designed? 2. Learners understand program purpose? 3. Program working? 4. Students have prerequisite skills? If not, what is being done? 5. Inservice needed? 6. Parents' input

Concepts from Stufflebeam, Daniel L. et al. (1971). *Educational Evaluation and Decision Making* (Itasca, IL: F. E. Peacock Publishers, Inc.) and Vogel, Paul G., and Seefeldt, Vern D. (September 1987). "Redesign of Physical Education Programs: A Procedural Model That Leads to Defensible Programs." *Journal of Physical Education, Recreation and Dance 58* (7): 65–69.

in the same school, or by guesstimates by administrators, teachers, parents, students, and community members working together. Preassessment scores of current students provide guidelines for developing standards. When students fail to achieve the standards, the program can be revised to produce the desired achievement, the objectives can be changed, or the program can be thrown out and a new one created.

Relative standards are those reflected by alternative programs. In other words, the program is compared with other programs to determine which one has the best outcomes. National norms for fitness and skill are available from the American Alliance for Health, Physical Education, Recreation and Dance. These norms tell how students compare with other students nationally. Locally constructed norms can be used to evaluate how students compare with students previously completing the program. Some difficulties are inherent in comparing two programs that look alike, since each may have some unique purposes the evaluation process may overlook. Thus, there may be no significant differences in the quantitative data when there are differences in the qualitative data. Both quantitative and qualitative data are necessary to overcome this deficiency.[7]

Essential standards in all evaluation studies are (1) validity—the extent to which the evaluation provides the information it is supposed to provide; (2) reliability—the degree to which the data collected are the same on different trials of the test; (3) objectivity—the extent to which the data are the same regardless of who administers the test; (4) cost-effectiveness in terms of the time, energy and money invested; and (5) timeliness—in time to make a decision.

Step 4—*Describe the information needed to make the decisions.*

Prior to evaluating the achievement of program objectives, the objectives should be analyzed to determine whether they are worthwhile and will produce the intended outcomes.

Periodic program evaluation helps administrators, teachers, and students to reach program goals.
© Dennis Mac Donald/Unicorn Stock Photos

Empirical analysis should include information from other groups or specialists to determine essential objectives. However, agreement with the objectives or methods used in other curricula does not mean that the objectives are worthwhile. In chapter 14, a list of guidelines for evaluating curricular goals and objectives was included (see pages 499 and 500). Evaluators should review these guidelines to determine whether the goals and objectives need revision.

Information on achievement of the objectives can be gained from students, teachers, parents, and outside observers, using both formal and informal evaluation techniques. Some commonly used techniques include (1) controlled research, (2) structured external evaluation, (3) standardized tests, (4) teacher-constructed evaluation techniques, (5) subjective judgment, and (6) informal analysis.

Controlled research involves the use of randomization to assign control and experimental groups, and then the construction and testing of hypotheses. In this way the program results can be compared with a different or preceding program or the posttest results can be compared with the pretest results to see if they are statistically significant.

Structured external evaluation was one of the earliest methods used to evaluate the total physical education program. The first scorecard was developed by William Ralph LaPorte in the 1930s. Since that time a number of scorecards have been developed by various state departments of education. They are often used by evaluation teams from accrediting associations. The *Assessment Guide for Secondary School Physical Education Programs*,[8] created by AAHPERD, provides standards for evaluating the physical education program in the areas of (1) administration, (2) the instructional program, (3) the intramural program, and (4) the athletic program. A sample of the criteria in the areas of administration and the instructional program is shown in figures 16.1 and 16.2. Two new program appraisal checklists have been created by the Middle and Secondary School Physical Education Council of the National Association for Sport and Physical Education.[9] Each checklist asks the evaluators to rate a number of statements relating to program goals; the curriculum; the teacher; student health and safety; scheduling, time allotment, and class size; and facilities, equipment, and supplies. A more comprehensive checklist for evaluating physical education programs prepared as part of the Michigan Exemplary Physical Education Programs Project is included in *Evaluation of K–12 Physical Education Programs: A Self-Study Approach*.[10] This checklist includes 33 categories divided into five parts dealing with the quality of the school-community environment; the program; instruction; personnel; and facilities, equipment, and safety.

AAHPERD has developed *standardized tests* to evaluate psychomotor skills and has adopted the *Prudential Fitnessgram*[11] to assess physical fitness. Several problems exist when using standardized tests for program evaluation. One is the selection of inappropriate instruments for the program being evaluated. Tests must have content validity; that is, they must test the objectives specified in the program. Since most standardized tests are directed toward lower-level cognitive and psychomotor skills, other instruments may be needed in addition to standardized tests if the program is to be evaluated fairly. Validity, reliability, and appropriate norms for the group to be tested must also be assessed prior to adoption. Teaching to the test is another problem with standardized tests. For a new program, teachers should not see the test before it is given. With regard to the standardized tests, Worthen and Sanders pointed out that "in all the history of evaluation in education it has proven exceedingly difficult to demonstrate the superiority of *any* procedure in terms of test performance."[12]

Teacher-constructed evaluation techniques are useful for assessing student achievement, along with student participation in extra-class or leisure-time activities, attendance, tardiness,

Criteria	Response (Circle)		Notes
6. Instructional program areas that are designed to meet objectives focusing on the organization, development, and refinement of skillful movement include the following units in *prescribed elective* courses:			
A. Sport, dance, and exercise activities offered at progressive skill levels.	Yes	No	
B. Students grouped for instruction according to grade level or ability.	Yes	No	
C. Formal instruction (coeducational whenever possible) provided in team sports, individual and dual sports, aquatics, dance, and lifetime / leisure time activities.	Yes	No	
D. Adapted program that is an integral part of the regular program that provides instruction compatible with physical disabilities (goal to successfully integrate students into regular classes).	Yes	No	
7. Instructional program areas that are designed to meet objectives focusing on knowledge of the basic theoretical concepts of human movement behavior as they relate to sport, dance, and exercise include the following areas in *required* theoretical course work and / or cognitive unit objectives within activity coursework:			

Figure 16.1 A sample of the evaluative criteria for instruction.
Source: From the Assessment Guide for Secondary School Physical Education Programs, developed by the National Association for Sport and Physical Education of the American Alliance for Health, Physical Education, Recreation and Dance, 1977.

discipline, dropouts, awards, assignments completed, library books checked out on a given subject, and choices made in selective activities. Parent and community involvement through attendance at parent-teacher association meetings, back-to-school nights, parent-teacher conferences, board of education meetings, and school visits can also be recorded.

Questionnaires, rating scales, and inventories can be constructed to determine student progress toward affective objectives. In general, assessment might include (1) whether student attitudes are positive or negative toward physical education or the specific activity engaged in, and how well students are applying the principles of appropriate social behavior such as good teamwork or sportspersonship, (2) whether students appear willing to approach physical education or an activity as readily at the end of course instruction as when they began, and (3) what activities appeal to students.

Criteria	Response (Circle)		Notes
A. Biomechanical and kinesiological concepts.	Yes	No	
B. Psychological concepts related to motor performance.	Yes	No	
C. Exercise physiology.	Yes	No	
D. Philosophy of human movement.	Yes	No	
E. Sports medicine/athletic injury.	Yes	No	
F. Historical development of sport, dance, and exercise forms.	Yes	No	
G. Rules and strategies of sport forms.	Yes	No	
H. Motor learning principles.	Yes	No	
I. Motor development.	Yes	No	
J. Sport sociology.	Yes	No	
K. Humanities and sciences subject matter relationships to movement forms.	Yes	No	
8. Written course outlines are followed by instructors and available to students. These outlines include:	Yes	No	
A. Rationale for inclusion in instructional program	Yes	No	
B. Behavioral objectives.	Yes	No	
C. Prescribed evaluation procedures based upon stated behavioral objectives.	Yes	No	
D. Sequential skill progressions.	Yes	No	

Figure 16.1 (*Continued*)

For students to answer honestly on affective evaluation instruments, they must trust that results will not be used against them. To achieve this, use questions that require checking or circling the responses instead of writing, tell students not to put their names on the papers, and have students collect the papers and tabulate the responses, or ask for papers to be placed in a box in a nonthreatening place. Sample questionnaire items might include the following:

Student goals and interests

1. Indicate your interest in physical fitness *before* taking this class: highly interested/ interested/ neutral/ less interested/ highly uninterested.
2. How long do you plan to continue your present exercise program? throughout life/ throughout school years/ until school is out this year/this term only/ I don't plan to continue.

	Response (Circle)			
Criteria	Instruc-tional Program	Intramural Program	Athletic Program	Notes
16. Written department policies are available concerning standard operating procedures involving:				
A. Uniforms, lockers, towels, locks, lost and found.	Yes No	Yes No	Yes No	
B. Emergencies and location of first aid supplies.	Yes No	Yes No	Yes No	
C. Facility problems or hazardous conditions.	Yes No	Yes No	Yes No	
D. Teacher evaluation.	Yes No	Yes No	Yes No	
E. Absences, excuses and attendance.	Yes No	Yes No	Yes No	
F. Legal responsibilities of personnel.	Yes No	Yes No	Yes No	
G. Scheduling.	Yes No	Yes No	Yes No	
H. Facility supervision.	Yes No	Yes No	Yes No	
I. Purchase of equipment and supplies.	Yes No	Yes No	Yes No	
J. Maintenance and management of facilities, equipment, and supplies.	Yes No	Yes No	Yes No	
17. Secretarial and support personnel are available to meet program needs.	Yes No	Yes No	Yes No	
18. Allotment of time and facilities for all programs are equitable and meet program needs.	Yes No	Yes No	Yes No	
19. Number of available indoor and outdoor teaching stations meet all programs needs. They:				
A. Are conducive to quality instruction.	Yes No	Yes No	Yes No	
B. Are adequate to handle peak hour loads.	Yes No	Yes No	Yes No	
C. Contain adequate office space.	Yes No	Yes No	Yes No	
20. Community facilities are utilized to avoid costly duplication, to expand program offerings, and to make use of superior facilities.	Yes No	Yes No	Yes No	

Figure 16.2 A sample of the evaluative criteria for administration.
Source: From the Assessment Guide for Secondary School Physical Education Programs, developed by the National Association for Sport and Physical Education of the American Alliance for Health, Physical Education, Recreation and Dance, 1977.

3. If you were asked to give a short talk about your favorite school subject, which subject would you talk about?
4. I took this class for the following reasons:

I was curious   _____
It was required   _____
I needed the challenge   _____
I've always liked it   _____
I wanted to learn something new   _____
I needed some easy credit or an easy A   _____
Nothing else was available and I needed
    an elective   _____
I don't know   _____

Student's perceptions of the curriculum

1. I learned more this semester because I was able to take the activities I wanted. yes/no
2. I like being able to select the teacher I want. yes/no
3. There should be a limit on the number of times a student can take a given activity. yes/no
4. With regard to activities, I wish we had a class in _____ .
5. In which of the following did you participate?

intramurals   _____
extramurals   _____
varsity sports   _____
none of these   _____

6. How do you prefer intramural teams be picked?

by homerooms   _____
by physical education class   _____
by personal selection   _____

7. If physical education were not required, would you still have taken it this year? yes/no

Rating scales usually include from three to nine choices. The number is based on the complexity of the information required. Fewer choices yield more reliable data. More choices provide more information. Generally an odd number is used so the midpoint will be a neutral category. Several types of scales exist. One form of scale is the continuum, on which the rater places a mark as shown in this question:

Has positive attitudes toward self:

| Very positive | Positive | Neutral | Negative | Very negative |

Another type has boxes to check:

| Very positive | Positive | Neutral | Negative | Very negative |

Inventories are rating scales designed to yield two or more scores by grouping items in certain prespecified ways. Attitude inventories generally contain three types of questions. The first type is the following:

	Agree	Disagree
1. Physical education is a waste of time. (2.00)	_____	_____
2. Physical education is helpful in one's life. (8.00)	_____	_____
3. Physical activity is important to my mental, physical, and emotional fitness. (9.00)	_____	_____
4. Physical fitness is no longer essential in today's world. (3.00)	_____	_____

The student's score is an average of the scale factors (in parentheses) for all of the questions marked "agree."

The second type of question looks like this:

	Strongly Agree	Agree	Uncertain	Disagree	Strongly Disagree
1. I need a lot of exercise to stay in good physical condition.	( )	( )	( )	( )	( )
2. Following game rules helps me be a better citizen in the community.	( )	( )	( )	( )	( )
3. I prefer to engage in activities that require a minimum of physical activity.	( )	( )	( )	( )	( )

The third type of question consists of bipolar adjectives. An example of this type of question is the following:

Physical education is:

Pleasant	: : : : : : :	Unpleasant
Good	: : : : : : :	Bad
Active	: : : : : : :	Passive

Another type of inventory is the interest or valued activities inventory. Examples are shown in figures 16.3 and 16.4. To score, simply tally the responses for each activity.

Adjective checklists differ slightly from inventories. Students select adjectives that apply to themselves or others from a list provided, such as the following:

Circle each of the words that tell how you feel about physical education:

interesting	dull	boring
fun	useful	very important
too hard	exciting	too easy
useless	tiring	

To score, compare the number of positive and negative words circled.

<table>
<tr><td colspan="5">Instructions: Circle the symbol representing your interest in each of the following activities.</td></tr>
<tr><td></td><td>Strong interest</td><td>OK</td><td>Neutral</td><td>Don't like</td></tr>
<tr><td>Archery</td><td>SI</td><td>OK</td><td>N</td><td>DL</td></tr>
<tr><td>Badminton</td><td>SI</td><td>OK</td><td>N</td><td>DL</td></tr>
<tr><td>Basketball</td><td>SI</td><td>OK</td><td>N</td><td>DL</td></tr>
<tr><td>Bicycling</td><td>SI</td><td>OK</td><td>N</td><td>DL</td></tr>
<tr><td>Bowling</td><td>SI</td><td>OK</td><td>N</td><td>DL</td></tr>
<tr><td>Others (list)</td><td></td><td></td><td></td><td></td></tr>
<tr><td>_____</td><td>SI</td><td>OK</td><td>N</td><td>DL</td></tr>
<tr><td>_____</td><td>SI</td><td>OK</td><td>N</td><td>DL</td></tr>
</table>

Figure 16.3 An interest or valued activities inventory.

INSTRUCTIONS: Each activity is followed by a number of symbols. Circle all of the symbols for the words that describe you.

Sport	Spectator	Occasional participant	Frequent participant	Low skill	Average skill	High skill
Chess	Ⓢ	ⓄⓅ	FP	ⓁⓈ	AS	HS
Archery	S	OP	FP	LS	AS	HS
Badminton	S	OP	FP	LS	AS	HS
Basketball	S	OP	FP	LS	AS	HS
Bicycling	S	OP	FP	LS	AS	HS
Others (list)						
_____	S	OP	FP	LS	AS	HS

Figure 16.4 An activity checklist.

Ranking involves arranging items on a list in order of personal preference or some other specified quality. Usually the number of items to be ranked is limited to about 10. Two examples of ranking are shown here:

Example 1: List all the subjects you are now taking and then rank them in order from most interesting to least interesting. (1 is best)

Example 2: Rank order the following activities by placing a 1 by the activity you like to play best, 2 next, and so on down to number 6:

Archery	_____	Folk dance	_____
Badminton	_____	Golf	_____
Basketball	_____	Gymnastics	_____

Do you dislike the activity you rated last? ____Yes ____ No
If yes, why?

To score, total the ranks from all students. The rank with the lowest score indicates the highest interest. One major disadvantage of ranking is that there is no way of knowing how much difference exists between items in adjacent ranks. Group scores, however, can provide valuable data.

Subjective judgment by teachers, administrators, parents, students, and community members can provide valuable information. Annual interviews or meetings to discuss goals and objectives, assess achievement of objectives, and predict needs and problems might deal with such questions as the following: Are goals and objectives appropriate? Should anything be added to or deleted from the program? Why or why not? What is not going well? and How could it be improved?

Teachers and administrators can use *informal analysis* to assess the effects of the program on faculty and staff. Adverse effects can result in physical and emotional deterioration, resulting in a less effective program for teachers and students. Chapter 13 discussed some techniques for informal analysis.

All program evaluations should use a variety of evaluation instruments. Failure to do so can result in a biased interpretation of program effectiveness. Each technique is selected to correspond with the objective and the group to be evaluated.

A schedule or work plan is formulated to keep the evaluation proceeding on schedule. The plan describes who will do what, with what instruments, using what population sample, and by what date. A suggested format appears in figure 16.5.

Step 5—*Obtain, record, and analyze information.*

Obtain and record the information specified in Step 4, including such areas as student experiences, student gains and losses, unintended outcomes, and program costs in terms of time, money, and other resources. Determine a format for classifying and recording the information. Analyze the information by using appropriate statistical methods.

Step 6—*Interpret data in terms of standards.*

The purpose of program evaluation is to determine the worth or value of the program. Thus, after all the data have been collected, a judgment must be made as to whether the program has been successful. As in the other phases of curriculum design, many people should be involved in making these judgments, including students, parents, faculty, administrators, the board of education, and community and professional leaders. Conclusions should be drawn concerning the program effectiveness and student progress.

Two questions must be answered when interpreting the information collected: (1) Were the objectives achieved? and (2) Was there a logical connection between entry behaviors, learning activities, and desired outcomes? Achievement of program objectives is determined by comparing the data with the standards specified in Step 3.

OBJECTIVE	ACTION BY	METHOD	POPULATION	DEADLINE
1. Pass five mastery tests.	Mr. Ames	Mastery tests.	All students in the school.	January and June
2. Complete contract.	Miss Jones	Count of completed contracts, analyze uncompleted contracts for problem areas.	All students in the school.	January and June
3. Take fitness appraisal.	Mr. Sims	Fitness appraisals recorded on class record sheets.	All students in the school.	January and June
4. Increase fitness.	Mrs. Garcia	Computer analysis of fitness appraisals.	All students in the school.	January and June
5. Positive feelings of students toward the unit; toward fitness.	Mr. Platt	Inventory of student feelings.	Random samples of 100 students.	January and June
6. Comparison with current program.	Mrs. Garcia	Computer analysis of fitness appraisals.	Test random sample of students in regular program and statistics from Step 4.	January and June

Figure 16.5 An evaluation work plan for Fitness for Life.

To interpret the relationship among entry behaviors, learning activities, and desired outcomes, pretest and posttest data must be analyzed. When students score high on the pretest, the instruction may be unnecessary. When students score low on the pretest and low on the posttest, the instruction was inadequate and needs revision or an alternative program should be adopted. Low pretest scores accompanied by high posttest scores demonstrate that sound instruction has occurred and students are learning as planned.

Step 7—*Make decisions and formulate recommendations.*

Once the data have been evaluated, decisions must be made concerning whether to retain or discontinue the program, adopt a new program, or change various facets of the program such as the budget, staff, facilities, or instructional strategies. The persons identified in Step 2 as those responsible for the program must evaluate the data by the criteria listed in Step 3. If the standards have all been met, the decision will be easy—to retain the program as is. If none of the standards have been met, the program will undoubtedly be replaced. However, when some of the criteria have been met and others have not been met, decisions will have to be made concerning whether the objectives are valid, whether the program can be changed in some way to achieve the objectives, or whether to adopt a new approach.

Recommendations provide a basis for administrative action in the form of further implementation, modification, or revision. The evaluation results, with accompanying recommendations, should be communicated to the faculty, administration, students, parents, and other interested community members.

An Example of Program Evaluation

Step 1—Describe the program to be evaluated.

The Fitness for Life program is an individualized program designed to help students write and apply their own fitness programs during school and throughout their lives. Students contract with an instructor to do the following:

1. Pass five mastery tests on (a) how to write programs for cardiovascular endurance, weight control, and strength and flexibility; (b) how to measure cardiovascular endurance, strength, and flexibility; and (c) fitness concepts.
2. Complete a nine-week contract for cardiovascular endurance according to the specifications on the course handout.
3. Take a fitness appraisal before and after completion of the contract and show progress.

Students complete the contract on their own time and check with the instructor for assistance as needed or to take mastery checks. A fourth outcome desired in the program is that students will have positive feelings about fitness activities and about the unit.

Step 2—Identify the purposes of the evaluation.

Some concerns about the Fitness for Life program included:

1. Did students actually increase physical fitness during the nine-week contract?
2. Did students have positive feelings about physical fitness and about the unit?
3. Were the instructors satisfied with the program?
4. Was the new program better than the existing program?
5. What administrative problems existed?

Step 3—Establish criteria for judging quality and making decisions.

The following absolute standards in the form of objectives were selected at the beginning of the Fitness for Life program. Eighty percent of the students will do the following:

1. Achieve good or excellent on the 1.5-mile run.
2. Achieve a percent body fat of 20 percent or below for girls and 15 percent or below for boys.
3. Obtain a score of 80 percent or better on all five tests of fitness concepts.
4. Complete a fitness contract for nine weeks at the contracted level of exercise.
5. Have positive attitudes toward participation in physical fitness activities.

Objective 2 was later increased from 20 percent to 22 percent due to the incidence of anorexia among girls.

With regard to relative standards, a comparison with the AAHPERD norms revealed that students in the Fitness for Life program were below the national average prior to participating in the program.

Step 4—Describe the information needed to make the decisions.

The following measures were considered to provide the information needed to evaluate the program. The Cooper 1.5-mile run and percent fat measured by skinfold calipers were used to evaluate fitness. Students in Fitness for Life classes were tested and found to improve significantly more in physical fitness than students who were enrolled in regular physical education classes at the same time. Therefore, it was concluded that the Fitness for Life program was better than the regular program for achieving fitness.

An attitude inventory was constructed to assess attitudes toward fitness. A questionnaire measured continued participation in fitness programs several years later. Another questionnaire requested feedback on preferred instructional methods.

An external evaluation team was invited to assess program effectiveness. They interviewed teachers, obtained questionnaire responses from students, and interviewed students who dropped the class.

Students in the fitness program were required to log in each time they requested individual help. Dates on which tests were taken were recorded. A contract was required on which students recorded their weekly participation in selected activities.

A continuous dialogue between teachers and students in the program helped to provide feedback on what was or was not working. Teachers met weekly to discuss the progress of the program.

In the Fitness for Life program, teachers were frustrated by student procrastination in taking written tests. Students also complained about the need to log in each week.

Step 5—Obtain, record, and analyze information.

The faculty decided that a coordinator would be assigned to take responsibility for collecting each portion of the data. The final evaluation would take place by the entire faculty one month prior to the end of the school year. Figure 16.6 shows the data collected during the evaluation of the Fitness for Life program. Note that only a sample of the total students participating in the program took the pretest on the mastery tests and completed the attitude inventory and instructional methods questionnaires. This was done by randomly assigning a few students in each class to each section of the inventory or questionnaire rather than by having all students complete all of the sections. This conserved student time and resulted in students being more attentive than they might have been to a long evaluation instrument. Since the fitness tests were used as a basis for the individual contracts, most of the students took them. The number of students achieving the 80 percent criterion on the mastery tests and the percentage achieving mastery are shown in the figure.

Step 6—Interpret data in terms of standards.

Analysis of the data in figure 16.6 revealed that more than 80 percent of the students achieved the three unit objectives with one exception. In test 3, only 75 percent of the students achieved mastery. Data from the questionnaire revealed that some test questions were confusing to students. An analysis of the test showed that questions 6 and 10 were consistently missed. One solution was better instruction in the area of planning the weight control program. Another solution was to clarify the questions on the test.

The data showed that students in the Fitness for Life program achieved significant increases in all four fitness components. The differences in fitness between students in the regular program and the fitness program were also significant. Students appeared to be positive toward the instruction and toward physical fitness, with the exceptions noted. Some revisions in the program were made to resolve these problems.

Step 7—Make decisions and formulate recommendations.

In the Fitness for Life program, the following recommendations were made:

1. The program should be retained.
2. The grading system should be changed to an "A-pass-fail" system in which students can get an "A" grade or a "pass grade" (B or C equivalent) or a "fail" to provide more challenge to students to excel.
3. The test and the handout on weight control should be rewritten.
4. Students in the "good" or above categories must log in only every other week. This will provide more time for students needing help.
5. Test deadlines for each test will be posted to reduce procrastination.
6. A meeting should be held in December to evaluate the changes.

Cautions in Program Evaluation

Program evaluators must be careful to use a variety of techniques to evaluate the curriculum. Exclusive reliance on quantitative assessment techniques may limit programs to outcomes that can be stated in precise terms and for which objective tests exist. Some of the most important goals of physical education cannot be stated as performance objectives or evaluated while students are still in school. Only after many years can we determine, for example, whether physical fitness has been maintained or lifetime skills applied throughout one's life. Short-term objectives, however, along with a variety of assessment techniques, can give us indicators of success or failure within the curriculum to help us adjust our course during the race.

The Curriculum Merry-Go-Round

Several years ago, Cassidy proposed a curriculum merry-go-round on which one could climb at any point in the curriculum design process and ride around until one's purposes were accomplished. The advantage of this concept is that curriculum design is perceived as a continuous

OBJECTIVE	PRETEST DATA		
	Number of Students	Number Achieving Criterion	%
1. Pass five mastery tests.			
Test 1	20	2	10%
Test 2	20	1	5%
Test 3	20	0	0%
Test 4	20	1	5%
Test 5	20	3	15%
Total			
2. Complete contract.	✕		
3. Take fitness appraisals.	200	200	100%

4. Increase fitness.	PRETEST MEAN Girls	PRETEST MEAN Boys
Percent fat.	19.48	15.10
1.5-mile run.	14:36	13:24

5. Positive feelings of students.	FAVORABLE	UNFAVORABLE
Orientation session.	|||| ||||		||||
Mastery tests.	|||| |||| ||	|||
Contract.	|||| ||||	||||
Fitness appraisals.	|||| |||| ||||		
Grading system.	||||	|||| ||||	
Instructor assistance.	||||		||||
Toward fitness.	|||| |||| ||||	

6. Comparison with current program.	CURRENT PROGRAM		
	Number of Students	Number Achieving Criterion	%
Concept tests.	800	111	13.9
Percent fat.	800	500	62.5
1.5-mile run.	800	436	54.5

Figure 16.6 A recording form for the Fitness for Life program data.

| POST-TEST DATA | | | | |
Number of Students	Number Achieving Criterion	%	CRITERION MET Yes	No
200	180	90.0%	X	
200	185	92.5%	X	
200	150	75.0%		X
200	190	95.0%	X	
200	195	97.5%	X	
200	165	82.5%	X	
200	192	96.0%	X	

POST-TEST MEAN Girls	POST-TEST MEAN Boys	SIGNIFICANT Yes	No
16.7	12.28	X	
13.27	12.11	X	

COMMENTS

Great!

Too easy, except Test 3, which had confusing questions.

Want ABC system.

Too busy to talk, too many log-ins.

| FITNESS FOR LIFE PROGRAM | | | | |
Number of Students	Number Achieving Criterion	%	CRITERION MET Yes	No
200	150	75	X	
200	152	76	X	
200	181	90.5	X	

Figure 16.6 (*Continued*)

process.[13] A crucial step in this process is evaluating whether program objectives have been achieved. The evaluation provides new information with which to begin the cycle over again. Objectives must be reevaluated to see whether they are desirable within the constantly changing environment. Curriculum patterns and teaching and learning strategies must be revised so that student achievement more nearly approximates the objectives that have been established. Thus, the cycle of design, plan, implement, and evaluate begins again with redesign, plan. . . .

Review Questions

1. Define and give an example of:
   a. Formative evaluation
   b. Summative evaluation
   c. Absolute standards
   d. Relative standards
   e. Controlled research
   f. Structured external evaluation
   g. Standardized tests
   h. Teacher-constructed evaluation techniques
   i. Subjective judgment
   j. Informal analysis

References

1. Rog, J. A. (1982, October). Will (should) your physical education program survive? *NASPE News,* 6.
2. Vogel, P. G., & Seefeldt, V. D. (1987, September). Redesign of physical education programs: A procedural model that leads to defensible programs. *Journal of Physical Education, Recreation and Dance, 58*(7), 65–69.
3. Hill, J. (1985, February). Curriculum evaluation—Practical approaches to dealing with the pitfalls. *NASSP Bulletin, 69*(478), 1–6.
4. Vogel & Seefeldt, Redesign of physical education programs, 65–69.
5. Stufflebeam, D. L., Foley, W. J., Gephart, W. J., Guba, E. G., Hammond, R. L., Merriam, H. O., and Provus, M. M. (1971). *Educational evaluation and decision making.* Itasca, IL: Peacock.
6. Hill, J. C. (1986). *Curriculum evaluation for school improvement.* Springfield, IL: Thomas.
7. Hill, Curriculum evaluation, 2.
8. American Alliance for Health, Physical Education and Recreation. (1977). *Assessment guide for secondary school physical education programs.* Washington, DC: Author.
9. Middle and Secondary School Physical Education Council of the National Association for Sport and Physical Education. (1991). *Program appraisal checklist for middle school physical education programs* and *Program appraisal checklist for secondary school physical education programs.* Reston, VA: AAHPERD.
10. Dummer, G. M., Reuschlein, P. L., Haubenstricker, J. L., Vogel, P. G., & Cavanaugh, P. L. (1993). *Evaluation of K–12 physical education programs: A self-study approach.* Dubuque, IA: Brown & Benchmark.
11. Information can be obtained from Cooper Institute for Aerobics Research, 12330 Preston Rd., Dallas, TX 75230, (214) 701–8001.
12. Worthen, B. R., & Sanders, J. R. (1973). *Educational evaluation: Theory and practice.* Worthington, OH: Jones.
13. Cassidy, R. (1954). *Curriculum development in physical education.* New York: Harper & Row.

Index